Lecture Notes in Artificial Intelligence   3171

Edited by J. G. Carbonell and J. Siekmann

Subseries of Lecture Notes in Computer Science

T0180891

Ana L.C. Bazzan   Sofiane Labidi (Eds.)

Advances in Artificial Intelligence – SBIA 2004

17th Brazilian Symposium on Artificial Intelligence
São Luis, Maranhão, Brazil
September 29 – October 1, 2004
Proceedings

 Springer

Series Editors

Jaime G. Carbonell, Carnegie Mellon University, Pittsburgh, PA, USA
Jörg Siekmann, University of Saarland, Saarbrücken, Germany

Volume Editors

Ana L.C. Bazzan
Universidade Federal do Rio Grande do Sul
Depto. de Informática Teórica, Instituto de Informática
Caixa Postal 15064, 91501-970 Porto Alegre, RS, Brazil
E-mail: bazzan@inf.ufrgs.br

Sofiane Labidi
Federal University of Maranhão UFMA
Intelligent Systems Laboratory LSI
Center of Technology
Bacanga Campus, 65080-040 São Luis, MA, Brazil
E-mail: labidi@uol.com.br

Library of Congress Control Number: 2004112252

CR Subject Classification (1998): I.2, F.4.1, F.1, H.2.8

ISSN 0302-9743
ISBN 3-540-23237-0 Springer Berlin Heidelberg New York

Springer is a part of Springer Science+Business Media

springeronline.com

© Springer-Verlag Berlin Heidelberg 2004
Printed in Germany

Typesetting: Camera-ready by author, data conversion by Olgun Computergrafik
Printed on acid-free paper   SPIN: 11316800   06/3142   5 4 3 2 1 0

Preface

SBIA, the Brazilian Symposium on Artificial Intelligence, is a biennial event intended to be the main forum of the AI community in Brazil. The SBIA 2004 was the 17th issue of the series initiated in 1984. Since 1995 SBIA has been accepting papers written and presented only in English, attracting researchers from all over the world. At that time it also started to have an international program committee, keynote invited speakers, and proceedings published in the Lecture Notes in Artificial Intelligence (LNAI) series of Springer (SBIA 1995, Vol. 991, SBIA 1996, Vol. 1159, SBIA 1998, Vol. 1515, SBIA 2000, Vol. 1952, SBIA 2002, Vol. 2507).

SBIA 2004 was sponsored by the Brazilian Computer Society (SBC). It was held from September 29 to October 1 in the city of São Luis, in the northeast of Brazil, together with the Brazilian Symposium on Neural Networks (SBRN). This followed a trend of joining the AI and ANN communities to make the joint event a very exciting one. In particular, in 2004 these two events were also held together with the IEEE International Workshop on Machine Learning and Signal Processing (MMLP), formerly NNLP.

The organizational structure of SBIA 2004 was similar to other international scientific conferences. The backbone of the conference was the technical program which was complemented by invited talks, workshops, etc. on the main AI topics.

The call for papers attracted 209 submissions from 21 countries. Each paper submitted to SBIA was reviewed by three referees. From this total, 54 papers from 10 countries were accepted and are included in this volume. This made SBIA a very competitive conference with an acceptance rate of 25.8%. The evaluation of this large number of papers was a challenge in terms of reviewing and maintaining the high quality of the preceding SBIA conferences. All these goals would not have been achieved without the excellent work of the members of the program committee – composed of 80 researchers from 18 countries – and the auxiliary reviewers.

Thus, we would like to express our sincere gratitude to all those who helped make SBIA 2004 happen. First of all we thank all the contributing authors; special thanks go to the members of the program committee and reviewers for their careful work in selecting the best papers. Thanks go also to the steering committee for its guidance and support, to the local organization people, and to the students who helped with the website design and maintenance, the papers submission site, and with the preparation of this volume. Finally, we would like to thank the Brazilian funding agencies and Springer for supporting this book.

Porto Alegre, September 2004

Ana L.C. Bazzan
(Chair of the Program Committee)
Sofiane Labidi
(General Chair)

Organization

SBIA 2004 was held in conjunction with SBRN 2004 and with IEEE MMLP 2004. These events were co-organized by all co-chairs involved in them.

Chair

Sofiane Labidi (UFMA, Brazil)

Steering Committee

Ariadne Carvalho (UNICAMP, Brazil)
Geber Ramalho (UFPE, Brazil)
Guilherme Bitencourt (UFSC, Brazil)
Jaime Sichman (USP, Brazil)

Organizing Committee

Allan Kardec Barros (UFMA)
Aluízio Araújo (UFPE)
Ana L.C. Bazzan (UFRGS)
Geber Ramalho (UFPE)
Osvaldo Ronald Saavedra (UFMA)
Sofiane Labidi (UFMA)

Supporting Scientific Society

SBC   Sociedade Brasileira de Computação

Program Committee

Luis Otavio Alvares	Univ. Federal do Rio Grande do Sul (Brazil)
Analia Amandi	Universidad Nacional del Centro de la Provincia de Buenos Aires (Argentina)
John Atkinson	Universidad de Concepcin (Chile)
Bráulio Coelho Avila	Pontifícia Universidade Católica, PR (Brazil)
Flávia Barros	Universidade Federal de Pernambuco (Brazil)
Guilherme Bittencourt	Universidade Federal de Santa Catarina (Brazil)
Olivier Boissier	École Nationale Superieure des Mines de Saint-Etienne (France)
Rafael H. Bordini	University of Liverpool (UK)
Dibio Leandro Borges	Pontifícia Universidade Católica, PR (Brazil)
Bert Bredeweg	University of Amsterdam (The Netherlands)
Jacques Calmet	Universität Karlsruhe (Germany)
Mario F. Montenegro Campos	Universidade Federal de Minas Gerais (Brazil)
Fernando Carvalho	Universidade Federal do Ceará (Brazil)
Francisco Carvalho	Universidade Federal de Pernambuco (Brazil)
Cristiano Castelfranchi	Institute of Psychology, CNR (Italy)
Carlos Castro	Univ. Técnica Federico Santa María (Chile)
Stefano Cerri	Université Montpellier II (France)
Ibrahim Chaib-draa	Université Laval (Canada)
Helder Coelho	Universidade de Lisboa (Portugal)
Vincent Corruble	Université Pierre et Marie Curie (France)
Ernesto Costa	Universidade de Coimbra (Portugal)
Anna Helena Reali Costa	Universidade de São Paulo (Brazil)
Antônio C. da Rocha Costa	Universidade Católica de Pelotas (Brazil)
Augusto C.P.L. da Costa	Universidade Federal da Bahia (Brazil)
Evandro de Barros Costa	Universidade Federal de Alagoas (Brazil)
Kerstin Dautenhahn	University of Hertfordshire (UK)
Keith Decker	University of Delaware (USA)
Marco Dorigo	Université Libre de Bruxelles (Belgium)
Michael Fisher	University of Liverpool (UK)
Peter Flach	University of Bristol (UK)
Ana Cristina Bicharra Garcia	Universidade Federal Fluminense (Brazil)
Uma Garimella	AP State Council for Higher Education (India)
Lúcia Giraffa	Pontifícia Universidade Católica, RS (Brazil)
Claudia Goldman	University of Massachusetts, Amherst (USA)
Fernando Gomide	Universidade Estadual de Campinas (Brazil)
Gabriela Henning	Universidad Nacional del Litoral (Argentina)
Michael Huhns	University of South Carolina (USA)
Nitin Indurkhya	University of New South Wales (Australia)
Alípio Jorge	University of Porto (Portugal)
Celso Antônio Alves Kaestner	Pontifícia Universidade Católica, PR (Brazil)

Franziska Klügl   Universität Würzburg (Germany)
Sofiane Labidi   Universidade Federal do Maranhão (Brazil)
Lluis Godo Lacasa   Artificial Intelligence Research Institute (Spain)
Marcelo Ladeira   Universidade de Brasília (Brazil)
Nada Lavrac   Josef Stefan Institute (Slovenia)
Christian Lemaitre   Lab. Nacional de Informatica Avanzada (Mexico)
Victor Lesser   University of Massachusetts, Amherst (USA)
Vera Lúcia Strube de Lima   Pontifícia Universidade Católica, RS (Brazil)
Jose Gabriel Pereira Lopes   Universidade Nova de Lisboa (Portugal)
Michael Luck   University of Southampton (UK)
Ana Teresa Martins   Universidade Federal do Ceará (Brazil)
Stan Matwin   University of Ottawa (Canada)
Eduardo Miranda   University of Plymouth (UK)
Maria Carolina Monard   Universidade de São Paulo at São Carlos (Brazil)
Valérie Monfort   MDT Vision (France)
Eugenio Costa Oliveira   Universidade do Porto (Portugal)
Tarcisio Pequeno   Universidade Federal do Ceará (Brazil)
Paolo Petta   Austrian Research Institut for Artificial
                                     Intelligence (Austria)
Geber Ramalho   Universidade Federal de Pernambuco (Brazil)
Solange Rezende   Universidade de São Paulo at São Carlos (Brazil)
Carlos Ribeiro   Instituto Tecnológico de Aeronáutica (Brazil)
Francesco Ricci   Istituto Trentino di Cultura (Italy)
Sandra Sandri   Artificial Intelligence Research Institute (Spain)
Sandip Sen   University of Tulsa (USA)
Jaime Simão Sichman   Universidade de São Paulo (Brazil)
Carles Sierra   Institut d'Investigació en Intel. Artificial (Spain)
Milind Tambe   University of Southern California (USA)
Patricia Tedesco   Universidade Federal de Pernambuco (Brazil)
Sergio Tessaris   Free University of Bozen-Bolzano (Italy)
Luis Torgo   University of Porto (Portugal)
Andre Valente   Knowledge Systems Ventures (USA)
Wamberto Vasconcelos   University of Aberdeen (UK)
Rosa Maria Vicari   Univ. Federal do Rio Grande do Sul (Brazil)
Renata Vieira   UNISINOS (Brazil)
Jacques Wainer   Universidade Estadual de Campinas (Brazil)
Renata Wasserman   Universidade de São Paulo (Brazil)
Michael Wooldridge   University of Liverpool (UK)
Franco Zambonelli   Università di Modena Reggio Emilia (Italy)
Gerson Zaverucha   Universidade Federal do Rio de Janeiro (Brazil)

Sponsoring Organizations

By the publication of this volume, the SBIA 2004 conference received financial support from the following institutions:

CNPq	Conselho Nacional de Desenvolvimento Científico e Tecnológico
CAPES	Fundação Coordenação de Aperfeiçoamento de Pessoal de Nível Superior
FAPEMA	Fundação de Amparo à Pesquisa do Estado do Maranhão
FINEP	Financiadora de Estudos e Projetos

Additional Reviewers

Mara Abel
Nik Nailah Bint Abdullah
Diana Adamatti
Stephane Airiau
João Fernando Alcântara
Teddy Alfaro
Luis Almeida
Marcelo Armentano
Dipyaman Banerjee
Dante Augusto Couto Barone
Gustavo Batista
Amit Bhaya
Reinaldo Bianchi
Francine Bica
Waldemar Bonventi
Flávio Bortolozzi
Mohamed Bouklit
Paolo Bouquet
Carlos Fisch de Brito
Tiberio Caetano
Eduardo Camponogara
Teddy Candale
Henrique Cardoso
Ariadne Carvalho
André Ponce de Leon F. de Carvalho
Ana Casali
Adelmo Cechin
Luciano Coutinho
Damjan Demsar
Clare Dixon
Fabrício Enembreck
Paulo Engel
Alexandre Evsukoff
Anderson Priebe Ferrugem
Marcelo Finger
Ricardo Freitas
Leticia Friske
Arjita Ghosh
Daniela Godoy
Alex Sandro Gomes
Silvio Gonnet
Marco Antonio Insaurriaga Gonzalez
Roderich Gross
Michel Habib

Juan Heguiabehere
Emilio Hernandez
Benjamin Hirsch
Jomi Hübner
Ullrich Hustadt
Alceu de Souza Britto Junior
Branko Kavsek
Alessandro Lameiras Koerich
Boris Konev
Fred Koriche
Luís Lamb
Michel Liquière
Peter Ljubic
Andrei Lopatenko
Gabriel Lopes
Emiliano Lorini
Teresa Ludermir
Alexei Manso Correa Machado
Charles Madeira
Pierre Maret
Graça Marietto
Lilia Martins
Claudio Meneses
Claudia Milaré
Márcia Cristina Moraes
Álvaro Moreira
Ranjit Nair
Marcio Netto
André Neves
Julio Cesar Nievola
Luis Nunes
Maria das Graças Volpe Nunes
Valguima Odakura
Carlos Oliveira
Flávio Oliveira
Fernando Osório
Flávio Pádua
Elias Pampalk
Marcelino Pequeno
Luciano Pimenta
Aloisio Carlos de Pina
Joel Plisson
Ronaldo Prati
Carlos Augusto Prolo

Table of Contents

Logics, Planning, and Theoretical Methods

Search, Reasoning, and Uncertainty

Knowledge Representation and Ontologies

Natural Language Processing

Machine Learning, Knowledge Discovery, and Data Mining

Evolutionary Computation, Artificial Life, and Hybrid Systems

Robotics and Computer Vision

Autonomous Agents and Multi-agent Systems

On Modalities for Vague Notions

Mario Benevides[1,2], Carla Delgado[2], Renata P. de Freitas[2],
Paulo A.S. Veloso[2], and Sheila R.M. Veloso[2]

[1] Instituto de Matemática
[2] Programa de Engenharia de Sistemas e Computação, COPPE
Universidade Federal do Rio de Janeiro, Caixa Postal 68511, 21945-970
Rio de Janeiro, RJ, Brasil
{mario,delgado,naborges,veloso,sheila}@cos.ufrj.br

Abstract. We examine modal logical systems, with generalized operators, for the precise treatment of vague notions such as 'often', 'a meaningful subset of a whole', 'most', 'generally' etc. The intuition of 'most'
as "all but for a 'negligible' set of exceptions" is made precise by means
of filters. We examine a modal logic, with a new modality for a local
version of 'most' and present a sound and complete axiom system. We
also discuss some variants of this modal logic.

Keywords: Modal logic, vague notions, most, filter, knowledge representation.

1 Introduction

We examine modal logical systems, with generalized operators, for the precise
treatment of assertions involving some versions of vague notions such as 'often',
'a meaningful subset of a whole', 'most', 'generally' etc. We wish to express these
vague notions and reason about them.

Vague notions, such as those mentioned above, occur often in ordinary language and in some branches of science, some examples being "most bodies ex-
pand when heated" and "typical birds fly". Vague terms such as 'likely' and
'prone' are often used in more elaborate expressions involving 'propensity', e.g.
"A patient whose genetic background indicates a certain propensity is prone
to some ailments". A precise treatment of these notions is required for reasoning about them. Generalized quantifiers have been employed to capture some
traditional mathematical notions [2] and defaults [10]. A logic with various generalized quantifiers has been suggested to treat quantified sentences in natural
language [1] and an extension of first-order logic with generalized quantifiers for
capturing a sense of 'generally' is presented in [5]. The idea of this approach
is formulating 'most' as 'holding almost universally'. This seems quite natural,
once we interpret 'most' as "all, but for a 'negligible' set of exceptions".

Modal logics are specification formalisms which are simpler to be handled
than first-order logic, due to the hiding of variables and quantifiers through the
modal operators (box and diamond). In this paper we present a modal counterpart of filter logic, internalizing the generalized quantifier through a new

A.L.C. Bazzan and S. Labidi (Eds.): SBIA 2004, LNAI 3171, pp. 1–10, 2004.

modality ∇ whose behavior is intermediate between those of the classical modal operators $\square$ and $\lozenge$. Thus one will be able to express "a reply to a message will be received almost always": ∇receive-reply, "eventually a reply to a message will be received almost always": $\lozenge\nabla$receive-reply, "the system generally operates correctly": ∇correct-operation, etc.

An important class of problems involves the stable property detection. In a more concrete setting consider the following situation. A stable property is one which once it becomes true it remains true forever: deadlock, termination and loss of a token are examples. In these problems, processes communicate by sending and receiving messages. A process can record its own state and the messages it sends and receives, nothing else.

Many problems in distributed systems can be solved by detecting global states. An example of this kind of algorithm is the Chandy and Lamport Distributed Snapshots algorithm for determining global states of distributed systems [6]. Each process records its own state and the two processes that a channel is incident on cooperate in recording the channel state. One cannot ensure that the states of all processes and channels will be recorded at the same instant, because there is no global clock, however, we require that the recorded process and channel states form a *meaningful* global state. The following text illustrates this problem [6]: "The state detection algorithm plays the role of a group of photographers observing a panoramic, dynamic scene, such as a sky filled with migrating birds – a scene so vast that it cannot be captured by a single photograph. The photographers must take several snapshots and piece the snapshots together to form a picture of the overall scene. The snapshots cannot all be taken at precisely the same instant because of synchronization problems. Furthermore, the photographers should not disturb the process that is being photographed; (...) Yet, the composite picture should be meaningful. The problem before us is to define 'meaningful' and then to determine how the photographs should be taken."

If we take the modality ∇ to capture the notion of meaningful, then the formula $\nabla\phi$ means: "ϕ is true in a meaningful set of states". Returning to the example of Chandy and Lamport Algorithm, the formula:

$$(\nabla(\bigwedge_{i,j=1..n} (\phi_i \wedge \psi_j \wedge \theta_{ij})) \rightarrow \square\gamma)$$

would mean "if in a meaningful set of states, for each pair of processes i and j, the snapshot of process i's local state has property ϕ_i, snapshot of process j has property ψ_j and the snapshot of the state of channel ij has property θ_{ij}, then it is always the case that global stable property γ holds forever". So we can express relationships among local process states, global system states and distributed computation's properties even if we cannot perfectly identify the global state at each time; for the purpose of evaluating stable properties, a set of meaningful states that can be figured out from the local snapshots collected should suffice.

Another interesting example comes from Game Theory. In Extensive Games with Imperfect Information (well defined in [9]), a player may not be sure about the complete past history that has already been played. But, based on a meaningful part of the history he/she has in mind, he/she may still be able to decide which action to choose. The following formula can express this fact

$$\Box((\mathsf{turn}_i \wedge \nabla(\phi_1 \wedge \cdots \wedge \phi_n)) \rightarrow \mathsf{perform\text{-}action}(a))$$

The formula above means: "it is always the case that, if it is player's i turn and properties $\phi_1, \cdots, \phi_n$ are true in a meaningful part of his/her history, then player i should choose action a to perform". This is in fact the way many absent-minded players reason, especially in games with lots of turns like 'War', Chess, or even a financial market game.

We present a sound and complete axiomatization for generalized modal logic as a first step towards the development of a modal framework for generalized logics where one can take advantage of the existing frameworks for modal logics extending them to these logics.

The structure of this paper is as follows. We begin by motivating families, such as filters, for capturing some intuitive ideas of 'generally'. Next, we briefly review a system for reasoning about generalized assertions in Sect. 3. In Sect. 4, we introduce our modal filter logic. In Sect. 5 we comment on how to adapt our ideas to some variants of vague modal logics. Sect. 6 gives some concluding remarks.

2 Assigning Precise Meaning to Generalized Notions

We now indicate how one can arrive at the idea of filters [4] for capturing some intuitive ideas of 'most', 'meaningful', etc. Our approach relies on the familiar intuition of 'most' as "all but for a 'negligible' set of exceptions" as well as on some related notions. We discuss, trying to explain, some issues in the treatment of 'most', and the same approach can be applied in treating 'meaningful', 'often', etc.

2.1 Some Accounts for 'Most'

Various interpretations seem to be associated with vague notions of 'most'. The intended meaning of "most objects have a given property" can be given either directly, in terms of the set of objects having the property, or by means of the set of exceptions, those failing to have it. In either case, a precise formulation hinges on some ideas concerning these sets. We shall now examine some proposals stemming from accounts for 'most'.

Some accounts for 'most' try to explain it in terms of relative frequency or size. For instance, one would understand "most Brazilians like football" as the "the Brazilians that like football form a 'likely' portion", with more than, say, 75% of the population, or "the Brazilians that like football form a 'large' set", in that their number is above, say, 120 million. These accounts of 'most' may be termed "metric", as they try to reduce it to a measurable aspect, so to speak. They seek to explicate "most people have property φ" as "the people having φ form a 'likely' (or 'large') set", i.e. a set having 'high' relative frequency (or cardinality), with 'high' understood as above a given threshold. The next example shows a relaxed variant of these metric accounts.

Example 1. Imagine that one accepts the assertions "most naturals are larger than fifteen" and "most naturals do not divide twelve" about the universe of natural numbers. Then, one would probably accept also the assertions:

($\vee$) "Most naturals are larger than fifteen or even"
($\wedge$) "Most naturals are larger than fifteen and do not divide twelve"

Acceptance of the first two assertions, as well as inferring ($\vee$) from them, might be explained by metric accounts, but this does not seem to be the case with assertion ($\wedge$). A possible account for this situation is as follows. Both sets F, of naturals below fifteen, and T, of divisors of twelve, are finite. So, their union still form a finite set.

This example uses an account based on sizes of the extensions: it explains "most naturals have property φ" as "the naturals failing to have φ form a 'small' set", where 'small' is taken as finite. Similarly, one would interpret "most reals are irrational" as "the rational reals form a 'small' set", with 'small' now understood as (at most) denumerable. This account is still quantitative, but more relaxed. It explicates "most objects have property φ" as "those failing to have φ form a 'small' set", in a given sense of 'small'.

As more neutral names encompassing these notions, we prefer to use 'sizable', instead of 'large' or 'likely', and 'negligible' for 'unlikely' or 'small'. The previous terms are vague, the more so with the new ones. This, however, may be advantageous. The reliance on a – somewhat arbitrary – threshold is less stringent and they have a wider range of applications, stemming from the liberal interpretation of 'sizable' as carrying considerable weight or importance. Notice that these notions of 'sizable' and 'negligible' are relative to the situation. (In "uninteresting meetings are those attended only by junior staff", the sets including only junior staff members are understood as 'negligible'.)

2.2   Families for 'Most'

We now indicate how the preceding ideas can be conveyed by means of families, thus leading to filters [4] for capturing some notions of 'most'. One can understand "most birds fly" as "the non-flying birds form a 'negligible' set". This indicates that the intended meaning of "most objects have φ" may be rendered as "the set of objects failing to have φ is negligible", in the sense that it is in a given family of negligible sets. The relative character of 'negligible' (and 'sizable') is embodied in the family of negligible sets, which may vary according to the situation. Such families, however, can be expected to share some general properties, if they are to be appropriate for capturing notions of 'sizable', such as 'large' or 'likely'. Some properties that such a family may, or may not, be expected to have are illustrated in the next example.

Example 2. Imagine that one accepts the assertions:

(β) "Most American males like beer"

(σ) "Most American males like sports" and

(ϵ) "Most American are Democrats or Republicans"

In this case, one is likely to accept also the two assertions:

($\supseteq$) "Most American males like beverages"

($\cap$) "Most American males like beer and sports"

Acceptance of ($\supseteq$) should be clear. As for ($\cap$), its acceptance may be explained by exceptions. (As the exceptional sets of non beer-lovers and of non-sports-lovers have negligibly few elements, it is reasonable to say that "negligibly few American males fail to like beer *or* sports", so "most American males like beer *and* sports".) In contrast, even though one accepts (ϵ), neither one of the assertions "most American males are Democrats" and "most American males are Republicans" seems to be equally acceptable.

This example hinges on the following ideas: if $B \subseteq W$ and B has 'most' elements, then W also has 'most' elements; if both $\overline{B}$ and $\overline{S}$ have 'negligibly few' elements, then $\overline{B} \cup \overline{S}$ will also have 'negligibly few' elements; a union $D \cup R$ may have 'most' elements, without either D or R having 'most' elements.

We now postulate reasonable properties of a family $\mathcal{N} \subseteq \mathcal{P}(V)$ of negligible sets (in the sense of carrying little weight or importance) of a universe V.

($\subseteq$) $X \in \mathcal{N}$ if $X \subseteq N \in \mathcal{N}$, "subsets of negligible sets are negligible".

($\emptyset$) $\emptyset \in \mathcal{N}$, "the empty set $\emptyset$ is negligible".

(V) $V \notin \mathcal{N}$, "the universe V is not negligible".

($\cup$) $N' \cup N'' \in \mathcal{N}$ if $N', N'' \in \mathcal{N}$, "unions of negligible sets are negligible".

These postulates can be explained by means of a notion of 'having about the same importance' [12]. Postulates ($\emptyset$) and (V) concern the non-triviality of our notion of 'negligible'. Also, ($\cup$) is not necessarily satisfied by families that may be appropriate for some weaker notions, such as 'several' or 'many'. In virtue of these postulates, the family $\mathcal{N}$ of negligible sets is non-empty and proper as well as closed under subsets and union, thus forming an ideal. Dually, a family of sizable sets – of those having 'most' elements – is a proper filter (but not necessarily an ultrafilter [4]).

Conversely, each proper filter gives rise to a non-trivial notion of 'most'. Thus, the interpretation of "most objects have property φ" as "the set of objects failing to have φ is negligible" amounts to "the set of objects having φ belongs to a given proper filter". The properties of the family $\mathcal{N}$ are intuitive and coincide with those of ideals. As the notion of 'most' was taken as the dual of 'negligible', it is natural to explain families of sizeable sets in terms of filters (dual of ideals). So, generalized quantifiers, ranging over families of sets [1], appear natural to capture these notions.

3 Filter Logic

Filter logic extends classical first-order logic by a generalised quantifier ∇, whose intended interpretation is 'generally'. In this section we briefly review filter logic: its syntax, semantics and axiomatics.

Given a signature ρ, we let $\mathsf{L}(\rho)$ be the usual first-order language (with equality $\cong$) of signature ρ and use $\mathsf{L}^\nabla(\rho)$ for the extension of $\mathsf{L}(\rho)$ by the new operator ∇. The formulas of $\mathsf{L}^\nabla(\rho)$ are built by the usual formation rules and a new variable-binding formation rule for generalized formulas: for each variable v, if φ is a formula in $\mathsf{L}^\nabla(\rho)$, then so is $\nabla v\varphi$.

Example 3. Consider a signature λ with a binary predicate L (on persons). Let $L(x,y)$ stand for "x loves y". Some assertions expressed by sentences of $\mathsf{L}^\nabla(\lambda)$ are: "people generally love everybody" – $\nabla x\forall yL(x,y)$, "somebody loves people in general" – $\exists x\nabla yL(x,y)$, and "people generally love each other" – $\nabla x\nabla yL(x,y)$. Let $L(x,y)$ be "y is taller than x". We can express "people generally are taller than x" by $\nabla yL(x,y)$ and "x is taller than people in general" by $\nabla yL(y,x)$.

The semantic interpretation for 'generally' is provided by enriching first-order structures with families of subsets and extending the definition of satisfaction to the quantifier ∇.

A *filter structure* $\mathcal{A}^\mathcal{F} = \langle \mathcal{A}, \mathcal{F}\rangle$ for a signature ρ consists of a usual structure $\mathcal{A}$ for ρ together with a filter $\mathcal{F}$ over the universe A of $\mathcal{A}$. We extend the usual definition of *satisfaction* of a formula in a structure under assignment $\underline{a}$ to its (free) variables, using the extension $\mathcal{A}^\mathcal{K}[\varphi(\underline{a}, z)] := \{b \in \mathsf{A} : \mathcal{A}^\mathcal{K} \models \varphi(\underline{u}, z)[\underline{a}, b]\}$, as follows: for a formula $\nabla z\varphi(\underline{u}, z)$, $\mathcal{A}^\mathcal{K} \models \nabla z\varphi(\underline{u}, v)[\underline{a}]$ iff $\mathcal{A}^\mathcal{K}[\varphi(\underline{a}, z)]$ is in $\mathcal{K}$.

As usual, satisfaction of a formula hinges only on the realizations assigned to its symbols. Thus, satisfaction for purely first-order formulas (without ∇) does not depend on the family of subsets. Other semantic notions, such as reduct, model ($\mathcal{A}^\mathcal{K} \models \Gamma$) and validity, are as usual [4, 7]. The behavior of ∇ is intermediate between those of the classical $\forall$ and $\exists$.

A deductive system for the logic of 'generally' is formalized by adding axiom schemata, coding properties of filters, to a calculus for classical first-order logic. To set up a deductive system for filter logic one takes a sound and complete deductive calculus for classical first-order logic, with Modus Ponens (MP) as the sole inference rule (as in [7]), and extend its set A of axiom schemata by adding a set Φ^f of new axiom schemata (coding properties of filters), to form $A^f := A \cup \Phi^f$. This set Φ^f consists of all the generalizations of the following five schemata (where φ, ψ and θ are formulas of $\mathsf{L}^\nabla(\rho)$):

[$\forall\nabla$] $\forall v\varphi \to \nabla v\varphi$;

[$\nabla\exists$] $\nabla v\varphi \to \exists v\varphi$;

[$\to \nabla$] $\forall v(\psi \to \theta) \to (\nabla v\psi \to \nabla v\theta)$;

[$\nabla\wedge$] $(\nabla v\psi \wedge \nabla v\theta) \to \nabla v(\psi \wedge \theta)$;

[$\nabla\alpha$] $\nabla v\varphi \to \nabla u\varphi[v := u]$, for a new variable u not occurring in φ.

These schemata express properties of filters, the last one covering alphabetic variants. Other usual deductive notions, such as (maximal) consistent sets, witnesses and conservative extension [4, 7], can be easily adapted. So, filter derivability amounts to first-order derivability from the filter schemata: $\Gamma \vdash^f \varphi$ iff $\Gamma \cup A^f \vdash \varphi$. Hence, we have monotonicity of $\vdash^f$ and substitutivity of equivalents.

This deductive system is sound and complete for filter logic, which is a proper conservative extension of classical first-order logic. It is not difficult to see that we have a conservative extension of classical logic: $\Delta \vdash \varphi$ iff $\Delta \vdash^f \varphi$, for Δ and

φ without ∇. We have a proper extension of classical logic, because sentences, such as $\exists u \nabla z u \cong z$, cannot be expressed without ∇.

4 Serial Local Filter Logic

In this section, we examine modal logics to deal with vague notions. As pointed out in Sect. 1, these notions play an important role in computing, knowledge representation, natural language processing, game theory, etc.

In order to introduce the main ideas, consider the following situation. Imagine we wish to examine properties of animals and their offspring. For this purpose, we consider a universe of animals and binary relation corresponding to "being an offspring of". Suppose we want to express "every offspring of a black animal is dark"; this can be done by the modal formula black → □dark. Similarly, black → ◊dark expresses "some offsprings of black animals are dark". Now, how do we express the vague assertion "most offsprings of black animals are dark"? A natural candidate would be black → ∇dark, where ∇ is the vague modality for 'most'. Here, we interpret ∇dark as "a sizable portion of the offsprings is dark". Thus, ∇ captures a notion of "most states among the reachable ones". This is a local notion of vagueness. (In the FOL version, sorted generalized quantifiers were used for local notions.) One may also encounter global notions of vagueness. For instance, in "most animals are herbivorous", 'most' does not seem to be linked to the reachable states (see also Sect. 6).

The *alphabet* of *serial local filter logic* (SLF) is that of basic modal logic with a new modality ∇. The *formulas* are obtained by closing the set of formulas of basic modal logic by the rule: $\alpha := \nabla \alpha$.

Frames, models and rooted models of SLF are much as in the basic modal logic. For each $s \in S$, we denote by $_sR = \{t \in S : R(s,t)\}$ the set of states in the frame that are accessible from s. Semantics of the ∇-operator is given by a family of filters $\{F_s\}_{s \in S}$, one for each state in a frame. A model of SLF is 4-tuple $\mathcal{M} = \langle S, R, F, V \rangle$, where $\mathcal{F} = \langle S, R \rangle$ is a serial frame (R is serial, i.e., $_sR \neq \emptyset$, for all $s \in S$), V is a valuation, as usual, and $F = \{F_s\}_{s \in S}$ with $F_s \subseteq 2^{_sR}$, a filter over S, for each $s \in S$.

Satisfaction of a formula α in a rooted arrow model $\langle \mathcal{M}, s \rangle$, denoted by $\mathcal{M}, s \models \alpha$, is defined as in the basic modal logic, with the following extra clause:

$$\mathcal{M}, s \models \nabla \alpha \text{ iff } {_sR} \cap \mathcal{M}[\alpha] \in F_s,$$

with $\mathcal{M} = \langle S, R, \{F_s\}_{s \in S}, V \rangle$ and $\mathcal{M}[\varphi] = \{s \in S : \mathcal{M}, s \models \varphi\}$ being the set of states that satisfies a formula φ in a model $\mathcal{M}$. A formula α is a *consequence* of a set of formulas Γ in SLF, denoted by $\Gamma \models \alpha$, when $\mathcal{M}, s \models \Gamma$ implies $\mathcal{M}, s \models \alpha$, for every rooted arrow model $\langle \mathcal{M}, s \rangle$, as usual.

A deductive system for SLF is obtained by extendind the deductive system for normal modal logic [14] with the axiom $[\Diamond \top] := \Diamond \top$ for seriality and the following modal versions of the axioms for filter first-order logic:

$$[\Box\nabla]\Box\varphi \to \nabla\varphi \qquad\qquad (S \in F_s)$$
$$[\nabla\Diamond]\nabla\varphi \to \Diamond\varphi \qquad\qquad (\emptyset \notin F_s)$$
$$[\to \nabla]\Box(\varphi \to \psi) \to (\nabla\varphi \to \nabla\psi) \quad (F_s \text{ up-closed})$$
$$[\nabla\wedge]\nabla\varphi \wedge \nabla\psi \to \nabla(\varphi \wedge \psi) \qquad (F_s \cap\text{-closed})$$

We write $\Gamma \vdash \alpha$ to express that formula α is derivable from set Γ, in SLF. The notion of derivability is defined as usual, considering the rules of necessitation and Modus Ponens.

Completeness

It is an easy exercise to prove that the Soundness Theorem for SFL, i. e., $\vdash \subseteq \models$. We now prove the Completeness Theorem for SLF, i. e., $\models \subseteq \vdash$. We use the canonical model construction.

We start with the canonical model $\mathcal{M}^C = \langle S^C, R^C, V^C \rangle$ of basic modal logic [3][1]. Since we have axiom $[\Diamond\top]$, model $\mathcal{M}^C$ is a serial model[2].

It remains to define a family F^C of filters over S^C. For this purpose, we will introduce some notation and obtain a few preliminary results.

Define $[\varphi] = \{\Sigma \in S^C : \varphi \in \Sigma\}$, $_\Sigma[\varphi] = {_\Sigma}R \cap [\varphi]$, and $K_\Sigma = \{_\Sigma[\varphi] \subseteq S^C : \nabla\varphi \in \Sigma\}$.

Proposition 1. *For every $\Sigma \in S^C$, (i) $_\Sigma R \in K_\Sigma$, (ii) $\emptyset \notin K_\Sigma$, and (iii) K_Σ is closed under intersection.*

Proof. (i) For all $\Sigma \in S^C$, $\top \in \Sigma$ (as Σ is an MCS). Thus, $_\Sigma[\top] = {_\Sigma}R \cap [\top] = {_\Sigma}R$. Given $\Sigma \in S^C$, by Necessitation and $[\Box\nabla]$, we have $\nabla\top \in \Sigma$. Thus $_\Sigma R \in K_\Sigma \neq \emptyset$. (ii) Assume $\emptyset \in K_\Sigma$. Then, for some formula φ, we have $_\Sigma[\varphi] = \emptyset$, i. e., $\nabla\varphi \in \Sigma$, for some φ. By $(\Diamond\nabla)$, we have $\Diamond\varphi \in \Sigma$, i. e., there is some $\Delta \in {_\Sigma}R$ with $\varphi \in \Sigma$. But since $_\Sigma[\varphi] = \emptyset$, for all $\Delta \in {_\Sigma}R$, $\varphi \notin \Delta$, a contradiction. (iii) From $[\nabla\wedge]$ we have $_\Sigma[\varphi] \cap {_\Sigma}[\psi] = {_\Sigma}[\varphi \wedge \psi]$. ∎

As a result, each family K_Σ has the finite intersection property. Now, let F_Σ be the closure of K_Σ under supersets. Note that F_Σ is a proper filter over $_\Sigma R$.

Proposition 2. $_\Sigma[\theta] \in K_\Sigma$ *iff* $_\Sigma[\theta] \in F_\Sigma$.

Proof. ($\Longrightarrow$) Clear. ($\Longleftarrow$) Suppose $_\Sigma[\theta] \in F_\Sigma$. Then, $_\Sigma[\theta] \supseteq {_\Sigma}[\varphi]$, for some $_\Sigma[\varphi] \in K_\Sigma$ (i. e., $_\Sigma[\theta] \supseteq {_\Sigma}[\varphi]$ and $\nabla\varphi \in \Sigma$, for some φ.) Now, $\Box(\varphi \to \theta) \in \Sigma$ [3]. Thus, by $[\to \nabla]$ and $\nabla\varphi \in \Sigma$, we have $\nabla\theta \in \Sigma$. Hence, $_\Sigma[\theta] \in K_\Sigma$. ∎

Define F^C to be $\{F_\Sigma : \Sigma \in S^C\}$. Define the canonical SLF model to be $\mathcal{M}^F = \langle S^C, R^C, F^C, V^C \rangle$. Then we can prove the Satisfiability Lemma ($\mathcal{M}^F, \Sigma \models \phi$ iff $\phi \in \Sigma$), by induction on formulas. Completeness is an easy corollary.

---

[1] S^C is the set of maximal consistent sets of formulæ.

[2] Recall that $R^C(\Gamma, \Delta)$ iff $\forall\varphi, \varphi \in \Delta \Longrightarrow \Diamond\varphi \in \Gamma$ and $_\Gamma R = \{\Delta \in S^C : R^C(\Gamma, \Delta)\}$. Also, given $\Gamma \in S^C$, if $\Diamond\varphi \in \Gamma$, then there is some $\Delta \in {_\Gamma}R$ s. t. $\varphi \in \Delta$ [3].

[3] If $_\Sigma[\theta] \supseteq {_\Sigma}[\varphi] \in K_\Sigma$, then $\Box(\varphi \to \theta) \in \Sigma$, for if $\Box(\varphi \to \theta) \notin \Sigma$, then there exists $\Delta \in {_\Sigma}R$ s. t. $\varphi \to \theta \notin \Delta$. Thus $\varphi \wedge \neg\theta \in \Delta$ (by consistency and maximality), i. e., $\varphi \in \Delta$ and $\theta \notin \Delta$. Thus we have $\Delta \in {_\Sigma}[\varphi] \subseteq {_\Sigma}[\theta]$, as $\varphi \in \Delta$ and $\Delta \in {_\Sigma}R$. Hence $\theta \in \Delta$, a contradiction.

5   Variants of Vague Modal Logics

We now comment on some variants of vague modal logics.

Variants of Local Filter Logics. First note that the choice of serial models is a natural one, in the presence of $[\Box\nabla]$ and $[\nabla\Diamond]$, i. e., $[\Box\nabla], [\nabla\Diamond] \vdash \Box\phi \rightarrow \Diamond\phi$, whence $\Box\top \vdash \Diamond\top$. An alternative choice would be non-serial local filter logics where one takes a filter over the extended universe ${}_sR^0 = \{s\} \cup {}_sR$, for each $s \in S$ and the corresponding axiom system $\{[\rightarrow \nabla], [\nabla\wedge], [\rightarrow \Box], [\Box\Diamond]\} + \{[\Box\nabla'], [\nabla\Diamond']\}$, where $[\Box\nabla'] := \Box\phi \wedge \phi \rightarrow \nabla\phi$, $[\nabla\Diamond'] := \nabla\phi \rightarrow \phi \vee \Diamond\phi$, and $[\Box\Diamond] := \Box\phi \rightarrow \Diamond\phi$, with $\mathcal{M}, s \models \nabla\alpha$ iff ${}_sR^0 \cap \mathcal{M}[\alpha]$. Soundness and completeness can be obtained in analogous fashion.

Other Local Modal Logics. Serial local filter axioms encodes properties of filters through $[\rightarrow \nabla]$ – closed under supersets, $[\nabla\wedge]$ – closed under intersections, and $[\nabla\Diamond]$ – non-emptyness axioms. Our approach is modular being easily adapted to encode properties of other structures, e. g., to encode families that are up-closed, one removes axiom $[\nabla\wedge]$, to encode lattices one replaces $[\rightarrow \nabla]$ axiom by the $[\nabla\vee]$, where $[\nabla\vee] := \nabla\phi \wedge \nabla\psi \rightarrow \nabla(\phi \vee \psi)$. For those systems one obtains soundness and completeness results with respect to semantics of the ∇-operator being given by a family of up-closed sets and a family of lattices, respectively, along the same lines we provided for SLF logics.(In these cases, one takes $F_\Sigma = K_\Sigma$ in the construction of the canonical model.)

6   Conclusions

Assertions and arguments involving vague notions, such as 'generally', 'most' and 'typical' occur often in ordinary language and in some branches of science. Modal logics are specification mechanisms simpler to handle than first-order logic.

We have examined a modal logic, with a new generality modality for expressing and reasoning about a local version of 'most' as motivated by the hereditary example in Sect. 4. We presented a sound and complete axiom system for local generalized modal logic, where the locality aspect corresponds to the intended meaning of the generalized modality: "most of the reachable states have the property". (We thank one of the referees for an equivalent axiomatization for SLF. It seems that it works only for filters, being more difficult to adapt to other structures.)

Some global generalized notions could appear in ordinary language, for instance; "most black animals will have most offspring dark". The first occurrence of 'most' is global (among all animals) while the second is a local one (referring to most offspring of each black animal considered). In this case one could have two generalized operators: a global one, $\underline{\nabla}$, and a local one, ∇. Semantically $\underline{\nabla}$ would refer to a filter (over the set of states) in a way analogous to the universal modality [8].

Other variants of generalized modal logics occur when one considers multi-modal generalized logics as motivated by the following example. In a chess game setting, a state is a chessboard configuration. States can be related by different ways, depending on which piece is moved. Thus, one would have $Q(s,t)$ for: t is a chessboard configuration resulting from a queen's move (in state s), $P(s,t)$ for: t is the chessboard configuration resulting from a pawn's move (in state s), etc. This suggests having ∇_P, ∇_Q, etc. Note that with pawn's moves one can reach fewer states of the chessboard than with queen's moves, i. e., $\{t \in S : Q(s,t)\}$ is (absolutely) large, while $\{t \in S : P(s,t)\}$ is not. Thus, we would have $\underline{\nabla}_Q\top$ holding in all states and $\neg\underline{\nabla}_P\top$ not holding in all states. On the other hand, among the pawn's moves many may be good, that is: $\{t \in S : P(s,t), \mathsf{good}(t)\}$ is large within $\{t \in S : P(s,t)\}$ (i. e. $\{t \in S : P(s,t), \mathsf{good}(t)\} \in K_s^P$.)

In this fashion one has a wide spectrum of new modalities and relations among them to be investigated. We hope the ideas presented in this paper provide a first step towards the development of a modal framework for generalized logics where vague notions can be represented and be manipulated in a precise way and the relations among them investigated (e. g. relate important with very important, etc.). By setting this analysis in a modal environment one can further take advantage of the machinery for modal logics [3], adapting it to these logics for vague notions.

References

1. Barwise, J., Cooper, R.: Generalized quantifiers and natural language. *Linguistics and Philosophy* **4** (1981) 159–219
2. Barwise, J., Feferman, S.: *Model-Theoretic Logics*, Springer, New York (1985)
3. Blackburn, P., de Rijke, M., Venema, Y.: *Modal Logic*, Cambridge University Press, Cambridge (2001)
4. Chang, C., Keisler, H.: *Model Theory*, North-Holland, Amsterdam (1973)
5. Carnielli, W., Veloso, P.: Ultrafilter logic and generic reasoning. In *Abstr. Workshop on Logic, Language, Information and Computation*, Recife (1994)
6. Chandy, K., Lamport, L.: Distributed Snapshot: Determining Global States of Distributed Systems. *ACM Transactions on Computer Systems* **3** (1985) 63–75
7. Enderton, H.: *A Mathematical Introduction to Logic*, Academic Press, New York (1972)
8. Goranko, V., Passy, S.: Using the Universal Modality: Gains and Questions. *Journal of Logic and Computation* **2** (1992) 5–30
9. Osborne, M., Rubinstein, A.: *A Course in Game Theory*, MIT, Cambrige (1998)
10. Schelechta, K.: Default as generalized quantifiers. *Journal of Logic and Computation* **5** (1995) 473–494
11. Turner, W.: *Logics for Artificial Intelligence*, Ellis Horwood, Chichester (1984)
12. Veloso, P.: On 'almost all' and some presuppositions. *Manuscrito XXII* (1999) 469–505
13. Veloso, P.: On modulated logics for 'generally'. In *EBL'03* (2003)
14. Venema, Y.: A crash course in arrow logic. In Marx, M., Pólos, L., Masuch, M. (eds.), *Arrow Logic and Multi-Modal logic*, CSLI, Stanford (1996) 3–34

Towards Polynomial Approximations
of Full Propositional Logic

Marcelo Finger*

Departamento de Ciência da Computação, IME-USP
mfinger@ime.usp.br

Abstract. The aim of this paper is to study a family of logics that approximates classical inference, in which every step in the approximation can be decided in polynomial time. For clausal logic, this task has been shown to be possible by Dalal [4, 5]. However, Dalal's approach cannot be applied to full classical logic. In this paper we provide a family of logics, called *Limited Bivaluation Logics*, via a semantic approach to approximation that applies to full classical logic. Two approximation families are built on it. One is parametric and can be used in a depth-first approximation of classical logic. The other follows Dalal's spirit, and with a different technique we show that it performs at least as well as Dalal's polynomial approach over clausal logic.

1 Introduction

Logic has been used in several areas of Artificial Intelligence as a tool for modelling an intelligent agent reasoning capabilities. However, the computational costs associated with logical reasoning have always been a limitation. Even if we restrict ourselves to classical propositional logic, deciding whether a set of formulas logically implies a certain formula is a co-NP-complete problem [9].

To address this problem, researchers have proposed several ways of approximating classical reasoning. Cadoli and Schaerf have proposed the use of approximate entailment as a way of reaching at least partial results when solving a problem completely would be too expensive [13]. Their influential method is *parametric*, that is, a set S of atoms is the basis to define a logic. As we add more atoms to S, we get "closer" to classical logic, and eventually, when S contains all propositional symbols, we reach classical logic. In fact, Schaerf and Cadoli proposed two families of logic, intending to approximate classical entailment from two ends. The S_3 family approximates classical logic from below, in the following sense. Let $\mathcal{P}$ be a set of propositions and $\varnothing \subseteq S' \subseteq S'' \subseteq \ldots \subseteq \mathcal{P}$; let $\models^3_S$ indicate the set of the entailment relation of a logic in the family. Then:

$$\models^3_\varnothing \subseteq \models^3_{S'} \subseteq \models^3_{S''} \subseteq \ldots \subseteq \models^3_\mathcal{P} = \models_{\mathrm{CL}}$$

where CL is classical logic.

* Partly supported by CNPq grant PQ 300597/95-5 and FAPESP project 03/00312-0.

A.L.C. Bazzan and S. Labidi (Eds.): SBIA 2004, LNAI 3171, pp. 11–20, 2004.

Approximating a classical logic from below is useful for efficient theorem proving. Conversely, approximating classical logic from above is useful for *disproving theorems*, which is the satisfiability (SAT) problem and has a similar formulation. In this work we concentrate only in theorem proving and approximations from below.

The notion of approximation is also related with the notion of an *anytime decision procedure*, that is, an algorithm that, if stopped anytime during the computation, provides an approximate answer, that is, an answer of the form "up to logic L_i in the family, the result is/is not provable". This kind of anytime algorithms have been suggested by the proponents of the Knowledge Compilation approach [14, 15], in which a theory was transformed into a set of polynomially decidable Horn-clause theories. However, the compilation process is itself NP-complete.

Dalal's approximation method [4] was the first one designed such that each reasoner in an approximation family can be decided in polynomial time. Dalal's initial approach was algebraic only. A model-theoretic semantics was provided in [5]. However, this approach was restricted to clausal form logic only.

In this work, we generalize Dalal's approach. We create a family of logics of *Limited Bivalence* (LB) that approximates full propositional logic. We provide a model-theoretic semantics and two entailment relations based on it. The entailment $\models_\Sigma^{\mathsf{LB}}$ is a parametric approximation on the set of formulas Σ and follows Cadoli and Schaerf's approximation paradigm. The entailment $\models_k^{\mathsf{LB}}$ follows Dalal's approach and we show that for clausal form theories, the inference $\models_k^{\mathsf{LB}}$ is polynomially decidable and serves as a semantics for Dalal's inference $\vdash_k^{\mathsf{BCP}}$.

This family of approximations is useful in defining families of efficiently decidable formulas with increasing complexity. In this way, we can define the set $\Gamma_k = \{\alpha |\models_k^{\mathsf{LB}} \alpha \text{ and } k\}$ of tractable theorems, such that $\Gamma_k \subseteq \Gamma_{k+1}$.

This paper proceeds as follows. Next section briefly presents Dalal's approximation strategy, its semantics and discuss its limitations. In Section 3 we present the family $\mathsf{LB}(\Sigma)$ of Limited Bivaluation Logics; the semantics for full propositional $\mathsf{LB}(\Sigma)$ is provided in Section 3.1; a parametric entailment $\models_\Sigma^{\mathsf{LB}}$ is presented in Section 3.2. The entailment $\models_k^{\mathsf{LB}}$ is presented in Section 3.4 and the soundness and completeness of Dalal's $\vdash_k^{\mathsf{BCP}}$ with respect to $\models_k^{\mathsf{LB}}$ is Shown in Sections 3.3 and 3.4.

Notation: Let $\mathcal{P}$ be a countable set of propositional letters. We concentrate on the classical propositional language $\mathcal{L}_C$ formed by the usual boolean connectives $\rightarrow$ (implication), $\wedge$ (conjunction), $\vee$ (disjunction) and $\neg$ (negation).

Throughout the paper, we use lowercase Latin letters to denote propositional letters, α, β, γ denote formulas, φ, ψ denote clauses and λ denote a literal. Uppercase Greek letters denote sets of formulas. By atoms(α) we mean the set of all propositional letters in the formula α; if Σ is a set of formulas, atoms(Σ) = $\bigcup_{\alpha \in \Sigma}$ atoms(α).

Due to space limitations, some proofs of lemmas have been omitted.

2 Dalal's Polynomial Approximation Strategy

Dalal specifies a family of anytime reasoners based on an equivalence relation between formulas [4]. The family is composed of a sequence of reasoners $\vdash_0, \vdash_1$,..., such that each $\vdash_i$ is tractable, each $\vdash_{i+1}$ is at least as complete (with respect to classical logic) as $\vdash_i$, and for each theory there is a complete $\vdash_i$ to reason with it.

The equivalence relation that serves as a basis for the construction of a family has to obey several restrictions to be *admissible*, namely it has to be *sound, modular, independent, irredundand* and *simplifying* [4].

Dalal provides as an example a family of reasoners based on the classically sound but incomplete inference rule known as BCP (Boolean Constraint Propagation) [12], which is a variant of unit resolution [3]. For the initial presentation, no proof-theoretic or model-theoretic semantics were provided for BCP, but an algebraic presentation of an equivalence relation $=_{\text{BCP}}$ was provided. For that, consider a theory as a set of clauses, where a disjunction of zero literals is denoted by $\mathbf{f}$ and the conjunction of zero clauses is denoted $\mathbf{t}$. Let $\neg p$ denote the negation of the atom p, and let $\sim\psi$ be the *complement* of the formula ψ obtained by pushing the negation inside in the usual way using De Morgan's Laws until the atoms are reached, at which point $\sim p = \neg p$ and $\sim \neg p = p$.

The equivalence relation $=_{\text{BCP}}$ is then defined as:

$$\{\mathbf{f}\} \cup \Gamma =_{\text{BCP}} \{\mathbf{f}\}$$
$$\{\lambda, \sim\lambda \vee \lambda_1 \vee \ldots \vee \lambda_n\} \cup \Gamma =_{\text{BCP}} \{\lambda, \lambda_1 \vee \ldots \vee \lambda_n\} \cup \Gamma$$

where λ, λ_i are literals.

The idea is to use an equivalence relation to generate an inference in which ψ can be inferred from Γ if $\Gamma \cup \{\sim\psi\}$ is equivalent to an inconsistency. In this way, the inference $\vdash_{\text{BCP}}$ is defined as $\Gamma \vdash_{\text{BCP}} \psi$ iff $\Gamma \cup \{\sim\psi\} =_{\text{BCP}} \{\mathbf{f}\}$.

Dalal presents an example[1] in which, for the theory $\Gamma_0 = \{p \vee q, p \vee \neg q, \neg p \vee s \vee t, \neg p \vee s \vee \neg t\}$ we both have $\Gamma_0 \vdash_{\text{BCP}} p$ and $\Gamma_0, p \vdash_{\text{BCP}} s$ but $\Gamma_0 \nvdash_{\text{BCP}} s$.

This example shows that $\vdash_{\text{BCP}}$ is unable to use a previously inferred clause p to infer s. Based on this fact comes the proposal of an anytime family of reasoners.

2.1 The Family of Reasoners

Dalal defines a family of incomplete reasoners $\vdash_0^{\text{BCP}}, \vdash_1^{\text{BCP}}$,..., where each $\vdash_k^{\text{BCP}}$ is given by the following:

$$1.\ \frac{\Gamma \vdash_{\text{BCP}} \varphi}{\Gamma \vdash_k^{\text{BCP}} \varphi} \qquad 2.\ \frac{\Gamma \vdash_k^{\text{BCP}} \psi \qquad \Gamma, \psi \vdash_k^{\text{BCP}} \varphi}{\Gamma \vdash_k^{\text{BCP}} \varphi} \text{ for } |\psi| \le k$$

where the size of a clause ψ, $|\psi|$ is the number of literals it contains.

---

[1] This example is extracted from [5].

The first rule tells us that every $\vdash_{\mathrm{BCP}}$-inference is also a $\vdash_k^{\mathrm{BCP}}$-inference. The second rule tells us that if ψ was inferred from a theory and it can be used as a further hypothesis to infer φ, and the size of ψ is at most k, then φ is can also be inferred from the theory.

Dalal shows that this is indeed an anytime family of reasoners, that is, for each k, $\vdash_k^{\mathrm{BCP}}$ is tractable, $\vdash_{k+1}^{\mathrm{BCP}}$ is as complete as $\vdash_k^{\mathrm{BCP}}$ and if you remove the restriction on the size of ψ in rule 2, then $\vdash_k^{\mathrm{BCP}}$ becomes complete, that is, for each classically inferable $\Gamma \vdash \varphi$ there is a k such that $\Gamma \vdash_k^{\mathrm{BCP}} \varphi$.

2.2   Semantics

In [5], Dalal proposed a semantics for $\vdash_k^{\mathrm{BCP}}$ based on the notion of k-*valuations*, which we briefly present here.

Dalal's semantics is defined for sets of clauses. Given a clause ψ, the *support set* of ψ, $S(\psi)$ is defined as the set of all literals occurring in ψ. Support sets ignore multiple occurrences of the same literal and are used to extend valuations from atoms to clauses. According to Dalal's semantics, a propositional valuation is a function $v : \mathcal{P} \to [0,1]$; note that the valuation maps atoms to real numbers. A valuation is then extended to literals and clauses in the following way:

1. $v(\neg p) = 1 - v(p)$ for any atom $p \in \mathcal{P}$.
2. $v(\psi) = \sum_{\lambda \in S(\psi)} v(\lambda)$, for any clause ψ.

Valuations of literals are real numbers in $[0,1]$, but valuations of clauses are non-negative real numbers that can exceed 1. A valuation v is a *model* of ψ if $v(\psi) \geq 1$. A valuation is a countermodel of ψ if $v(\psi) = 0$. Therefore it is possible for a formula to have neither a model nor a countermodel. For instance, if $v(p) = v(q) = 0.2$, then $p \vee q$ has neither a model nor a countermodel. A valuation is a model of a theory (set of clauses) if it is a model of all clauses in it.

Define $\Gamma \approx \psi$ iff no model of the theory Γ is a countermodel of ψ.

Proposition 1 ([5]). *For every theory Γ and every clause ψ, $\Gamma \vdash_{\mathrm{BCP}} \psi$ iff $\Gamma \approx \psi$.*

So $\vdash_{\mathrm{BCP}}$ is sound and complete with respect to $\approx$. The next step is to generalize this approach to obtain a semantics of $\vdash_k^{\mathrm{BCP}}$. For that, for any $k \geq 0$, a set V of valuations is a k-*valuation* iff for each clause ψ of size at most k, if V has a non-model of ψ then V has a countermodel of ψ. V is a k-*model* of ψ if each $v \in V$ is a model of ψ; this notion extends to theories as usual.

It is then possible to define $\Gamma \approx_k \psi$ iff there is no countermodel of ψ in any k-model of Γ.

Proposition 2 ([5]). *For every theory Γ and every clause ψ, $\Gamma \vdash_k^{\mathrm{BCP}} \psi$ iff $\Gamma \approx_k \psi$.*

Thus the inference $\vdash_k^{\mathrm{BCP}}$ is sound and complete with respect to $\approx_k$.

2.3 Analysis of $\vdash_k^{BCP}$

Dalal's notion of a family of anytime reasoners has very nice properties. First, every step in the approximation is sound and can be decided in polynomial time. Second, the approximation is guaranteed to converge to classical inference. Third, every step in the approximation has a sound and complete semantics, enabling an anytime approximation process.

However, the method based on $\vdash_k^{BCP}$-approximations also has its limitations:

1. It only applies to clausal form formulas. Although every propositional formula is classically equivalent to a set of clauses, this equivalence may not be preserved in any of the approximation steps. The conversion of a formula to clausal form is costly: one either has to add new propositional letters (increasing the complexity of the problem) or the number of clauses can be exponential in the size of the original formula. With regards to complexity, BCP is a form of resolution, and it is known that there are theorems that can be proven by resolution only in exponentially many steps [2].

2. Its non-standard semantics makes it hard to compare with other logics known in the literature, specially other approaches to approximation. Also, the semantics presented is based on support sets, which makes it impossible to generalize to non-clausal formulas.

3. The proof-theory for $\vdash_k^{BCP}$ is poor in computational terms. In fact, if we are trying to prove that $\Gamma \vdash_k^{BCP} \varphi$, and we have shown that $\Gamma \nvdash_{BCP} \varphi$, then we would have to guess a ψ with $|\psi| \leq k$, so that $\Gamma \vdash_k^{BCP} \psi$ and $\Gamma, \psi \vdash_k^{BCP} \varphi$. Since the BCP-approximations provide no method to guess the formula ψ, this means that a computation would have to generate and test all the $O((2n)^k)$ possible clauses, where n is the number of propositional symbols occurring in Γ and φ.

In the rest of this paper, we address problems 1 and 2 above. That is, we are going to present a family of anytime reasoners for the full fragment of propositional logic, in which every approximation step has a semantics and can be decided in polynomial time. Problem 3 will be treated in further work.

3 The Family of Logics LB(Σ)

We present here the family of logics of *Limited Bivalence*, LB(Σ). This is a parametric family that approximates classical logic, in which every approximation step can be decided in polynomial time. Unlike $\vdash_k^{BCP}$, LB(Σ) is parameterized by a set of formulas Σ; when Σ contains all formulas of size at most k, LB(Σ) can simulate an approximation step of $\vdash_k^{BCP}$.

The family LB(Σ) can be applied to the full language of propositional logic, and not only to clausal form formulas, with an alphabet consisting of a countable set of propositional letters (atoms) $\mathcal{P} = \{p_0, p_1, \ldots\}$, and the connectives $\neg$, $\wedge$, $\vee$ and $\rightarrow$, and the usual definition of well-formed propositional formulas; the set of all well-formed formulas is denoted by $\mathcal{L}$. The presentation of LB is made in terms of a model theoretic semantics.

3.1   Semantics of LB(Σ)

The semantics of LB(Σ) is based of a three-level lattice, $(L, \sqcap, \sqcup, 0, 1)$, where L is a countable set of elements $L = \{0, 1, \varepsilon_0, \varepsilon_1, \varepsilon_2, \ldots\}$, $\sqcup$ is the least upper bound, $\sqcap$ is the gratest lower bound, and $\sqsubseteq$ is defined, as usual, as $a \sqsubseteq b$ iff $a \sqcup b = b$ iff $a \sqcap b = a$; 1 is the $\sqsubseteq$-top and 0 is the $\sqsubseteq$-bottom. L is subject to the conditions: (i) $0 \sqsubseteq \varepsilon_i \sqsubseteq 1$, for every $i < \omega$; and (ii) $\varepsilon_i \not\sqsubseteq \varepsilon_j$ for $i \neq j$. This three-level lattice is illustrated in Figure 3.1(a).

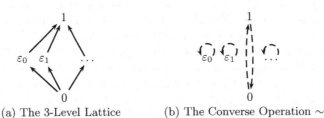

(a) The 3-Level Lattice   (b) The Converse Operation $\sim$

This lattice is enhanced with a *converse operation*, $\sim$, defined as: $\sim 0 = 1$, $\sim 1 = 0$ and $\sim \varepsilon_i = \varepsilon_i$ for all $i < \omega$. This is illustrated in Figure 3.1(b).

We next define the notion of an *unlimited valuation*, and then we present its limitations. An unlimited propositional valuation is a function $v_\Sigma : \mathcal{P} \to L$ that maps atoms to elements of the lattice. We extend v_Σ to all propositional formulas, $v_\Sigma : \mathcal{L} \to L$, in the following way:

$$v_\Sigma(\neg \alpha) = \sim v_\Sigma(\alpha)$$
$$v_\Sigma(\alpha \wedge \beta) = v_\Sigma(\alpha) \sqcap v_\Sigma(\beta)$$
$$v_\Sigma(\alpha \vee \beta) = v_\Sigma(\alpha) \sqcup v_\Sigma(\beta)$$
$$v_\Sigma(\alpha \to \beta) = (\sim v_\Sigma(\alpha)) \sqcup v_\Sigma(\beta)$$

A formula can be mapped to any element of the lattice. However, the formulas that belong to the set Σ are bivalent, that is, they can only be mapped to the top or the bottom element of the lattice. Therefore, a *limited valuation* must satisfy the restriction of Limited Bivalence given by, for every $\alpha \in \mathcal{L}$:

$$v_\Sigma(\alpha) = 0 \text{ or } v_\Sigma(\alpha) = 1, \text{ if } \alpha \in \Sigma.$$

In the rest of this work, by a valuation v_Σ we mean a limited valuation subject to the condition above.

A valuation v_Σ *satisfies* α if $v_\Sigma(\alpha) = 1$, and α is said *satisfiable*; a set of formulas Γ is satisfied by v_Σ if all its formulas are satisfied by v_Σ. A valuation v_Σ *contradicts* α if $v_\Sigma(\alpha) = 0$; if α is neither satisfied nor contradicted by v_Σ, we say that v_Σ is *neutral* with respect to α. A valuation is *classical* if it assigns only 0 or 1 to all proposition symbols, and hence to all formulas.

For example, consider the formula $p \to q$, and $\Sigma = \emptyset$. Then

- if $v_\Sigma(p) = 1$, then $v_\Sigma(p \to q) = v_\Sigma(q)$;
- if $v_\Sigma(p) = 0$, then $v_\Sigma(p \to q) = 1$;

- if $v_\Sigma(q) = 0$, then $v_\Sigma(p \to q) = v_\Sigma(p)$;
- if $v_\Sigma(q) = 1$, then $v_\Sigma(p \to q) = 1$;
- if $v_\Sigma(p) = \varepsilon_p$ and $v_\Sigma(q) = \varepsilon_q$, then $v_\Sigma(p \to q) = 1$;

The first four valuations coincide with a classical behavior. The last one shows that if p and q are mapped to distinct neutral values, then $p \to q$ will be satisfiable. Note that, in this case, $p \lor q$ will also be satisfiable, and that $p \land q$ will be contradicted.

3.2   LB-Entailment

The notion of a parameterized LB-Entailment, $\models_\Sigma^{\mathsf{LB}}$ follows the spirit of Dalal's entailment relation, namely $\Gamma \models_\Sigma^{\mathsf{LB}} \alpha$ if it is not possible to satisfy Γ and contradict α at the same time. More specifically, $\Gamma \models_\Sigma^{\mathsf{LB}} \alpha$ if no valuation v_Σ such that $v_\Sigma(\Gamma) = 1$ also makes $v_\Sigma(\alpha) = 0$. Note that since this logic is not classic, if $\Gamma \models_\Sigma^{\mathsf{LB}} \alpha$ and $v_\Sigma(\Gamma) = 1$ it is possible that the $c\alpha$ is either neutral or satisfied by v_Σ.

For example, we reconsider Dalal's example, where $\Gamma_0 = \{p \lor q, p \lor \neg q, \neg p \lor s \lor t, \neg p \lor s \lor \neg t\}$ and make $\Sigma = \varnothing$. We want to show that $\Gamma_0 \models_\Sigma^{\mathsf{LB}} p$, $\Gamma_0, p \models_\Sigma^{\mathsf{LB}} s$ but $\Gamma_0 \not\models_\Sigma^{\mathsf{LB}} s$.

To see that $\Gamma_0 \models_\Sigma^{\mathsf{LB}} p$, suppose there is a v_Σ such that $v_\Sigma(p) = 0$. Then we have $v_\Sigma(p \lor q) = v_\Sigma(q)$ and $v_\Sigma(p \lor \neg q) = {\sim} v_\Sigma(q)$. Since it is not possible to satisfy both, we cannot have $v_\Sigma(\Gamma_0) = 1$, so $\Gamma_0 \models_\Sigma^{\mathsf{LB}} p$.

To show that $\Gamma_0, p \models_\Sigma^{\mathsf{LB}} s$, suppose there is a v_Σ such that $v_\Sigma(s) = 0$ and $v_\Sigma(p) = 1$. Then $v_\Sigma(\neg p \lor s \lor t) = v_\Sigma(t)$ and $v_\Sigma(\neg p \lor s \lor \neg t) = {\sim} v_\Sigma(t)$. Again, it is not possible to satisfy both, so $\Gamma_0, p \models_\Sigma^{\mathsf{LB}} s$.

Finally, to see that $\Gamma_0 \not\models_\Sigma^{\mathsf{LB}} s$, take a valuation v_Σ such that $v_\Sigma(s) = 0, v_\Sigma(p) = \varepsilon_p, v_\Sigma(q) = \varepsilon_q, v_\Sigma(t) = \varepsilon_t$. Then $v_\Sigma(\Gamma_0) = 1$. However, if we make $\Sigma = \{p\}$ then we have only two possibilities for $v_\Sigma(p)$. If $v_\Sigma(p) = 1$, we have already seen that no valuation that contradicts s will satisfy Γ_0. If $v_\Sigma(p) = 0$, we have also seen that no valuation that contradicts s will satisfy Γ_0. So for $p \in \Sigma$, we obtain $\Gamma_0 \models_\Sigma^{\mathsf{LB}} s$.

This example indicates that $\models_\varnothing^{\mathsf{LB}}$ behave in a similar way to $\vdash_{\mathsf{BCP}}$, and that by adding an atom to Σ we have a behavior similar to $\vdash_1^{\mathsf{BCP}}$. We now have to demonstrate that this is not a mere coincidence.

An Approximation Process. As defined in [8], a family of logics, parameterized with a set, Σ, is said to be an approximation of classical logic "from below" if, for increasing size of the parameter set Σ we get closer to classical logic. That is, for $\varnothing \subseteq \Sigma' \subseteq \Sigma'' \subseteq \ldots \subseteq \mathcal{L}$ we have that,

$$\models_\varnothing^{\mathsf{LB}} \subseteq \models_{\Sigma'}^{\mathsf{LB}} \subseteq \models_{\Sigma''}^{\mathsf{LB}} \subseteq \ldots \subseteq \models_{\mathcal{L}}^{\mathsf{LB}} = \models_{\mathsf{CL}}$$

Lemma 1. *The family of logics* LB(Σ) *is an approximation of classical logic from below.*

Note that for a given pair (Γ, α) the approximation of $\Gamma \models \alpha$ can be done in a finite number of steps. In fact, if $\beta, \gamma \in \Sigma$ any formula made up of β and γ has the property of bivalence. In particular, if all atoms of Γ and α are in Σ, then only classical valuations are allowed.

An approximation method as above is not in the spirit of Dalal's approximation, but follows the paradigm of Cadoli and Schaerf [13, 1], also applied by Massacci [11, 10] and Finger and Wassermann [6–8].

We now show how Dalal's approximations can be obtained using LB.

3.3 Soundness and Completeness of $\vdash_{\mathrm{BCP}}$ with Respect to $\models_{\varnothing}^{\mathsf{LB}}$

For the sake of this section and the following, let Γ be a set of clauses and let ψ and φ denote clauses, and $\lambda, \lambda_1, \lambda_2, \ldots$ denote literals. We now show that, for $\Sigma = \varnothing$, $\Gamma \vdash_{\mathrm{BCP}} \psi$ iff $\Gamma \models_{\varnothing}^{\mathsf{LB}} \psi$.

Lemma 2. *Suppose BCP transforms a set of clauses Γ into a set of clauses Δ, then $v_\Sigma(\Gamma) = 1$ iff $v_\Sigma(\Delta) = 1$.*

Lemma 3. $\Gamma =_{\mathrm{BCP}} \{\mathbf{f}\}$ *iff for all valuations $v_\varnothing$, $v_\varnothing(\Gamma) \neq 1$.*

Theorem 1. *Let Γ be a set of clauses and ψ a clause. Then $\Gamma \vdash_{\mathrm{BCP}} \psi$ iff $\Gamma \models_{\varnothing}^{\mathsf{LB}} \psi$.*

Proof. $\Gamma \models_{\varnothing}^{\mathsf{LB}} \psi$ iff for no $v_\varnothing$, $v_\varnothing(\Gamma) = 1$ and $v_\varnothing(\psi) = 0$ iff for no $v_\varnothing$, $v_\varnothing(\Gamma \cup \neg\psi) = 1$ iff, by Lemma 3, $\Gamma \cup \neg\psi =_{\mathrm{BCP}} \{\mathbf{f}\}$ iff $\Gamma \vdash_{\mathrm{BCP}} \psi$.

Lemma 4 (Deduction Theorem for $\vdash_{\mathrm{BCP}}$). *Let Γ be a set of clauses, λ a literal and ψ a clause. Then the following are equivalent statements:*

$$\text{(a) } \Gamma, \lambda \vdash_{\mathrm{BCP}} \psi; \quad \text{(b) } \Gamma \vdash_{\mathrm{BCP}} \neg\lambda \vee \psi; \quad \text{(c) } \Gamma \vdash_{\mathrm{BCP}} \lambda \to \psi.$$

3.4 Soundness and Completeness of $\vdash_k^{\mathrm{BCP}}$

As mentioned before, the family of entailment relations $\models_\Sigma^{\mathsf{LB}}$ does not follow Dalal's approach to approximation, so in order to obtain a sound and complete semantics for $\vdash_k^{\mathrm{BCP}}$ we need to provide another entailment relation based on $\models_\Sigma^{\mathsf{LB}}$, which we call $\models_{\mathbb{S}}^{\mathsf{LB}}$.

For that, let $\mathbb{S}$ be a set of sets of formulas and define $\Gamma \models_{\mathbb{S}}^{\mathsf{LB}} \psi$ iff there exists a set $\Sigma \in \mathbb{S}$ such that $\Gamma \models_\Sigma^{\mathsf{LB}} \psi$. We concentrate on the case where Γ is a set of clauses, ψ is a clause and each $\Sigma \in \mathbb{S}$ is a set of atoms. We define $\mathbb{S}_k = \{\Sigma \subseteq \mathcal{P} | \; |\Sigma| = k\}$.

That is, $\mathbb{S}_k$ is a set of sets of atoms of size k. Note that if we restrict our attention to n atoms, $|\mathbb{S}_k| = \binom{n}{k} = O(n^k)$ sets of k atoms. For a fixed k, we only have to consider a polynomial number of sets of k atoms.

We then write $\models_k^{\mathsf{LB}}$ to mean $\models_{\mathbb{S}_k}^{\mathsf{LB}}$.

Theorem 2. *Let Γ be a set of clauses and ψ a clause. Then $\Gamma \vdash_k^{\mathrm{BCP}} \psi$ iff $\Gamma \models_k^{\mathsf{LB}} \psi$.*

Proof. ($\Rightarrow$) By induction on the number of uses of rule 2 in the definition of $\vdash_k^{\mathrm{BCP}}$. For the base case, Theorem 1 gives us the result. Assume that $\Gamma \vdash_k^{\mathrm{BCP}} \psi$ due to $\Gamma \vdash_k^{\mathrm{BCP}} \varphi$ and $\Gamma, \varphi \vdash_k^{\mathrm{BCP}} \varphi$. Suppose for contradiction that $\Gamma \not\models_k^{\mathrm{LB}} \psi$, then for all $\Sigma \subseteq \mathcal{P}$, $|\Sigma| \leq k$, there exists v_Σ such that $v_\Sigma(\Gamma) = 1$ and $v_\Sigma(\psi) = 0$. By the induction hypothesis, $\Gamma \models_k^{\mathrm{LB}} \varphi$, which implies $v_\Sigma(\varphi) \neq 0$, and $\Gamma, \varphi \models_k^{\mathrm{LB}} \varphi$, which implies $v_\Sigma(\varphi) \neq 1$. So $v_\sigma(\varphi) = \varepsilon_i$, for some $i < \omega$, which implies that atoms$(\varphi) \cap \Sigma = \varnothing$, but this cannot hold for all Σ, a contradiction. So $\Gamma \models_k^{\mathrm{LB}} \psi$.

($\Leftarrow$) Suppose $\Gamma \models_k^{\mathrm{LB}} \psi$. Then for some Σ with $|\Sigma| \leq k$, $\Gamma \models_\Sigma^{\mathrm{LB}} \psi$ and suppose that Σ is a smallest set with such property. Therefore, for all with v_Σ with $v_\Sigma(\Gamma) = 1$ we have $v_\Sigma(\psi) \neq 0$. Choose one such v_Σ and define the set of literals $\Lambda = \{\lambda$ is a literal whose atom is in $\Sigma | v_\Sigma(\lambda) = 1\}$.

We first show that $\Gamma \models_\Sigma^{\mathrm{LB}} \lambda$ for every $\lambda \in \Lambda$. Suppose for contradiction that for some $\lambda \in \Lambda$, $\Gamma \not\models_\Sigma^{\mathrm{LB}} \lambda$, then there is a v'_Σ with $v'_\Sigma(\Gamma) = 1$ and $v'_\Sigma(\psi) \neq 0$ but $v'_\Sigma(\lambda) = 0$. Let atoms$(\lambda) = \{p\}$. If p does not occur in ψ, then $\Gamma \models_{\Sigma - \{p\}}^{\mathrm{LB}} \psi$, which contradicts the minimality of Σ. So $\psi = p \vee \chi'$ or $\psi = \neg p \vee \chi''$. Consider a $v_{\Sigma - \{p\}}$ such that $v_{\Sigma - \{p\}}(\Gamma) = 1$; if $v_{\Sigma - \{p\}}$ maps p to 0 or 1 it is a v_Σ, so $v_{\Sigma - \{p\}}(\psi) \neq 0$; if $v_{\Sigma - \{p\}}(p) = \varepsilon_i$ for some i, then clearly we have that $v_{\Sigma - \{p\}}(\psi) \neq 0$, so $\Gamma \models_{\Sigma - \{p\}}^{\mathrm{LB}} \psi$, which contradicts the minimality of Σ. It follows that $\Gamma \models_\Sigma^{\mathrm{LB}} \Lambda$.

We now show that $\Gamma \cup \Lambda \vdash_{\mathrm{BCP}} \psi$. Suppose for contradiction that $\Gamma \cup \Lambda \not\vdash_{\mathrm{BCP}} \psi$. Then, by Theorem 1, $\Gamma \cup \Lambda \not\models_\varnothing^{\mathrm{LB}} \psi$, that is, there exists $v_\varnothing$ such that $v_\varnothing(\Gamma \cup \Lambda) = 1$ and $v_\varnothing(\psi) = 0$. However, such $v_\varnothing$ maps all atoms of Σ to 0 or 1, so it is actually a v_Σ that contradicts $\Gamma \models_\Sigma^{\mathrm{LB}} \psi$. So $\Gamma \cup \Lambda \vdash_{\mathrm{BCP}} \psi$.

If $\Gamma \vdash_{\mathrm{BCP}} \psi$ then clearly $\Gamma \vdash_k^{\mathrm{BCP}} \psi$. So suppose $\Gamma \not\vdash_{\mathrm{BCP}} \psi$. In this case, we show that $\Gamma \vdash_k^{\mathrm{BCP}} \bigwedge \Lambda$. Let $\Lambda = \{\lambda_1, \ldots, \lambda_m\}$, we prove by induction that for $1 \leq i \leq m$, $\Gamma, \lambda_1, \ldots, \lambda_{i-1} \vdash_{\mathrm{BCP}} \lambda_i$. From $\Gamma \not\vdash_{\mathrm{BCP}} \psi$ and Theorem 1 we know that there is a valuation $v_\varnothing$ such that $v_\varnothing(\Gamma) = 1$ and $v_\varnothing(\psi) = 0$. From $\Gamma \cup \Lambda \vdash_{\mathrm{BCP}} \psi$ we infer that there must exist a $\lambda \in \Lambda$ such that $v_\varnothing(\lambda) \neq 1$; without loss of generality, let $\lambda = \lambda_m$. Suppose for contradiction that $\Gamma, \lambda_1, \ldots, \lambda_{m-1} \not\vdash_{\mathrm{BCP}} \lambda_m$. Then there exists a valuation $v'_\varnothing$ such that $v'_\varnothing(\Gamma, \lambda_1, \ldots, \lambda_{m-1}) = 1$ but $v'_\varnothing(\lambda_m) = 0$, which contradicts $\Gamma \models_\Sigma^{\mathrm{LB}} \Lambda$. So $\Gamma, \lambda_1, \ldots, \lambda_{m-1} \vdash_{\mathrm{BCP}} \lambda_m$.

Now note that for $1 < i \leq m$, $\Gamma, \lambda_i, \ldots, \lambda_m \not\vdash_{\mathrm{BCP}} \psi$, otherwise the minimality of Σ would be violated. From Theorem 1 we know that there is a valuation $v_\varnothing$ such that $v_\varnothing(\Gamma, \lambda_i, \ldots, \lambda_m) = 1$ and $v_\varnothing(\psi) = 0$. From $\Gamma \cup \Lambda \vdash_{\mathrm{BCP}} \psi$ we infer that there must exist a $\lambda \in \{\lambda_1, \ldots, \lambda_{i-1}\}$ such that $v_\varnothing(\lambda) \neq 1$; without loss of generality, let $\lambda = \lambda_{i-1}$. Suppose for contradiction that $\Gamma, \lambda_1, \ldots, \lambda_{i-2} \not\vdash_{\mathrm{BCP}} \lambda_{i-1}$. Then there exists a valuation $v'_\varnothing$ such that $v'_\varnothing(\Gamma, \lambda_1, \ldots, \lambda_{i-2}) = 1$ but $v'_\varnothing(\lambda_{i-1}) = 0$, but this contradicts $\Gamma \models_\Sigma^{\mathrm{LB}} \Lambda$. So $\Gamma, \lambda_1, \ldots, \lambda_{i-2} \vdash_{\mathrm{BCP}} \lambda_{i-1}$.

Thus we have that $\Gamma \vdash_{\mathrm{BCP}} \lambda_1$; $\Gamma, \lambda_1 \vdash_{\mathrm{BCP}} \lambda_2$; $\ldots$; $\Gamma, \lambda_1, \ldots, \lambda_{m-1} \vdash_{\mathrm{BCP}} \lambda_m$. It follows that $\Gamma \vdash_k^{\mathrm{BCP}} \bigwedge \Lambda$ as desired. Finally, from $\Gamma \cup \Lambda \vdash_{\mathrm{BCP}} \psi$ and $\Gamma \vdash_k^{\mathrm{BCP}} \bigwedge \Lambda$ we obtain that $\Gamma \vdash_k^{\mathrm{BCP}} \psi$, and the result is proved.

The technique above differs considerably from Dalal's use of the notion of *vividness*. It follows from Dalal's result that each approximation step $\models_k^{\mathrm{LB}}$ is decidable in polynomial time.

4   Conclusions and Future Work

In this paper we presented the family of logics LB(Σ) and provided it with a lattice-based semantics. We showed that it can be a basis for both a parametric and a polynomial clausal approximation of classical logic. This semantics is sound and complete with respect to Dalal's polynomial approximations $\vdash_k^{BCP}$.

Future work should extend polynomial approximations to non-clausal logics. It should also provide a proof-theory for these approximations.

References

1. Marco Cadoli and Marco Schaerf. The complexity of entailment in propositional multivalued logics. *Annals of Mathematics and Artificial Intelligence*, 18(1):29–50, 1996.
2. Alessandra Carbone and Stephen Semmes. *A Graphic Apology for Symmetry and Implicitness*. Oxford Mathematical Monographs. Oxford University Press, 2000.
3. C. Chang and R. Lee. *Symbolic Logic and Mechanical Theorem Proving*. Academic Press, London, 1973.
4. Mukesh Dalal. Anytime families of tractable propositional reasoners. In *International Symposium of Artificial Intelligence and Mathematics AI/MATH-96*, pages 42–45, 1996.
5. Mukesh Dalal. Semantics of an anytime family of reasponers. In *12th European Conference on Artificial Intelligence*, pages 360–364, 1996.
6. Marcelo Finger and Renata Wassermann. Expressivity and control in limited reasoning. In Frank van Harmelen, editor, *15th European Conference on Artificial Intelligence (ECAI02)*, pages 272–276, Lyon, France, 2002. IOS Press.
7. Marcelo Finger and Renata Wassermann. The universe of approximations. In Ruy de Queiroz, Elaine Pimentel, and Lucilia Figueiredo, editors, *Electronic Notes in Theoretical Computer Science*, volume 84, pages 1–14. Elsevier, 2003.
8. Marcelo Finger and Renata Wassermann. Approximate and limited reasoning: Semantics, proof theory, expressivity and control. *Journal of Logic And Computation*, 14(2):179–204, 2004.
9. M. R. Garey and D. S. Johnson. *Computers and Intractability: A Guide to the Theory of NP-Completeness*. Freeman, 1979.
10. Fabio Massacci. Anytime approximate modal reasoning. In Jack Mostow and Charles Rich, editors, *AAAI-98*, pages 274–279. AAAIP, 1998.
11. Fabio Massacci. *Efficient Approximate Deduction and an Application to Computer Security*. PhD thesis, Dottorato in Ingegneria Informatica, Università di Roma I "La Sapienza", Dipartimento di Informatica e Sistemistica, June 1998.
12. D. McAllester. Truth maintenance. In *Proceedings of the Eighth National Conference on Artificial Intelligence (AAAI-90)*, pages 1109–1116, 1990.
13. Marco Schaerf and Marco Cadoli. Tractable reasoning via approximation. *Artificial Intelligence*, 74(2):249–310, 1995.
14. Bart Selman and Henry Kautz. Knowledge compilation using horn approximations. In *Proceedings AAAI-91*, pages 904–909, July 1991.
15. Bart Selman and Henry Kautz. Knowledge compilation and theory approximation. *Journal of the ACM*, 43(2):193–224, March 1996.

Using Relevance to Speed Up Inference
Some Empirical Results

Joselyto Riani and Renata Wassermann

Department of Computer Science
Institute of Mathematics and Statistics
University of São Paulo, Brazil
{joselyto,renata}@ime.usp.br

Abstract. One of the main problems in using logic for solving problems is the high computational costs involved in inference. In this paper, we propose the use of a notion of relevance in order to cut the search space for a solution. Instead of trying to infer a formula α directly from a large knowledge base K, we consider first only the most relevant sentences in K for the proof. If those are not enough, the set can be increased until, at the worst case, we consider the whole base K.

We show how to define a notion of relevance for first-order logic with equality and analyze the results of implementing the method and testing it over more than 700 problems from the TPTP problem library.

Keywords: Automated theorem provers, relevance, approximate reasoning.

1 Introduction

Logic has been used as a tool for knowledge representation and reasoning in several subareas of Artificial Intelligence, from the very beginning of the field. Among these subareas, we can cite Diagnosis [1], Planning [2], Belief Revision [3], etc.

One of the main criticisms against the use of logic is the high computational costs involved in the process of making inferences and testing for consistency. Testing satisfiability of a set of formulas is already an NP-complete problem even if we stay within the realms of propositional logic [4]. And propositional logic is usually not rich enough for most problems we want to represent. Adding expressivity to the language comes at the cost of adding to the computational complexity.

In the area of automatic theorem proving [5], the need for heuristics that help on average cases has long been established. Recently, there have been several proposals in the literature of heuristics that not only help computationally, but are also based on intuitions about human reasoning. In this work, we concentrate on the ideas of approximate reasoning and the use of relevance notions.

Approximate reasoning consists in, instead of attacking the original problem directly, performing some simplification such that, if the simplified problem is

A.L.C. Bazzan and S. Labidi (Eds.): SBIA 2004, LNAI 3171, pp. 21–30, 2004.

solved, the solution is also a solution for the original problem. If no solution is found, then the process is restarted for a problem with complexity lying between those of the original and the simplified problem.

That is, we are looking for a series of deduction mechanisms $\{\vdash_1, \vdash_2, ...\}$, with $\vdash_i$ computationally less expensive than $\vdash_j$ for $i < j$, such that if $Th(\vdash_i)$ represents the theorems which can be proved using $\vdash_i$, and $\vdash$ is a sound and complete deduction mechanism for classical logic, we get: $Th(\vdash_1) \subseteq Th(\vdash_2) \subseteq \ldots \subseteq Th(\vdash)$

An example of such kind of system is Schaerf and Cadoli's "Approximate Entailment" [6] for propositional logic. The idea behind their work is that at each step of the approximation process, only some atoms of the language are considered.

Given a set S of propositional letters, their system S_3 disconsiders those atoms outside S by allowing both p and $\neg p$ to be assigned the truth value 1 when p is not in S. If p is in S, then its behavior is classic, i.e., p is assigned the truth value 1 if and only if $\neg p$ is assigned 0. The system S_3 is sound but incomplete with respect to classical logic. This means that for any S, if a formula is an S_3 consequence of a set of formulas, it is also a classical consequence. Since the system is incomplete, the fact that a formula does not follow from the set according to S_3 does not give us information about its classical status.

There are several other logical systems found in the literature which are also sound and incomplete, such as relevant [7] and paraconsistent logics [8].

In this work, we present a sound an incomplete system based on a notion of relevance. We try to prove that a sentence α follows from a set of formulas K by first considering only those elements of K which are most relevant to α. If this fails, we can add some less relevant elements and try again. In the worst case, we will end up adding all the elements of K, but if we are lucky, we can prove α with less.

The system presented here is based on the one proposed in [9]. The original framework was developed for propositional logic. In this paper, we extend it to deal with first order logic and show some empirical results.

The paper proceeds as follows: in the next section, we present the idea of using a relevance graph to structure the knowledge base, proposed in [9]. In Section 3, we introduce a particular notion of relevance, which is based purely on the syntactical analysis of the knowledge base. In Section 4, we show how these ideas were implemented and the results obtained. We finally conclude and present some ideas for future work.

2   The Relevance Graph Approach

In this section, we assume that the notion of relevance which will be used is given and show some general results proven in [9]. In the next section, we consider a particular notion of relevance which can be obtained directly from the formulas considered, without the need of any extra-logical resources.

Let $\mathcal{R}$ be a relation between two formulas with the intended meaning that $\mathcal{R}(\alpha, \beta)$ if and only if the formulas α and β are directly relevant to each other.

Given such a relatedness relation, we can represent a knowledge base (a set of formulas) as a graph where each node is a formula and there is an edge between φ and ψ if and only if $\mathcal{R}(\varphi, \psi)$. This graph representation gives us immediately a notion of degrees of relatedness: the shorter the path between two formulas of the base is, the closer related they are. Another notion made clear is that of connectedness: the connected components partition the graph into unrelated "topics" or "subjects". Sentences in the same connected component are somehow related, even if far apart (see Figure 1).

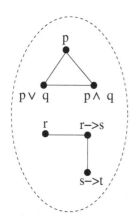

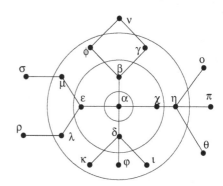

Fig. 1. Structured Knowledge Base   **Fig. 2.** Degrees of Relevance

Definition 1. *[9] Let K be a knowledge base and $\mathcal{R}$ be a relation between formulas. A $\mathcal{R}$-path between two formulas φ and ψ in K is a sequence $P = (\varphi_0, \varphi_1, ..., \varphi_n)$ of formulas such that:*

1. *$\varphi_0 = \varphi$ and $\varphi_n = \psi$*
2. *$\{\varphi_1, ..., \varphi_{n-1}\} \subseteq K$*
3. *$\mathcal{R}(\varphi, \varphi_1), \mathcal{R}(\varphi_1, \varphi_2), ...,$ and $\mathcal{R}(\varphi_n, \psi)$.*

If it is clear from the context to which relation we refer we will talk simply about a path in K.

We represent the fact that P is a path between φ and ψ by $\varphi \overset{P}{\leadsto} \psi$.

The length of a path $P = (\varphi_0, \varphi_1, ..., \varphi_n)$ is $l(P) = n$

Note that the extremities of a path in K are not necessarily elements of K.

Definition 2. *[9] Let K be a knowledge base and $\mathcal{R}$ a relation between formulas of the language. We say that two formulas φ and ψ are related in K by $\mathcal{R}$ if and only if there is a path P such that $\varphi \overset{P}{\leadsto} \psi$.*

Given two formulas φ and ψ and a base K, we can use the length of the shortest path between them in K as the degree of unrelatedness of the formulas. If the formulas are not related in K, the degree of unrelatedness is set to infinity. Formulas with a shorter path between them in K are closer related in K.

Definition 3. *[9] Let K be a knowledge base, $\mathcal{R}$ a relation between formulas of the language and φ and ψ formulas. The unrelatedness degree of φ and ψ in K is given by:*

$$u(\varphi, \psi) = \begin{cases} 0 & \text{if } \varphi = \psi \text{ and } \varphi \in K \\ min\{l(P)|\varphi \overset{P}{\leadsto} \psi\} & \text{if } \varphi \text{ and } \psi \text{ are related in } K \text{ by } \mathcal{R} \\ \infty & \text{otherwise} \end{cases}$$

We now show, given the structure of a knowledge base, how to retrieve the set of formulas relevant for a given formula α:

Definition 4. *[9] The set of formulas of K which are relevant for α with degree i is given by:*

$$\Delta^i(\alpha, K) = \{\varphi \in K | u(\alpha, \varphi) = i\} \text{ for } i \geq 0$$

Definition 5. *[9]*

The set of formulas of K which are relevant for α up to degree n is given by:

$$\Delta^{\leq n}(\alpha, K) = \bigcup_{0 \leq i \leq n} \Delta^i(\alpha, K) \text{ for } n \geq 0$$

We say that $\Delta^{\leq \omega}(\alpha, K) = \bigcup_{i \geq 0} \Delta^i(\alpha, K)$ is the set of relevant formulas for α.

In Figure 2, we see an example of a structured knowledge base $K = \{\alpha, \beta, \gamma, \delta, \varepsilon, \eta, \theta, \iota, \kappa, \lambda, \mu, \nu, o, \pi, \rho, \sigma, \phi, \varphi, \chi\}$. The dotted circles represent different levels of relevance for α. We have:

$\Delta^0(\alpha, K) = \{\alpha\}$
$\Delta^1(\alpha, K) = \{\beta, \chi, \delta, \varepsilon\}$
$\Delta^2(\alpha, K) = \{\gamma, \eta, \iota, \varphi, \kappa, \lambda, \mu, \phi\}$
$\Delta^3(\alpha, K) = \{\nu, o, \pi, \theta, \rho, \sigma\}$
$\Delta^{\leq \omega}(\alpha, K) = \Delta^0(\alpha, K) \cup \Delta^1(\alpha, K) \cup \Delta^2(\alpha, K) \cup \Delta^3(\alpha, K) = K$

We can now define our notion of relevant inference as:

Definition 6. *$K \vdash_i \alpha$ if and only if $\Delta^{\leq i}(\alpha, K) \vdash \alpha$*

Since $\Delta^{\leq i}(\alpha, K)$ is a subset of K, it is clear that if for any i, $K \vdash_i \alpha$, then $K \vdash \alpha$. Note however that if $K \nvdash_i \alpha$, we cannot say anything about whether $K \vdash \alpha$ or not.

An interesting point of the framework above is that it is totally independent on which relevance relation is chosen. In the next section, we explore one particular notion of relevance, which can be used with this framework.

3   Syntactical Relevance

We have seen that, given a relevance relation, we can use it to structure a set of formulas so that the most relevant formulas can be easily retrieved. But where does the relevance relation come from? Of course, we could consider very sophisticated notions of relevance. But in this work, our main concern is to find a notion that does not require that any extra information is added to the set K.

In [9], a notion of syntactical relevance is proposed (for propositional logic), which makes $\mathcal{R}(\alpha, \beta)$ if and only if the formulas α and β share an atom. It can be argued that this notion is very simplistic, but it has the advantage of being very easy to compute (this is the relation used in Figure 1). We can also see that it gives intuitive results. Consider the following example, borrowed from [10][1].

Example 1. Consider Paul, who is finishing school and preparing himself for the final exams. He studied several different subjects, like Mathematics, Biology, Geography. His knowledge base contains (among others) the beliefs in Figure 3.

When Paul gets the exam, the first question is: *Do cows have molar teeth?*

Of course Paul cannot reason with all of his knowledge at once. First he recalls what he knows about cows and about molar teeth:

> *Cows eat grass.*
>
> *Mammals have canine teeth or molar teeth.*

From these two pieces of knowledge alone, he cannot answer the question. Since all he knows (explicitly) about cows is that they eat grass, he recalls what he knows about animals that eat grass:

Triangles are polygons.
Triangles with one right angle are Pythagorean.
Rectangles are polygons.
Rectangles have four right angles.
Cows eat grass.
Dogs are carnivore.
Animals that eat grass do not have canine teeth.
Carnivorous animals are mammals.
Mammals have canine teeth or molar teeth.
Animals that eat grass are mammals.
Mammals are vertebrate.
Vertebrates are animals.
Brazil is in South America.
Volcanic soil is fertile.

Fig. 3. Student's knowledge base

Animals that eat grass do not have canine teeth.
Animals that eat grass are mammals.

From these, Paul can now derive that cows are mammals, that mammals have canine teeth or molar teeth, but that cows do not have canine teeth, hence cows have molar teeth.

The example shows that usually, a system does not have to check its whole knowledge base in order to answer a query. Moreover, it shows that the process of retrieving information is made gradually, and not in a single step. If Paul had to go too far in the process, he would not be able to find an answer, since the time available for the exam is limited. But this does not mean that if he was given more time later on, he would start reasoning from scratch: his partial (or approximate) reasoning would be useful and he would be able to continue from more or less where he stopped.

Using the syntactical notion of relevance, the process of creating the relevance graph can be greatly simplified. The graph can be implemented as a bipartite graph, where some nodes are formulas and some are atoms. The list of atoms is organized in lexicographic order, so that it can be searched efficiently. For every formula which is added to the graph, one only has to link it to the atoms

---

[1] The example is based on an example of [6].

occurring in it. In this way, it will be automatically connected to every other formula with which it shares an atom.

This notion of relevance gives us a "quick and dirty" method for retrieving the most relevant elements of a set of formulas.

Epstein [11] proposes some desiderata for a binary relation intended to represent relevance. Epstein's conditions are:

R1 - $\mathcal{R}(\varphi, \varphi)$
R2 - $\mathcal{R}(\varphi, \psi)$ iff $\mathcal{R}(\neg\varphi, \psi)$
R3 - $\mathcal{R}(\varphi, \psi)$ iff $\mathcal{R}(\psi, \varphi)$
R4 - $\mathcal{R}(\varphi, \gamma \to \psi)$ iff $\mathcal{R}(\varphi, \gamma)$ or $\mathcal{R}(\varphi, \psi)$
R5 - $\mathcal{R}(\varphi, \gamma \land \psi)$ iff $\mathcal{R}(\varphi, \gamma \to \psi)$.

It is easy to see that syntactical relevance satisfies Epstein's desiderata. Moreover, Rodrigues [12] has shown that this is actually the smallest relation satisfying the conditions given in [11].

Unfortunately, propositional logic is very often not enough to express many problems found in Artificial Intelligence. We would like to move to first-order logic. As is well known, this makes the inference problem much harder. On the other hand, having a problem which is hard enough is a good reason to abandon completeness and try some heuristics.

In what follows, we adapt the definition of syntactical relevance relation to deal with full first-order logic with equality.

Definition 7. *Let α be a formula. Then $C(\alpha)$ is the set of non-logical constants (constants, predicate, and function names) which occur in α.*

Definition 8 (tentative). *Let ρ be a binary relation defined as:*
$\rho(\alpha, \beta)$ *if and only if* $C(\alpha) \cap C(\beta) \neq \emptyset$

It is easy to see that this relation satisfies Epstein's desiderata.

One problem with the definition above is that we very often have predicates, functions or constants that appear in too many formulas of the knowledge base, and could make all formulas seem relevant to each other. In this work, we consider one such case, which is the equality predicate ($\sim$).

Based on the work done by Epstein on relatedness for propositional logic, Krajewski [13] has considered the difficulties involved in extending it to first-order logic. He notes that the equality predicate should be dealt with in a different way and presents some options. The option we adopt here is that of handling equality as a connective, i.e., not considering it as a symbol which would contribute for relevance:.

Definition 9. *Let ρ be a binary relation defined as:*
$\rho(\alpha, \beta)$ *if and only if* $(C(\alpha) \cap C(\beta)) \setminus \{\sim\} \neq \emptyset$

We can now use ρ as the relatedness relation needed to structure the relevance graph, and instantiate the general framework.

In the next section, we describe how this approximate inference has been implemented and some results obtained, which show that the use of the relatedness relation ρ does bring some gains in the inference process.

4 Implementation and Results

In this section, we show how the framework for approximate inference based on syntactical relevance has been implemented and the results which were obtained.

The idea is to have the knowledge base structured by the relatedness relation ρ and to use breadth-first search in order to retrieve the most relevant formulas. The algorithm receives as input the knowledge base K, the formula α which we are trying to prove, the relation ρ, a global limit Λ of resources (time, memory) for the whole process, a local limit λ which will be used at each step of the approximation process, an inference engine I, which will be called at each step and a function H which decides whether it is time to move to the next approximation step.

The basic algorithm is as follows:

Input: K, α, ρ, Λ (Global limit of resources), λ (Local limit of resources), I (inference engine, returns Yes, No, or Fail), H (function that decides whether to apply next inference step).

Output: Yes, No or Fail.

Data Structures: Q (a queue), K^i (a subset of K)

1. $i = 1$; $Q = \emptyset$; $K^i = \emptyset$.
2. Enqueue(Q, α); Mark(α);
3. While ($Q \neq \emptyset$) and (used resources $< \Lambda$) do
    3.1. β = Dequeue(Q);
    3.2. For all φ such that $\rho(\beta, \varphi)$ and φ is not marked, do
        3.2.1. Enqueue(Q, φ); Mark(φ);
        3.2.2. $K^i = K^i \cup \{\varphi\}$;
        3.2.3. If $H(K, K^i, i, \alpha)$ then
            3.2.3.1 If $I(K^i, \alpha, \lambda)$ = Yes, then return Yes;
            3.2.3.2 $i = i + 1$; $K^i = K^{(i-1)}$;
4. If used resources $< \Lambda$ then return $I(K^i, \alpha, \lambda)$;
        else return Fail.

In our tests, the inference engine used (the function I) was the theorem prover OTTER [14]. OTTER is an open-source theorem prover for first-order logic written in C. The code and documentation can be obtained from http://www-unix.mcs.anl.gov/AR/OTTER. OTTER was modified so that it could receive as a parameter the maximum number of sentences to be considered at each step. It was also modified to build the relevance graph after reading the input file. We call the modified version RR-OTTER (Relevance-Reasoning OTTER). The algorithm was implemented in C and the code and complete set of tests are available in [15].

The function H looks at the number of formulas retrieved at each step. At the first step, only the 25 most relevant formulas are retrieved, i.e., for $i = 1$, when $|K^i| = 25$, H returns true.

In order to test the algorithm, two knowledge bases were created, putting together problems of the TPTP[2] (Thousands of Problems for Theorem Provers) benchmark. Base 1 was obtained by putting together the axioms of the problems in the domains "Set theory", "Geometry", and "Management", and it contained 1029 clauses. Base 2 was obtained adding to Base 1 the axioms of the problems in "Group Theory", "Natural Language Processing", and "Logic Calculi", yielding 1781 clauses. Only problems in which the formula was a consequence of the base were considered.

Two sets of tests were run. The first one (Tests 1) contained 285 problems from the "Set Theory" domain, and used as the knowledge base Base 1 described above. The function H was set to try to solve the problems with 25, then 50, 100, 200, 250, 300, 350, 400, 450, 500, 550, and 600 clauses at each step. For each step, the maximum time allowed was 12.5 seconds. This gives a global time limit of 150 seconds.

The second set of tests (Tests 2) contained 458 problems from the "Group Theory" domain and used Base 2. It was tested with 25, 50, 100, 200, 250, 300, 350, 400, 450, and 500 clauses at each step, with the time limit at each step being 15 seconds. Again, the global limit was 150 seconds.

In order to compare the results obtained, each problem was also given to the original implementation of OTTER, with the time limit of 150 seconds.

The table below shows the results for six problems from the set Tests 1.

Problem	Time OTTER (s)	Time RR-OTTER (s)	# of sentences used
SET003-1	-	13.06	50
SET018-1	-	63.21	300
SET024-6	0.76	12.96	50
SET031-3	0.71	0.45	25
SET183-6	-	98.46	400
SET296-6	0.74	38.08	200

We can see that for the problems SET003-1, SET018-1, and SET183-6, which OTTER could not solve given the limit of 150 seconds, RR-OTTER could find a solution, considering 50, 300 and 400 clauses respectively. In this cases, it is clear that limiting the attention to relevant clauses brings positive results. For problem SET031-3, the heuristic proposed did not bring any significant gain. And for problems SET024-6 and SET296-6, we can see that OTTER performed better than RR-OTTER. These last two problems illustrate the importance of choosing a good function H. Consider problem SET024-6. RR-OTTER spent the first 12.5 seconds trying to prove it with 25 clauses and failed. Once it started with 50 clauses, it took 0.46 seconds. The same happened in problem SET296-6, where the first 37.5 seconds were spent with unsuccessful steps.

The following is a summary of the results which were obtained:

---

[2] http://www.tptp.org/

	Tests 1 (285 problems)	Tests 2 (458 problems)
Solutions found by OTTER	111	212
Solutions found by RR-OTTER	196	258
Average time 1 OTTER	93 sec	128 sec
Average time 1 RR-OTTER	61 sec	138 sec
Average time 2 OTTER	3.04 sec	11.6 sec
Average time 2 RR-OTTER	6.9 sec	23.07 sec

We can see that, given the global limit of 150 seconds, RR-OTTER solved more problems than the original OTTER. The lines "Average time 1" consider the average time for all the problems, while "Average time 2" takes into account only those problems in which the original version of OTTER managed to find a solution.

An interesting fact which can be seen from the tests is the influence of a bad choice of function H. For the problems in Tests 1, if we had started with 50 sentences instead of 25, the Average time 2 of RR-OTTER would have been 3.1 instead of 6.9 (for the whole set of results, please refer to [15]).

As it would be expected, when RR-OTTER manages to solve a problem considering only a small amount of sentences, the number of clauses it generates is much lower than what OTTER generates, and therefore, the time needed is also shorter. As an example, the problem SET044-5 is solved by RR-OTTER at the first iteration (25 sentences) in 0.46 seconds, generating 29 clauses, while OTTER takes 9.8 seconds and generates 3572 new clauses. This shows that, at least for simple problems, the idea of restricting attention to relevant sentences helps to avoid the generation of more irrelevant data and by doing so, keeps the search space small.

5   Conclusions and Future Work

In this paper, we have extended the framework proposed in [9] to deal with first-order logic and showed how it can be used to perform approximate theorem proving.

The method was implemented, using the theorem prover OTTER. Although the implementation is still naive, we could see that in many cases, we could obtain some gains. The new method, RR-OTTER, managed to solve some problems that OTTER could not prove, given a time limit.

The tests show that the strategy of considering the most relevant sentences first can be fruitful, by keeping the search space small.

Future work includes more tests in order to better determine the parameters of the method, such as the function H, and improving the implementation. Instead of external calls to OTTER, we plan to use otterlib [16], a C library developed by Flavio Ribeiro. The idea is that we could then keep the inference state after each step of the approximation (for example, all the clauses that were generated), instead of restarting from scratch.

Acknowledgements

Renata Wassermann is partly supported by the Brazilian Research Council (CNPq), grant PQ 300196/01-6. This work has been supported by FAPESP project 03/00312-0.

References

1. Hamscher, W., Console, L., de Kleer, J., eds.: Readings in Model-Based Diagnosis. Morgan Kaufmann (1992)
2. Allen, J., Hendler, J., Tare, A., eds.: Readings in Planning. Morgan Kaufmann Publishers (1990)
3. Gärdenfors, P.: Knowledge in Flux - Modeling the Dynamics of Epistemic States. MIT Press (1988)
4. Garey, M.R., Johnson, D.S.: Computers and Intractability: A Guide to the Theory of NP-Completeness. Freeman (1979)
5. Robinson, J.A., Voronkov, A., eds.: Handbook of Automated Reasoning. MIT Press (2001)
6. Schaerf, M., Cadoli, M.: Tractable reasoning via approximation. Artificial Intelligence **74** (1995) 249–310
7. Anderson, A., Belnap, N.: Entailment: The Logic of Relevance and Necessity, Vol. 1. Princeton University Press (1975)
8. da Costa, N.C.: Calculs propositionnels pour les systémes formels inconsistants. Comptes Rendus d'Academie des Sciences de Paris **257** (1963)
9. Wassermann, R.: Resource-Bounded Belief Revision. PhD thesis, Institute for Logic, Language and Computation — University of Amsterdam (1999)
10. Finger, M., Wassermann, R.: Expressivity and control in limited reasoning. In van Harmelen, F., ed.: 15th European Conference on Artificial Intelligence (ECAI02), Lyon, France, IOS Press (2002) 272–276
11. Epstein, R.L.: The semantic foundations of logic, volume 1: Propositional Logic. Nijhoff International Philosophy Series. Kluwer Academic Publishers (1990)
12. Rodrigues, O.T.: A Methodology for Iterated Information Change. PhD thesis, Imperial College, University of London (1997)
13. Krajewski, S.: Relatedness logic. Reports on Mathematical Logic **20** (1986) 7–14
14. McCune, W., Wos, L.: Otter: The cade-13 competition incarnations. Journal of Automated Reasoning (1997)
15. Riani, J.: Towards an efficient inference procedure through syntax based relevance. Master's thesis, Department of Computer Science, University of São Paulo (2004) Available at http://www.ime.usp.br/~joselyto/mestrado.
16. Ribeiro, F.P.: otterlib – a C library for theorem proving. Technical Report RT-MAC 2002-09, Computer Science Department, University of São Paulo (2002) Available from http://www.ime.usp.br/~fr/otterlib/.

A Non-explosive Treatment of Functional Dependencies Using Rewriting Logic*

Gabriel Aguilera, Pablo Cordero, Manuel Enciso,
Angel Mora, and Inmaculada Perez de Guzmán

E.T.S.I. Informática, Universidad de Málaga, 29071, Málaga, Spain
amora@ctima.uma.es

Abstract. The use of rewriting systems to transform a given expression into a simpler one has promoted the use of rewriting logic in several areas and, particularly, in Software Engineering. Unfortunately, this application has not reached the treatment of Functional Dependencies contained in a given relational database schema. The reason is that the different sound and complete axiomatic systems defined up to now to manage Functional Dependencies are based on the transitivity inference rule. In the literature, several authors illustrate different ways of mapping inference systems into rewriting logics. Nevertheless, the explosive behavior of these inference systems avoids the use of rewriting logics for classical FD logics. In a previous work, we presented a novel logic named $\mathbf{SL}_{FD}$ whose axiomatic system did not include the transitivity rule as a primitive rule. In this work we consider a new complexity criterion which allows us to introduce a new minimality property for FD sets named *atomic-minimality*. The $\mathbf{SL}_{FD}$ logic has allowed us to develop the heart of this work, which is the use of Rewriting Logic and Maude 2 as a logical framework to search for atomic-minimality.

Keywords: Knowledge Representation, Reasoning, Rewriting Logic, Redundancy Removal

1 Introduction

E.F. Cood introduces the *Relational Model* [1] having both, a formal framework and a practical orientation. Cood's database model is conceived to store and to manage data in an efficient and smart way. In fact, its formal basis is the main reason of their success and longevity in Computer Science. In this formal framework the notion of *Functional Dependency* (FD) plays an outstanding role in the way in which the Relational Model stores, recovers and manages data.

FDs were introduced in the early 70's and, after an initial period in which several authors study in depth their power, they fell into oblivion, considering that the research concerning them had been completed. Recently, some works have proved that there is still a set of FDs problems which can be revisited in a successful way with novel techniques [2, 3].

---

* This work has been partially supported by TIC-2003-08687-CO2-01.

A.L.C. Bazzan and S. Labidi (Eds.): SBIA 2004, LNAI 3171, pp. 31–40, 2004.

On the other hand, rewriting systems have been used in databases for database query optimization, analysis of binding propagation in deductive databases [4], and for proposing a new formal semantics for active databases [5]. Nevertheless, we have not found in the literature any work which uses rewriting logic (RL) to tackle an FD problem. FD problems can be classified in two classes according to one dimension: their abstraction level. So, we have instance problems (for example the extraction of all the FD which are satisfied in a given instance relation) and schema problems (for example the construction of all the FDs which are inferred from a given set of FDs). The first kind of problems are being faced successfully with Artificial Intelligence techniques. Schema problems seem to be suitable to be treated with RL.

There are some authors who introduce several FDs logics [6–8]. All of these logics are cast in the same mold. In fact, they are strongly based on Armstrong's Axioms [6], a set of expressions which illustrates the semantics of FDs. These FD logics cited above were created to formally specify FDs and as a metatheoretical tool to prove FD properties. Unfortunately, all of these FD axiomatic systems have a common heart: the transitivity rule. The strong dependence with respect to the transitivity inference rule avoids its executable implementation into RL.

The most famous problem concerning FDs is the *Implication Problem*: we have a set of FDs Γ and we would like to prove if a given FD can be deduced from Γ using the axiomatic system. If we incorporate any of these axiomatic systems into RL, the exhaustive use of the inference rule would make this rewrite system unapplicable, even for trivial FD sets. This limitation caused that a set of indirect methods with polinomial cost were created to solve the Implication Problem. Furthermore, other well-known FD problems are also tackled with indirect methods [9].

As the authors says about Maude in [10]:"The same reasons that make it a good semantic framework at the computational level make it also a good logical framework at the logical level, that is, a metalogic in which many other logics can be naturally represented and implemented". To do that, we need a new FD logic, which does not have the transitivity rule in its axiomatic system. Such a logic was presented in [11] and we named it the *Functional Dependencies Logic with Substitution* ($\mathbf{SL}_{FD}$). In this work we use for the first time RL to manage FDs. Particularly, we apply Maude as a metalogical framework for representing FD logics illustrating that "Maude can be used to create executable environments for different logics" [10].

The main novelty of $\mathbf{SL}_{FD}$ is the replacement of the transitivity rule by another inference rule, named *Substitution rule*[1] with a non-explosive behavior. This rule preserves equivalence and reduce the complexity of the original expression in linear time. Substitution rule allows the design of a new kind of FD logic with a sound and complete inference system. These characteristics allow the development of some FD preprocessing transformations which improve the use of indirect methods (see [12]) and open the door to the development of a future automated theorem prover for FDs.

---

[1] We would like to remark that our novel rule does not appear in the literature either like a primitive rule nor a derived rule.

The implication problem for FDs was motivated by the search for sets of FDs with less size, where the measure is the number of FDs[2]. In this work we introduce another criterion for FD complexity. We present the notion of atomic-minimality and we show how the Substitution rule may be used to develop a rewriting system which receives a set of FDs and produces an atomic-minimal FD set. As a general conclusion, we show that Rewriting Logic and Maude are very appropriate to tackle this problem.

The work is organized as follows: In Section 2 we show the implication problem for FDs and the classical FD logics. Besides, we provide a Maude 2 implementation of Paredaens FD logic. Section 3 introduces the atomic-minimality concept, a novel criterion to detect redundancy. Atomic-minimality can be used to design a rewriting system to depurate FDs sets. In Section 4 we use RL and Maude 2 to develop such a system. We conclude this section with several illustrative examples. The work ends with the conclusions and future work section.

2 The Implication Problem for FDs

The problem of removing redundancy in FD sets is presented exhaustively in [7]. In this paper, the authors illustrate the strong relation between the implication problem and redundancy removal. Thus, they introduce the notion of *minimality*, a property of FD sets which ensures that every FD contained in the set can not be deduced from the others i.e. it is not redundant. As P. Atzeni and V. de Antonellis cite [7], the soundness and completeness of the inference rules for FDs guaranteed the decidability of the implication problem: given Γ a set of FDs, we can exhaustively apply the inference rules to generate the closure of Γ. This new set of FDs is used to test whether a given FD is implied by Γ. Obviously, the method is not used in practice, because the size of this set of FDs is exponential with respect to the cardinality of Γ. This situation is due to both the axiom and the transitivity that are shown below.

We select FD Paredaens Logic (with no loss of generality) to illustrate its explosive behavior:

Definition 1 (The $\mathbf{L}_{Par}$ language). [3] *Let Ω be an infinite enumerable set of atoms (attributes) and let $\mapsto$ be a binary connective, we define the language*

$$\mathcal{L}_{FD} = \{X \mapsto Y \mid X, Y \in 2^{\Omega} \text{ and } X \neq \varnothing\}$$

Definition 2 (The $\mathcal{S}_{Par}$ axiomatic system). $\mathbf{L}_{Par}$ *is the logic given by the pair $(\mathcal{L}_{FD}, \mathcal{S}_{Par})$ where $\mathcal{S}_{Par}$, has one axiom scheme and two inference rules:*

$$
\begin{array}{lll}
\lfloor Ax_{Par} \rfloor : & \vdash_{\mathcal{S}_{Par}} X \mapsto Y & \text{if } Y \subseteq X \\
\lfloor Trans \rfloor & X \mapsto Y \ Y \mapsto Z \vdash_{\mathcal{S}_{Par}} X \mapsto Z & \textbf{Transitivity Rule} \\
\lfloor Augm \rfloor & X \mapsto Y \vdash_{\mathcal{S}_{Par}} X \mapsto XY & \textbf{Augmentation Rule}
\end{array}
$$

---

[2] The treatment of a set of FDs is normally focussed on the reduction of the size of the set. Nevertheless, we would like to remark that this treatment is not deterministic.

[3] As usual, XY is used as the union of sets X, Y; $X \subseteq Y$ as X included in Y; $Y - X$ as the set of elements in Y that are not in X (difference) and $\top$ as the empty set.

In $\mathcal{S}_{Par}$ we have the following derived rules (these rules appear in [8]):

$\lfloor Union \rfloor$ $X{\mapsto}Y,\ X{\mapsto}Z \vdash_{\mathcal{S}_{Par}} X{\mapsto}YZ$ **Union Rule**

$\lfloor Comp \rfloor$ $X{\mapsto}Y,\ W{\mapsto}Z \vdash_{\mathcal{S}_{Par}} XW{\mapsto}YZ$ **Composition Rule**

$\lfloor Inters \rfloor$ $X{\mapsto}Y,\ X{\mapsto}Z \vdash_{\mathcal{S}_{Par}} X{\mapsto}Y \cap Z$ **Intersection Rule**

$\lfloor Reduc \rfloor$ $X{\mapsto}Y \vdash_{\mathcal{S}_{Par}} X{\mapsto}Y\text{-}X$ **Reduction Rule**

$\lfloor Frag \rfloor$ $X{\mapsto}YZ \vdash_{\mathcal{S}_{Par}} X{\mapsto}Y$ **Fragmentation Rule**

$\lfloor gAugm \rfloor$ $X{\mapsto}Y \vdash_{\mathcal{S}_{Par}} U{\mapsto}V$, where $X \subseteq U$ and $V \subseteq XY$

                    Generalized Augmentation Rule

$\lfloor gTrans \rfloor$ $X{\mapsto}Y,\ Z{\mapsto}U \vdash_{\mathcal{S}_{Par}} V{\mapsto}W$, where $Z \subseteq XY$, $X \subseteq V$ and $W \subseteq UV$

                    Generalized Transitivity Rule

Unfortunately, $\mathcal{S}_{Par}$ and all the other classical FD axiomatic systems are not suitable tools to develop automated deduction techniques, because all of them are based on the transitivity rule, which has an inherent *explosive* behavior. This is a well-known problem in other deduction methods, like *tableaux*-like methods, based on a distribution rule which limits their use.

Primitive rules of $\mathcal{S}_{Par}$ have been implemented in Maude 2 [13]. It is remarkable the direct translation of the inference rules into conditional equations. Some basic modules in Maude 2 have been necessary for the implementation[4]: *ostring.maude* (this module is defined for ordered strings management), *dependency.maude* (this module defines the sort *Dep* (dependency) and related operators and sorts) and *subgenerator.maude* (this module produces all the dependencies generated by the axiom through the operators *subdeps* and *subfrag*).

The axiom $\lfloor Ax_{Par} \rfloor$ has been implemented by way of two equations called "raxiom" and "laxiom". The first one adds all the dependencies of the form $X{\mapsto}Y$ if $Y \subseteq X$. The second one does the same but applied to the right part of any dependency. The corresponding module in Maude is shown below. As it is cited in [10], "Maude's equational logic is so expressive as to offer very good advantages as a logical framework".

```
fmod PARADAENS is
    protecting SUBGENERATOR .
    op < _ > : SetofDeps -> SetofDeps .
    vars T V W X Y Z : String .
    var LR : ListofDeps .
--- Augmentation
    ceq [Augm] : < {(X |--> Y), LR} > = < {(X |--> (X Y)),(X |--> Y), LR} >
    if (not ((X |--> (X Y)) in {(X |--> Y), LR})) .
--- Transitivity
    ceq [Trans] : < {(X |--> Y),(Y |--> Z),LR} > = < {(X |--> Z),(X |--> Y),(Y |--> Z), LR} >
    if (((X =/= Y) and (Y =/= Z)) and (not ((X |--> Z) in {LR}))) .
--- rAxiom
    ceq [rAxiom] : < {(X |--> Y), LR} > = < {subdeps(X),(X |--> Y), LR} >
    if not ({subdeps(X)} c {(X |--> Y), LR}) .
--- lAxiom
    ceq [lAxiom] :  < {(X |--> Y), LR} > = < {subdeps(Y),(X |--> Y), LR} >
    if not ({subdeps(Y)} c {(X |--> Y), LR}) .
endfm
```

The application of this Maude 2 code to a given set of FDs produces all the inferrable FDs. The cardinality of this equivalent output set grows in an

---

[4] The complete specification is available at
http://www.satd.uma.es/gabri/fd/sources.htm.

exponential way. This is an unsurprising result due to the inherent exponentiality of the problem. Even for trivial examples (up to two FDs), the execution of this rewriting module generates a huge FDs set. It is clear that this situation requires us to investigate in another direction.

If we are looking for an efficient method to solve the implication problem, we do not use $\mathcal{S}_{Par}$. Instead of that, a closure operator for attributes is used. Thus, if we have to prove if $X \mapsto Y$ is a consequence of Γ, we compute X^+ (the closure of X in Γ) and we test if Y is a subset of X^+. In the literature there are several algorithms to compute the closure attribute operator in linear time (see [7, 9] for further details). This ensures that we can solve the implication problem in polinomial time.

Nevertheless, this efficient method has a very important disadvantage: it does not allow giving an explanation about the answer. When we use an indirect method we are not able to translate the final solution into an inference chain to explain the answer in terms of the inference system. This limits the use of the indirect methods, because we cannot apply them in artificial intelligence environments, where the explanation is as important as the final answer.

3   The Minimality and the Optimality Problems. A New Intermediate Solution

The number of FDs in a set is a critical measure, because it is directly related to the cost of every problem concerning FD. The search for a set of FDs with minimal cardinality that is equivalent to a given one it is known as *Minimality problem*.

Nevertheless, as Atzeni et al. [7] remark, the problem is not always the number of FDs in the set but it is sometimes the number of attributes of the FD set. This second approach of the size of a FD set conduces to the *Optimality problem*.

Firstly, we define formally the concept of size of an FD set.

Definition 3. *Let $\Gamma \subseteq \mathcal{L}_{FD}$ be finite. We define the size of Γ as*

$$\|\Gamma\| = \sum_{X \mapsto Y \in \Gamma} |X| + |Y| \qquad \text{(where $|X|$ denotes the cardinality of X)}$$

Secondly, we outline problems mentioned before as follows.

- **Minimality:** the search for a set equivalent to Γ such that any set of FDs with lower cardinality is non-equivalent to Γ.
- **Optimality:** the search for a set equivalent to Γ such that any set of FDs with lower size is non-equivalent to Γ.

As they demonstrate, optimality implies minimality and, while minimality can be checked in polinomial time using indirect algorithms, optimality is NP-hard. Besides, the exponential cost of optimality is due, particularly, to the need of testing cycles in the FD graph.

Now we formalize these problems and a new non NP-Hard problem more useful than minimality. We will show in section 4 that this new problem has linear cost. Moreover, we propose the use of RL to solve this new problem.

Definition 4. *Let $\Gamma \subseteq \mathcal{L}_{FD}$ be finite. We say that Γ is **minimal** if the following condition holds*

$$\text{If } |\Gamma'| \leq |\Gamma| \text{ and } \Gamma' \equiv_{S_{Par}} \Gamma \text{ then } |\Gamma'| = |\Gamma|.$$

*We say that Γ is **optimal** if the following condition holds*

$$\text{If } \|\Gamma'\| \leq \|\Gamma\| \text{ and } \Gamma' \equiv_{S_{Par}} \Gamma \text{ then } \|\Gamma'\| = \|\Gamma\|.$$

The minimality condition is in practise unapproachable with the axiomatic system and the optimality condition take us to an NP-hard problem. We are interested in an intermediate point between minimality and optimality. To this end we characterize the minimality using the following definition.

Definition 5. *We define* Union *to be a rewriting rule which is applied $\lfloor Union \rfloor$ to condense FDs with the same left-hand side. That is, if $\Gamma \subseteq \mathcal{L}_{FD}$ is finite,* Union *systematically makes the following transformation:*

$$\text{If } X \mapsto Y, X \mapsto Z \in \Gamma \text{ then replace } X \mapsto Y \text{ and } X \mapsto Z \text{ by } X \mapsto YZ.$$

Therefore, when we say that a set is minimal, we mean that this set is a minimal element of its equivalence class. In this case we use the order given by the inclusion of sets. However, when we say that a set is optimal, we refer to the "minimality" in the preorder given by $\Gamma_1 \preccurlyeq \Gamma_2$ if and only if $\|\Gamma_1\| \leq \|\Gamma_2\|$. Now we define a new order to improve the concept of minimality.

Definition 6. *Let Γ_1 and Γ_2 be finite subsets of $\mathcal{L}_{FD}$. We define the **atomic inclusion**, denoted by $\sqsubseteq$, as follows: we say that $\Gamma_1 \sqsubseteq \Gamma_2$ if and only if*

$$\text{for all } X \mapsto Y \in \Gamma_1 \text{ there exists } X' \mapsto Y' \in \Gamma_2 \text{ such that } X \subseteq X' \text{ and } Y \subseteq Y'$$

Obviously, this relation is an order[5]. Now, we introduce a new concept of minimality based on this order.

Definition 7. *Let $\Gamma \subseteq \mathcal{L}_{FD}$ be finite. We say that Γ is **atomic-minimal** if the following conditions hold*

- Union$(\Gamma) = \Gamma$.
- *If $\Gamma' \sqsubseteq \Gamma$ and $\Gamma' \equiv_{S_{Par}} \Gamma$ then* Union$(\Gamma') = \Gamma$.

Example 1. Let us consider the following sets of FDs:

$$\Gamma_1 = \{ab \mapsto de, de \mapsto ac, c \mapsto ab, c \mapsto de, adef \mapsto g\}$$
$$\Gamma_2 = \{ab \mapsto de, de \mapsto ac, c \mapsto ab, adef \mapsto g\}$$
$$\Gamma_3 = \{ab \mapsto de, de \mapsto c, c \mapsto ab, def \mapsto g\}$$
$$\Gamma_4 = \{ab \mapsto de, de \mapsto c, c \mapsto ab, cf \mapsto g\}$$

---

[5] Note that, if we extend this relation to all subsets of $\mathcal{L}_{FD}$ (finite and infinite subsets), this relation is a preorder but not an order.

These sets are equivalent in Paredaen's logic and we have that: Γ_4 is optimal. Γ_3 is not optimal because $\|\Gamma_3\| = \|\Gamma_4\| + 1$ (the FD $def \rightarrow g$ of Γ_3 has been replaced by $cf \rightarrow g$ in Γ_4). Γ_3 is atomic-minimal. Γ_2 is not atomic-minimal because $\Gamma_3 \sqsubseteq \Gamma_2$ and $\text{Union}(\Gamma_3) = \Gamma_3 \neq \Gamma_2$ (notice the FDs $de \rightarrow ac$ and $adef \rightarrow g$ of Γ_2 and their corresponding $de \rightarrow c$ and $def \rightarrow g$ in Γ_3). Γ_2 is minimal because there are no superfluous FDs. Finally, Γ_1 is not minimal because $c \rightarrow de$ can be obtained by transitivity from $c \rightarrow ab$ and $ab \rightarrow de$. The relation among these sets is depicted in the following table:

	Γ_1	Γ_2	Γ_3	Γ_4
Minimal		✓	✓	✓
Atomic-minimal			✓	✓
Optimal				✓

Finally, we remark that $|\Gamma_1| = 5 > |\Gamma_2| = |\Gamma_3| = |\Gamma_4| = 4$.
However, $\|\Gamma_1\| = 19 > \|\Gamma_2\| = 16 > \|\Gamma_3\| = 14 > \|\Gamma_4\| = 13$

Let us remark that a set Γ is minimal if we cannot obtain an equivalent set by removing some FD of Γ. Therefore, we may design an algorithm to obtain minimal sets through elimination of redundant FDs. In the same way, Γ is atomic-minimal if we cannot obtain an equivalent set by removing an attribute of one FD belonging to Γ. This fact guide the following results.

Definition 8. *Let $\Gamma \subseteq \mathcal{L}_{FD}$ and $\varphi = X \mapsto Y \in \Gamma$.*

- *φ is **superfluous** in Γ if $\Gamma \smallsetminus \{\varphi\} \vdash_{S_{Par}} \varphi$.*
- *φ is **l-redundant** in Γ if there exist $\varnothing \neq Z \subseteq X$ such that*

$$(\Gamma \smallsetminus \{\varphi\}) \cup \{(X\text{-}Z) \mapsto Y\} \vdash_{S_{Par}} \varphi$$

- *φ is **r-redundant** in Γ if there exist $\varnothing \neq U \subseteq Y$ such that*

$$(\Gamma \smallsetminus \{\varphi\}) \cup \{X \mapsto (Y\text{-}U)\} \vdash_{S_{Par}} \varphi$$

The following theorem is directly obtained from Definition 8.

Theorem 1. *Let $\Gamma \subseteq \mathcal{L}_{FD}$ be a finite set of FDs such that $\text{Union}(\Gamma) = \Gamma$. Then Γ is atomic-minimal if and only if there not exist $\varphi \in \Gamma$ such that φ is superfluous, l-redundant or r-redundant in Γ.*

This theorem relates atomic-minimality and the three situations included in Definition 8. The question is, what situations in Definition 8 are not covered with minimality? The superfluous FDs are covered trivially.

In the literature, the algorithms which treat with sets of FDs consider a preprocessing transformation which renders FDs with only one attribute in the right-hand side. This preprocessing transformation applies exhaustively the $\lfloor Frag \rfloor$ rule in Definition 2.

In these algorithms, r-redundant attributes are captured as superfluous FDs. The l-redundant attribute situation is a novel notion in the literature and the classical FDs algorithms do not deal with it.

4   The Search for Atomic-Minimality

In Section 2 the implication problem cannot be solved using directly Paredaens logic. Thus, we use a novel logic, the $\mathbf{SL}_{FD}$ logic presented in [11] which avoids the disadvantages of classical FD logics. The axiomatic system of $\mathbf{SL}_{FD}$ logic is more appropriate to automate.

Definition 9. *We define the* $\mathbf{SL}_{FD}$ *logic as the pair* $(\mathcal{L}_{FD}, \mathcal{S}_{FDS})$ *where* $\mathcal{S}_{FDS}$ *has one axiom scheme:* $\lfloor Ax_{FDS} \rfloor :$ $\vdash X \mapsto Y$, *where* $Y \subseteq X$. *Particulary,* $X \mapsto \top$ *is an axiom scheme.*

The inferences are the following:

$\lfloor Frag \rfloor$	$X \mapsto Y \vdash_{\mathcal{S}_{FDS}} X \mapsto Y'$ if $Y' \subseteq Y$	**Fragmentation rule**
$\lfloor Comp \rfloor$	$X \mapsto Y,\ U \mapsto V \vdash_{\mathcal{S}_{FDS}} XU \mapsto YV$	**Composition rule**
$\lfloor Subst \rfloor$	$X \mapsto Y,\ U \mapsto V \vdash_{\mathcal{S}_{FDS}} (U\text{-}Y) \mapsto (V\text{-}Y)$ if $X \subseteq U,\ X \cap Y = \varnothing$	
		Substitution rule

Theorem 2. *The* $\mathcal{S}_{Par}$ *and* $\mathcal{S}_{FDS}$ *systems are equivalent.*

The proof of this equivalence and the advantages of the $\mathbf{SL}_{FD}$ were shown in [11]. $\mathcal{S}_{FDS}$ is sound and complete (see [11]), thus, we have all the derived rules presented in $\mathcal{S}_{Par}$. Besides that, we have the following novel derived rule:

$$\lfloor rSust \rfloor \qquad X \mapsto Y, U \mapsto V \vdash_{\mathcal{S}_{FDS}} U \mapsto (V\text{-}Y) \qquad \text{if } X \subseteq UV, X \cap Y = \varnothing$$

r-Substitution Rule

Obviously, $\mathcal{S}_{FDS}$ does not avoid the exponential complexity of the problem of searching for all the inferrable FDs. Nevertheless, the replacement of the transitivity law by the substitution law allows us to design a rewriting method to search for atomic-minimality in a FDs set.

Next, we show how to use Maude to create an executable environment to search for **atomic-minimal** FD sets. The $\mathbf{SL}_{FD}$ inference system can be directly translated to a rewriting system which allows a natural implementation of FD sets transformations. This rewriting view is directly based on the following theorem.

Theorem 3. *Given* $X, Y, Z, U, V \in 2^{\Omega}$, *we have the following* $\mathcal{S}_{FDS}$-*equivalences:*

Reduction $\{X \mapsto Y\} \equiv_{\mathcal{S}_{FDS}} \{X \mapsto (Y\text{-}X)\}$
Union $\{X \mapsto Y, X \mapsto Z\} \equiv_{\mathcal{S}_{FDS}} \{X \mapsto YZ\}$
Fi *If* $X \subseteq U$ *then* $\{X \mapsto Y, U \mapsto V\} \equiv_{\mathcal{S}_{FDS}} \{X \mapsto Y, (U\text{-}Y) \mapsto (V\text{-}Y)\}$
Fi-r *If* $X \nsubseteq U$ *and* $X \subseteq UV$ *then* $\{X \mapsto Y, U \mapsto V\} \equiv_{\mathcal{S}_{FDS}} \{X \mapsto Y, U \mapsto (V\text{-}Y)\}$

These equivalences[6] are used to rewrite the FD set into a simpler one. Atomic-minimality induces the application of these equivalences from left to right. **Fi** and **Fi-r** are only applied when they render a proper reduction, i.e.:

---

[6] It is easily proven that the reduction rule and the union rule are $\mathcal{S}_{FD}$-*equivalence* transformations.

- If $U \cap Y \neq \varnothing$ or $V \cap Y \neq \varnothing$ then **Fi** is applied to eliminate l-redundant or r-redundant atoms of $U \mapsto V$.
- If $V \cap Y \neq \varnothing$ then **Fi-r** is applied to eliminate r-redundant atoms of $U \mapsto V$.

Now, we give the corresponding rewriting rules in Maude.

```
fmod RED-SLFD is
    protecting DEPENDENCY .
    op > _ < : SetofDeps -> SetofDeps .
    vars  T V W X Y Z : String .
    var LR : ListofDeps .
--- Axiom
    ceq [Axiom] : > {(X |--> Y), LR} < = > {LR} < if (Y c X) .
--- Reduction
    ceq [Reduction] : > {(X |--> Y), LR} < = > {(X |--> (Y - X)), LR} <
    if not ((X /\ Y) == "") .
--- Fi
    ceq [Fi] : > {(X |--> Y), (Z |--> V),LR} < = > {((Z - Y) |--> (V - Y)), (X |--> Y), LR} <
    if (X c Z)  and not (((Z /\ Y) == "")  and  ((V /\ Y) == "")) .
--- Fi-r
    ceq [Fi-r] : > {(X |--> Y), (Z |--> V), LR} < = > {(Z |--> (V - Y)), (X |--> Y), LR}  <
    if not (X c Z) and not ((V /\ Y) == "")  and  (X c (Z V)) .
--- Union
    eq [Union] : > {(X |--> Y),(X |--> Z),LR} < = > {(X |--> (Y Z)),LR} <  .
endfm
```

Let Γ be a FD set. Since the size of Γ is reduced in every rewrite, the number of rewrites is linear in the size of Γ.

Below, some examples are shown. We reduce several set of FDs and we show the results that offers Maude 2. The low cost of these reductions is remarkable.

Example 2. This example is used in [14]. The size of the FD set decrease from 26 to 18.

```
reduce in RED-SLFD : > {("b" |--> "e"),("b" |--> "f"), ("c" |-->
"a"),("ad" |--> "c"),("bc" |--> "d"),("be" |--> "c"), ("cd" |-->
"e"),("ce" |--> "af"),"cf" |--> "bd"} < .
rewrites: 111650 in 130ms cpu (130ms real) (858846 rewrites/second)
result SetofDeps: > {("ad" |--> "c"),("b" |--> "cdf"), ("c" |-->
"a"),("cd" |--> "e"),("ce" |--> "f"),"cf" |--> "b"} <
```

Example 3. This example is depurated in [9] using 16 $^+$-closures. Our reduction in RL and Maude obtains the same result without using a closure operator.

```
reduce in RED-SLFD : > {("b" |--> "a"),("b" |--> "g"), ("b" |-->
"h"),("d" |--> "a"),("bn" |--> "h"),("ab" |--> "d"), ("ab" |-->
"e"),("ab" |--> "f"),("ab" |--> "g"),("abc" |--> "d"), ("abc" |-->
"j"),"abc" |--> "k"} < .
rewrites: 102222 in 120ms cpu (120ms real) (851850 rewrites/second)
result SetofDeps:
> {("b" |--> "defgh"),("bc"|--> "jk"),"d" |--> "a"} <
```

5   Conclusions and Future Work

In this work we have studied the relation between RL and the treatment of sets of FDs. We have illustrated the difficulties to face the implication problem with a method directly based on FDs logics. We have introduced the notion of atomic-minimality, which guides the treatment of sets of FDs in a rewriting style. Given Γ a set of FDs, we rewrite Γ into an equivalent and more depurated FD set. This goal has been reached using $\mathbf{SL}_{FD}$. This axiomatic system avoids the use of transitivity paradigm and introduces the application of substitution paradigm. $\mathbf{SL}_{FD}$ axiomatic system ($\mathcal{S}_{FDS}$) is easily translated to RL and Maude 2.

The implementation of $\mathcal{S}_{FDS}$ in Maude 2 allows us to have an executable rewriting system to reduce the size of a given FDs set in the direction guided by atomic-minimality. Thus, we open the door to the use of RL and Maude 2 to deal with FDs.

As a short-term future work, our intention is to develop a Maude 2 system to get atomic-minimality FDs sets. As a medium-term future work, we will use Maude *strategies* to fully treat the redundancy contained in FDs sets.

References

1. Codd, E.F.: The relational model for database management: Version 2. reading, mass. Addison Wesley (1990)
2. Bell, D.A., Guan, J.W.: Computational methods for rough classifications and discovery. J. American Society for Information Sciences. Special issue on Data Minig **49** (1998)
3. Stumme, G., Taouil, R., Bastide, Y., Pasquier, N., Lakhal, L.: Functional and embedded dependency inference: a data mining point of view. Information Systems **26 (7)** (2002) 477–506
4. Han, J.: Binding propagation beyond the reach of rule / goal graphs. Information Processing Letters **42 (5)** (1992 Jul 3) 263–268
5. Montesi, D., Torlone, R.: Analysis and optimization of active databases. Data & Knowledge Engineering **40 (3)** (2002 Mar) 241–271
6. Armstrong, W.W.: Dependency structures of data base relationships. Proc. IFIP Congress. North Holland, Amsterdam (1974) 580–583
7. Atzeni, P., Antonellis, V.D.: Relational Database Theory. The Benjamin/Cummings Publishing Company Inc. (1993)
8. Paredaens, J., De Bra, P., Gyssens, M., Van Gucht, D.: The structure of the relational database model. EATCS Monographs on TCS (1989)
9. Diederich, J., Milton, J.: New methods and fast algorithms for database normalization. ACM Transactions on Database Systems **13 (3)** (1988) 339–365
10. Clavel, M., Durán, F., Eker, S., Lincoln, P., Martí-Oliet, N., Meseguer, J., Quesada, J.F.: Maude: specification and programming in rewriting logic. Theoretical Computer Science (TCS) **285 (2)** (2002) 187–243
11. Cordero, P., Enciso, M., Guzmán, I.P.d., Mora, Á.: Slfd logic: Elimination of data redundancy in knowledge representation. (Advances in AI, Iberamia 2002. LNAI 2527 141-150. Springer-Verlag.)
12. Mora, Á., Enciso, M., Cordero, P., Guzmán, I.P.d.: An efficient preprocessing transformation for funtcional dependencies set based on the substitution paradigm. CAEPIA 2003. To be published in LNAI. (2003)
13. Clavel, M., Durán, F., Eker, S., Lincoln, P., Martí-Oliet, N., Meseguer, J., Quesada, J.: A Maude Tutorial. SRI International. (2000)
14. Ullman, J.D.: Database and knowledge-base systems. Computer Science Press (1988)

Reasoning About Requirements Evolution Using Clustered Belief Revision

Odinaldo Rodrigues[1], Artur d'Avila Garcez[2], and Alessandra Russo[3]

[1] Dept. of Computer Science, King's College London, UK
odinaldo@dcs.kcl.ac.uk
[2] Department of Computing, City University London, UK
aag@soi.city.ac.uk
[3] Department of Computing, Imperial College London, UK
ar3@doc.ic.ac.uk

Abstract. During the development of system requirements, software system specifications are often inconsistent. Inconsistencies may arise for different reasons, for example, when multiple conflicting viewpoints are embodied in the specification, or when the specification itself is at a transient stage of evolution. We argue that a formal framework for the analysis of evolving specifications should be able to *tolerate* inconsistency by allowing reasoning in the presence of inconsistency without trivialisation, and *circumvent* inconsistency by enabling impact analyses of potential changes to be carried out. This paper shows how *clustered belief revision* can help in this process.

1 Introduction

Conflicting viewpoints inevitably arise in the process of requirements analysis. Conflict resolution, however, may not necessarily happen until later in the development process. This highlights the need for requirements engineering tools that support the management of inconsistencies [12, 17].

Many formal methods of analysis and elicitation rely on classical logic as the underlying formalism. Model checking, for example, typically uses temporal operators on top of classical logic reasoning [10]. This facilitates the use of well-behaved and established proof procedures. On the other hand, it is well known that classical logic theories trivialise in the presence of inconsistency and this is clearly undesirable in the context of requirements engineering, where inconsistency often arises [6].

Paraconsistent logics [3] attempt to ameliorate the problem of theory trivialisation by weakening some of the axioms of classical logic, often at the expense of reasoning power. While appropriate for concise modelling, logics of this kind are too weak to support practical reasoning and the analysis of inconsistent specifications.

Clustered belief revision [15] takes a different view and uses theory prioritisation to obtain plausible (i.e., non trivial) conclusions from an inconsistent theory, yet exploiting the full power of classical logic reasoning. This allows the

A.L.C. Bazzan and S. Labidi (Eds.): SBIA 2004, LNAI 3171, pp. 41–51, 2004.

requirements engineer to analyse the results of different possible prioritisations by reasoning classically, and to evolve specifications that contain conflicting viewpoints in a principled way. The analysis of user-driven cluster prioritisations can also give stakeholders a better understanding of the impact of certain changes in the specification.

In this paper, we investigate how clustered belief revision can support requirements analysis and evolution. In particular, we have developed a tool for clustered revision that translates requirements given in the form of "if then else" rules into the (more efficient) disjunctive normal form (DNF) for classical logic reasoning and cluster prioritisation. We have then used a simplified version of the light control case study [9] to provide a sample validation of the clustered revision framework in requirements engineering.

The rest of the paper is organised as follows. In Section 2, we present the clustered revision framework. In Section 3, we apply the framework to the simplified light control case study and discuss the results. In Section 4, we discuss related work and, in Section 5, we conclude and discuss directions for future work.

2   Clustered Belief Revision

Clustered belief revision [15] is based on the main principles of the well established field of belief revision [1, 7], but has one important feature not present in the original work: the ability to group sentences with a similar *role* into a *cluster*. As in other approaches [11, 8], extra-logical information is used to help in the process of conflict resolution. Within the context of requirements evolution, such extra-logical information is a (partial) ordering relation on sentences, expressing the relative level of preference of the engineer on the requirements being formalised. In other words, less preferred requirements are the ones the engineer is prepared to give up first (as necessary) during the process of conflict resolution.

The formalism uses sentences in DNF in order to make the deduction and resolution mechanisms more efficient. The resolution extends classical deduction by using the extra-logical information to decide how to solve the conflicts. A cluster can be resolved and simplified into a single sentence in DNF. Clusters can be embedded in other clusters and priorities between clusters can be specified in the same way as priorities can be specified within a single cluster. The embedding allows for the representation of complex structures which can be useful in the specification of requirements in software engineering. The behaviour of the selection procedure in the deduction mechanism – that makes the choices in the resolution of conflicts – can be tailored according to the ordering of individual clusters and the intended local interpretation of that ordering.

Our approach has the following main characteristics: *i)* it allows users to specify clusters of sentences associated with some (possibly incomplete) priority information; *ii)* it resolves conflicts within a cluster by taking into account the priorities specified by the user and provides a consistent conclusion whenever possible; *iii)* it allows clusters to be embedded in other clusters so that complex priority structures can be specified; and finally *iv)* it combines the reasoning about the priorities with the deduction mechanism itself in an intuitive way.

In the resolution of a cluster, the main idea is to specify a deduction mechanism that reasons with the priorities and computes a *conclusion* based on these priorities. The priorities themselves are used only when conflicts arise, in which case sentences associated with higher priorities are preferred to those with lower priorities. The *prioritisation principle* (PP) used here is that *"a sentence with priority x cannot block the acceptance of another sentence with priority higher than x"*. In the original AGM theory of belief revision, the prioritisation principle exists implicitly but is only applied to the new information to be incorporated.

We also adopt the *principle of minimal change* (PMC) although to a limited extent. In the original AGM theory PMC requires that old beliefs should not be given up unless this is strictly necessary in order to repair the inconsistency caused by the new belief. In our approach, we extend this idea to cope with several levels of priority by stating that *"information should not be lost unless it causes inconsistency with information conveyed by sentences with higher priority"* (PMC$_\leq$). As a result, when a cluster is provided without any relative priority between its sentences, the mechanism behaves in the usual way and computes a sentence whose models are logically equivalent to the models of the (union of) the maximal consistent subsets of the cluster. On the other extreme, if the sentences in the cluster are linearly prioritised, the mechanism behaves in a way similar to Nebel's *linear prioritised belief bases* [11].

Unfortunately, we do not have enough space to present the full formalism of clustered belief revision and its properties here. Further details can be found in [15]. The main idea is to associate labels of set $\mathcal{J}$ to propositional formulae via a function f and define a partial order $\leq$ on $\mathcal{J}$ according to the priorities one wants to express. $\leq$ is then extended to the power set of $\mathcal{J}$ in the following way[1].

Definition 1. *Let* $\mathsf{B} = \langle \mathcal{J}, \leq, f \rangle$ *be a cluster of sentences and* $X, Y \in 2^{\mathcal{J}}$. $X \preceq Y$ *iff either* i) $Y = \emptyset$; *or* ii) $\exists x \in X$, $\exists y \in Y$, *s.t.* $x \leq y$ *and* $X - \{x\} \preceq Y - \{y\}$; *or* iii) $\exists x \in X$, $\exists Y' \subseteq Y$, *s.t.* $Y' \neq \emptyset$ *and* $\forall y \in Y'.x < y$ *and* $X - \{x\} \preceq Y - Y'$.

The ordering above is intended to extend the user's original preference relation $\leq$ on the set of requirements to the power set of these requirements. This allows one to compare how subsets of the original requirements relate to each other with respect to the preferences stated by the user on the individual requirements. Other extensions of $\leq$ to $\mathcal{J}$ could be devised according to the needs of specific applications.

A separate mechanism selects some sets in $2^{\mathcal{J}}$ according to some criteria. For our purposes here, this mechanism calculates the sets in $2^{\mathcal{J}}$ that are associated

---

[1] In the full formalism, the function f can map an element x of J to another cluster as well, creating nested revision levels, i.e., when the object mapped to x by f, namely $f(x)$, is not a sentence, $f(x)$ is recursively resolved first.

with *consistent* combination of sentences[2]. In order to choose the *best* consistent sets (according to $\leq$), we use the ordering $\preceq$, i.e., we take the minimal elements in $2^{\mathcal{J}}$ that are consistent. Since $\preceq$ forms a lattice on $2^{\mathcal{J}}$, where $\mathcal{J}$ is always the minimum, if the labelled belief base is consistent, then the choice of the best consistent sets will give just $\mathcal{J}$ itself. Otherwise, this choice will identify some subsets of $\mathcal{J}$ according to $\leq$. The search for consistent combinations of sentences and minimal elements of $\preceq$ can be combined and optimised (see [14]).

Example 1. Consider the cluster $\mathcal{C}$ defined by the set $\mathcal{J} = \{x, w, y, z\}$; the partial order $\leq$ on $\mathcal{J}$ given in the middle of Figure 1, where an arrow from a to b indicates priority of a over b; and the following function f: $f(x) = p \wedge q$, $f(w) = \neg p \vee r$, $f(y) = \neg r \vee \neg s$ and $f(z) = \neg q \vee s$.

The sentences above taken conjunctively are inconsistent, so we look for consistent subsets of the base. It can be shown that the maximal consistent subsets of $\{p \wedge q, \neg p \vee r, \neg r \vee \neg s, \neg q \vee s\}$ will be those associated with the labels in the sets $\{x, w, y\}$, $\{x, y, z\}$, $\{x, w, z\}$ and $\{w, y, z\}$. According to the ordering $\preceq$, amongst these $\{x, w, y\}$ and $\{x, y, z\}$ are the ones which best verify PMC$_\leq$. The sets $\{w, y, z\}$ and $\{x, w, z\}$ do not verify PP. In fact, $\{w, y, z\}$ has lower priority even than $\{x\}$ since it does not contain the label x associated with the most important sentence in $\mathcal{J}$. $\{x, w, z\}$ on the other hand is strictly worse than $\{x, w, y\}$, since the latter contains y which is strictly better than z according to $\leq$. The resolution of $\mathcal{C}$ would produce a result which accepts the sentences associated with x and y and includes the consequences of the disjunction of the sentences associated with w and z. This signals that whereas it is possible to consistently accept the sentences associated with x and y, it is not possible to consistently include both the sentences associated with w and z. Not enough information is given in $\leq$ in order to make a choice between w and z and hence their disjunction is taken instead.

3   The Light Control Example

In what follows, we adapt and simplify the Light Control Case Study (LCS) [13] in order to illustrate the relevant aspects of our revision approach. LCS describes the behaviour of light settings in an office building. We consider two possible light scenes: the *default* light scene and the *chosen* light scene. Office lights are set to the default level upon entry of a user, who can then override this setting to a chosen light scene.

If an office is left unoccupied for more than t_1 minutes, the system turns the office's lights off. When an unoccupied office is reoccupied within t_2 minutes, the light scene is re-established according to its immediately previous setting. The value of t_1 is set by the facilities' manager whereas the value of t_2 is set by the office user [9]. For simplicity, our analysis does not take into account how these two times relate.

---

[2] As suggested about the extension of $\leq$, this selection procedure can be tailored to fit other requirements. One may want for instance to select amongst the subsets of $\mathcal{J}$ those that satisfy a given requirement.

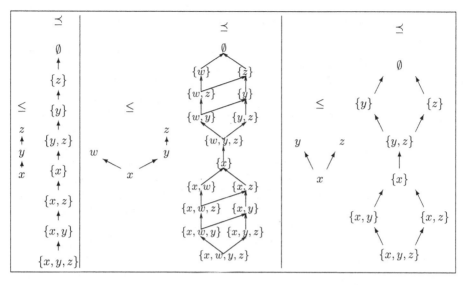

Fig. 1. Examples of orderings $\leq$ and the corresponding final ordering $\preceq$.

Table 1. Dictionary of symbols used in the specification.

prop.	meaning	prop.	meaning
occ	the office is occupied	ui	a user enters an unoccupied office
uo	a user leaves an office unoccupied	e_t_i	t_i minutes have elapsed
t_unocc	unoccupied office for $t < t_2$ mins	$unocc$	unoccupied office for $t \geq t_1$ mins
us_lig	office lights as set by the user	df_lig	office lights in default setting
alm	the alarm is activated	$dark$	office lights are off
$glux_1$	day light level is greater or equal to the light level required by the chosen or default light scene (lux_1)		
$glux_2$	day light level is greater or equal to the maximum luminosity achievable by the office lights (lux_2)		

A dictionary of the symbols used in the LCS case study is given in Table 1. As usual, unprimed literals denote properties of a given state of the system, and primed literals denote properties of the state immediately after (e.g., occ denotes that the office is occupied at time t and occ' that the office is occupied at time $t + 1$).

A partial specification of the LCS is given below:

Behaviour rules

$r_1 : ui \rightarrow occ'$

$r_2 : occ \wedge uo \wedge \neg e\_t_2 \rightarrow t\_unocc'$

$r_3 : t\_unocc \wedge e\_t_1 \rightarrow unocc'$

$r_4 : t\_unocc \wedge ui \rightarrow occ'$

$r_5 : unocc \rightarrow dark'$

$r_6 : t\_unocc \wedge ui \rightarrow us\_lig'$

$r_7 : ui \rightarrow df\_lig'$

Safety rules

$s_1 : alm \wedge \neg e\_t_3 \rightarrow df\_lig'$

$s_2 : alm \wedge e\_t_3 \rightarrow dark'$

$s_3 : df\_lig \leftrightarrow \neg dark$

$s_4 : df\_lig' \leftrightarrow \neg dark'$

Economy rules

$e_1 : glux_1 \wedge (us\_lig \vee df\_lig) \rightarrow dark'$

$e_2 : glux_2 \rightarrow dark'$

We assume that LCS should satisfy two types of properties: *safety* properties and *economy* properties.

The following are safety properties: *i)* the lights are not off in the default light scene; *ii)* if the fire alarm (alm) is triggered, the default light scene must be re-established in all offices; and *iii)* t_3 minutes after the alarm is triggered, all lights must be turned off (i.e., only emergency lights must be on). The value of t_3 is set by the facilities manager. The above requirements are represented by rules s_1 to s_4.

The economy properties include the fact that, whenever possible, the system ought to use natural light to achieve the light levels required by the office light scenes. Sensors can check *i)* whether the luminosity coming from the outside is enough to surpass the luminosity required by the current light scene; and *ii)* whether the luminosity coming from the outside is greater than the maximum luminosity achievable by the office lights. The latter is useful because it can be applied independently of the current light scene in an office. Let lux_1 denote the luminosity required by the current light scene, and lux_2 the maximum luminosity achievable by the office lights. *i)* if the natural light is at least lux_1 ($glux_1$) and the office is in the chosen or default light scene, then the lights must be turned off; and *ii)* if the natural light is at least lux_2 ($glux_2$), then the lights must be turned off. This is represented by rules e_1 and e_2.

Now, consider the following scenario. On a bright Summer's day, John is working in his office when suddenly the fire alarm goes off. He leaves the office immediately. Once outside the building, he realises that he left his briefcase behind and decides to go back to fetch it. By the time he enters his office, more than t_3 minutes have elapsed. This situation can be formalised as follows:

i_1: John enters the office (ui), i_2: the alarm is sounding (alm)
i_3: t_3 minutes or more have elapsed since the alarm went off (e_t_3)
i_4: daylight provides luminosity enough to dispense with artificial lighting ($glux_2$)

We get inconsistency in two different ways:

1. Because John walks in the office (i_1), lights go to the default setting (r_7). By s_4, the lights must be on in this setting. This contradicts s_2, which states that lights should be turned off t_3 minutes after the alarm goes off.

   ui (i_1), alm (i_2), e_t_3 (i_3), $df\_lig' \rightarrow \neg dark'$ (s_4), $ui \rightarrow df\_lig'$ (r_7), $alm \wedge e\_t_3 \rightarrow dark'$ (s_2)

2. Similarly, as John walks in the office (i_1), lights go to the default setting (r_7). Therefore lights are turned on (s_4). However, by e_2, this is not necessary, since it is bright outside and the luminosity coming through the window is higher the maximum luminosity achievable by the office lights ($glux_2$).

   ui (i_1), $glux_2$ (i_4), $df\_lig' \rightarrow \neg dark'$ (s_4), $ui \rightarrow df\_lig'$ (r_7), $glux_2 \rightarrow dark'$ (e_2)

This is a situation where inconsistency on the light scenes occur due to violations of safety and economy properties. We need to reason about how to resolve the inconsistency. Using clustered belief revision, we can arrange the components of the specification in different priority settings, by grouping rules in clusters, e.g., a safety cluster, an economy cluster, etc. It is possible to prioritise the clusters *internally* as well, but this is not considered here for reasons of space and simplicity.

The organisation of the information in each cluster can be done independently but the overall prioritisation of the clusters at the highest level requires input from all stakeholders. For example, in the scenario described previously, we might wish to prioritise safety rules over the other rules of the specification and yet not have enough information from stakeholders to decide on the relative strength of economy rules. In this case, we would ensure that the specification satisfies the safety rules but not necessarily the economy ones.

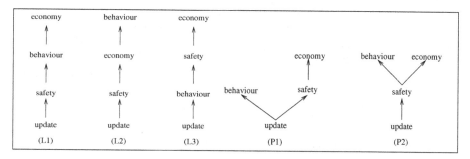

Fig. 2. Linearly (L1, L2 and L3) and partially (P1 and P2) ordered clusters.

Let us assume that sensor and factual information is correct and therefore not subject to revision. We combine this information in a cluster called "update" and give it highest priority. In addition, we assume that safety rules must have priority over economy rules. At this point, no information on the relative priority of behaviour rules is available. With this in mind, it is possible to arrange the clusters with the update, safety, behaviour and economy rules as depicted in Figure 2. Prioritisations L1, L2 and L3 represent all possible linear arrangements of these clusters with the assumptions mentioned above, whereas prioritisations P1 and P2 represent the corresponding partial ones.

The overall result of the clustered revision will be consistent as long as the cluster with the highest priority (factual and sensor information) is not itself inconsistent. When the union of the sentences in all clusters is indeed inconsistent, in order to restore consistency, some rules may have to be withdrawn. For example, take prioritisation L1. The sentences in the safety cluster are consistent with those in the update cluster; together, they conflict with behaviour rule r_7 (see Figure 3). Since r_7 is in a cluster with lower priority in L1, it cannot be consistently kept and it is withdrawn from the intermediate result. The final step is to incorporate what can be consistently accepted from the economy cluster. For example, rule e_1 is consistent with the (partial) result given in Figure 3 and is therefore included in the revised specification, and similarly for rule e_2.

Notice however, that r_7 might be kept given a different arrangement of the priorities. The refinement process occurs by allowing one to reason about these

---

update + safety include (in DNF): $ui \wedge alm \wedge e\_t_3 \wedge glux_2 \wedge dark' \wedge \neg df\_lig'$

behaviour includes (in DNF): $\qquad \neg ui \vee df\_lig'$

---

result 1: $ui \wedge alm \wedge e\_t_3 \wedge glux_2 \wedge dark' \wedge \neg df\_lig'$

Fig. 3. Conflict with behaviour rule r_7.

different arrangements and the impact on the rules in the specification, without trivialising the results. Eventually, one aims to reach a final specification that is consistent regardless of the priorities between the clusters, i.e., consistent in the classical logic sense, although this is not essential in our framework.

Prioritisations L2 and P2 give the same results as L1, i.e., withdrawal of r_7 is recommended. On the other hand, in prioritisation L3, the sentence in the behaviour cluster is consistent with those in the update cluster; together, they conflict with safety rule s_4 (see Figure 4). Since the safety cluster is given lower priority in L3, both sentences s_2 and s_4 cannot be consistently kept. One has to give up either s_2 or s_4. However, if s_4 were to be kept, then e_2 would also have to be withdrawn. Minimal change to the specification forces us to keep s_2 instead, as it allows for the inclusion of e_2.

---

update + behaviour include (in DNF): $ui \wedge alm \wedge e\_t_3 \wedge glux_2 \wedge df\_lig'$

safety includes (in DNF): $\qquad ((\neg df\_lig' \wedge dark') \vee (\neg df\_lig' \wedge \neg alm) \vee$
$(\neg dark' \wedge \neg alm) \vee (\neg df\_lig' \wedge \neg e\_t_3) \vee$
$(\neg dark' \wedge \neg e\_t_3))$

---

result 2: $ui \wedge alm \wedge e\_t_3 \wedge glux_2 \wedge df\_lig' \wedge dark'$

Fig. 4. Conflict with safety rule s_4.

Finally, prioritisation P1 offers a choice between the sets of clusters {update, safety, economy} and {update, behaviour, economy}. The former corresponds to withdrawing r_7 (reasoning in the same way as for L1, L2 and P2), whereas the latter corresponds to withdrawing s_4 as in the case of L3.

In summary, from the five different cluster prioritisations analysed, a recommendation was made to withdraw a behaviour rule in three of them, to withdraw a safety rule in one of them, and to withdraw either a behaviour or a safety rule in one of them. From these results and the LCS context, the withdrawal of behaviour rule r_7 seems more plausible. In more complicated cases, a decision support system could be used to help the choice of recommendations made by the clustered revision framework.

4   Related Work

A number of logic-based approaches for handling inconsistency and evolving requirements specifications have been proposed in the literature. Zowghi and Offen [18] proposed belief revision for default theories as a formal approach for resolving inconsistencies. Specifications are formalised as default theories where each requirement may be defeasible or non-defeasible, each kind assumed to be consistent within itself. Inconsistencies introduced by an evolutionary change are resolved by performing a revision operation over the entire specification. Defeasible information that is inconsistent with non-defeasible information is not used in the reasoning process and thus does not trigger a revision. Similarly, in our approach, requirements with lower priority that are inconsistent with requirements with higher priority are not considered in the computation of the revised specification. However, in our approach, the use of different levels of priority enables the engineer to fine-tune the specification and reason with different levels of defeasibility.

In [16], requirements are assumed to be defeasible, having an associated *preference ordering relation*. Conflicting defaults are resolved not by changing the specification but by considering only scenarios or models of the inconsistent specification that satisfy as much of the preferrable information as possible. Whereas Ryan's representation of priorities is similar to our own, we use classical logic entailment as opposed to Ryan's *natural entailment* and the priorities in our framework are used only in the solution of conflicts. Moreover, the use of clusters in our approach provides the formalisation of requirements with additional dimensions, enabling a more refined reasoning process about inconsistency.

In [4], a logic-based approach for reasoning about requirements specifications based on the construction of goal tree structures is proposed. Analyses of the consequences of alternative changes are carried out by investigating which goals would be satisfied and which would not, after adding or removing facts from a specification. In a similar fashion, our approach supports the evaluation of consequences of evolutionary changes by checking which requirements are lost and which are not after adding or deleting a requirement.

Moreover, other techniques have been proposed for managing inconsistency in specifications. In [2], priorities are used but only in subsets of a knowledge base which are responsible for inconsistency. Some inference mechanisms are proposed for locally handling inconsistent information using these priorities. Our approach differs from that work in that the priorities are defined independently of the inconsistency and thus facilitating a richer impact analysis on the overall specification. Furthermore, in [2] priorities can only be specified at the same level within the base, whereas we allow for more complex representations (e.g., between and within sub-bases).

Finally, a lot of work has focused on consistency checking, analysis and action based on pre-defined inconsistency handling rules. For example, in [5], consistency checking rules are combined with pre-defined lists of possible actions, but with no policy or heuristics on how to choose among alternative actions. The entire approach relies on taking decisions based on an analysis of the history of the development process (e.g., past inconsistencies and past actions). Differently, our approach provides a formal support for analysing the impact of changes over the specification by allowing the engineer to perform *if* questions on possible changes and to check the effect that these changes would have in terms of requirements that are lost or preserved.

5   Conclusions and Future Work

In this paper, we have shown how clustered belief revision can be used to analyse the results of different prioritisations on requirements reasoning classically, and to evolve specifications that contain conflicting viewpoints in a principled way. A simplified version of the light control case study was used to provide an early validation of the framework. We believe that this approach gives the engineer more freedom to make appropriate choices on the evolution of the requirements, while at the same time offering rigourous means for evaluating the consequences that such choices have on the specification.

Our approach provides not only a technique for revising requirements specifications using priorities, but also a methodology for handling evolving requirements. The emphasis of the work is on the use of priorities for reasoning about potentially inconsistent specifications. The same technique can be used to check the consequences of a given specification and to reason about "what if" questions that arise during evolutionary changes.

A number of heuristics about the behaviour of the ordering $\preceq$ have been investigated in [14]. The use of DNF greatly simplifies the reasoning, but the conversion to DNF sometimes generates complex formulae making the reasoning process computationally more expensive. To improve scalability of the approach, these formulae should be as simple as possible. This simplification could be achieved by using Karnaugh maps to find a "minimal" DNF of a sentence.

References

1. C. A. Alchourrón and D. Makinson. On the logic of theory change: Contraction functions and their associated revision functions. *Theoria*, 48:14–37, 1982.
2. S. Benferhat and L. Garcia, *Handling Locally Stratified Inconsistent Knowledge Bases*, Studia Logica, 70:77–104, 2002.
3. N. C. A. da Costa, On the theory of inconsistent formal systems. Notre Dame Journal of Formal Logic, 15(4):497–510, 1974.
4. D. Duffy et al., A Framework for Requirements Analysis Using Automated Reasoning, CAiSE95, LNCS 932, Springer, 68–81, 1995.
5. S. Easterbrook and B. Nuseibeh, Using ViewPoints for Inconsistency Management. In Software Engineering Journal, 11(1): 31-43, BCS/IEE Press, January 1996.
6. A. Finkelstein et. al, Inconsistency handling in multi-perspective specifications, IEEE Transactions on Software Engineering, 20(8), 569-578, 1994.
7. Peter Gärdenfors. *Knowledge in Flux: Modeling the Dynamics of Epistemic States.* The MIT Press, Cambridge, Massachusetts, London, England, 1988.
8. P. Gärdenfors and D. Makinson. Revisions of knowledge systems using epistemic entrenchment. TARK II, pages 83–95. Morgan Kaufmann, San Francisco, 1988.
9. C. Heitmeyer and R. Bharadwaj, Applying the SCR Requirements Method to the Light Control Case Study, Journal of Universal Computer Science, Vol.6(7), 2000.
10. M. R. Huth and M. D. Ryan. Logic in Computer Science: Modelling and Reasoning about Systems. Cambridge University Press, 2000.
11. B Nebel. Syntax based approaches to belief revision. *Belief Revision*, 52–88, 1992.

12. B. Nuseibeh, J. Kramer and A. Finkelstein, A Framework for Expressing the Relationships Between Multiple Views in Requirements Specification, IEEE Transactions on Software Engineering, 20(10): 760-773, October 1994.
13. S. Queins et al., The Light Control Case Study: Problem Description. Journal of Universal Computer Science, Special Issue on Requirements Engineering: the Light Control Case Study, Vol.6(7), 2000.
14. Odinaldo Rodrigues. *A methodology for iterated information change.* PhD thesis, Department of Computing, Imperial College, January, 1998.
15. O. Rodrigues, Structured Clusters: A Framework to Reason with Contradictory Interests, Journal of Logic and Computation, 13(1):69–97, 2003.
16. M. D. Ryan. Default in Specification, IEEE International Symposium on Requirements Engineering (RE93), 266–272, San Diego, California, January 1993.
17. G. Spanoudakis and A. Zisman. Inconsistency Management in Software Engineering: Survey and Open Research Issues, Handbook of Softawre Engineering and Knowledge Engineering, (ed.) S.K. Chang, pp. 329-380, 2001.
18. D. Zowghi and R. Offen, A Logical Framework for Modeling and Reasoning about the Evolution of Requirements, Proc. 3rd IEEE International Symposium on Requirements Engineering RE'97, Annapolis, USA, January 1997.

Analysing AI Planning Problems in Linear Logic – A Partial Deduction Approach

Peep Küngas

Norwegian University of Science and Technology
Department of Computer and Information Science
peep@idi.ntnu.no

Abstract. This article presents a framework for analysing AI planning problem specifications. We consider AI planning as linear logic (LL) theorem proving. Then the usage of partial deduction is proposed as a foundation of an analysis technique for AI planning problems, which are described in LL. By applying this technique we are able to investigate for instance why there is no solution for a particular planning problem. We consider here !-Horn fragment of LL, which is expressive enough for representing STRIPS-like planning problems. Anyway, by taking advantage of full LL, more expressive planning problems can be described, Therefore, the framework proposed here could be seen as a step towards analysing both, STRIPS-like and more complex planning problems.

1 Introduction

Recent advancements in the field of AI planning together with increase of computers' computational power have established a solid ground for applying AI planning in mainstream applications. Mainstream usage of AI planning is especially emphasised in the light of the Semantic Web initiative, which besides other factors, assumes that computational entities in the Web embody certain degree of intelligence and autonomy. Therefore AI planning could have applications in automated Web service composition, personalised assistant agents and intelligent user interfaces, for instance.

However, there are issues, which may become a bottleneck for a wider spread of AI planning technologies. From end-user's point of view a planning problem has to be specified in the simplest way possible, by omitting many details relevant at AI planning level. Thus a planning system is expected to reason about missing information and construct a problem specification, which still would provide expected results.

Another issue is that there exist problems, where quite often a complete solution to a declaratively specified problem may not be found. Anyway, system users would be satisfied with an approximate solution, which could be modified later manually. Thus, if there would be no solution for a planning problem, a planner could modify the problem and announce the user about the situation. An example of such applications includes automated Web service composition. It may happen that no service satisfying completely user requirements could be

A.L.C. Bazzan and S. Labidi (Eds.): SBIA 2004, LNAI 3171, pp. 52–61, 2004.
© Springer-Verlag Berlin Heidelberg 2004

composed. However, there might be a solution available which at least partially satisfies user requirements.

Similar problems may arise in dynamically changing systems as well, since it is sometimes hard to foresee, the exact planning problem specification, which would be really needed. Therefore, while computational environments are changing, specifications should alter as well. Anyway, the planner should follow certain criteria while changing specifications. Otherwise the planning process may easily loose its intended purpose.

Finally, humans tend to produce errors even to small pieces of code. Hence a framework for debugging planning specification and identifying users about potential mistakes would be appreciated. One way of debugging could be runtime analysis of planning problems. If no solution to a problem is found, a reason may be a bug in the planning problem specification.

Masseron et al [13], besides others, demonstrated how to apply linear logic (LL) theorem proving for AI planning. We have implemented an AI planner [8], which applies LL theorem proving for planning. Experimental results indicate that on certain problems the performance of our planner is quite close to the current state-of-the-art planners like TALPlanner, SHOP2 and TLPlan.

In this paper we present a framework for applying partial deduction to LL theorem proving in order to extend applicability of AI planning. Our approach to analysing AI planning problems provides a framework, which could assist users while debugging planning specifications. Additionally, the framework allows autonomous systems, given predefined preferences, to adapt themselves to rapidly changing environments.

The rest of the paper is organised as follows. In Section 2 we present an introduction to LL and PD. Additionally we show how to encode planning problems in LL such that LL theorem proving could be used for AI planning. Section 3 describes a motivating example and illustrates how PD in LL could be applied for AI planning. Section 4 sketches theorems about completeness and soundness of PD in LL. Section 5 reviews related work. The last section concludes the paper and discusses future work.

2   Formal Basics and Definitions

2.1   Linear Logic

LL is a refinement of classical logic introduced by J.-Y. Girard to provide means for keeping track of "resources". In LL two assumptions of a propositional constant A are distinguished from a single assumption of A. This does not apply in classical logic, since there the truth value of a fact does not depend on the number of copies of the fact. Indeed, LL is not about truth, it is about computation.

In the following we are considering !-Horn fragment [5] of LL (HLL) consisting of multiplicative conjunction ($\otimes$), linear implication ($\multimap$) and "of course" operator (!). In terms of resource acquisition the logical expression $A \otimes B \vdash C \otimes D$ means that resources C and D are obtainable only if both A and B are obtainable. After the sequent has been applied, A and B are consumed and C and D are produced.

While implication $A \multimap B$ as a computability statement clause in HLL could be applied only once, $!(A \multimap B)$ may be used an unbounded number of times. Therefore the latter formula could be represented with an extralogical LL axiom $\vdash A \multimap B$. When $A \multimap B$ is applied, then literal A becomes deleted from and B inserted to the current set of literals. If there is no literal A available, then the clause cannot be applied. In HLL ! cannot be applied to other formulae than linear implications.

Since HLL could be encoded as a Petri net, theorem proving complexity of HLL is equivalent to the complexity of Petri net reachability checking and therefore decidable [5]. Complexities of many other LL fragments have been summarised by Lincoln [11].

2.2   Representing STRIPS-Like Planning Problems in LL

While considering AI planning within LL, one of the intriguing issues is how to represent planning domains and problems. This section reflects a resource-conscious representation of STRIPS-like operators as adopted by several researchers [13, 4, 3, 6] for LL framework.

Since we do not use negation in our subset of LL, there is no notion of truth-value for literals. All reasoning is reduced to the notion of resource – the *number* of occurrences of a literal determines whether an operator can be applied or not. Moreover, it is crucial to understand that absence or presence of a literal from any state of a world does not determine literal's truth-value.

While LL may be viewed as a resource consumption/generation model, the notion of STRIPS *pre-* and *delete-*lists overlap, if we translate STRIPS operators to LL. This means that a LL planning operator may be applied, if resources in its *delete-*list form a subset of resources in a given state of the world. Then, if the operator is applied, all resources in the *delete-*list are deleted from the particular state of the world and resources in the *add-*list are inserted to the resulting state. Therefore, all literals, which have to be preserved from the *pre-*list, should be presented in the *add-*list. For instance, let us consider the STRIPS operator in Figure 1. An appropriate extralogical LL axiom representing semantics of that operator is

$$\vdash \forall x.(BALL(x) \otimes NEAR(x) \multimap BALL(x) \otimes IN(x) \otimes MOVE\_OK).$$

Thus every element in the *pre-*list of a STRIPS operator is inserted to the left hand side of linear implication $\multimap$. Additionally, all elements of the *delete-*list, which do not already exist there already, are inserted. To the right hand side of $\multimap$, the *add-*list elements are inserted plus all elements from the *pre-*list, which have to be preserved. This is due to the resource-consciousness property of LL, meaning literally that everything in the left hand side of $\multimap$ would become consumed and resources in the right hand side of $\multimap$ would become generated.

Definition 1. *Planning operator is an extralogical axiom* $\vdash \forall \underline{x}.(D \multimap A)$, *where* D *is the delete-list,* A *is the add-list, and* $\underline{x}$ *is a set of variables, which are free in* D *and* A. D *and* A *are multiplicative conjunctions.*

```
Get(x) :
    pre : BALL(x), NEAR(x)
  delete : NEAR(x)
    add : IN(x), MOVE_OK
```

Fig. 1. A STRIPS operator.

It should be noted that due to resource consciousness several instances of the same predicate may be involved in a state of the world. Thus, in contrast to classical logic and informal STRIPS semantics, in LL formulae $ON(a, b)$ and $ON(a, b) \otimes ON(a, b)$ are distinguished.

Definition 2. *A state is a multiplicative conjunction.*

Definition 3. *A planning problem is represented with a LL sequent $\Gamma; S \vdash G$, where S is the initial state and G is the goal state of the planning problem. Both, S and G, are multiplicative conjunctions consisting of ground literals. Γ represents a set of planning operators as extralogical LL axioms.*

From theorem proving point of view the former LL sequent represents a theorem, which has to be proved. If the theorem is proved, a plan is extracted from the proof.

2.3   Partial Deduction and LL

Partial deduction (PD) (or partial evaluation of logic programs, first introduced in [7]) is known as one of optimisation techniques in logic programming. Given a logic program, partial deduction derives a more specific program while preserving the meaning of the original program. Since the program is more specialised, it is usually more efficient than the original program, if executed. For instance, let A, B, C and D be propositional variables and $A \multimap B$, $B \multimap C$ and $C \multimap D$ computability statements in LL. Then possible partial deductions are $A \multimap C$, $B \multimap D$ and $A \multimap D$. It is easy to notice that the first corresponds to forward chaining (from initial to goal state), the second to backward chaining (from goal to initial state) and the third could be either forward or backward chaining. Partial deduction in logic programming is often defined as unfolding of program clauses.

Although the original motivation behind PD was to deduce specialised logic programs with respect to a given goal, our motivation for PD is a bit different. We are applying PD for determining planning subtasks, which cannot be performed by the planner, but still are possibly closer to a solution than an initial task. This means that given a state S and a goal G of a planning problem we compute a new state S' and a new goal G'. This information is used for planning problem adaptation or debugging. Similar approach has been applied by Matskin and Komorowski [14] in automatic software synthesis. One of their motivations was debugging of declarative software specifications.

PD steps for back- and forward chaining in our framework are defined with the following rules.

Definition 4. *First-order forward chaining PD step $\mathcal{R}_f(L_i(\underline{x}))$ is a rule*

$$\frac{B \otimes C \vdash G}{A \otimes C \vdash G} \; \mathcal{R}_f(L_i(\underline{x}))$$

Definition 5. *First-order backward chaining PD step $\mathcal{R}_b(L_i(\underline{x}))$ is a rule*

$$\frac{S \vdash A \otimes C}{S \vdash B \otimes C} \; \mathcal{R}_b(L_i(\underline{x}))$$

In the both preceding definitions $L_i(\underline{x})$ is defined as $\vdash \forall \underline{x}.(A' \multimap_{L_i(\underline{x})} B')$. A, B, C are first-order LL formulae. Additionally we assume that $\underline{a} \overset{def}{=} a_1, a_2, \ldots$ is an ordered set of constants, $\underline{x} \overset{def}{=} x_1, x_2, \ldots$ is an ordered set of variables, $[\underline{a}/\underline{x}]$ denotes substitution, and $X = X'[\underline{a}/\underline{x}]$. When substitution is applied, elements in $\underline{a}$ and $\underline{x}$ are mapped to each other in the order they appear in the ordered sets. These sets must have the same number of elements.

PD steps $\mathcal{R}_f(L_i(\underline{x}))$ and $\mathcal{R}_b(L_i(\underline{x}))$, respectively, apply planning operator $L_i(\underline{x})$ to move the initial state towards the goal state or vice versa. In $\mathcal{R}_b(L_i(\underline{x}))$ step formulae $B \otimes C$ and $A \otimes C$ denote respectively a goal state G and a modified goal state G'. Thus the step encodes that, if there is a planning operator $\vdash \forall \underline{x}.(A' \multimap_{L_i(\underline{x})} B')$, then we can change goal state $B \otimes C$ to $A \otimes C$. Analogously, in the inference figure $\mathcal{R}_f(L_i(\underline{x}))$ formulae $B \otimes C$ and $A \otimes C$ denote respectively an initial state S and its modification S'. And the rule encodes that, if there is a planning operator $\vdash \forall \underline{x}.(A' \multimap_{L_i(\underline{x})} B')$, then we can change the initial state $A \otimes C$ to $B \otimes C$.

3   A Motivating Example

To illustrate the usage of PD in AI planning, let us consider the following planning problem in the blocks world domain. We have a robot who has to collect two red blocks and place them into a box. The robot has two actions available – $getBlock(x)$ and $fillBox(x, y)$. The first action picks up a red block, while the other places two blocks into a box. The planning operators are defined in the following way:

$$\Gamma = \begin{array}{l} \vdash \forall x.(Block(x) \otimes Red(x) \multimap_{getBlock(x)} In(x)), \\ \vdash \forall x, y.(In(x) \otimes In(y) \multimap_{fillBox(x,y)} Filled). \end{array}$$

We write $\multimap_L$ to show that a particular linear implication represents planning operator L. The planning problem is defined in the following way:

$$\Gamma; Block(a) \otimes Red(a) \otimes Block(b) \otimes Black(b) \vdash Filled.$$

In the preceding Γ is the set of available planning operators as we defined previously. The initial state is encoded with formula

$$Block(a) \otimes Red(a) \otimes Block(b) \otimes Black(b).$$

The goal state is encoded with formula *Filled*. Unfortunately, one can easily see that there is only one red block available in the initial state. Therefore, there is no solution to the planning problem.

However, by applying PD we can find at least a partial plan and notify the user about the situation. Usage of PD on the particular problem is demonstrated below:

$$\cfrac{\cfrac{In(a) \otimes Block(b) \otimes Black(b) \vdash \forall x, y.(In(x) \otimes In(y))}{In(a) \otimes Block(b) \otimes Black(b) \vdash Filled} \; \mathcal{R}_b(\mathit{fillBox}(x, y))}{Block(a) \otimes Red(a) \otimes Block(b) \otimes Black(b) \vdash Filled} \; \mathcal{R}_f(\mathit{getBlock}(a))$$

This derivation represents plan $\{getBlock(a), X, \mathit{fillBox}(x, y)\}$, where X represents a part of the plan, which could not be computed. The derivation could be derived further through LL theorem proving:

$$\cfrac{\cfrac{\cfrac{\overline{In(a) \vdash In(a)} \; Id}{In(a) \vdash \forall x.In(x)} \; R\forall \quad \overline{Block(b) \otimes Black(b) \vdash \forall y.In(y)}}{In(a), Block(b) \otimes Black(b) \vdash \forall x, y.(In(x) \otimes In(y))} \; R\otimes}{In(a) \otimes Block(b) \otimes Black(b) \vdash \forall x, y.(In(x) \otimes In(y))} \; L\otimes$$

The sequent $Block(b) \otimes Black(b) \vdash \forall y.In(y)$ could be sent to user now, who would determine what to do next. The partial plan and the achieved planning problem specification could be processed in some domains further automatically. In this light, one has to implement a selection function for determining literals in the planning problem specification which could be modified by the system.

4   Formal Results for PD

Definition 6 (Partial plan). *A partial plan* $\vdash I \multimap O$ *of a planning problem* $\Gamma; S \vdash G$ *is a sequence of planning operator instances such that state* O *is achieved from state* I *after applying the operator instances.*

One should note that a partial plan $\vdash A \multimap A$ is an empty plan, while symmetrically, a partial plan $\vdash S \multimap G$ of a planning problem $\Gamma; S \vdash G$ is a complete plan, since it encodes that the plan leads from the initial state S to the goal state G.

Definition 7 (Resultant). *A resultant is a partial plan*

$$\vdash I \multimap_{\lambda a_1, \dots, a_n . f} O, n \geq 0,$$

where f is a term representing the function, which generates O from I by applying potentially composite functions over $a_1, \ldots, a_n$, which represent planning operators in the partial plan.

Definition 8 (Derivation of a resultant). *Let $\mathcal{R}$ be any predefined PD step. A derivation of a resultant R_0 is a finite sequence of resultants: $R_0 \Rightarrow_{\mathcal{R}} R_1 \Rightarrow_{\mathcal{R}} R_2 \Rightarrow_{\mathcal{R}} \ldots \Rightarrow_{\mathcal{R}} R_n$, where $\Rightarrow_{\mathcal{R}}$ denotes to an application of a PD step $\mathcal{R}$.*

Definition 9 (Partial deduction). *A partial deduction of a planning problem $\Gamma; S \vdash G$ is a set of all possible derivations of a complete plan $\vdash S \multimap G$ from any resultant R_i. The result of PD is a multiset of resultants R_i.*

One can easily denote that this definition of PD generates a whole proof tree for a planning problem $\Gamma; S \vdash G$.

Definition 10 (Executability). *A planning problem $\Gamma; S \vdash G$ is executable, iff given Γ as a set of operators, resultant $\vdash S \multimap_{\lambda a_1, \ldots, a_n.f} G, n \geq 0$ can be derived such that derivation ends with resultant R_n, which equals to $\vdash A \multimap A$ and where A is an arbitrary state.*

Soundness and completeness are defined through executability of planning problems.

Definition 11 (Soundness of PD of a planning problem). *A partial plan $\vdash S' \multimap G'$ is executable, if a complete plan $\vdash S \multimap G$ is executable in a planning problem $\Gamma; S \vdash G$ and there is a derivation $\vdash S \multimap G \Rightarrow_{\mathcal{R}} \ldots \Rightarrow_{\mathcal{R}} \vdash S' \multimap G'$.*

Completeness is the converse:

Definition 12 (Completeness of PD of a planning problem). *A complete plan $\vdash S \multimap G$ is executable, if a partial plan $\vdash S' \multimap G'$ is executable in a planning problem $\Gamma; S' \vdash G'$ and there is a derivation $\vdash S \multimap G \Rightarrow_{\mathcal{R}} \ldots \Rightarrow_{\mathcal{R}} \vdash S' \multimap G'$.*

Our proofs of soundness and completeness are based on proving that derivation of a partial plan is a derivation in a planning problem using PD steps, which were defined as inference figures in HLL.

Proposition 1. *First-order forward chaining PD step $\mathcal{R}_f(L_i(\underline{x}))$ is sound with respect to first order LL rules.*

Proof.

$$
\cfrac{
\cfrac{A \otimes C \vdash A \otimes C \ ^{Id} \quad \cfrac{}{\vdash \forall \underline{x}.(A' \multimap_{L_i(\underline{x})} B')} \ ^{Axiom}}{A \otimes C \vdash A \otimes C \otimes \forall \underline{x}.(A' \multimap_{L_i(\underline{x})} B')} \ ^{R\otimes}
\quad
\cfrac{
\cfrac{
\cfrac{
\cfrac{C \vdash C \ ^{Id} \quad \cfrac{\cfrac{A \vdash A \ ^{Id} \quad B \vdash B \ ^{Id}}{A, (A \multimap_{L_i(\underline{a})} B) \vdash B} \ ^{L\multimap}}{A \otimes (A \multimap_{L_i(\underline{a})} B) \vdash B} \ ^{L\otimes}}{C, A \otimes (A \multimap_{L_i(\underline{a})} B) \vdash B \otimes C} \ ^{R\otimes}}{A \otimes C \otimes (A \multimap_{L_i(\underline{a})} B) \vdash B \otimes C} \ ^{L\otimes}}{A \otimes C \otimes \forall \underline{x}.(A' \multimap_{L_i(\underline{x})} B') \vdash B \otimes C} \ ^{L\forall}
\quad B \otimes C \vdash G}{A \otimes C \otimes \forall \underline{x}.(A' \multimap_{L_i(\underline{x})} B') \vdash G} \ ^{Cut}}{A \otimes C \vdash G} \ ^{Cut}
$$

Proposition 2. *First-order backward chaining PD step $\mathcal{R}_b(L_i(\underline{x}))$ is sound with respect to first order LL rules.*

Proof. The proof in LL is the following

$$
\cfrac{
\cfrac{S \vdash A \otimes C \qquad \vdash \forall\underline{x}.(A' \multimap_{L_i(\underline{x})} B')}{S \vdash A \otimes C \otimes \forall\underline{x}.(A' \multimap_{L_i(\underline{x})} B')} \; R\otimes
\qquad
\cfrac{
\cfrac{
\cfrac{C \vdash C \;\; Id \quad \cfrac{\cfrac{A \vdash A \;\; Id \quad B \vdash B \;\; Id}{A, (A \multimap_{L_i(\underline{a})} B) \vdash B} \; L\multimap}{A \otimes (A \multimap_{L_i(\underline{a})} B) \vdash B} \; L\otimes}{C, A \otimes (A \multimap_{L_i(\underline{a})} B) \vdash B \otimes C} \; R\otimes}{A \otimes C \otimes (A \multimap_{L_i(\underline{a})} B) \vdash B \otimes C} \; L\otimes}{A \otimes C \otimes \forall\underline{x}.(A' \multimap_{L_i(\underline{x})} B') \vdash B \otimes C} \; L\forall
}{S \vdash B \otimes C} \; Cut
$$

(with $S \vdash A \otimes C$ and $\vdash \forall\underline{x}.(A' \multimap_{L_i(\underline{x})} B')$ derived by *Axiom*)

Theorem 1 (Soundness). *PD for LL in first-order HLL is sound.*

Proof. Since all PD steps are sound, PD for LL in HLL is sound as well. The latter derives from the fact that, if there exists a derivation $\vdash S \multimap G \Rightarrow_{\mathcal{R}}$ $\ldots \Rightarrow_{\mathcal{R}} \vdash S' \multimap G'$, then the derivation is constructed by PD in a formally correct manner.

Theorem 2 (Completeness). *PD for LL in first-order HLL is not complete.*

Proof. In the general case first-order HLL is undecidable. Therefore, since PD applies HLL inference figures for derivation, PD in first-order HLL is not complete. With other words – a derivation $\vdash S \multimap G \Rightarrow_{\mathcal{R}} \ldots \Rightarrow_{\mathcal{R}} \vdash S' \multimap G'$ may not be found in a finite time, even if there exists such derivation. Therefore PD for LL in first-order HLL fragment of LL is not complete.

Kanovich and Vauzeilles [6] determine certain constraints, which help to reduce the complexity of theorem proving in first-order HLL. By applying those constraints, theorem proving complexity could be reduced to PSPACE. However, in the general case theorem proving complexity in first-order HLL is still undecidable.

5   Related Work

Several works have considered theoretical issues of LL planning. The multiplicative conjunction ($\otimes$) and additive disjunction ($\oplus$) have been employed in [13], where a demonstration of a robot planning system has been given. The usage of ? and !, whose importance to AI planning is emphasised in [1], is discussed there, but not demonstrated.

Influenced by [13], LL theorem proving has been used by Jacopin [4] as an AI planning kernel. Since only the multiplicative conjunction $\otimes$ is used in formulae there, the problem representation is almost equivalent to presentation in STRIPS-like planners – the left hand side of a LL sequent represents a STRIPS *delete*-list and the right hand side accordingly an *add*-list. In [2] a formalism has been proposed for deductively generating recursive plans in LL. This advancement is a step further to more general plans, which are capable to solve instead of a single problem a class of problems.

Although PD was first introduced by Komorowski [7], Lloyd and Shepherd-son [12] were first ones to formalise PD for normal logic programs. They showed PD's correctness with respect to Clark's program completion semantics. Since then several formalisations of PD for different logic formalisms have been developed. Lehmann and Leuschel [10] developed a PD method capable of solving planning problems in the fluent calculus. A Petri net reachability checking algorithm is used there for proving completeness of the PD method. However, they do not consider how to handle partial plans.

Matskin and Komorowski [14] applied PD to automated software synthesis. One of their motivations was debugging of declarative software specification. The idea of using PD for debugging is quite similar to the application of PD in symbolic agent negotiation [9]. In both cases PD helps to determine computability statements, which cannot be solved by a system.

6   Conclusions

In this paper we described a PD approach for analysing AI planning problems. Generally our method applies PD to the original planning problem until a solution (plan) is found. If no solution is found, one or many modified planning problems are returned. User preferences could be applied for filtering out essential modifications.

We have implemented a planner called RAPS, which is based on a fragment of linear logic (LL). RAPS applies constructive theorem proving in multiplicative intuitionistic LL (MILL). First a planning problem is described with LL sequents. Then LL theorem proving is applied to determine whether the problem is solvable. And if the problem is solvable, finally a plan is extracted from a proof.

By combining the planner with PD approach we have implemented a symbolic agent negotiation [9]. The main idea is that, if one agent fails to find a solution for a planning problem, it engages other agents who possibly help to develop the partial plan further. As a result the system implements distributed AI planning. The main focus of the current paper, however, has been set to analysing planning problems, not to cooperative problem solving as presented in [9].

Acknowledgements

This work was partially supported by the Norwegian Research Foundation in the framework of Information and Communication Technology (IKT-2010) program – the ADIS project. The author would like to thank anonymous referees for their comments.

References

1. S. Brüning, S. Hölldobler, J. Schneeberger, U. Sigmund, M. Thielscher. Disjunction in Resource-Oriented Deductive Planning. Technical Report AIDA-93-03, Technische Hochschule Darmstadt, Germany, 1994.

2. S. Cresswell, A. Smaill, J. Richardson. Deductive Synthesis of Recursive Plans in Linear Logic. In Proceedings of the Fifth European Conference on Planning, pp. 252–264, 1999.
3. G. Grosse, S. Hölldobler, J. Schneeberger. Linear Deductive Planning. Journal of Logic and Computation, Vol. 6, pp. 232–262, 1996.
4. É. Jacopin. Classical AI planning as theorem proving: The case of a fragment of Linear Logic. In AAAI Fall Symposium on Automated Deduction in Nonstandard Logics, Palo Alto, California, AAAI Press, pp. 62–66, 1993.
5. M. I. Kanovich. Linear Logic as a Logic of Computations. Annals of Pure and Applied Logic, Vol. 67, pp. 183–212, 1994.
6. M. I. Kanovich, J. Vauzeilles. The Classical AI Planning Problems in the Mirror of Horn Linear Logic: Semantics, Expressibility, Complexity. Mathematical Structures in Computer Science, Vol. 11, No. 6, pp. 689–716, 2001.
7. J. Komorowski. A Specification of An Abstract Prolog Machine and Its Application to Partial Evaluation. PhD thesis, Technical Report LSST 69, Department of Computer and Information Science, Linkoping University, Linkoping, Sweden, 1981.
8. P. Küngas. Resource-Conscious AI Planning with Conjunctions and Disjunctions. Acta Cybernetica, Vol. 15, pp. 601–620, 2002.
9. P. Küngas, M. Matskin. Linear Logic, Partial Deduction and Cooperative Problem Solving. In Proceedings of the First International Workshop on Declarative Agent Languages and Technologies (in conjunction with AAMAS 2003), DALT'2003, Melbourne, Australia, July 15, 2003, Lecture Notes in Artificial Intelligence, Vol. 2990, 2004, Springer-Verlag.
10. H. Lehmann, M. Leuschel. Solving Planning Problems by Partial Deduction. In Proceedings of the 7th International Conference on Logic for Programming and Automated Reasoning, LPAR'2000, Reunion Island, France, November 11–12, 2000, Lecture Notes in Artificial Intelligence, Vol. 1955, pp. 451–467, 2000, Springer-Verlag.
11. P. Lincoln. Deciding Provability of Linear Logic Formulas. In J.-Y. Girard, Y. Lafont, L. Regnier (eds). Advances in Linear Logic, London Mathematical Society Lecture Note Series, Vol. 222, pp. 109–122, 1995.
12. J. W. Lloyd, J. C. Shepherdson. Partial Evaluation in Logic Programming. Journal of Logic Programming, Vol. 11, pp. 217–242, 1991.
13. M. Masseron, C. Tollu, J. Vauzeilles. Generating plans in Linear Logic I–II. Theoretical Computer Science, Vol. 113, pp. 349–375, 1993.
14. M. Matskin, J. Komorowski. Partial Structural Synthesis of Programs. Fundamenta Informaticae, Vol. 30, pp. 23–41, 1997.

Planning with Abduction: A Logical Framework to Explore Extensions to Classical Planning*

Silvio do Lago Pereira and Leliane Nunes de Barros

Institute of Mathematics and Statistics – University of São Paulo
{slago,leliane}@ime.usp.br

Abstract. In this work we show how a planner implemented as an abductive reasoning process can have the same performance and behavior as classical planning algorithms. We demonstrate this result by considering three different versions of an abductive event calculus planner on reproducing some important comparative analyses of planning algorithms found in the literature. We argue that a logic-based planner, defined as the application of general purpose theorem proving techniques to a general purpose action formalism, can be a very solid base for the research on extending the classical planning approach.

Keywords: abduction, event calculus, theorem proving, planning.

1 Introduction

In general, in order to cope with domain requirements, any extension to STRIPS representation language would require the construction of complex planning algorithms, whose soundness cannot be easily proved. The so called practical planners, which are said to be capable of solving complex planning problems, are constructed in an *ad hoc* fashion, making difficult to explain why they work or why they present a successful behavior. The main motivation for the construction of logic-based planners is the possibility to specify planning systems in terms of general theories of action and implement them as general purpose theorem provers, having a guarantee of soundness. Another advantage is that a planning system defined in this way has a close correspondence between specification and implementation. There are several works aiming the construction of sound and complete logic-based planning systems [1], [2],[3]. More recent research results [4] demonstrate that a good theorectical solution can coexist with a good practical solution, despite of contrary widespread belief [5].

In this work, we report on the implementation and analysis of three different versions of an abductive event calculus planner, a particular logic-based planner which uses *event calculus* [6] as a formalism to reason about actions and change and *abduction* [7] as an inference rule. By reproducing some important results on comparative analyses of planning algorithms [8] [9], and including experiments with the corresponding versions of the abductive event calculus planner, we show that there is a close correspondence between well known planning algorithms and

---

* This work has been supported by the Brazilian sponsoring agencies Capes and CNPq.

A.L.C. Bazzan and S. Labidi (Eds.): SBIA 2004, LNAI 3171, pp. 62–72, 2004.

logic-based planners. We also show that the efficiency results observed with a logic-based planner that adopts abductive event calculus and theorem proving can be comparable to that observed with some practical planners. We claim that one should start from an efficient logical implementation in order to make further extensions towards the specification of non-classical planners.

2   Abductive Reasoning in the Event Calculus

Abduction is an inference principle that extends deduction, providing hypothetical reasoning. As originally introduced by [10], it is an unsound inference rule that resembles a reverse modus ponens: if we observe a fact β, and we know $\alpha \rightarrow \beta$, then we can accept α as a possible explanation for β. Thus, abduction is a weak kind of inference in the sense that it only guarantees that the explanation is plausible, not that it is true.

Formally, given a set of sentences $\mathcal{B}$ describing a domain (*background theory*) and a sentence Γ describing an observation, the abduction process consists of finding a set of sentences Δ (*residue* or *explanation*) such that $\mathcal{B} \cup \Delta$ is consistent and $\mathcal{B} \cup \Delta \models \Gamma$. Clearly, depending on $\mathcal{B}$, for the same observed fact we can have multiple possible explanations. In general, the definition of *best explanation* depends on the context, but it is almost always related to some notion of minimallity. In practice, we should prefer explanations that postulates the minimum number of causes [11]. Furthermore, abduction is, by definition, a kind of nonmonotonic reasoning, *i.e.* an explanation consistent, w.r.t. a determined knowledge state, can become inconsistent when new information is taken into account [7].

Next, we present the event calculus as the formalism used to describe the background theory on planning domains and we show how the planning task can be understood as an abductive process in the event calculus.

2.1   The Event Calculus Formalism

The event calculus [12] is a formalism designed to model and reason about scenarios described as sets of events whose occurrences have the effect of starting or terminating the truth of determined properties (*fluents*) of the world. There are many versions of event calculi [13]. In this work, we use a version defined in [6], whose axiomatization is the following:

$$holdsAt(F,T) \leftarrow initially_p(F) \wedge \neg clipped(0,F,T) \tag{Ec1}$$

$$holdsAt(F,T) \leftarrow happens(A,T_1,T_2) \wedge initiates(A,F,T_1) \wedge (T_2 \prec T) \wedge \tag{Ec2}$$
$$\neg clipped(T_1,F,T)$$

$$\neg holdsAt(F,T) \leftarrow initially_n(F) \wedge \neg declipped(0,F,T) \tag{Ec3}$$

$$\neg holdsAt(F,T) \leftarrow happens(A,T_1,T_2) \wedge terminates(A,F,T_1) \wedge (T_2 \prec T) \wedge \tag{Ec4}$$
$$\neg declipped(T_1,F,T)$$

$$clipped(T_1,F,T_2) \leftrightarrow \exists A, T_3, T_4[happens(A,T_3,T_4) \wedge (T_1 \prec T_3) \wedge (T_4 \prec T_2) \wedge \tag{Ec5}$$
$$[terminates(A,F,T_3) \vee releases(A,F,T_3)]]$$

$$declipped(T_1,F,T_2) \leftrightarrow \exists A, T_3, T_4[happens(A,T_3,T_4) \wedge (T_1 \prec T_3) \wedge (T_4 \prec T_2) \wedge \tag{Ec6}$$
$$[initiates(A,F,T_3) \vee releases(A,F,T_3)]]$$

$$happens(A,T_1,T_2) \rightarrow T_1 \leq T_2 \tag{Ec7}$$

Table 1. Predicates of the event calculus

predicate	description
$holdsAt(F,T)$	fluent F holds at time T
$initially_p(F)$	fluent F holds from time 0
$initially_n(F)$	fluent F does not hold from time 0
$happens(A,T_1,T2)$	event A starts at T_1 and finishes at T_2
$initiates(A,F,T)$	event A starts fluent F at time T
$terminates(A,F,T)$	event A finishs fluent F at time T
$releases(A,F,T)$	event A releases fluent F at time T
$clipped(T_1,F,T_2)$	fluent F ceased to hold in $[T_1,T_2]$
$declipped(T_1,F,T_2)$	fluent F started to hold in $[T_1,T_2]$

In the event calculus, the frame problem is overcome through circumscription. Given Σ a domain description expressed as a conjunction of formulae that does not include the predicates *initially* or *happens*; Δ a narrative of actions expressed as a conjunctions of formulae that does not include the predicates *initiates*, *terminates* or *releases*; Ω a conjunction of uniqueness-of-names axioms for actions and fluents; and EC a conjunction of the axioms of the event calculus, we have to consider the following formula as the background theory on the abductive event calculus planning:

$$\text{CIRC}[\Sigma; initiates, terminates, releases] \wedge \text{CIRC}[\Delta; happens] \wedge \Omega \wedge EC,$$

where $\text{CIRC}[\Sigma; \rho_1, \ldots, \rho_n]$ means the circumscription of Σ with relation to the predicates $\rho_1, \ldots, \rho_n$. By circumscribing *initiates*, *terminates* and *releases* we are imposing that the known effects of actions are the only effects of actions, and by circumscribing *happens* we assume that there are no unexpected event occurrences. An extended discussion about the frame problem and its solution through circumscription can be found in [14].

2.2 An Abductive Event Calculus Planner

Planning in the event calculus is naturally handled as an abduction process [2]. In this setting, given a domain description Σ, the task of planning a sequence of actions Δ in order to satisfy a given goal Γ corresponds to an abductive process expressed by:

$$\text{CIRC}[\Sigma; initiates, terminates, releases] \wedge \text{CIRC}[\Delta; happens] \wedge \Omega \wedge EC \models \Gamma,$$

where Δ – *the abductive explanation* – is a plan for the goal Γ. In [4] a planning system based on this idea is presented as a PROLOG abductive meta-interpreter. This meta-interpreter is specialized for the event calculus by compiling the EC axioms into its meta-clauses. The main advantage of this compilation is to allow an extra level of control to the planner. In particular, it allows us to define an ordering in which subgoals can be achieved, improving efficiency and giving special treatment to predicates that represent incomplete information. By incomplete information we mean predicates for which we do not assume its closure, *i.e.* we cannot use negation as failure to prove their negations, since they can be abduced. The solution to this problem is to give a special treatment for negated literals with incomplete information at the meta-level. In the case of partial order planning, we have incomplete information about the predicate *before*, allowing the representation of partial order plans. Thus, when the meta-interpreter finds a literal $\neg before(X, Y)$, it tries to prove it by adding $before(Y, X)$ to the plan (*abductive residue*) and checking its consistency.

In the abductive event calculus planner – AECP – a planning problem is given by a *domain* description represented by a set of clauses *initiates*, *terminates* and *releases*, an *initial state* description represented by a set of clauses $initially_p$ and $initially_n$, and a *goal* description represented by a list of literals *holdsAt*. As solution, the planner returns an abductive residue composed by literals *happens* and *before* (the partial order plan) and a negative residue composed of literals *clipped* and *declipped* (the causal links of the partial order plan).

3 Classical Planning in the Event Calculus

In order to perform a fair comparative analysis with STRIPS-like planning algorithms, some modifications have to be done in the AECP, which are related to the following assumptions in classical planning: (*i*) atomic time, (*ii*) deterministic effects and (*iii*) omniscience. From (*i*) follows that we need to change the predicate $happens(A, T1, T2)$ to a binary version. Thus, $happens(A, T)$ means that the action A happens at time T and, by doing this change, the axiom EC7 will be no longer necessary. From (*ii*) follows that there is no need for the predicate *releases* and, finally, from (*iii*) (remembering the fact that STRIPS's action representation does not allow negative preconditions), follows that there is no need for predicate $initially_n$ neither the axioms EC3, EC4 and EC6. With these changes, we specify a simplified axiomatization of the event calculus containing only its relevant aspects to the classical planning:

$holdsAt(F, T) \leftarrow initially(F) \land \neg clipped(0, F, T)$ (SEC1)

$holdsAt(F, T) \leftarrow happens(A, T_1) \land initiates(A, F, T_1) \land (T_1 \prec T) \land$ (SEC2)
    $\neg clipped(T_1, F, T)$

$clipped(T_1, F, T_2) \leftrightarrow \exists A, T[happens(A, T) \land (T_1 \prec T) \land (T \prec T_2) \land$ (SEC3)
    $terminates(A, F, T)]$

3.1 The ABP Planning System

Based on this simplified axiomatization, we have implemented the ABP planning system. This planner uses *iterative deepening search* (IDS) and *first-in, first-out* (FIFO) goal ordering, while AECP uses *depth first search* (DFS) and *last-in, first-out* (LIFO) strategies. Using IDS, we turn out the method complete and we increase the possibility to find minimal explanations. It is important to notice that in the original version of the AECP, both properties did not hold. Next, we explain the details of the knowledge representation and control knowledge decisions made in our implementations that are relevant on the comparative analysis presented in the next section.

Action Representation. In the event calculus, the predicates *initiates* and *terminates* are used to describe the effects of an action. For instance, consider the predicate $walk(X,Y)$ representing the act of walking from x to y. The effects of this action can be described as:

$$initiates(walk(X,Y), at(Y), T) \leftarrow holdsAt(at(X), T) \wedge X \neq Y$$
$$terminates(walk(X,Y), at(X), T) \leftarrow holdsAt(at(X), T) \wedge X \neq Y$$

In the AECP's meta-level, the above clauses are represented by the predicate $axiom(H, B)$, where H is the head of the clause and B is its body, that is:

```
axiom(initiates(walk(X,Y),at(Y),T),[holdsAt(at(X),T),X\=Y]).
axiom(terminates(walk(X,Y),at(X),T),[holdsAt(at(X),T),X\=Y]).
```

Similarly, the STRIPS representation of this action is:

```
oper(walk(X,Y),[at(X),X\=Y],[at(Y)],[at(X)]).
```

Note that, in the STRIPS representation, the first parameter of the predicate `oper` is the action's name, while in the EC representation, the first parameter of the predicate `axiom` is `initiates` or `terminates`. Since PROLOG's indexing method uses the first parameter as the searching key, finding an action with the predicate `oper` would take constant time, while a search with the predicate `axiom` would take time proportional to the number of clauses for this predicate included in the knowledge base. Thus, in order to establish a suitable correspondence between both approaches, in the implementation of the ABP, the clauses of the form `axiom(initiates(`α, ϕ, T`),B)` are represented at the meta-level as `initiates(`α, ϕ, T, B`)`. In analogous way, the clauses `axiom(terminates(`α, ϕ, T`),B)` are represented as `terminates(`α, ϕ, T, B`)`.

Abducible and Executable Predicates. In the AECP [4], the meta-predicates `abducible` and `executable` are used to establish which are the abducible predicates and the executable actions, repectively. The declaration of the abducible predicates is important to the planner, as it needs to know the predicates with incomplete information that can be added to the residue. By restricting the facts that can be abduced, we make sure that only basic explanations are computed (*i.e.* those explanations that cannot be formulated in terms of others effects). On the other hand, the declaration of executable actions only makes sense in *hierarchical task network* planners (HTN), where it is important to distinguish between primitive and compound actions. Since in this work we only want to compare the logical planner with partial order planners, we can assume that all the actions in the knowledge base are executable and that the only abducible predicates are `happens` and `before` (the same assumption is made in STRIPS-like partial order planners).

Codesignation Constraints. Since the AECP uses the PROLOG's unification procedure as the method to add codesignations constraints to the plan, it is difficult to compare it with STRIPS-like planning algorithms (which have a special procedure implemented for this purpose). So, we have implemented ABP as a propositional planner, as is commonly done in most of the performance analyses in the planning literature. As we will see, this change has positively affected the verification of the consistency of the negative residue.

Consistency of the Negative Residue. In the AECP, the negative residue (*i.e.* facts deduced through negation as failure) has to be checked for consistency every time the positive residue H (*i.c.* facts obtained through abduction) is modified. This behavior corresponds to an interval protection strategy for the predicate `clipped` (in a way equivalent to *book-keeping* in partial order planning). However, in the case of a propositional planner, we have only to check for consistency a new literal `clipped` (added to the negative residue) with respect to the actions already in the positive residue, and a new literal `happens` (added to the positive residue) with respect to the intervals already in the negative residue. Thus, in contrast with the performance presented by the AECP, the conflict treatment in the ABP is incremental and has a time complexity of $O(|H|)$. In addition, when an action in the plan is selected as the establisher of a subgoal, only the new added literal `clipped` has to be protected.

3.2   Systematicity and Redundancy

In order to analyse the performance of the abductive event calculus planner, we have implemented three different planning strategies:

- ABP: abductive planner (equivalent to POP [15]);
- SABP: systematic version of ABP (equivalent to SNLP [16]);
- RABP: redundant version of ABP (equivalent to TWEAK [17]).

Systematicity. A systematic version of the ABP, called SABP, can be obtained by modifying the event calculus axiom SEC3 to consider as a "threat" to a fluent F not only an action that terminates it, but also an action that initiates it:

$$clipped(T_1, F, T_2) \leftrightarrow \exists A, T[happens(A, T) \wedge (T_1 \prec T) \wedge (T \prec T_2) \wedge \qquad \text{(SEC3')}$$
$$[terminates(A, F, T) \vee initiates(A, F, T)]]$$

With this simple change, we expect that SABP will have the same performance of systematic planners, like SNLP [16], and the same trade-off performance with the corresponding redundant version of the ABP planner.

Redundancy. A redundant version of the ABP, called RABP, does not require any modification in the *EC* axioms. The only change that we have to make is in the goal selection strategy. In the ABP, as well in the SABP, subgoals are selected and then eliminated from the list of subgoals as soon as they are satisfied. This can be safely done because those planners apply a causal link protection strategy.

A MTC – *modal truth criterion* – strategy for goal selection can be easily implemented in the RABP by performing a temporal projection. This is done by making the meta-interpreter to "execute" the current plan, without allowing any modification on it. This process returns as output the first subgoal which is not necessarily true.

Another modification is on the negative residue: the RABP does not need to check the consistency of negative residues every time the plan has been modified. So, in the RABP, the negative literals of the predicate `clipped` does not have a special treatment by the meta-interpreter. As in TWEAK [17], this will make the RABP to select the same subgoal more than once but, on the other hand, it can plan for more than one subgoal with a single goal establishment.

4   The Comparative Analysis

In order to show the correspondence between abductive planning and partial order planning, we have implemented the abductive planners (ABP, SABP and RABP) and three well known partial order planning algorithms (POP, SNLP and TWEAK). All these planners have been implemented in PROLOG and all the cares necessary to guarantee the validity of the comparisons have been taken (*e.g.* all the planners shared common data structures and procedures). A complete analysis of these results is presented in [18] and [19].

We have performed two experiments with these six planners: (*i*) evaluation of the correspondence between abductive planning in the event calculus and partial order planning and (*ii*) evaluation of systematicity/redundancy obtained with different goal protection strategies.

4.1   Experiment I: Correspondence Between POP and ABP

In order to evaluate the relative performance of the planners POP and ABP, we have used the artificial domains family $D^m S^n$ [15]. With this, we ensure that the empirical results we have obtained were independent of the idiosyncrasies of a particular domain.

Based on these domains, we have performed two tests: in the first, we observe how the size of the search space explored by the systems increases as we increase the number of subgoals in the problems; in the second, we observe how the average CPU-time consumed by the systems increases as we increase the number of subgoals in the problems. In figure 1, we can observe that the ABP and POP explore identical search spaces. Therefore, we can conclude that they implement the same planning strategies (*i.e.* they examine the same number of plans, independently of the fact that they implement different approaches). This result extends the work presented in [4], which verifies the correspondence between abductive planning in the event calculus (AECP) and partial order planning (POP) only in an informal way, by inspecting the code. In figure 2, we can observe that, for all problems solved, the average CPU-time consumed by both planners is approximately the same. This shows that the necessary inferences in the logical planners do not increase the time complexity of the planning task.

Therefore, through this first experiment, we have corroborated the conjecture that abductive planning in the event calculus is isomorphic to partial order

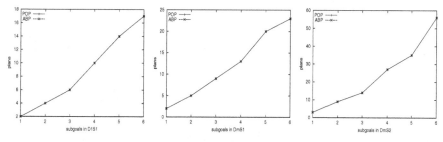

Fig. 1. Search space size to solve problems in $D^m S^n$

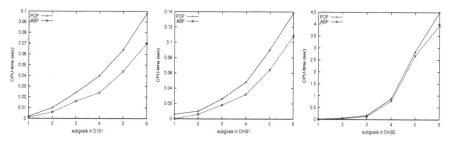

Fig. 2. Average CPU-time to solve problems in $D^m S^n$

planning [4]. Also, we have showed that, using abduction as inference rule and event calculus as formalism to reasoning about actions and chance, a logical planning system can be as efficient as a partial order planning system, with the advantage that its specification is "directly executable".

4.2   Experiment II: Trade-Off Between Systematicity and Redundancy

There was a belief that by decreasing redundancy it would be possible to improve planning efficiency. So, a systematic planner, which never visits the same plan twice in its search space, would be more efficient than a redundant planner [16]. However, [20] has shown that there is a trade-off between redundancy elimination and least commitment: redundancy is eliminated at the expense of increasing commitment in the planner. Therefore, the performance of a partial order planner is better predicted based on the way it deals with the trade-off between redundancy and commitment than on the systematicity of its search.

In order to show the effects of this trade-off, Kambhampati chose two well known planning algorithms: TWEAK and SNLP. TWEAK does not keep track of which goals were already achieved and which remains to be achieved. Therefore, TWEAK may achieve and clobber a subgoal arbitrarily many times, having a lot of redundancy on its search space. On the other hand, SNLP achieves systematicity by keeping track of the causal links of the plans generated during search, and ensuring that each branch of the search space commits to and protects mutually exclusive causal links for the partial plans, *i.e.* it protects already established goals from negative or positive threats. Such protection corresponds to a strong

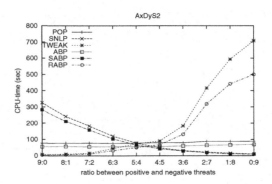

Fig. 3. Average CPU-time to solve problems in $A^x D^y S^2$

form of premature commitment (by imposing ordering constraints on positive threats) which can increase the amount of backtracking as well as the solution depth, having an adverse effect on the performance of the planner.

Kambhampati's experimental analyses show that there is a spectrum of solutions to the trade-off between redundancy and commitment in partial order planning, in which the SNLP and TWEAK planners fall into opposite extremes. To confirm this result, and to show that it is valid to abductive planners too, we created a new family of artificial domains, called $A^x D^y S^2$ [19], through which we can accurately control the ratio between the number of positive threats x (*i.e.* distinct actions that contribute with one same effect) and negative threats y (*i.e.* distinct actions that contribute with opposing effects) in each domain. To observe the behavior of the compared planners, as we vary the ratio between the number of positive and negative threats in the domains, we keep constant the number of subgoals in the solved problems. Then, as a consequence of this fact and of the characteristics of the domains in the family $A^x D^y S^2$, the number of steps in all solutions stays always the same.

The results of this second experiment (figure 3), show that the systematic and redundant versions of the abductive planner (SABP and RABP) have the same behavior of its corresponding algorithmic planners (SNLP and TWEAK).

So, we have extended the results of the previous experiment and show that the isomorphism between abductive reasoning in the event calculus and partial order planning can be preserved for systematic and redundant methods of planning. Moreover, we also corroborate the conjecture that the performance of a systematic or redundant planner is strongly related to the ratio between the number of positive and negative threats in the considered domain [8] and that this conjecture remains valid to abductive planning in the event calculus.

5   Conclusion

The main contribution of this work is: (*i*) to propose a formal specification of different well-known algorithms of classical planning and (*ii*) to show how a planner based on theorem proving can have similar behavior and performance to those observed in partial order planners based on STRIPS. One extra advantage of our formal specification is its close relationship with a PROLOG implementation, which can provide a good framework to test extensions to the classical approach, as well to the integration of knowledge-based approaches for planning.

It is important to note that the original version of the AECP proposed in [4] does not guarantee completeness neither minimal plan solution. However, the abductive planners we have specified and implemented guarantee these properties by using IDS (iterative deepening search) and FIFO goal ordering strategies.

We are currently working on the idea proposed in [21] which aims to build, on the top of our abductive planners, a high-level robot programming language for applications in cognitive robotics. First, we have implemented a HTN version of the abductive event calculus planner to cope with the idea of high-level specifications of robotic tasks. Further, we intend to work with planning and execution with incomplete information.

References

1. Green, C.: Application of theorem proving to problem solving. In: International Joint Conference on Artificial Intelligence. Morgan Kaufmann (1969) 219–239
2. Eshghi, K.: Abductive planning with event calculus. In: Proc.of the 5th International Conference on Logic Programming. MIT Press (1988) 562–579
3. Missiaen, L., Bruynooghe, M., Denecker, M.: Chica, an abductive planning system based on event calculus (1994)
4. Shanahan, M.P.: An abductive event calculus planner. In: The Journal of Logic Programming. (2000) 44:207–239
5. Russell, S., Norvig, P.: Artificial Intelligence: A Modern Approach (second edition). Prentice-Hall, Englewood Cliffs, NJ (2003)
6. Shanahan, M.: A circumscriptive calculus of events. Artificial Intelligence **77** (1995) 249–284
7. Kakas, A.C., Kowalski, R.A., Toni, F.: Abductive logic programming. Journal of Logic and Computation **2** (1992) 719–770
8. Knoblock, C., Yang, Q.: Evaluating the tradeoffs in partial-order planning algorithms (1994)
9. Kambhampati, S., Knoblock, C.A., Yang, Q.: Planning as refinement search: A unified framework for evaluating design tradeoffs in partial-order planning. Artificial Intelligence **76** (1995) 167–238
10. Peirce, C.S.: Collected Papers of Charles Sanders Peirce. Harvard University Press (1931-1958)
11. Cox, P.T., Pietrzykowski, T.: Causes for events: their computation and applications. In: Proc. of the 8th international conference on Automated deduction, Springer-Verlag New York, Inc. (1986) 608–621
12. Kowalski, R.A., Sergot, M.J.: A logic-based calculus of events. In: New Generation Computing 4. (1986) 67–95
13. Santos, P.E.: Formalising the common sense of a mobile robot (1998)
14. Shanahan, M.P.: Solving the Frame Problem: A Mathematical Investigation of the Common Sense Law of Inertia. MIT Press (1997)

15. Barrett, A., Weld, D.S.: Partial-order planning: Evaluating possible efficiency gains. Artificial Intelligence **67** (1994) 71–112
16. MacAllester, D., Rosenblitt, D.: Systematic nonlinear planning. In: Proc. 9th National Conference on Artificial Intelligence. MIT Press (1991) 634–639
17. Chapman, D.: Planning for conjunctive goals. Artificial Intelligence **32** (1987) 333–377
18. Pereira, S.L., Barros, L.N.: Efficiency in abductive planning. In: Proceedings of 2nd Congress of Logic Applied to Technology. Senac, São Paulo (2001) 213–222
19. Pereira, S.L.: Abductive Planning in the Event Calculus. Master Thesis, Institute of Mathematics and Statistics - University of Sao Paulo (2002)
20. Kambhampati, S.: On the utility of systematicity: Understanding tradeoffs between redundancy and commitment in partial-ordering planning. In: Foundations of Automatic Planning: The Classical Approach and Beyond: Papers from the 1993 AAAI Spring Symposium, AAAI Press, Menlo Park, California (1993) 67–72
21. Barros, L.N., Pereira, S.L.: High-level robot programs based on abductive event calculus. In: Proceedings of 3rd International Cognitive Robotics Workshop. (2002)

High-Level Robot Programming:
An Abductive Approach Using Event Calculus

Silvio do Lago Pereira and Leliane Nunes de Barros

Institute of Mathematics and Statistics – University of São Paulo
{slago,leliane}@ime.usp.br

Abstract. This paper proposes a new language that can be used to build high-level robot controllers with high-level cognitive functions such as plan specification, plan generation, plan execution, perception, goal formulation, communication and collaboration. The proposed language is based on GOLOG, a language that uses the situation calculus as a formalism to describe actions and deduction as an inference rule to synthesize plans. On the other hand, instead of situation calculus and deduction, the new language uses event calculus and abductive reasoning to synthesize plans. As we can forsee, this change of paradigm allows the agent to reason about partial order plans, making possible a more flexible integration between deliberative and reactive behaviors.

Keywords: cognitive robotics, abduction, event calculus, planning.

1 Introduction

The area of cognitive robotics is concerned with the development of agents with autonomy to solving complex tasks in dynamic environments. This autonomy requires high-level cognitive functions such as reasoning about actions, perceptions, goals, plans, communication, collaboration, etc. As we can guess, to implement these functions using a conventional programming language can be a very difficult task. On the other hand, by using a logical formalism to reason about actions and change, we can have the necessary expressive power to provide these capabilities.

A logical programming language designed to implement autonomous agents should have two important characteristics: (*i*) to allow a programmer to specify a robot control program, as easily as possible, using high-level actions as primitives and (*ii*) to allow a user to specify goals and provide them to an agent with the ability to plan a correct course of actions to achieve these goals. The GOLOG [1] programming language for agents, developed by the Group of Cognitive Robotics of the University of Toronto, was designed to attend this purpose: (*i*) it is a high-level agent programming language, in which standard programming constructs (*e.g. sequence, choice* and *iteration*) are used to write the agent control program and (*ii*) it can effectively represent and reason about the actions performed by agents in dynamic environments. The emerging success of GOLOG has shown that, by using a logical approach, it is possible to solve complex robotic tasks

A.L.C. Bazzan and S. Labidi (Eds.): SBIA 2004, LNAI 3171, pp. 73–82, 2004.

efficiently, despite of the contrary widespread belief [2]. However, GOLOG uses a planning strategy based on situation calculus, a logical formalism in which plans are represented as a totally ordered sequence of actions and, therefore, it inherits the well known deficiencies of this approach [3].

In this work, we argue that a partial order plan representation can be better adapted to different planning domains, being more useful in robotic applications (notice that a least commitment strategy on plan step ordering can allow a more flexible interleaving of reactive and deliberative behavior). We also propose a new high-level robot programming language called ABGOLOG. This language is based on GOLOG (*i.e.* has same sintax and semantic), but it uses event calculus as the formalism to describe actions and abductive reasoning to synthesize plans, which corresponds to partial order planning [4]. So, based on our previous work on implementation and analysis of abductive event calculus planning systems [5], we show how it is possible to modify ABGOLOG's implementation to improve its efficiency, according to specific domain characteristics.

This paper is organized as follows: in Section 2, we briefly review the basis of situation calculus and how it is used in the GOLOG language; in Section 3, we present the event calculus and how it can be used to implement three versions of an abductive event calculus planner that can serve as a kernel in ABGOLOG; we also show how the different versions of the abductive planner can be used by this language, depending on the characteristics of the robotics application; finally, in Section 4, we discuss important aspects of the proposed language ABGOLOG.

2   Robot Programming with GOLOG

GOLOG [1] is an attempt to combine two different styles of knowledge representation – *declarative* and *procedural* – in the same programming language, allowing the programmer to cover the whole spectrum of possibilities from a pure reactive agent to a pure deliberative agent. In contrast to programs written in standard programming languages, when executed, GOLOG programs are decomposed into primitives which correspond to the agent's actions. Furthermore, since these primitives are described through situation calculus axioms, it is possible to reason logically about their effects.

2.1   The Situation Calculus Formalism

The situation calculus [6] is a logical formalism, whose ontology includes *situations*, which are like "snapshots" of the world; *fluents*, which describe properties of the world that can change their truth value from one situation to another one; and *actions*, which are responsible for the actual change of a situation into another. In the situation calculus, which is a dialect of the first order predicate logic, the constant s_0 denotes the *initial situation*; the function $do(\alpha, \sigma)$ denotes the *resulting situation* after the execution of the action α in the situation σ; the predicate $poss(\alpha, \sigma)$ means that it is possible to execute the action α in the situation σ and, finally, the predicate $holds(\phi, \sigma)$ means that the fluent ϕ holds in the situation σ.

Given a specification of a planning domain in the situation calculus formalism, a solution to a planning problem in this domain can be found through theorem proving. Let $\mathcal{A}$ be a set of axioms describing the agent's actions, $\mathcal{I}$ a set of axioms describing the initial situation and $\mathcal{G}$ a logical sentence describing a planning goal. Thus, a constructive proof of $\mathcal{A} \wedge \mathcal{I} \models (\exists S).legal(S) \wedge \mathcal{G}(S)$, where $legal(S) \equiv poss(\alpha_1, s_0) \wedge \ldots \wedge poss(a_n, do(\alpha_{n-1}, do(\ldots, do(\alpha_1, s_0))))$, causes the variable S to be instanciated to a term of the form $do(\alpha_n, do(\ldots, do(\alpha_1, s_0)))$. Clearly, the sequence of actions $\langle \alpha_1, \ldots, \alpha_n \rangle$ corresponding to this term is a plan that, when executed by the agent from the initial situation s_0, leads to a situation that satisfy the planning goal.

2.2 The GOLOG Interpreter

GOLOG programs are executed by a specialized theorem prover (figure 1). The user has to provide an axiomatization $\mathcal{A}$, describing the agent's actions (*declarative knowledge*), as well a control program c, specifying the desired behavior of the agent (*procedural knowledge*). After that, to execute the program corresponds to prove that exists a situation σ such that $\mathcal{A} \models exec(c, s_0, \sigma)$. Thus, if the situation σ found by the theorem prover is a term of the form $do(a_n, do(\ldots, do(a_1, s_0)))$, the corresponding sequence of actions $\langle a_1, \ldots, a_n \rangle$ is executed by the agent.

```
:- op(950,xfy,[&]). % sequence
:- op(500,xfy,[?]). % test (temporal projection)
:- op(960,xfy,[|]). % non-deterministic choice
:- op(960,xfy,[~]). % negation as failure

exec(A1 & A2,S1,S3) :- exec(A1,S1,S2), exec(A2,S2,S3).
exec(P?,S,S):- holds(P,S).
exec(A1 | A2,S1,S2) :- exec(A1,S1,S2); exec(A2,S1,S2).
exec(if(P,A1,A2),S1,S2) :- exec(P? & A1 | ~P? & A2,S1,S2).
exec(star(E),S1,S2) :- S1=S2; copy(E,E1), exec(E & star(E1),S1,S2).
exec(while(P,A),S1,S2) :- copy(P,P1), exec(star(P? & A) & ~P1?,S1,S2).
exec(A,S1,S2) :- proc(A,A1), exec(A1,S1,S2).
exec(A,S,do(A,S)) :- prim(A), poss(A,S).

holds(A=A,_).
holds(~P,S) :- not holds(P,S).
holds(P,do(A,S)) :- holds(P,S), not affects(A,P). % frame axiom
```

Fig. 1. A very simplified implementation of GOLOG in PROLOG

For instance, consider the following situation calculus axiomatization for the *elevator domain* [1], where the agent's actions are *open, close, turnoff, up* e *down*:

```
holds(curfloor(4),s0).
holds(on(3),s0).
holds(on(5),s0).

poss(open,_).
poss(close,_).
poss(up(N),S)  :- holds(curfloor(C),S), C<N.
poss(down(N),S) :- holds(curfloor(C),S), C>N.
poss(turnoff(N),S) :- holds(on(N),S).

holds(curfloor(N),do(up(N),S)).
holds(curfloor(N),do(down(N),S)).

affects(up(N),curfloor(M)) :- N\=M.
affects(down(N),curfloor(M)) :- N\=M.
affects(turnoff(N),on(N)).

prim(open).
prim(close).
prim(up(_)).
prim(down(_)).
prim(turnoff(_)).
```

In this domain, the agent's goal is to attend all calls[1], represented by the fluent $on(n)$, and its behavior can be specified by the following GOLOG program:

```
proc(control,
    while(on(N), serve(N)) &
    park).
proc(serve(N),
    curfloor(C)? &
    if(C=N,
        open & turnoff(N) & close,
        up(N) | down(N))).
proc(park,
    curfloor(C)? &
    if(C=0,
        open,
        down(0) & open)).
```

Once the domain axiomatization and the control program are provided, we can execute the GOLOG interpreter as follows:

```
?- exec(control,s0,S).

S = do(open, do(down(0), do(close, do(turnoff(5), do(open, do(up(5),
do(close, do(turnoff(3), do(open, do(down(3), s0)))))))))))
```

3   Abductive Reasoning in the Event Calculus

Abduction is an inference principle that extends deduction, providing hypothetical reasoning. As originally introduced by [7], it is an unsound inference rule

---

[1] There is no distinction between calls made from inside or outside the elevator.

that resembles a reverse *modus ponens*: if we observe a fact β, and we know $\alpha \rightarrow \beta$, then we can accept α as a possible explanation for β. Thus, abduction is a weak kind of inference in the sense that it only guarantees that the explanation is plausible, not that it is true.

Formally, given a set of sentences $\mathcal{B}$ describing a domain (*background theory*) and a sentence Γ describing an observation, the abduction process consists of finding a set of sentences Δ (*residue* or *explanation*) such that $\mathcal{B} \cup \Delta$ is consistent and $\mathcal{B} \cup \Delta \models \Gamma$. Clearly, depending on the background theory, for the same observed fact we can have multiple possible explanations. In general, the definition of *best explanation* depends on the context, but it is almost always related to some notion of minimallity. In practice, we should prefer explanations which postulates the minimum number of causes [8]. Furthermore, by definition, abduction is a kind of nonmonotonic reasoning, *i.e.* an explanation consistent, w.r.t. a determined knowledge state, can become inconsistent when new information is considered [9].

Next, we present the event calculus as the logical formalism used to describe the background theory in ABGOLOG programs and we show how abduction can be used to synthesize partial order plans in this new language.

3.1   The Event Calculus Formalism

The event calculus [10] is a temporal formalism designed to model and reason about scenarios described as a set of *events* whose occurrences on *time* have the effect of starting or terminating the validity of *fluents* which denote properties of the world [11]. Note that event calculus emphasize the dynamics of the world and not the statics of the situations, as the situation calculus does. The basic idea of events is to establish that a fluent *holds* in a time point t_1 if it holds *initially* or if it is *initiated* in some previous time point t_0, by the occurrence of an action, and it is not *terminated* by the occurrence of another action between t_0 and t_1. A simplified axiomatization to this formalism is the following:

$holdsAt(F, T) \leftarrow$ [SEC1]
    $initially(F) \wedge \neg clipped(0, F, T)$

$holdsAt(F, T) \leftarrow$ [SEC2]
    $happens(A, T') \wedge initiates(A, F, T') \wedge (T' \prec T) \wedge \neg clipped(T', F, T)$

$clipped(T_1, F, T_2) \leftrightarrow$ [SEC3]
    $\exists A, T [happens(A, T) \wedge (T_1 \prec T) \wedge (T \prec T_2) \wedge terminates(A, F, T)]$

In the event calculus, the frame problem is overcome through circumscription. Given Σ a domain description expressed as a conjunction of formulae that does not include the predicates *initially* or *happens*; Δ a narrative of actions expressed as a conjunctions of formulae that does not include the predicates *initiates* or *terminates*; Ω a conjunction of uniqueness-of-names axioms for actions and fluents; and EC a conjunction of the axioms of the event calculus, we have to consider the following formula as the background theory on the abductive event calculus planning:

$\text{CIRC}[\Sigma; initiates, terminates] \wedge \text{CIRC}[\Delta; happens] \wedge \Omega \wedge EC,$

where $\text{CIRC}[\Sigma; \rho_1, \ldots, \rho_n]$ means the circumscription of Σ w.r.t. the predicate symbols $\rho_1, \ldots, \rho_n$. By circumscribing *initiates* and *terminates* we are imposing that the known effects of actions are the only effects of actions, and by circumscribing *happens* we assume that there are no unexpected event occurrences. An extended discussion about the frame problem and its solution through circumscription can be found in [11].

Besides the domain independent axioms [SEC1]-[SEC3], we also need axioms to describe the fluents that are initially true, specified by the predicate *initially*, as well the positive and negative effects of the domain actions, specified by the predicates *initiates* and *terminates*, respectively. Remembering the elevator domain example, we can write:

$initially(curfloor(4))$
$initially(on(3))$
$initially(on(5)$

$initiates(up(N), curfloor(N), T) \leftarrow holdsAt(curfloor(C), T), C < N$
$initiates(down(N), curfloor(N), T) \leftarrow holdsAt(curfloor(C), T), C > N$

$terminates(up(N), curfloor(C), T) \leftarrow holdsAt(curfloor(C), T), C < N$
$terminates(down(N), curfloor(C), T) \leftarrow holdsAt(curfloor(C), T), C > N$
$terminates(turnoff(N), on(N), T) \leftarrow holdsAt(on(N), T)$

In the event calculus, a partial order plan is represented by a set of facts *happens*, establishing the occurrence of actions in time, and by a set of temporal constraints $\prec$, establishing a partial order over these actions. For instance, $\pi := \{happens(down(3), t_1), happens(up(5), t_2), t_1 \prec t_2\}$ is a partial order plan. Given a set of facts *happens* e $\prec$, representing a partial order plan, the axioms [SEC1]-[SEC3] and the domain description, we can find the truth of the domain fluents at any time point. For instance, given the plan π, we can conclude that $holdsAt(curfloor(5), t_2)$ is true, which is the effect of the action $up(5)$; and that $holdsAt(on(3), t_2)$ is also true, which is a property that persists in time, from the instant 0. In fact, the axioms [SEC1]-[SEC3] capture the *temporal persistence* of fluents and, therefore, the event calculus does not require persistence axioms.

3.2   The ABP Planning System

As [12] has shown, planning in event calculus is naturally handled as an abductive process. In this setting, planning a sequence of actions that satisfies a given goal Γ, w.r.t. a domain description Σ, is equivalent to finding an abductive explanation Δ (narrative or plan) such that:

$\text{CIRC}[\Sigma; initiates, terminates] \wedge \text{CIRC}[\Delta; happens] \wedge EC \wedge \Omega \models \Gamma$

Based on this idea, we have implemented the ABP [4] planning system. This planner is a PROLOG abductive interpreter specialized to the event calculus formalism. An advantage of this specialized interpreter is that predicates with incomplete information can receive a special treatment in the meta-level. For instance, in partial order planning, we have incomplete information about the predicate *before*, used to sequencing actions. Thus, when the interpreter finds a negative literal $\neg before(X, Y)$, it tries to prove it by showing that $before(Y, X)$ is consistent w.r.t. the plan being constructed.

3.3   Systematicity and Redundancy in the ABP Planning System

An interesting feature of the abductive planning system ABP is that we can modify its planning strategy, according to the characteristics of the application domain [5]. By making few modifications in the ABP specification, we have implemented two different planning strategies: SABP, a systematic partial order planner, and RABP, a redundant partial order planner.

A *systematic* planner is one that never visits the same plan more than once in its search space (*e.g.* SNLP [13]). A systematic version of the ABP, called SABP, can be obtained by modifying the axiom [SEC3] to consider as a *threat* to a fluent F not only an action that terminates it, but also an action that initiates it:

$$clipped(T_1, F, T_2) \leftrightarrow \qquad\qquad\qquad\qquad \text{[SEC3']}$$
$$\exists A, T [happens(A, T) \wedge (T_1 \prec T) \wedge (T \prec T_2) \wedge$$
$$(terminates(A, F, T) \vee initiates(A, F, T))]$$

A *redundant* planner is one that does not keep track of which goals were already achieved and which remains to be achieved and, therefore, it may establish and clobber a subgoal arbitrarily many times (*e.g.* TWEAK [14]). A redundant version of the ABP, called RABP, does not require any modification in the *EC* axioms. The only change that we have to make is in the goal selection strategy. In the ABP, as well in the SABP, subgoals are selected and then eliminated from the list of subgoals as soon as they are satisfied. This can be safely done because those planners apply a causal link protection strategy.

A MTC – *modal truth criterion* – strategy for goal selection can be easily implemented in the RABP by performing a temporal projection. This is done by making the meta-interpreter to "execute" the current plan, without allowing any modification on it. This process returns as output the first subgoal which is not necessarily true.

Another modification is on the negative residue: the RABP does not need to check the consistency of negative residues every time the plan has been modified. So, in the RABP, the negative literals of the predicate `clipped` does not have a special treatment by the meta-interpreter. As in TWEAK [14], this will make the RABP to select the same subgoal more than once but, on the other hand, it can plan for more than one subgoal with a single goal establishment.

3.4   Selecting the Best Planner: ABP, SABP or RABP

In our previous publication [4], we have demonstrated that, by varying the ratio r between positive and negative threats on a planning domain, the abductive planners exhibit different behavior: when $r > 1$, the systematic version is dramatically better than the redundant version; on the other hand, when $r < 1$, the systematic version is dramatically worse than the redundant version. This result provides a foundation for predicting the conditions under which different planning systems will perform better, depending on different characteristics of the domain. In other words, this result allows that someone building a planning system or a robotic control program can select the appropriate goal protection strategy, depending on the characteristics of the problem being solved.

By running the same experiment presented in [15], using our three implementations of the abductive planner, we can observe that these planners show behaviors significantly similar to the well known STRIPS-based planners POP, SNLP and TWEAK (see figure 2). Therefore, we can conclude that the logical and the algorithmic approaches implement the same planning strategies and present the same performance.

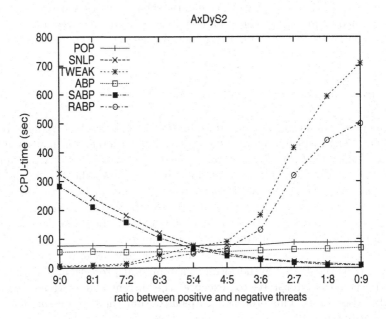

Fig. 2. The performance of the planners, depending on the domains characteristics

4   The New Programming Language Proposed

As we guess, GOLOG is a programming language that could be used to implement deliberative and reactive agents. However, as we have tested, GOLOG computes (in *off-line* mode) a complete total order plan that is submitted to an agent to execute it (in *on-line* mode). The problem with this approach is that it does not work well in many real dynamic applications. In the example of the elevator domain, this can be noticed by the fact that the agent cannot modify its plan in order to attend new serving requests. This is a case where we need to interleave the theorem prover with the executive module that controls the actions of the elevator, which is not possible with GOLOG.

Although our first implementation of the ABGOLOG (omitted here due to space limitation) suffered from the same problem, we foresee many ways of how we can change both, the ABGOLOG interpreter and the abdutive planner, in order to allow the agent to re-plan when relevant changes in the environment occur. These modifications are currently under construction but, to illustrate the idea, consider the following situation: *The elevator is parked in the 5th floor and there are two calls: the first one is from the 9th floor and the second one from the 2nd floor.* Thus, the agent generates a plan to serve these floors and initiates its execution, going first to the 9th floor. However, in the way up, a new call from the 8th floor is made by a user. Because of the occurrence of this new event, the agent should react to *fix* its execution plan, in order to also take care of to this new call. As we know, a partial order planner can modify its plan with a relative ease, since it keeps track of the causal links informations about plan's steps (*clipped* predicate in the abductive planner).

5   Conclusions

Traditionally, the notion of agents in Artificial Intelligence has been close related with the capability to think about actions and its effects in a dynamic environment [6], [16]. In this last decade, however, the notion of a purely rational agent, which ignores almost completely its interaction with the environment, gives place to the notion of an agent which must be capable of react to the perceptions received from its environment [17].

In this work, we consider a new logical programming language, especially guided for programming of robotic agents, which aims at to conciliate deliberation and reactivity. This language, based on GOLOG [1], uses the event calculus as the formalism to describe actions and to reason about its effects, and uses abduction as the mechanism for the synthesis of plans. Therefore, the main advantage of the ABGOLOG language is to be based on a more flexible and expressive action formalism, when compared to the situation calculus.

Our future work on ABGOLOG's implementation includes exploring aspects of compound actions (HTN planning), domain constraints involving the use of metric resources, conditional effects and durative actions.

References

1. Levesque, H.J., Reiter, R., Lesperance, Y., Lin, F., Scherl, R.B.: GOLOG: A logic programming language for dynamic domains. Journal of Logic Programming **31** (1997) 59–83
2. Russell, S., Norvig, P.: Artificial Intelligence: A Modern Approach (second edition). Prentice-Hall, Englewood Cliffs, NJ (2003)
3. Weld, D.S.: An introduction to least commitment planning. AI Magazine **15** (1994) 27–61

4. Pereira, S.L.: Abductive Planning in the Event Calculus. Master Thesis, Institute of Mathematics and Statistics - University of Sao Paulo (2002)
5. Pereira, S.L., Barros, L.N.: Efficiency in abductive planning. In: Proceedings of 2nd Congress of Logic Applied to Technology. Senac, São Paulo (2001) 213–222
6. McCarthy, J.: Situations, actions and causal laws. Technical Report Memo 2 - Stanford University Artificial Intelligence Laboratory (1963)
7. Peirce, C.S.: Collected Papers of Charles Sanders Peirce. Harvard University Press (1931-1958)
8. Cox, P.T., Pietrzykowski, T.: Causes for events: their computation and applications. In: Proc. of the 8th international conference on Automated deduction, Springer-Verlag New York, Inc. (1986) 608–621
9. Kakas, A.C., Kowalski, R.A., Toni, F.: Abductive logic programming. Journal of Logic and Computation **2** (1992) 719–770
10. Kowalski, R.A., Sergot, M.J.: A logic-based calculus of events. In: New Generation Computing 4. (1986) 67–95
11. Shanahan, M.P.: Solving the Frame Problem: A Mathematical Investigation of the Common Sense Law of Inertia. MIT Press (1997)
12. Eshghi, K.: Abductive planning with event calculus. In: Proc.of the 5th International Conference on Logic Programming. MIT Press (1988) 562–579
13. MacAllester, D., Rosenblitt, D.: Systematic nonlinear planning. In: Proc. 9th National Conference on Artificial Intelligence. MIT Press (1991) 634–639
14. Chapman, D.: Planning for conjunctive goals. Artificial Intelligence **32** (1987) 333–377
15. Knoblock, C., Yang, Q.: Evaluating the tradeoffs in partial-order planning algorithms (1994)
16. Green, C.: Application of theorem proving to problem solving. In: International Joint Conference on Artificial Intelligence. Morgan Kaufmann (1969) 219–239
17. Brooks, R.A.: A robust layered control system for a mobile robot. IEEE Journal of Robotics and Automation **2** (1986) 14–23

Word Equation Systems: The Heuristic Approach

César Luis Alonso[1,*], Fátima Drubi[2],
Judith Gómez-García[3], and José Luis Montaña[3]

[1] Centro de Inteligencia Artificial, Universidad de Oviedo
Campus de Viesques, 33271 Gijón, Spain
calonso@aic.uniovi.es
[2] Departamento de Informática, Universidad de Oviedo
Campus de Viesques, 33271 Gijón, Spain
[3] Departamento de Matemáticas, Estadística y Computación
Universidad de Cantabria
montana@matesco.unican.es

Abstract. One of the most intricate algorithms related to words is
Makanin's algorithm for solving word equations. Even if Makanin's algorithm is very complicated, the solvability problem for word equations remains NP-hard if one looks for short solutions, i. e. with length bounded
by a linear function w. r. t. the size of the system ([2]) or even with constant bounded length ([1]). Word equations can be used to define various
properties of strings, e. g. characterization of imprimitiveness, hardware
specification and verification and string unification in PROLOG-3 or
unification in theories with associative non-commutative operators. This
paper is devoted to propose the heuristic approach to deal with the problem of solving word equation systems provided that some upper bound
for the length of the solutions is given. Up to this moment several heuristic strategies have been proposed for other NP-complete problems, like
3-SAT, with a remarkable success. Following this direction we compare
here two genetic local search algorithms for solving word equation systems. The first one consists of an adapted version of the well known
WSAT heuristics for 3-SAT instances (see [9]). The second one is an improved version of our genetic local search algorithm in ([1]). We present
some empirical results which indicate that our approach to this problem
becomes a promising strategy. Our experimental results also certify that
our local optimization technique seems to outperform the WSAT class
of local search procedures for the word equation system problem.

Keywords: Evolutionary computation, genetic algorithms, local search
strategies, word equations.

1   Introduction

Checking if two strings are identical is a rather trivial problem. It corresponds to
test equality of strings. Finding patterns in strings is slightly more complicated.

---

* Partially supported by the spanish MCyT and FEDER grant TIC2003-04153.

A.L.C. Bazzan and S. Labidi (Eds.): SBIA 2004, LNAI 3171, pp. 83–92, 2004.

It corresponds to solve word equations with a constant side. For example:

$$xx01x1y = 010010101000110101010 . \qquad (1)$$

where x, y are variable strings in $\{0,1\}^*$. Equations of this type are not difficult to solve. Indeed many cases of this problem have very efficient algorithms in the field of pattern matching.

In general, try to find solutions to equations where both sides contain variable strings, like for instance:

$$x01x1y = 1y0xy . \qquad (2)$$

where x, y are variables in $\{0,1\}^*$ or show it has none, is a surprisingly difficult problem.

The satisfiability problem for word equations has a simple formulation: Find out whether or not an input word equation (like that in example (2)) has a solution. The decidability of the problem was proved by Makanin ([6]). His decision procedure is one of the most complicated algorithms in theoretical computer science. The time complexity of this algorithm is $2^{2^{P(n)}}$ nondeterministic time, where $P(n)$ is a single exponential function of the size of the equation n ([5]). In recent years several better complexity upper bounds have been obtained: EXPSPACE ([4]), NEXPTIME ([8]) and PSPACE ([7]). A lower bound for the problem is NP ([2]). The best algorithms for NP-hard problems run in single exponential deterministic time. Each algorithm in PSPACE can be implemented in single exponential deterministic time, so exponential time is optimal in the context of deterministic algorithms solving word equations unless faster algorithms are developed for NP-hard problems.

In the present paper we compare the performance of two new evolutionary algorithms which incorporate some kind of local optimization for the problem of solving systems of word equations provided that an upper bound for the length of the solutions is given. The first strategy proposed here is inspired in the well known local search algorithms GSAT an WSAT to find a satisfying assignment for a set of clauses (see [9]). The second one is an improved version, including random walking in hypercubes of the kind $\{0,1\}^m$, of the flipping genetic local search algorithm announced in ([1]). As far as we know there are no references in the literature for solving this problem in the framework of heuristic strategies involving local search. The paper is organized as follows: in section 2 we explicitly state the WES problem with bounds; section 3 describes the evolutionary algorithms with the local search procedures; in section 4, we present the experimental results, solving some word equation systems randomly generated forcing solvability; finally, section 5 contains some conclusive remarks.

2 The Word Equation Systems Problem

Let A be an alphabet of constants and let Ω be an alphabet of variables. We assume that these alphabets are disjoint. As usual we denote by A^* the set of words on A, and given a word $w \in A^*$, $|w|$ stands for the length of w; ε denotes the empty word.

Definition 1. *A word equation over the alphabet A and variables set Ω is a pair $(L, R) \in (A \cup \Omega)^* \times (A \cup \Omega)^*$, usually denoted by $L = R$. A word equation system (WES) over the alphabet A and variables set Ω is a finite set of word equations $S = \{L_1 = R_1, \ldots, L_n = R_n\}$, where, for $i \in \{1, \ldots, n\}$, each pair $(L_i, R_i) \in (A \cup \Omega)^* \times (A \cup \Omega)^*$.*

Definition 2. *Given a WES over the alphabet A and variables set Ω, $S = \{L_1 = R_1, \ldots, L_n = R_n\}$, a solution of S is a morphism $\sigma : (A \cup \Omega)^* \to A^*$ such that $\sigma(a) = a$, for $a \in A$, and $\sigma(L_i) = \sigma(R_i)$, for $i \in \{1, \ldots, n\}$.*

The WES problem, in its general form, is stated as follows: given a word equation system as input find a solution if there exists anyone or determine the no existence of solutions otherwise. The problem we are going to study in this contribution is not as general as stated above, but it is also a NP-complete problem (see Theorem 5 below). In our formulation of the problem also an upper bound d for the length of the variable values in a solution is given. We name this variation the d-WES problem.

d-WES Problem: Given a WES over the alphabet A with variables set Ω, $S = \{L_1 = R_1, \ldots, L_n = R_n\}$, find a solution $\sigma : (A \cup \Omega)^* \to A^*$ such that $|\sigma(x)| \leq d$, for each $x \in \Omega$, or determine the no existence otherwise.

Example 3. (see [1]) For each $d \geq 1$, let F_d and $WordFib_d$ be the d-th Fibonacci number and the d-th Fibonacci word over the alphabet $A = \{0, 1\}$, respectively. For any $d \geq 2$ let S_d be the word equation system over the alphabet $A = \{0, 1\}$ and variables set $\Omega = \{x_1, \ldots, x_{d+1}\}$ defined as:

$$x_1 = 0$$

$$x_2 = 1$$

$$01x_1x_2 = x_1x_2x_3$$

$$\cdots$$

$$01x_1x_2x_2x_3 \ldots x_{d-1}x_d = x_1x_2x_3 \ldots x_{d+1}.$$

Then, for any $d \geq 2$, the morphism $\sigma_d : (A \cup \Omega)^* \to A^*$, defined by

$$\sigma_d(x_i) = FibWord_i,$$

for $i \in \{1, \ldots, d+1\}$, is the only solution of the system S_d. This solution satisfies $|\sigma(x_i)| = F_i \leq F_{d+1}$, for each $i \in \{1, \ldots, d+1\}$. Recall that $FibWord_1 = 0$, $FibWord_2 = 1$ and $FibWord_i = FibWord_{i-2}FibWord_{i-1}$ if $i > 2$.

Remark 4. Example 3 is quite meaningful itself. It shows that any exact deterministic algorithm which solves the WES problem in its general form (or any heuristic algorithm solving all instances S_d) must have, at least, exponential worst-case complexity. This is due to the fact that the system S_d has polynomial size in d and the only solution of S_d, namely σ_d, has exponential length w.r.t d, because it contains, as a part, the d-th Fibonacci word, $WordFib_d$. Note that $WordFib_d$ has size equal to the d-th Fibonacci number, F_d, which is exponential w.r.t d.

A problem which does not allow to exhibit the exponential length argument for lower complexity bounds is the d-WES problem stated above. But this problem remains NP-complete.

Theorem 5. *(c. f. [1]) For any $d \geq 2$ the d-WES problem is NP-complete.*

3   The Evolutionary Algorithm

Given an alphabet A and some string over A, $\alpha \in A^*$, for any pair of positions i, j, $1 \leq i \leq j \leq |\alpha|$, in the string α, $\alpha[i, j] \in A^*$ denotes the substring of α given by the extraction of $j - i + 1$ consecutive many letters i through j from string α. In the case $i = j$, we denote by $\alpha[i]$ the single letter substring $\alpha[i, i]$, which represents the i-th symbol of the string α.

3.1   Individual Representation

Given an instance for the d-WES problem, that is, a word equation system $S = \{L_1 = R_1, \ldots, L_n = R_n\}$ with n equations and m variables, over the alphabet $A = \{0, 1\}$ and variables set $\Omega = \{x_1, \ldots, x_m\}$, if a morphism σ is candidate solution for S, then for each $i \in \{1, \ldots, m\}$, the size of the value of any variable x_i, $|\sigma(x_i)|$, must be less than or equal to d. This motivates the representation of a chromosome as a list of m strings $\{\alpha_1, \ldots, \alpha_m\}$ where, for each $i \in \{1, \ldots, m\}$, α_i is a word over the alphabet $A = \{0, 1\}$ of length $|\alpha_i| \leq d$, such that the value of the variable x_i, is represented in the chromosome by the string $\alpha_i \in A^*$.

3.2   Fitness Function

First, we introduce a notion of distance between strings which extends Hamming distance to the case of non-equal size strings. This is necessary because the chromosomes (representing candidate solutions for our problem instances) are variable size strings.

Given to strings α, $\beta \in A^*$ the generalized Hamming distance between them is defined as follows:

$$H(\alpha, \beta) = Max\{|\alpha|, |\beta|\} - \sharp\{k \in \{1, \ldots, min\{|\alpha|, |\beta|\}\} : \alpha[k] = \beta[k]\}.$$

Given a word equation system $S = \{L_1 = R_1, \ldots, L_n = R_n\}$ over the alphabet $A = \{0, 1\}$ with set variables $\Omega = \{x_1, \ldots, x_m\}$ and a chromosome $\bar{\alpha} = \{\alpha_1, \ldots, \alpha_m\}$, representing a candidate solution for S, the fitness of $\bar{\alpha}$ is computed as follows:

First, in each equation, we substitute, for $j \in \{1, \ldots, m\}$, every variable x_j for the corresponding string $\alpha_j \in A$, and, after this replacement, we get the expressions $\{L_1(\bar{\alpha}) = R_1(\bar{\alpha}), \ldots, L_n(\bar{\alpha}) = R_n(\bar{\alpha})\}$ where $\{L_i(\bar{\alpha}), R_i(\bar{\alpha})\} \subset A^*$ for all $i \in \{1, \ldots, n\}$.

Then, the fitness of the chromosome $\bar{\alpha}$, $f(\bar{\alpha})$, is defined as:

$$f(\bar{\alpha}) = \sum_{i=1}^{n} H(L_i(\bar{\alpha}), R_i(\bar{\alpha})).$$

Proposition 6. *Let $S = \{L_1 = R_1, \ldots, L_n = R_n\}$ be a word equation system over the alphabet $A = \{0, 1\}$ with set variables $\Omega = \{x_1, \ldots, x_m\}$ and let $\bar{\alpha} = \{\alpha_1, \ldots, \alpha_m\}$ be a chromosome representing a candidate solution for S. Define the morphism $\sigma : (A \cup \Omega)^* \to A^*$ as $\sigma(x_i) = \alpha_i'$, for each $i \in \{1, \ldots, m\}$. Then the morphism σ is a solution of system S if and only if the fitness of the chromosome $\bar{\alpha}$ is equal to zero, that is $f(\bar{\alpha}) = 0$.*

Remark 7. According to Proposition 7, the goal of our evolutive algorithm is to minimize the fitness function f. By means of this fitness function, we propose a measure of the quality of an individual which distinguishes between individuals that satisfy the same number of equations. This last objective cannot be reached by other fitness functions like, for instance, the number of satisfied equations in the given system.

3.3   Genetic Operators

selection: We make use of the roulette wheel selection procedure (see [3]).

crossover: Given two chromosomes $\bar{\alpha} = \{\alpha_1, \ldots, \alpha_m\}$ and $\bar{\beta} = \{\beta_1, \ldots, \beta_m\}$, the result of a crossover is a chromosome constructed applying a local crossover to every of the corresponding strings α_i, β_i. Fixed $i \in \{1, \ldots m\}$, the crossover of the strings α_i, β_i, denoted as cr_i, is given as follows. Assume $a_i = |\alpha_i| \leq |\beta_i|$ then, the substring $cr_i[1, a_i]$ is the result of applying uniform crossover ([3]) to the strings $\alpha_i \in A^*$ and $\beta_i[1, a_i]$. Next, we randomly select a position $k_i \in \{a_i + 1, \ldots, d\}$ and define $cr_i[a_i + 1, k_i] = \beta_i[a_i + 1, min\{k_i, |\beta_i|\}]$.
We clarify this local crossover by means of the following example:

Example 8. Let $\alpha_i = 01$ and $\beta_i = 100011$ be the variable strings. In this case, we apply uniform crossover to the first two symbols. Let us suppose that 11 is the resulting substring. This substring is the first part of the resulting child. Then, if the selected position were, for instance, position 4, the second part of the child would be 00, and the complete child would be 1100.

mutation: We apply mutation with a given probability p. The concrete value of p in our algorithms is given in Section 4 below. Given a chromosome $\bar{\alpha} = \{\alpha_1, \ldots, \alpha_m\}$, the mutation operator applied to $\bar{\alpha}$ consists in replacing each gene of each word α_i with probability $\frac{1}{d}$, where d is the given upper bound.

3.4   Local Search Procedures

Given a word equation system $S = \{L_1 = R_1, \ldots, L_n = R_n\}$ over the alphabet $A = \{0, 1\}$ with set variables $\Omega = \{x_1, \ldots, x_m\}$ and a chromosome

$\bar{\alpha} = (\alpha_1, \ldots, \alpha_m)$, representing a candidate solution for S, for any $k \geq 0$ we define the k-neighborhood of $\bar{\alpha}$ with respect to the generalized Hamming distance as follows:

$$U_k(\bar{\alpha}) := \{\bar{\beta} : \; Maximum_{1 \leq i \leq m} \; H(\alpha_i, \beta_i) \leq k\}$$

Local Search 1 (LS1) First, we present our adapted version of the local search procedure WSAT which will be sketched below. The local search procedure takes as input a chromosome $\bar{\alpha} = (\alpha_1, \ldots, \alpha_m)$ and, at each step, yields a chromosome $\bar{\beta} = (\beta_1, \ldots, \beta_m)$, which satisfies the following properties. With probability p, $\bar{\beta}$ is a random chromosome in $U_1(\bar{\alpha})$ and with probability $1 - p$, $\bar{\beta}$ is a chromosome in $U_1(\bar{\alpha})$ with minimal fitness. In this last case $\bar{\beta}$ cannot be improved by adding or flipping any single bit from $\bar{\alpha}$ (because their components are at Hamming distance at most one). This process iterates until a given specified maximum number of flips is reached. We call the parameter p probability of noise.

Below, we display the pseudo-code of this local search procedure taking as input a chromosome with m string variables of size bounded by d (one for each variable).

```
Input system S, chromosome cr, Maxflips M, probability p;
Procedure Local_Search1
begin
    for j=1 to M do
    begin
        if cr satisfies S then  return cr;
        cr1:= select (S,cr,p);
    end
    return cr1
end
```

```
Input system S, chromosome cr, probability p;
Procedure Select
begin
    u:= minimal fitness in U1(cr);
    if u=0 then
            cr1:= chromosome with minimal fitness in U1(cr)
    else
            with probability p:
                cr1:= a random chromosome in U1(cr);
            with probability 1-p:
                cr1:= chromosome with minimal fitness in U1(cr);
            end
    return cr1
end
```

Local Search 2 (LS2) Suppose we are given a chromosome $\bar{\alpha} = (\alpha_1, \ldots, \alpha_m)$. At each iteration step, the local search generates a random walk inside the truncated hypercube $U_k(\bar{\alpha})$ and at each new generated chromosome makes a flip (or modifies its length by one unit if possible) if there is a gain in the fitness. This process iterates until there is no gain. Here k is the number of genes of the chromosome $\bar{\alpha}$, that is $k = \sum_{1 \le i \le m} |\alpha_i|$.

For each chromosome $\bar{\alpha}$ and each pair (i, j) such that, $1 \le i \le m$ and $1 \le j \le |\alpha_i|$ (representing the gene at position j in the i-component α_i of chromosome $\bar{\alpha}$) we define the set $U_{(i,j)}(\bar{\alpha})$ trough the next two properties:

- $U_{(i,j)}(\bar{\alpha}) \subset U_1(\bar{\alpha})$ and
- Any element $\bar{\beta} \in U_{(i,j)}(\bar{\alpha})$ satisfies: for all pair (i', j'), $1 \le i' \le m$; $1 \le j' \le |\alpha_i|$, if $(i', j') \ne (i, j)$ then $\alpha_{i'}[j'] = \beta_{i'}[j']$.

Note that any element in $U_{(i,j)}(\bar{\alpha})$ can be obtained in one of the following ways: if $j < |\alpha_i|$ by flipping the gene (i, j) in $\bar{\alpha}$; if $j = |\alpha_i|$ adding a new gene at the end of the component α_i of $\bar{\alpha}$, or deleting the gene (i, j) of the component α_i or flipping gene (i, j). In the pseudo-code displayed below we associate a gen g with a pair (i, j) and a chromosome cr with an element $\bar{\alpha}$. Then, notation $Ug(cr)$ denotes a subset of the type $U_{(i,j)}(\bar{\alpha})$.

```
Input chromosome cr;
Procedure Local_search2
begin
    H:=gens(cr);
    repeat
        cr_aux:=cr
        repeat
            g:= an element of H uniformly generated;
            cr:= chromosome with minimal fitness in Ug(cr);
            H:=H-{g}
        until empty H
    until cr=cr_aux
end
```

Summarizing, the pseudo-code of our evolutionary algorithms is the following:

```
begin
    Generation := 0;
    Population := initial_population;
    evaluate(Population);
    while (not_termination_condition) do
    begin
        Best := best_individual(Population);
        New_population := {Best};
        while (|New_population| < |Population|) do
        begin
            Pair := select_parents(Population);
```

```
            Child := crossover(Pair);
            Child := mutation(Child, probability);
            Child := local_search(Child);
            New_population := insert(Child, New_population);
        end
        Population := New_population;
        Generation := Generation + 1
    end
end
```

Remark 9. The initial population is randomly generated. The procedure evaluate(population) computes the fitness of all individuals in the population. The procedure local_search(Child) can be either LS1 or LS2. Finally, the termination condition is true when a solution is found (the fitness at some individual equals zero) or the number of generations attains a given value.

4   Experimental Results

We have performed our experiments over problem instances having n equations, m variables and a solution of maximum variable length q, denoted as pn-m-q. We run our program for various upper bounds of variable length $d \geq q$. Let us note that, m variables and d as upper bound for the length of a variable, determine a search space of size $(\sum_{i=0}^{d} 2^i)^m = (2^{d+1} - 1)^m$.

Since we have not found in the literature any benchmark instance for this problem, we have implemented a program for random generate word equation systems with solutions, and we have applied our algorithm to these systems[1].

All runs where performed over a processor AMD Athlom XP 1900+; 1,6 GHz and 512 Mb RAM. For a single run the execution time ranges from two seconds, for the simplest problems, to five minutes, for the most complex ones. The complexity of a problem is measured through the average number of evaluations to solution.

4.1   Probability of Mutation and Size of the Initial Population

After some previous experiments, we conclude that the best parameters for the LS2 program are **population size** equals 2 and **probability of mutation** equals 0.9. This previous experimentation was reported in ([1]). For the LS1 program we conclude that the best parameters are Maxflips equals 40 and probability of noise equals 0.2. We remark that these parameters correspond to the best results obtained in the problems reported in Table 1.

4.2   LS1 vs. LS2

We show the local search efficiency executing some experiments with both local search procedures. In all the executions, the algorithm stops if a solution is found

---

[1] Available on line in http://www.aic.uniovi.es/Tc/spanish/repository.htm

Table 1. Experimental results for various sizes of search space (S.S.). We have run for the instances the evolutionary algorithm with LS1 (SR1 & AES1) and with LS2 (SR2 & AES2). The elements of column U.B. are the different upper bounds.

P. instance	U.B.	S.S.	SR2	SR1	AES2	AES1
p10-8-3	3	2^{32}	100%	100%	3164.24	20930.6
p25-8-3	3	2^{32}	100%	100%	473.46	7304.34
p10-8-3	4	2^{40}	100%	100%	5121.25	41141.9
p25-8-3	5	2^{48}	100%	100%	1002.26	16824.5
p25-8-3	6	2^{56}	100%	100%	2193	25628.2
p5-15-3	3	2^{60}	100%	100%	16459.25	54459
p10-15-3	3	2^{60}	100%	100%	8124.48	55379.3
p15-12-4	4	2^{60}	100%	100%	479.63	4187.68
p10-8-3	7	2^{64}	100%	100%	168344	300204
p25-8-3	8	2^{72}	100%	100%	3567.86	69748
p10-8-3	10	2^{88}	85%	86%	405326	682543
p5-15-3	5	2^{90}	100%	96%	156365.52	546898
p10-15-3	5	2^{90}	100%	86%	258556	399374
p10-15-5	5	2^{90}	100%	100%	95457.93	180146
p25-23-4	4	2^{115}	100%	58%	412375	592463
p25-23-4	5	2^{138}	81%	34%	389630	858080
p15-25-5	5	2^{150}	98%	96%	278782.36	444430
p5-15-3	10	2^{165}	8%	0%	557410.58	–
p25-8-3	20	2^{168}	100%	78%	24221	689104

or the limit of 1500000 evaluations is reached. The results of our experiments are displayed in Table 1 based on 50 independent runs for each instance. As usually, the performance of the algorithm is measured first of all by the *Success Rate (SR)*, which represents the portion of runs where a solution has been found. Moreover, as a measure of the time complexity, we use the *Average number of Evaluations to Solution (AES)* index, which counts the average number of fitness evaluations performed up to find a solution in successful runs. Comparing the two local search procedures, we observe that the improved version of our local search algorithm (LS2) is significantly better than the adapted version to our problem (LS1) of the WSAT strategies. This can be confirmed by looking at the respective Average number of Evaluations to Solution reported in our table of experiments. The comparatione between the evolutionary local-search strategy an the pure genetic approach was already reported in ([1]) using a preliminary version of (LS2) that does not use random walks. We observed there a very bad behavior of the pure genetic algorithm.

5   Conclusions, Summary and Future Research

The results of the experiments reported in Table 1, indicate that the use of evolutive algorithms is a promising strategy for solving the d-WES problem, and that our algorithms have a good behavior also dealing with large search space sizes.

Nevertheless, these promising results, there are some hard problems, as p5-15-3, over which our algorithms have some difficulties trying to find a solution and in other ones, as for example p25-8-3, the program always finds just the same. In both cases, the found solution agrees with that proposed by the random problem generator. In this sense, we have not a conclusion about the influence either of the number of equations or of the ratio size of the system/number of variables, on the difficulty of the problem. For the two compared local search algorithms we conclude that LS2 seems to outperform LS1, that is, the WSAT extension of local search procedures for the word equation system problem. Nevertheless it would be convenient to execute new experiments over problem instances with higher size of search space and to adjust for each instance, the parameters of Maxflips and probability of noise in procedure LS1. The most important limitation of our approach is the use of upper bounds on the size of the variables when looking for solutions. In a work in progress, we are developing an evolutionary algorithm for the general problem of solving systems of word equations (WES) that profits a logarithmic compression of the size of a minimal solution of a word equation via Lempel–Ziv encodings of words. We think that this will allow to explore much larger search spaces and avoiding the use of the upper bound on the size of the solutions.

References

1. Alonso C. L., Drubi F., Montana J. L.: An evolutionary algoritm for solving Word Equation Systems. Proc. CAEPIA-TTIA'2003. To appear in Springer L.N.A.I.
2. Angluin D.: Finding patterns common to a set of strings, J. C. S. S. 21(1) (1980) 46-62
3. Goldbert, D. E.: Genetic Algorithms in Search Optimization & Machine Learning. Addison Wesley Longmann, Inn. (1989)
4. Gutiérrez, C.: Satisfiability of word equations with constants is in exponential space. in Proc. FOCS'98, IEEE Computer Society Press, Palo Alto, California (1998)
5. Koscielski, A., Pacholski, L.: Complexity of Makanin's algorithm, J. ACM 43(4) (1996) 670-684
6. Makanin, G.S.: The Problem of Solvability of Equations in a Free Semigroup. Math. USSR Sbornik 32 (1977) 2 129-198
7. Plandowski, W.: Wojciech Plandowski: Satisfiability of Word Equations with Constants is in PSPACE. FOCS'99 495-500 (1999)
8. Plandowski, W., Rytter, W.: Application of Lempel-Ziv encodings to the Solution of Words Equations. Larsen, K.G. et al. (Eds.) L.N.C.S. 1443 (1998) 731-742
9. Selman, B., Levesque H., Mitchell: A new method for solving hard satisfiability problems. Pro. of the Tenth National Conference on Artificial Intelligence, AAAI Press, California (1992) 440-446

A Cooperative Framework Based on Local Search and Constraint Programming for Solving Discrete Global Optimisation

Carlos Castro, Michael Moossen*, and María Cristina Riff**

Departamento de Informática
Universidad Técnica Federico Santa María
Valparaíso, Chile
{Carlos.Castro,Michael.Moossen,Maria-Cristina.Riff}@inf.utfsm.cl

Abstract. Our research has been focused on developing cooperation techniques for solving large scale combinatorial optimisation problems using Constraint Programming with Local Search. In this paper, we introduce a framework for designing cooperative strategies. It is inspired from recent research carried out by the Constraint Programming community. For the tests that we present in this work we have selected two well known techniques: Forward Checking and Iterative Improvement. The set of benchmarks for the Capacity Vehicle Routing Problem shows the advantages to use this framework.

1 Introduction

Solving Constraint Satisfaction Optimisation Problems (CSOP) consists in assigning values to variables in such a way that a set of constraints is satisfied and a goal function is optimised [15]. Nowadays, complete and incomplete techniques are available to solve this kind of problems. On one hand, Constraint Programming is an example of complete techniques where a sequence of Constraint Satisfaction Problems (CSP) [10] is solved by adding constraints that impose better bounds on the objective function until an unsatisfiable problem is reached. On the other hand, Local Search techniques are incomplete methods where an initial solution is repeatedly improved considering neighborg solutions. The advantages and drawbacks of each of these techniques are well-known: complete techniques allow to get, when possible, global optimum but they show a poor scalability to solve very large problems, thus they do not give an optimal solution. Incomplete methods gives solutions very quickly but they remains local.

Recently, the integration of both complete and incomplete approaches to solve Constraint Satisfaction Problems has been studied and it has been recognized that an cooperative approach should give good results when none is able to solve a problem. In [13], Prestwich proposes a hybrid approach that sacrifies

---

* The first and the second authors have been partially supported by the Chilean National Science Fund through the project FONDECYT 1010121
** She is supported by the project FONDECYT 1040364

A.L.C. Bazzan and S. Labidi (Eds.): SBIA 2004, LNAI 3171, pp. 93–102, 2004.

completeness of backtracking methods to achieve the scalability of local search, this method outperforms the best Local Search algorithms. In [8], Jussien & Lhomme present a hybrid technique where Local Search performs over partial assignments instead of complete assignments, and uses constraint propagation and conflict- based heuristics to improve the search. They applied their approach to open-shop scheduling problems obtaining encouraging results. In the metaheuristics community various hybrid approaches combining Local Search and Constraint Programming have been proposed. In [5], Focacci et al. present a good state of the art of hybrid methods integrating both Local Search and Constraint Programming techniques.

On the other hand, solver cooperation is a hot research topic that has been widely investigated during the last years [6, 11, 12]. Nowadays, very efficient constraint solvers are available and the challenge is to integrate them in order to improve their efficiency or to solve problems that cannot be treated by an elementary constraint solver. In the last years, we have been interested in the definition of cooperation languages allowing to define elementary solvers and to integrate several solvers in a flexible and efficient way [4, 3, 2].

In this work, we concentrate our attention on to solve CSOP instead of CSP. We introduce a framework for designing cooperative strategies using both kinds of techniques: Constraint Programming and Local Search. The main difference of our framework with respect to existing hybrid methods is that, using a cooperation of solvers point of view, we build a new solver based on elementary ones. In this case, elementary solvers implement Local Search and Constraint Programming techniques independently, each of them as a black-box. Thus, in this sense, this work does not have to be considered as a hybrid algorithm. In this framework, all cooperation scheme must not lose completeness. The motivation for this work is that we strongly believe that local search carried out, for example, by a Hill-Climbing algorithm, should allow us to reduce the search space by adding more constraints on the bounds for applying the Constraint Programming approach. Preliminary results on a classical hard combinatorial optimisation problem, the Capacity Vehicle Routing Problem, using simplifications of the Solomon benchmarks [14], show that in our approach Hill-Climbing really helps Forward Checking and it becomes able to find better solutions.

This paper is organised as follows: in section 2, we briefly present both complete and incomplete techniques. In section 3, we introduce the framework for design cooperative hybrid strategies. In section 4, we present the test solved using Forward Checking as complete technique and Iterative Improvement as incomplete technique and we evaluate and compare the results. Finally, in section 5, we conclude the paper and give further research lines.

2   Constraint Programming and Local Search for CSOP

Constraint Programming evolved from research carried out during the last thirty years on constraint solving. Techniques used for solving CSPs are generally classified in: Searching, Problem Reduction, and Hybrid Techniques [9]. *Searching* consists of techniques for systematic exploration of the space of all solutions. *Problem reduction* techniques transform a CSP into an equivalent problem by reducing the set of values that the variables can take while preserving the set of solutions. Finally, *hybrid* techniques integrate problem reduction techniques into an exhaustive search algorithm in the following way: whenever a variable is instantiated, a new CSP is created; then a constraint propagation algorithm is applied to remove local inconsistencies of these new CSPs [16]. Many algorithms that essentially fit the previous format have been proposed. *Forward Checking*, *Partial Lookahead*, and *Full Lookahead*, for example, primarily differ in the degree of local consistency verification performed at the nodes of the search tree [7, 9, 16].

Constraint Programming deals with optimisation problems, CSOPs, using the same basic idea of verifying the satisfiability of a set of constraints that is used for solving CSPs. Asuming that one is dealing with a minimisation problem, the idea is to use an upper bound that represents the best possible solution obtained so far. Then we solve a sequence of CSPs each one giving a better solution with respect to the optimisation function. More precisely, we compute a solution s to the original set of constraints C and we add the constraint $f < f(s)$, where f represents the optimisation function and $f(s)$ represents the evaluation of f in the solution s. Adding this constraint restricts the set of possible solutions to those that give better values for the optimisation function always satisfying the original set of constraints. When, after adding such a constraint, the problem becomes unsatisfiable, the last feasible solution so far obtained represents the global optimal solution [1]. Very efficient hybrid techniques, such as Forward Checking, Full Lookahead or even more specialised algorithms, are usually applied for solving the sequence of CSPs. The next figure presents this basic optimisation scheme.

Procedure Basic Optimisation in Constraint Programming
Begin
s = GenerateFeasibleSolution(C)
best-solution = s
solution-value = $f(s)$
While Problem has solution
s = GenerateFeasibleSolution(C & $f < solution - value$)
best-solution = s
solution-value = $f(s)$
EndWhile
End /* Procedure */

Fig. 1. Basic Constraint Programming Algorithm for CSOP

Local Search is a general approach, widely used, to solve hard combinatorial optimisation problems. Roughly speaking, a local search algorithm starts off with an initial solution and then repeatedly tries to find better solutions by searching neighborhoods, the algorithm is shown in figure 2.

Procedure Basic Iterated Local Search
Begin
s = GenerateInitialSolution
best-solution = s
solution-value = $f(s)$
Repeat
s = Perturbation(best-solution, history)
best-solution = AcceptanceCriterion(best-solution, s, history)
Until termination condition met
End /* Procedure */

Fig. 2. Basic Local Search Algorithm for CSOP

A basic version of Local Search is Iterative Improvement or Hill-Climbing procedures. Iterative Improvement starts with some initial solution that is constructed by some other algorithm, or just generated randomly, and from then on it keeps moving to a better neighborg, as long as there is one, until finally it finishes at a locally optimal solution, one that does not have a better neighborg. Iterative Improvement can apply either first improvement, in which the current solution is replaced by the first cost-improving solution found by the neighborhood search, or best improvement in which the current solution is replaced by the best solution in its neighborhood. Empirically, local search heuristics appear to converge usually rather quickly, within low-order polynomial time. However, they are only able to find near-optimal solutions, i.e., in general, a local optimum might not coincide with a global optimum. In this paper, we analise the cooperation between Forward Checking, for solving the sequence of CSPs, and Iterative Improvement using a best improvement strategy to carry out a local search approach.

3   A Framework for Design Cooperative Hybrid Strategies

Our idea to make an incomplete solver to cooperate with a complete one is to take advantage of the efficiency of incomplete techniques to find a new bound and, given it to the complete approach, to continue searching the global optimum. For the next, we will call the incomplete solver as *i-solver* and the complete one as *c-solver*. In our approach, *c-solver* could begin solving a CSP, after this the solution so obtained gives a bound for the optimal value of the problem. In case of *c-solver* is stucked trying to find a solution, the collaborative algorithm detects this situation and gives this information to a ι-solver method, that is charged to find quickly a new feasible solution.

The communication between *c-solver* and *i-solver* depends on the direction of the communication. Thus, when the algorithm gives the control from *c-solver* to *i-solver*, *i-solver* receives the variable values previously found by *c-solver* and it works trying to find a new better solution applying some heuristics. When the control is from *i-solver* to *c-solver*, *i-solver* gives information about the local optima that it found. This information modifies the bound of the objective function constraint, and *c-solver* works trying to find a solution for this new problem configuration.

Roughly speaking, we expect that using *i-solver*, *c-solver* will reduce its search tree cutting some branches using the new bound for the objective function. On the other hand, *i-solver* focuses its search when it uses an instantiation previously found by *c-solver* on an area of the search space where it is more probably to obtain the optimal value.

In figure 3, we ilustrate the general cooperation approach proposed in this work.

```
Procedure Cooperating Solvers (f, C, c − solver, i − solver)
Begin /* Procedure Cooperating Solvers */
While (Not OK-Global-Solution)
   While ((Not condition max-stuck-c-solver) and
          (Not OK-CSP-Solution))
      pre-solution-from-c-solver = c − solver(C)
      If (Not OK-CSP-solution)
         While ((Not condition max-stuck-i-solver) and
                (Not OK-CSP-Solution))
            P = pre-solution-from-c-solver
            near-optimal-solution-i-solver = i-solver(P, f)
            Bound = near-optimal-solution-i-solver
         EndWhile
      Else Bound = pre-solution-from-c-solver
      C = C  &  f < Bound
   EndWhile
EndWhile
End /* Procedure */
```

Fig. 3. Cooperating Solvers Strategy

The goal is to find the solution named `Global-Solution` of a constrained optimisation problem with the objective function $Min\ f$, and its constraints represented by C. The cooperating strategy is an iterative process that begins trying to solve the CSP associated to the optimisation problem using a complete `c-solver`. This algorithm has associated an stuck condition criteria, i.e., when it becomes enable to find a complete instantiation in a reasonable either time or number of iterations. The `pre-solution-from-c-solver` corresponds to the variables values instantiated until now. When `c-solver` is stopped because it accomplished the stuck condition another algorithm, `i-solver`, which does an incomplete search, continues taking as input the `pre-solution-from-c-solver`. `i-solver` uses it to find a near-optimal-solution for the optimisation problem until it accomplishes to a stuck condition. A new CSP is defined including the new constraint that indicates that the objective function value must be lower than the value found either by `c-solver` with a complete instantiation or by `i-solver` with the near optimal solution. This framework is a general cooperation between complete and incomplete techniques.

4   Evaluation and Comparison

In this section, we first explain the problems that we will use as benchmarks and then we present results obtained using our cooperative approach.

4.1   Tested Problems

In order to test our schemes of cooperation, we use the classical Capacity Vehicle Routing Problem (CVRP). In the basic Vehicle Routing Problem (VRP), m identical vehicles initially located at a depot are to deliver discrete quantities of goods to n customers, each one having a demand for goods. A vehicle has to make only one tour starting at the depot, visiting a subset of customers, and returning to the depot. In CVRP, each vehicle has a capacity, extending in this way the VRP. A solution to a CVRP is a set of tours for a subset of vehicles such that all customers are served only once and the capacity constraints are respected. Our objective is to minimise the total distance travelled by a number fixed of vehicles to satisfy all customers.

Our problems are based in instances $C101$, $R101$ and $RC101$, proposed by Solomon, [14], belonging to classes $C1$, $RC1$, $R1$, respectively. Each class defines a different topology. Thus, in $C1$ the location of customers are clustered. In $R1$, the location of customers are generated randomly. In $RC1$, instances are generated considering clustered groups of randomly generated locations of customers. These instances are modified including capacity constraints. We named the so obtained problems as instances $c1$, $r1$, and $rc1$. These problems are hard to solve for a complete approach. We remark that the goal of our tests are to evaluate and to compare the search made by a complete algorithm in contrast to its behaviour when another algorithm, which does an incomplete search that is incorporated into the search process.

4.2   Evaluating Forward Checking with Iterative Improvement

For the test we have selected two very known techniques: Forward Checking (FC) from Constraint Programming and Hill Climbing or Iterative Improvement from Local Search. Forward Checking is a technique specially designed to solve CSP, it is based on a backtracking procedure but it includes filtering to eliminate values that the variables cannot take in any solution to the set of constraints. Some heuristics have been proposed in the literature to improve the search of FC. For example, in our tests we include the minimum domain criteria to select variables.

On the other hand, local search works with complete instantiations. We select iterative improvement which is particular to solve CVRP. The characteristics of our iterative improvement algorithm are:

- The Initial Solution is obtained from FC.
- The moves are 2-opt proposed by Kernighan.
- The acceptance criterium is best improvement.
- It works only with feasible neighbourhood.

The first step in our research was to verify the performance of applying a standard FC algorithm to solve problems $c1$, $r1$, and $rc1$ as defined previously. Table 1 presents the obtained results, where, for each instance, we show all partial solutions found during the execution, the time (t), in milliseconds, at which the partial solution has been found, and the value of the objective function (z) evaluated in the corresponding partial solution.

Table 1. Application of Forward Checking

	r1		rc1		c1	
#	t	z	t	z	t	z
1	30	431,39	29803	383,32	37063	248,36
2	180	431,38	31545	367,00	37754	245,53
3	210	431,16	35200	364,61	40629	234,44
4	260	425,41	109537	359,83	40719	233,90
5	270	418,62	111180	357,78	40719	231,78
6	410	414,20				
7	560	404,92				
8	560	398,13				
9	1091	392,03				
10	38014	391,76				
11	38014	385,21				
12	38014	383,53				
13	51694	377,33				
14	51694	375,66				
15	106854	375,66				

Thus, reading the last row of columns t and z for the $r1$ instance, we can see that the best value of $z = 375,66$ is obtained for the objective function after 15 instantiations in 106854 seconds. In the same way, we can see that for instance $rc1$, the best value obtained by the application of FC is $z = 357,78$ after 5 instantiations in 111180 seconds, and for instance $c1$, the value $z = 231,78$ is also obtained after 5 instantiations but in 40719 seconds. For all applications of FC in this work, we consider a limit of 100 minutes to find the optimal solution and carry out optimality proofs. This table only show the results of applying FC for solving each instance, we cannot infer any thing about these results because we are solving three differents problems.

Our idea to make these two solvers cooperate is to help Forward Checking when the problem became too hard for this algorithm, and take advantage of Hill-Climbing that could be able to find a new bound for the search of the optimal solution. In our approach, Forward Checking could begin solving a CSP, after this solution gives a bound for the optimal value of the problem. In case of Forward Checking is stucked trying to find a solution, the collaborative algorithm detects this situation and gives this information to a Hill-Climbing method that is charged to find quickly a new feasible solution. The communication between Forward Checking and Hill-Climbing depends on the direction of communication. Thus, when the algorithm gives the control to Hill-Climbing from Forward Checking, Hill-Climbing receives the variable values previously found by Forward Checking, at it works trying to find a new better solution applying some heuristics and accepting using a strong criteria, that is selecting the best feasible solution on the neighborhood defined by the move.

When the control is from Hill-Climbing to Forward Checking, Hill-Climbing gives information about the local optima that it found. This information modifies the bound of the objective function constraint, and Forward Checking works trying to find a solution for this new problem configuration.

Roughly speaking, we expect that using Hill-Climbing, Forward Checking will reduce its search tree cutting some branches using the new bound for the objective function. On the other hand, Hill-Climbing focuses its search when it uses an instantiation previously found by Forward Checking on an area of the search space where it is more probably to obtain the optimal value.

The first scheme of cooperation that we have tried consists in:

1. We first try to apply FC looking for an initial solution.
2. Once a solution has been obtained, we try to apply HC until it cannot be applied any more, i.e., a local optimum has been reached.
3. Then, we try again both algorithms in the same order until the problem becomes unsatisfiable or a limit time is achieved.

The results of applying this scheme are presented in table 2.

Table 2. Trying Hill-Climbing inmediately after Forward Checking

	r1			rc1			c1		
#	s	t	z	s	t	z	s	t	z
1	FC	30	431,39	FC	29803	383,32	FC	37063	248,36
2	HC	470	392,03	HC	30023	341,42	HC	37344	211,22
3	HC	820	379,62	HC	30214	294,99	HC	37654	197,30
4	HC	1090	358,99				HC	38090	194,07
5	HC	1360	353,66				HC	38330	191,05
6							HC	38580	189,05
7							HC	38810	187,44

In order to verify the effect of applying HC immediately after the application of FC, we try the same cooperation scheme but we give the possibility to FC to be applied several times before trying HC. The idea was to analyse the possibility of improve bounds just by the application of FC. As we know that FC can need too much time to get a new solution, we establish a limit of two seconds, if this limit was reached and FC has not yet return a solution, we try to apply HC. The results of this second scheme of cooperation are presented in table 3.

We can make the following remarks concerning these results:

– Surprisenly, when solving each instance, both cooperation schemes found the same best value.

Table 3. Trying Hill-Climbing two seconds after Forward Checking

#	r1			rc1			c1		
	s	t	z	s	t	z	s	t	z
1	FC	30	431,39	FC	29803	383,32	FC	37063	248,36
2	FC	180	431,38	FC	31545	367,00	FC	37754	245,53
3	FC	210	431,16	FC	33200	364,61	FC	39629	234,44
4	FC	260	425,41	HC	35491	294,99	FC	40719	233,90
5	FC	270	418,62				FC	40729	231,78
6	FC	410	414,20				HC	43165	197,89
7	FC	560	404,92				HC	43465	194,86
8	FC	560	398,13				HC	43795	191,45
9	FC	1091	392,03				HC	44025	189,45
10	HC	3803	379,62				HC	44265	187,85
11	HC	4083	358,99				HC	44505	187,44
12	HC	4374	353,66						

- The first scheme of cooperation (table 2) always takes less time than the second one (table 3). In fact, the total time is mainly due to the time expended by FC.
- In general, applying both cooperations schemes, the results are better, in terms of z, than applying FC isolated.

5   Conclusions

The main contribution of this work is that we have presented a framework for design cooperative hybrid strategies integrating complete methods with incomplete for solving combinatorial optimisation problems. The results tested shown that Hill Climbing can help Forward Checking by adding bounds during the search procedure. This is based on the well-known idea that adding constraints, in general, can improve the performance of Constraint Programming. We are currently working on using other complete and incomplete methods. In case of good news, we plan to try solving other combinatorial optimisation problems to validate this cooperation scheme.

It is important to note that the communication between the methods use for testing in this paper has been carried out by communicating information about bounds. In case of we were interested in communicating more information we should to address the problem of representation, because complete and incomplete generally do not use the same codification. In order to prove optimality the use of an incomplete technique is not useful, so, as further work, we are interested in using other techniques to improve optimality proofs. We think that the research already done on overconstrained CSPs could be useful because when an optimal solution has been found the only task is to prove that the remaining problem has become unsatisfiable, i.e., an overconstrained CSP.

Nowadays, considering that the research carried out by each community separately has produced good results, we strongly believe that in the future the work will be in the integration of both approaches.

References

1. Alexander Bockmayr and Thomas Kasper. Branch-and-Infer: A unifying framework for integer and finite domain constraint programming. *INFORMS J. Computing*, 10(3):287–300, 1998. Also available as Technical Report MPI-I-97-2-008 of the Max Planck Institut für Informatik, Saarbrücken, Germany.
2. C. Castro and E. Monfroy. A Control Language for Designing Constraint Solvers. In *Proceedings of Andrei Ershov Third International Conference Perspective of System Informatics, PSI'99*, volume 1755 of *Lecture Notes in Computer Science*, pages 402–415, Novosibirsk, Akademgorodok, Russia, 2000. Springer-Verlag.
3. Carlos Castro and Eric Monfroy. Basic Operators for Solving Constraints via Collaboration of Solvers. In *Proceedings of The Fifth International Conference on Artificial Intelligence and Symbolic Computation, Theory, Implementations and Applications, AISC 2000*, volume 1930 of *Lecture Notes in Artificial Intelligence*, pages 142–156, Madrid, Spain, July 2000. Springer-Verlag.
4. Carlos Castro and Eric Monfroy. Towards a framework for designing constraint solvers and solver collaborations. *Joint Bulletin of the Novosibirsk Computing Center (NCC) and the A. P. Ershov Institute of Informatics Systems (IIS). Series: Computer Science. Russian Academy of Sciences, Siberian Branch.*, 16:1–28, December 2001.
5. Filippo Focacci, François Laburthe, and Andrea Lodi. *Constraint and Integer Programming: Toward a Unified Methodology*, chapter 9, Local Search and Constraint Programming. Kluwer, November 2003.
6. L. Granvilliers, E. Monfroy, and F. Benhamou. Symbolic-Interval Cooperation in Constraint Programming. In *Proceedings of the 26th International Symposium on Symbolic and Algebraic Computation (ISSAC'2001)*, pages 150–166, University of Western Ontario, London, Ontario, Canada, 2001. ACM Press.
7. Robert M. Haralick and Gordon L. Elliot. Increasing Tree Search Efficiency for Constraint Satisfaction Problems. *Artificial Intelligence*, 14:263–313, 1980.
8. Jussien and Lhomme. Local search with constraint propagation and conflict-based heuristics. *Artificial Intelligence*, 139:21–45, 2002.
9. Vipin Kumar. Algorithms for Constraint-Satisfaction Problems: A Survey. *Artificial Intelligence Magazine*, 13(1):32–44, Spring 1992.
10. Alan K. Mackworth. Consistency in Networks of Relations. *Artificial Intelligence*, 8:99–118, 1977.
11. Philippe Marti and Michel Rueher. A Distributed Cooperating Constraints Solving System. *International Journal of Artificial Intelligence Tools*, 4(1-2):93–113, 1995.
12. E. Monfroy, M. Rusinowitch, and R. Schott. Implementing Non-Linear Constraints with Cooperative Solvers. In K. M. George, J. H. Carroll, D. Oppenheim, and J. Hightower, editors, *Proceedings of ACM Symposium on Applied Computing (SAC'96), Philadelphia, PA, USA*, pages 63–72. ACM Press, February 1996.
13. Prestwich. Combining the scalability of local search with the pruning techniques of systematic search. *Annals of Operations Research*, 115:51–72, 2002.
14. M. Solomon. Algorithms for the vehicle routing and scheduling problem with time window constraints. *Operations Research*, pages 254–365, 1987.
15. Edward Tsang. *Foundations of Constraint Satisfaction*. Academic Press, 1993.
16. Martin Zahn and Walter Hower. Backtracking along with constraint processing and their time complexities. *Journal of Experimental and Theoretical Artificial Intelligence*, 8:63–74, 1996.

Machine Learned Heuristics
to Improve Constraint Satisfaction[*]

Marco Correia and Pedro Barahona

Centro de Inteligência Artificial, Departamento de Informática
Universidade Nova de Lisboa, 2829-516 Caparica, Portugal
{mvc,pb}@di.fct.unl.pt

Abstract. Although propagation techniques are very important to solve constraint solving problems, heuristics are still necessary to handle non trivial problems efficiently. General principles may be defined for such heuristics (e.g. first-fail and best-promise), but problems arise in their implementation except for some limited sources of information (e.g. cardinality of variables domain). Other possibly relevant features are ignored due to the difficulty in understanding their interaction and a convenient way of integrating them. In this paper we illustrate such difficulties in a specific problem, determination of protein structure from Nuclear Magnetic Resonance (NMR) data. We show that machine learning techniques can be used to define better heuristics than the use of heuristics based on single features, or even than their combination in simple form (e.g majority vote). The technique is quite general and, with the necessary adaptations, may be applied to many other constraint satisfaction problems.

Keywords: constraint programming, machine learning, bioinformatics

1 Introduction

In constraint programming, the main role is usually given to constraint propagation techniques (e.g. [1, 2]) that by effectively narrowing the domain of the variables significantly decrease the search.

However non trivial problems still need the adoption of heuristics to speed up search, and find solutions with an acceptable use of resources (time and/or space). Most heuristics follow certain general principles, namely the first-fail principle for variable selection (enumerate difficult variables first) and the best promise heuristic for value selection (choose the value that more likely belongs to a solution) [3].

The implementation of these principles usually depends on the specificities of the problems or even problem instances, and is more often an art than a science. A more global view of the problem can be used, by measuring its potential by means of global indicators (e.g. the kappa indicator [4]), but such techniques

---

[*] This work was supported by Fundação para a Ciência e Tecnologia, under project PROTEINA, POSI/33794/SRI/2000

A.L.C. Bazzan and S. Labidi (Eds.): SBIA 2004, LNAI 3171, pp. 103–113, 2004.

do not take into account all the possible relevant features. Many other specific features could possibly be taken into account, but they interact in such unpredictable ways that it is often difficult to specify an adequate form of combining them.

This paper illustrates one such problem, determination of protein structure given a set of distance constraints between atom pairs extracted from Nuclear Magnetic Resonance (NMR) data. Previous work on the problem led us to adopt first-fail, best promise heuristics, selecting from the variables with smaller domains those halfs that interact least with other variables. However, many other interesting features can be specified (various forms of volumes, distances, constraint satisfaction promise, etc.) but their use was not tried before.

In this paper we report on the first experiments that exploit the rich information that was being ignored. We show that none of the many heuristics that can be considered always outperforms the others. Hence, a combination of the various features would be desirable, and we report on various possibilities of such integration. Eventually, we show that a neural network based machine learning approach is the one that produces the best results.

The paper is organised as follows. In section 2 we briefly describe PSICO, developed to predict protein structure from NMR data. The next section discusses profiling techniques to measure the performance of PSICO. Section 4 presents a number of features that can be exploited in search heuristics, and shows the potential of machine learning techniques to integrate them. Section 5 briefly shows a preliminary evaluation of the improvements obtained with such heuristics. Last section presents the main conclusions and directions for further research.

2   The PSICO Algorithm

PSICO (Processing Structural Information with Constraint programming and Optimisation) [5, 6] is a constraint based algorithm to predict the tri-dimensional structure of proteins from the set of atom distances found by NMR, a technique that can only estimate lower and higher bounds for the distance between atoms not too far apart. The goal of the algorithm is to take the list of bounded distances as input and produce valid 3D positions for all atoms in the protein.

2.1   Definition as a CSP

This problem can be modeled as a constraint satisfaction problem assuming the positions of the atoms as the (tri-dimensional) variables and the allowed distances among them as the constraints. The domain of each variable is represented by one *good* cuboid (allowed region) resulting from the intersection of several cubic *in* constraints (see below), containing a number (possibly zero) of *no-good* cuboids (forbidden regions) representing the union of one or more cubic *out* constraints. Spherical distance constraints are implemented based on the following relaxation:

$$in(d) \; : \; |x_1 - x_2| \leq d \wedge |y_1 - y_2| \leq d \wedge |z_1 - z_2| \leq d$$

$$out(d) \; : \; |x_1 - x_2| \geq \frac{d}{\sqrt{3}} \vee |y_1 - y_2| \geq \frac{d}{\sqrt{3}} \vee |z_1 - z_2| \geq \frac{d}{\sqrt{3}}$$

2.2   Algorithm

We will focus on the first phase of the PSICO algorithm, which is a depth first search with full look ahead using an AC-3 variant for consistency enforcement. Variables are pruned in round robin by eliminating one half of the cuboid at each enumeration. Two heuristics are used for variable and value selection. After variable enumeration, arc-consistency is enforced by constraint propagation.

Whenever a domain becomes empty the algorithm backtracks, but backtracking is seldom used. The number of enumerations between an incorrect enumeration and the enumeration where the inconsistency is found is prohibitively large and recovering from bad decisions has a profound impact on execution time. While better alternatives to standard backtracking are being pursued, the first phase of the PSICO algorithm is used only for providing good approximations of the solution, relying on the promise of both variable and value enumeration heuristics to do so. When domains are small enough (usually less than 1Å^3) search terminates with success and PSICO algorithm moves on to second phase (see [5]).

3   Profiling

3.1   Sample Set

The set of proteins used for profiling the impact of heuristics on search is composed of seven samples (proteins) ordered from the smallest (sample 1) to the largest (sample 7) chosen sparsely over the range of NMR solved structures in the BMRB database [7]. The corresponding structural data was retrieved from the PDB database [8]. The number of constraints per variable and the constraint tightness does not vary significantly with the size of the problems [9].

3.2   Profiling Techniques

Common performance measures like the number of nodes visited, average path length, and many others, are not adequate for this problem, given the limited use of backtracking. Instead, in this paper, the algorithm performance is estimated by the RMS (Root Mean Square) distance between the solution found by the algorithm (molecule) and a known solution for the problem (the oracle), once properly aligned [5].

3.3   Probabilistic Analysis of Value Ordering

Tests were made to access the required performance of a value enumeration heuristic. Final RMS distance was averaged over several runs of all test samples by using a probabilistic function for selecting the correct half of the domain at each enumeration. Fig. 1 shows that an heuristic must make correct predictions 80% of the times for achieving a good solution for the first phase of the algorithm (4Å or less).

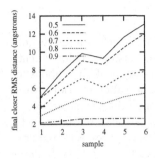

Fig. 1. Final RMS distance at the end of search using a value enumeration with a given probability of making the correct choice. Results are displayed for all samples.

4 Domain Region Features

A number of features that characterize different regions of the domain of the variable to enumerate given the current state of the problem may help in suggesting which region is most likely to contain the solution. They were grouped according to their source of information: (a) Volumes, (b) Distances, (c) No-good information and (d) Constraint minimization vectors.

Fig. 2. Illustrates two sources of features. The spotted cuboid is the domain d_1 of the variable to enumerate. Geometrical properties of other domains (exterior cuboids) $d_2 \ldots d_N$ can help choosing which half R of d_1 will be selected. The set of no-goods $ng_1 \ldots ng_{NG}$ (interior cuboids) is another source of features being used.

In the following functions, N is the number of atoms, d_1 is the domain of the variable to enumerate, $d_2 \ldots d_N$ are the domains of the other variables in the problem, and R is a region inside d_1, typically one half of the cubic domain (see fig. 2). For the first group, the following measures were considered:

$$\sum_{i=2}^{N} volume\left(d_i \cap R\right) \quad \text{(loc-a1)}$$

$$\sum_{i=2}^{N} \frac{volume^2\left(d_i \cap R\right)}{volume\left(d_i\right)} \quad \text{(loc-a3)}$$

$$\sum_{i=2}^{N} \frac{volume\left(d_i \cap R\right)}{volume\left(d_i\right)} \quad \text{(loc-a2)}$$

$$\sum_{i=2}^{N} \left(d_i \cap R > 0\right) \quad \text{(loc-a4)}$$

The first function is the sum of the volumes of all domains intersected with the considered region. Function loc-a2 accumulates the fraction of each domain inside region R, to account for the small cuboid intersections largely ignored by the previous function. The third function assigns more weight to the intersection value. The last function simply counts the number of domains that intersect the considered region.

The second group of features considers distances between the center of the cubic domains:

$$\sum_{i=2}^{N} distance\left[center\left(R\right), center\left(A\right)\right] \quad \text{(loc-b1,loc-b2,loc-b3)}$$

Function loc-b1 $(A = d_i)$ accumulates the distances between the center of region R and the center of all the other domains. Function loc-b2 $(A = d_i \cap R)$ sums the distances between the center of the considered region and the center of the intersections between the region and the other domains. Function loc-b3 $(A = d_i \cap d_1)$ is similar but considers the center of the intersection with the entire domain d_1 instead.

The third group of features is based on the set of NG no-goods of the domain of the variable to enumerate, each represented by ng_i (see fig. 2):

$$\sum_{i=1}^{NG} volume\,(ng_i \cap R) \qquad\qquad \text{(loc-c1)}$$

$$\sum_{i=1}^{NG} distance\,[center\,(ng_i)\,, center\,(R)] \qquad\qquad \text{(loc-c2)}$$

They represent respectively the sum of the no-good volume inside region R and the sum of distances between the center of each no-good and the region R.

The last set considers constraint information features, where $c_{1,i}$ represents a constraint from a set of C_1 constraints involving variable v_1 to enumerate:

$$\sum_{i=1}^{C_1} violated\,(c_{1,i}) \qquad \text{(loc-d1)}$$

$$\sum_{c_{in}(1,i)} \overrightarrow{n_{c_{in}(1,i)}} \qquad \text{(loc-d2-1)}$$

$$\frac{1}{C_1}\sum_{c(1,i)} \overrightarrow{n_{c(1,i)}} \qquad \text{(loc-d2-2)}$$

$$\sum_{c_{out}(1,i)} \overrightarrow{n_{c_{out}(1,i)}} \qquad \text{(loc-d2-3)}$$

$$\frac{1}{C_1}\sum_{c(1,i)} \overrightarrow{m_{c(1,i)}} \qquad \text{(loc-d3)}$$

The first function counts the number of constraints violated considering the center of the region R and the center of the other domains involved. Feature loc-d2 has three variations. For each violated constraint $c(1, i)$ between variables v_1 and v_i, $\overrightarrow{n_{c(1,i)}}$ is a vector applied from $center\,(d_1)$ to $center\,(d_i)$, with magnitude

$$\left\|\overrightarrow{n_{c(1,i)}}\right\| = |distance\,[center\,(d_1)\,, center\,(d_i)] - c(1, i)|$$

and direction defined by $sign\,(distance\,[center\,(d_1)\,, center\,(d_i)] - c(1, i))$.

Features loc-d2-1 and loc-d2-3 are respectively the sums of these vectors for *in* and *out* constraints over v_1. Feature loc-d2-2 averages the vectors for all constraints affecting v_1. Feature loc-d3 is a special case of loc-d2-2, as it does not consider vectors for constraints which are not being violated (by the domain centers).

4.1   Isolated Features as Value Enumeration Heuristics

An interval enumeration heuristic can be generally seen as a function g which selects the domain region R most likely to contain the solution(s) from several candidate domain regions $R_1 \ldots R_n$ [1]. The most straightforward method to incorporate each feature f presented above in a value enumeration heuristic is by using a function $g_{isol(f)}$ that selects R based on a simple relation ($>$ or $<$) among the output of the feature for each $R_1 \ldots R_n$.

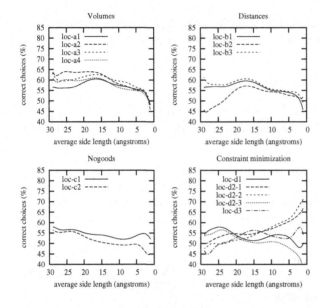

Fig. 3. Value ordering heuristic performance averaged over all samples. Each point represents the percent of correct choices for an average domain side length and was averaged over 100 independent runs.

Figure 3 shows the percentage of correct choices of each isolated feature averaged over all test samples. As can be seen, some features are best suited for early stages of search (e.g. features based on volumes) and others for final stages (features based on constraint minimization vectors). This did not come as a complete surprise since at the beginning of search most domains are very large and overlapping making volume based features meaningful and constraint vectors useless. At the end of search, domains are sparsely distributed, uniformly sized and smaller, thus turning constraint minimization vectors more informative.

All these value heuristics based on isolated features clearly underperform the lower bound estimated on section 3.3 to obtain good approximate solutions.

4.2 Feature Combination

Since none of the heuristics dominates the others, we considered their combination, by the following methods:

Ad-Hoc Selection of Best Feature. Analysis of the charts of figure 3 suggest that feature loc-a2 is used for average side length above 10Å and loc-d2-2 for those bellow. This heuristic is referred to as g_{sel}.

---

[1] It this approach only two regions (halves) of the domain are being considered at each enumeration. For an explanation of why this is a better option refer to [9].

Majority Voting. In this case an odd number of heuristics based on isolated features vote on the region most likely to contain the solutions, and the region with more votes is selected. The heuristic, $g_{maj(f)}$ is based on three presented heuristics, $g_{isol(loc-a2)}, g_{isol(loc-b3)}$ and $g_{isol(loc-d2-2)}$, taken from three different classes (volumes, distances, and constraints).

Neural Network. Features were also combined using a two-layer, feed-forward neural network [10], representing a function h that combines all features evaluated in both domain halves R_1, R_2 plus the average domain side length s

$$h(R_1, R_2, s) : [f_1(R_1) - f_1(R_2), \ldots, f_{14}(R_1) - f_{14}(R_2), s] \to]0, 1[$$

Training (with usual backpropagation) and testing data was collected by doing several runs of the test samples using a random variable enumeration heuristic and at each enumeration recording the feature vector plus a boolean indicating the correct half. The optimal value enumeration heuristic was used. Data was then arranged in seven partitions, where each partition p included a training set made of data collected from runs of all samples except sample p, and a test set with only data collected from runs of sample p for ensuring the generalization ability of the learned function. For more details concerning training/network see [9].

The output of the learned function h is filtered and used in an heuristic g_{nn},

$$g_{nn1(r)}(R_1, R_2, s) = \begin{cases} R_1 \Leftarrow h(R_1, R_2, s) \geq 1 - r \\ R_2 \quad \Leftarrow h(R_1, R_2, s) < r \end{cases}$$

where $r \in [0, 0.5]$ is a constant denoting the risk associated with the prediction. Note that this function may be undefined for a given feature vector if $r < 0.5$.

Table 1. Train and test performance of $g_{nn1(0.5)}, g_{nn1(0.3)}$ and $g_{nn1(0.2)}$ for each partition. Column "Qual." represents the number of correct predictions over all enumerations for which g_{nn1} is defined. Column "Def." displays the percentage of test samples for which g_{nn1} is defined, over all enumerations. The "MSE" column stands for Mean Square Error (see [10]).

| | r=0.5 | | | | r = 0.3 | | r = 0.2 | |
| | Train | | Test | | Test | | | |
Partition	MSE	Qual. (%)	MSE	Qual. (%)	Qual. (%)	Def. (%)	Qual. (%)	Def. (%)
1	0.67	68	0.67	70	83	16	87	5
2	0.66	67	0.68	61	76	28	80	9
3	0.67	66	0.70	60	78	27	87	11
4	0.67	67	0.68	67	80	41	87	20
5	0.66	68	0.68	60	69	27	65	12
6	0.67	66	0.69	63	76	26	77	10
7	0.66	64	0.65	68	83	37	87	20

Training and test performance of the neural network used in $g_{nn1(0.5)}$ and test results of the learned function $g_{nn1(0.3)}$ and $g_{nn1(0.2)}$ are displayed on table 1. Figure 4 shows a comparison of the performance of the g_{sel}, g_{maj}, $g_{nn1(0.5)}$, $g_{nn1(0.3)}$ and $g_{nn1(0.2)}$ heuristics.

These results show that, as expected, predictions with less risk associated occur fewer times than those made with higher risk. They also show that heuristics based on neural networks with smaller associated risk perform better than the others, and $g_{nn1(0.2)}$ can actually guess the correct half of the domain 80% of the times, which has been shown to be a lower bound for an acceptable final solution quality (see section 3.3).

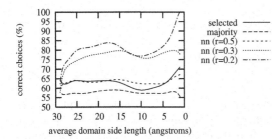

Fig. 4. Runtime performance comparison of the methods presented for feature combination, averaged over all partitions.

Neural Network Trained with Noisy Data. Since in this problem backtracking is not an option, the value enumeration heuristic must be robust and account for early mistakes so that a good approximation to the solution may still be found. It is therefore important that inconsistent states be included in the training data of the neural networks.

The $g_{nn1(r)}$ neural network was then trained with data collected from several runs driven by a probabilistic value ordering heuristic with 90% probability of making the correct choice. For enumerations where the solution was already outside the domain because of earlier mistakes, the correct choice was considered the half whose center was closer to the solution.

Figure 5 shows the performance of both networks when classifying noisy data. As expected, the neural network trained with noisy data outperforms the neural network trained with *clean* data, if not by much. The chart on the right shows that safe decisions with noisy data are much more rare than with *clean* data.

5   Application

In this section the enumeration heuristics presented above were integrated with search and the final results produced were compared. The results for the heuristics based on neural networks were obtained by using networks trained with noisy data.

The variable enumeration heuristic used with g_{sel} and g_{maj} always selects the variable with smaller domain, which has been shown to maximize overall

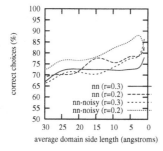 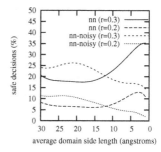

Fig. 5. The graphic on the left shows the percentage of correct choices over the total number of choices considered "safe" by the $g_{nn1(0.2)}$ and $g_{nn1(0.3)}$ heuristics trained with normal and noisy data. The graphic on the right shows the percentage of decisions considered "safe" over all decisions made by the heuristics. Results were averaged over all partitions.

search promise (see [9]). Since the $g_{nn1(r)}$ heuristic may be undefined for a given enumeration with a given r, a modified version was used instead,

$$g_{nn2}(R_1, R_2, s) = \begin{cases} R_1, 1 - r & \Leftarrow h(R_1, R_2, s) \geq 0.5 \\ R_2, r & \Leftarrow h(R_1, R_2, s) < 0.5 \end{cases}$$

which is always defined. This version gives a hint on the correct region plus the risk associated with the prediction, a valuable information that was used to define the variable enumeration order. This was done by evaluating g_{nn2} for all domains at each enumeration and choosing the variable for which the prediction with smallest risk can be made.

As errors accumulate, the information provided by the features degrades, since they are measured from an already inconsistent state of the problem. To estimate the influence on the overall performance of the above described heuristics, tests were made where the first 10 and 20 value selection errors were corrected (fig. 6), with a view on exploiting a limited form of backtracking (e.g. limited discrepancy search [11]) since full exploitation of backtracking is unfeasible due to the sheer size of the search space.

The solutions obtained with the neural network are consistently much better than those obtained with the ad-hoc heuristics selection or majority vote, which justifies the use of this technique. Moreover, the quality of the solutions provided is quite promising. The RMSD above 5Å for the smallest proteins was reduced to less than 4Å if the first 10 wrong value choices are corrected. For the larger proteins tha effect is more visible with correction of 20 wrong choices, where the RMSD decreases from around 10Å to less than 6Å. Notwithstanding further improvements, these results already provide quite acceptable starting points for the second phase of PSICO.

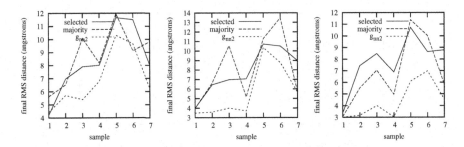

Fig. 6. Final RMS distance between the solution found and a known solution using the value heuristics described. The three charts show the results when correcting the first 0 *(left)*, 10 *(center)* and 20 *(right)* mistakes of the heuristics.

6   Conclusion

In this paper we show that machine learning techniques can be used to integrate various features, and that they outperform heuristics based on single features or on simple feature combination. Notwithstanding the specificity of the problem under consideration, the approach should be easily adapted to handle other difficult problems (notice that none of the domain features considered conveys any specific biochemical information).

In the determination of protein structure from NMR data, these heuristics made the constraint satisfaction phase of our algorithm to reach results with much lower RMSD deviations than previously achieveable.

We are now considering the tuning of the heuristics selection, not only by including biochemical information (e.g. amino-acid hidrophobicity), but also by incorporating other advanced propagation techniques for rigid (sub-)structures, as well as developing a controlled form of backtracking (e.g. limited discrepancy search), that may efficiently exploit the correction of the first wrong value choice decisions.

References

1. Beldiceanu, N., Contejean, E.: Introducing global constraints in CHIP. Mathl. Comput. Modelling **20** (1994) 97–123
2. Krippahl, L., Barahona, P.: Propagating N-ary rigid-body constraints. In: ICCP: International Conference on Constraint Programming (CP), LNCS. (2003)
3. Beck, J., Prosser, P., Wallace, R.: Toward understanding variable ordering heuristics for constraint satisfaction problems. In: Procs. of the Fourteenth Irish Artificial Intelligence and Cognitive Science Conference (AICS03). (2003)
4. Gent, I.P., MacIntyre, E., Prosser, P., Walsh, T.: The constrainedness of search. In: AAAI/IAAI, Vol. 1. (1996) 246–252
5. Krippahl, L., Barahona, P.: PSICO: Solving protein structures with constraint programming and optimization. Constraints **7** (2002) 317–331
6. Krippahl, L.: Integrating Protein Structural Information. PhD thesis, FCT/UNL (2003)

7. Seavey, B., Farr, E., Westler, W., Markley, J.: A relational database for sequence-specific protein nmr data. J. Biomolecular NMR **1** (1991) 217–236
8. Noguchi, T., Onizuka, K., Akiyama, Y., Saito, M.: PDB-REPRDB: A database of representative protein chains in PDB (Protein Data Bank). In: Procs. of the 5th International Conference on Intelligent Systems for Molecular Biology, Menlo Park, AAAI Press (1997) 214–217
9. Correia, M.: Heuristic search for protein structure determination. Master's thesis, FCT/UNL (Submitted March/2004)
10. Haykin, S.: Neural Networks: A comprehensive Foundation. Macmillan College Publishing Company, Inc. (1994)
11. Harvey, W., Ginsberg, M.: Limited discrepancy search. In Mellish, C., ed.: IJCAI'95: Procs. Int. Joint Conference on Artificial Intelligence, Montreal (1995)

Towards a Natural Way of Reasoning

José Carlos Loureiro Ralha and Célia Ghedini Ralha

Departamento de Ciência da Computação
Instituto de Ciências Exatas
Universidade de Brasília
Campus Universitário Darcy Ribeiro
Asa Norte Brasília DF 70.910–900
{ralha,ghedini}@cic.unb.br

Abstract. It is well known that traditional quantifiers $\forall$ and $\exists$ are not suitable for expressing common sense rules such as 'birds fly.' This sentence expresses the defeasible idea that 'most birds fly,' and not 'all birds fly.' Another defeasible rule is exemplified by 'many Americans like American football.' Noun phrases such as 'most birds, many birds,' or even 'some birds' are recognized by semanticists as natural language generalized quantifiers. From a non-monotonic reasoning perspective, one can divide the class of linguistic generalized quantifiers into two categories. The first partition includes categorical quantifiers such as 'all birds.' The other one includes the defeasible quantifiers such as 'most birds' and 'many birds.' It is clear that the semantics of defeasible quantifiers leaves room for exceptions. The exceptional elements licensed by defeasible generalized quantifiers are usually the 'non flying birds' that non-monotonic logics deal with.

Keywords: generalized quantifiers, non-monotonic reasoning, defeasible reasoning, argumentative systems.

1   Generalized Quantifiers and Non-monotonic Reasoning

It is common knowledge that *mammals don't lay eggs*. However, there are some recalcitrant mammals that do lay eggs. Actually, there are only three species of monotreme[1] in the world – the platypus and two species of echidna known as spiny anteaters. This knowledge, which is properly and easily expressed through natural language sentences as in (1), can not be formalized so easily. Only through the use of sophisticated logic systems this common sense knowledge can be grasped by formal systems based on universal and existential quantifiers ([1], [12], [18], [19]).

(1) a – Most mammals don't lay eggs.
    b – Few mammals lay eggs.

In English and other natural languages, quantifying determiners like *all, no, every, some, most, many, few, all but two*, are always accompanied by nominal expressions that seem to restrict the universe of discourse to individuals to which the nominal applies. Although quantification in ordinary logic bears a connection with quantification in English, such a connection is not straightforward. Nominals like *man* in (2) are usually represented by a predicate in ordinary logic.

---

[1] Monotreme is the order of mammals that lay eggs.

A.L.C. Bazzan and S. Labidi (Eds.): SBIA 2004, LNAI 3171, pp. 114–123, 2004.
© Springer-Verlag Berlin Heidelberg 2004

Ideas employed in (4) can be applied to other quantification structures as long as we take (i) full noun phrases, NPs, (determiner + nominal), as logical quantifiers and (ii) sets of sets as the semantic objects interpreting NPs.

The previous discussion made a point toward moving from determiners as quantifiers, as it occurs in ordinary logic, to full NPs as quantifiers; full NPs as quantifiers is also known as *generalized quantifiers*, GQ.

One remarkable feature of GQ is the notational uniformity of its formulas. As (3.a), (3.b), (4.c), and (4.f) exemplified, GQ formulas can be expressed by $[det\, x : P(x)]Q(x)$ schema. This uniformity makes the development of formal systems and automatic theorem provers easier. It is worth to note that the parallel between natural language and formal language induced by the compositional principle – the uniformity referred to before – makes even easier the translation between them.

2 GQ Notation

Although GQ notation, conforming to the schema $[det\, x : P(x)]Q(x)$, have some advantages when compared to traditional notations, it can be pushed even further when considering theorem proving implementation issues.

From now on, the general schema $P\langle det, x\rangle \,\|\, Q\langle det, x\rangle$ replaces the previous GQ notation. There are many reasons to stick to the new notation introduced by the authors in this paper. First, it makes clear the nature of the quantified variable as pointed out by $\langle det, x\rangle$. $\langle det, x\rangle$ says on a naïve basis that variable x belongs to the class of *det*. *This nature could be used to determine what kind of inference ought to be (or has been) used.* Determiners such as *all*, and *any* allow categorical deductions while *most, almost, fewer... than*, etc. allow only defeasible deductions. So, if there exists a relationship amongst GQs, they implicitly carry into them such relationship. Therefore, we don't have to assign degrees to the common sense rules as many non-monotonic systems usually do[4]. Second, GQ notation sticks to the compositional criteria. The same is not true for Fregean systems as pointed out on sect. 1. At last, but not least, it seems not difficult to develop deduction systems using such notation. And this is a desirable feature since it allows the development of efficient natural deduction automatic theorem provers as well as resolution based ones ([14], [5], [12]).

3 A Few Comments on Inference Rules

It seems clear that non-monotonic systems ought to relay on non-monotonic inference rules in order to keep inconsistency away.

For traditional[5] systems, the most common inference rules are the *defeasible modus ponens*, the *penguin principle*, and the *Nixon diamond*. Basically, the *defeasible modus ponens* says that one is granted to (defeasibly) infer Ψ from Φ and $\Phi \rightarrow \Psi$ *but only* in the absence of contrary evidence. *Penguin Principle* expresses a specificity relationship

---

[4] This is akin in spirit to [5] where they say "....We believe that common sense reasoning should be defeasible in a way that is not explicitly programmed."

[5] Understand traditional the logic systems, monotonic or not, build upon $\forall$ and $\exists$.

between conditions; it says that one should pick up more specific rules. *Nixon Diamond* rule states that opposite conclusions should not be allowed on a system if they were drawn on inference chains of same specificity. These three principles try to overcome the problem brought to traditional logics by the choice of $\forall$, and $\exists$ as the only quantifiers.

Suppose we adopt NPs as quantifying expressions. For each NP, if one looks at the core determiner, one can recognize specific (common sense) inference patterns which can be divided into two categories. Some inference patterns are *categorical* as exemplified by *all*. But most patterns are *defeasible* as exemplified by *most*[6].

Defeasible inference patterns induced by "defeasible NPs" get their strength from human communication behavior. People involved in a communicative process work in a collaborative way. If someone says "most birds fly", and "Tweety is a bird", the conversation partners usually take as granted that "Tweety flies". The inferred knowledge comes from the use of (defeasible) modus ponens. Only when someone has a better knowledge about Tweety's flying abilities, one is supposed to introduce that knowledge to the partners. The better (or more specific) knowledge acquainted by one defeats the previous knowledge. The remarkable point about getting better knowledge is the way it is done; it is done in a *dialectical argumentative* way resembling to game theoretical systems ([10], [16], [4], [7]).

4   Argumentative Approach

The naïve idea behind argumentation could be summarized through the motto "contrary evidence should be provided by the opponent". Therefore, argumentative theories could be seen as a two challengers game where both players try to rebutt the opponent conclusions.

The game is played in turns by challengers Ch_1 and Ch_2 in the following fashion: if player Ch_1 comes to a defeasible conclusion, the opponent Ch_2 takes a turn trying to defeat Ch_1's result. The easiest way to do so is assuming the opponent's opposite argument hopping to arrive at opposite conclusion. If Ch_2 succeeds and the *derivation path* does not include any defeasible quantifier, then the defeasible conclusion of player Ch_1 was successfully defeated by the opponent Ch_2. If Ch_2 succeeds but the derivation path includes a defeasible argument, then both players loose the game.

Literature presents different argumentative strategies which can be seen as polite or greedy ones. Examples in the present paper conform to a polite approach since the adversary keeps himself quiet to the end of his opponent deduction. A greedy strategy is based on the monitoring the adversary deduction stopping him when he uses a defeasible argument or rule.

Figure 1 and Fig. 2 show the argumentation process at work. For these figures, Challenger Ch_2 wins in the first example while both players loose in the second one. To understand these figures, one has to know: (i) that for these and all subsequent figures in the paper, the first column enumerates each formula in a deduction chain; the second column is the GQ-formula proper and the third column is a retro-referential system, i.e., the explanation for deriving such a formula; (ii) how the inference rules work.

---

[6] These patterns corresponds to [5]'s *strict* and *defeasible* rules, respectively.

Next section presents GQ inference rules in a setup suitable for the development of dialectical argumentative systems.

5   GQ Inference Rules

Robinson's Resolution rule [17] can be adapted, in a similar way found in [3], to become the GQ-resolution rule. GQ-resolution is shown in (5).

$$
(5) \quad \frac{\begin{array}{c} R_1\langle det_1, x_1\rangle \ ||\ Q_1\langle det_1, x_1\rangle \vee Q_2\langle det_1, x_1\rangle \\ R_2\langle det_2, x_2\rangle \ ||\ \neg Q_1\langle det_2, x_2\rangle \end{array}}{R_1\langle det, x_1\rangle \wedge R_2\langle det, x_2\rangle \wedge x_1 = x_2 \ ||\ Q_2\langle det, x_2\rangle}
$$

where $det = det_1$ if either both det_1 and det_2 belongs to the same category[7] or det_1 is defeasible and det_2 is categorical.

GQ-resolution means that one can mix categorical and defeasible knowledge. It also means that defeasible knowledge "weakens" the GQ-resolvent. This is accomplished by making the weakest determiner between det_1 and det_2 the determiner on the GQ-resolvent. Notice also that the weakness process gets propagated through the inference chain making possible the conclusion's rebuttal as presented on section 4. Examples (6), and (7) shed light into the subject.

$$
(6) \quad \frac{\begin{array}{c} bird\langle most, x\rangle \ ||\ fly\langle most, x\rangle \\ ||\ \neg fly\langle cte, Tux\rangle \end{array}}{bird\langle most, Tux\rangle \ ||\ \square}
$$

First line of (6) says that *most birds fly*; this clause is defeasible as emphasized by $\langle most, x\rangle$. Second line says that *Tux doesn't fly*. This categorical clause is characterized by the proper name 'Tux' taken as a categorical determiner denoted as $\langle cte, Tux\rangle$. Both clauses GQ-resolve delivering the GQ-resolvent $bird\langle most, Tux\rangle \ ||\ \square$. Notice however that

- $\langle most, x\rangle$ weakens $\langle cte, Tux\rangle$.
- The GQ-resolvent is a defeasible clause. Defeasibility is stressed by using *most* in $bird\langle most, Tux\rangle$. Notice also that $bird\langle most, Tux\rangle \ ||\ \square$ is GQ-satisfiable iff there is evidence supporting *Tux is a bird*.

$$
(7) \quad \frac{\begin{array}{c} penguin\langle all, x\rangle \ ||\ \neg fly\langle all, x\rangle \\ ||\ fly\langle cte, Tux\rangle \end{array}}{penguin\langle cte, Tux\rangle \ ||\ \square}
$$

---

[7] Recall that *all*, *some* and *cte* are taken as categorical while *most* is taken as defeasible.

(7) shows the case for categorical determiners. Now, the GQ-resolvent is a categorical clause $penguin\langle cte, Tux\rangle \parallel \Box$ is GQ-satisfiable iff there is evidence supporting *Tux is a penguin*.

Traditional resolution systems define the *empty clause* $\Box$. GQ-clauses such as $R_1\langle det_1, x_1\rangle \wedge \ldots R_n\langle det_k, x_k\rangle \parallel \Box$ could be seen as GQ-quasi_empty clause. Opposed to $\Box$, which is unsatisfiable, no one can take for sure the unsatisfiability of GQ-quasi_empty clauses. In order to show the unsatisfiability of GQ-quasi_empty clauses, one has to make sure that the "left hand side", i.e., what comes before $\parallel$, is unsatisfiable. This is accomplished through the $\parallel shift$ (admissible) rule informally stated in (8).

(8) Let $\Gamma \parallel \Box$ be an arbitrary GQ-formula and Δ an arbitrary derivation tree. If $\Gamma \parallel \Box$ occurs in Δ, then $\parallel \neg\Gamma$ can be adjoined to Δ.

6   GQ Reasoner at Work

It should not be difficult to develop an argumentative refutation style defeasible theorem prover based on generalized quantifiers. For the sake of space and simplicity, we explain the GQ-reasoning in the context of a polite argumentation approach.

Deductions using GQ-resolution resort on the idea of "marking" and "propagating" the kind of determiner been used. This seems easily achievable from the inspection on the notation adopted for variables, $\langle det, var\rangle$. For defeasible $dets$, the new derived clause is defeasible. Therefore, all subsequent clauses, including GQ-quasi_empty clauses, derived from defeasible clauses are defeasible. The main point here is that combinations between defeasible and categorical clauses lead to defeasible clauses. This point is exemplified by entry 7 in Fig. 1. Clause 7 was inferred by using rule 2a, which is categoric, over argument 6, which was arrived at on a defeasible inference chain. Therefore, argument on entry 7 must be marked as defeasible. The mark goes to the det entry of $\langle det, term\rangle$.

Entry 5 in Fig. 1 deserves special attention. Note that the system inferred $bird\langle most, Tux\rangle \parallel \Box$. This clause is not the classical empty clause, i.e. $\Box$, because

1	$bird\langle most, x\rangle \parallel fly\langle most, x\rangle$	defeasible axiom (da)
2a	$penguin\langle all, x\rangle \parallel bird\langle all, x\rangle$	categorical axiom (ca)
2b	$penguin\langle all, x\rangle \parallel \neg fly\langle all, x\rangle$	ca
3	$\parallel penguin\langle cte, Tux\rangle$	ca
4	$\parallel \neg fly\langle cte, Tux\rangle$	Ch_1 argument
5	$bird\langle most, Tux\rangle \parallel \Box$	(4,1,GQ-resolution, most)
6	$\parallel \neg bird\langle most, Tux\rangle$	(5,$\parallel$shift,GQ-resolution, most)
7	$\parallel \neg penguin\langle most, Tux\rangle$	(6,2a,GQ-resolution, most)
8	$\parallel \Box$	(7,3,GQ-resolution, most)
4'	$\parallel fly\langle cte, Tux\rangle$	Ch_2 rebutt
5'	$\parallel \neg penguin\langle cte, Tux\rangle$	(4',2b,$\parallel$shift,GQ-resolution, cte)
6'	$\parallel \Box$	(5',3,GQ-resolution, cte)

Fig. 1. Defeasible argumentation game for Penguin Principle

1	$quaker\langle most, x\rangle \parallel pacifist\langle most, x\rangle$	da
2	$republican\langle most, x\rangle \parallel \neg pacifist\langle most, x\rangle$	da
3	$\parallel quaker\langle cte, Nixon\rangle$	ca
4	$\parallel republican\langle cte, Nixon\rangle$	ca
5	$\parallel pacifist\langle cte, Nixon\rangle$	Ch_1 argument
6	$\parallel \neg republican\langle most, Nixon\rangle$	(5,2,$\parallel$shift,GQ-resolution, most)
7	$\parallel \square$	(6,4,$\parallel$shift,GQ-resolution, most)
5′	$\parallel \neg pacifist\langle cte, Nixon\rangle$	Ch_2 argument
6′	$\parallel \neg quaker\langle most, Nixon\rangle$	(5′,1,$\parallel$shift,GQ-resolution, most)
7′	$\parallel \square$	(6′,3,$\parallel$shift,GQ-resolution, most)

Fig. 2. Defeasible argumentation game for Nixon diamond

there is a restriction to be achieved, namely $bird\langle most, Tux\rangle$. Therefore, the system must verify if restrictions can be met (cf. [3], [12], [2]). The easiest way to do so is pushing the restrictions to the opposite side of $\parallel$ negating the material being pushed over. This move is based on rule (8) and makes possible to arrive to the GQ-empty clause $\parallel \square$ when there is a refutation for the argument under dispute.

Suppose now that two players engage themselves on a dispute trying to answer the question *Does Silvester lay eggs?* Suppose also they share the following knowledge: (i) all cats are not monotremes; (ii) all cats are mammals; (iii) few mammals lay eggs; (iv) only[8] monotremes are mammals that lay eggs; (v) Silvester is a cat. The winner is the player sustaining that *Silvester does not lay eggs*, i.e., Ch_2. The dispute is shown in fig. 3 where $c\,a$, and $d\,a$ stand for categorical axiom and defeasible axiom.

It is worth notice that Ch_2 lose the game in the absence of the very specific knowledge expressed by 'only monotremes are mammals that lay eggs'. In this situation, Ch_1 wins the game but his argument could be defeated as soon as new knowledge is brought to them.

Rebuttals are started whenever a GQ-empty clause $\parallel \square$ is drawn. The winner, if any, is the one who has arrived to the GQ-empty clause under a categorical inference chain. If no player wins the game, both arguments go to a *controversial* list ([12]'s control set). This is the case for Nixon diamond (see Fig. 2). In this case, $pacifist$ and $\neg pacifist$ go to the controversial list and can not be used on any other deduction chain. This is the dead-end entry in Fig. 4 and is known as ambiguity propagation.

Since "Nixon diamonds" will be put on the controversial list, before trying to unify a literal, the system should consult the list. If the literal is there, the system should try another path. If there are no options available, the current player gives up and the opponent should try to prove his/her rebutting argument. This process goes on in a recursive fashion and the winner will be, as already pointed out before, the one who has arrived to the empty clause under (i) a categorical inference chain, or (ii) defeasible inference chain provided the opponent can not rebut the argument under dispute. The last situation occurs when one player has a "weak argument" – a defeasible argument, but the opponent has none. "Nixon diamonds" are not covered by either (i) or (ii). In

---

[8] Only is not a determiner, it is an adverb and therefore not in the scope of the present work. However, it seems reasonable to accept the translation given wrt the example given.

1	$cat\langle all, x\rangle \,\|\, \neg monotreme\langle all, x\rangle$	ca
2	$cat\langle all, x\rangle \,\|\, mammal\langle all, x\rangle$	ca
3	$mammal\langle few, x\rangle \,\|\, lay\_eggs\langle few, x\rangle$	da
4	$mammal\langle all, x\rangle \wedge \neg monotreme\langle all, x\rangle \,\|\, \neg lay\_eggs\langle all, x\rangle$	ca
5	$\| cat\langle cte, Silvester\rangle$	ca
6	$\| \neg lay\_eggs\langle cte, Silvester\rangle$	Ch_1 argument
7	$mammal\langle few, Silvester\rangle \,\|\, \square$	$(6, 3, few)$
8	$\| \neg mammal\langle few, Silvester\rangle$	$(7, \| shift)$
9	$cat\langle few, Silvester\rangle \,\|\, \square$	$(8, 2, few)$
10	$\| \neg cat\langle few, Silvester\rangle$	$(9, \| shift)$
11	$\| \square$	$(10, 5, few)$
6'	$\| lay\_eggs\langle cte, Silvester\rangle$	Ch_2 argument
7'	$mammal\langle cte, Silvester\rangle \wedge \neg monotreme\langle cte, Silvester\rangle \,\|\, \square$	$(6', 4, all)$
8'	$\| \neg(mammal\langle cte, Silvester\rangle \wedge \neg monotreme\langle cte, Silvester\rangle)$	$(7', \| shift)$
9'	$\| \neg mammal\langle cte, Silvester\rangle \vee monotreme\langle cte, Silvester\rangle$	$(8', \neg)$
10'	$cat\langle cte, Silvester\rangle \,\|\, monotreme\langle cte, Silvester\rangle$	$(9', 2, all)$
11'	$cat\langle cte, Silvester\rangle \wedge cat\langle cte, Silvester\rangle \,\|\, \square$	$(10', 1, all)$
12'	$cat\langle cte, Silvester\rangle \,\|\, \square$	$(11', \wedge)$
13'	$\| \neg cat\langle cte, Silvester\rangle$	$(12', \| shift)$
14'	$\| \square$	$(13', 5, all)$

Fig. 3. The monotreme dispute

this case, both players arrived at mutually defeasible conclusons; therefore both players loose the game.

The strategy described is clearly algorithmic and its implementation straightforward; however, its complexity measures are not dealt with in the present paper.

7 Conclusions and Further Developments

In the paper we claimed that natural language generalized quantifiers *most*, and *all* could be used as natural devices for dealing with non-monotonic automated defeasible reasoning systems.

Non-monotonicity could be achieved through (i) defeasible logics exemplified by [11], [15], and [1] or (ii) defeasible argumentative systems as [4], [20], and [16]. As Simari states in [5], "...in most of these formalisms, a priority relation among rules must be explicitly given with the program in order to decide between rules with contradictory consequents." Anyway, what all non-monotonic formalisms try to explain (and deal with) is the meaning of vague concepts exemplified by 'generally'. A different approach can be found in Veloso(s)' work ([18], [19]). In these papers, the authors characterize 'generally' in terms of filter logics (FL) *being faithfully embedded into a first-order theory of certain predicates*. In this way, they provide a framework where semantic intuitions of filter logics could capture the naïve meaning of 'most', for instance. Their framework supports theorem proving in FL via proof procedures and theorem provers for classical first-order logic (via faithful embedding). In this way, Velosos' work deal with defeasibility in a monotonic fashion. However, in order to de-

1	$quaker\langle most, x\rangle$ $\|$ $pacifist\langle most, x\rangle$	da
2	$republican\langle most, x\rangle$ $\|$ $\neg pacifist\langle most, x\rangle$	da
3	$republican\langle most, x\rangle$ $\|$ $footballfan\langle most, x\rangle$	da
4	$pacifist\langle most, x\rangle$ $\|$ $antimilitarist\langle most, x\rangle$	da
5	$footballfan\langle most, x\rangle$ $\|$ $\neg antimilitarist\langle most, x\rangle$	da
6	$\|$ $quaker\langle cte, Nixon\rangle$	ca
7	$\|$ $republican\langle cte, Nixon\rangle$	ca
8	$\|$ $\neg antimilitarist\langle cte, Nixon\rangle$	Ch_1 argument
9	dead end due to pacifist & $\neg pacifist$	Nixon$\Diamond$
$8'$	$\|$ $antimilitarist\langle cte, Nixon\rangle$	Ch_2 rebutt
$9'$	$\|$ $\neg footballfan\langle most, Nixon\rangle$	($8'$,5,$\|$shift,GQ-res, most)
$10'$	$\|$ $\neg republican\langle cte, Nixon\rangle$	($9'$,3,$\|$shift,GQ-res, most)
$11'$	$\|$ $\Box$	($10'$,7,$\|$shift,GQ-res, most)

Fig. 4. Ambiguity propagation

velop a theorem prover for 'generally' they have to embed FL into first-order logic (of certain predicates).

The main advantage of GQ approach proposed in this paper is the clear separation between categorical and defeasible knowledge and their interaction given by, for example, *most, few*, and *all*. Of course, such separation improves the understanding of what makes common sense knowledge processing so hard. Most importantly, the approach introduced in the paper could be further expanded by introducing new natural language quantifiers. The natural rank amongst quantifiers would be used to control their interactions in a way almost impossible to be achieved on traditional non-monotonic systems.

As a future development, logical properties of generalized quantifiers ([13], [6]) should be used in order to set up a GQ-framework dealing with a bigger class of defeasible determiners. This should improve the inference machinery of future GQ-theorem provers.

Acknowledgments

The authors would like to thank anonymous referees for suggestions and comments that helped to improve the structure of the first version of this paper.

References

1. G. Antoniou, D. Bilington, G. Governatori, and M. Maher. Representation results for defeasible logic. *ACM Transactions on Computational Logic*, 2(2):255–287, April 2001.
2. G. Antoniou, D. Billington, G. Governatori, M. J. Maher, and A. Rock. A family of defeasible reasoning logics and its implementation. In *Proceedings of European Conference on Artificial Intelligence*, pages 459–463, 2000.
3. Hans-Jürgen Bürckert, Bernard Hollunder, and Armin Laux. On skolemization in constrained logics. Technical Report RR-93-06, DFKI, March 1993.
4. C. I. Chesñevar, A. Maguitman, and R. Loui. Logical models of argument. *ACM Computing Surveys*, 32(4):343–387, 2000.

5. Alejandro J. Garcia and Guillermo R. Simari. Defeasible logic programming: An argumentative aproach. Article downloaded on May 204 from http://cs.uns.edu.ar/~grs/Publications/index-publications.html. To appear in Theory and Practice of Logic Programming.

6. Peter Gärdenfors, editor. *Generalized Quantifiers, Linguistic and Logical Approaches*, volume 31 of *Studies in Linguistics and Philosophy*. Reidel, Dordrecht, 1987.

7. Jaakko Hintikka. *Quantifiers in Natural Language: Game-Theoretical Semantics*. D. Reidel, 1979. pp. 81–117.

8. Edward L. Keenan. The semantic of determiners. In Shalom Lappin, editor, *The Handbook of Contemporary Semantic Theory*, pages 41–63. Blackwell Plublishers Inc., 1996.

9. Jan Tore Lønning. Natural language determiners and binary quantifiers. Handout, August 1993. Handout on Generalized Quantifiers presented at the fifth European Summer School on Logic, Language and Information.

10. Paul Lorenzen. *Metamatemática*. Madrid: Tecnos, 1971, 1962. [Spanish translator: Jacobo Muñoz].

11. Donald Nute. Defeasible logic. In D. M. Gabbay, C. J. Hogger, and J. A. Robinson, editors, *Handbook of Logic in Artificial Intelligence and Logic Programming*, volume 3, pages 355–395. Oxford University Press, 194.

12. Sven Eric Panitz. Default reasoning with a constraint resolution principle. Ps file downloaded on January 2003 from http://www.ki.informatik.uni-frankfurt.de/persons/panitz/paper/bbt.ps.gz. The article was presented at the LPAR 1993 in St Petersburg.

13. Stanley Peters and Dag Westerståhl. Quantifiers, 2002. Pdf file downloadable on May 2003 from http://www.stanford.edu/group/nasslli/courses/peter-wes/PWbookdraft2-3.pdf.

14. John L. Pollock. Natural deduction. Pdf file downloadable on December 2002 from Oscar's home page http://oscarhome.soc-sci.arizona.edu/ftp/OSCAR-web-page/oscar.html.

15. H. Prakken. Dialectical proof theory for defeasible argumentation with defeasible priorities. In *Proceedings of the [th] ModelAge Workshop 'Formal Models of Agents'*, Lecture Notes in Artificial Intelligence, Berlin, 1999. Springer Verlag.

16. Henry Prakken and Gerard Vreeswijk. Logics for defeasible argumentation. In D. Gabbay and F. Guenthner, editors, *Handbook of Philosophical Logic*, volume 4, pages 218–319. Kluwer Academic Publishers, Dordrecht, 2002.

17. J. A. Robinson. A machine-oriented logic based on the resolution principle. *J. ACM*, 12(1):23–41, 1965.

18. P. A. S. Veloso and W. A. Carnielli. Logics for qualitative reasoning. CLE e-prints, Vol. 1(3), 2001 (Section Logic) available at http://www.cle.unicamp.br/e-prints/abstract_3.htm. To appear in "Logic, Epistemology and the Unity of Science" edited by Shahid Rahman and John Symons, Kluwer, 2003.

19. P. A. S. Veloso and S. R. M. Veloso. On filter logics for 'most' and special predicates. Article downloaded on May 2004 from http://www.cs.math.ist.utl.pt/comblog04/abstracts/veloso.pdf.

20. G. A. W. Vreeswijk. Abstract argumentation systems. *Artficial Intelligence*, 90:225–279, 1997.

Is Plausible Reasoning a Sensible Alternative for Inductive-Statistical Reasoning?*

Ricardo S. Silvestre[1] and Tarcísio H.C. Pequeno[2]

[1] Department of Philosophy, University of Montreal
2910 Édouard-Montpetit, Montréal, QC, H3T 1J7, Canada
(Doctoral Fellow, CNPq, Brazil)
ricardo.silvestre@umontreal.ca
[2] Department of Computer Science, Federal University of Ceará
Bloco 910, Campus to Pici, Fortaleza-Ceará, 60455-760, Brazil
thcp@ufc.br

Abstract. The general purpose of this paper is to show a practical instance of how philosophy can benefit from some ideas, methods and techniques developed in the field of Artificial Intelligence (AI). It has to do with some recent claims [4] that some of the most traditional philosophical problems have been raised and, in some sense, solved by AI researchers. The philosophical problem we will deal with here is the representation of non-deductive intra-theoretic scientific inferences. We start by showing the flaws with the most traditional solution for this problem found in philosophy: Hempel's Inductive-Statistical (I-S) model [5]. After we present a new formal model based on previous works motivated by reasoning needs in Artificial Intelligence [11] and show that since it does not suffer from the problems identified in the I-S model, it has great chances to be successful in the task of satisfactorily representing the non-deductive intra-theoretic scientific inferences.

1 Introduction

In the introduction of a somewhat philosophical book of essays on Artificial Intelligence [4], the editors spouse the thesis that in the field of AI "traditional philosophical questions have received sharper formulations and surprising answers", adding that "… important problems that the philosophical tradition overlooked have been raised and solved [in AI]". They go as far as claiming that "Were they reborn into a modern university, Plato and Aristotle and Leibniz would most suitably take up appointments in the department of computer science." Even recognizing a certain amount of over enthusiasm and exaggeration in those affirmations, the fact is that there are evident similarities and parallels between some problems concretely faced in AI practice with some classic ones dealt with within philosophical investigation. However, although there is some contact between AI and philosophy in fields like philosophy of mind and philosophy of language, the effective contribution of ideas, methods and tech-

---

* This work is partially supported by CNPq through the LOCIA (Logic, Science and Artificial Intelligence) Project.

A.L.C. Bazzan and S. Labidi (Eds.): SBIA 2004, LNAI 3171, pp. 124–133, 2004.
© Springer-Verlag Berlin Heidelberg 2004

niques from AI to philosophy is still something hard to be seen. In this paper we continue a project started in a previous work [14] and present what we believe to be a bridge between these two areas of knowledge that, in addition to its own interest, can also serve as an example and an illustration of a whole lot of connections we hope to come over.

The study of non-deductive inferences has played a fundamental role in both artificial intelligence (AI) and philosophy of science. While in the former it has given rise to the development of *nonmonotonic logics* [9], [10], [13], as AI theorists have named them, in the later it has attracted philosophers, for over half century, in the pursuit of a so-called *logic of induction* [2], [6], [7]. Perhaps because the technical devices used by these areas were quite different, the obvious fact that both AI researches and philosophers were dealing with the *same* problem has been during all these years of formal investigation of non-deductive reasoning remained almost unnoticed. The first observations about the similarities between these two domains appeared in print as late as about the end of the eights [8], [11], [12], [15]. More than a surprising curiosity, the mentioned connection is important because, being concerned with the same problem of formalizing non-deductive patterns of inference, at least in principle, computer scientists and philosophers can benefit from the results achieved by each other. It is our purpose here to lay down what we believe to be an instance of such a sort of contribution from the side of AI to philosophy of science.

One of the problems that have motivated philosophers of science to engage in the project of developing a logic of induction was the investigation of what we can call *intra-theoretic scientific inference*, that is to say, the inferences performed inside a scientific theory already existent and formalized in its basic principles. This kind of inference thus goes from the theory's basic principles to the derived ones, in opposition to the inductive inferences which go from particulars facts in order to establish general principles. Intra-theoretic inferences play an important role, for example, in the explanation of scientific laws and singular facts as well as in the prediction of non-observed facts.

The traditional view concerning intra-theoretic scientific inferences states that scientific arguments are of two types: *deductive* and *inductive/probabilistic*. This deductive/inductive-probabilistic view of intra-theoretic scientific inferences was put forward in its most precise form by Carl Hempel's models of scientific explanation [5]. In order to represent the *non-deductive* intra-theoretic scientific inferences, Hempel proposed a probabilistic-based model of scientific explanation named by him Inductive-Statistical (I-S) model. However, in spite of its intuitive appeal, this model was unable to solve satisfactorily the so-called problem of *inductive ambiguities*, which is surprisingly similar to the problem of anomalous extensions that AI theorists working with nonmonotonic logics are so familiar with.

Our purpose in this paper is to show how a logic which combines nonmonotonicity (in the style of Reiter's default logic [13]) with paraconsistency [3] regarding nonmonotonically derived formulae is able to satisfactorily express reasoning under these circumstances, dealing properly with the mentioned inconsistency problems that undermined Hempel's project. The structure of the paper is as follows. First of all we introduce Hempel's I-S model and show, through some classical examples, how it fails in treating properly some very simple cases. This is done in the Section 2. Our nonmonotonic and paraconsistent logical system is presented in Section 3, were we also show how it is able to avoid the problems that plagued Hempel's proposal.

2 Hempel's I-S Model and the Problem of Inductive Inconsistencies

According to most historiographers of philosophy, the history of the philosophical analysis of scientific explanation began with the publication of 'Studies in the Logic of Explanation' in 1948 by Carl Hempel and Paul Oppenheim. In this work, Hempel and Oppenheim propose their deductive-nomological (D-N) model of scientific explanation where scientific explanations are considered as being deductive arguments that contain essentially at least one general law in the premises. Later, in 1962, Hempel presented his inductive-statistical (I-S) model by which he proposed to analyze the statistical scientific explanations that clearly could not be fitted into the D-N model. (These papers were reprinted in [5].)

Because of his emphasis on the idea that explanations are arguments and his commitment to a numerical approach, Hempel's models perfectly exemplify the deductive-inductive/probabilistic view of intra-theoretic scientific inferences. According to Hempel's I-S model, the general schema of non-deductive scientific explanations is the following:

$$\frac{\begin{array}{c} P(G, F) = r \\ Fb \end{array}}{Gb\,.} \quad [r]$$

Here the first premise is a statistical law asserting that the relative frequency of Gs among Fs is r, r being close to 1, the second stands for b having the property F, and the expression '[r]' next to the double line represents the degree of inductive probability conferred on the conclusion by the premises. Since the law represented by the first premise is not a universal but a statistical law, the argument above is inductive (in Carnap's sense) rather than deductive.

If we ask, for instance, why John Jones (to use Hempel's preferred example) recovered quickly from a streptococcus infection we would have the following argument as the answer:

$$\frac{\begin{array}{c} P(G, F \wedge H) = r \\ Fb \end{array}}{Gb\,.} \quad [r] \tag{1}$$

where F stands for having a streptococcus infection, H for administration of penicillin, G for quick recovery, b is John Jones, and r is a number close to 1. Given that penicillin was administered in John Jones case (Hb) and that most (but not all) streptococcus infections clear up quickly when treated with penicillin ($P(G,F \wedge H) = r$), the argument above constitutes the explanation for John Jones's quick recovery.

However, it is known that certain strains of streptococcus bacilli are resistant to penicillin. If it turns out that John Jones is infected with such a strain of bacilli, then the probability of his quick recovery after treatment of penicillin is low. In that case, we could set up the following inductive argument:

$$P(G, F \wedge H \wedge J) = r' \quad \text{or, equivalently,} \quad P(\neg G, F \wedge H \wedge J) = 1 - r'$$

$$\frac{Fb \wedge Hb \wedge Jb}{Gb} \, [r'] \qquad\qquad \frac{Fb \wedge Hb \wedge Jb}{\neg Gb} \, [1-r'] \quad (2)$$

J stands for the penicillin-resistant character of the streptococcus infection and r' is a number close to zero (consequently $1 - r'$ is a number close to 1.)

This situation exemplifies what Hempel calls the problem of explanatory or *inductive ambiguities*. In the case of John Jones's penicillin-resistant infection, we have two inductive arguments where the premises of each argument are logically compatible and the conclusion is the same. Nevertheless, in one argument the conclusion is strongly supported by the premises, whereas in the other the premises strongly undermine the same conclusion.

In order to solve this sort of problem, Hempel proposed his *requirement of maximal specificity*, or RMS. It can be explained as follows. Let *s* be the conjunction of the premises of the argument and *k* the conjunction of all statements accepted at the given time (called knowledge situation). Then, according to Hempel, "to be rationally acceptable" in that knowledge situation the explanation must meet the following condition: If $s \wedge k$ implies that *b* belongs to a class F_1, and that F_1 is a subclass of F, then $s \wedge k$ must also imply a statement specifying the statistical probability of G in F_1, say, $P(G, F_1) = r'$. Here, r' must equal r unless the probability statement just cited is a theorem of mathematical probability theory.

The RMS intends basically to prevent that the property or class F to be used in the explanation of Gb has a subclass whose relative frequency of Gs is different from $P(G,F)$. In order to explain Gb through Fb and a statistical law such as $P(G, F) = 0.9$, we need to be sure that, for all sets $F_1 \in F$ such that $F_1 b$, the relative frequency of Gs among F_1s is the same as that among Fs, that is to say, $P(G, F_1) = 0.9$. In other words, in order to be used in an explanation, the class F must be a *homogeneous* one with respect to G. (All these observations are valid for the new version of the RMS proposed in 1968 and called RMS* [5].)

The RMS was proposed of course because of I-S model's inability to solve the problem of ambiguities. Since the I-S model allows the appearance of ambiguities and gives no adequate treatment for them, without RMS it is simply useless as a model of intra-theoretical scientific inferences. But we can wonder: Is the situation different with the RMS?

First of all, in its new version the I-S model allows us to classify arguments as authentic scientific inferences able to be used for explaining or predicting only if they satisfy the RMS. It is not difficult to see that this restriction is too strong to be satisfied in practical circumstances. Suppose that we *know* that most streptococcus infections clear up quickly when treated with penicillin, but we *do not* know whether this statistical law is applicable to all kinds of streptococcus bacillus taken separately (that is, we do not know if the class in question is a homogeneous one). Because of this incompleteness of our knowledge, we are not entitled to use argument (1) to explain (or predict) the fact that John Jones had (or will have) a quick recovery. Since when making scientific prediction, for example, we have nothing but imprecise and incomplete knowledge, the degree of knowledge required by the RMS is clearly incompatible with actual scientific practice.

Second, the only cases that the RMS succeeds in solving are those that involve class specificity. In other words, the only kind of ambiguity that the RMS prevents consists of that that comes from a conflict arising *inside* a certain class (that is, a conflict taking place between the class and one of its subclasses.) Suppose that John Jones has contracted HIV. As such, the probability of his quick recovery (from any kind of infection) will be low. But given that he took penicillin and that most streptococcus infections clear up quickly when treated with penicillin, we will still have the conclusion that he will recover quickly. Thus an ambiguity will arise. However, as the class of HIV infected people who have an infection does not belong to the class of individuals having a streptococcus infection which were treated with penicillin (and nor vice-versa), the RMS will not be able to solve the conflict.

Third, sometimes the policy of preventing all kinds of contradictions may not be the best one. Suppose that the antibiotic that John Jones used in his treatment belongs to a recently developed kind of antibiotic that its creators guarantee to cure even the known penicillin-resistant infection. The initial statistics showed a 90% of successful cases. Even though this result cannot be considered as definitive (due to the always-small number of cases considered in initial tests), it must be taken into account. Now, given argument (2), the same contradiction will arise. But here we do not know yet which of the two 'laws' has priority over the other: maybe the penicillin-resistant bacillus will prove to be resistant even to the new antibiotic or maybe not. Anyway, if we reject the contradiction as the I-S model does and do not allow the use of these inferences, we will loss a possibly relevant part of the total set of information that could be useful or even necessary for other inferences.

3   A Nonmonotonic and Paraconsistent Solution to the Problem of Inductive Inconsistencies

Compared to the traditional probabilistic-statistical view of non-deductive intra-theoretical scientific inferences, our proposal's main shift can be summarized as follows. First, we import from AI some techniques often used there in connection to nonmonotonic reasoning to express non-deductive scientific inferences. Second, in order to prevent the appearance of ambiguities we provide a mechanism by which *exceptions* to laws can be represented. This mechanism has two main advantages over Hempel's RMS: it can prevent the class specificity ambiguities without rejecting both arguments (as Hempel's does), being also able to treat properly those cases of ambiguity that do not involve class specificity (that remained uncovered by Hempel's system.) Finally, in order to consider the cases where the ambiguities are due to the very nature of the knowledge to be formalized and, as such, cannot be prevented, we supply a *paraconsistent* apparatus by which those ambiguities can be tolerated and sensibly reasoned out, without trivializing the whole set of conclusions. Consequently, even in the presence of contradictions we can make use of all available information, achieving just the reasonable conclusions.

Our proposal takes the form of a logical system consisting of two different logics, organically connected, which are intended to operate in two different levels of reasoning. At one level, the nonmonotonic one, there is a logic able to perform non-deductive inferences. This logic is conceived in a style which resembles Reiter's default logic [13], but incorporates a very important distinction: it is able to generate extensions including contradictory conclusions obtained through the use of default rules. By this reason, it is called *Inconsistent Default Logic* (IDL) [1], [11]. The conclusions achieved by means of nonmonotonic inferences do not have the same epistemic status of the ones deductively derived from known facts and assumed principles. They are taken as just *plausible* (in opposition to certain, as far as the theory and the observations are themselves so taken). In order to explicitly recognize this epistemic fact, and thus make it formally treatable in the reasoning system, they are marked with a modal sign (?), where α? means "α is plausible." In this way, differently from traditional nonmonotonic logics, IDL is able to distinguish revisable formulae obtained though nonmonotonic inferences from non-refutable ones, deductively obtained.

At the second level, operates a deductive logic. But here again, not a classic one, but one able to properly treat and make sensible deductions in the theory that comes out from the first level, *even if it is inconsistent*, as it may very well be. This feature makes this logic a paraconsistent one, but, again, not one of the already existent paraconsistent logics, as the ones proposed by da Costa and his collaborators [3], but one specially conceived to reason properly under the given circumstances. It is called the *Logic of Epistemic Inconsistencies* (LEI) [1], [11]. In this logic, a distinction is made between *strong contradictions,* a contradiction involving at least one occurrence of deductive, non-revisable knowledge, from *weak contradictions*, of the form $\neg (\alpha)? \wedge \alpha$?, which involves just plausible conclusions. This second kind of contradictions are well tolerated and do not trivialize the theory, as the first kind still do, just as in classical logic.

The general schema of an IDL default rule is $\alpha \supset_\varphi \beta$, which can be read as "$\beta$ can be nonmonotonically inferred from α unless φ." Adopting Reiter's terminology, α represents the prerequisite, β the consequent, and φ the negation of the justification, here called exception. One important difference between Reiter's logic and ours is that the consistency of the consequent does not need to be explicitly stated in φ: it is internally guaranteed by the definition of extension. Translating Reiter's normal and semi-normal defaults to our notation, for example, would produce respectively $\alpha \supset \beta$ and $\alpha \supset_\varphi \beta$, where $\alpha \supset \beta$ is an abbreviation for $\alpha \supset_{P(t1, ..., tn) \wedge \neg P(t1, ..., tn)} \beta$. Other difference is that the consequent is added to the extension necessarily with the plausibility mark ? attached to it. The definition of IDL theory is identical to default logic's one. Above it follows the definition of IDL extension.

Let S be a set of closed formulae and <W, D> a closed IDL theory. $\Gamma(S)$ is the smallest set satisfying the following conditions:

(i) $W \subseteq \Gamma(S)$;

(ii)   If $\Gamma(S) \vdash_? \alpha$, then $\alpha \in \Gamma(S)$;

(iii) If $\alpha \supset_\varphi \beta \in D$, $\alpha \in \Gamma(S)$, $\varphi \notin S$, and $\beta? \cup S$ is ?-consistent, then $\beta? \in \Gamma(S)$.

A set of formulae E is an *extension* of <W, D> iff $\Gamma(E) = E$, that is, iff E is a fixed point of the operator Γ.

The symbol $\vdash_?$ refers to the inferential relation defined by the deductive and para-consistent logic LEI, according to which weak inconsistencies do not trivialize the theory. Similarly, the expression "?-consistent" refers to consistency or non-trivialization under such relation. Above we show the axiomatic of LEI. Latin letters represent ?-free formulae and ~ is a derived operator defined as follows: $\sim\!\alpha =_{\text{def}} \alpha \rightarrow$ $(P(t_1, ..., t_n) \wedge \neg P(t_1, ..., t_n))$, where $P(t_1, ..., t_n)$ is any atomic ?-free formula.

1. $\alpha \rightarrow (\beta \rightarrow \alpha)$.
2. $(\alpha \rightarrow \beta) \rightarrow ((\alpha \rightarrow (\beta \rightarrow \gamma)) \rightarrow (\alpha \rightarrow \gamma))$.
3. $\alpha, \alpha \rightarrow \beta \vdash \beta$.
4. $\alpha \wedge \beta \rightarrow \alpha$.
5. $\alpha \wedge \beta \rightarrow \beta$.
6. $\alpha \rightarrow (\beta \rightarrow (\alpha \wedge \beta))$.
7. $\alpha \rightarrow (\alpha \vee \beta)$.
8. $\beta \rightarrow (\alpha \vee \beta)$.
9. $(\alpha \rightarrow \gamma) \rightarrow ((\beta \rightarrow \gamma) \rightarrow (\alpha \vee \beta \rightarrow \gamma))$.
10. $((\alpha \rightarrow \beta) \rightarrow \alpha) \rightarrow \alpha$.
11. $\forall x\alpha \rightarrow \alpha(x|t)$, where t is free for x in α.
12. $\forall x(\alpha \rightarrow \beta) \rightarrow (\forall x\alpha \rightarrow \forall x\beta)$.
13. $\alpha \rightarrow \forall x\alpha$, where x is not free in α.
14. $\alpha \vdash^x \forall x\alpha$, where x is a varying object.
15. $\alpha(x|t) \rightarrow \exists x\alpha$, where t is free for x in α.
16. $\forall x(\alpha \rightarrow \beta) \rightarrow (\exists x\alpha \rightarrow \exists x\beta)$.
17. $\exists x\alpha \rightarrow \alpha$, where x is not free in α.
18. $\neg\forall x\alpha \leftrightarrow \exists x\neg\alpha$.
19. $\neg\exists x\alpha \leftrightarrow \forall x\neg\alpha$.
20. $\neg(\alpha \rightarrow \beta) \leftrightarrow (\alpha \wedge \neg\beta)$.
21. $\neg(\alpha \wedge \beta) \leftrightarrow (\neg\alpha \vee \neg\beta)$.
22. $\neg(\alpha \vee \beta) \leftrightarrow (\neg\alpha \wedge \neg\beta)$.
23. $\neg\neg\alpha \leftrightarrow \alpha$.
24. $(\alpha \rightarrow B) \rightarrow ((\alpha \rightarrow \neg B) \rightarrow \neg\alpha)$.
25. $(\alpha? \rightarrow \beta?)? \rightarrow (\alpha? \rightarrow \beta?)$.
26. $(\alpha \vee \beta)? \rightarrow (\alpha? \vee \beta?)$.
27. $(\neg\alpha)? \leftrightarrow \neg(\alpha?)$.
28. $\alpha \rightarrow \alpha?$.
29. $\alpha?? \rightarrow \alpha?$.
30. $(\exists x\alpha)? \rightarrow \exists x(\alpha?)$.
31. $\alpha? (\sim\!\sim\!\alpha)?$.
32. $\alpha? \wedge \sim\!(\beta?) \rightarrow (\alpha \wedge \sim\!\beta)?$.
33. $\alpha \vdash^? \sim\!((\sim\!\alpha)?)$, where ? is a varying object.

Axiom schema 24, which is a weaker version of the *reductio ad absurdum* axiom, is the key of LEI's paraconsistency. By restricting its use only to situations where B is ?-free, it prevents that from weak contradictions we derive everything; at the same time that allows ?-free formulae to have a classical behaviour. Axiom schema 27 is another important one in LEI's axiomatic. It allows for the internalization and exter-nalization of ? and $\neg$ with respect to each other and represents, in our view, one of the main differences between the notions of possibility and plausibility. The varying object restriction present in some axiom schemas is needed to guarantee the univer-sality of the deduction theorem. For more details about LEI's axiomatic (and seman-tics) see [11].

Turning back to the problem of inductive inconsistencies, as Hempel himself ac-knowledged [5], the appearance of ambiguities is an inevitable phenomenon when we deal with non-deductive inferences. Surprisingly enough, all cases of inductive ambi-guities identified by Hempel are not due to this suggested connection between ambiguity and induction, but to the incapacity of his probabilistic approach to represent properly the situations in question.

Consider again John Jones's example. The situation exposed in section 2 can be formalized in IDL as follows:

$$Fx \wedge Hx \supset_{Jx} Gx .\qquad(3)$$

$$Fb \wedge Hb .\qquad(4)$$

Here (3) is a default schema that says that if someone has a streptococcus infection and was treated with penicillin, then it is plausible that it will have a quick recovery unless it is verified that the streptococcus is a penicillin resistant one. (4) states that John Jones has a streptococcus infection and that he took penicillin. Given W = {Fb∧Hb} and D = {Fb∧Hb $\supset_{Jb}$ Gb} as the IDL-theory, we will have E = Th$_?$({Fb∧Hb, Gb?) as the only extension of <W,D>, where Th$_?$(A) is the set of all formulae that can be inferred from A through ⊢$_?$.

Suppose now that we have got the new information that John Jones's streptococcus is a penicillin resistant one. We represent this through the following formula:

$$Fb \wedge Hb \wedge Jb .\qquad(4')$$

Like in Hempel's formalism, if someone is infected with a penicillin-resistant bacillus, it is not plausible that he will have a quick recovery after the treatment of penicillin (unless we know that he will recover quickly). This can be represented by the following default schema:

$$Fx \wedge Hx \wedge Jx \supset \neg Gx\qquad(5)$$

Given W' = {Fb∧Hb∧Jb} and D'= D ∪ {Fb∧Hb∧Jb ⊃ ¬Gb} as our new IDL-theory, we will have E' = Th$_?$({Fb∧Hb∧Jb, Gb?}) as the only extension of <W',D'>.

Since in Hempel's approach there is no connection between laws (1) and (2), the conclusion of ¬Gb has no effect upon the old conclusion Gb. Here however it is being represented the priority that we know law (5) must have over law (3): the clauses Jx in the exception of (3) and Jx in the prerequisite of (5) taken together mean that if (5) can be used for inferring, for example ¬Gb?, (3) cannot be used for inferring Gb?. So, if after using law (3) we get new information that enable us to use law (5), since in the light of the new state of knowledge law (3)'s utilization is not possible, we have to give up the previous conclusion got from this law. So, since Jb∈ E', we are no longer entitled to infer Gb? from (3). The only plausible fact that we can conclude from (3) and (5) is ¬Gb?. As such, in contrast to Hempel's approach, we do not have the undesirable consequence that it is plausible (or in Hempel's approach, high probable) that John will quickly recover and it is plausible that he will not.

As we have said, in this specific case we know that law (5) has a kind of priority over law (3), in the sense that if (5) holds, (3) does not hold. Like we did in Section 2, suppose now that the antibiotic that John Jones used in his treatment belongs to a recently developed kind of antibiotic that its creators guarantee to cure even the known penicillin-resistant infection. The initial statistics showed a 90% of successful cases but due to the always-small number of initial cases, this result cannot be considered as definitive. Even so, we can set up the following tentative law:

$$Fx \wedge H'x \supset Gx \ . \tag{6}$$

Here H' stands for administration of the new kind of antibiotic. To complete the formalization we have the two following formulae:

$$Fb \wedge H'b \wedge Jb \ . \tag{4'}$$

$$\forall x(H'x \rightarrow Hx) \ . \tag{7}$$

Given W'' = {Fb∧H'b∧Jb ,∀x(H'x →Hx)} and D''= {Fb∧Hb∧Jb ⊃ ¬Gb , Fb∧H'b ⊃ Gb} (laws (5) and (6)) as our new IDL-theory, we have that the extension of <W'',D''> is E'' = Th₂({Fb∧H'b∧Jb , ¬Gb?, Gb?}.

In this case, we do not know which of the two 'laws' has priority over the other. Maybe the penicillin-resistant bacillus will prove to be resistant even to the new antibiotic or maybe not. Instead of rejecting both conclusions, as I-S model with its RMS would do, we defend that a better solution is to keep reasoning even in the presence of such ambiguity, but without allowing that we deduce everything from it. Formally this is possible because of the restriction imposed by the already shown LEI's axiom of non-contradiction. However, if a modification that resolves the conflict is made in the set of facts (a change in (5) representing the definitive success of the new kind of penicillin, for example) the IDL's nonmonotonic inferential mechanism will update the extension and exclude one of the two contradictory conclusions.

Finally, the HIV example can be easily solved in the following way.

$$Fx \wedge Hx \supset_{Ax} Gx \ . \tag{3'}$$

$$Ax \wedge Ix \supset \neg Gx \ . \tag{8}$$

$$\forall x(Fx \rightarrow Ix) \tag{9}$$

$$Ab \wedge Hb \wedge Fb \tag{10}$$

Here A stands for having contracted HIV and I for having an infection. The solution is similar to our first example. Since (7) has priority over (3'), we will be able to conclude only ¬Gb? and consequently the ambiguity will not arise.

We have shown therefore that our formalism solves the three problems identified in Hempel's I-S model. One consideration remains to be done. Hempel's main intention with the introduction of the I-S model was to analyze the scientific inferences which contain *statistical laws*. At a first glance, it is quite fair to conclude that in those cases where something akin to a relative frequency is involved, a qualitative approach like ours will not have the same representative power as a quantitative one. However, there are several ways we can "turn" our qualitative approach into a quantitative one in such a way as to represent how much plausible a formula is. For instance, we could drop axiom 29 as to allow the weakening of the "degree of plausibility" of formulae: α? would represent the highest plausibility status a formulae may have, which could be weakened by additional ?'s. In this way, a default could represent the statistical probability of a law by changing the quantity of ?'s attached to its conclusion. A somehow inverse path could also be undertaken. In LEI's semantic, it is used a Kripke possible worlds structure (in our case we call them plausible worlds) to evaluate sentences in such a way that α? is true iff α is true in at least one plausible world [11]. We could define then $\alpha?_1$ as α?, $\alpha?_2$ as $(\alpha \wedge p)? \wedge (\alpha \wedge \neg p)?$, $\alpha?_3$ as $(\alpha \wedge p)? \wedge (\alpha \wedge \neg p)? \wedge (\alpha \wedge q)?$, $\alpha?_4$ as $(\alpha \wedge p)? \wedge (\alpha \wedge \neg p) \wedge (\alpha \wedge q)? \wedge (\alpha \wedge \neg q)?$, where p and q are different ?-free atomic formulae, and so on, in such a way that the index n at the abbreviation $\alpha?_n$ says in how many plausible worlds α is true.

References

1. Buchsbaum, A. Pequeno, T., Pequeno, M.: The Logical Expression of Reasoning. To appear in: Béziau, J., Krause, D. (eds.): New Threats in Foundations of Science. Papers Dedicated to the Eightieth Birthday of Patrick Suppes. Kluver, Dordrecht (2004).
2. Carnap, R.: Logical Foundations of Probability. U. of Chicago Press, Chicago (1950)
3. da Costa, N. C. A.: On the Theory of Inconsistent Formal Systems. Notre Dame Journal of Formal Logic 15 (1974) 497–510.
4. Ford, M. , Glymour, C., Hayes, P. (eds.): Android Epistemology. The MIT Press (1995).
5. Hempel, C. G.: Aspects of Scientific Explanation and Other Essays in the Philosophy of Science. Free Press, New York (1965)
6. Hintikka, J.: A Two-Dimensional Continuum of Inductive Methods. In: Hintikka, J., Suppes P. (eds.): Aspects of Inductive Logic. North Holland, Amsterdam (1966).
7. Kemeny, J.: Fair Bets and Inductive Probabilities. Journal of Symbolic Logic 20 (1955) 263–273.
8. Kyburg, H.: Uncertain Logics. In: Gabbay, D., Hogge D., Robinson, J. (eds.): Handbook of Logic in Artificial Intelligence and Logic Programming, Vol. 3, Nonmonotonic Reasoning and Uncertain Reasoning. Oxford University Press, Oxford (1994).
9. McCarthy, J.: Applications of Circumscription to Formalizing Commonsense Knowledge. Artificial Intelligence 26 (1986) 89–116.
10. Moore, R.: Semantic Considerations on Nonmonotonic Logic. Artificial Intelligence 25 (1985) 75–94.
11. Pequeno, T., Buchsbaum, A.: The Logic of Epistemic Inconsistency. In: Allen, J., Fikes, R., Sandewall, E. (eds.): Principles of Knowledge Representation and Reasoning: Proceedings of Second International Conference. Morgan Kaufmann, San Mateo (1991) 453-460.
12. Pollock, J. L: The Building of Oscar. Philosophical Perspectives 2 (1988) 315–344
13. Reiter, R.: A Logic for Default Reasoning. Artificial Intelligence 13 (1980) 81–132
14. Silvestre, R., Pequeno, T: A Logical Treatment of Scientific Anomalies. In: Arabnia, H, Joshua, R., Mun, Y. (eds.): Proceedings of the 2003 International Conference on Artificial Intelligence, CSRA Press, Las Vegas (2003) 669-675.
15. Tan, Y. H.: Is Default Logic a Reinvention of I-S Reasoning? Synthese 110 (1997) 357–379.

Paraconsistent Sensitivity Analysis for Bayesian Significance Tests

Julio Michael Stern

BIOINFO and Computer Science Dept., University of São Paulo
jstern@ime.usp.br

Abstract. In this paper, the notion of degree of inconsistency is introduced as a tool to evaluate the sensitivity of the Full Bayesian Significance Test (FBST) value of evidence with respect to changes in the prior or reference density. For that, both the definition of the FBST, a possibilistic approach to hypothesis testing based on Bayesian probability procedures, and the use of bilattice structures, as introduced by Ginsberg and Fitting, in paraconsistent logics, are reviewed. The computational and theoretical advantages of using the proposed degree of inconsistency based sensitivity evaluation as an alternative to traditional statistical power analysis is also discussed.

Keywords: Hybrid probability / possibility analysis; Hypothesis test; Paraconsistent logic; Uncertainty representation.

1 Introduction and Summary

The Full Bayesian Significance Test (FBST), first presented in [25] is a coherent Bayesian significance test for sharp hypotheses. As explained in [25], [23], [24] and [29], the FBST is based on a possibilistic value of evidence, defined by coherent Bayesian probability procedures. To evaluate the sensitivity of the FBST value of evidence with respect to changes in the prior density, a notion of degree of inconsistency is introduced and used. Despite the possibilistic nature of the uncertainty given by the degree of inconsistency defined herein, its interpretation is similar to standard probabilistic error bars used in statistics. Formally, however, this is given in the framework of the bilattice structure, used to represent inconsistency in paraconsistent logics. Furthermore, it is also proposed that, in some situations, the degree of inconsistency based sensitivity evaluation of the FBST value of evidence, with respect to changes in the prior density, be used as an alternative to traditional statistical power analysis, with significant computational and theoretical advantages. The definition of the FBST and its use are reviewed in Section 2. In Section 3, the notion of degree of inconsistency is defined, interpreted and used to evaluate the sensitivity of the FBST value of evidence, with respect to changes in the prior density. In Section 4, two illustrative numerical examples are given. Final comments and directions for further research are presented in Section 5. The bilattice structure, used to represent inconsistency in paraconsistent logics is reviewed in the appendix.

A.L.C. Bazzan and S. Labidi (Eds.): SBIA 2004, LNAI 3171, pp. 134–143, 2004.

2   The FBST Value of Evidence

Let $\theta \in \Theta \subseteq \mathcal{R}^p$ be a vector parameter of interest, and $L_x = L(\theta \mid x)$ the likelihood associated to the observed data x, a standard statistical model. Under the Bayesian paradigm the posterior density, $p_x(\theta)$, is proportional to the product of the likelihood and a prior density $p(\theta)$. That is,

$$p_x(\theta) \propto p(\theta)L(\theta \mid x).$$

The (null) hypothesis H states that the parameter lies in the null set Θ_H, defined by

$$\Theta_H = \{\theta \in \Theta \mid g(\theta) \leq 0 \wedge h(\theta) = 0\},$$

where g and h are functions defined in the parameter space. Herein, however, interest will rest particularly upon sharp (precise) hypotheses, i.e., those for which $\dim(\Theta_H) < \dim(\Theta)$.

The posterior surprise, $s(\theta)$, relative to a given reference density $r(\theta)$, is given by

$$s(\theta) = p_x(\theta)/r(\theta).$$

The relative surprise function, $s(\theta)$, was used by several others statisticians, see [19], [20] and [13]. The supremum of the relative surprise function over a given subset Θ_H of the parameter space, will be denoted by $s^*(\Theta_H, p, L_x, r)$, that is,

$$s^*(\Theta_H, p, L_x, r) \;=\; \sup_{\theta \,\in\, \Theta_H} s(\theta)$$

Despite the importance of making a conceptual distinction between the statement of a statistical hypothesis, H, and the corresponding null set, Θ_H, one often relax the formalism and refers to the hypothesis Θ_H, instead of $H : \theta \in \Theta_H$. In the same manner, when some or all of the argument functions, p, L_x and r, are clear from the context, they may be omitted in a simplified notation and $s^*(\Theta_H)$ or even $s^*(H)$ would be acceptable alternatives for $s^*(\Theta_H, p, L_x, r)$.

The contour or level sets, $C(\varphi, p, L_x, r)$, of the relative surprise function, and the Highest Relative Surprise Set (HRSS), $D(\varphi, p, L_x, r)$, at a given level φ, are given by

$$C(\varphi, p, L_x, r) \;=\; \{\theta \in \Theta \mid s(\theta) = \varphi\} \;,\quad D(\varphi, p, L_x, r) \;=\; \{\theta \in \Theta \mid s(\theta) > \varphi\}$$

The FBST value of evidence against a hypothesis H, $\mathrm{Ev}(H)$ or $\mathrm{Ev}(\Theta_H)$, is defined by

$$\mathrm{Ev}(\Theta_H, p, L_x, r) = \int_{T(\Theta_H, p, L_x, r)} p_x(\theta)\, d\theta \; , \text{ where}$$
$$T(\Theta_H, p, L_x, r) = D(s^*(\Theta_H), p, L_x, r)$$

The tangential HRSS $T(\Theta_H)$, or $T(H)$, contains the points in the parameter space whose surprise, relative to the reference density, is higher than that of

(2) a – Every man snores.

  b – $\forall x[man(x) \rightarrow snore(x)]$

  c – Some man snores.

  d – $\exists x[man(x) \wedge snore(x)]$

However, such representations do not emphasize the intuition that nominals like *man* do play, indeed, quite a different role from predicates like *snore*. Moreover, ordinary logic's formulas change not only the quantifier but also the connective in a complex formula over which the quantifier has scope. The companion connective for $\forall$ is $\rightarrow$; for $\exists$ is $\wedge$. In contrast, the English sentences differ only in the quantifying expression used. (3) shows a way to make the dependence of the quantifier on the nominal explicit with the further advantage of making clear the need for no connectives when considering simple sentences as those in (2)[2].

(3) a – $[\forall x : man(x)]\, snore(x)$

  b – $[\exists x : man(x)]\, snore(x)$

Logics using this kind of quantification impose that the range of quantifiers be restricted to those individuals satisfying the formula immediately following the quantifying expression. The quantifiers are then interpreted as usual requiring that all (3.a) or some (3.b) of the assignments of values to *x* satisfying the restricting formula must also satisfy what follows.

Both approaches work equally well for traditional quantifiers as those in (2). However, quantifiers like *most*, and *few* which can not be represented in ordinary logic, are easily accounted for in the restricted quantification approach. Example (4.c) is true *iff* more than half assignments from the restricted domain of *mammals* are also assignments for which *lay_eggs* is false[3]. On the other hand, if one takes *few* as the opposite of *most*, then example (4.f) is true *iff* less than half assignments from the restricted domain of *mammals* are also assignments for which *lay_eggs* is true. (4.b) and (4.e) are dead-ends since there are no combination between most assignments and few assignments, respectively, and connectives $\rightarrow$, $\wedge$, $\neg$ capable to express (4.a) and (4.d) in ordinary logic.

(4) a – most mammals don't lay eggs.

  b – ? $x[mammal(x)\ ?\ \neg lay\_eggs(x)]$

  c – $[most\ x : mammal(x)]\ \neg lay\_eggs(x)$

  d – Few mammals lay eggs.

  e – ? $x[mammal(x)\ ?\ lay\_eggs(x)]$

  f – $[few\ x : mammal(x)]\ lay\_eggs(x)$

---

[2] Notation in (3) was first seen by the authors at the Fifth European Summer School in Logic, Language and Information, Jan Tore Lønning's reader on Generalized Quantifiers. The same kind of notation can be found in ([8, page 42]).

[3] The semantics presented for *most* as more than half successful assignments is oversimplified. One can argue for *most As are Bs*, as [9] does, the following possibilities: (i) $\mid A \cap B \mid > k \mid A - B \mid$ for some specified $k \geq 1$; (ii) $\mid A \cap B \mid > k \mid A \mid$; (iii) in terms of a measure.

any other point in the null set Θ_H. When the uniform reference density, $r(\theta) \propto 1$, is used, $T(\Theta_H)$ is the Posterior's Highest Density Probability Set (HDPS) tangential to the null set Θ_H.

The role of the reference density in the FBST is to make $\mathrm{Ev}(H)$ implicitly invariant under suitable transformations of the coordinate system. Invariance, as used in statistics, is a metric concept. The reference density is just a compact and interpretable representation for the reference metric in the original parameter space. This metric is given by the geodesic distance on the density surface, see [7] and [24]. The natural choice of reference density is an uninformative prior, interpreted as a representation of no information in the parameter space, or the limit prior for no observations, or the neutral ground state for the Bayesian operation. Standard (possibly improper) uninformative priors include the uniform and maximum entropy densities, see [11], [18] and [21] for a detailed discussion.

The value of evidence against a hypothesis H has the following interpretation: "Small" values of $\mathrm{Ev}(H)$ indicate that the posterior density puts low probability mass on values of θ with high relative surprise as compared to values of $\theta \in \Theta_H$ thus providing weak evidence against hypothesis H. On the other hand, if the posterior probability of $T(\Theta_H)$ is "large", that is for "large" values of $\mathrm{Ev}(H)$, values of θ with high relative surprise as compared to values of $\theta \in \Theta_H$, have high posterior density. The data provides thus strong evidence against the hypothesis H. Furthermore, the FBST is "Fully" coherent with the Bayesian likelihood principle, that is, that the information gathered from observations is represented by (and only by) the likelihood function.

3   Prior Sensitivity and Inconsistency

For a given likelihood and reference density, let, $\eta = \mathrm{Ev}(\Theta_H, p, L_x, r)$ denote the value of evidence against a hypothesis H, with respect to prior p. Let $\eta', \eta'' \ldots$ denote the evidence against H with respect to priors $p', p'' \ldots$. The degree of inconsistency of the value of evidence against a hypothesis H, induced by a set of priors, $\{p, p', p'' \ldots\}$ can be defined by the index

$$I\{\eta, \eta', \eta'' \ldots\} \;=\; \max\{\eta, \eta', \eta'' \ldots\} - \min\{\eta, \eta', \eta'' \ldots\}$$

This intuitive measure of inconsistency can be made rigorous in the context of paraconsistent logic and bilattice structures, see the appendix. If $\eta = \mathrm{Ev}(H)$ is the value of evidence against H, the value of evidence in favor of H is defined by $\overline{\eta} = \overline{\mathrm{Ev}}(H) = 1 - \mathrm{Ev}(H)$. The point $x = \langle \overline{\eta}, \eta \rangle$ in the unit square bilattice, represents herein a single evidence, see the appendix. Since $\mathrm{BI}(x) = 0$, such a point is consistent. It is also easy to verify that for the multiple evidence values, the definition of degree of inconsistency given above, is the degree of inconsistency of the knowledge join of all the single evidence points in the unit square bilattice,

$$I(\eta, \eta', \eta'' \ldots) \;=\; \mathrm{BI}\left(\langle \overline{\eta}, \eta \rangle \sqcup_k \langle \overline{\eta}', \eta' \rangle \sqcup_k \langle \overline{\eta}'', \eta'' \rangle \ldots \right) .$$

As shown in [29], the value of evidence in favor of a composite hypothesis $H = A \vee B$, is the most favorable value of evidence in favor of each of its terms, i.e., $\overline{\text{Ev}}(H) = \max\{\overline{\text{Ev}}(A), \overline{\text{Ev}}(B)\}$. This makes $\overline{\text{Ev}}$ a possibilistic (partial) support structure coexisting with the probabilistic support structure given by the posterior probability measure in the parameter space, see [10] and [29]. The degree of inconsistency for the evidence against H induced by multiple changes of the prior can be used as an index of imprecision or fuzziness of the value of evidence $\text{Ev}(H)$. Moreover, it can also be interpreted within the possibilistic context of the partial support structure given by the evidence. Some of the alternative ways of measuring the uncertainty of the value of evidence $\text{Ev}(H)$, such as the empirical power analysis have a dual possibilistic / probabilistic interpretation, see [28] and [22]. The degree of inconsistency has also the practical advantage of being "inexpensive", i.e., given a few changes of prior, the calculation of the resulting inconsistency requires about the same work as computing $\text{Ev}(H)$. In contrast, an empirical power analysis requires much more computational work than it is required to compute a single evidence.

4   Numerical Examples

In this paper we will concentrate on two simple model examples: the Hardy-Weinberg (HW) Equilibrium Law model and Coefficient of Variation model. The HW Equilibrium is a genetic model with a sample of n individuals, where x_1 and x_3 are the two homozygote sample counts and $x_2 = n - x_1 - x_3$ is the hetherozygote sample count. The parameter vector for this trinomial model is $\theta = [\theta_1, \theta_2, \theta_3]$ and the parameter space, the null hypothesis set, the prior density, likelihood function and the reference density are given by:

$$\Theta = \{\theta \geq 0 \mid \theta_1 + \theta_2 + \theta_3 = 1\} \quad , \quad \Theta_H = \{\theta \in \Theta \mid \theta_3 = (1 - \sqrt{\theta_1})^2\}$$

$$p(\theta) \propto 1 \quad , \quad L(\theta \mid x) \propto \theta_1^{x_1} \theta_2^{x_2} \theta_3^{x_3} \quad , \quad r(\theta) \propto 1$$

For the Coefficient of Variation model, a test for the coefficient of variation $C = \mu\sqrt{\rho}$, of a normal variable with mean μ and precision $\rho = 1/\sigma^2$, the parameter space, the null hypothesis set, the maximum entropy prior, the reference density, and the likelihood density are given by:

$$\Theta = \{\theta = [\mu, \rho] \in \mathcal{R} \times \mathcal{R}_+\} \quad , \quad \Theta_H = \{\theta \in \Theta \mid \mu\sqrt{\rho} = c\}$$

$$p(\theta) \propto 1/\rho \quad , \quad r(\theta) \propto 1$$

$$L_x(\theta \mid x) \propto \sqrt{\rho} \, \exp\left(-\frac{n}{2}\rho(\mu - m)^2\right) \, \exp\left(-\frac{n}{2}v\rho\right)\rho^a$$

$$x = [x_1 \ldots x_n] \quad , \quad m = \frac{1}{n}\sum_{i=1}^{n} x_i \quad , \quad v = \frac{1}{n}\sum_{i=1}^{n}(x_i - m)^2 \quad , \quad a = \frac{n-1}{2}$$

Figure 1 displays the elements of a value of evidence against the hypothesis, computed for the HW (Left) and Coefficient of Variation (Right) models. The null set, Θ_H, is represented by a dashed line. The contour line of the posterior, delimiting the tangencial set, $T(\Theta_H)$, is represented by a solid line. The posterior unconstrained maximum is represented by "o" and the posterior maximum constrained to the null set is represented by "*".

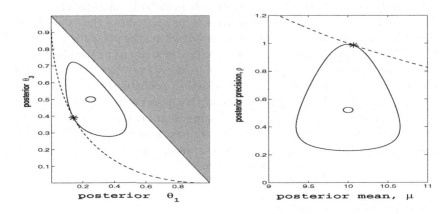

Fig. 1. FBST for Hardy-Weinberg (L) and Coefficient of Variation (R)

In order to perform the sensitivity analysis several priors have to be used. Uninformative priors are used to represent no previous observations, see [16], [21] and [31] for a detailed discussion.

For the HW model we use as uniformative priors the uniform density, that can be represented as $[0, 0, 0]$ observation counts, and also the standard maximum entropy density, that can be represented as $[-1, -1, -1]$ observation counts. Between these two uninformative priors, we also consider perturbation priors corresponding to $[-1, 0, 0]$, $[0, -1, 0]$ and $[0, 0, -1]$ observation counts. Each of these priors can be interpreted as the exclusion of a single observation of the corresponding type from the data set, $x_1, \ldots x_n$.

Finally, we consider the dual perturbation priors corresponding to $[1, 0, 0]$, $[0, 1, 0]$ and $[0, 0, 1]$ observation counts. The term dual is used meaning that instead of exclusion, these priors can be interpreted as the inclusion of a single artificial observation of the corresponding type, x_{n+1}, in the data set.

The examples in the top part of Table 1 are given by size and proportions, $[x_1, x_2, x_3] = n * [0.25, 0.5, 0.25]$, where the HW hypothesis is true.

For the Coefficient of Variation model we use as uninformative priors the uniform density, for the mean, and either the standard maximum entropy density, $p(\theta) \propto 1/\rho$, or the uniform, $p(\theta) \propto 1$, for the precision. We also consider (with uniform prior) perturbations by the inclusion in the data set of an artificial observation, x_{n+1}, at fixed quantiles of the predictive posterior, in this case, at three standard deviations below or above the mean, $x_{n+1} = m \pm 3\sigma$.

The examples in the bottom part of Table 2 are given by $cv = 0.1$, size n, and the sufficient statistics $m = 10$ and $std = 1.2$, where the hypothesis is false.

Table 1. HW and CV models, Ev(H) for several priors and sample sizes

HW model; sample $= n[1/4, 1/2, 1/4]$; H: equilibrium, true										
$p(\theta) \setminus n =$	8	16	32	64	128	$p(\theta) \setminus n =$	8	16	32	64	128
$[0,0,0]$	0.00	0.00	0.00	0.00	0.00	$[-1,-1,-1]$	0.13	0.04	0.02	0.01	0.00
$[1,0,0]$	0.05	0.03	0.02	0.01	0.00	$[-1,0,0]$	0.12	0.04	0.02	0.01	0.00
$[0,1,0]$	0.07	0.03	0.02	0.01	0.00	$[0,-1,0]$	0.09	0.04	0.02	0.01	0.00
$[0,0,1]$	0.05	0.03	0.02	0.01	0.00	$[0,0,-1]$	0.12	0.04	0.02	0.01	0.00

CV model; suff.stat: $m = 10, std = 1.2$; H: $cv = 0.1$, false										
$p(\rho) \setminus n =$	16	32	64	128	256	$x_{n+1} \setminus n =$	16	32	64	128	256
$\propto 1$	0.45	0.69	0.91	0.99	1.00	$m + 3\sigma$	0.38	0.66	0.89	0.99	1.00
$\propto 1/\rho$	0.64	0.79	0.94	0.99	1.00	$m - 3\sigma$	0.55	0.75	0.92	0.99	1.00

In order to get a feeling of the asymptotic behavior of the evidence and the inconsistency, the calculations are repeated for the same sufficient statistics but for sample sizes, n, taking values in a convenient range. In Figure 2, the maximum and minimum values of evidence against the hypothesis H, among all choices of priors used in the sensitivity analysis, are given by the interpolated dashed lines. For the HW model, Table 1 and Figure 2 top, the sample size ranged from $n = 8$ to $n = 128$. For the Coefficient of Variation model, Table 1 and Figure 2 bottom, the sample size ranged from $n = 16$ to $n = 256$. In Figure 2, the induced degree of inconsistency is given by the vertical distance between the dashed lines. The interpretation of the vertical interval between the lines in Figure 2 (solid bars) is similar to that of the usual statistical error bars. However, in contrast with the empirical power analysis developed in [28] and [22], the uncertainty represented by these bars does not have a probabilistic nature, being rather a possibilistic measure of inconsistency, defined in the partial support structure given by the FBST evidence, see [29].

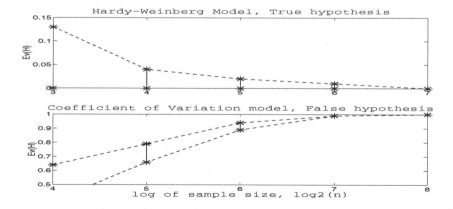

Fig. 2. Sensitivity Analysis for Ev(H)

5 Directions for Further Research and Acknowledgements

For complex models, the sensitivity analysis in the last section can be generalized using perturbations generated by the inclusion of single artificial observations created at (or the exclusion of single observations near) fixed quantiles of some convenient statistics, $t(x)$, of the predictive posterior. Perturbations generated by the exclusion of the most extreme observations, according to some convenient criteria, could also be considered. For the sensitivity analysis consistency when the model allows the data set to be summarized by some sufficient statistics in the form of L-estimators, see [4], section 8.6. The asymptotic behavior of the sensitivity analysis for several classes of models and perturbations is the subject of forthcoming articles.

Finally, perturbations to the reference density, instead of to the prior, could be considered. One advantage of this approach is that, when computing the evidence, only the integration limit, i.e. the threshold s^*, is changed, while the integrand, i.e. the posterior density, remains the same. Hence, when computing $Ev(H)$, only little additional work is required for the inconsistency analysis.

The author has benefited from the support of FAPESP, CNPq, BIOINFO, the Computer Science Department of São Paulo University, Brazil, and the Mathematical Sciences Department at SUNY-Binghamton, USA. The author is grateful to many of his colleges, most specially, Jair Minoro Abe, Wagner Borges, Joseph Kadane, Marcelo Lauretto, Fabio Nakano, Carlos Alberto de Bragança Pereira, Sergio Wechsler, and Shelemyahu Zacks. The author can be reached at *jstern@ime.usp.br* .

References

1. Abe,J.M. Avila,B.C. Prado,J.P.A. (1998). *Multi-Agents and Inconsistence.* IC-CIMA'98. 2nd International Conference on Computational Intelligence and Multimidia Applications. Traralgon, Australia.

2. Alcantara,J. Damasio,C.V. Pereira,L.M. (2002). Paraconsistent Logic Programs. JELIA-02. 8th European Conference on Logics in Artificial Intelligence. *Lecture Notes in Computer Science,* 2424, 345–356.

3. Arieli,O. Avron,A. (1996). Reasoning with Logical Bilattices. *Journal of Logic, Language and Information,* 5, 25–63.

4. Arnold,B.C. Balakrishnan,N. Nagaraja,H.N. (1992). *A First Course in Order Statistics.* NY: Wiley.

5. C.M.Barros, N.C.A.Costa, J.M.Abe (1995). Tópicos de Teoria dos Sistemas Ordenados. *Lógica e Teoria da Ciência,* 17,18,19. IEA, Univ. São Paulo.

6. N.D.Belnap (1977). A useful four-valued logic, pp 8–37 in G.Epstein, J.Dumm. *Modern uses of Multiple Valued Logics.* Dordrecht: Reidel.

7. Boothby,W. (2002). *An Introduction to Differential Manifolds and Riemannian Geometry.* Academic Press, NY.

8. N.C.A.Costa, V.S.Subrahmanian (1989). Paraconsistent Logics as a Formalism for Reasoning about Inconsistent Knowledge Bases. *Artificial Inteligence in Medicine,* 1, 167–174.

9. Costa,N.C.A. Abe,J.M. Subrahmanian,V.S. (1991). Remarks on Annotated Logic. *Zeitschrift für Mathematische Logik und Grundlagen der Mathematik*, 37, 561–570.

10. Darwiche,A.Y. Ginsberg,M.L. (1992). *A Symbolic Generalization of Probability Theory*. AAAI-92. 10th Natnl. Conf. on Artificial Intelligence. San Jose, USA.

11. Dugdale,J.S. (1996). *Entropy and its Physical Meaning*. Taylor-Francis,London.

12. Epstein,G. (1993). *Multiple-Valued Logic Design*. Inst.of Physics, Bristol.

13. M.Evans (1997). Bayesian Inference Procedures Derived via the Concept of Relative Surprise. *Communications in Statistics*, 26, 1125–1143.

14. M. Fitting (1988). Logic Programming on a Topological Bilattice. *Fundamentae Informaticae*, 11, 209–218.

15. Fitting,M. (1989). Bilattices and Theory of Truth. *J. Phil. Logic*, 18, 225–256.

16. M.H.DeGroot (1970). *Optimal Statistical Decisions*. NY: McGraw-Hill.

17. Ginsberg,M.L. (1988). Multivalued Logics. *Computat. Intelligence*, 4, 265–316.

18. Gokhale,D.V. (1999). On Joint Conditional Enptropies. *Entropy Journal*,1,21–24.

19. Good,I.J. (1983). *Good Thinking*. Univ. of Minnesota.

20. Good,I.J. (1989). Surprise indices and p-values. *J. Statistical Computation and Simulation*, 32, 90–92.

21. Kapur,J.N.(1989). *Maximum Entropy Models in Science Engineering*. Wiley, NY.

22. Lauretto,M. Pereira,C.A.B. Stern,J.M. Zacks,S. (2004). Comparing Parameters of Two Bivariate Normal Distributions Using the Invariant FBST. To appear, Brazilian Journal of Probability and Statistics.

23. Madruga,M.R. Esteves,L.G. Wechsler,S. (2001). On the Bayesianity of Pereira-Stern Tests. *Test*, 10, 291–299.

24. Madruga,M.R. Pereira,C.A.B. Stern,J.M. (2003). Bayesian Evidence Test for Precise Hypotheses. *Journal of Statistical Planning and Inference,* 117,185–198.

25. Pereira,C.A.B. Stern,J.M. (1999). Evidence and Credibility: Full Bayesian Significance Test for Precise Hypotheses. *Entropy Journal*, 1, 69–80.

26. Pereira,C.A.B. Stern,J.M. (2001). Model Selection: Full Bayesian Approach. *Environmetrics*, 12, 559–568.

27. Perny,P. Tsoukias,A. (1998). *On the Continuous Extension of a Four Valued Logic for Preference Modelling*. IPMU-98. 7th Conf. on Information Processing and Management of Uncertainty in Knowledge Based Systems. Paris, France.

28. Stern,J.M. Zacks,S. (2002). Testing the Independence of Poisson Variates under the Holgate Bivariate Distribution, The Power of a new Evidence Test. *Statistical and Probability Letters*, 60, 313–320.

29. Stern,J.M. (2003). Significance Tests, Belief Calculi, and Burden of Proof in Legal and Scientific Discourse. Laptec-2003, 4th Cong. Logic Applied to Technology. *Frontiers in Artificial Intelligence and its Applications*, 101, 139–147.

30. Zadeh,L.A. (1987). *Fuzzy Sets and Applications*. Wiley, NY.

31. Zellner,A. (1971). *Introduction to Bayesian Inference in Econometrics*. NY:Wiley.

Appendix: Bilattices

Several formalisms for reasoning under uncertainty rely on ordered and lattice structures, see [5], [6], [8], [9], [14], [15], [17], [30] and others. In this section we recall the basic bilattice structure, and give an important example. Herein, the presentations in [2] and [3], is followed.

Given two complete lattices, $\langle C, \leq_c \rangle$, and $\langle D, \leq_d \rangle$, the bilattice $B(C, D)$ has two orders, the knowledge order, $\leq_k$, and the truth order, $\leq_t$, given by:

$$B(C, D) = \langle C \times D, \leq_k, \leq_t \rangle$$
$$\langle c_1, d_1 \rangle \leq_k \langle c_2, d_2 \rangle \Leftrightarrow c_1 \leq_c c_2 \text{ and } d_1 \leq_d d_2$$
$$\langle c_1, d_1 \rangle \leq_t \langle c_2, d_2 \rangle \Leftrightarrow c_1 \leq_c c_2 \text{ and } d_2 \leq_d d_1$$

The standard interpretation is that C provides the "credibility" or "evidence in favor" of a hypothesis (or statement) H, and D provides the "doubt" or "evidence against" H. If $\langle c_1, d_1 \rangle \leq_k \langle c_2, d_2 \rangle$, then we have more information (even if inconsistent) about situation 2 than 1. Analogously, if $\langle c_1, d_1 \rangle \leq_t \langle c_2, d_2 \rangle$, then we have more reason to trust (or believe) situation 2 than 1 (even if with less information).

For each of the bilattice orders we define a join and a meet operator, based on the join and the meet operators of the single lattices orders. More precisely, $\sqcup_t$ and $\sqcap_t$, for the truth order, and $\sqcup_k$ and $\sqcap_k$, for the knowledge order, are defined by the folowing equations:

$$\langle c_1, d_1 \rangle \sqcup_t \langle c_2, d_2 \rangle = \langle c_1 \sqcup_c c_2, d_1 \sqcap_d d_2 \rangle \quad,$$
$$\langle c_1, d_1 \rangle \sqcap_t \langle c_2, d_2 \rangle = \langle c_1 \sqcap_c c_2, d_1 \sqcup_d d_2 \rangle$$
$$\langle c_1, d_1 \rangle \sqcup_k \langle c_2, d_2 \rangle = \langle c_1 \sqcup_c c_2, d_1 \sqcup_d d_2 \rangle \quad,$$
$$\langle c_1, d_1 \rangle \sqcap_k \langle c_2, d_2 \rangle = \langle c_1 \sqcap_c c_2, d_1 \sqcap_d d_2 \rangle$$

Negation type operators are not an integral part of the basic bilattice structure. Ginsberg (1988) and Fitting (1989) require of possible "negation", $\neg$ and "conflation", $-$, operators to be compatible with the bilattice orders, and to satisfy the double negation property:
Ng1: $x \leq_k y \Rightarrow \neg x \leq_k \neg y$, Ng2: $x \leq_t y \Rightarrow \neg y \leq_t \neg x$, Ng3: $\neg \neg x = x$.
Cf1: $x \leq_k y \Rightarrow -y \leq_k -x$, Cf2: $x \leq_t y \Rightarrow -x \leq_t -y$, Cf3: $- -x = x$.
Hence, negation should reverse trust, but preserve knowledge, and conflation should reverse knowledge, but preserve trust. If the double negation property is not satisfied (Ng3 or Cf3) the operators are called weak (negation or conflation).

The "unit square" bilattice, $\langle [0, 1] \times [0, 1], \leq, \leq \rangle$ has been routinely used to represent fuzzy or rough pertinence relations, logical probabilistic annotations, etc. Examples can be found in [1], [9], [12], [27], [30] and others. The lattice $\langle [0, 1], \leq \rangle$ is the standard unit interval, where the join and meet, $\sqcup$ and $\sqcap$ coincide with the max and min operators. The standard negation and conflation operators are defined by $\neg \langle c, d \rangle = \langle d, c \rangle$, $- \langle c, d \rangle = \langle 1 - c, 1 - d \rangle$.

In the unit square bilattice the "truth", "false", "inconsistency" and "indetermination" extremes are t, f, $\top$, $\bot$, whose coordinates are given in Table 3. As a simple example, let region R be the convex hull of the four vertices n, s, e and w, given in Table 3. Points kj, km, tj and tm are the knowledge and truth join and meet, over $r \in R$.

In the unit square bilattice, the degree of trust and degree of inconsistency for a point $x = \langle c, d \rangle$ are given by a convenient linear reparameterization of $[0, 1]^2$, to $[-1, +1]^2$ defined by

Table 2. Coordinates $\langle c, d \rangle$ and $\langle \text{BT}, \text{BI} \rangle$ for example A1

	f	$\perp$	$\top$	t	w	n	s	e	tm	km	kj	tj
c	0	0	1	1	1/4	1/2	1/2	3/4	1/4	1/4	3/4	3/4
d	1	0	1	0	1/2	3/4	1/4	1/2	3/4	1/4	3/4	1/4
BT	−1	0	0	1	−1/4	−1/4	1/4	1/4	−1/2	0	0	1/2
BI	0	−1	1	0	−1/4	1/4	−1/4	1/4	0	−1/2	1/2	0

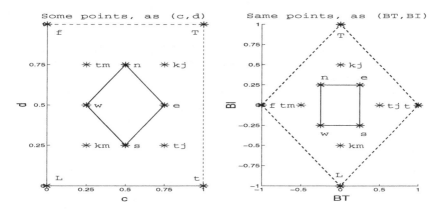

Fig. 3. Points in Table 3, using (c, d) and (BT, BI) coordinates

$$\text{BT}\left(\langle c, d \rangle\right) = c - d \ , \quad \text{BI}\left(\langle c, d \rangle\right) = c + d - 1 \ .$$

Figure 3 shows the points in Table 3 in the unit square bilattice, also using the trust-inconsistency reparameterization.

An Ontology for Quantities in Ecology

Virgínia Brilhante

Computing Science Department, Federal University of Amazonas
Av. Gen. Rodrigo O. J. Ramos, 3000, Manaus – AM, 69060-020, Brazil
virginia@dcc.ufam.edu.br

Abstract. Ecolingua is an ontology for ecological quantitative data, which has been designed through reuse of a conceptualisation of quantities and their physical dimensions provided by the EngMath family of ontologies. A hierarchy of ecological quantity classes is presented together with their definition axioms in first-order logic. An implementation-level application of the ontology is discussed, where conceptual ecological models can be synthesised from data descriptions in Ecolingua through reuse of existing model structures.

Keywords: Ontology reuse, engineering and application; ecological data; model synthesis.

1   Introduction

The Ecolingua ontology brings a contribution towards a conceptualisation of the Ecology domain by formalising properties of ecological quantitative data that typically feed simulation models. Building on the EngMath family of ontologies [6], data classes are characterised in terms of physical dimensions, which are a fundamental property of physical quantities in general. The ontology has been developed as part of a research project on model synthesis based on metadata and ontology-enabled reuse of model designs [1].

We start by briefly referring to other works on ontologies in the environmental sciences domain in Sect. 2, followed by a discussion on the reuse of the EngMath ontology in the development of Ecolingua in Sect 3. Section 4 is the core of the paper, presenting the concepts in upper-level Ecolingua. In Section 5 we give a summary description of an application of Ecolingua in the synthesis of conceptual ecological models with the desirable feature of consistency with respect to the properties of their supporting data. Finally, conclusions and considerations on future work appear in Sect. 6.

2   Environmental Ontologies

There has been little research on the intersection between ontologies and environmental sciences despite the need for a unifying conceptualisation to reconcile conflicts of meaning amongst the many fields – biology, geology, law, computing science, etc. – that draw on environmental concepts. The work by B.N. Niven

A.L.C. Bazzan and S. Labidi (Eds.): SBIA 2004, LNAI 3171, pp. 144–153, 2004.

[9, 10] proposes a formalisation of general concepts in animal and plant ecology, such as environment, niche and community. Although taxonomies have been in use in the field for a long time, this work is the earliest we are aware of where concepts are defined in the shape of what we call today a formal ontology. Other developments have been EDEN, an informal ontology of general environmental concepts designed to give support to environmental information retrieval [7], and an ontology of environmental pollutants [13], built in part through reuse of a chemical elements ontology. These more recent ontologies have a low degree of formality, lacking axiomatic definitions.

3 Quantities in Ecology and EngMath Reuse

The bulk of ecological data consists of numeric values representing measurements of attributes of entities and processes in ecological systems. The most intrinsic property of such a measurement value lies on the physical nature, or dimension, of what the value quantifies [3]. For example, a measure of weight is intrinsically different from a measure of distance because they belong to different physical dimensions, mass[1] and length respectively. The understanding of this fundamental relation between ecological measurements and physical dimensions drew our attention towards the EngMath family of ontologies, which is publicly available in the Ontolingua Server [11]. All defined properties in EngMath's conceptualisation of constant, scalar, physical quantities are applicable to ecological measurements:

1. Every ecological measurement has an intrinsic physical dimension – e.g. vegetation biomass is of the mass dimension, the height of a tree is of the length dimension;
2. The physical dimension of an ecological measurement can be a composition of other dimensions through multiplication and exponentiation to a real power – e.g. the amount of a fertiliser applied to soil every month has the composite dimension mass/time;
3. Ecological measurements can be dimensionless – e.g. number of individuals in a population; and can be non-physical – e.g. profit from a fishing harvest;
4. Comparisons and algebraic operations (including unit conversion) can be meaningfully applied to ecological measurements, provided that their dimensions are homogeneous – e.g. you could add or compare an amount of some chemical to an amount of biomass (both of the mass dimension).

Also relevant to Ecolingua is the EngMath conceptualisation of units of measure, which are also physical quantities, but established by convention as an absolute amount of something to be used as a standard reference for quantities of the same dimension. Therefore, one can identify the physical dimension of a quantity from the unit of measure in which it is expressed [8]. Being Ecolingua an ontology for description of ecological data, instantiation of its terms, as we shall

---

[1] Or force, if rigorously interpreted (see Sect. 4.4).

see in Sect. 4, requires the specification of a quantity's unit of measure. In this way, describing a data set in Ecolingua does not demand additional effort in the sense that it is of course commonplace to have the units of measure of the data on hand, whereas the data's physical dimensions are not part of the everyday vocabulary of ecologists and modellers. Lower-level Ecolingua, available in [1], includes a detailed axiomatisation of units and scales of measurement, including their dimensions, base and derived units, and the SI system (Système International d'Unités), which allows for automatic elicitation of a quantity's physical dimension from the unit or scale in which it is specified.

4   Quantity Classes

Ecolingua's class hierarchy can be seen in Fig. 1. The hierarchy comprises Ecolingua classes and external classes defined in other ontologies, namely, Physical-Quantities and Standard-Dimensions of the EngMath family of ontologies, and Okbc-Ontology and Hpkb-Upper-Level, all of which are part of the Ontolingua Server's library of ontologies. External classes are denoted Class@Ontology, a notation we borrow from the Ontolingua Server. The arcs in the hierarchy represent subclass relations, bottom up, e.g. the 'Weight of' class is a subclass of the 'Quantity' class. We distinguish two different types of subclass relations, indicated by the bold and dashed arcs in Fig. 1. Bold arcs correspond to full, formal subclass relations. Dashed arcs correspond to relations we call *referential* between Ecolingua classes and external classes, mostly of the EngMath family of ontologies, in that they do not hold beyond the conceptual level, i.e., definitions that the (external) class involves are not directly incorporated by the (Ecolingua) subclass. In the forthcoming definitions of Ecolingua classes, textual and axiomatic KIF [5] definitions of their referential classes are given as they appear in the Ontolingua Server. Ecolingua axioms defining quantity classes incorporate the physical dimension, when specified, of its referential class in EngMath through the unit of measure concept, as explained in Sect. 3, and contextualises the quantity in the ecology domain through concepts such as ecological entity, compatibility between materials and entities, etc.

Forms of Ecolingua Concept Definitions. Ecolingua axioms are represented as first-order logic, well-formed formulae of the form $Cpt \rightarrow Ctt$. That is, if Cpt holds then Ctt must hold, where Cpt is an atomic sentence representing an Ecolingua concept and Ctt is a logical sentence that constrains the interpretation of Cpt. The Cpt sentences make up Ecolingua vocabulary. One describes an ecological data set by instantiating these sentences.

4.1   Amount Quantity

Many quantities in ecology represent an amount of something contained in a thing or place, for example, carbon content in leaves, water in a lake, energy stored in an animal's body.

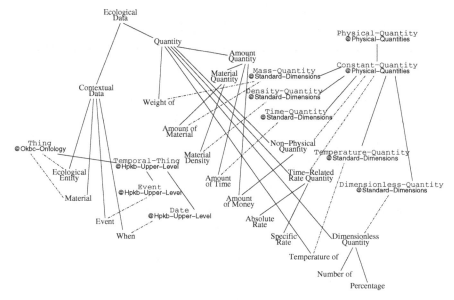

Fig. 1. Ecolingua class hierarchy

Material Quantity. Quantities that represent an amount of material things are of the mass dimension (intuitively a 'quantity of matter' [8]). For such quantities the amount of material class is defined as a referential subclass of the `Mass-Quantity@Standard-Dimensions` class defined in the Ontolingua Server as:

$(\Leftrightarrow$ `(Quantity.Dimension ?X Mass-Dimension) (Mass-Quantity ?X))`

- **Amount of Material** class – *If A identifies a measure of amount of material Mt in E specified in U then Mt is a material, E is an entity which is compatible with Mt, and U is a unit of mass:*

  amt_of_mat$(A, Mt, E, U) \rightarrow$
  material(Mt) ∧ eco_entity(E) ∧ compatible(Mt, E) ∧ mass_unit(U)

A material Mt is anything that has mass and can be contained in an ecological entity (e.g. biomass, chemicals, timber). An ecological entity E is any distinguishable thing, natural or artificial, with attributes of interest in an ecological system (e.g. vegetation, water, an animal, a population, a piece of machinery), the system itself (e.g. a forest, a lake), or its boundaries (e.g. atmosphere). Ecological quantities usually consist of measurements of attributes of such entities (e.g. carbon content of vegetation, temperature of an animal's body, birth rate of a population, volume of water in a lake). A material and an entity are compatible if it occurs in nature that the entity contains the material. For example, biomass is only thought of in relation to living entities (plants and animals), not in relation to inorganic things.

Other quantities represent measurements of amount of material in relation to space, e.g. amount of biomass in a crop acre, or of timber harvested from a hectare of forest. The dimension of such quantities is mass over some power of length. For these quantities, we define the material density class as a referential subclass of the Density-Quantity@Standard-Dimensions class defined in the Ontolingua Server as:

(⇔ (Density-Quantity ?XO) (Quantity.Dimension ?XO Density-Dimension))

- **Material Density** class – *If A identifies a measure of density of Mt in E specified in U then Mt is a material, E is an entity which is compatible with Mt, and U is equivalent to an expression Um/Ul, where Um is a unit of mass and Ul is a unit of some power of length:*

$$\text{mat\_dens}(A, Mt, E, U) \rightarrow$$
$$\text{material}(Mt) \wedge \text{eco\_entity}(E) \wedge \text{compatible}(Mt, E) \wedge$$
$$\exists\ Um, Ul\ .\ \text{eqv\_expr}(U, Um/Ul) \wedge \text{mass\_unit}(Um) \wedge \text{length}^n\text{\_unit}(Ul)$$

Amount of Time. Quantities can also represent amounts of immaterial things, time being a common example. The duration of a sampling campaign and the gestation period of females of a species are examples of ecological quantities of the amount of time class. The class is a referential subclass of the Time-Quantity@Standard-Dimensions class defined in the Ontolingua Server as:

(⇔ (Quantity.Dimension ?X Time-Dimension) (Time-Quantity ?X))

- **Amount of Time** class – *If A identifies a measure of an amount of time of Ev specified in U then Ev is an event and U is a unit of time:*

$$\text{amt\_of\_time}(A, Ev, U) \rightarrow \text{event}(Ev) \wedge \text{time\_unit}(U)$$

where an event Ev is any happening of ecological interest with a time duration (e.g. seasons, sampling campaigns, harvest events, etc.).

Non-physical Quantity. Despite the name, the 'physical quantity' concept in EngMath allows for so-called non-physical quantities. These are quantities of new or non-standard dimensions, such as the monetary dimension, which can be defined preserving all the properties of physical quantities, as already defined in the ontology (Sect. 3). The class of non-physical quantities is a referential subclass of Constant-Quantity@Physical-Quantities class defined in the Ontolingua Server as: "A Constant-Quantity is a constant value of some Physical-Quantity, like 3 meters or 55 miles per hour. ..." Ecological data often involve measurements of money concerning some economical aspect of the system-of-interest, e.g. profit given by a managed natural system.

- **Amount of Money** class – *If A identifies a measure of amount of money in E specified in U then E is an entity and U is a unit of money:*

$$\text{amt\_of\_money}(A, E, U) \rightarrow \text{eco\_entity}(E) \wedge \text{money\_unit}(U)$$

4.2   Time-Related Rate Quantity

In general, rates express a quantity in relation to another. In ecology, rates commonly refer to instantaneous measures of processes of movement or transformation of something occurring over time, for example, decay of vegetation biomass every year, consumption of food by an animal each day. Ecolingua defines a class of rate quantities of composite physical dimension including time, as a referential subclass of the `Constant-Quantity@Physical-Quantities` class in the Ontolingua Server, which is a generalisation of dimension-specific quantity classes (see Fig. 1). The absolute rate class is for measures of processes where an amount of some material is processed over time. These quantities have a composite dimension of mass, mass/length^n or money (the dimensions of amount quantities with the exception of time) over the time dimension. To the mass or mass/length^n dimensions will correspond adequate units of measure (e.g. kg, ton/ha) which we call units of material.

– **Absolute Rate** class – *If R identifies a measure of the rate of processing Mt from E_{from} to E_{to} specified in U then Mt is a material, E_{from} and E_{to} are entities which are different from each other and compatible with Mt, and U is equivalent to an expression Ua/Ut, where Ua is a unit of material and Ut is a unit of time:*

$$\text{abs\_rate}(R, Mt, E_{\text{from}}, E_{\text{to}}, U) \rightarrow$$
$$\text{material}(Mt) \wedge \text{eco\_entity}(E_{\text{from}}) \wedge \text{eco\_entity}(E_{\text{to}}) \wedge$$
$$E_{\text{from}} \neq E_{\text{to}} \wedge \text{compatible}(Mt, E_{\text{from}}) \wedge \text{compatible}(Mt, E_{\text{to}}) \wedge$$
$$\exists\, Ua, Ut\ .\ \text{eqv\_expr}(U, Ua/Ut) \wedge$$
$$(\text{mat\_unit}(Ua) \vee \text{money\_unit}(Ua)) \wedge \text{time\_unit}(Ut)$$

Sometimes, processes are measured in relation to an entity involved in the process. We call these measures specific rates. For example, a measure given in, say, g/g/day is a specific rate meaning how much food in grams per gram of the animal's weight is consumed per day.

– **Specific Rate** class – *If R identifies a measure of a specific rate, related to R_{abs}, of processing Mt specified in U then: R_{abs} measures the absolute rate of processing Mt from E_{from} to E_{to} specified in U_{abs}, which is an expression equivalent to Ua/Ut where Ua is a unit of measure of material; and U is equivalent to an expression $Ub/Uc/Ut$ where both Ub and Uc are units of measure of material and are of the same dimension D:*

$$\text{spf\_rate}(R, R_{\text{abs}}, Mt, U) \rightarrow \exists\, E_{\text{from}}, E_{\text{to}}, U_{\text{abs}}, Ua, Ut\ .$$
$$\text{abs\_rate}(R_{\text{abs}}, Mt, E_{\text{from}}, E_{\text{to}}, U_{\text{abs}}) \wedge \text{eqv\_expr}(U_{\text{abs}}, Ua/Ut) \wedge \text{mat\_unit}(Ua) \wedge$$
$$\exists\, Ub, Uc, D\ .\ \text{eqv\_expr}(U, Ub/Uc/Ut) \wedge \text{mat\_unit}(Ub) \wedge \text{mat\_unit}(Uc) \wedge$$
$$\text{unit\_dimension}(Ub, D) \wedge \text{unit\_dimension}(Uc, D)$$

4.3   Temperature Quantity

Another fundamental physical dimension is *temperature*, which has measurement scales rather than units [8]. Temperature in a green house or of water in a pond, are two examples of temperature quantities in ecological data sets. The referential superclass of the class below is Temperature-Quantity@Standard-Dimensions defined in the Ontolingua Server as:

> ($\Leftrightarrow$ (Temperature-Quantity ?X0)
> (Quantity.Dimension ?X0 Thermodynamic-Temperature-Dimension))

– **Temperature of** class – *If T identifies a measure of the temperature of E specified in S then E is an entity and S is a scale of temperature:*

$$\text{temperature\_of}(T, E, S) \rightarrow \text{eco\_entity}(E) \wedge \text{temperature\_scale}(S)$$

4.4   Weight Quantity

Strictly speaking weight is a force, a composite physical dimension of the form mass × length × time^{-2}. But in ecology, as in many other contexts, people colloquially refer to 'weight' meaning a quantity of mass. For example, the weight of an animal, the weight of a fishing harvest. It is in this everyday sense of weight that we define a class of weight quantities. It has Mass-Quantity@Standard-Dimensions as referential superclass defined in the Ontolingua Server.

– **Weight of** class – *If W identifies a measure of the weight of E specified in U then E is an entity and U is a unit of mass:*

$$\text{weight\_of}(W, E, U) \rightarrow \text{eco\_entity}(E) \wedge \text{mass\_unit}(U)$$

Note that for quantities of both this class and the Amount of Material class the specified unit must be a unit of mass. But the intuition of a measure of weight does not bear a containment relationship between a material and an entity like the intuition of an amount of material does.

4.5   Dimensionless Quantity

Another paradoxically named concept in the EngMath ontology is that of dimensionless quantities. They do have a physical dimension but it is the identity dimension. Real numbers are an example. The class of dimensionless quantities has a referential superclass of the same name, Dimensionless-Quantity@Physical-Quantities, defined in the Ontolingua Server as:

> ($\Leftrightarrow$ (Dimensionless-Quantity ?X)
> (And (Constant-Quantity ?X)
> (= (Quantity.Dimension ?X) Identity-Dimension)))

This concept applies to quantities in ecology that represent counts of things, such as number of individuals in a population or age group.

– **Number of** class – *If N measures the number of E specified in U then E is an entity and N is a dimensionless quantity specified in U:*

$$\text{number\_of}(N, E, U) \rightarrow \text{eco\_entity}(E) \wedge \text{dimensionless\_qtty}(N, U)$$

Percentages can also be defined as dimensionless quantities. Food assimilation efficiency of a population, mortality and birth rates are examples of ecological quantities expressed as percentages.

– **Percentage** class – *If P is a percentage that quantifies an attribute of E specified in U then E is an entity and P is a dimensionless quantity specified in U:*

$$\text{percentage}(P, E, U) \rightarrow \text{eco\_entity}(E) \wedge \text{dimensionless\_qtty}(P, U)$$

5   A Practical Application of Ecolingua

In ecological modelling, as in other domains, using data derived from observation to inform model design adds credibility to model simulation results. Also, a common methodological approach that facilitates understanding of complex systems is to firstly design a conceptual (or qualitative) model which is later used as a framework for specification of a quantitative model. However, data sets given to support modelling of ecological systems contain mainly quantitative data which, in its low representational level, do not directly connect to high-level model conceptualisation. In this context, an ontology of properties of domain data can play the role of a conceptual vocabulary for representation of data sets, by way of which the data's level of abstraction is raised to facilitate connections with conceptual models. Ecolingua was initially built to support an application of synthesis of conceptual system dynamics models [4] stemming from data described in the ontology, where existing models are reused to guide the synthesis process. The application is depicted in Fig. 2 and is briefly discussed in the sequel; a complete description including an evaluation of the synthesis system on the run time efficiency criterion and examples of syntheses of actual and fictitious models can be found in [1].

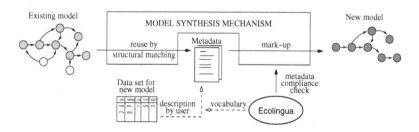

Fig. 2. Application of Ecolingua in model synthesis through reuse

Figure 2 shows the synthesis process starting with a given modelling data set to support the design of a conceptual ecological model. Ecolingua vocabulary is then manually employed to describe the data set yielding metadata (e.g. amt_of_mat(t, timber, tree, kg) is an instance of metadata). The synthesis mechanism tries and matches the structure (or topology) of the existing model with the metadata set, whose content marks up the structure to give a new model that is consistent with the given metadata. This is done by solving constraint rules that represent modelling knowledge in the mechanism. Matching the existing model with metadata means to reduce its structure to the concepts in Ecolingua. It all comes down to how similar the two data sets – the new model's described in Ecolingua, and the data set that once backed up the existing model – are with respect to ontological properties. The more properties they share, the more of the existing model's structure will be successfully matched with the new model's metadata.

5.1   Automatically Checking for Ecolingua-Compliant Metadata

Besides providing a vocabulary for description of ecological data by users, Ecolingua is employed by the synthesis system to check compliance of the manually specified metadata with the underlying ontology axioms, ensuring that only compliant metadata are carried forward into the model synthesis process. Since in the synthesis system the $Cpt \rightarrow Ctt$ axioms are only reasoned upon when a metadata term C_{term} with logical value true unifies with Cpt, the use of the axiom can be reduced to solving Ctt, as its logical value alone will correspond to the logical value of the whole expression. Therefore, each Ecolingua axiom can be represented in the synthesis systems as a clause of the form c_ctt(Cpt, Ctt). The following Ecolingua compliance checking mechanism is thus defined.

Let C_{term} be an instance of an Ecolingua concept Cpt. As defined by the Ecolingua axioms formula, C_{term} being true and unified with Cpt implies that the consequent constraint Ctt must be true. If however, the concept in question is one that lacks an axiomatic definition, it suffices to verify that C_{term} unifies with an Ecolingua concept:

$$\text{onto\_check}(C_{term}) \leftarrow \text{c\_ctt}(C_{term},\ Ctt) \wedge Ctt$$
$$\text{onto\_check}(C_{term}) \leftarrow \neg\ \text{c\_ctt}(C_{term},\ \_Ctt) \wedge \text{eco\_concept}(C_{term})$$

6   Concluding Remarks

We have defined classes of quantitative data in ecology, using the well-known formalism of first-order logic. The definitions draw on the EngMath ontology to characterise quantity classes with respect to their physical dimension, which can be captured through the unit of measure in which instances of the quantity classes are expressed in. The ontology has been employed to enable a technique of synthesis of conceptual ecological models from metadata and reuse of existing models. The synthesis mechanism that implements the technique involves proofs over the ontology axioms written in Prolog in order to validate metadata that is given to substantiate the models. This is an application where an ontology is not used at a conceptual level only, as we commonly see, but at a practical, implementational level, adding value to a knowledge reuse technique. As the ontology is founded on the universal concept of physical dimensions, its range of application can be widened. However, while the definitions presented here have been validated by an ecological modelling expert at the Institute of

Ecology and Resource Management, University of Edinburgh, Ecolingua's concepts and axioms are not yet fully developed. Quantities of space, energy and frequency dimensions, for example, as well as precise definitions, with axioms where possible, of contextual ecological concepts such as ecological entity, event, the compatibility relation between entities and materials, are not covered and will be added as the ontology evolves. We would also like to specify Ecolingua using state-of-the-art ontology languages, such as DAML+OIL [2] or OWL [12], and make it publicly available so as to allow its cooperative development and diverse applications over the World Wide Web.

Acknowledgements

The author wishes to thank FAPEAM (Fundação de Amparo a Pesquisa do Estado do Amazonas) for its partial sponsorship through the research project Metadata, Ontologies and Sustainability Indicators integrated to Environmental Modelling.

References

1. Brilhante, V.: Ontology and Reuse in Model Synthesis. PhD thesis, School of Informatics, University of Edinburgh (2003)
2. DARPA Agent Markup Language. http://www.daml.org/2001/03/, Defense Advanced Research Projects Agency (2001) (last accessed on 10 Mar 2004)
3. Ellis, B.: Basic Concepts of Measurement (1966) Cambridge University Press, London
4. Ford, A.: Modeling the Environment: an Introduction to System Dynamics Modeling of Environmental Systems (1999) Island Press
5. Genesereth, M., Fikes, R.: Knowledge Interchange Format, Version 3.0, Reference Manual, Logic-92-1 (1992) Logic Group, Computer Science Department, Stanford University, Stanford, California
6. Gruber, T., Olsen, G.: An Ontology for Engineering Mathematics. In Proceedings of the Fourth International Conference on Principles of Knowledge Representation and Reasoning (1994) Bonn, Germany, Morgan Kaufmann
7. Kashyap, V.: Design and Creation of Ontologies for Environmental Information Retrieval. In Proceedings of the Twelfth International Conference on Knowledge Acquisition, Modeling and Management (1999) Banff, Canada
8. Massey, B.: Measures in Science and Engineering: their Expression, Relation and Interpretation (1986) Ellis Horwood Limited
9. Niven, B.: Formalization of the Basic Concepts of Animal Ecology. Erkenntnis **17** (1982) 307–320
10. Niven, B.: Formalization of Some Concepts of Plant Ecology. Coenoses **7(2)** (1992) 103–113
11. Ontolingua Server. http://ontolingua.stanford.edu, Knowledge Systems Laboratory, Department of Computer Science, Stanford University (2002) (last accessed on 10 Mar 2004)
12. Ontology Web Language. http://www.w3.org/2001/sw/WebOnt, WebOnt Working Group, W3C (2004) (last accessed on 10 Mar 2004)
13. Pinto, H.: Towards Ontology Reuse. Papers from the AAAI-99 Workshop on Ontology Management, WS-99-13, (1999) 67–73. Orlando, Florida, AAAI Press

Using Color to Help
in the Interactive Concept Formation

Vasco Furtado and Alexandre Cavalcante

University of Fortaleza – UNIFOR, Av. Washington Soares 1321, Fortaleza – CE, Brazil
vasco@unifor.br, alex@sspds.ce.gov.br

Abstract. This article describes a technique that aims at qualifying a concept hierarchy with colors, in such a way that it can be feasible to promote the interactivity between the user and an incremental probabilistic concept formation algorithm. The main idea behind this technique is to use colors to map the concept properties being generated, to combine them, and to provide a resulting color that will represent a specific concept. The intention is to assign similar colors to similar concepts, thereby making it possible for the user to interact with the algorithm and to intervene in the concept formation process by identifying which approximate concepts are being separately formed. An operator for interactive merge has been used to allow the user to combine concepts he/she considers similar. Preliminary evaluation on concepts generated after interaction has demonstrated improved accuracy.

1 Introduction

Incremental concept formation algorithms accomplish the concept hierarchy construction process from a set of observations – usually an attribute/value paired list – that characterizes an observed entity. By using these algorithms, learning occurs gradually over a period of time.

Different from non-incremental learning (where all observations are presented at the same time), incremental systems are capable of changing the hierarchical structure constructed as new observations become available for processing. These systems, besides closely representing the manner in which humans learn, they present the disadvantage that the quality of the generated concepts depends on the presentation order of the observations.

This work proposes a strategy to help in the identification of bad concept formation, making it possible to initiate an interaction process. The resource that makes this interaction possible is a color-based data visualization technique. The idea is to help users recognize similarities or differences in the conceptual hierarchies being formed. The basic assumption of this strategy is to match up human strengths with those of computers. In particular, by using the human visual perceptive capacity in identifying color patterns, it seeks to aid in the identification of poor concept formation.

The proposed solution consists of mapping colors to concept properties and then mixing them to obtain a concept color. The probability of an entity, represented by a concept, having a particular property assumes a fundamental role in the mixing process mentioned above, thereby directly influencing the final color of the concept. At the end of the process, each concept of the hierarchy will be qualified by a color. An

A.L.C. Bazzan and S. Labidi (Eds.): SBIA 2004, LNAI 3171, pp. 154–163, 2004.
© Springer-Verlag Berlin Heidelberg 2004

operator for the interactive merge has been defined to allow the user to combine concepts he/she considers similar. Preliminary evaluations on generated concepts, after such an interaction, have demonstrated that the conceptual hierarchy accuracy has improved considerably.

2 Incremental Probabilistic Concept Formation

Incremental probabilistic concept formation systems accomplish a process of concept hierarchy formation that generalizes observations contained in the node in terms of the conditional probability of their characteristics.

The task that these systems accomplish does not require a "teacher" to pre-classify objects, but such systems use an evaluation function to discover classes with "good" conceptual descriptions. Generally, the most common criterion to qualify how good is a concept is its capacity to make inferences about unknown properties of new entities.

Most of the recent work on this topic is built on the work of Fisher (1987) and the COBWEB algorithm, which forms probabilistic concepts (CP) defined in the following manner. Let: $A=\{a_1,a_2,a_3,.....a_n\}$ be the set of all attributes and $v(a_n) = \{v_{n1},v_{n2},v_{n3},......v_{nm}\}$ be the set of all values of an attribute $a_n \in A$, that describes a concept CP where $CP = \{(a_n,\{(v_{nm},P(v(a_n)=v_{nm}|C))\})|v_{nm} \in v(a_n),0 \langle m \ \langle \ Card(v(a_n))$ $,0 \langle n \langle \ Card(A)\}$. $P(v(a_n)=v_{nm}|C)$ indicates the probability of an entity possessing an attribute a_n with the value v_{nm} given that this entity is a member of class C (extent of CP). Then, consider the pair $p_{nm}=(a_n,v_{nm})$ as being a property of the concept CP.

The incremental character of processing observations causes the presentational order of these observations to influence the concept formation process. Consider the set of observations in the domain of animals in Table 1:

Table 1. Set of observations.

	Body Cover	Heart	Body Temp.	Fertiliz	Olfact	
1	Hair	4	Reg.	Int.	Good	Mammal1
2	Scales	2	Unreg.	Ext.	Hybrid	Fish2
3	Hair	4	Reg.	Int.	Medium	Mammal2
4	Feather	4	Reg.	Ext.	Sensitive	Bird1
5	Scales	2	Unreg.	Ext.	None	Fish1

When processing the observations with COBWEB in the order of 1,3,4,5, and 2, it may be noticed that the concept hierarchy formed does not reflect an ideal hierarchy for the domain since the two mammals are not in the same class, as it can be seen in Figure 1.

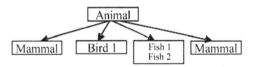

Fig. 1. Hierarchical structure generated in a bad order by Cobweb.

3 Modeling Colors

In 1931, the CIE *(Comission Internationale de L'Eclairage)* defined its first model of colors. An evolution of this first CIE color model led the CIE to define two other models: the CIELuv and the CIELab, which represented that the Euclidean distance between two coordinates represents two colors, and the same distance between two coordinates represents other two colors, agreeing on the same difference in visual perception (Wyszecki, 1982).

The CIELab standard began to influence new ways for the measurement of visual differences between colors, such as the CIELab94 and the CMC (Sharma & Trussell, 1997). For this work, similarity between colors is the first key point for the solution, and it will be used extensively in the color mixture algorithm.

On the other hand, the color models may also be used to define colors according to their properties. These properties are luminosity (L), hue (H), which is the color that an object is perceived (green, blue, etc.) and saturation (S) or chrome (C), indicating the depth in which the color is either vivid or diluted (Fortner & Meyer, 1997). These color spaces are denominated HLS or HLC, and they will be further applied in this work to map colors to properties.

4 Mixing Color in Different Proportions

We defined a color-mixing algorithm following the assumption that the resulting mixture of two colors must be perceptually similar to the color being mixed that carries the higher weight in the mixing process.

The proposed algorithm considers the CIELab94 metric as a measure of similarity/dissimilarity between colors. We define the function $CIELab94(R_1, R_2)$, which measures the extent to which the color $R1$ and the color $R2$ resemble each other in accordance with the CIELab94 model. The range of results points out that the smaller the calculated result of the CIELab94 metric is, the greater the similarity between the colors involved will be.

4.1 Mixing Two Colors

When mixing two colors, consider that the set CLAB = $\{(L,a,b)^1 \mid L, a \text{ and } b$ are coordinates of the CIELab model. The colors R_1 and $R_2 \in$ CLAB, and the weights p_1 and p_2, associated with the colors R_1 and R_2, are such that, $p_1+p_2=1$. The color R_r, the mixture result of R_1 and R_2, is then calculated in the following manner:

```
function Mix2Colors(R1,R2,p2)
1.Let RG be the color corresponding to the medium
point in the line between R1 and R2
2. Let SimRG be the similarity between RG and R1
3. Let SimRR be  p2  x similarity between R1 and R2
```

---

[1] L stands for luminosity, a stands for the red/green aspect of the color, and b stands for the yellow/blue aspect.

```
4. If SimRG equals SimRR then Return RG
5. If SimRG is greater than SIMRR then
   Let R₂ be RG
   else Let R₁ be RG
6. Go to 1
```

It should be underscored that a color is a point in a three dimensional space. That is why it is necessary to compute the medium point between two colors. The function *Mix2colors* searches for the color represented by this medium point, so that its similarity with the first color that participated in the mixture is equal to the weight p_2 multiplied by the similarity between the colors that are being mixed.

4.2 Mixing n Colors

To mix n colors, first, it is necessary to mix two colors, and the result obtained is mixed with the third color. This procedure is extended for n colors. The weight by which each color influences the result of the mixture is proportional to the order in which the color participates in the mixing process. For instance, the first two colors, when mixed, participate with 0.5 each. The third color, participates with 0.33, since the first two will already have influenced 0.66 of the final color. Generalizing, let i be the order that a color is considered in the process of mixing n colors, the influence of each color in the process is given by $1/i^2$. Different order of color mixture can produce

The function to mix n colors has the following steps: let RT={$R_1,R_2,R_3,....R_n$} be the set of colors to be mixed, where each color $R_n \in$ CLAB, and the mixture of the colors of the set RT will be accomplished by the following function:

```
function Mixncolor (RT)
    1. Let M be R₁
    2. For i=2 to n
       Let M be  Mix2colors (M,Ri,(1/i))
 return  M
```

The Mixncolor function accepts, as a parameter, a set of colors to be mixed (set RT), and returns a single color belonging to the set CIELab. It calls the Mix2colors function with three parameters: (i) the color R_i of the set RT, (ii) the result of the mixture (M) obtained from the two previous colors, and (iii) a weight $1/i$ for a color R_i.

5 Aiding the Identification of Poor Concept Hierarchy Formations Using Colors

The strategy developed to aid in the identification of poor concept hierarchy formation is done in two phases. The first one maps the initial colors to concept properties and the second phase mixes these colors, concluding with the resulting color of the concept.

---

[2] Different order of color mixture can produce different results, but this won't be a problem, since the same process will be applied to every concept.

5.1 Initial Color Mapping of Probabilistic Concept Properties

The initial color mapping attributes, to each property $p_{nm}=(a_n,v_{nm})$ of a probabilistic concept, a color $R_{nm} \in CLAB$, so that, at the end of this procedure, a set denominated RM will be obtained, made up of all these mapped colors. To carry out this task, we have as parameters: (i) the set of properties $CR = \{(a_n,v_{nm}),| \ v_{nm} \in v(a_n)\}$, formed by all of the properties of CP, (ii) the value for minimum luminosity, L_{ini}, and, (iii) the value for maximum luminosity, L_{fim}. In this work, we used values between 50 and 98 for these latter parameters in order not to generate excessively dark color patterns.

The procedure initiates going through all the attributes a_n of set A, which will receive a coordinate H of the color that is being mapped. Knowing that, coordinate H of the HLC model varies from 0° to 360°, we have for the set of observations in table 1, the following values for H: 72, 144, 216, and 288.

The second step seeks to attribute the coordinates L and C, for each value of attribute a_n. First, for each value $v(a_n)$ of a_n a value of L is calculated. The third column in table 2 shows the coordinates L calculated for the set of observations in table 1. Finally, coordinate C is calculated so that its value is the biggest possible, whose transformation of all the values of H given a same L, returns only valid RGB values[3] (R>=0 and <=255,G>=0 and <=255,B >=0 and <= 255).

Table 2 describes the mapping of H, L and C for the two first attributes of the example in Table 1.

Table 2. Example of HLC color mapping from Table 1.

Atr/Valor	H	L	C	Color
n,m=1,1	0°	50	34	
n,m=1,2	0°	74	39	
n,m=1,3	0°	98	2	
n,m=2,1	72°	50	34	
n,m=2,2	72°	98	2	

5.2 Processing Mapped Colors

In order to complete the color qualification process of the hierarchical structure, we will consider the following parameters: (i) the RM set of the initial mapping, (ii) the conditional probabilities of the properties $P(a=v|C)$. The conditional probability of each property will function as the weight that the function *Mix2Colors* needs. As a final product, we will have set RT (input of the *Mixncolor* function). The algorithm to generate RT and its explanation follows:

```
function GenerateColorforAttr
   1. for each attribute a of a probabilistic concept
      Let Rr be the color of the first value v1 of a
      Let Pacum be  P(a= v1|C)
```

---

[3] That heuristic aims at having RGB valid for all lines for the H, L and C being chosen.

```
for I=2 to number of values of a
    Let P₂ be P(a= vᵢ|C)
    Let Rᵣ be Mix2Colors (Rᵣ,Rᵢ, P₂/(Pₐcᵤₘ+P₂))
    Let Pₐcᵤₘ beP₂ + Pₐcᵤₘ
    Insert Rᵣ into the set RT
Return RT
```

To calculate the color R_r of an attribute, we mix, two by two, the colors of each value of this attribute. For such, the variable R_r is initialized with the color of the first value v_1 of attribute a. P_{acum} is set up with the conditional probability of the attribute a, which is equal to v_1 given class C. After this, the procedure enters in a loop that treats each color of the values of the attributes a, using the *Mix2colors* function. It uses the partial result R_r and the color R_i that is being processed. The parameter $P_2/(P_{acum}+P_2)$ normalizes the accumulated weight of the values so far considered and the weight of the current property P_2, so that $P_{acum} + P_2 = 1$, as the *Mix2colors* function requires.

Finally, the generated set *RT* feeds the *Mixncolor* function resulting in the final color of the concept. This process is repeated for each concept of the hierarchy.

Figure 2 shows the colored concept hierarchy for the example described in section 2. Note that the colors aid the user in perceiving the need to restructure the hierarchy since the two mammals, which did not form a single class, have a similar resulting color in the eyes of the user:

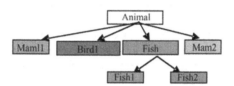

Fig. 2. Hierarchical structure qualified with colors.

6   Evaluation of the Color Heuristic

We have defined an evaluation method, which seeks to prove that two things will take place:

1. Highly similar concepts will result in highly similar colors;
2. Concepts of low similarity will result in colors also of low similarity.

It is important to state that the proposed method will qualify each pair of equal concepts with equal colors. However, it cannot guarantee that similar concepts will receive similar colors, but in most cases, this will be true[4]. The evaluation process will use two basic functions. One function aims to measure the similarity between two probabilistic concepts and the other one aims to measure the similarity between two colors that represent these same concepts. The first was defined in (Talavera & Béjar,

---

[4] The proposed method doesn't guarantee this because the color space is not linear and sometimes little variation produces big color perception variation.

1998), which considers two probabilistic concepts as similar if their probabilistic distributions[5] are highly intersecting. The second is the $CIELab94(C_1,C_2)$ function already seen in this article.

The basic idea is to generate a concept hierarchy with associated colors and to evaluate the similarity between the concepts, two by two, in terms of similarity of content and of color. The ranges of similarities of concepts were defined as ten by ten, and for each band the average of the similarity values among the colors of the compared concepts was calculated. Three databases were considered in the tests. The first two databases are composed of animal observations, with 105 and 305 observations, and the third is the Mushrooms base (UCI, 2003), composed of 1000 observations.

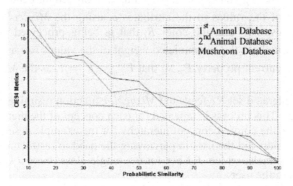

Fig. 3. Evolution of probabilistic similarity versus similarity among colors.

Figure 3 shows the analysis defined in the previous paragraphs for the three bases considered. Note that for all bases there is a decrease of metric CIE94 as the measure of probabilistic similarity among them increases. This evidence reveals that the heuristic strategy we have defined for the concept qualification with colors reaches its main goal that is to generate similar colors for similar concepts in the greatest number of cases possible.

7 Interacting with the Concept Formation Process

The main goal of the strategy developed to qualify a hierarchical structure with colors is to make interaction between the structure and the user feasible. Thus, it is possible to improve the quality of the concept hierarchy easily because instead of accessing the probabilistic values of each concept in order to compare them one by one, the user can use his/her visual ability to have a global view of the conceptual structure and to identify similarities. The interaction is simple and intuitive because the user only has to identify two similar colors, comparing the probabilistic distribution of the concepts, and proceeds with the merge of the two colored concepts, if he/she considers interesting. To do that, we define an operator called *I-merge* similar to COBWEB's original merge operator. Unlike COBWEB's merge that only combines concepts in the same

---

[5] A probabilistic distribution of a concept is the set of its properties associated to its conditional probabilities.

hierarchical level, with I-merge it is possible to merge concepts, which are in different levels of the hierarchy. The algorithm below explains the steps of *I-merge*:

```
function  I-Merge (NodeOrigin, NodeTarget)
   Subtract probabilities of nodes in the path from the
      NodeOrigin to root
   Merge NodeOrigin and NodeTarget (as COBWEB)
   Add probabilities of nodes in the path from the
      merged node to root
```

The original node counters will be used to subtract the counters from the hierarchical nodes, starting at the parent node of the original node until the root node is reached. Once that is accomplished, a merge node, resultant of the juxtaposing of the original and destination nodes, is created, and it will be hierarchically superior to the destination node, accumulating the counters of the two clustered nodes. Finally, the node counters will be updated beginning with the parent node of this node cluster, until the root node is reached.

8 Accuracy Evaluation

To evaluate whether the method proposed here has improved the accuracy of the probabilistic concept formation, an animal database with 105 observations was used. This set of observations was divided into 80 training observations and 25 test observations. The accuracy test consists in modifying a test observation by ignoring an attribute and classifying this observation in a previously built concept hierarchy. From the concept found, the algorithm must suggest a value for the attribute based on the attribute value with higher predictability. This process is performed for each attribute of each test observation. The higher the number of correct suggestions, the better the concept hierarchy is, in terms of prediction.

The procedure begins with the application of COBWEB and the visualization of the hierarchical structure formed by means of a tool that we developed to visualize colored concept hierarchies called *SmartTree*. The initial shape of the hierarchical structure is shown in figure 4 where each colored square represents a concept.

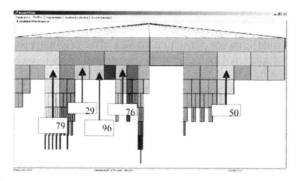

Fig. 4. Conceptual structure for ANIMALS database.

For that initial structure, the inference test is carried out using the test set of 25 observations, with 47% of errors observed. The performance of the user begins at this moment. He/She observes that node 29 has a color similar to node 50. The user then asks *SmartTree* about the probabilistic similarity between them to finally decide to merge them. In this example, 3 mergers were carried out, linking the following nodes: 29 to 50, 76 to 96, and the result of the latter to node 79. The application of the inference tests on the structure, after each merge, indicates the following evolution in the accuracy of the hierarchical structure:

- After the 1st merge: 43% of errors;
- After the 2nd merge: 38% of errors;
- After the 3rd merge: 32% of errors;

Figure 5 shows the format of the resulting tree. Besides a substantial increase in terms of accuracy, it may be verified that the resultant tree presents more uniformity with more clustered concepts.

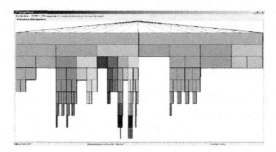

Fig. 5. Resultant tree after the interactive merge process.

A second test was done with the Mushrooms database composed of 1000 observations. We use 900 training observations and 100 for testing. The initial accuracy indicated 28.2% of errors. After the first *I-merge,* that rate decreased to 25.9% and after a second *I-merge,* that rate still reduced to 25.2%.

9 Related Work

Proposals to solve the order problem are based on algorithmic alternatives implemented in the original concept formation model. The original proposal of Fisher (1987) has already considered two operators (*merge* and *split*) in an attempt to minimize the problem. Along the same lines, ARACHNE (McKusick & Langley, 1991) included two others in an attempt to adjust the hierarchy generated. The problem with these alternatives is that restructuring the tree is only done at the local partition level. Further, to reduce problems in the order of time complexity, operators only act upon the two best nodes of the partition.

Fisher et al. (1992) showed that a database that contains consecutive dissimilar observations, based on Euclidean distance, tend to form a good hierarchy. Biswas *et al.* (1994) adapted that study in the ITERATE algorithm. Later, Fisher (1996) suggested minimizing the effects of the order through an interactive optimization process running in the background.

Another line of study is based on the mingling of non-incremental techniques with those of the incremental approach. This work is exemplified in (Atlintas 1995), where

instances already added to the hierarchy are reprocessed together with the new observation until a measure of structural stability is attained. Upon concluding this phase,
the process continues incrementally following the models already commented on.

10 Conclusion

We have defined a heuristic method to give colors to probabilistic concepts to allow a
user to interact with the conceptual structure. Moreover, we have defined a way to
user interaction via the I-merge operator, and we showed that improvements on the
accuracy of concepts could be easily obtained as a result of this interaction.

This work is innovative and multidisciplinary, since it combines resources of Graphics Computation – in this case, color technology – with concept formation from
Artificial Intelligence. It has demonstrated that topics related to the concept formation
process, as a problem of dependence on observational presentation order, can be dealt
with this focus.

Other alternatives of the use of this approach are being investigated for combining
concepts, which are produced via distributed data mining in grid computing architectures. Improvements on SmartTree for elaborating different strategies for concept
visualization are also in development.

References

1. Altintas, I., N.:Incremental Conceptual Clustering without Order Dependency. Master's
   Degree Thesis, Middle East Technical University (1995)
2. Biswas, G., Weiberg, J., & Li, C.:ITERATE: A conceptual clustering method for knowledge discovery in databases. In Innovative Applications of Artificial Intelligence in the Oil
   and Gas Industry, Editions Technip (1994)
3. Fisher, D. H.: Knowledge Acquisition via Incremental Conceptual Clustering. Machine
   Learning, 2 (1987) 139-172
4. Fisher, D., Xu, L., & Zard, N.:Order effects in clustering. Proceedings of the Ninth International Conference on Machine Learning. Aberdeen, UK: Morgan Kaufmann (1992) 163-
   168
5. Fisher, D.:Iterative optimization and simplification of hierarchical clusterings. Journal of
   Artificial Intelligence and Research, 4 (1996) 147-179
6. Fortner, B., Meyer, T. E.: Number by Colors: A Guide to Using Color to Understand
   Technical Data. Springer, ISBN 0-387-94685-3 (1997)
7. McKusick, K., & Langley, P.:Constraints on Tree Structure in Concept Formation, Proceedings of the 12th International Joint Conference on Artificial Intelligence, (pp. 810-
   816), Sydney, Australia (1991)
8. Sharma, G., & Trussell, H. J.:Digital Color Imaging, IEEE Transactions on Image Processing, Vol.6, No.7 (1997)
9. Talavera, L., Béjar, J.:Efficient and Comprehensible Hierarchical Clusterings in Proceedings of the First Catalan Conference on Artificial Intelligence, CCIA98. Tarragona, Spain,
   ACIA Bulletin, no 14-15, (1998) 273-281
10. UCI. In http://www.ics.uci.edu /~mlearn/MLSummary.html/01/03/ (2003)
11. Wyszecki G., and Stiles, W. S.: Color Science: Concepts and Methods Quantitative Data
    and Fornulae, 2nd Ed. New York, Wiley (1982)

Propositional Reasoning
for an Embodied Cognitive Model

Jerusa Marchi and Guilherme Bittencourt

Departamento de Automação e Sistemas
Universidade Federal de Santa Catarina
88040-900 - Florianópolis - SC - Brazil
{jerusa,gb}@das.ufsc.br

Abstract. In this paper we describe the learning and reasoning mechanisms of
a cognitive model based on the systemic approach and on the autopoiesis theory. These mechanisms assume perception and action capabilities that can be
captured through propositional symbols and uses logic for representing environment knowledge. The logical theories are represented by their conjunctive and
disjunctive normal forms. These representations are enriched to contain annotations that explicitly store the relationship among the literals and (dual) clauses
in both forms. Based on this representation, algorithms are presented that learn a
theory from the agent's experiences in the environment and that are able to determine the robustness degree of the theories given an assignment representing the
environment state.

Keywords: cognitive modeling, automated reasoning, knowledge representation.

1 Introduction

In recent years the interest in logical models applied to practical problems such as planning [1] and robotics [21] has been increasing. Although the limitations of the *sense-
model-plan-act* have been greatly overcome, the gap between the practical *had hoc*
path to "behavior-based artificial creatures situated in the world" [6] and the logical
approach is yet to be filled. A promising way to build such a unified approach is the
autopoiesis and enaction theory of Humberto Maturana and Francisco Varela [15] that
connect cognition and action stating that "all knowing is doing and all doing is knowing". A cognitive autopoietic system is a system whose organization defines a domain
of interactions in which it can act with relevance to the maintenance of itself, and the
process of cognition is the actual acting or behaving in this domain.

In this paper we define the learning and reasoning mechanisms of a generic model
for a cognitive agent that is based on the *systemic* approach [16] and on the cognitive
autopoiesis theory [25]. These mechanisms belong to the cognitive level of a three level
architecture presented by Bittencourt in [2].

2 Framework

In the proposed model, the *cognitive agent* is immersed in an unknown environment,
its *domain* according to the autopoiesis theory nomenclature. The agent interaction

A.L.C. Bazzan and S. Labidi (Eds.): SBIA 2004, LNAI 3171, pp. 164–173, 2004.

with this environment is only possible through a set of *primitive* propositional symbols. Therefore, the *states of the world*, from the agent point of view, are defined as the possible truth assignments to this set of propositional symbols. We also suppose that, as time goes by, the environment drifts along the possible states (i.e., assignments) through flips of the primitive propositional symbols truth values. The primitive propositional symbols can be of three kinds: *controllable, uncontrollable* and *emotional*. Roughly, uncontrollable symbols correspond to *perceptions* and controllable ones to *actions*. Controllable and uncontrollable symbols are "neutral", in the sense that, a priori, they have no semantic value from the agent point of view.

Emotional symbols correspond to *internal perceptions*, i.e. properties of the agent that are not directly controllable but can be "felt", such as pleasure, hunger or cold[1]. In a first approximation, we assume that emotional symbols are either "good" or "bad", in the sense that the agent has the *intention* that good emotional symbols be true and bad ones false. From the agent point of view, all semantic value is directly or indirectly derived from primitive emotional symbols.

The goal of the agent's cognitive capability is to recognize, memorize and predict "objects" or "situations" in the world, i.e, propositional symbols assignments, that relate, in a *relevant* way, these three kind of symbols.

To apply the proposed cognitive model to some experimental situation, the first step would be to define the emotional symbols and build the non cognitive part of the agent in such a way that the adopted emotional symbols suitable represent the articulation between the agent and the external environment, in terms of agent structure maintenance and functional goals. Emotional symbols may include *trustful peer* communication, i.e., symbols whose truth value in a given situation (as described by controllable and uncontrollable symbols) is determined by an external entity (e.g., another agent) that meaningfully communicates with the agent.

Example 1. Consider a simple agent-environment setting that consists of floor and walls. The agent is a robot that interacts with the environment through 3 uncontrollable propositional symbols associated with left, front and right sensors (S_l, S_f and S_r) and 2 controllable symbols associated with left and right motors (M_l and M_r). A possible emotional symbol would be *Move*, that is true when the robot is not blocked by some obstacle in the environment. The goal of the cognitive agent is to discover the relation between its actions (movements) and the actions consequences (collisions or non collisions), in order to connect the symbols and to find a semantical meaning for them.

The working hypothesis is that the agent's cognitive capabilities are supported by a set of non contradictory logical theories that represent its knowledge about these relations. These theories are the agent *structure*, according to the autopoiesis theory and the cognitive *organization* is such as to construct and maintain this structure according to the interaction with the environment. The goal of this paper is to describe two aspects of this *organization*: (i) the learning mechanism that determines how logical theories constructed with controllable and uncontrollable propositional symbols are related with emotional propositional symbols and (ii) a robustness [10] verification mechanism that

---

[1] The name *emotional* is derived from Damasio's notion of "somatic marker", presented in [7].

determines what would be the effect, on the validity of one of these theories, of any change in the assignments to propositional symbols, i.e., what is the minimal set of flips in propositional symbol truth values that should be made to maintain the satisfiability of the theory when the present assignment is modified.

3 Theory Representation

Let $P = \{P_1, \ldots, P_n\}$ be a set of propositional symbols and $L = \{\phi_1, \ldots, \phi_{2n}\}$ the set of their associated literals, where $\phi_i = P_j$ or $\phi_i = \neg P_j$. A *clause* C is a *generalized disjunction* [9] of literals: $C = [\phi_1, \ldots, \phi_{k_C}] \equiv \phi_1 \vee \cdots \vee \phi_{k_C}$ and a *dual clause* is a *generalized conjunction* of literals: $D = \langle \phi_1, \ldots, \phi_{k_D} \rangle \equiv \phi_1 \wedge \cdots \wedge \phi_{k_D}$.

Given a propositional theory $\mathcal{L}(P)$ represented by an *ordinary formula* W, there are algorithms for converting it into a *conjunctive normal form (CNF)*: $W_c = \langle C_1, \ldots, C_m \rangle$, defined as a generalized conjunction of clauses, or into a *disjunctive normal form (DNF)*: $W_d = [D_1, \ldots, D_w]$, defined as a generalized disjunction of dual clauses, such that $W \Leftrightarrow W_c \Leftrightarrow W_d$, e.g., [23].

Alternatively, a special case of CNF and DNF formula can be the prime implicates and prime implicants, that consist of the smallest sets of clauses (or terms) closed for inference, without any subsumed clauses (or terms), and not containing a literal and its negation. In the sequel, conjunctions and disjunctions of literals, clauses or terms are treated as sets.

A clause C is an *implicate* [12] of a formula W iff $W \models C$, and it is a *prime implicate* iff for all implicates C' of W such that $C' \models C$, we have $C \models C'$, or syntactically [20], for all literals $L \in C$, $W \not\models (C - \{L\})$. We define PI_W as a conjunction of prime implicates of W such that $W \equiv PI_W$. A term D is an *implicant* of a formula W iff $D \models W$, and it is a *prime implicant* iff for all implicants D' of W such that $D \models D'$, we have $D' \models D$, or syntactically, for all literals $L \in D$, $(D - \{L\}) \not\models W$. We define IP_W as a disjunction of prime implicants of W such that $W \equiv IP_W$.

To transform a formula from one clause form to the other, what we call *dual transformation (DT)*, only the distributivity of the logical operators $\vee$ and $\wedge$ is needed. In propositional logic, implicates and implicants are dual notions, in particular, an algorithm that calculates one of them can also be used to calculate the other [5, 24].

To represent these normal forms, we introduce the concept of a *quantum*, defined as a pair (ϕ, F), where ϕ is a literal and $F \subseteq W_c$ is its set of *coordinates* that contains the subset of clauses in W_c to which the literal ϕ belongs. A quantum is noted ϕ^F, to remind that F can be seen as a function $F : L \rightarrow 2^L$. The rationale behind the choice of the name *quantum* is to emphasize that the minimal semantical unity in the proposed model is not the value of propositional symbol, but the value of a propositional symbol with respect to the theory in which it occurs.

Any dual clause $D = \langle \phi_1, \ldots, \phi_k \rangle$ in the DNF W_d can be represented by a set of quanta: $\langle \phi_1^{F_1}, \ldots, \phi_k^{F_k} \rangle$ such that $\cup_{i=1}^k F_i = W_c$, i.e., D contains at least one literal that belongs to each clause in W_c, spanning a path through W_c, and no pair of contradictory literals, i.e., if a literal belongs to D, its negation is excluded. A dual clause D is minimal, if the following condition is also satisfied: $\forall i \in \{1, \ldots, k\}, F_i^* = F_i - \cup_{j=1, i \neq j}^k F_j \neq \emptyset$. This condition states that each literal in D should represent *alone* at least one clause in W_c, otherwise it would be redundant and could be deleted. The notation is symmetric, i.e., a clause $C = [\phi_1, \ldots, \phi_k]$ in the CNF W_c can be associated with a set of quanta: $[\phi_1^{F_1}, \ldots, \phi_k^{F_k}]$ such that $\cup_{i=1}^{k} F_i = W_d$, with no tautological literals allowed. Again the minimality condition for C is expressed by $\forall i \in \{1, \ldots, k\}, F_i^* = F_i - \cup_{j=1, i \neq j}^{k} F_j \neq \emptyset$.

The quantum notation is an enriched representation of the minimal normal forms, in the sense that the quantum representation explicitly contains the relation between literals in one form and the (dual) clauses in the other form. The CNF and DNF, from a syntactical point of view, are totally symmetric and each one of them contains all the information about the theory, but we propose that the agent should store its theories in both minimal normal forms. We belief that this 'holographic' representation can be used in others tasks of the agent, such as verification (as presented in the section 5) and belief changes [4], among others[2].

4 Learning

Theories can be learned by perceiving and acting in the environment, while keeping track of the truth value of a specific emotional propositional symbol. This symbol can be either a primitive emotional symbol or an abstract emotional symbol represented by a theory that also contains controllable and uncontrollable symbols, but ultimately depends on some set of primitive emotional symbols. The primitive emotional symbols may also depend on a communication from another agent that can be *trustfully* used as an oracle to identify its truth value.

The proposed learning mechanism has some analogy with the reinforcement learning method [11], where the agent acts in the environment monitoring a given *utility* function. Directly learning the relevant assignments can be thought of as a *practical* learning.

Example 2. Consider the robot of example 1. To learn the relation between the primitive emotional symbol *Move* and the controllable (M_l, M_r) and uncontrollable (S_l, S_f, S_r) symbols, it may randomly act in the world, memorizing the situations in which the *Move* symbol is assigned the value true. After, trying all $2^5 = 32$ possible truth assignments, it concludes that the propositional symbol *Move* is satisfied only by the 12 assignments[3]:

$[\langle S_l, S_f, \neg S_r, M_l, \neg M_r\rangle, \langle S_l, \neg S_f, S_r, M_l, M_r\rangle, \langle S_l, \neg S_f, \neg S_r, M_l, M_r\rangle, \langle S_l, \neg S_f, \neg S_r,$
$M_l, \neg M_r\rangle, \langle \neg S_l, S_f, S_r, \neg M_l, M_r\rangle, \langle \neg S_l, S_f, \neg S_r, M_l, \neg M_r\rangle, \langle \neg S_l, S_f, \neg S_r, \neg M_l, M_r\rangle,$
$\langle \neg S_l, \neg S_f, S_r, M_l, M_r\rangle, \langle \neg S_l, \neg S_f, S_r, \neg M_l, M_r\rangle, \langle \neg S_l, \neg S_f, \neg S_r, M_l, M_r\rangle, \langle \neg S_l, \neg S_f,$
$\neg S_r, M_l, \neg M_r\rangle, \langle \neg S_l, \neg S_f, \neg S_r, \neg M_l, M_r\rangle],$

The dual transformation (DT), applied on the dual clauses associated with the good assignments, returns the clauses of the minimal CNF (PI_W). A further application of

---

[2] The authors presently investigate others properties of the normal forms.

[3] To simplify the notation, an assignment is noted as a set of n literals, where n is the number of propositional symbols that appear in the theory, such that $\langle \phi_1, \ldots, \phi_i, \ldots, \phi_n\rangle$ represents the assignment $\epsilon(P_i) = true$ if $\phi_i = P_i$ or $\epsilon(P_i) = false$ if $\phi_i = \neg P_i$, and $\epsilon : P \rightarrow \{true, false\}$ is the semantic function that maps propositional symbols into truth values.

the dual transformation in this CNF returns the minimal DNF (IP_W)[4]. The minimal forms and their relation can be represented by the following sets of quanta:

PI_W	IP_W
$0 : [M_r^{\{0,3,4\}}, M_l^{\{1,2,3\}}]$	$0 : \langle \neg M_l^{\{2,3\}}, M_r^{\{0,1\}}, \neg S_l^{\{4,5,6\}} \rangle$
$1 : [\neg S_r^{\{1,2\}}, M_r^{\{0,3,4\}}]$	$1 : \langle \neg M_r^{\{2,4\}}, M_l^{\{0,6\}}, \neg S_r^{\{1,3,5\}} \rangle$
$2 : [\neg M_r^{\{1\}}, \neg M_l^{\{0\}}, \neg S_f^{\{2,3,4\}}]$	$2 : \langle M_l^{\{0,6\}}, \neg S_r^{\{1,3,5\}}, \neg S_f^{\{2,3,4,5\}} \rangle$
$3 : [\neg S_r^{\{1,2\}}, \neg M_l^{\{0\}}, \neg S_f^{\{2,3,4\}}]$	$3 : \langle M_l^{\{0,6\}}, M_r^{\{0,1\}}, \neg S_f^{\{2,3,4,5\}} \rangle$
$4 : [\neg S_l^{\{0,4\}}, \neg M_r^{\{1\}}, \neg S_f^{\{2,3,4\}}]$	$4 : \langle M_r^{\{0,1\}}, \neg S_l^{\{4,5,6\}}, \neg S_f^{\{2,3,4,5\}} \rangle$
$5 : [\neg S_r^{\{1,2\}}, \neg S_l^{\{0,4\}}, \neg S_f^{\{2,3,4\}}]$	
$6 : [\neg S_l^{\{0,4\}}, M_l^{\{1,2,3\}}]$	

It should be noted that IP_W contains less dual clauses than the original number of assignments, nevertheless each assignment satisfies at least one of this dual clauses. The application of the dual transformation provides a conjunctive characterization of the theory that, because of the local character of the clauses, can be used as a set of rules for decision making.

To formalize the proposed learning mechanism, we define an entailment relation $\models_\heartsuit$ that connect semantically neutral propositional symbols (controllable and uncontrollable) to emotional symbols. Let Γ be a neutral propositional formula and P an emotional symbol, this entailment relation has the following properties.

- If $\Gamma \models_\heartsuit P$ then $\neg \Gamma \not\models_\heartsuit P$.
- If $\Gamma_i \models \Gamma_j$ and $\Gamma_j \models_\heartsuit P$ then $\Gamma_i \models_\heartsuit P$.

In practice, learning is always incremental, that is, the agent begins with an empty theory $\mathcal{W}_0$ and incrementally constructs a sequence of theories $\mathcal{W}_0, \mathcal{W}_1, \ldots, \mathcal{W}_n$ such that $\mathcal{W}_n$ correctly captures the intended emotional propositional symbol P. According to the properties above, we have that $\mathcal{W}_i \models_\heartsuit P, i = 1, \ldots, n$ and $\mathcal{W}_j \models \mathcal{W}_i, i < j$. The algorithm to obtain $\mathcal{W}_{i+1}$, represented by its CNF and DNF, PI_W^{i+1} and IP_W^{i+1}, given $P, \mathcal{W}_i$ and the assignment ϵ is the following:

Learn($P, \epsilon, \mathcal{W}_i$)
if $D_\epsilon \models_\heartsuit P$ and $D_\epsilon \not\models \mathcal{W}_i$ **then**
  $PI_W^{i+1} \leftarrow DT(IP_W^i \cup [D_\epsilon]), IP_W^{i+1} \leftarrow DT(PI_W^i)$

where D_ϵ is the n literals dual clause such that $\epsilon(D) = true$ and DT is the dual transformation[5].

A similar algorithm may be used to incrementally compute the sequence of theories $\mathcal{W}_i'$, such that $\mathcal{W}_i' \not\models_\heartsuit P, i = 1, \ldots, m$ and $\mathcal{W}_j' \models \mathcal{W}_i', i < j$. The theories in this sequence are descriptions of those situations that do not entail the emotional symbol P. During learning, when the agent has already tried i theories entailing P and j not entailing it, the theory $\neg(\mathcal{W}_i \vee \mathcal{W}_j')$ captures those situations that were not yet experienced by the agent and can be used in the choice of future interactions. Its DNF can

---

[4] In fact, this second application is not necessary, because, once the prime implicants are known, there are polynomial time algorithms to calculate the prime implicates [8].

[5] As specified in the Section 3.

be computed by flipping all literals in $DT(IP_W^i) \cup DT(W_d'^i)$. If learning is complete, then $W_n \vee W_m' \models \top$.

Although nothing directly associated with the CNF occurs in the environment, if its contents can be communicated by another agent, then a theory can be taught by stating a CNF that represents it. In this case, the trustful oracle would communicate all the relevant rules that define the theory. This transmission of rules can be thought of as an *intellectual* learning, because it does not involve any direct experience in the environment.

5   Verification and Robustness

As stated above, we assume that the agent stores, for each theory, both normal forms.

5.1   Conjunctive Memory

With the CNF, the agent can verify whether an assignment satisfies a theory using the following method: given an assignment: $\langle \phi_1, \ldots, \phi_n \rangle$, the agent, using the DNF coordinates of the quanta (that specify in which clauses of the CNF each literal occurs), constructs the following set of quanta: $\langle \phi_1^{F_1}, \ldots, \phi_n^{F_n} \rangle$.

If $\cup_{i=1}^{n} F_i = PI_W$ then the assignment satisfies the theory, otherwise it does not satisfy it. In the case the assignment satisfies the theory, the number of times a given coordinate appears in the associated set of quanta informs how robust is the assignment with respect to changes in the truth value of the propositional symbol associated with it. The smaller this number, more *critical* is the clause denoted by the coordinate. If a given coordinate appears only once, then flipping the truth value of the propositional symbol associated with it will cause the assignment not to satisfy the theory anymore. In this case, the other literals in the critical rule represent additional changes in the assignment that could lead to a new satisfying assignment.

Example 3. Consider the theory of example 2 and the following assignment: $\langle \neg S_l, \neg S_f, \neg S_r, M_l, M_r \rangle$. The DNF coordinates (that refer to the CNF) of the literals in the assignment are: $\langle \neg S_l^{\{4,5,6\}}, \neg S_f^{\{2,3,4,5\}}, \neg S_r^{\{1,3,5\}}, M_l^{\{0,6\}}, M_r^{\{0,1\}} \rangle$.

The union of all coordinates is equal to the complete clause set: $\{0, 1, 2, 3, 4, 5, 6\}$ and, therefore, the assignment satisfies the theory. The only coordinate that appears only once is 2. This means that, if the truth assignment to the propositional symbols S_f is changed, then the resulting assignment will not satisfy clause 2 and therefore will not satisfy the theory anymore. On the other hand, the truth assignments to the other propositional symbols can be changed and the resulting assignment would still satisfy the theory. This is according to the intuition: the robot is moving forward (M_l and M_r true) and the three sensors are off (S_l, S_f and S_r false). In this situation the only event that would affect the possibility of moving is the frontal sensor to become on (S_f become true) and in this case, in order to satisfy again clause 2, $[\neg M_r, \neg M_l, \neg S_f]$, one of the two motors should be turned off (M_l or M_r false).

5.2   Disjunctive Memory

With the DNF, the agent can verify whether an assignment satisfies a theory using the following method: given an assignment: $\langle \phi_1, \ldots, \phi_n \rangle$, the agent should determines whether one of the dual clauses in the DNF is included in the assignment. To facilitate the search for such a dual clause, it constructs the following set of quanta: $\langle \phi_1^{F_1}, \ldots, \phi_n^{F_n} \rangle$ where the F_i are the CNF coordinates (that specify in which dual clauses of the DNF each literal occurs). The number of times a given coordinate appears in this set of quanta informs how many literals the dual clauses denoted by the coordinate shares with the assignment. If this number is equal to the number of literals in the dual clause then it is satisfied by the assignment. Dual clauses that do not appear in $\cup_{i=1}^n F_i$ need not to be checked for inclusion. If a dual clause is not satisfied by the assignment, it is possible to determine the set of literals that should be flipped, in the assignment, to satisfy it.

Example 4. Consider the theory of example 2 and the assignment: $\langle \neg S_l, S_f, \neg S_r, M_l, \neg M_r \rangle$. The CNF coordinates of the literals are: $\langle \neg S_l^{\{0,4\}}, S_f^{\{\}}, \neg S_r^{\{1,2\}}, M_l^{\{1,2,3\}}, \neg M_r^{\{1\}} \rangle$. The coordinates determine which dual clauses share which literals with the assignment:

$Dual clause$	$Share$	$Need$	$Don'tcare$
1	$\{\neg S_r, M_l, \neg M_r\}$	$\{\}$	$\{\neg S_l, S_f\}$
2	$\{\neg S_r, M_l\}$	$\{\neg S_f\}$	$\{\neg S_l, \neg M_r\}$
4	$\{\neg S_l\}$	$\{\neg S_f, M_r\}$	$\{\neg S_r, M_l\}$
0	$\{\neg S_l\}$	$\{\neg M_l, M_r\}$	$\{\neg S_r, S_f\}$
3	$\{M_l\}$	$\{\neg S_f, M_r\}$	$\{\neg S_l, \neg S_r\}$

In this case, except for literals $\neg S_l, S_f$, any change will affect the satisfiability of the theory. The robot is turning right and the right sensor is off, clearly the state of left and frontal sensors are irrelevant.

5.3   Models and Supermodels

In the proposed framework, robustness is the main concern because the agent should know how to modify its controllable symbols in order to maintain the satisfiability of its theories, given any possible change in the uncontrollable symbols. In [10], Ginsberg et al. introduce the concept of supermodels to measure the inherent degree of robustness associated with a model. This concept is defined as follows: *An (S_1^a, S_2^b)-supermodel is a model such that, if we modify the values taken by the variables in a subset of S_1^a of size at most a, another model can be obtained by modifying the values of the variables in a disjoint subset of S_2^b of size at most b.*

They also show that deciding whether a propositional theory has a (a, b)-*supermodel* [6] or not is NP-complete and provide an encoding for the more specific notion of $(1, 1)$-*supermodel* that allows to find out if a given theory has such a supermodel using standard SAT solvers. In our case, we are interested in the (S_1^a, S_2^b)-*supermodel* case, because we have controllable and uncontrollable symbols. We formalize the intuitive notions of the previous sections in the algorithms below.

Although each algorithm uses just one normal form, they require the minimal form, what implies, whether the theory is obtained through practical or intellectual learning,

---

[6] An (a, b)-*supermodel* is a (S_1^a, S_2^b)-*supermodel* in which the sets S_1^a and S_2^b are the set of all propositional symbols.

the calculation of the dual transformation. The algorithms receive as input a literal[7] to be flipped ($S_1^a = \{\phi\}$), a satisfying assignment (ϵ) represented as a dual clause (D_ϵ) and one of the normal forms (either PI_W or IP_W). They return, either "Prime implicate", if ϕ is a *unary prime implicate (UPI)* of the theory, or the set of literals (S_2^b) that should be flipped in order to restore satisfiability after ϕ is flipped. The algorithms are non deterministic and each choice would produce a different S_2^b set. Any S_2^b set returned by algorithm Super$_d$ has the minimal b, because this algorithm always chooses one of the $Need_k$ sets that has minimal size. The algorithm Super$_c$ only returns a set with minimal b if the choice of the ϕ_k's is such that they form one of the dual clauses with minimal size associated with the theory whose CNF is given by $\{C - \{\phi\} \mid C \in F^c, C \notin F_i^c, \phi \neq \phi_i\}$. These minimal dual clauses can be obtained by the application of the dual transformation to this (small) theory.

Super$_c(\phi, D_\epsilon, PI_W)$
Let $D_\epsilon = \langle \phi_1^{F_1^c}, \ldots, \phi_n^{F_n^c} \rangle, F_i^c \subseteq PI_W$ and $\phi^{F^c} \in D_\epsilon$
if $\mid F^c \mid = 1$ and $\mid C \mid = 1, C \in F^c$
  then Return(Prime Implicate) **else**
  Let $D_\epsilon' \leftarrow D_\epsilon \cup \{\overline{\phi}\} - \{\phi\}$
  if $\forall C \in F^c, \exists F_i^c, C \in F_i^c, \phi \neq \phi_i$ **then** Return($\emptyset$) **else**
    forall $C \in F^c, C \notin F_i^c, \phi \neq \phi_i$
      choose $\phi_k \in C - \{\phi\}$ **and do**
      $D_\epsilon' \leftarrow D_\epsilon' \cup \{\phi_k\} - \{\overline{\phi_k}\}, R \leftarrow R \cup \{\phi_k\}$
      if D_ϵ' is a model, i.e. $\cup_j F_j^c = PI_W, \phi_j^{F_j^c} \in D_\epsilon'$
      then Return(R)

Super$_d(\phi, D_\epsilon, IP_W)$
Let $IP_W = \{D_1, \ldots, D_m\}$ and
  $D_\epsilon = \langle \phi_1^{F_1^d}, \ldots, \phi_n^{F_n^d} \rangle, F_i^d \subseteq IP_W$ and $\phi^{F^d} \in D_\epsilon$
if $F^d = IP_W$ **then** Return(Prime Implicate) **else**
  Let $D_\epsilon' \leftarrow D_\epsilon \cup \{\overline{\phi}\} - \{\phi\}$ and
    $Share_k \leftarrow D_k \cap D_\epsilon'$ and $Need_k \leftarrow D_k - D_\epsilon'$
  if $\exists k, \mid Share_k \mid = \mid D_k \mid$ **then** Return($\emptyset$) **else**
    choose k such that $\phi \notin D_k$ and $\mid Need_k \mid$ is minimal
    $D_\epsilon' \leftarrow D_\epsilon' \cup Need_k - \{\overline{\phi_k} \mid \phi_k \in Need_k\}$
    Return($Need_k$)

The dual transformation, i.e. finding one minimal normal form given its dual non minimal form, is NP-complete and is as hard as the SAT problem [26], but the fact that the number of minimal dual clauses is always less (or in the worst case equal) than the number of models indicates that searching only for minimal dual clauses can be a good heuristic for a SAT solver [3]. Once the minimal normal form is available, both supermodel algorithms are polynomial. For a theory with n symbols and m (dual) clauses, both algorithms are $O(nm)$.

The dual transformation has been implemented for first-order and propositional logic and the results reported elsewhere. The algorithms presented above have been implemented in Common Lisp and applied to the theories in the SATLIB benchmark

---

[7] We note $\overline{\phi}$ the flipped form of literal ϕ.

(http://www.satlib.org/). Some results for supermodels with $\mid S_1^a \mid = 1$, obtained with the random 3SAT theories with 50 propositional symbols and 218 clauses, are shown in the table below:

	$\mid PI_W \mid$	$\mid IP_W \mid$	$\mid UPI \mid$	$\mid Pure \mid$	$\mid S_2^b \mid$
Max	83,695	929	50	50	19.51
Min	46	1	2	4	1
Mean	1892,10	40.26	32.29	36.09	5.95

For theories in the *critical region* the size of the S_2^b sets for those literals in S_2^a that are not UPI's nor pure are usually quite big, but some of them can be as small as 1.

6   Related Work

This work is rooted in the logicist school [18] and inscribe itself in the *Cognitive Robotics* domain [13, 14, 22]. We try to apply the, seemingly underexplored, properties of the minimal normal forms of logical theories to the several challenges of the domain: environment learning and modeling, reasoning about change, planning, abstraction and generalization. Because of its focus on normal forms, this work is also related with the SAT research concerned with the syntactical properties of the theories [17, 19]. A particularity of this work is that it searches for semantic grounds for logical theories in the autopoiesis theory [15], instead of in a pure model theoretical account.

7   Conclusion

The paper describes learning and robustness verification of logical theories that represent the knowledge of a cognitive agent. The semantics of these theories, instead of being a mapping from syntactic expressions to an outside world reality, is represented by the holographic relation between the two syntactic normal forms of theories that represent relevant interaction properties with the environment. This paper is part of a cognitive representation project.

Acknowledgments

The authors express their thanks to the Brazilian research support agency "Fundação Coordenação de Aperfeiçoamento de Pessoal de Nível Superior (Capes)" (project number 400/02) for the partial support of this work.

References

1. W. Bibel. Let's plan it deductively. In *Proceedings of IJCAI 15, Nagoya, Japan, August 23-29*, pages 1549–1562. Morgan Kaufmann (ISBN 1-55860-480-4), 1997.
2. G. Bittencourt. In the quest of the missing link. In *Proceedings of IJCAI 15, Nagoya, Japan, August 23-29*, pages 310–315. Morgan Kaufmann (ISBN 1-55860-480-4), 1997.

3. G. Bittencourt and J. Marchi. A syntactic approach to satisfaction. In Boris Konev and Renate Schmidt, editors, *Proceedings of the 4th International Workshop on the Implementation of Logics*, pages 18–32. University of Liverpool and University of Manchester, 2003.

4. G. Bittencourt, L. Perrussel, and J. Marchi. A syntactical approach to revision. Accepted to ECAI'04.

5. G. Bittencourt and I. Tonin. An algorithm for dual transformation in first-order logic. *Journal of Automated Reasoning*, 27(4):353–389, 2001.

6. R. A. Brooks. Intelligence without representation. *Artificial Intelligence (Special Volume Foundations of Artificial Intelligence)*, 47(1-3):139–159, January 1991.

7. A. R. Damasio. *Descartes' Error: Emotion, Reason, and the Human Brain*. G.P. Putnam's Sons, New York, NY, 1994.

8. A. Darwiche and P. Marquis. A perspective on knowledge compilation. In *IJCAI*, pages 175–182, 2001.

9. M. Fitting. *First-Order Logic and Automated Theorem Proving*. Springer Verlag, New York, 1990.

10. M. L. Ginsberg, A. J. Parkes, and A. Roy. Supermodels and robustness. In *Proceedings of AAAI-98*, pages 334–339, 1998.

11. L. P. Kaelbling, M. L. Littman, and A.W. Moore. Reinforcement learning: A survey. *Journal of Artificial Intelligence Research*, 4:237–285, 1996.

12. A. Kean and G. Tsiknis. An incremental method for generating prime implicants/implicates. *Journal of Symbolic Computation*, 9:185–206, 1990.

13. Y. Lespérance, H. J. Levesque, F. Lin, D. Marcu, R. Reiter, and R. B. Scherl. A logical approach to high level robot programming – a progress report. In B. Kuipers, editor, *Working notes of the 1994 AAAI fall symposium on Control of the Physical World by Intelligent Systems*, New Orleans, LA, November 1994.

14. H. Levesque, F. Pirri, and R. Reiter. Foundations for the situation calculus, 1998.

15. H. R. Maturana and F. J. Varela. Autopoiesis and cognition: The realization of the living. In Robert S. Cohen and Marx W. Wartofsky, editors, *Boston Studies in the Philosophy of Science*, volume 42. Dordecht (Holland): D. Reidel Publishing Co., 1980.

16. E. Morin. *La Méthode 4, Les Idées*. Editions du Seuil, Paris, 1991.

17. N. Murray, A. Ramesh, and E. Rosenthal. The semi-resolution inference rule and prime implicate computations. In *Proc. Fourth Golden West International Conference on Intelligent Systems, San Fransisco, CA, USA*, pages 153–158, 1995.

18. A. Newell. The knowledge level. *Artificial Intelligence*, 18:87–127, 1982.

19. A. J. Parkes. Clustering at the phase transition. In *AAAI/IAAI*, pages 340–345, 1997.

20. A. Ramesh, G. Becker, and N. V. Murray. CNF and DNF considered harmful for computing prime implicants/implicates. *Journal of Automated Reasoning*, 18(3):337–356, 1997.

21. R. Scherl and H. J. Levesque. Knowledge, action, and the frame problem. *Artificial Intelligence*, 1(144):1–39, March 2003.

22. M. Shanahan. Explanation in the situation calculus. In Ruzena Bajcsy, editor, *Proceedings of the Thirteenth International Joint Conference on Artificial Intelligence*, pages 160–165, San Mateo, California, 1993. Morgan Kaufmann.

23. J.R. Slagle, C.L. Chang, and R.C.T. Lee. A new algorithm for generating prime implicants. *IEEE Transactions on Computing*, 19(4):304–310, 1970.

24. R. Socher. Optimizing the clausal normal form transformation. *Journal of Automated Reasoning*, 7(3):325–336, 1991.

25. F. J. Varela. *Autonomie et Connaissance: Essai sur le Vivant*. Editions du Seuil, Paris, 1989.

26. L. Zhang and S. Malik. The quest for efficient boolean satisfiability solvers. In *Proceedings of 8th International Conference on Computer Aided Deduction(CADE 2002)*, 2002. Invited Paper.

A Unified Architecture
to Develop Interactive Knowledge Based Systems

Vládia Pinheiro, Elizabeth Furtado, and Vasco Furtado

Universidade de Fortaleza – UNIFOR
Av. Washington Soares 1321 – Edson Queiroz - Fortaleza – CE - Brasil - Cep: 60811-905
vladiacelia@zaz.com.br, {elizabet,vasco}@unifor.br

Abstract. A growing need related to the use of knowledge-based systems (KBSs) is that these systems provide ways of adaptive interaction with the user. A comparative analysis of approaches to develop KBSs allowed us to identify a high functional quality level and a lack of integration of human factors in their frameworks. In this article, we propose an approach to develop adaptive and interactive KBSs that integrate works from the Knowledge Engineering and HCI areas, through the definition of a unified software architecture. A contribution of this work is the use of interaction patterns in order to define the interaction flow according to the user profile. These interaction patterns are defined for different kinds of interaction, such as, explanation, cooperation, argumentation or criticism. The reusable architecture components were implemented using Java and Protégé-2000, and they were used in a KBS for assessment of installments of tax debts.

Keywords: Knowledge-based systems, reusable components, interaction patterns.

1 Introduction

The Knowledge Engineering area has evolved since the art of building Expert Systems began until now, thus, providing methods, technologies, and patterns for the development of Knowledge-Based Systems (KBS). These systems are used in various domains to solve problems that involve the human reasoning process.

Some of the Knowledge Engineering works concentrate in providing problem solving methods (PSM) libraries. A PSM describes the reasoning steps and the knowledge roles used during the problem solving process, independent of the domain, allowing its reuse in many applications [1].

A growing need related to the use of KBSs is that these systems provide ways of interaction with the user. Moulin et al [2] analyze that kind of user-KBS interaction, such as, explanation, cooperation, argumentation, or criticism, allows a better level of acceptance from users related to the solutions proposed by the system.

McGraw [3] observes that novice users do not understand complex reasoning strategies. This is true mainly due to the fact that KBSs are developed based on PSMs developed according to the vision that experts have about the problem. That is, the

A.L.C. Bazzan and S. Labidi (Eds.): SBIA 2004, LNAI 3171, pp. 174–183, 2004.

development of KBSs does not consider the end-users knowledge level, neither their point of view of the problem. Therefore, it is important that the user-KBS interaction is adaptive according to users and to the context of use.

The Human-Computer Interaction (HCI) area develops methods and techniques to build adaptive interactive systems. The focus of HCI researches is on the people who use the system, which tasks they execute, their ability level, preferences, and external factors, such as organizational and environmental factors.

A comparative analysis of approaches to develop KBSs allowed us to identify a high functional quality level, and, on the other hand, there is a lack of integration of human factors in their frameworks.

As a solution, we propose an approach to develop adaptive and interactive KBSs that integrate works from the Knowledge Engineering and HCI areas, through the definition of a unified software architecture. In this article, we show the implementation of the proposed architecture components, describing how they were used in a KBS to evaluate the concession of installments of tax debts.

2   HCI Aspects for KBS Development

We studied some approaches on KBS development verifying how they treat aspects related to HCI. The HCI aspects used in model-based user interface design are: user modeling, context of use modeling, user tasks modeling, and adaptability.

These aspects are particularly relevant in the interactive KBS context. Kay [4] affirms that user modeling allows adapting the presentation of the information according to users, and facilitates the definition of the type of intervention that can be made during the user-system collaborative processes. User tasks modeling, which tasks are performed through the system interface, allows the analysis of the interaction based on the users' point of view and identifies the information they need, as well as their goals.

CommonKADS [5] defines phases in its methodology that consist on the construction of its models: Organization Model, Task Model, Knowledge Model, Agent Model, and Communication Model. Specifically, the Agent Model, which describes the abilities of the stakeholders when executing tasks, and the Communication Model, which models how the agents communicate, already consider user modeling in its phases. However, it does not use models for the user-interaction design, neither for the adaptation of the user-interaction.

Sengès [6] proposes an extension of CommonKADS to allow the user-KBS cooperation during the system execution. She proposes a new model: the cooperation model, which structures the sequence of resolution steps and the exchange of information according to the users' knowledge level and to the organizational context. However, the adaptation of the cooperation is defined by generating a cooperation model for each kind of user during the KBS development. Therefore, this adaptation is static, that is, the system is not capable of dynamically adapting itself to a new kind of user.

Unified Problem-Solving Method Description Language (UPML) [7] describes different KBS software components by integrating two important research lines in Knowledge Engineering: components reusability and ontologies. UPML, besides being an architecture, also is a KBS development framework because it describes components, adaptors, architecture restrictions, development guidelines, and tools. The architecture components are: (i) Task, that defines the problem that should be solved by the KBS; (ii) PSM, that defines the reasoning process of a KBS; (iii) Domain Model, that describes the domain knowledge of the KBS; (iv) Ontologies, that provide the terminology used in the other elements; (v) Bridges, that models the relationships between two UPML components; and (vi) Refiners, that can be used to specialize an component. Each component in the UPML is described independently to enable reusability. For instance, problem-solving methods can be reused for different tasks and domains. This is possible because of the fifth element – bridges.

The comparative analysis of how HCI aspects are considered in the studied KBS development approaches demonstrated that the model-based user interface design is not taken into account by any of the approaches. However, CommonKADS and Sengès already consider aspects such as user modeling, user task modeling, and context of use modeling, although, with some disadvantages. UPML does not consider any HCI aspect and only the approach proposed by Sengès for cooperative KBSs uses interaction modeling through the cooperation model.

3   A Unified Architecture for Interactive KBSs

The analysis of the integration of HCI aspects in the KBS development approaches lead us to the definition of a software architecture that integrates works from the Knowledge Engineering and HCI areas, aiming at attending the following requirements for interactive KBSs: knowledge modeling from reusable components for problem-solving, user modeling, context of use modeling, and user task modeling for adaptability.

This unified architecture integrates components of a KBS architecture, such as UPML, and from the interactive systems architecture defined in [8], thus, providing components that consider the user point of view during the KBS development.

A major contribution of our approach is the use of interaction patterns in order to define the interaction flow according to the user profile. The interactive tasks performed by the users, such as, require and receive explanations, cooperate with the KBS, are defined by means of design patterns [9] aiming at reducing the development effort [10].

3.1   Architecture Description

The architecture components, presented in Figure 1, are separately described according to their responsibilities.

User-KBS Dialogue Control

- Functional Core: it contains the PSM functionalities and the domain knowledge.
- Dialogue Controller, Interface Toolkit, and Adaptors: these components are responsible for controlling the interaction flow and presenting the information to the user. The Dialogue Patterns Model, which is part of the Dialogue Controller, implements the dialogue patterns identified during the system user interface design [11]. Dialogue patterns are ways to present information and to allow interaction according to the task to be performed, the user profile, data types, etc.

Construction of the Models

- PSMs Library: library that contains problem-solving methods.
- Interaction Patterns Library: library that contains patterns for various forms of user-KBS interaction, such as, explanation, cooperation, argument, and criticism.
- Organization Model: it models the functional staff of the organization, in which each function is associated to rules that define the behavior of users who perform such function.
- User Model: it represents characteristics of users, being individuals or grouped in stereotypes. These characteristics can be: expertise level, domain concepts known by the user, goals, etc.

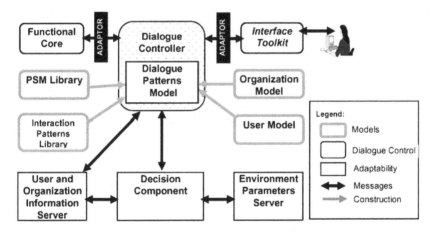

Fig. 1. A Unified Architecture for Interactive KBSs.

Adaptability

Adaptability requires a dynamic user and context of use modeling, as well as the choice of appropriate dialogue patterns. In order to provide adaptation during the system execution, two servers work in the acquisition of dynamic information. They are: the User and Organization Information Server and the Environment Parameters Server.

The User and Organization Information Server contains the logic to infer information about the user model and the organization model, such as, identifying which concepts are known by users, allowing the adaptation of the type of explanation to be provided. The Environment Parameters Server contains the logic to infer data about the context of use, before and during the execution.

The information inferred by these servers is provided to the Decision Component, which selects the appropriate dialogue patterns. For example, a dialogue pattern of the plan text type is more appropriate to present the explanation content to novice users.

Table 1 presents the activities supported by the architecture components aiming at attending the requirements for interactive KBS.

Table 1. Activities supported by the architecture components.

Responsibility	Activity	Component
Dialogue control	Knowledge modeling	Functional Core
	Dialogue separation	Dialogue Controller
Construction of models	User modeling	User Model
	User task modeling	Interaction Patterns Library
	Context of use modeling	Organization Model
Adaptability	Dynamic user modeling	User and Organization Server
	Dynamic context modeling	Environment Parameters Server
	Dialogue patterns choice	Decision Component

4 Implementation of the Architecture Components

The generic architecture components were implemented using Java and using Protégé-2000 [12] as the UPML editor. This implementation focus on reusability and, therefore, these components can be reused in other applications. Following, we detail the implementation of each component:

Functional Core
For this component, we implemented the elements of the UPML architecture in the Java classes: *BridgeComponent, PSMComponent, TaskComponent,* and *Domain-Component.* The reason to use the UPML framework is because this approach makes the reasoning process explicit by implementing the PSM as part of the application. This enhances, for instance, the quality of the explanation to be given to the user because it allows a greater control of the reasoning steps. This implementation was done according to the design patterns for translation of the UPML in Java defined in [7].

The *PSMComponent* Java class contains the generic methods that execute the mapping of domain-PSM and task-PSM, and that are responsible for the communication of the knowledge roles among the other UPML elements, and for the execution of the sub-tasks associated to the PSM. These methods are defined in the Java interface *BridgeComponent*. For example, its method executeSubTask receives the name of a sub-task as parameter; searches for the object related to that sub-task, and calls the execute() method of this object. Figure 2 shows the Java implementation of this method.

According to the definition of the design pattern for the UPML implementation, each PSM can be implemented as a subclass of the *PSMComponent* class and the subtasks of the PSM as methods.

The *TaskComponent* Java class is an abstract class responsible for providing the knowledge roles necessary in each subclass. The PSM subtasks are implemented as subclasses of this class and each subclass implements the abstract execute() method.

The *DomainComponent* Java class is responsible for defining the properties and methods common to the various PSM knowledge roles. The ontology of the problem-solving method is implemented as subclasses of this class.

```
public void executeSubTask(String SubTaskName){
    TaskComponent task=(TaskComponent)tasks.get(SubTaskName);
    savePSMLog(task,null,null,"execute()",null);
    task.execute();
}
```

Fig. 2. Java implementation of the executeSubTask method from the *PSMComponent* super class.

Interaction Patterns Library

This component contains design patterns, called interaction patterns, which define how the interaction functionalities should be implemented in a KBS. In this article, is described the implementation of an interaction pattern for explanation composed of two classes: *Explanation* and *PSMLog*. The *Explanation* class represents the explanation to be provided to the user that is defined by operations that answer the questions: What (is this)?, How (did this happen)?, Why (did this happen)?. The *PSMLog* class represents the KBS reasoning steps during the search for a solution to the problem. The operations in this class are responsible for associating values to the attributes that characterize each reasoning step.

Figure 3 presents the sequence diagram in Unified Model Language (UML) representing the implementation of the interaction pattern for explanation. The interaction flow is the following one: (i) the User requests an explanation and the DialogueController receives the object to be explained and the explanation type; (ii) the DialogueController requests the user and organization profiles to the UserOrganizationServer; (iii) the UserOrganizationServer infers about UserModel and OrganizationModel and answers to the DialogueController and to the DecisionComponent; (iv) the DialogueController requests the explanation sending the object to be explained, the explanation type and the user and organization informations; (v) the Explanation defines the explanation adapted to the UserModel and to the OrganizationModel. The Explanation executes a method according to the explanation type; (vi) the DialogueController requests a dialogue pattern to the DecisionComponent and shows the explanation using the dialogue pattern.

The same Figure 3 presents an example of an algorithm in English that represents a implementation of the explainWhat() method of the *Explanation* class responsible for defining the explanation of the type What (is this)? This method defines the explanation according to the object type (a Method, a Field, a Class or an Instance). For instance, when the object to be explained is an instance of a class, this method defines the description from the domain concepts known by the user, which are modeled in the UserModel.

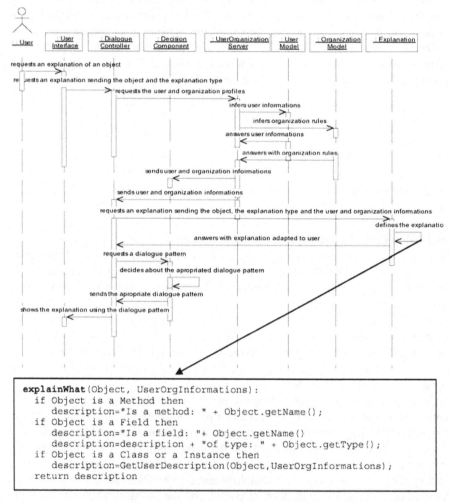

```
explainWhat(Object, UserOrgInformations):
    if Object is a Method then
        description="Is a method: " + Object.getName();
    if Object is a Field then
        description="Is a field: "+ Object.getName()
        description=description + "of type: " + Object.getType();
    if Object is a Class or a Instance then
        description=GetUserDescription(Object,UserOrgInformations);
    return description
```

Fig. 3. UML sequence diagram of the interaction pattern for explanation and an algorithm in English of the implementation of the explainWhat() method.

Organization Model

The Java classes that implement this component are: (i) *Organization Model*, which represents the generic rules applied for all users in the organization; (ii) *Organiza-*

tionFunction, which represents the specific rules of each function in the organization applied for the users who perform such function; (iii) *OrganizationRule,* which represents the organizational rules that are associated to the other two classes as generic or specific rules.

User Model
The implemented user model represents the users' stereotypes. According to Sengès [6], we identified that KBS users can be classified as: domain expert users, expert users in other knowledge domains, and general public users. The *UserModel* Java class implements the user model, which is composed of three other classes *FunctionUser, ObjectiveUser,* and *DomainComponentUser.* These classes represent parts of the user model and contain, respectively, the expertise level according to the user function in the organization, users' goals, and domain concepts known by users.

Adaptability Components and Dialogue Controller
The components responsible for Adaptability and Dialogue Controller were implemented in the following Java classes: *UserOrganizationServer, EnvironmentServer, DecisionComponent,* and *DialogueController.*

5 An Example of Adaptive Interaction in a KBS

In order to demonstrate how the use of the architecture generic components facilitates the development of adaptive interactions, we used the example of user-KBS interaction to evaluate the concession of installments of tax debts, in which there is a dialogue for explanation about the evaluation process of the installments of tax debts. One requirement is that this KBS provides explanations adapted to the users.

This knowledge-based application evaluates a set of criteria based on the taxpayer data and on the installment request. After the criteria evaluation, the system must decide whether or not to provide the installment plan request.

The functional core of this KBS was implemented as subclasses of the UPML generic classes. The abstract-and-match PSM for assessment tasks was implemented as subclasses of the *PSMComponent* class. The tax installment plan domain model was implemented as subclasses of the *DomainComponent* class.

The users of this KBS are tax auditors or directors, experts on the tax domain, or the actual taxpayers who request installments of their debts through the Internet. Therefore, we identified two user stereotypes: domain experts and general public users. The User Model of this application is mapped to the domain model of the UPML Architecture through a *bridge.* This way, the domain concepts known by users and the domain concepts known by experts are related.

In this KBS, the heuristic used to adapt the explanation is the following one: general public users receive simple explanations with the terminology known by them, and the domain expert users receive contextual explanations that show the hierarchy of the knowledge involved.

Figure 4 presents the explanation dialogue during the evaluation process with a general public user (a) and a domain expert user (b). The question is: What is the tax evasion level?. This expert concept "tax evasion level" is mapped to the "tax fraud level" concept from the user model for general public users. Notice that the explanation given about the same concept for a domain expert user is presented in a dialogue pattern interactive tree, which facilitates the knowledge hierarchy organization. Besides this, the description presented about the concept is different because it was recovered from the user model for domain expert users.

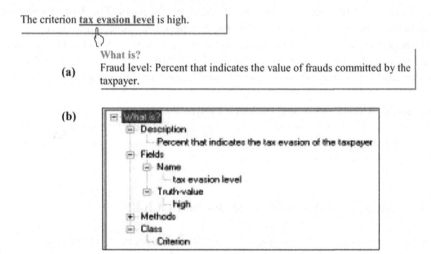

Fig. 4. An example of adaptive explanation for a general public user (a) and for a domain expert user (b).

6 Conclusion

In this article, based on the growing need for knowledge–based systems to allow interaction with its final users, we evaluated how some KBS development approaches consider HCI aspects. This analysis pointed out the lack of an approach that completely considers aspects such as: knowledge modeling from reusable components for problem-solving, user modeling, context of use modeling, user task modeling, use of usability patterns, and adaptability.

Therefore, we defined components of a software architecture for interactive KBSs that unifies a KBS development architecture, such as UPML, and an architecture for interactive systems. Two characteristics are in this architecture: interaction adaptation based on user modeling and organizational context modeling, and the construction of the user-KBS dialogue based on interaction patterns. Interaction patterns provide a solution to implement interaction adaptation to various users, independent of the domain.

Another contribution of this work was the implementation of generic components of the architecture in Java. This way, the architecture components are available to be reused in others interactive knowledge-based applications. In this article, we exemplified the use of the architecture in adapting user-KBS interaction to evaluate the concession of installments of tax debts. Specifically, the interaction consists of dialogues for explanations to various kinds of KBS users about the installment evaluation process and about the domain concepts.

As future work, we intend to apply this architecture in the development of other interactive applications, as a way to enhance its validation and maturity. An important extension for this work is the development of plug-ins in Protégé for the architecture generic components. Thus, the architecture can be integrated with a powerful modeling and knowledge acquisition tool.

References

1. Fensel, D. and Benjamins, V.R., Key Issues for Automated Problem-Solving Methods Reuse.13th European Conference on Artificial Intelligence, ECAI98, Wiley & Sons Pub, 1998.
2. Moulin, B., et al. Explanation and Argumentation Capabilities: Towards the Creation of More Persuasive Agents. Artificial Intelligence Review, Kluwer Academic Publishers, 17: 169-222, 2002.
3. McGraw, K.L., Designing and evaluating User Interface for Knowledge-Based Systems. Ellis Hordwood series in Interactive Information Systems, 1993.
4. Kay, J. User Modeling for Adaptation. User Interfaces for All – Concepts, Methods and Tools, LEA Publishers. London. 271-294, 2001.
5. Schreiber et al., Knowledge Engineering and Management: The CommonKADS Methodology. The MIT Press. Cambridge, MA, 2000.
6. Senges, V., Coopération Homme-Machine dans lês Systèmes à Base de Connaissances. Thèse de l'Universitè Toulouse, 1994.
7. Fensel, D. et al., The Unified Problem-Solving Method Development Language UPML. Knowledge and Information Systems, An International Journal, 5, 83-127, 2003.
8. Savidis, A. and Stephanidis, C., The Unified User Interface Software Architecture. User Interfaces for All – Concepts, Methods and Tools, LEA Publishers. London. 389-415, 2001.
9. Gamma, E., Helm, R., Johnson, R., and Vlissides, J., Design Patterns: Elements of Reusable Object-Oriented Software. Reading, MA, Addison-Wesley, 1995.
10. Pinheiro, V. Furtado, V. An Architecture for Interactive Knowledge-Based Systems. ACM International Conference Proceeding Series, Proceedings of the Latin American conference on Human-computer interaction, Rio de Janeiro, Brazil, 2003.
11. Savidis, A., Akoumianakis, D., Stephanidis, C., The Unified User Interface Design Method. User Interfaces for All – Concepts, Methods and Tools, LEA Publishers. London. 417-440, 2001.
12. Eriksson H, Fergerson R.W., Shahar Y, Musen M.A. Automatic generation of ontology editors. In Proceedings of the 12th Banff Knowledge Acquisition for Knowledge-based Systems Workshop. Banff, Alberta, Canada. 1999.

Evaluation of Methods for Sentence and Lexical Alignment of Brazilian Portuguese and English Parallel Texts

Helena de Medeiros Caseli,
Aline Maria da Paz Silva, and Maria das Graças Volpe Nunes

NILC-ICMC-USP, CP 668P, 13560-970 São Carlos, SP, Brazil
{helename,alinepaz,gracan}@icmc.usp.br
http://www.nilc.icmc.usp.br

Abstract. Parallel texts, i.e., texts in one language and their translations to other languages, are very useful nowadays for many applications
such as machine translation and multilingual information retrieval. If
these texts are aligned in a sentence or lexical level their relevance increases considerably. In this paper we describe some experiments that
have being carried out with Brazilian Portuguese and English parallel
texts by the use of well known alignment methods: five methods for sentence alignment and two methods for lexical alignment. Some linguistic
resources were built for these tasks and they are also described here. The
results have shown that sentence alignment methods achieved 85.89% to
100% precision and word alignment methods, 51.84% to 95.61% on corpora from different genres.

Keywords: Sentence alignment, Lexical alignment, Brazilian Portuguese

1 Introduction

Parallel texts – texts with the same content written in different languages – are
becoming more and more available nowadays, mainly on the Web. These texts
are useful for applications such as machine translation, bilingual lexicography
and multilingual information retrieval. Furthermore, their relevance increases
considerably when correspondences between the source and the target (source's
translation) parts are tagged.

One way of identifying these correspondences is by means of alignment. Aligning two (or more) texts means to find correspondences (translations) between
segments of the source text and segments of its translation (the target text).
These segments can be the whole text or its parts: chapters, sections, paragraphs,
sentences, words or even characters. In this paper, the focus is on sentence and
lexical (or word) alignment methods.

The importance of sentence and word aligned corpora has increased mainly
due to their use in Example Based Machine Translation (EBMT) systems. In
this case, parallel texts can be used by machine learning algorithms to extract
translation rules or templates ([1], [2]).

A.L.C. Bazzan and S. Labidi (Eds.): SBIA 2004, LNAI 3171, pp. 184–193, 2004.

The purpose of this paper is to report the results of experiments carried out on sentence and lexical alignment methods for Brazilian Portuguese (BP) and English parallel texts. As far as we know this is the first work on aligners involving BP. Previous work on sentence alignment involving European Portuguese has shown similar values to the experiment for BP described in this paper. In [3], for example, the Translation Corpus Aligner (TCA) has shown 97.1% precision on texts written in English and European Portuguese.

In a project carried out to evaluate sentence and lexical alignment systems, the ARCADE project, twelve sentence methods have been evaluated and it was achieved over 95% precision while the five lexical alignment methods have achieved 75% precision ([4]).

The lower precision for lexical alignment is due to its hard nature and it still remains problematic as shown in previous evaluation tasks, such as ARCADE. Most alignment systems deal with the stability of the order of translated segments, but this property does not stand to lexical alignment due to the syntactic difference between languages[1].

This paper is organized as following: Section 2 presents an overview of alignment methods, with special attention to the five sentence alignment methods and the two lexical alignment methods considered in this paper. Section 3 describes the linguistic resources developed to support these experiments and Section 4 reports the results of the seven alignment methods evaluated on BP-English parallel corpora. Finally, in Section 5 some concluding remarks are presented.

2   Alignment Methods

Parallel text alignment can be done on different levels: from the whole text to its parts (paragraphs, sentences, words, etc). In the sentence level, given two parallel texts, a sentence alignment method tries to find the best correspondences between source and target sentences. In this process, the methods can use information about sentences' length, cognate and anchor words, POS tags and other clues. These information stands for the alignment criteria of these methods.

In the lexical level, the alignment can be divided into two steps: a) the identification of word units in the source and in the target texts; b) the establishment of correspondences between the identified units. However, in practice the modularization of these tasks is not quite simple considering that a single unit can correspond to a multiword unit. A multiword unit is a word group that expresses ideas and concepts that can not be explained or defined by a single word, such as phrasal verbs (e.g., "turn on") and nominal compounds (e.g., "telephone box").

In both sentence and lexical alignments the most frequent alignment category is 1-1, in which one unit (sentence or word) in the source text is translated exactly to one unit (sentence or word) in the target text. However, there are other alignment categories, such as omissions (1-0 or 0-1), expansions (n-m, with n < m; n, m >= 1), contractions (n-m, with n > m; n, m >= 1) or unions

---

[1] Gaussier, E., Langé, J.-M.: Modèles statistiques pour l'extraction de lexiques bilingues. T.A.L. 36 (1–2) (1995) 133–155 apud [5].

(n-n, with n > 1). In the lexical level, categories different from 1-1 are more frequent than in the sentence level as can be exemplified by multiword units.

2.1 Sentence Alignment Methods

The sentence alignment methods evaluated here were named: GC ([6], [7]), GMA and GSA+ ([8], [9]), Piperidis et al. ([10]) and TCA ([11]).

GC (its authors' initials) is a sentence alignment method based on a simple statistical model of sentence lengths, in characters. The main idea is that longer sentences in the source language tend to have longer translations in the target language and that shorter sentences tend to be translated into shorter ones. GC is the most referenced method in the literature and it presents the best performance considering its simplicity.

GMA and GSA+ methods use a pattern recognition technique to find the alignments between sentences. The main idea is that the two halves of a bitext – source and target sentences – are the axes of a rectangular bitext space where each token is associated with the position of its middle character. When a token at the position x in the source text and a token at the position y in the target text correspond to each other, it is said to be a point of correspondence (x, y).

These methods use two algorithms for aligning sentences: SIMR (Smooth Injective Map Recognizer) and GSA (Geometric Segment Alignment). The SIMR algorithm produces points of correspondence (lexical alignments) that are the best approximation of the correct translations (bitext maps) and GSA aligns the segments based on these resultant bitext maps and information about segment boundaries. The difference between GMA and GSA+ methods is that, in the former, SIMR considers only cognate words to find out the points of correspondence, while in the latter a bilingual anchor word list[2] is also considered.

The Piperidis et al.'s method is based on a critical issue in translation: meaning preservation. Traditionally, the four major classes of content words (or open class words) – verb, noun, adjective and adverb – carry the most significant amount of meaning. So, the alignment criterion used by this method is based on the semantic load of a sentence[3], i.e., two sentences are aligned if, and only if, the semantic loads of source and target sentences are similar.

Finally, TCA (Translation Corpus Aligner) relies on several alignment criteria to find out the correspondence between source and target sentences, such as a bilingual anchor word list, words with an initial capital (candidates for proper nouns), special characters (such as question and exclamation marks), cognate words and sentence lengths.

---

[2] An anchor word list is a list of words in source language and their translations in the target language. If a pair source_word/target_word that occurs in this list appears in the source and target sentence respectively, it is taken as a point of correspondence between these sentences.

[3] Semantic load of a sentence is defined, in this case, as the union of all open classes that can be assigned to the words of this sentence ([10]).

2.2   Lexical Alignment Methods

The lexical alignment methods evaluated here were: SIMR ([12], [9], [13]) and LWA ([14], [15], [16]).

The SIMR method is the same used in sentence alignment task (see Section 2.1). This method considers only single words (not multiword units) in its alignment process.

The LWA (Linköping Word Aligner) is based on co-occurrence information and some linguistic modules to find correspondences between source and target lexical units (words and multiwords). Three linguistic modules were used by this method: the first one is responsible for the categorization of the units, the second one deals with multiword units using multiword unit lists and the last one establishes an area (a correspondence window) within the correspondences will be looked for.

3   Linguistic Resources

3.1   Linguistic Resources for Sentence Alignment

The required linguistic resources for sentence alignment methods can be divided into two groups: corpora and anchor word lists ([17]). For testing and evaluation purposes, three BP-English parallel corpora of different genres – scientific, law and journalistic – were built: CorpusPE, CorpusALCA and CorpusNYT.

CorpusPE is composed of 130 authentic (non-revised) academic parallel texts (65 abstracts in BP and 65 in English) on Computer Science. A revised (by a human translator) version of this corpora was also generated. They were named authentic CorpusPE and pre-edited CorpusPE respectively.

Authentic CorpusPE has 855 sentences, 21432 words and 7 sentences per text on average. Pre-edited CorpusPE has 849 sentences, 21492 words and also 7 sentences per text on average. These two corpora were used to investigate the methods' performance on texts with (authentic) and without (pre-edited) noise (grammatical and translation errors).

CorpusALCA is composed of 4 official documents of Free Trade Area of the Americas (FTAA)[4] written in BP and in English with 725 sentences, 22069 words and 91 sentences per text on average.

Finally, CorpusNYT is composed of 8 articles in English and their translation to BP from the journal "The New York Times"[5]. It has 492 sentences, 11516 words and 30 sentences per text on average.

To test and evaluate the methods, two corpora were built (test and reference) based on the four previous corpora. Texts in the test corpora were given as input for the five sentence alignment methods. Reference corpora – composed of correctly aligned parallel texts – were built in order to calculate precision and recall metrics for the texts of test.

---

[4] Available in http://www.ftaa-alca.org/alca_e.asp.
[5] Available in http://www.nytimes.com (English version) and
   http://ultimosegundo.ig.com.br/useg/nytimes (BP version).

The texts of test and reference corpora have been tagged to distinguish paragraphs and sentences. Tags for aligned sentences were also manually introduced in the reference corpora. A tool for aiding this pre-processing was especially implemented [18].

Most of the alignments in the reference corpora (94%), as expected, are of type 1-1 while omissions, expansions, contractions and unions are quite rare.

Other linguistic resources developed include an anchor word list for each corpus genre: scientific, law and journalistic. Examples of BP/English anchor words found in these lists are: "abordagem/approach", "algoritmo/algorithm" (in scientific list); "adoção/adoption", "afetado/affected" (in law list) and "armas/weapons", "ataque/attack" (in journalistic list).

3.2 Linguistic Resources for Lexical Alignment

The linguistic resources for lexical alignment methods can be divided into two groups: corpora and multiword unit lists.

For testing and evaluation purposes, three corpora were used: pre-edited CorpusPE[6], CorpusALCA and CorpusNYT, the same corpora built for the sentence alignment task (see Section 3.1). Texts in the test corpora were automatically tagged with word boundaries and reference corpora were also built with alignments of words and multiwords.

Multiword unit lists contain the multiwords that have to be considered during the lexical alignment process. For the extraction of these lists, were used the following corpora: texts on Computer Science from the ACM Journals (704915 English words); academic texts from Brazilian Universities (809708 BP words); journalistic texts from the journal "The New York Times" (48430 English words and 17133 BP words) and official texts from ALCA documentation (251609 English words and 254018 BP words).

The multiword unit lists were built using automatic extraction algorithms followed by a manual analysis done by a human expert. The algorithms used for automatic extraction of multiword units were NSP (N-gram Statistic Package)[7] and another which was implemented based on the Mutual Expectation technique [19]. Through this process, three lists (for each language) were generated by each algorithm and the final English and BP multiword lists have 240 and 222 units respectively.

Some examples of multiwords in these lists are: "além disso", "nações unidas" and "ou seja" for BP; "as well as", "there are" and "carry out" for English[8].

4   Evaluation and Results

The experiments described in this paper used the precision, recall and F-measure metrics to evaluate the alignment methods. Precision stands for the number of

---

[6] It is important to say that CorpusPE was evaluated with 64 pairs rather than 65 because we note that one of them was not parallel at lexical level.

[7] Available in http://www.d.umn.edu/ tdeperse/code.html.

[8] For more details of automatic extraction of multiword units lists see [20].

correct alignments per the number of proposed alignments; recall stands for the number of correct alignments per the number of alignments in the reference corpus; and F-measure is the combination of these two previous metrics [4].

The values for these metrics range between 0 and 1 where a value close to 0 indicates a bad performance of the method while a value close to 1 indicates that the method performed very well.

4.1   Evaluation and Results of Sentence Alignment Methods

Precision, recall and F-measure for each corpus of test corpora (see Section 3.1) are shown in Table 1.

Table 1. Precision, Recall and F-measure of Sentence Alignment Methods

Corpus	Metric	GC	GMA	GSA+	Piperidis et al.	TCA
Authentic	Precision	0.9125	0.9485	0.9507	0.8589	0.9017
CorpusPE	Recall	0.9012	0.9556	0.9531	0.8716	0.9062
	F-measure	0.9068	0.9520	0.9519	0.8652	0.9039
Pre-edited	Precision	0.9759	0.9904	0.9904	0.9784	0.9420
CorpusPE	Recall	0.9736	0.9928	0.9928	0.9784	0.9375
	F-measure	0.9747	0.9916	0.9916	0.9784	0.9398
	Precision	0.9917	0.9876	0.9876	0.9833	1.0000
CorpusALCA	Recall	0.9890	0.8788	0.8788	0.9725	1.0000
	F-measure	0.9903	0.9300	0.9300	0.9778	1.0000
	Precision	-	0.8788	0.8832	-	0.9190
CorpusNYT	Recall	-	0.8571	0.8571	-	0.9507
	F-measure	-	0.8678	0.8700	-	0.9346

It is important to say that only GMA, GSA+ and TCA methods were evaluated on CorpusNYT because this corpus was evaluated later and only the methods which had had better performance where considered in this last experiment.

It can be noticed that precision ranges between 85.89% and 100% and recall is between 85.71% and 100%. The best methods considering these metrics were GMA/GSA+ for CorpusPE (authentic and pre-edited) and TCA for CorpusALCA and CorpusNYT.

Taking into account these results, it is possible to notice that all methods performed better on pre-edited CorpusPE than on the authentic one, as already evidenced by other experiments [21]. These two corpora have some features which distinguish them from the other two. Firstly, the average text length (in words) in the former two is much smaller than in the latter two (BP=175, E=155 on authentic CorpusPE and BP=173, E=156 on pre-edited CorpusPE versus BP=2804, E=2713 on CorpusALCA and BP=772, E=740 on CorpusNYT). Secondly, texts in CorpusPE have more complex alignments than those in law and journalistic corpora. For example, CorpusPE contains six 2-2 alignments while 99.7% and 96% of all alignments in CorpusALCA and CorpusNYT, respectively, are 1-1.

These differences between authentic/pre-edited CorpusPE and CorpusALCA /CorpusNYT probably causes the differences in methods' performance on these corpora. It is important to say that text lengths affected the alignment task since the greater the number of sentences are, the greater will be the number of combinations among sentences to be tried during alignment.

Besides the three metrics, the methods were also evaluated by considering the error rate per alignment category. The major error rate was in 2-3, 2-2 and omissions (0-1 and 1-0) categories. The error rate in 2-3 alignments was of 100% in all methods (i.e., none of them correctly aligned the unique 2-3 alignment in authentic CorpusPE). In 2-2 alignments, the error rate for GC and GMA was 83.33% while for the remaining methods it was 100%.

TCA had the lowest error rate in omissions (40%), followed by GMA and GSA+ (80% each), while the other methods had 100% of error in this category. It can be noticed that only the methods that consider cognate words as an alignment criterion had success in omissions. In [7], Gale and Church had already mentioned the necessity of considering language-specific methods to deal adequately with this alignment category and this point was confirmed by the results reported in this paper.

As expected, all methods worked performed better on 1-1 alignments and their error rate in this category was between 2.88% and 5.52%.

4.2 Evaluation and Results of Lexical Alignment Methods

Precision, recall and F-measure for each corpus of test corpora (see Section 3.2) are shown in Table 2.

SIMR method had a better precision (91.01% to 95.61%) than LWA (51.84% to 62.15%), but its recall was very low (16.79% to 20%) what can be a problem for many applications such as bilingual lexicography. The high precision, on the other hand, can be explained by its very accurate alignment criterion based only on cognate words.

LWA had a better distribution between precision and recall: 51.84% to 62.15% and 59.38% and 65.14% respectively. These values are quite different from that obtained in an experiment carried out on English-Swedish pair in which LWA has achieved 83.9% to 96.7% precision and 50.9% to 67.1% recall ([15]) but are close to that obtained in another experiment carried out on English-French pair in which LWA has achieved 60% precision and 57% recall ([4]). So, for languages with common nature like French and BP the values were very close.

The LWA's partially correct link proposals were also evaluated using the metrics proposed in [22]. With these metrics precision improved 12% to 16% (from 51.84%–62.15% considering only totally correct alignments to 66.87%–74.86% considering also partially correct alignments) while recall improved almost 1% (from 59.38%–65.14% to 59.81%–65.82% considering totally and partially correct alignments respectively).

Table 2. Precision, Recall and F-measure of Lexical Alignment Methods

Corpus	Metric	SIMR	LWA
Pre-edited	Precision	0.9383	0.5888
CorpusPE	Recall	0.1832	0.6514
	F-measure	0.3065	0.6185
	Precision	0.9561	0.6215
CorpusALCA	Recall	0.2000	0.5983
	F-measure	0.3308	0.6097
	Precision	0.9101	0.5184
CorpusNYT	Recall	0.1679	0.5938
	F-measure	0.2835	0.5535

5 Some Conclusions

This paper has described some experiments carried out on five sentence alignment methods and two lexical alignment methods for BP-English parallel texts.

The obtained precision and recall values for all sentence alignment methods in almost all corpora are above 95%, which is the average value related in the literature [4]. However, due to the very similar performances of the methods, at this moment it is not possible to choose one of them as the best sentence alignment method for BP-English parallel texts. More tests are necessary (and will be done) to determine the influence of the alignment categories, the text lengths and genre on methods' performance.

For lexical alignment, SIMR was the method that presented the best precision, but its recall was very low and it does not deal with multiwords. LWA, on the other hand, achieved a better recall and it is able to deal with multiwords, but its precision was not so good as SIMR's one. Considering multiword units, the literature has not yet established an average value for precision and recall, but it has been clear and this work has stressed that corpus size and the pair of language have great influence on the aligners' performance ([15], [4]).

The results for sentence alignment methods have stressed the values related in the literature while the results for lexical alignment methods have demonstrated that there are still some improvement to be achieved.

In spite of this, this work has specially contributed to researches on computational linguistic involving Brazilian Portuguese by implementing, evaluating and distributing a great number of potential resources which can be useful for important applications such as machine translation and information retrieval.

Acknowledgments

We would like to thank FAPESP, CAPES and CNPq for financial support.

References

1. Carl, M.: Inducing probabilistic invertible translation grammars from aligned texts. In: Proceedings of CoNLL-2001, Toulouse, France (2001) 145–151
2. Menezes, A., Richardson, S.D.: A best-first alignment algorithm for automatic extraction of transfer mappings from bilingual corpora. In: Proceedings of the Workshop on Data-driven Machine Translation at 39th Annual Meeting of the Association for Computational Linguistics (ACL'01), Toulouse, France (2001) 39–46
3. Santos, D., Oksefjell, S.: An evaluation of the translation corpus aligner, with special reference to the language pair English-Portuguese. In: Proceedings of the 12th "Nordisk datalingvistikkdager", Trondheim, Departmento de Lingüística, NTNU (2000) 191–205
4. Véronis, J., Langlais, P.: Evaluation of parallel text alignment systems: The AR-CADE project. In Véronis, J., ed.: Parallel text processing: Alignment and use of translation corpora, Kluwer Academic Publishers (2000) 369–388
5. Kraif, O.: From translation data to constrative knowledge: Using bi-text for bilingual lexicons extraction. International Journal of Corpus Linguistic 8:1 (2003) 1–29
6. Gale, W.A., Church, K.W.: A program for aligning sentences in bilingual corpora. In: Proceedings of the 29th Annual Meeting of the Association for Computational Linguistics (ACL), Berkley (1991) 177–184
7. Gale, W.A., Church, K.W.: A program for aligning sentences in bilingual corpora. Computational Linguistics 19 (1993) 75–102
8. Melamed, I.D.: A geometric approach to mapping bitext correspondence. In: Proceedings of the Conference on Empirical Methods in Natural Language Processing, Philadelphia, Pennsylvania (1996) 1–12
9. Melamed, I.D.: Pattern recognition for mapping bitext correspondence. In Véronis, J., ed.: Parallel text processing: Alignment and use of translation corpora, Kluwer Academic Publishers (2000) 25–47
10. Piperidis, S., Papageorgiou, H., Boutsis, S.: From sentences to words and clauses. In Véronis, J., ed.: Parallel text processing: Alignment and use of translation corpora, Kluwer Academic Publishers (2000) 117–138
11. Hofland, K.: A program for aligning English and Norwegian sentences. In Hockey, S., Ide, N., Perissinotto, G., eds.: Research in Humanities Computing, Oxford, Oxford University Press (1996) 165–178
12. Melamed, I.D.: A portable algorithm for mapping bitext correspondence. In: Proceedings of the 35th Annual Meeting of the Association for Computational Linguistics. (1997) 305–312
13. Melamed, I.D., Al-Adhaileh, M.H., Kong, T.E.: Malay-English bitext mapping and alignment using SIMR/GSA algorithms. In: Malaysian National Conference on Research and Development in Computer Science (REDECS'01), Selangor Darul Ehsan, Malaysia (2001)
14. Ahrenberg, L., Andersson, M., Merkel, M.: A simple hybrid aligner for generating lexical correspondences in parallel texts. In: Proceedings of Association for Computational Linguistics. (1998) 29–35
15. Ahrenberg, L., Andersson, M., Merkel, M.: A knowledge-lite approach to word alignment. In Véronis, J., ed.: Parallel text processing: Alignment and use of translation corpora. (2000) 97–116

16. Ahrenberg, L., Andersson, M., Merkel, M.: A system for incremental and interactive word linking. In: Third International Conference on Language Resources and Evaluation (LREC 2002), Las Palmas (2002) 485–490
17. Caseli, H.M., Nunes, M.G.V.: A construção dos recursos lingüísticos do projeto PESA. Série de Relatórios do NILC NILC-TR-02-07, NILC, http://www.nilc.icmc.usp.br/nilc/download/NILC-TR-02-07.zip (2002)
18. Caseli, H.M., Feltrim, V.D., Nunes, M.G.V.: TagAlign: Uma ferramenta de pré-processamento de textos. Série de Relatórios do NILC NILC-TR-02-09, NILC, http://www.nilc.icmc.usp.br/nilc/download/NILC-TR-02-09.zip (2002)
19. Dias, G., Kaalep, H.: Automtic extraction of multiword units for Estonian: Phrasal verbs. In Metslang, H., Rannut, M., eds.: Languages in Development. Number 41 in Linguistic Edition, Lincom-Europa, München (2002)
20. Silva, A.M.P., Nunes, M.G.V.: Extração automática de multipalavras. Série de Relatórios do NILC NILC-TR-03-11, NILC, http://www.nilc.icmc.usp.br/nilc/download/NILC-TR-03-11.zip (2003)
21. Gaussier, E., Hull, D., Aït-Mokthar, S.: Term alignment in use: Machine-aided human translation. In Véronis, J., ed.: Parallel text processing: Alignment and use of translation corpora, Kluwer Academic Publishers (2000) 253–274
22. Ahrenberg, L., Merkel, M., Hein, A.S., Tiedemann, J.: Evaluation of word alignment systems. In: Proceedings of 2nd International Conference on Language Resources & Evaluation (LREC 2000). (2000) 1255–1261

Applying a Lexical Similarity Measure to Compare Portuguese Term Collections

Marcirio Silveira Chaves and Vera Lúcia Strube de Lima

Pontifícia Universidade Católica do Rio Grande do Sul - PUCRS
Faculdade de Informática - FACIN
Programa de Pós-Graduação em Ciência da Computação - PPGCC
Av. Ipiranga, 6681 - Partenon - Porto Alegre - RS
CEP 90619-900
{mchaves,vera}@inf.pucrs.br

Abstract. The number of ontologies publicly available and accessible through the web has increased in the last years, so that the task of finding similar terms[1] among these structures becomes mandatory. We depict the application and the evaluation of a new similarity measure for comparing Portuguese Ontological Structures (OSs) called Lexical Similarity (LS). This paper describes contributions to the study and application of mapping between terms present in multidomain OSs. In order to approach this mapping we combine preliminar similarity measures and heuristics. Our measure uses a stemmer, it is established upon String Matching (SM) proposed in [1] and it was evaluated by means of a comparison to human evaluation. Finally, we concentrate on the application of LS measure to terms belonging to same domain thesauri and discuss the results obtained.

Keywords: Lexical Similarity Measure, Mapping, Ontological Structures

1 Introduction

The automatic mapping between Ontological Structures (OSs) has been a continuous concern as a task of integration and reuse of knowledge. However, the manual execution of such task is quite tedious and slow, so it is important to automate it, at least partially.

In this work, OSs are understood as sets of pre-defined terms explicitly connected by semantic relations in a format, which is readable by humans and machines. This notion is suitable for collections of vocabularies as well as for collections of concepts.

Several efforts have been reported in the literature to mapping different OSs in English language [2–4] and in German language [1]. However, other works that deal with Portuguese OSs have not been found. We concentrate our efforts on

---

[1] The words "terms" and "concepts" will be used with the same meaning in this article.

A.L.C. Bazzan and S. Labidi (Eds.): SBIA 2004, LNAI 3171, pp. 194–203, 2004.

Portuguese OSs, developing, testing, validating and evaluating a proper measure to help detecting similar terms between OSs, which are projected independently using preview studies [1, 3].

This paper is further organized as follows. Section 2 describes the SM measure [1]. Section 3 details the similarity measure proposed in this paper. The experiments accomplished over multidomain Portuguese OSs are presented in Section 4. Section 5 presents the experiments with thesauri belonging to the same domain. Finally, Section 6 gives an outlook on future work.

2   Maedche and Staab Measure

Maedche and Staab [1] present a two layer approach, first lexical and then conceptual, to measure the similarity between terms of different OSs. At the lexical level, they consider the Edit Distance (ED) formulated by Levenshtein [5]. This distance contemplates the minimum number of insertions, deletions or substitutions (reversals) necessary to transform one string into another using a dynamic programming algorithm. The contribution of Maedche and Staab consists of the String Matching (SM) measure given by:

$$SM(T_i, T_j) := max\left(0, \frac{min(|\,T_i\,|, |\,T_j\,|) \; - \; ED(T_i, T_j)}{min(|\,T_i\,|, |\,T_j\,|)}\right) \; \in \; [0, 1]\,. \qquad (1)$$

The SM measure calculates the similarity between two terms (Ti, Tj). The length in characters of the shortest term is represented by $min(|Ti|, |Tj|)$. For example, to obtain the similarity between the terms (comerciario, comerciante) the minimum length is 11 and $ED(Ti, Tj)$ is 3 (changes "r" by "n" and inserts "t" and "e"). Thus, the resulting value for SM(comerciario, comerciante) is 0.73.

This measure always returns a value between 0 and 1, where 1 stands for perfect match and zero indicates absence of match. Maedche and Staab worked with German language OSs from tourism domain. However, while applying SM measure to Portuguese OSs, many terms were mapped inconsistently. In order to get better results we developed a proper measure, which was validated and evaluated[2].

3   Lexical Similarity Measure

We propose an alternative to SM measure which is based on the radicals[3] of the words. Generally, these radicals are the most representative part of a word in Portuguese, and they can be extracted with the help of a stemmer. We used a stemmer that was specifically developed for Portuguese by Orengo and Huyck,

---

[2] Detailed results, experiments, validation and evaluation can be found in [6].

[3] The term radical as used in this article represents the initial character string of a word and not necessarily the linguistic concept of radical.

which presented good performance when compared [7] to Porter algorithm or other [8]. Our proposal is named Lexical Similarity (LS) and it is expressed by the equation in 2, where terms are represented by T_i and T_j, and index i points to the terms in OS_A while index j refers to terms in OS_B.

$$LS(T_i, T_j) = min\{\Delta_{ij}^1, \Delta_{ij}^2, \ldots, \Delta_{ij}^k\} \in [0, 1] . \tag{2}$$

Terms can be formed by single-words, or by more than one word. LS measure, in contrast to SM measure, considers only the radical of each word, instead of the complete string of characters. The symbol Δ represents the value obtained by SM measure under the following conditions:

$$\Delta_{ij}^k = \begin{cases} SM(Rad_i^k, Rad_j^k) & if\ ED(Rad_i^k, Rad_j^k) = 0 \\ SM(Rad_i^k, Rad_j^k) - 0.1 & if\ ED(Rad_i^k, Rad_j^k) = 1 \\ SM(Rad_i^k, Rad_j^k) - 0.2 & if\ ED(Rad_i^k, Rad_j^k) = 2 \\ 0 & if\ ED(Rad_i^k, Rad_j^k) \geq 3 \end{cases} \tag{3}$$

The radical of a word that is part of a term T is represented by Rad_i^k, where k indicates the position of this word in T and i indicates the OS to which this term belongs. When T_i and T_j are multiword terms, the index k reaches the value of the amount of words of the term with the minimum number of words, so that LS measure calculates the similarity between the first k pairs of radicals (Rad_i^k, Rad_j^k) in the terms being compared.

The result returned by LS measure is the minimum value produced by equation 3, which depends on the Edit Distance. As the radical of a term owns a strong semantic weight, the result obtained by ED is decremented according to the conditions stated in equation 3. The highest is the ED, the highest is the penalty used. The penalty values (0.1 and 0.2) were obtained from empirical studies with SM measure. We assume that, if ED $\geq$ 3 the value returned by SM is zero and, consequently, LS is zero, too. What means, three or more changes in the radical of a word suggest a low degree of similarity.

For example, in order to check the similarity between the terms **areaEstrategica** and **armaEstrategica**, the words of the each term are processed by a stemming algorithm, which produces the stems "are" and "arm", "estrateg" and "estrateg", so that:

$$LS(areaEstrategica, armaEstrategica) = min\{SM(are, arm),$$
$$SM(estrateg, estrateg)\} .$$

To calculate SM*(are, arm)*, we obtain the length of the shortest term, in this case 3. Then ED*(are, arm)* is calculated, which gives 1, since the letter "e" is changed to "m" to transform the string "are" into "arm". So, SM*(are, arm)* is solved as:

$$max\left(0, \frac{3-1}{3}\right) = 0.67 .$$

As in this case $ED = 1$, the penalty to be applied is 0.1. So, the resultant similarity is 0.57.

The next result to be obtained is the similarity between SM(*estrateg, estrateg*) that is 1. In this case ED(*estrateg, estrateg*) is zero, (since the strings are in perfect match). Thus:

$$LS(areaEstrategica, armaEstrategica) = min\{0.57, 1\} = 0.57 .$$

We did not find other works in the literature that provide a study on semantic weighting for each single-word in a multiword term, which would be suitable for Portuguese language as well as for several other languages such as Spanish, French and so on. In our proposal, as the reader can observe, words with the lowest lexical similarity value may perform an important role on similarity detection.

4   Multidomain Experiment

The OSs we used in this experiment come from two distinct sources[4]. Their terms belong to one of two groups: single-word terms or multiword terms[5].

The experiments were organized in two steps: testing and validation[6] of LS measure, followed by its evaluation. The terms in OS_A were categorized into two sets for each phase, while terms in OS_B remained without categorization during both validation and evaluation phases. The terms were placed in alphabetical order and an algorithm was developed to randomly distribute them through validation and evaluation experiment groups.

We also disclosed a heuristic to tune the mappings generated by LS measure. In Portuguese language, the semantic weight of the first characters in a term is apparently strong, which gives rise to the heuristic that is stated as:

$$If \ Rad[1]_i^k \neq Rad[1]_j^k \ then \ SM(Rad_i^k, Rad_j^k) = 0 \qquad (4)$$

According to LS measure (equation 2), let the index inside the brackets be the position of the first character in the radical of the word in a term. If the two radicals Rad_i^k, Rad_j^k being compared have a different first letter, the value returned by SM measure will be zero. Consequently, LS will be zero, too.

For the evaluation phase, we used 1,823 single-word terms of Senate OS, while the USP OS remained with its original 7,039 single-word terms. We selected 4,701 multiword terms of Senate OS and kept 16,986 multiword terms of USP. The aim of the experiments in this phase was to check the agreement among LS and SM measures according to the results given by a human analysis of similarity.

---

[4] Namely: Brazilian Senate Thesaurus (OS_A) and São Paulo University - USP Thesaurus (OS_B).

[5] For the experiments with multiword terms, OSs were first preprocessed in order to eliminate blanks. Moreover, the first character of each word was capitalized, except for the first word in a term. This procedure is necessary to compare results with those in English [3] and German [1] experiments.

[6] Details on the experiments carried out in testing and validation can be found in [9].

In order to examine in detail the 2,887 pairs of terms and the corresponding system-computed or human confirmed analysis, we split them into seven groups. These groups are presented in Table 1, where **G1** to **G7** stand for the respective group[7].

Table 1. Composition of the groups according to a human point of view

	$SM \geq 0.75$ $LS \geq 0.75$	$SM \geq 0.75$ $LS < 0.75$	$SM < 0.75$ $LS \geq 0.75$
Terms estimated as similar by human analysis	G1	G2	G3
Terms estimated as unlike by human analysis	G4	G5	G6
Doubt		G7	

Human analysts pointed the pairs of terms as "similar", "unlike" or "doubtful". This result was compared with the automatically processed combinations. We choose Group G5 in Table 1 deemed as the most representative to be described in detail in the next section.

4.1   Analysis of Group G5

This group contains terms whose are deemed similar by SM measure and unlike by LS measure as well as by the human analysis. Moreover, in G5 there are most of the pairs analyzed during the evaluation phase, that is, about 73% which corresponds to 907 single-word terms and 1,211 multiword terms. We show an extract of these terms in Table 2.

Table 2 contemplates single-word (first five lines) and multiword (next five lines) terms. At first, let's analyze single-word terms. Most of them belonging to this group have the same suffix, that is, the final string is a perfect match of characters. As SM equally weights the strings belonging to the radical or to the suffix, a high value of similarity was observed between the terms having same suffix. However, this policy is not yet confirmed for Portuguese.

Otherwise, in the multiword terms, at least one word of the term has the same suffix. As the reader may note, all terms in Table 2 seem to be unlike, despite SM measure detects them as similar. We can increase the threshold from 0.75 to 0.8 in order to get a more consistent mapping by SM. However, this higher threshold is not enough to deem the terms belonging to G5 as dissimilar, once just some pairs of terms have similarity value under 0.8.

As this group represents most of the terms analyzed in evaluation phase and, taking into account the results generated by SM measure, it is possible to question if this measure is really proper to treat Portuguese terms. Specifically for multiword terms, we believe that the best performance of LS measure is due to the fact that it considers each constituent word individually.

---

[7] We used the threshold 0.75 in our experiments. This value is also used in [1].

Table 2. Extract of group G5: single-word and multiword terms

OS_A	OS_B	SM	LS
tuberculose	tuberculos	0.90	0.5
terceiros	terreiros	0.89	0.65
atentado	atestado	0.88	0.70
corretor	corredor	0.88	0.65
desarmamento	desmatamento	0.75	0
delitoFiscal	debitoFiscal	0.92	0.70
ensinoMedico	ensinoMedio	0.91	0.65
policiaAdministrativa	politicaAdministrativa	0.90	0.65
direitoPenalEcologico	direitoPenalEconomico	0.90	0.47
direitoAVida	direitoAVoto	0.75	0.13

As a following step toward experimentation, we concentrate our efforts in mapping of terms belonging to the same domain. We apply the SM and LS measures to these terms through the experiment described in the next section.

5   Same Domain Experiment

In this experiment we verify the similarity among 2,083 terms from GEODESC Thesaurus[8] and 429 terms from USP Thesaurus, which belong to the Geosciences domain. In order to carry out this experiment, we do not consider the cases where there is a perfect matching of characters, because these ones do not help to evaluate any of the measures. Moreover, we use the first letter heuristic to help us obtain better results.

After running the algorithm with the two measures, 91 mappings were found between the two thesauri representing 4.36% of the terms of GEODESC Thesaurus and 21.21% of the terms of USP Thesaurus. In order to analyze these mappings, we split them into 2 groups. In Group A (GA) these are the terms considered similar by LS measure, while the Group B (GB) includes the terms deemed as similar by SM and dissimilar by LS. Table 3 shows these groups considering similar terms with similarity value ≥ 0.75.

Table 3. Groups composed after same domain experiment

Group	Conditions	
GA	SM < 0.75	LS ≥ 0.75
	SM ≥ 0.75	LS ≥ 0.75
GB	SM ≥ 0.75	LS < 0.75

Table 3 presents the combinations between SM and LS similarity measures. These cases are explained as follows:

---

[8] Available by ftp://ftp.cprm.gov.br/pub/pdf/didote/geodesc.pdf

5.1   Analysis of Group A

This group contains those terms which are considered similar by LS measure. The analysis was broken into two tables, comparing our LS measure with Maedche and Staab's SM measure. Only 4 mappings were detected while considering SM < 0.75 and LS ≥ 0.75, as is shown in Table 4. In our point of view just the first mapping (between the terms sais and sal) can be considered correct by LS. In order to evaluate the remaining mappings it is necessary to know the semantic relations among the terms and to take into account the meaning of each term.

Table 4. Pairs of terms considered dissimilar by SM and similar by LS

GEODESC	USP	CC	LS
sais	sal	0.33	1.00
arqueamento	arqueano	0.63	1.00
meteorito	meteoritica	0.67	0.76
vulcanicas	vulcanismo	0.70	1.00

In Group A, when both measures consider the terms being compared as similar (SM ≥ 0.75 and LS ≥ 0.75) we have the terms presented in Table 5. Lines 1 to 5 show terms with number variation and they are correctly deemed as similar by both measures. The remaining pairs of terms, such as those in Table 4, do not present a unique characteristic and it is difficult to perform an evaluation of the results generated.

Table 5. Pairs of terms considered similar by SM and LS

GEODESC	USP	CC	LS
lava	lavas	0.75	1.00
aguaSubterranea	aguasSubterraneas	0.87	1.00
depositosGlaciais	depositoGlacial	0.80	1.00
fumarola	fumarolas	0.88	1.00
oolitos	oolito	0.83	1.00
andesina	andesito	0.75	0.76
dolomita	dolomito	0.88	1.00
metamorficas	metamorfismo	0.75	1.00
metassomaticas	metassomatismo	0.79	0.79
prospeccaoGeotermal	prospeccaoGeotermica	0.84	1.00

5.2   Analysis of Group B

This group presents most of the mappings found in our experiment. We split these pairs of terms into two tables, the former composed by only one word terms and the latter by multiword terms.

The single-word terms are shown in Table 6. Despite all these pairs of terms have high lexical similarity, their meanings are different. So, in the context of mapping of similar terms between OSs we consider they should not be mapped.

Table 6. Single word pairs of terms

GEODESC	USP	CC	LS	GEODESC	USP
bioestratigrafia	litoestratigrafia	0.88	0.66	bioestratigraf	litoestratigraf
biologia	geologia	0.75	0.47	biolog	geolog
cosalita	sodalita	0.75	0.51	cosalit	sodalit
gemologia	geologia	0.88	0.73	gemolog	geolog
hamarita	hematita	0.75	0.51	hamarit	hematit
paleoecologia	paleontologia	0.85	0.62	paleoecolog	paleontolog
pedologia	geologia	0.75	0.47	pedolog	geolog
pinita	pirita	0.83	0.70	pinit	pirit
reologia	geologia	0.88	0.73	reolog	geolog
teleprocessamento	geoprocessamento	0.81	0	teleprocess	geoprocess

In this moment it is important to stress a contribution of our measure. According to the literature studied, just the SM measure has been used to map terms among OSs. In this work, when we apply SM measure to single-word terms the reader can note its low performance, while our measure seems to attribute a suitable similarity value to the same pairs of terms. So, LS measure contributes to avoid detection of dissimilar terms like similar.

Still in this group, we analyze the multiword terms. The pairs of terms in this case are depicted in Table 7.

Table 7. Multiword pairs of terms

GEODESC	USP	CC	LS
faciesSedimentares	rochasSedimentares	0.78	0
geologiaAplicada	hidrologiaAplicada	0.75	0
geologiaEconomica	geologiaIsotopica	0.76	0
geologiaEstrutural	petrologiaEstrutural	0.83	0
geologiaFisica	geodesiaFisica	0.79	0
prospeccaoGeoquimica	prospeccaoBioquimica	0.90	0.51
sistemasOperacionais	sistemasDeposicionais	0.75	0

The reader may note that these pairs are considered similar by SM measure mainly due to the fact of dealing with them as a single string. As oppose to the LS measure, SM does not verify the similarity among individual words. The multiword terms belonging to Geosciences domain are generally composed by more than 10 characters. So, the value returned by ED does not generate sufficient impact to reduce the final similarity value of SM of the full term.

On the other hand, our measure considers individually the words belonging to the terms. This fact helps reducing the final similarity value, once the shortest term has a lower value than the one used by SM. So, the result of ED has a greater impact in the equation, decreasing the value of LS measure.

It is important to observe in Table 7 that most of the values generated by LS measure is zero. This occurs because those pairs have 3 or more distinct characters in the radical of the words.

Table 8. Contribution of the penalties

GEODESC	USP	CC	LS
bioestratigrafia	litoestratigrafia	0.88	0.66
lazurita	azurita	0.86	0.73
litoestratigrafia	bioestratigrafia	0.88	0.66
reologia	geologia	0.88	0.73

Finally, it is worth noting the contribution of the penalties introduced in equation 2, as expressed in Table 8.

These penalties allow decreasing the value of LS measure and, consequently, considering terms as dissimilar (maintaining threshold 0.75), in opposite to SM measure. For example, the similarity between the pair of terms bioestratigrafia and litoestratigrafia by LS measure without penalties would be 0.86. This value allows us to consider it as similar, however, introducing the penalties (in this case 0.2) we have the final similarity value 0.66, which is under the threshold established. In fact, this pair is not really similar likewise the remaining ones in Table 8. Thus, they should not be mapped in the context of our analysis.

6   Final Remarks and Future Work

This work is the first effort towards the detection of similar terms between Portuguese OSs. LS measure was evaluated based on human evaluation of similarity, even though we find difficulties to evaluate similarity measures in agreement with a human point of view. A full description and analysis of the results obtained with LS measure are given in [6]. We believe that our measure contributes to help the ontology engineers reuse the information contained in the ontological structures, since the reuse is one of the main concerns in the context of the semantic web.

We carried out experiments with terms belonging to multidomain as well as to the same domain structures, and we commented the main results obtained. In spite of being them preliminary results, they are encouraging.

The next step is the application of LS measure to other languages, such as English or Spanish. In this situation a proper stemming algorithm, suitable for each different language, should be used. Besides, the similarity measures presented in this article can be used in order to aid on the task of union or alignment of ontological structures. It could also be connected to specific interface to help the ontologists detect terms suggested as similar.

Acknowledgements

Marcirio Silveira Chaves was supported by the research center HP-CPAD (Centro de Processamento de Alto Desempenho HP Brasil-PUCRS).

References

1. Alexander Maedche and Steffen Staab. Measuring Similarity between Ontologies. In *Proceedings of the European Conference on Knowledge Acquisition and Management - (EKAW-2002). Madrid, Spain, October 1-4*, pages 251–263, 2002.
2. AnHai Doan, Jayant Madhavan, Pedro Domingos, and Alon Halevy. Learning to Map between Ontologies on the Semantic Web. In *Proceedings of the World-Wide Web Conference (WWW-2002), Honolulu, Hawaii, USA*, May 2002.
3. Natalya Fridman Noy and Mark A. Musen. Anchor-PROMPT: Using Non-Local Context for Semantic Matching. In *Proceedings of the Workshop on Ontologies and Information Sharing at the Seventeenth International Joint Conference on Artificial Intelligence (IJCAI-2001), Seattle, WA*, August 2001.
4. Sushama Prasad, Yun Peng, and Timothy Finin. Using Explicit Information To Map Between Two Ontologies. In *Proceedings of the 1st International Joint Conference on Autonomous Agents and Multi-Agent Systems - Workshop on Ontologies in Agent Systems (OAS) - Bologna, Italy. 15-19 July*, 2002.
5. Vladimir Levenshtein. Binary Codes Capable of Correcting Deletions, Insertions and Reversals. *Cybernetics and Control Theory*, 10(8):707–710, 1966.
6. Marcirio Silveira Chaves. Comparação e Mapeamento de Similaridade entre Estruturas Ontológicas. Master's thesis, PUCRS-FACIN-PPGCC, 2004.
7. Viviane Moreira Orengo and Christian Huyck. A Stemming Algorithm for Portuguese Language. In *Proceedings of Eigth Symposium on String Processing and Information Retrieval (SPIRE-2001)*, pages 186–193, 2001.
8. Marcirio Silveira Chaves. Um Estudo e Apreciação sobre Dois Algoritmos de Stemming para a Língua Portuguesa. Jornadas Iberoamericanas de Informática. Cartagena de Indias - Colômbia (CD-ROM), August 11-15, 2003.
9. Marcirio Silveira Chaves and Vera Lúcia Strube de Lima. *Looking for Similarity between Portuguese Ontological Structures*. In: António Branco, Amália Mendes, Ricardo Ribeiro (editors). Edições Colibri, Lisboa, 2004 (to appear).

Dialog with a Personal Assistant

Fabrício Enembreck[1] and Jean-Paul Barthès[2]

[1] PUCPR, Pontifícia Universidade Católica do Paraná
PPGIA, Programa de Pós-Graduação em Informática Aplicada
Rua Imaculada Conceição, 1155, Curitiba PR, Brasil
fabricio@ppgia.pucpr.br
[2] UTC – Université de Technologie de Compiègne
HEUDIASYC – Centre de Recherches Royallieu
60205 Compiègne, France
barthes@utc.fr

Abstract. This paper describes a new generic architecture for dialog systems enabling communication between a human user and a personal assistant based on speech acts. Dialog systems are often domain-related applications. That is, the system is developed for specific applications and cannot be reused in other domains. A major problem concerns the development of scalable dialog systems capable to be extended with new tasks without much effort. In this paper we discuss a generic dialog architecture for a personal assistant. The assistant uses explicit task representation and knowledge to achieve an "intelligent" dialog. The independence of the dialog architecture from knowledge and from tasks allows the agent to be extended without needing to modify the dialog structure. The system has been implemented in a collaborative environment in order to personalize services and to facilitate the interaction with collaborative applications like e-mail clients, document managers or design tools.

Keywords: Dialog Systems, Natural Language, Personal Assistants

1 Introduction

While using our computers to work or to communicate, we observe three major trends: (i) the user's environment becomes increasingly complex; (ii) cooperative work is growing; (iii) knowledge management is spreading rapidly. Because of the increasing complexity of their environment, users are frequently overwhelmed with tasks that they must accomplish through many different tools (e-mail managers, web browsers, word processors, etc.). The resulting cognitive overload leads to some disorganization, which has negative impacts, in particular when the information is shared among different people. A major issue is thus to develop better and more intuitive interfaces.

We are currently developing a Personal Assistant Agent in a project called AACC[1], for supporting collaboration between French and American groups of

---

[1] The AACC (Agents d'Aide à la Conception Coopérative) project is a collaborative project involving the CNRS HEUDIASYC laboratory of UTC, and the LaRIA laboratory of UPJV in France.

A.L.C. Bazzan and S. Labidi (Eds.): SBIA 2004, LNAI 3171, pp. 204–213, 2004.
© Springer-Verlag Berlin Heidelberg 2004

students, located at UTC (Université de Technologie de Compiègne) and at ISU (Iowa State University). The students must design electro-mechanical devices using assistant agents. In this paper, we focus on the Personal Assistant (PA), discussing how a Natural Language interface allows the user to interact with the Assistant efficiently, and how this interaction can be used to increase the agent knowledge of the user. We developed a generic dialog system using several models: dialog model, tasks models, domain knowledge model and user model. We focus in this paper the construction of the dialog model and show how speech acts can be used to make the dialog model independent of domain data (tasks and knowledge).

The paper is organized as follows: Section 2 presents some theory on natural language and dialog systems; Section 3 describes the architecture of our system. The deployment and evaluation are discussed in section 4. We discuss related work in section 5. Finally, Section 6 concludes with our observations.

2 Natural Language and Dialog Systems

Communications using natural language (NL) have been proposed in the past. Early attempts were done at the end of the sixties, early seventies. Szolovits et al. [1] or Goldstein and Roberts [6] developed formalisms and languages for representing the knowledge contained in English utterances. The internal language would support inferences in order to produce answers. In the first project (OWL language) the application was to draw inferences on an object database. In the second one (FRL-0 language), the goal was to schedule meetings. The internal language was used to represent knowledge and to translate utterances. Such an approach can simplify the representations and inferences, because only very specific applications are considered. However, for new domains, a major part of the application must be rewritten, which is unfortunate in an environment involving several tasks (like collaborative work) when part of the dialog must be recoded each time a new task is added to the system. Later, sophisticated knowledge representation techniques were proposed by several researchers, including Schank and Abelson [13], Sowa [16] or Riesbeck and Martin [12], for handling natural language and representing meaning. They allowed expressing complex relationships between objects. The main difficulty with such techniques however, is to define the right level of granularity for the representation, because even very simple utterances can produce very complex structures. Moreover, modeling concepts and utterances is a very time consuming non-trivial task. The field of NL and machine understanding has expanded since the early attempts, however, the techniques being used are fairly complex and most of the time unnecessary for the purpose of conducting dialogs, in particular goal-oriented dialogs, since "it is not necessary to understand in order to act."

Like NL techniques, dialog systems generally use internal but simpler structures to represent knowledge, e.g., ontologies, semantic nets, or frames systems. The emphasis however is not on the adequacy of the knowledge representation, but rather on the dialog coordination by a dialog manager. In addition, the dialog systems are designed so that they can be used in other domains without the necessity of changing the dialog structure, in order to save development time.

Many dialog systems implementing NL interfaces have been developed in applications like speech-to-speech translation [8], meeting schedule, travel books [2] [15], telephone information systems, transportation and traffic information, tutorial systems, etc. Flycht-Eriksson [5] has classified dialog systems into query/answer systems and task-oriented systems. Query/answer systems include consultation systems like tourist information, time information, traveling, etc. Task-oriented systems guide the user through a dialog to execute a task. Tasks range from very simple tasks like "find a document" to complex tasks decomposed into several subtasks. We argue that a dialog system for supporting collaborative work must be both of query/answer and task-oriented type because user problems can involve questions ("Where does Robert work?", "What does electrostatic mean?") and tasks ("Find a document for me", "Send a message to the project leader"). We present our approach in next section.

3   A Personal Assistant That Participates in Dialogs

We discuss the different models that compose our dialog system paying a special attention to the dialog model.

```
 1  User:    Send a mail to Marco for me.
 2  System:  Who are the Carbon Copy receivers?
 3  User:    What is Leila's address?
 4  System:  The address of Leila is "25 rue de Paris".
 5  System:  Who are the Carbon Copy receivers?
 6  User:    none
 7  System:  What is the subject?
 8  User:    Ohh I'm sorry I made mistake!
 9  System:  Who are the Carbon Copy receivers?
10  User:    Mary's husband.
11  System:  What is the subject?
...
```

Fig. 1. Open Dialog.

3.1   Dialog Model

Our approach uses a speech act system. According to Searle [14], the speech act is the basic unit of language used to express meaning through an utterance that expresses an intention of doing something (to act). In our system, the users' utterances express questions and requests. Then, a PA starts a dialog to reach a state where an action is triggered according to the intention of the user. The dialog states are nodes of a dialog graph in which most speech acts are available at all times. For instance, consider the dialog on Fig. 1onfoo. In lines 1-5, the user requests the task "send mail" and the system asks for additional information. The user enters a new question during the task dialog (lines 3-4), the system answers it and returns to the previous dialog context. To accomplish this, the system keeps a stack of states. When a new task is requested the system pushes a number of states in the stack equal to number of slots required to accomplish the task. When a slot is successfully filled, the system marks it as "poped." This strategy also allows the user to return to previous states (Fig. 1 lines 5-10).

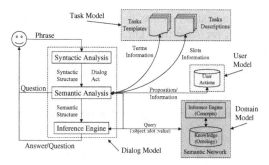

Fig. 2. Model-Based Architecture.

Our system (architecture Fig. 2) has been developed for dialog-based and question/answer interaction. In task-oriented dialog the system asks the user to fill slots of a given task (like *send e-mails* or *locate documents*). Then the system runs the task and presents the result. In question/answer interaction, the user asks the system for information. In this case the assistant uses its knowledge base for providing correct answers.

Fig. 2 shows that when the system receives a simple question or information the syntactic analyzer produces a syntactic representation. The representation gives the grammatical structure of the sentence (verbal phrase, nominal phrase, prepositional phrase, etc). We developed a grammatical rule base, where each rule refers to a single dialog act. The semantic analyzer uses this structure to build requests. The role of the semantic analyzer is to identify objects, properties, values and actions in the syntactic structure using the object hierarchy and relations defined in the domain model. The information is used to create a formal query. During the semantic analysis the system can ask the user for confirmation or request additional information to resolve conflicts. Finally, the inference engine uses the resulting formal query to retrieve the required information and the system presents it to user.

Whenever a task-oriented dialog starts, the semantic analyzer first tries to determine if a known task is concerned. If it is the case, it verifies the slots initially filled with information and continues the dialog to acquire important information for executing the task. To identify the task and concerned slots, the analyzer retrieves information from task models (see Section 3.3). The recursive stack strategy allows the user to use relations and concepts defined in the domain model (see Fig. 1, line 10) at all times.

In our system, the dialog coordination depends on the type of utterances denoted by speech acts. Schank and Abelson [13] proposed a categorization of messages, of which we keep the following:

- *Assertive*: message that affirms something or gives an answer (e.g., "Paul is professor of AI at UTC.", "Mary's husband");
- *Directive*: gives a directive (e.g., "Find a document for me.");
- *Explicative*: ask for explanation (e.g. "Why?");
- *Interrogative*: ask for a solution (e.g., "Where does Paul work?").

To maintain a terminological coherence, the previous categories will be referred to by speech acts: Assert act for Assertive; Directive act for Directive; Explain act for Explicative and WH/Question (where, what or which) or Y-N/Question (yes-no) for Interrogative. Speech acts are used to classify nodes of the dialog state graph. The dialog graph represents a discussion between the user and the system where nodes are the user's utterances and arcs are the classification given to the node.

To improve communications we introduced new specialized speech acts:

- *Confirm*: used by the system to ask the user to confirm a given value;
- *Go-back*: used by the user to go to the previous node of the dialog, for instance when the user made a mistake;
- *Abort*: used by the user to terminate the dialog;
- *Propose*: used by the system to propose a value to a question. This act can be followed by a Confirm act.

Fig. 3 shows the functional architecture of the dialog coordination. Fig. 3 shows how we implemented the semantic interpretation for each speech act. The interaction with the user starts always with the "Ask" system act. The default question is "What can I do for you?" Then, the user can ask for information or start a task. Based on the user phrase the Task Recognizer classifies the user phrase as a "General Utterance" or a "Task-Related Utterance." The task recognizer compares the verbs and nouns of the verbal and nominal parts of the utterance with the linguistic information stored previously into task templates (section 3.3).

A general utterance is simply analyzed by the semantic analyzer taking into account the speech act recognized during syntactic analysis. Four types of speech acts are possible: Assertive (assert act), Explicative (explain act), Directive (directive act) and Interrogative (wh/question or y-n/question acts). Finally the Inference Engine can ask the knowledge base for the answer. Inference engine does a top-down search into the concepts hierarchy, identifying classes and subclasses of concepts, properties and values filtering the concepts that satisfy the constraints specified into the queries.

The interpretation of a task-related utterance is more complex. First the Task Recognizer locates the correct task based on the terms present on the nominal phrases using the terminological representation (Task Template on Section 3.3) about the tasks. Next the task recognizer matches the modifiers of these nominal phrases with information about the parameters for filling the slots referred in the phrase. Then, the Task Engine will ask the user about other parameters sequentially. For each parameter an *Ask* act is executed by the system. At this point the user can: simply answer the question (in this case the task engine fills the slot and passes to the next one), ask for *Explanation*, *Go-back* to the last slot or *Abort* the dialog. When a user asks for *Explanation*, the Task Explainer presents the information coded on the task description concerning the current parameter (*params-explains* on Section 3.3) and the task engine restarts the dialog concerning the current parameter. The *Go-back* act simply makes the task engine roll back the dialog flow to the last parameter filled. When the user enters an *Abort* act the Task Eraser reinitializes variables concerning the current task and the system goes back to the default prompt or to the top task of the task stack.

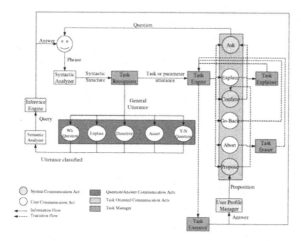

Fig. 3. Functional Architecture.

The system can also ask for confirmation and propose values with *Confirm* and *Propose* speech acts respectively. To confirm a given value the system shows a default question like "Confirm the value?" and waits for a valid answer. If a positive answer is given, the system confirms the value and the dialog continues. Otherwise, the task engine asks the question concerning the current parameter again. The *Propose* act is executed before the *Ask* act. The User Profile Manager looks at the user model for a value to propose to the user. If a value if found, it is presented to the user and the system ask the user for a confirmation executing a *Confirm* act.

Finally, when no more information is needed the Task Executor executes the task and presents the solution or a feedback to the user. It also sends information to User Profile Manager that saves the current task in the user model.

3.2 How to Interpret the User's Utterances

In our approach, we use a simple English regular grammar extended from Allen [1]. We divided the syntactic and semantic processing into two steps. The algorithm uses nominal and prepositional phrases to locate known objects and properties. We implemented an algorithm that analyzes the syntactic representation and the domain ontology and generates well-formed requests. The semantic analysis is complemented by a linguistic analysis of the phrase, where we try to identify if an action, e.g., "leave", or some general modifier, e.g., "time (when), quantity (how many)" is being asked using a list of verbs denoting actions and modifiers. Finally, the inference engine takes the resulting formal query and does the filtering. The query is a conjunction of atomic queries. The format of each query can be "(:Object O :slot S :value V)" for object selection or "(:Object O :slot S)" for slot-value verification. "O" and "V" can be complex recursive structures.

3.3 Task Model

We divide a task into two parts: *template* and *description*. To identify the task requested by the user and the information related to parameters, the semantic analyzer uses the template part of the task. The template contains linguistic terms related to the parameters and the verbs used to start the task. The task description describes all the information required for the task execution. The data required in the task structure definition are:

- *Params*: the parameters of the task;
- Params-values: the values given by the user as parameters;
- Semantic-value: the specification of a function that must be executed on the value given by the user. For instance the function "e-mail" can give the value "carvalho@utc.fr" for the term "carlos" given by the user;
- Params-confirm: it is true if a confirmation for the value given by the user is necessary;
- Params-labels: the question presented to the user;
- Params-save: the specification if the values of the parameters are used to generate the user model (see next Section);
- Params-explains: if true (for a parameter) an explanation is given to the user;
- Global-confirm: if true a global confirmation for the task execution is made.

3.4 User Model (UM)

We use a dynamic UM generation process. All the tasks and query executions are saved within the user model. Values are predicted with a weighted frequency-based technique. We use UM dynamic generation to avoid manual modeling of users. The main idea is to minimize the user's work during the execution of repetitive dialogs predicting values and decreasing the needs for feedback. A more elaborated discussed about user model in dialog systems is out of the scope of this paper.

3.5 Domain Model

To allow the system to identify users' problems and provide answers to particular questions it is necessary to keep a knowledge base within the assistant. The knowledge of the agent is used to identify objects, relations and values required by the user. Such objects can represent instances of various object classes (*People, Task, Design,* etc.) and have a number of synonyms. Therefore, it is quite important to use efficient tools to represent objects, synonyms and a hierarchical structure of concepts. In our approach, we use the MOSS system proposed by Barthès [4] to represent knowledge. MOSS allows object indexing by terms and synonyms. Several objects can share the same index. MOSS has been developed at the end of seventies for representing and manipulating LISP objects. The objects can be versioned and modified simultaneously by several users. The MOSS concepts have been further used in object-oriented databases.

```
 1  User:    Joe is a professor of Artificial Intelligence at UTC.
 2  System:  OK.
 3  User:    What does Joe do?
 4  System:  Joe is a professor of Artificial Intelligence at UTC.
 5  User:    What is Joe's profession?
 6  System:  Joe is a professor of Artificial Intelligence at UTC.
 7  User:    Where does Joe works?
 8  System:  At UTC
 9  User:    Is Joe a professor of Artificial Intelligence?
10  System:  Yes
11  User:    Is Joe a professor of artificial intelligence at UTC?
12  System:  Yes
13  User:    Is Joe a professor of artificial intelligence at PUC?
14  System:  I don't know. None information about this.
15  User:    What does Joe teaches?
16  System:  Artificial Intelligence
```

Fig. 4. Intelligent Dialog.

Knowledge is important because it increases the capability of the system to produce rational answers. Consider the dialog reproduced Fig. 4. Initially, the system has no information on Joe's occupation. The user starts the dialog with an "Assert" dialog act stating Joe's occupation. Afterwards, the user asks several questions related to the initial utterance and the system is able to answer them. The system can identify and interpret correctly very different questions related to the same concepts (lines 3 and 5) and answer questions about them. This is possible because the semantic meanings of the slots are explored in the queries. Thus, a slot can play a role that is referenced in different ways.

4 Deployment and Evaluation

We currently develop a personal assistant (PA) in the AACC project. We hope to use the mechanisms discussed on this paper to improve the interaction with the actual assistant prototype. Then, students will have an assistant for executing services and for helping them with mechanical engineering tasks, and capable of answering questions using natural language.

The current state of the prototype did not allow its immediate application because the current interface is not good enough. The interface is being redesigned for testing our dialogue approach during the mechanical engineering courses given to students. During the Spring semester of 2004 we will evaluate the results of students using or not using the assistant and we will measure the quality of the information provided by the assistant. A formal evaluation of the system can be accomplished for instance with the criteria presented by Allen et al. [2], however, for us, the main criterion is the acceptation or the non acceptation of the system by the students.

5 Related Work

Grosz and Sidner [7] discuss the importance of an explicit task representation for the understanding of a task-oriented dialogue. According to the authors, the discourse is a composite of three elements: (i) linguistics (utterances); (ii) intentions and (iii) attentional states (objects, properties, relations and intentions salient at any given point of the discourse). Our system presents some very close elements like linguistic information (template of tasks), intentions (given by speech acts) and specific information about tasks and tasks properties. Very often, assistants communicate using ACLs (Agent Communication Languages) like KQML or FIPA ACL[2]. However, such messages are based into *Performatives* rather *speech acts*. A basic difference between performatives and speech acts is that they tell what to do when something is said (action) and do not express the meaning of what is said (intention). In other words, ACL messages cannot express a Go-back like speech act because there is no an explicit action into the utterance. Unlike most dialog systems the dialog flow implemented in Section 3.1 is completely generic. Thereby, new tasks and knowledge can be added to the system (Assistant) without changing or extending the dialog structure. Generic dialog systems are relatively rare. Usually the developer specifies state transition graphs where dialog flow should be coded entirely like the dialog model discussed by McRoy and Ali [10]. Kölzer [9] discusses a generic dialog system generator. In the Kölzer's system, the developer must specify the dialog flow using state charts. Such techniques make the development of real applications quite hard. In contrast, in our approach we need to specify only tasks structure and domain knowledge concerning. Rich and Sidner [11] also used the concept of generic dialog systems. The authors used the core of the COLLAGEN system for developing very different applications. COLLAGEN is based on a plan recognition algorithm and a complex model of collaborative discourse. The problem is that most part of the collaborative discourse must be coded using a language for modeling the semantic of communicative acts. The representation includes knowledge concerning the application. So the knowledge of the system is intermixed with the dialog discourse, which makes the application domain dependent. Allen et al. [3] used speech acts for modeling the behavior and the reasoning of a deliberative autonomous agent. Speech acts are separated into three groups: Interaction, Collaborative Problem Solving (CPS) and Problem Solving (PS). Assuming we do not intent to model interaction with the user like a problem solving process, PS and CPS speech acts proposed by Allen are not relevant to our work because they are domain-related. However the interactions acts are very similar with the speech acts that we proposed.

6 Conclusions

In this paper we addressed the problem of communication between User and Personal Assistant Agent (PA). In the AACC project, users need to communicate with a PA to do collaborative work. We argued that natural language should be used to provide a better interaction. A user assistant communication module was developed as a modular dialog system. To execute services and to ask for knowledge, the user enters a dialog with her PA. In this application the dialog coordination model should be generic for supporting the scalability of the system concerning the addition of new tasks

---

[2] FIPA – Foundations for Intelligent Physical Agents, http://www.fipa.org

without much effort. Then, we introduced a new generic model of dialog based on speech acts. Simple tasks and questions have been used to highlight the effectiveness of the system and the advantages in relation to traditional collaborative work tools.

References

1. Allen, J. F., *Natural Language Understanding*, The Benjamin/Cummings Publishing Company, Inc, Menlo Park, California, 1986. ISBN 0-8053-0330-8
2. Allen, J. F.; Miller, B. W. et al. *Robust Understanding in a Dialogue System*, Proc. 34 th. Meeting of the Association for Computational Linguistics, June, 1996.
3. Allen, J. ; Blaylock, N. ; Ferguson, G., *A Problem Solving Model for Collaborative Agents*, Proc. of AAMAS'02, pp. 774 – 781, ACM Press New York, NY, USA , 2002. ISBN 1-58113-480-0
4. Barthès, J-P. A., *MOSS 3.2*, Memo UTC/GI/DI/N 111, Université de Technologie de Compiègne, Mars, 1994.
5. Flycht-Eriksson, A., *A Survey of Knowledge Sources in Dialogue Systems*, Proceedings of the (IJCAI)-99 Workshop on Knowledge and Reasoning in Practical Dialogue Systems, International Joint Conference on Artificial Intelligence, Murray Hill, New Jersey, Jan Alexandersson (ed.), pp 41-48, 1999.
6. Goldstein, I. P.; Roberts, R. B., *Nudge, A Knowledge-Based Scheduling Program*, MIT AI memo 405, February, 23 pages, 1977.
7. Grosz, B. J., Sidner, C. L.. *Attention, intentions, and the structure of discourse*, Computational Linguistics, 12(3):175--204, 1986.
8. Kipp, M.; Alexandersson, J.; Reithinger, N., 1999. *Understanding Spontaneous Negotiation Dialogue*, Linköping University Electronic Press: Electronic Articles in Computer and Information Science, ISSN 1401-9841, vol. 4, n° 027.
9. Kölzer, A., *Universal Dialogue Specification for Conversational Systems*, Linköping University Electronic Press: Eletronic Articles in Computer and Information Science, ISSN 1401-9841, vol. 4, n° 028, 1999.
10. McRoy, S., Ali, S. S., *A practical, declarative theory of dialog*. Electronic Transactions on Artificial Intelligence, vol. 3, Section D, 1999, 18 pp.
11. Rich, C.; Sidner, C. L.; Lesh, N., *COLLAGEN: Applying Collaborative Discourse Theory to human-Computer Interaction*, AI Magazine, Special Issue on Intelligent User Interfaces, vol 22, issue 4, pp. 15-25, Winter 2001.
12. Riesbeck, C., Marlin, C., *Direct Memory Access Parsing*, Yale University Report 354, 1985.
13. Schank, R. C., Abelson, R. P., *Scripts, Plans, Goals and Understanding, Lawrence Erlbaum Associates*, Hillsdale, NJ, 1977.
14. Searle, J., *Speech Acts: An Essay in the Philosophy of Language*, Cambridge, Cambridge University Press, 1969.
15. Seneff, S.; Polifroni, J., *Formal and Natural Language Generation in the Mercury Conversational System*, Proc. 6th Int. Conf. on Spoken Language Processing, Beijing, China, October, 2000.
16. Sowa, J. F., *Conceptual Structures. Information Processing and Mind and Machine*, Addison Wesley, Reading Mass, 1984.
17. Szolovits, P; Hawkinson L. B.; Martin W. A., *An Overview of OWL, A Language for Knowledge Representation*, Technical Memo TM-86, Laboratory for Computer Science, MIT, 1977.

Applying Argumentative Zoning in an Automatic Critiquer of Academic Writing

Valéria D. Feltrim[1], Jorge M. Pelizzoni[1], Simone Teufel[2],
Maria das Graças Volpe Nunes[1], and Sandra M. Aluísio[1]

[1] University of São Paulo - ICMC/NILC
Av. do Trabalhador São Carlense, 400
13560-970, São Carlos - SP, Brazil
{vfeltrim,jorgemp,gracan,sandra}@icmc.usp.br
[2] University of Cambridge - Computer Laboratory
JJ Thomson Avenue, Cambridge CB3 0FD, UK
Simone.Teufel@cam.ac.uk

Abstract. This paper presents an automatic critiquer of Computer Science Abstracts in Portuguese, which formulates critiques and/or suggestions of improvement based on automatic argumentative structure recognition. The recognition is performed by an statistical classifier, similar to Teufel and Moens's Argumentative Zoning (AZ) [1], but ported to work on Portuguese abstracts. The critiques and suggestions made by the system come from a set of fixed critiquing rules based on corpus observations and guidelines for good writing from the literature. Here we describe the overall system and report on the AZ porting exercise, its intrinsic evaluation and application in the critiquer.

Keywords: Academic Writing Support Tools, Argumentative Zoning, Machine Learning

1 Introduction

It is well known that producing a "good" argumentative structure in academic writing is not an easy job, even for experienced writers. Besides dealing with the inherent complexities of any writing task, the writer has also to deal with those specific to the academic genre. More specifically, the academic audience expects to find in papers a certain kind of information presented in a certain way. However, novice writers are usually not quite aware of these expectations or demands and are believed to benefit a lot from established structure models.

Many such models have indeed been proposed for academic writing in various areas of Science [2–4], which one can in principle use as guide when preparing or correcting one's own text. Notwithstanding, there is a major pitfall to that: as these models view text as a sequence of "moves" or categories ascribed to textual segments, the burden falls upon the writer of having to identify these categories within their own text, which tends to be harder the less experienced the writer is. In consequence, "manual" application of such structure models by novices is prone to inefficiency. One significant improvement to that scenario

A.L.C. Bazzan and S. Labidi (Eds.): SBIA 2004, LNAI 3171, pp. 214–223, 2004.

Table 1. Example sentence for each category with lexical patterns underlined

---

1 BACKGROUND

"The research article (RA) or paper <u>is one of the most important</u> genres that both scientists and engineers will write."

2 GAP

"<u>When faced with</u> the tasks of reading and writing a complex technical paper, many nonnative scientists and engineers (...) <u>lack an</u> adequate knowledge of commonly used structural patterns at the discourse level."

3 PURPOSE

"<u>In this paper, we propose</u> a novel computer software tool that can assist these people in the understanding and construction of technical papers (...)."

4 METHODOLOGY

"<u>The software uses</u> a supervised learning approach, in which the system first "learns" the characteristic features of text structure in a particular discipline <u>using</u> a small number of training examples."

5 RESULTS

"<u>We can see that the system performs</u> consistently across the different data sets, with an average accuracy of 68%."

6 CONCLUSION

"The system is tested <u>using</u> research article abstracts <u>and is shown to be</u> fast, accurate, and useful aid in the reading and writing process."

7 OUTLINE

"<u>In the next section we present</u> the contextualization of this work and details about the used methodology."

---

would be having a computer aid, in the sense that there could be an artificial collaborator able to recognize the argumentative structure of an evolving text automatically, on which to base critiquing and suggestions.

In this paper, we present such an automatic critiquer of Computer Science Abstracts in Portuguese. As a reference structure model, we use a seven-category fixed-order scheme as illustrated in Table 1[1] and discussed in Section 2. The automatic category recognition is performed by an statistical classifier similar to Teufel and Moens's Argumentative Zoning (AZ) [1], but ported to work on Portuguese abstracts, for which reason it is called AZPort. The critiques/suggestions made by the system come from a fixed set of critiquing rules generated by corpus observations [6] and guidelines for good writing from the literature.

The critiquer was conceived to be part of a bigger system called SciPo, whose ultimate goal is to support novice writers in producing academic writing in Portuguese. SciPo was inspired by the Amadeus system [7] and its current functionality can be summarized thus: (a) a base of authentic thesis abstracts and introductions annotated according to our structure scheme; (b) browse and search facilities for this base; (c) support for building a structure that the writer can use as a starting point for the text; (d) critiquing rules that can be applied to such a structure; and (e) recovery of authentic cases that are similar to the writer's structure. Also, the existing lexical patterns (i.e. highly reusable segments) in the recovered cases are highlighted so that the writer can easily add these patterns to a previously built structure. Examples of lexical patterns are underlined in Table 1.

---

[1] The sentences in Table 1 (except the one for OUTLINE) were collected from [5]. Note that the texts in our corpus are in Portuguese, in contrast to this paper.

The major shortcoming of SciPo before the work described in this paper is that the writer is expected to explicitly state a schematic structure. Not only is that usually unnatural to many writers, but also it implies that they should master a common artificial language, i.e. they need to understand the meaning of all categories or else they will fail to communicate their intentions to the system. Our structure-sensitive critiquer is intended to overcome this by inverting the flow of interaction. Now the writer may just input a draft and benefit from all of SciPo's original features, because the schematic structure is elicited automatically.

In the following section we present our reference scheme and report a human annotation experiment to verify the reproducibility and stability of it. In Section 3 we report on the AZ porting exercise for Brazilian Portuguese. In Section 4 we comment on our critiquing rules and demonstrate the usage of the system.

2   Manual Annotation of Abstracts

As a starting point for our annotation scheme, we used three models: Swales' CARS [2] and those by Weissberg and Buker [3] and by Aluísio and Oliveira Jr. [8]. Although these works deal with introduction sections, we have found that the basic structure of their models could also be applied to abstracts. Thus, after some preliminary analysis, the scheme was modified to accommodate all the argumentative roles found in our corpus. Finally, in order to make it more reproducible, we simplified it, ending up with a scheme close to that presented by Teufel et al [9]. It comprehends the following categories: BACKGROUND (B), GAP (G), PURPOSE (P), METHODOLOGY (M), RESULT (R), CONCLUSION (C) and OUTLINE (O).

One of the main difficulties faced by the annotators was the high number of sentences with overlapping argumentative roles, which leads to doubt about the correct category to be assigned. Anthony [10] also reported on categories assignment conflicts when dealing with introductions of Software Engineering papers. We have tried to minimize this difficulty by stating specific strategies in the written guidelines to deal with frequent conflicts, such as, for example, PURPOSE vs. RESULT.

Experiments performed on the basis of our scheme and specific annotation guidelines (similar to AZ's) showed it to be reproducible and stable. To check reproducibility, we performed an annotation experiment with 3 human annotators who were already knowledgeable of the corpus domain and familiar with scientific writing. To check stability, i.e. the extent to which one annotator will produce the same classifications at different times, we repeated the annotation experiment with one annotator with a time gap of 3 months. We used the Kappa coefficient K [11] to measure reproducibility between k annotators on N items and stability for one annotator. In our experiment, items are sentences and the number of categories is n=7. The formula for the computation of Kappa is:

$$K = \frac{P(A) - P(E)}{1 - P(E)}$$

where P(A) is pairwise agreement and P(E) is random agreement. Kappa varies between -1 and 1. It is -1 for maximal disagreement, 0 for if agreement is only as would be expected by chance annotation following the same distribution as the observed distribution, and 1 for perfect agreement.

For the reproducibility experiment, we used 6 abstracts in the training stage, which was performed in three rounds, each round consisting of explanation, annotation, and discussion. After training, the annotators were asked to annotate 46 abstracts sentence by sentence, assigning exactly one category per sentence.

The results show our scheme to be reproducible (K=0.69, N=320, k=3), considering the subjectiveness of this kind of annotation and the literature recommendations. In a similar experiment, Teufel et al [9] reported the reproducibility of their scheme as slightly higher (K=0.71, N=4261, k=3). However, collapsing our categories METHODOLOGY, RESULTS and CONCLUSION as a single one (similar to Teufel et al's category OWN) increases our agreement significantly (K=0.82, N=320, k=3). We also found our scheme to be stable, as the same annotator produced very similar annotation at different times (K=0.79, N=320, k=2).

From this we conclude that trained humans can distinguish our set of categories and thus the data resulting from these experiments are reliable enough to be used as training material for an automatic classifier.

3   Automatic Annotation of Abstracts

AZ [1] – and thus AZPort – is a Naive Bayesian classifier that renders each input sentence a set of possible rhetorical roles with their respective estimated probabilities. As usual with machine learning algorithms, instead of dealing directly with the object to be classified (i.e. sentences), AZ receives sentences as feature vectors. *Feature extraction* is thus a crucial design step in such scenarios and hopefully will yield a set of features that *captures* the target categories, i.e., that correlates with them in patterns that the learning algorithm is able to identify. Here we report on AZPort's redesign of AZ's feature extraction.

3.1   Description of the Used Features

Our first step was to select the set of features to be applied in our experiment. We implemented a set of 8 features, derived from the 16 used by Teufel and Moens [1]: sentence length, sentence location, presence of citations, presence of formulaic expressions, verb tense, verb voice, presence of modal auxiliary and history.

The **Length** feature classifies a sentence as *short, medium* or *long* length, based on two thresholds (20 and 40 words) that were estimated using the average sentence length present in our corpus.

The **Location** feature identifies the position occupied by a sentence within the abstract. We use four values for this feature: *first, medium, 2ndlast* and *last.* Experiments showed that these values characterize common sentence locations for some specific categories of our scheme.

The **Citation** feature flags the presence or absence of citations in a sentence. As we are not working with full texts, it is not possible to parse the reference list and identify self-citations.

The **Formulaic** feature identifies the presence of a formulaic expression in a sentence and the scheme category to which an expression belongs. Examples of formulaic expressions are underlined text in Table 1. In order to recognize these expressions, we built a set of 377 regular expressions estimated to generate as many as 80,000 strings. The sources for these regular expressions were phrases mentioned in the literature, and corpus observations. We then performed a manual generalization to cover similar constructs.

Due to the productive inflectional morphology of Portuguese, much of the porting effort went into adapting verb-syntactic features. The **Tense**, **Voice** and **Modal** features report syntactic properties of the first finite verb phrase in indicative or imperative mood. **Tense** may assume 14 values, including *noverb* for verbless sentences. As verb inflection in Portuguese has a wide range of simple tenses – many of which are rather rare in general and even absent in our corpus – we collapsed some of them. As a result, we use one single value of past/future, to the detriment of the three/two morphological past/future tenses. In addition, mood distinction is neutralized. The **Voice** feature may assume *noverb*, *passive* or *active*. Passive voice is understood here in a broader sense, collapsing some Portuguese verb forms and constructs that are usually used to omit an agent, namely (i) regular passive voice (analogous to English, by means of auxiliary "*ser*" plus past participle), (ii) synthetic passive voice (by means of passivizating particle "*se*") and (iii) a special form of indeterminate subject (also by means of particle "*se*"). The **Modal** feature flags the presence of a modal auxiliary (if no verb is present, it assumes the value *noverb*).

The **History** feature takes into account the category of the previous sentence in the classification process. It is known that some argumentative zones tend to follow other particular zones [1, 5]. This property is even more apparent in self-contained texts such as abstracts [6]. In our corpus, some particular sequences of argumentative zones are very frequent. For example, the pattern BACKGROUND followed by GAP, with repetition or not, and then followed by PURPOSE, i.e. $((BG)|(GB)+)P$, occurs in 30.7% of the corpus. To determine the value of **History** for unseen sentences, we calculate it as a second pass process during testing, performing a beam search with width three among the candidate categories for the previous sentence to reach the most likely classification.

3.2   Automatic Annotation Results

Our training material was a collection of 52 abstracts from theses in Computer Science, containing 366 sentences (10,936 words). The abstracts were automatically segmented into sentences using XML tags. Citations in running text were also marked with a XML tag. The sentences were POS-tagged according to the partial NILC tagset[2]. The target categories for our experiment were provided by one of the subjects of the annotation experiment described in Section 2.

---

[2] http://www.nilc.icmc.usp.br/nilc/tools/nilctaggers.html

We implemented a simple Naive Bayesian classifier to estimate the probability that a sentence S has category C given the values of its features. The category with the highest probability is chosen as the output for the sentence.

The results of classification were compiled by applying 13-fold cross-validation to our 52 abstracts (training sets of 48 texts and testing sets of 4 texts). As Baseline 1, we considered a random choice of categories weighted by their distribution in the corpus. As Baseline 2, we consider classification as the most frequent category. The categories distribution in our corpus is BACKGROUND (21%), GAP (10%), PURPOSE (18%), METHODOLOGY (12%), RESULT (32%), CONCLUSION (5%) and OUTLINE (2%).

Comparing our Naive Bayesian classifier (trained with the full pool of features) to one human annotator, the agreement reaches K=0.65 (system accuracy of 74%). This is an encouragingly high amount of agreement when compared to Teufel and Moens' [1] figure of K=0.45. Our good result might be in part due to the fact that we are dealing with abstracts (instead of full papers) and that all of them fall into the same domain (Computer Science). This result is also much better than Baseline 1 (K=0 and accuracy of 20%) and Baseline 2 (K=0.26 and accuracy of 32%).

Further analysis of our results shows that, except for category OUTLINE, the classifier performs well on all other categories, cf. the confusion matrix in Table 2. We use the *F-measure*, defined as

$$\frac{2 * P * R}{P + R}$$

as a convenient way of reporting precision (P) and recall (R) in one value. The classifier performs worst for OUTLINE sentences (*F-measure*=0). This is no wonder, since we are dealing with an abstract corpus and thus there is not much OUTLINE-type training material[3] (total of 6 sentences in the whole corpus). Regarding the other categories, the best performance of the classifier is for PURPOSE sentences (*F-measure*=0.845), followed by RESULT sentences (*F-measure*=0.769), cf. Table 3. We attribute the high performance for PURPOSE to the presence of strong discourse markers on this kind of sentences (modelled by the **Formulaic** feature). As for RESULT, we ascribe the good performance to the high frequency of this kind of sentence in our corpus and to the presence of specific discourse markers as well.

Looking at the contribution of single features, we found the strongest feature to be **Formulaic**. We also observed that taking the context into account (**History** feature) is a helpful heuristic and improves the result significantly, by 12%. Syntactic features – **Tense**, **Voice** and **Modal** – and **Citation** are the weakest ones. We believe that the **Citation** feature would perform better in other kind of text than abstracts (e.g. introductions).

In Table 4, the second column gives the predictiveness of the feature on its own, in terms of Kappa between the classifier and one annotator. Apart from **Formulaic** and **History**, all other features are outperformed by both

---

[3] Many machine learning algorithms, including the Naive Bayes classifier, perform badly on infrequent categories due to the lack of sufficient training material.

Table 2. Confusion matrix: human vs. automatic annotation

	Category	B	G	P	M	R	C	O	Total
					Machine				
	B	**57**	10	2	1	7	0	0	77
	G	11	**23**	0	0	2	0	0	36
	P	6	1	**49**	0	8	1	0	65
Human	M	5	0	0	**26**	14	0	0	45
	R	2	2	0	9	**101**	3	0	117
	C	0	0	0	0	9	**10**	1	20
	O	0	0	0	0	5	1	**0**	6
	Total	81	36	51	36	146	15	1	366

Table 3. Precision, recall and F-measure per category

Category	Precision	Recall	F-Measure
BACKGROUND	0.704	0.74	0.722
GAP	0.639	0.639	0.639
PURPOSE	0.961	0.754	0.845
METHODOLOGY	0.722	0.578	0.642
RESULTS	0.692	0.863	0.768
CONCLUSION	0.667	0.5	0.571
OUTLINE	0	0	0

Table 4. Potential of individual features

Feature	Alone	Left out
Length	-0.106	0.62
Location	-0.047	0.624
Citation	-0.272	0.63
Formulaic	0.557	0.345
Tense	-0.166	0.642
Voice	-0.018	0.644
Modality	-0.287	0.65
History	0.251	0.54
Baseline 1 (random by distr.): K=0		
Baseline 2 (most freq. cat.): K=0.26		

baselines. The third column gives Kappa coefficients for experiments using all features except the given one. As shown, all features apart from the syntactic ones contribute some predictiveness in combination with others.

The results for automatic classification are reasonably in agreement with our previous experimental results for human classification. We also observed that the confusion classes of the automatic classification are similar to the confusion classes of our human annotators. As can be observed in Table 2, the classifier has some problems in distinguishing the categories METHODOLOGY, RESULT and CONCLUSION and so do our human annotators. As mentioned in Section 2, collapsing these three categories in one raises the human agreement considerably, which suggests distinction problems amongst these categories even for humans.

We can conclude that the performance of the classifier, although much lower than human, is promising and acceptable to be used as part of our automatic critiquer. In the next section, we describe the critiquer and how it works on unseen abstracts.

4   Automatic Critiquing of Abstracts

Once the schematic structure of an input has been recognized, it is checked against a fixed set of critiquing rules, which ultimately refer to our seven-category fixed-order model scheme. We focus on two kind of possible deviations: (i) lack of categories and (ii) bad flow (i.e. ordering) of categories.

Naturally, an abstract does not have to present all the categories predicted by this model, neither does its strict order have to be verified. However, some categories are considered obligatory (e.g. PURPOSE) and the lack of those and/or the unbalanced use of (optional and obligatory) categories may lead to very poor abstracts. As one major idea underlying our rules, we argue that a good abstract must provide factual and specific information about a work. Thus, our aim is to help writers to produce more "informative" abstracts, in which the reader is likely to learn quickly what is most characteristic of and novel about the work at hand.

Taking this into account, we find it reasonable to treat categories PURPOSE, METHODOLOGY and RESULT as obligatory. On the other hand, categories BACKGROUND, GAP and CONCLUSION are treated as optional and, in the event of their absence, the system only suggests their use to the writer. We consider OUTLINE an inappropriate category for abstracts and, when detected, the critiquer will recommend its removal. In fact, this category only appears in our scheme to reflect our corpus observations.

Regarding the flow of categories, the critiquer tries to avoid error-prone sequences, such as RESULT before PURPOSE, and awkward sequences, such as the use of BACKGROUND information separating two PURPOSEs, which is likely to confuse the reader.

Table 5 exemplifies the AZPort output for one of the abstracts used in our previous experiments[4]. We present the original English abstract, which is the direct translation of the Portuguese abstract. For illustration purposes, we include between parentheses the (correct) manual annotation in those cases in which the system disagreed; in agreement cases, we show a tick ($\sqrt{}$).

Note that the classifier made some mistakes (BACKGROUND vs. GAP), but that does not affect the resulting critiques in this specific example. Sometimes it may also confound very dissimilar categories, e.g. PURPOSE with BACKGROUND. However, we believe the latter to be a lesser problem because the writer is likely to perceive such mistakes and is encouraged to correct AZPort's output before submitting it to critiquing. A major problem is confusion between METHODOLOGY and RESULT, which does reflect directly in the critiquing stage. Although our experiments with human annotators showed that these categories are hard to distinguish in general texts, we believe that it is easier to make this distinction for authors in their own writing, after they received a critique of this writing from our system.

---

[4] Extracted from Simão, A.S.: "Proteum-RS/PN: Uma Ferramenta para a Validação de Redes de Petri Baseada na Análise de Mutantes". Master's Thesis, University of São Paulo (2000). Translation into English by the author.

Table 5. Sample AZPort output

BACKGROUND
Reactive Systems are characterized by continuously reacting to external as well as internal stimuli and controlling human activities. (✓)
GAP
In these systems, faults can result in large losses. (BACKGROUND) The use of rigorous methods and techniques for the specification of their behavior is essential to avoid inconsistencies and ambiguities. (BACKGROUND)
BACKGROUND
Petri Nets have been used for reactive-system specification. (✓) The test and validation of the underlying model are essential activities for the production of such systems. (✓) Thus, the Mutant Analysis – a fault-based criterion usually used for program testing – has been explored in the context of specification testing. (✓) The development of tools to support its application is necessary, since its manual application is unrealistic. (GAP)
PURPOSE
The objective of this work is the implementation of Proteum-RS/PN, a testing tool which supports the application of Mutant Analysis criterion to validate Petri-Nets based specifications. (✓)

Table 6. Critiquer's output for the abstract presented in Table 5

CRITIQUES AND SUGGESTIONS

Critique: Essential components are missing!
– Add Methodology
   It is important to inform the reader about the methodology used in your work
– Add Result
   It is important to inform the reader about the main findings of your work
Suggestion: You can enrich your abstract!
– You can add some Conclusions
   Conclusion sentences is a nice way to finish up an abstract as they make it look more self-contained and add to its cohesion

In Table 6, we present the critiquer's output for the previously classified abstract (Table 5). It is in accordance with the critiquing rules commented above and alerts the writer to the fact that no explicit methodology and result was found in the abstract. One might argue that the PURPOSE sentence already indicates both methodology and result. However, as this system was designed for writers of dissertations and theses (longer than journal/conference paper abstracts, which are usually written in English), it would be interesting to have more detailed abstracts, in which the methodology and results/contributions of the research are properly emphasized. Finally, the critiquer suggests the addition of the CONCLUSION component as a way to make the abstract more self-contained.

It is important to say that the system does not ensure that the final abstract will be a good one, as the system focuses only on the argumentative structure and there are other factors involved in the writing task. However, the system has been informally tested and offers potentially useful guidance towards more informative and genre-compliant abstracts.

5   Conclusion

We have reported on the experiment of porting Argumentative Zoning [1] from English to Portuguese, including its adaptation to a new purpose. We call this new classifier AZPort. The results showed that AZPort is suitable to be used in the context of an automatic abstract critiquer, despite some limitations. As future work, we intent to evaluate the critiquer inside a supportive writing system, called SciPo.

Acknowledgements

We would like to thank CAPES, CNPq and FAPESP for the financial support as well as the annotators for their precious work. Special thanks to Lucas Antiqueira for his invaluable help implementing SciPo.

References

1. Teufel, S., Moens, M.: Summarising scientific articles — experiments with relevance and rhetorical status. Computational Linguistics **28** (2002) 409–446
2. Swales, J. In: Genre Analysis: English in Academic and Research Settings. Chapter 7: Research articles in English. Cambridge University Press, Cambridge, UK (1990) 110–176
3. Weissberg, R., Buker, S.: Writing up Research: Experimental Research Report Writing for Students of English. Prentice Hall (1990)
4. Santos, M.B.d.: The textual organisation of research paper abstracts. Text **16** (1996) 481–499
5. Anthony, L., Lashkia, G.V.: Mover: A machine learning tool to assist in the reading and writing of technical papers. IEEE Transactions on Professional Communication **46** (2003) 185–193
6. Feltrim, V., Aluisio, S.M., Nunes, M.d.G.V.: Analysis of the rhetorical structure of computer science abstracts in portuguese. In Archer, D., Rayson, P., Wilson, A., McEnery, T., eds.: Proceedings of Corpus Linguistics 2003, UCREL Technical Papers, Vol. 16, Part 1, Special Issue. (2003) 212–218
7. Aluisio, S.M., Barcelos, I., Sampaio, J., Oliveira Jr., O.N.: How to learn the many unwritten "Rules of the Game" of the Academic Discourse: A Hybrid Approach Based on Critiques and Cases. In: Proceedings of the IEEE International Conference on Advanced Learning Technologies. (2001) 257–260
8. Aluisio, S.M., Oliveira Jr., O.N.: A detailed schematic structure of research papers introductions: An application in support-writing tools. Revista de la Sociedad Española para el Procesamiento del Lenguaje Natural (1996) 141–147
9. Teufel, S., Carletta, J., Moens, M.: An annotation scheme for discourse-level argumentation in research articles. In: Proceedings of the Ninth Meeting of the European Chapter of the Association for Computational Linguistics (EACL-99). (1999) 110–117
10. Anthony, L.: Writing research article introductions in software engineering: How accurate is a standard model? IEEE Transactions on Professional Communication **42** (1999) 38–46
11. Siegel, S., Castellan, N.J.J.: Nonparametric Statistics for the Behavioral Sciences. 2nd edn. McGraw-Hill, Berkeley, CA (1988)

DiZer: An Automatic Discourse Analyzer
for Brazilian Portuguese

Thiago Alexandre Salgueiro Pardo, Maria das Graças Volpe Nunes, and
Lucia Helena Machado Rino

Núcleo Interinstitucional de Lingüística Computacional (NILC)
CP 668 – ICMC-USP, 13.560-970 São Carlos, SP, Brasil
thiago@nilc.icmc.usp.br, gracan@icmc.usp.br
lucia@dc.ufscar.br
http://www.nilc.icmc.usp.br

Abstract. This paper presents DiZer, an automatic DIscourse analyZER for
Brazilian Portuguese. Given a source text, the system automatically produces its
corresponding rhetorical analysis, following Rhetorical Structure Theory – RST
[1]. A rhetorical repository, which is DiZer main component, makes the automatic analysis possible. This repository, produced by means of a corpus analysis, includes discourse analysis patterns that focus on knowledge about discourse markers, indicative phrases and words usages. When applicable,
potential rhetorical relations are indicated. A preliminary evaluation of the system is also presented.

Keywords: Automatic Discourse Analysis, Rhetorical Structure Theory

1 Introduction

Researches in Linguistics and Computational Linguistics have shown that a text is
more than just a simple sequence of juxtaposed sentences. Indeed, it has a highly
elaborated underlying discourse structure. In general, this structure represents how
the information conveyed by the text propositional units (that is, the meaning of the
text segments) correlate and make sense together.

There are several discourse theories that try to represent different aspects of discourse. The Rhetorical Structure Theory (RST) [1] is one of the most used theories
nowadays. According to it, all propositional units in a text must be connected by
rhetorical relations in some way for the text to be coherent. As an example of a rhetorical analysis of a text, consider Text 1 (adapted from [2]) in Figure 1 (with segments that express basic propositional units numbered) and its rhetorical structure in
Figure 2. The symbols N and S indicate the nucleus and satellite of each rhetorical
relation: in RST, the nucleus indicates the most important information in the relation,
while the satellite provides complementary information to the nucleus. In this structure, propositions 1 and 2 are in a CONTRAST relation, that is, they are opposing
facts that may not happen at the same time; proposition 3 is the direct RESULT (non
volitional) of the opposition between 1 and 2. In some cases, relations are multinu-
clear (e.g., CONTRAST relation), that is, they have no satellites and the connected
propositions are considered to have the same importance.

A.L.C. Bazzan and S. Labidi (Eds.): SBIA 2004, LNAI 3171, pp. 224–234, 2004.

[1] He wanted to play tennis with Jane, [2] but also wanted to have dinner with Susan. [3] This indecision drove him crazy.

Fig. 1. Text 1.

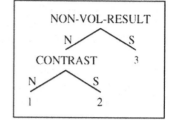

Fig. 2. Text 1 rhetorical structure.

The ability to automatically derive discourse structures of texts is of great importance to many applications in Computational Linguistics. For instance, it may be very useful for automatic text summarization (to identify the most important information of a text to produce its summary) (see, for instance, [2] and [3]), co-reference resolution (determining the context of reference in the discourse may help determining the referred term) (see, for instance, [4] and [5]), and for other natural language understanding applications as well. Some discourse analyzers are already available for both English and Japanese languages, (see, for example, [2], [6], [7], [8], [9], [22] and [23]).

This paper describes DiZer, an automatic DIscourse analyZER for Brazilian Portuguese. To our knowledge, it is the first proposal for this language. It follows those existing ones for English and Japanese, having as the main process a rhetorical analyzer, in accordance with RST. DiZer main resource is a rhetorical repository, which comprises knowledge about discourse markers, indicative phrases and words usages, and the rhetorical relations they may indicate, in the form of discourse analysis patterns. Such patterns were produced by means of a corpus analysis. When applied to an unseen text, they may identify the rhetorical relations between the propositional units. The rhetorical repository also comprises heuristics for helping determining some rhetorical relations, mainly those that are usually not superficially signaled in the text.

Next section presents some relevant aspects of other discourse analysis researches. Section 3 describes the corpus analysis and the repository of rhetorical information used in DiZer. Section 4 outlines DiZer architecture and describes its main processes. Section 5 shows some preliminary results concerning DiZer performance, while concluding remarks are given in Section 6.

2   Related Work

Automatic rhetorical analysis became a burning issue lately. Significant researches on such an issue have arisen that focus on different methodologies and techniques. This section sketches some of them.

Based on the assumption that cue-phrases and discourse makers are direct hints of a text underlying discourse structure, Marcu [6] was the first to develop a cue-phrase-based rhetorical analyzer for free domain texts in English. He used a corpus-driven methodology to identify discourse markers and information on their contextual occurrences and possible rhetorical relations. Marcu also proposed a complete formalization for RST in order to enable its computational manipulation according to his purposes. Later on, Marcu [2], Marcu and Echihabi [7] and Soricut and Marcu [8] proposed, respectively, a decision-based rhetorical analyzer, a Bayesian machine learning-based rhetorical analyzer and a sentence-level rhetorical analyzer using statistical models. In the first one, Marcu applied a shift-reduce parsing model to build rhetorical structures. He achieved better results than with the cue-phrase-based analyzer. In the second one, Marcu and Echihabi trained a Bayesian classifier only with the words of texts to identify four basic rhetorical relations. They achieved a high accuracy in their analysis. Finally, Soricut and Marcu made use of syntactic and lexical information extracted from discourse annotated lexicalized syntactic trees to train statistical models. With this method, in the sentence-level analysis, they achieved results near human performance.

Also based on Marcu's RST formalization, Corston-Oliver [9] developed a rhetorical analyzer for encyclopedic texts based on the occurrence of discourse markers in texts and syntactic realizations relating text segments. He investigated which syntactic features could help determining rhetorical relations, focusing on features like subordination and coordination, active and passive voices, the morphosyntactic categorization of words and the syntactic heads of constituents.

Following Marcu's analyzer [6], DiZer may also be classified as a cue-phrase-based rhetorical analyzer. However, differently from Marcu's analyzer, DiZer is genre specific. For this reason, it makes use of other knowledge sources (indicative phrases and words, heuristics) and adopts an incremental analysis method, as will be discussed latter in this paper. Next section describes the conducted corpus analysis for DiZer development.

3   Corpus Analysis and Knowledge Extraction

3.1   Annotating the Corpus

The corpus was composed of 100 scientific texts on Computer Science taken from the introduction sections of MsC. Dissertations (c.a. 53.000 words and 1.350 sentences). The scientific genre has been chosen for the following reasons: a) scientific texts are supposedly well written; b) they usually present more discourse makers and indicative phrases and words than other text genres; c) other works on discourse analysis for Brazilian Portuguese ([10], [11], [12], [13], [14]) have used the same sort of texts.

The corpus has been rhetorically annotated following Carlson and Marcu's discourse annotation manual [15]. Although this manual focuses on the English language, it may be also applied to Brazilian Portuguese, since RST rhetorical relations are theoretically language independent. The use of this manual has allowed a more systematic and mistake-free annotation. For annotating the texts, Marcu's adaptation of O'Donnel's RSTTool [16] was used. To guarantee consistency during the annotation process, the corpus has been annotated by only one expert in RST.

Initially, the original RST relations set has been used to annotate the corpus. When necessary, more relations have been added to the set. In the end, the full set amounts to 32 relations, as shown in Figure 3. The added ones are in bold face. Some of them (PARENTHETICAL and SAME-UNIT) are only used for organizing the discourse structure. The table also shows the frequency (in %) of each relation in the analyzed corpus.

Relation	*Freq.*	ENABLEMENT	1.09	NON-VOL-RES	0.78
ANTITHESIS	0.43	EVALUATION	0.31	OTHERWISE	0.04
ATTRIBUTION	3.81	EVIDENCE	0.31	**PARENTHETICAL**	7.42
BACKGROUND	2.33	**EXPLANATION**	0.62	PURPOSE	9.42
CIRCUMSTANCE	3.13	INTERPRETATION	0.29	RESTATEMENT	0.41
COMPARISON	0.23	JOINT	0	**SAME-UNIT**	8.10
CONCESSION	1.46	JUSTIFY	1.98	SEQUENCE	1.44
CONCLUSION	0.29	LIST	11.33	SOLUTIONHOOD	1.03
CONDITION	0.41	MEANS	1.36	SUMMARY	0.08
CONTRAST	1.83	MOTIVATION	0.39	VOL-CAUSE	1.71
ELABORATION	34.64	NON-VOL-CAUSE	1.36	VOL-RES	1.96

Fig. 3. DiZer rhetorical relations set.

The annotation strategy for each text was incremental, step by step, in the following way: initially, all propositions of each sentence were related by rhetorical relations; then, the sentences of each paragraph were related; finally, the paragraphs of the text were related. This annotation scheme takes advantage of the fact that the writer tends to put together (i.e., in the same level in the hierarchical organization of the text) the related propositions. For instance, if two propositions are directly related (e.g., a cause and its consequence), it is probable that they will be expressed in the same sentence or in adjacent sentences. This very same reasoning is used in DiZer for analyzing texts. More details about the corpus and its annotation may be found in [17] and [18].

3.2 Knowledge Extraction

Once completely annotated, the corpus has been manually analyzed in order to identify discourse markers, indicative phrases and words, and heuristics that might indicate rhetorical relations. Based on this, discourse analysis patterns for each rhetorical relation have been yielded, currently amounting to 840 patterns. These convey the main information repository of the system.

As an example, consider the discourse analysis pattern for the OTHERWISE rhetorical relation in Figure 4. According to it, an OTHERWISE relation connects two propositional units 1 and 2, with 1 been the satellite and 2 the nucleus and with the segment that expresses 1 appearing before the segment that expresses 2 in the text, if the discourse marker *ou, alternativamente,* (in English, 'or, alternatively,') be present in the beginning of the segment that expresses propositional unit 2.

The idea is that, when a new text is given as input to DiZer, a pattern matching process is carried out. If one of the discourse analysis patterns matches some portion of the text being processed, the corresponding rhetorical relation is supposed to occur between the appropriate segments.

The discourse analysis patterns may also convey morphosyntactic information, lemma and specific genre-related information. For instance, consider the pattern in Figure 5, which hypothesizes a PURPOSE relation. This pattern specifies that a PURPOSE rhetorical relation is found if there is in the text an indicative phrase composed by (1) a word whose lemma is *cujo* ('which', in English[1]), (2) followed by any word that indicates purpose (represented by the 'purWord' class, whose possible values are defined apart by the user), (3) followed by any adjective, (4) followed by a word whose lemma is *ser* (verb 'to be', in English). Based on similar features, any pattern may be represented. Complex patterns, possibly involving long distance dependencies, may also be represented by using a special character (*) to indicate jumps in the pattern matching process.

Relation	OTHERWISE
Order	satellite (S) before nucleus (N)
Marker1 in S	---
Position of marker1	---
Marker2 in N	*ou, alternativamente,*
Position of marker2	beginning

Fig. 4. Discourse analysis pattern for the OTHERWISE rhetorical relation.

Relation	PURPOSE
Order	satellite (S) before nucleus (N)
Marker1 in S	---
Position of marker1	---
Marker2 in N	*cujo_lem purWord _adj ser_lem*
Position of marker2	beginning

Fig. 5. Discourse analysis pattern for the PURPOSE rhetorical relation.

For relations that are not explicitly signaled in the text, like EVALUATION and SOLUTIONHOOD, it has been possible to define some heuristics to enable the discourse analysis, given the specific text genre under focus. For the SOLUTIONHOOD relation, for example, the following heuristic holds:

> if in a segment X, 'negative' words like 'cost' and 'problem' appear more than once and, in segment Y, which follows X, 'positive' words like 'solution' and 'development' appear more than once too, then a SOLUTIONHOOD relation holds between propositions expressed by segments X and Y, with X being the satellite and Y the nucleus of the relation

Next section describes DiZer and its processes, showing how and where the rhetorical repository is used.

---

[1] Although 'which' is invariable in English, its counterpart in Portuguese, *cujo*, may vary in gender and number.

4 DiZer Architecture

DiZer comprises three main processes: (1) the segmentation of the text into propositional units, (2) the detection of occurrences of rhetorical relations between propositional units and (3) the building of the valid rhetorical structures. In what follows,
each process is explained. Figure 6 presents the system architecture.

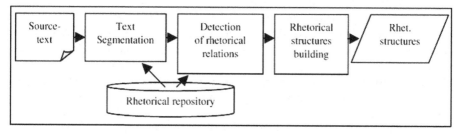

Fig. 6. DiZer architecture.

4.1 Text Segmentation

In this process, DiZer tries to determine the simple clauses in the source text, since
simple clauses usually express simple propositional units, which are assumed to be
the minimal units in a rhetorical structure. For doing this, DiZer initially attributes
morphosyntactic categories to each word in the text using a Brazilian Portuguese
tagger [19]. Then, the segmentation process is carried out, segmenting the text always
a punctuation signal (comma, dot, exclamation and interrogation points, etc.) or a
strong discourse maker or indicative phrase is found. By strong discourse maker or
indicative phrase we mean those words groups that unambiguously have a function in
discourse. According to this, words like *e* and *se* (in English, 'and' and 'if'[2], respectively) are ignored, while words like *portanto* and *por exemplo* (in English, 'therefore'
and 'for instance', respectively) are not. DiZer still verifies whether the identified
segments are clauses by looking for occurrences of verbs in them.

Although this process is very simple, it produces reasonable results (see Figure 7
for an example of segmentation). In some cases, the system can not distinguish embedded clauses, causing inaccurate segmentation, but this may be overcome in the
future by using a syntactic parser.

4.2 Detection of Rhetorical Relations

DiZer tries to determine at least one rhetorical relation for each two adjacent text
segments representing the corresponding underlying propositions. In order to do so, it
uses both discourse analysis patterns and heuristics. Initially, it looks for a relation
between every two adjacent segments of each sentence; then, it considers every two

---

[2] Although 'if' is rarely ambiguous in English, its counterpart in Portuguese, *se*, may assume
many roles in a text. See a comprehensive discussion about *se* possible roles in [20].

adjacent sentences of a paragraph; finally, it considers every two adjacent paragraphs. This processing order is supported by the premise that a writer organizes related information at the same organization level, as already discussed in this paper.

When more than one discourse analysis pattern apply, usually in occurrences of ambiguous discourse markers, all the possible patterns are considered. In this case, several rhetorical relations may be hypothesized for the same propositions. Because of this, multiple discourse structures may be derived for the same text.

In the worst case, when no rhetorical relation can be found between two segments, DiZer assumes a default heuristic: it adopts an ELABORATION relation between them, with the segment that appears first in the text being its nucleus. This is in accordance with what has been observed in the corpus analysis, in that the first segment is usually elaborated by following ones. Although this may cause some underspecification, or, maybe, inadequateness in the discourse structure, it is a plausible solution and it may even be the case that such relation really applies. ELABORATION was chosen as the default relation for being the most frequent relation in the corpus analyzed.

The system also keeps a record of the applied discourse analysis patterns and heuristics, so that it may be possible to identify later manually and/or computationally problematic/ambiguous cases in the discourse structure. In this way, it is possible to reengineer and improve the resulting discourse analysis.

4.3 Building the Rhetorical Structure

This step consists of determining the complete text rhetorical structure from the individual rhetorical relations between its segments. For this, the system makes use of the rule-based algorithm proposed in [6]. This algorithm produces grammar rules for each possible combination of segments by a rhetorical relation, in the form of a DCG (Definite-Clause Grammar) rule [21]. When the final grammar is executed, all possible valid rhetorical structures are built.

As a complete example of DiZer processing, Figures 7 and 8 present, respectively, a text (translated from Portuguese) already segmented by DiZer and one of the valid rhetorical structures built. One may verify that the structure is totally plausible. It is also worth noticing that paragraphs and sentences form complete substructures in the overall structure, given the adopted processing strategy.

Next section presents some preliminary results concerning DiZer performance.

5 Preliminary Evaluation

A preliminary evaluation of DiZer has been carried out taking into account five scientific texts on Computer Science (which are not part of the corpus analyzed for producing the rhetorical repository). These have been randomly selected from introductions of MsC. dissertations of the NILC Corpus[3], currently the biggest corpora of texts for Brazilian Portuguese. Each text had, in average, 225 words, 7 sentences, 17 propositional units and 16 rhetorical relations.

---

[3] www.nilc.icmc.usp.br/nilc/tools/corpora.htm

Once discourse-analyzed by DiZer, the resulting rhetorical structures have been verified in order to assess two main points: (I) the performance of the segmentation process and (II) the plausibility of the hypothesized rhetorical relations. Such features have been chosen for being the core of DiZer main processes. Only one expert in RST has analyzed those structures, using as reference one manually generated discourse structure for each text, which incorporated all plausible relations between the propositions. Table 1 presents the resulting recall and precision average numbers for DiZer. It also shows the results for a baseline method, which considers complete sentences as segments and always hypothesizes ELABORATION relations between them (since it is the most common and generic relation).

[1] Since its commercial opening at 1993, Internet became a powerful communication service [2] when permitted a user to get in touch with any other users in the world. [3] The electronic commerce is one of the new exploration niches in Internet, [4] because Internet makes it possible to realize global commercial transactions with inferior maintenance cost.

[5] The purpose of this work is to propose the project and implementation of an electronic commerce service on the JAMP platform. [6] This platform is a middleware implemented on Java/RMI for distributed multimedia applications development and, in particular, for World Wide Web applications, through service frameworks for these applications development support.

Fig. 7. Text 2.

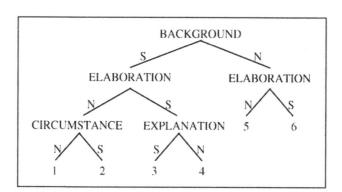

Fig. 8. Text 2 rhetorical structure.

For text segmentation, recall indicates how many segments of the reference discourse structure were correctly identified and precision indicates how many of the identified segments were correct; for rhetorical relations hypotheses, recall indicates how many relations of the reference discourse structure were correctly hypothesized (taking into account the related segments and their nuclearity – which segments were nuclei and satellites) and precision indicates how many of the hypothesized relations were correct. It is possible to see that the baseline method performed very poorly and that DiZer outperformed it.

Table 1. Evaluation results.

	DiZer		Baseline method	
	Recall	*Precision*	*Recall*	*Precision*
Text segmentation	81%	87%	16%	32%
Rhet. relations hypotheses	71%	76%	22%	50%

Some problematic issues might interfere in the evaluation, namely, the tagger performance and the quality of the source texts. If the tagger fails in identifying the morphosyntactic classes of the words, discourse analysis may be compromised. Also, if the source texts present a significant misuse of discourse markers, inadequate rhetorical structures may be produced. These problems have not been observed in the current evaluation, but they should be taken into account in future evaluations.

It is worth noticing that Marcu's cue-phrase-based rhetorical analyzer (which is presently the most similar analyzer to DiZer), achieved worse recall in both cases (51% and 47%), but better precision (96% and 78%) than DiZer. Although this direct comparison is unfair, given that the languages, test corpora and even the analysis methods differ, it gives an idea of the state of the art results in cue-phrase-based automatic discourse analysis.

6 Concluding Remarks

This paper presented DiZer, a knowledge intensive discourse analyzer for Brazilian Portuguese that produces rhetorical structures of scientific texts based upon the Rhetorical Structure Theory. To our knowledge, DiZer is the first discourse analyzer for such language and, once available, must be the basis for the development and improvement of other NLP tasks, like automatic summarization and co-reference resolution.

Although DiZer was developed for scientific texts analysis, it is worth noticing that it may also be applied for free domain texts, since, in general, discourse markers are consistently used across domains.

In a preliminary evaluation, DiZer has achieved very good performance. However, there is still room for improvements. The use of a parser and the development of new specialized analysis patterns and heuristics must improve its performance. In the near future, a statistical module should be introduced into the system, enabling it to determine the most probable discourse structure among the possible structures built, as well as to hypothesize rhetorical relations in the case that there are not discourse markers and indicative phrases and words present in some segment in the source text.

Acknowledgments

The authors are grateful to the Brazilian agencies FAPESP, CAPES and CNPq, and to Fulbright Commission for supporting this work.

References

1. Mann, W.C. and Thompson, S.A.: Rhetorical Structure Theory: A Theory of Text Organization. Technical Report ISI/RS-87-190 (1987).
2. Marcu, D.: The Theory and Practice of Discourse Parsing and Summarization. The MIT Press. Cambridge, Massachusetts (2000).
3. O'Donnell, M.: Variable-Length On-Line Document Generation. In the Proceedings of the 6th European Workshop on Natural Language Generation. Duisburg, Germany (1997).
4. Cristea, D.; Ide, N.; Romary, L.: Veins Theory. An Approach to Global Cohesion and Coherence. In the Proceedings of Coling/ACL. Montreal (1998).
5. Schauer, H.: Referential Structure and Coherence Structure. In the Proceedings of TALN. Lausanne, Switzerland (2000).
6. Marcu, D.: The Rhetorical Parsing, Summarization, and Generation of Natural Language Texts. PhD Thesis, Department of Computer Science, University of Toronto (1997).
7. Marcu, D. and Echihabi, A.: An Unsupervised Approach to Recognizing Discourse Relations. In the Proceedings of the 40th Annual Meeting of the Association for Computational Linguistics (ACL'02), Philadelphia, PA (2002).
8. Soricut, R. and Marcu, D.: Sentence Level Discourse Parsing using Syntactic and Lexical Information. In the Proceedings of the Human Language Technology and North American Association for Computational Linguistics Conference (HLT/NAACL), Edmonton, Canada (2003).
9. Corston-Oliver, S.: Computing Representations of the Structure of Written Discourse. PhD Thesis, University of California, Santa Barbara, CA, USA (1998).
10. Feltrim, V.D.; Aluísio, S.M.; Nunes, M.G.V.: Analysis of the Rhetorical Structure of Computer Science Abstracts in Portuguese. In the Proceedings of Corpus Linguistics (2003).
11. Pardo, T.A.S. and Rino, L.H.M.: DMSumm: Review and Assessment. In E. Ranchhod and N. J. Mamede (eds.), Advances in Natural Language Processing, (2002) pp. 263-273 (Lecture Notes in Artificial Intelligence 2389). Springer-Verlag, Germany.
12. Aluísio, S.M. and Oliveira Jr., O.N.: A Case-Based Approach for Developing Writing Tools Aimed at Non-native English Users. Lecture Notes in Computer Science, Vol. 1010, (1995) pp. 121-132.
13. Aluísio, S.M.; Barcelos, I.; Sampaio, J.; Oliveira J, O.N.: How to Learn the Many Unwritten 'Rules of the Game' of the Academic Discourse: A Hybrid Approach Based on Critiques and Cases to Support Scientific Writing. In the Proceedings of the IEEE International Conference on Advanced Learning Technologies. Madison, Wisconsin. Los Alamitos, CA: IEEE Computer Society, Vol. 1, (2001) pp. 257-260.
14. Rino, L.H.M. and Scott, D.: A Discourse Model for Gist Preservation. In the Proceedings of the XIII Brazilian Symposium on Artificial Intelligence (SBIA'96). Curitiba - PR, Brasil (1996).
15. Carlson, L. and Marcu, D.: Discourse Tagging Reference Manual. ISI Technical Report ISI-TR-545 (2001).
16. O'Donnell, M.: RST-Tool: An RST Analysis Tool. In the Proceedings of the 6th European Workshop on Natural Language Generation. Gerhard-Mercator University, Duisburg, Germany (1997).
17. Pardo, T.A.S. e Nunes, M.G.V.: A Construção de um Corpus de Textos Científicos em Português do Brasil e sua Marcação Retórica. Série de Relatórios Técnicos do Instituto de Ciências Matemáticas e de Computação - ICMC, Universidade de São Paulo, no. 212 (2003).

18. Pardo, T.A.S. e Nunes, M.G.V.: Relações Retóricas e seus Marcadores Superficiais: Análise de um Corpus de Textos Científicos em Português do Brasil. Relatório Técnico NILC-TR-04-03. Série de Relatórios do NILC, ICMC-USP (2004).
19. Aires, R.V.X.; Aluísio, S.M.; Kuhn, D.C.S.; Andreeta, M.L.B.; Oliveira Jr., O.N.: Combining Multiple Classifiers to Improve Part of Speech Tagging: A Case Study for Brazilian Portuguese. In the Proceedings of the Brazilian AI Symposium (SBIA'2000), (2000) pp. 20-22.
20. Martins, R.T.; Montilha, G.; Rino, L.H.M.; Nunes, M.G.V.: Dos Modelos de Resolução da Ambigüidade Categorial: O Problema do SE. In the Proceedings do IV Encontro para o Processamento Computacional da Língua Portuguesa Escrita e Falada, PROPOR'99, (1999) pp. 115-128. Évora, Portugal.
21. Pereira, F.C.N. and Warren, D.H.D.: Definite Clause Grammars for Language Analysis – A Survey of the Formalism and Comparison with Augmented Transition Networks. Artificial Intelligence, N. 13, (1980) pp. 231-278.
22. Schilder, F.: Robust discourse parsing via discourse markers, topicality and position. In J. Tait, B.K. Boguraev and C. Jacquemin (eds.), Natural Language Engineering, Vol. 8. Cambridge University Press (2002).
23. Sumita, K.; Ono, K.; Chino, T.; Ukita, T.; Amano, S.: A discourse structure analyzer for Japonese text. In the Proceedings of the International Conference on Fifth Generation Computer Systems, Vol. 2, (1992) pp. 1133-1140. Tokyo, Japan.

A Comparison of Automatic Summarizers of Texts in Brazilian Portuguese*

Lucia Helena Machado Rino[1], Thiago Alexandre Salgueiro Pardo[1],
Carlos Nascimento Silla Jr.[2], Celso Antônio Alves Kaestner[2], and Michael Pombo[1]

[1] Núcleo Interinstitucional de Lingüística Computacional (NILC/São Carlos)
DC/UFSCar – CP 676, 13565-905 São Carlos, SP, Brazil
thiago@nilc.icmc.usp.br, {michaelp,lucia}@dc.ufscar.br
http://www.nilc.icmc.usp.br
[2] Pontifícia Universidade Católica do Paraná (PUC-PR)
Av. Imaculada Conceição 1155, 80215-901 Curitiba, PR, Brazil
{silla,kaestner}@ppgia.pucpr.br

Abstract. Automatic Summarization (AS) in Brazil has only recently become a significant research topic. When compared to other languages initiatives, such a delay can be explained by the lack of specific resources, such as expressive lexicons and corpora that could provide adequate foundations for deep or shallow approaches on AS. Taking advantage of having commonalities with respect to resources and a corpus of texts and summaries written in Brazilian Portuguese, two NLP research groups have decided to start a common task to assess and compare their AS systems. In the experiment five distinct extractive AS systems have been assessed. Some of them incorporate techniques that have been already used to summarize texts in English; others propose novel approaches to AS. Two baseline systems have also been considered. An overall performance comparison has been carried out, and its outcomes are discussed in this paper.

1 Introduction

We definitely live in the information explosion era. A recent study from Berkeley [12] indicates there were 5 million terabytes of new information created via print, film, magnetic, and optical storage media in 2002, and the www alone contains about 170 terabytes of information on its surface. This is about twice the data generated in 1999, given an increasing rate at about 30% each year. Conversely, to use this information is very hard. Problems like information retrieval and extraction, and text summarization became important areas in Computer Science research.

Especially concerning Automatic Summarization (AS), we focus on extractive methods in order to produce extracts of texts written in Brazilian Portuguese. Extracts, in this context, are summaries produced automatically on the basis of superficial, empirical or statistical, techniques, broadly known as extractive methods [15]. These actually aim at producing summaries that consist entirely of material copied,

---

* The Brazilian Agencies FAPESP and PIBIC-CNPQ supported this research.

A.L.C. Bazzan and S. Labidi (Eds.): SBIA 2004, LNAI 3171, pp. 235–244, 2004.

usually sentences, from the source texts. Typically, extracts or summaries automatically generated have 10 to 30% of the original text length – being faster to read – but must contain enough information to satisfy the user's needs [13].

Five AS systems were assessed, all of them sharing the same linguistic resources, when applicable. Only precision (P) and recall (R) have been considered, for practical reasons: being extractive, all the summarizers under consideration could be automatically assessed to calculate P and R. The performance of those AS systems could thus be compared, in order to identify the features that apply better to a genre-specific text corpus in Brazilian Portuguese.

To calculate P and R, ideal summaries – extractive versions of the manual summaries – have been used, which have been automatically produced by a specific tool, a generator of ideal extracts (available in http://www.nilc.icmc.usp.br/~thiago). This tool is based upon the widely known vector space model and the cosine similarity measure [25], and works as follows: 1) for each sentence in the manual summary the most similar sentence in the text is obtained (through the cosine measure); 2) the most representative sentences are selected, yielding the corresponding ideal, extractive, summary. This procedure works as suggested by [14], i.e., it is based on the premise that ideal extracts should be composed of as many sentences (the most similar ones) as the ones in the corresponding manual summary.

As we shall see, some of the systems being assessed had to be trained. In this case, the very same pre-processing tools and data have been used by all of them. We chose TeMário [19] (available in_http://www.linguateca.pt/Repositorio/TeMario), a corpus of 100 newspaper texts (c.a. 613 words, or 1 to 2 ½ pages long) that has been built for AS purposes, as the only input for the assessment reported here. Those texts have been withdrawn from online regular Brazilian newspapers, the Folha de São Paulo (60 texts) and the Jornal do Brasil (40 texts) ones. They are equally distributed amongst distinct domains, namely, those respecting to free author views, critiques, world, politics, and foreign affairs. The summaries that come along with this corpus are those hand-produced by the consultant on the Brazilian Portuguese language.

Details of the considered systems and their assessment are given below. In Section 2, we outline the main features of each system under focus. In Section 3 we describe the experiment itself and a thorough discussion on their overall rating. Finally, in section 4 we address the outcomes of the reported assessment, concerning the potentialities to apply AS for Brazilian Portuguese texts of a particular genre.

2   Extractive AS Systems Under Focus

Each of the assessed AS systems tackles a particular AS strategy. Specially, three of them suggest novel approaches, as follows: (a) **Gist Summ**arizer (GistSumm) [20], focuses upon the matching of lexical items of the source text against lexical items of a gist sentence, supposed to be the sentence of the source text that best expresses its main idea, which is previously determined by means of a word frequency distribution; (b) **Term Frequency-Inverse Sentence Frequency-based Summ**arizer (TF-ISF-Summ) [9], adapts Salton's TF-IDF information retrieval measure [25] in that, instead of signaling the documents to retrieve, it pinpoints those sentences of a source text that must be included in a summary; (c) **Neural Summ**arizer (NeuralSumm) [21] is based upon a neural network that, after training, is capable of identifying relevant sentences in a source text for producing the extract. Added to those, we employ a classification system (ClassSumm) that produces extracts based on a Machine Learning (ML) approach, in which summarization is considered as a classification task. Finally, we use Text **Su**mmarization in **Por**tuguese (SuPor) [17], a system aiming at exploring alternative methodologies that have been previously suggested to summarize texts in English. Based on a ML technique, it allows the user to customize surface and/or linguistic features to be handled during summarization, permitting one to generate diverse AS engines. In the assessment reported in this paper, SuPor has been customized to just one AS system.

All the systems consistently incorporate language-specific resources, aiming at ensuring the accuracy of the assessment. The most significant tools already available for Brazilian Portuguese are a part-of-speech tagger [1], a parser [16], and a stemmer based upon Porter's algorithm [3]. Linguistic repositories include a lexicon [18], and a list of discourse markers, which is derived from the DiZer system [22]. Additionally, a stoplist (i.e., a list of stopwords, which are too common and, therefore, irrelevant to summarization) and a list of the commonest lexical items that signal anaphors are also used. Apart from the discourse markers and the lexical items lists, which are used only by ClassSumm, and the tagger and parser, which are not used by GistSumm and NeuralSumm, the other resources are shared amongst all the systems.

Text pre-processing is also common to all the systems. It involves text segmentation, through delimiting sentences by applying simple rules based on punctuation marks, case folding and stemming, and stopwords removal. In the following we briefly describe each AS system.

2.1 The GistSumm System

GistSumm is an automatic summarizer based on a novel extractive method, called gist-based method. For GistSumm to work, the following premises must hold: (a) every text is built around a main idea, namely, its gist; (b) it is possible to identify in a text just one sentence that best expresses its main idea, namely, the gist sentence. Based on them, the following hypotheses underlie GistSumm methodology: (I) through simple statistics the gist sentence or an approximation of it is determined; (II) by means of the gist sentence, it is possible to build coherent extracts conveying the gist sentence itself and extra sentences from the source text that complement it.

GistSumm comprises three main processes: text segmentation, sentence ranking, and extract production. Sentence ranking is based on the keywords method [11]: it scores each sentence of the source text by summing up the frequency of its words and the gist sentence is chosen as the most highly scored one. Extract production focuses on selecting other sentences from the source text to include in the extract, based on: (a) gist correlation and (b) relevance to the overall content of the source text. Criterion (a) is fulfilled by simply verifying co-occurring words in the candidate sentences and the gist sentence, ensuring lexical cohesion. Criterion (b) is fulfilled by sentences whose score is above a threshold, computed as the average of all the sentence scores, to guarantee that only relevant-to-content sentences are chosen. All the selected sentences above the cutoff are thus juxtaposed to compose the final extract.

GistSumm has already undergone several evaluations, the main one being DUC'2003 (Document Understanding Conference). According to this, Hypothesis I above has been proved to hold. Other methods than the keywords one were also used for sentence ranking. The keywords one outperformed all of them.

2.2 The TF-ISF-Summ System

TF-ISF-Summ is an automatic summarizer that makes use of the TF-ISF (Term-Frequency Inverse-Sentence-Frequency) metric to rank sentences in a given text and then extract the most relevant ones. Similarly to GistSumm, the approach used by this system has also three main steps: (1) text pre-processing (2) sentence ranking, and (3) extract generation. Differently from that, in order to rank the sentences, it calculates the mean TF-ISF of each sentence, as proposed in [9]: (1) each sentence is considered as a fragment of the text; (2) given a sentence, the TF-ISF metric for each term (similar to the TF-IDF metric [25]) is calculated: TF is the frequency of the term in the document and ISF is a function of the number of sentences in which the term appears; (3) finally, the TF-ISF for the whole sentence is computed as the arithmetic mean of all the TF-ISF values of its terms. Sentences with the highest mean-TF-ISF score and above the cutoff are selected to compose the output extract.

The method showed to be only as good as the random sentences approach in the experiments made by Larocca Neto [8] for documents in English.

2.3 The NeuralSumm System

NeuralSumm system makes use of a ML technique, and runs on four processes: (1) text segmentation, (2) features extraction, (3) classification, and (4) extract production. It is primarily unsupervised, since it is based on a self-organizing map (SOM) [6], which clusters information from the training texts. NeuralSumm produces two clusters: one that represents the important sentences of the training texts (and, thus, should be included in the extract) and another that represents the non-important sentences (and, thus, should be discarded). To our knowledge, it is the first time a SOM has been used to help determining relevant sentences in AS.

During AS, after analyzing the source text, features extraction focuses on each sentence, in order to collect the following features: (i) sentence length, (ii) sentence position in the source text, (iii) sentence position in the paragraph it belongs to, (iv) presence of keywords in the sentence, (v) presence of gist words in the sentence, (vi) sentence score by means of its words frequency, (vii) sentence score by means of TF-ISF and (viii) presence of indicative words in the sentence. It is worth noticing that keywords are limited to the two most frequent words in the text, gist words are the composing words of the gist sentence, and indicative words are genre-dependent and could be corresponding to, e.g., 'problem', 'solution', 'conclusion', or 'purpose', in scientific texts. Both feature (vi) and the gist sentence are calculated in the same way as they are in GistSumm. The rationale behind incorporating these features in NeuralSumm may be found in [21]. Sentence classification is carried out by considering every feature of each sentence, which is given as input to the SOM. This finally classifies the sentences as important or non-important, the important ones being selected and juxtaposed to compose the final extract.

NeuralSumm SOM was already compared to other ML techniques. It proved to be better than Naïve Bayes, decision trees and decision rules methods, with an error decreasing rate to the worst case of c.a. 10% [21].

2.4 The ClassSumm System

The Classification System was proposed by Larocca Neto et al. [10] and uses a ML approach to determine relevant segments to extract from source texts. Actually, it is based on a Naïve Bayes classifier.

To summarize a source text, the system performs the same four processes that NeuralSumm, as previously explained. Text pre-processing is similar to the one performed by TF-ISF-Summ. Features extracted from each sentence are of two kinds: statistical, i.e., based on measures and counting taken directly from the text components, and linguistic, in which case they are extracted from a simplified argumentative structure of the text, produced by a hierarchical text agglomerative clustering algorithm. A total of 16 features are associated to each sentence, to know: (a) mean-TF-ISF, (b) sentence length, (c) sentence position in the source text, (d) similarity to title, (e) similarity to keywords, (f) sentence-to-sentence cohesion, (g) sentence-to-centroid cohesion, (h) main concepts – the most frequent nouns that appear in the text, (i) occurrence of proper nouns, (j) occurrence of anaphors, (k) occurrence of non-essential information. Features (d), (e), (f) and (g) use the cosine measure to calculate similarity; features (h) and (i) use the POS Tagger; finally, features (j) e (k) use fixed lists, as mentioned before. The remaining are linguistic features, based on the binary tree that represents the argumentative structure of the text, where each leaf is associated to a sentence and the internal nodes are associated to partial clusters of sentences. These features are: (l) the depth of each sentence in the tree, and (m) four features that represent specific directions in a given level of the tree (height 1,2,3,4) that indicate, for each depth level, the direction taken by the path from the root to the leaf associated with the sentence.

Extract generation is considered as a two-valued classification problem: sentences should be classified as relevant-to-extract or not. According to the values of the features for each sentence, the classification algorithm must "learn" which ones must belong to the summary. Finally, the sentences to include in the extract will be those above the cutoff and, thus, those with the highest probabilities of belonging to it.

In the experiment reported in this article, the only unused feature was the keywords similarity, because the TeMário corpus does not convey a list of keywords. Compared to the other systems, ClassSumm uses two extra lists: one with indicators of main concepts and another with the commonest anaphors. Although there are no such fixed lists to Brazilian Portuguese, we followed Larocca Neto's [8] suggestions, incorporating to the current version of the system the corresponding pronoun anaphors for English, such as 'this', 'that', 'those', etc.

ClassSumm was evaluated on a TIPSTER corpus of 100 news stories for training, and two test procedures, namely, one that has used 100 automatic summaries and another that has used 30 manual extracts [10], in which it outperforms the "from-top" – those from the beginning of the source text, and random order baselines.

2.5 The SuPor System

Similarly to some of the above systems, SuPor also conveys two distinct processes: training and extracting based on a Bayesian method, following [7]. Unlike them, it embeds a flexible way to combine linguistic and non-linguistic constraints for extraction production. AS options include distinct suggestions originally aimed at texts in English, which have been adapted to Brazilian Portuguese. To configure an AS strategy, SuPor must thus be customized by an expert user [17].

In SuPor, relevant features for classification are (a) sentence length (minimum of 5 words); (b) words frequency [11]; (c) signaling phrases; (d) sentence location in the texts; and (e) occurrence of proper nouns. As a result of training, a probabilistic distribution is produced, which entitles extraction in SuPor. For this, only features (a), (b), (d) and (e) are used, along with lexical chaining [2]. Adaptations from the originals have been made for Portuguese, to know: (i) for lexical chaining computation, a thesaurus [4] for Brazilian Portuguese is used; (ii) sentence location (10% of the first and 5% of the last sentences of a source text are considered); (iii) proper nouns are those that are not abbreviations, occur more than once in the source text and do not appear at the beginning of a sentence; (iv) a minimum threshold has been set for the selection of the most frequent words: each term of the source text is frequency-weighed, and the total weight of the text is produced; then the average weight, along with its standard deviation is taken as the cutoff of frequent words.

SuPor works in the following way: firstly, the set of features of each sentence are extracted. Secondly, for each of the sets, the Bayesian classifier provides its probability, which will enable top-sentences to be included in the output extract.

SuPor performance has been previously assessed through two distinct experiments that also focused on newspaper articles and their ideal extracts, produced by the generator of ideal extracts already referred to. However, testing texts had nothing to do with TeMário. Both experiments addressed the representativeness of distinct groupings of features. Overall, the features grouping that have been most significant included lexical chaining, sentence length and proper nouns (avg.F-measure=40%).

3 Experiments and Results

We proceeded to a blackbox-type evaluation, i.e., only comparing the systems outputs. The main limitation imposed to the experiment was making it efficient: to compare the performance of the five systems, evaluation should be entirely automatic. As a result, only co-selection measures [23], more specifically P, R, and F-measure were used. We could not compare either automatic extracts with TeMário manual summaries because they are hand-built and do not allow for a viable automatic evaluation. For this reason, the corresponding ideal extracts were used, as described in Section 1.

In relation to the systems that need training, to assure non-biasing, a 10-fold cross validation has been used (each fold comprising 10 texts).

We also included in the evaluation two baseline methods: the one based just upon the selection of from-top sentences and the other that chooses them at random (hereafter, From-top and Random order methods, respectively). Following the same approach, the extracts contain as many sentences as the cutoff allows in this case.

In the AS context, the metrics under focus here are defined as follows: (a) compression rate is 30%. It has been chosen to conform to the sizes of both, the manual summaries (length ranging from 25 to 30%) and ideal extracts; (b) Let N be the total number of sentences in the output extract; M be the total number of sentences in the ideal extract; NR be the number of relevant sentences included in the output extract, i.e., the number of coinciding sentences between the output and its corresponding ideal extract; (c) precision and recall are defined by P=NR/N and R=NR/M, and F-measure is the balance metric between P and R, F=2*P*R/(P+R).

All the systems were independently run. Table 1 shows the averaged precision, recall and F-measure metrics of each system obtained in the experiments, with last column indicating the relative performance of each system as the percentage over the random order baseline method, i.e. (F-measure/F-measure-random-baseline - 1).

Table 1. Systems performance (in %).

Systems	Avg. P	Avg. R	Avg. F	% over random
SuPor	44.9	40.8	42.8	38
ClassSumm	45.6	39.7	42.4	37
From-top	42.9	32.6	37.0	19
TF-ISF-Summ	39.6	34.3	36.8	19
GistSumm	49.9	25.6	33.8	9
NeuralSumm	36.0	29.5	32.4	5
Random order	34.0	28.5	31.0	0

Overall, the combination of features that lead to SuPor performance is [location, words frequency, length, proper nouns, lexical chaining]. SuPor performance may well be due to the inclusion of lexical chaining, since this is its most distinctive feature. Meaningfully, training has also counted on signaling phrases, which has been considered only in SuPor. This, added to lexical chaining, may well be one of the reasons for SuPor outperformance. Lexical chaining also has a close relationship to the innovative features added to ClassSumm, the second topmost system. Especially, it focuses on the strongest lexical chains, whilst ClassSumm focuses on sentence-to-sentence and sentence-to-centroid for cohesion.

Close performance between SuPor and ClassSumm can also be explained through the relationship between the following features combinations, respectively: [words frequency, signaling phrases] and [mean TF-ISF, indicator of main concepts, similarity to title]. This is justified by acknowledging that the mean TF-ISF is based on words frequency and main concepts and titles may signal phrases that lead to decision patterns.

Both topmost systems include features that have been formerly indicated for good performance, when individually taken (see the generalization of Edmundson's [5] paradigm in [13]): sentences location and cue phrases (i.e., the referred signaling ones). Additionally, both have been trained through a Bayesian classifier, with a considerable overlap of features. Keywords, which have been considered the poorest in Edmundson's model [5], have not been considered in any of them. In all, they substantially differ only through the anaphors and non-essential information features, although location, in ClassSumm, addresses the argumentative tree of a source text, instead of its surface structure, as it is in SuPor.

TF-ISF-Summ, which has a worse performance than ClassSumm, coincides with that in the combination [words frequency, mean TF-ISF], for the same reasons given above. Although its performance is not substantially far from that of SuPor, its upperbound is a baseline. This may also suggest that what distinguishes SuPor is not the word frequency, neither is the mean TF-ISF measure in ClassSumm.

Not surprisingly, GistSumm performance is farther than the other systems referred to, for it is based mainly upon words distribution, which has been repeatedly evidenced as a non-expressive feature. However, evidences provided by the DUC'2003 evaluation show that GistSumm is effective in determining the gist sentence. In that evaluation, GistSumm scored 3.12 in a 0-4 scale for usefulness. This metric was presented to DUC judges in the following way: their score of any given summary should indicate how useful the summary was in retrieving the corresponding source text (0 indicating no use at all and 4, totally useful, i.e., as good as having the full text instead. So, the problem must be in the extraction module instead. Although this system achieved the best P, its R is the worst, even worse than the baselines. Recall could be improved, for example, if gist words were spread over the whole source text, which does not seem to be the case in newspaper texts, where the gist is usually in the lead sentences.

Although NeuralSumm is based on a combination of most of the features embedded in SuPor and ClassSumm, its performance is much worse. This may be due to its training on SOM, as well as on the means training has been carried out (e.g., a non-significant corpus) or, ultimately, on the features themselves, which also include word frequency.

The From-top method occupies, as expected, the 3rd position in the F-measure scale. Being composed of newspaper texts of varied domains, the test corpus has an expressive feature: lead sentences usually are the most relevant ones. Distinction between that and the other 2 topmost systems may be due to the sophistication of combining distinctive features. Since most of them coincide, but cohesive indicators, lexical chaining (SuPor) and sentence-to-sentence or sentence-to-centroid cohesion (ClassSumm) seem to be the key parameters for our outperforming systems.

It is important to notice that the described evaluation is not noise free. The ways ideal extracts are generated bring about a problem to our evaluation: since the generator relies on the cosine similarity measure, and this does not take into account the sentence size, there is no way to guarantee that compression rate is uniformly observed. Actually, there are ideal extracts in our reference corpus that are considerably longer than the extracts automatically generated. This poses an evaluation problem in that the comparison between both penalizes recall, whilst increasing precision.

These results are relatively similar to the ones obtained in the literature for texts in English, such as the ones of Teufel and Moens [26] (P=65% and R=44%), Kupiec et al. (P=R=42%) and Saggion and Lapalme [24] (P=20% and R=23%). Although the direct comparison between the results is not fair, due to different training, test corpora, and even language, it may indicate the general state of the art in extractive AS.

4   Final Remarks

Clearly, considering linguistic features and, thus, knowledge-based decisions, indicates a way of improving extractive AS. It is also worthy considering that the topmost evaluated systems are based on training, which means that, with more substantial training data, performance may be improved. Limitations usually addressed in the literature refer to the impossibility of, e.g., aggregating or generalizing information. SuPor and ClassSumm evaluations suggest that, although those procedures keep been inexistent in extractive approaches, a way of surpassing those difficulties is still to address the semantic-level through surface manipulation of text components. Another significant way of improving SuPor and ClassSumm is to make the input reference lists (e.g., stoplists and discourse markers) more expressive, by adding more terms to them. Also, substituting the language-dependent repositories that have been currently adapted (e.g., the thesaurus in SuPor) or building an argumentative tree in Class-Summ by other means may improve performance, since that will be likely to tune better the systems to Brazilian Portuguese.

After all, the common evaluation presented here made it possible to compare different systems, allowing fostering AS research especially concerning texts in Brazilian Portuguese and, more importantly, delineating future goals to pursue.

References

1. Aires, R.V.X., Aluísio, S.M., Kuhn, D.C.e.S., Andreeta, M.L.B., Oliveira Jr., O.N.: Combining classifiers to improve part of speech tagging: A case study for Brazilian Portuguese. In: Open Discussion Track Proceedings of the 15th Brazilian Symposium on AI. (2000) 227–236
2. Barzilay, R., Elhadad, M.: Using Lexical Chains for Text Summarization. In: Advances in Automatic Text Summarization. MIT Press (1999) 111–121
3. Caldas Jr., J., Imamura, C.Y.M., Rezende, S.O.: Evaluation of a stemming algorithm for the Portuguese language (in Portuguese). In: Proceedings of the 2nd Congress of Logic Applied to Technology. Volume 2. (2001) 267–274
4. Dias-da Silva, B., Oliveira, M.F., Moraes, H.R., Paschoalino, C., Hasegawa, R., Amorin, D., Nascimento, A.C.: The Building of an Electronic thesaurus for Brazilian Portuguese (in Portuguese). In: Proceedings of the V Encontro para o Processamento Computacional da Língua Portuguesa Escrita e Falada. (2000) 1–11
5. Edmundson, H.P.: New methods in automatic extracting. Journal of the Association for Computing Machinery 16 (1969) 264–285
6. Kohonen, T.: Self organized formation of topologically correct feature maps. Biological Cybernetics 43 (1982) 59–69

7. Kupiec, J., Pedersen, J., Chen, F.: A trainable document summarizer. In: Proc. of the 18th ACM-SIGIR Conference on Research & Development in Information Retrieval. (1995) 68–73

8. Larocca Neto, J.: Contribution to the study of automatic text summarization techniques (in Portuguese). Master's thesis, Pontifícia Universidade Católica do Paraná (PUC-PR), Graduate Program in Applied Computer Science (2002)

9. Larocca Neto, J., Santos, A.D., Kaestner, C.A.A., Freitas, A.A.: Document clustering and text summarization. In: Proc. 4th Int. Conf. Practical Applications of Knowledge Discovery and Data Mining. (2000) 41–55

10. Larocca Neto, J., Freitas, A.A., Kaestner, C.A.A.: Automatic text summarization using a machine learning approach. In: XVI Brazilian Symp. on Artificial Intelligence. Number 2057 in Lecture Notes in Artificial Intelligence (2002) 205–215

11. Luhn, H.: The automatic creation of literature abstracts. IBM Journal of Research and Development 2 (1958) 159–165

12. Lyman, P., Varian, H.R.: How much information. Retrieved from http://www.sims.berkeley.edu/how-much-info-2003 on [01/19/2004] (2003)

13. Mani, I.: Automatic Summarization. John Benjamin's Publishing Company (2001)

14. Mani, I., Bloedorn, E.: Machine learning of generic and user-focused summarization. In: Proc. of the 15th National Conf. on Artificial Intelligence (AAAI 98). (1998) 821–826

15. Mani, I., Maybury, M.T.: Advances in Automatic Text Summarization. MIT Press (1999)

16. Martins, R.T., Hasegawa, R., Nunes, M.G.V.: Curupira: a functional parser for Portuguese (in Portuguese). NILC Tech. Report NILC-TR-02-26 (2002)

17. Módolo, M.: Supor: an environment for exploration of extractive methods for automatic text summarization for portuguese (in Portuguese). Master's thesis, Departamento de Computação, UFSCar (2003)

18. Nunes, M.G.V., Vieira, F.M.V., Zavaglia, C., Sossolete, C.R.C., Hernandez, J.: The building of a Brazilian Portuguese lexicon for supporting automatic grammar checking (in Portuguese). ICMC-USP Tech. Report 42 (1996)

19. Pardo, T.A.S., Rino, L.H.M.: TeMário: A corpus for automatic text summarization (in Portuguese). NILC Tech. Report NILC-TR-03-09 (2003)

20. Pardo, T.A.S., Rino, L.H.M., Nunes, M.G.V.: GistSumm: A summarization tool based on a new extractive method. In: 6th Workshop on Computational Processing of the Portuguese Language – Written and Spoken. Number 2721 in Lecture Notes in Artificial Intelligence, Springer (2003) 210–218

21. Pardo, T.A.S., Rino, L.H.M., Nunes, M.G.V.: NeuralSumm: A connexionist approach to automatic text summarization (in Portuguese). In: Proceedings of the IV Encontro Nacional de Inteligência Artificial. (2003)

22. Pardo, T.A.S., Rino, L.H.M., Nunes, M.G.V.: DiZer: An automatic discourse analysis proposal to brazilian portuguese (in Portuguese). In: Proc. of the I Workshop em Tecnologia da Informação e da Linguagem Humana. (2003)

23. Radev, D.R., Teufel, S., Saggion, H., Lam, W., Blitzer, J., Qi, H., Çelebi, A., Liu, D., Drabek, E.: Evaluation challenges in large-scale document summarization. In: Proc. of the 41st Annual Meeting of the Association for Computational Linguistics. (2003) 375–382

24. Saggion, H., Lapalme, G.: Generating indicative-informative summaries with sumUM. Computational Linguistics 28 (2002) 497–526

25. Salton, G., Buckley, C.: Term-weighting approaches in automatic text retrieval. Information Processing and Management 24 (1988) 513–523

26. Teufel, S., Moens, M.: Summarizing scientific articles: Experiments with relevance and rhetorical status. Computational Linguistics 28 (2002) 409–445

Heuristically Accelerated Q–Learning: A New Approach to Speed Up Reinforcement Learning

Reinaldo A.C. Bianchi[1,2], Carlos H.C. Ribeiro[3], and Anna H.R. Costa[1]

[1] Laboratório de Técnicas Inteligentes
Escola Politécnica da Universidade de São Paulo
Av. Prof. Luciano Gualberto, trav. 3, 158. 05508-900, São Paulo, SP, Brazil
`rbianchi@fei.edu.br, anna.reali@poli.usp.br`
[2] Centro Universitário da FEI
Av. Humberto A. C. Branco, 3972. 09850-901, São Bernardo do Campo, SP, Brazil
[3] Instituto Tecnológico de Aeronáutica
Praça Mal. Eduardo Gomes, 50. 12228-900, São José dos Campos, SP, Brazil
`carlos@ita.br`

Abstract. This work presents a new algorithm, called Heuristically Accelerated Q–Learning (HAQL), that allows the use of heuristics to speed up the well-known Reinforcement Learning algorithm Q–learning. A heuristic function $\mathcal{H}$ that influences the choice of the actions characterizes the HAQL algorithm. The heuristic function is strongly associated with the policy: it indicates that an action must be taken instead of another. This work also proposes an automatic method for the extraction of the heuristic function $\mathcal{H}$ from the learning process, called Heuristic from Exploration. Finally, experimental results shows that even a very simple heuristic results in a significant enhancement of performance of the reinforcement learning algorithm.

Keywords: Reinforcement Learning, Cognitive Robotics

1 Introduction

The main problem approached in this paper is the speedup of Reinforcement Learning (RL), aiming its use in mobile and autonomous robotic agents acting in complex environments. RL algorithms are notoriously slow to converge, making it difficult to use them in real time applications. The goal of this work is to propose an algorithm that preserves RL advantages, such as the convergence to an optimal policy and the free choice of actions to be taken, minimizing its main disadvantage: the learning time.

For being the most popular RL algorithm and because of the large amount of data available in literature for a comparative evaluation, the Q–learning algorithm [11] was chosen as the first algorithm to be extended by the use of heuristic acceleration. The resulting new algorithm is named Heuristically Accelerated Q–Learning (HAQL) algorithm.

In order to describe this proposal in depth, this paper is organized as follows. Section 2 describes the Q–learning algorithm. Section 3 describes the HAQL and

A.L.C. Bazzan and S. Labidi (Eds.): SBIA 2004, LNAI 3171, pp. 245–254, 2004.

its formalization using a heuristic $\mathcal{H}$ function and section 4 describes the algorithm used to define the heuristic function, namely Heuristic from Exploration. Section 5 describes the domain where this proposal has been evaluated and the results obtained. Finally, Section 6 summarizes some important points learned from this research and outlines future work.

2   Reinforcement Learning and the Q–Learning Algorithm

Consider an autonomous agent interacting with its environment via perception and action. On each interaction step the agent senses the current state s of the environment, and chooses an action a to perform. The action a alters the state s of the environment, and a scalar reinforcement signal r (a reward or penalty) is provided to the agent to indicate the desirability of the resulting state.

The goal of the agent in a RL problem is to learn an action policy that maximizes the expected long term sum of values of the reinforcement signal, from any starting state. A policy $\pi : \mathcal{S} \to \mathcal{A}$ is some function that tells the agent which actions should be chosen, under which circumstances [8]. This problem can be formulated as a discrete time, finite state, finite action Markov Decision Process (MDP), since problems with delayed reinforcement are well modeled as MDPs. The learner's environment can be modeled (see [7,9]) by a 4-tuple $\langle \mathcal{S}, \mathcal{A}, \mathcal{T}, \mathcal{R} \rangle$, where:

- $\mathcal{S}$: is a finite set of states.
- $\mathcal{A}$: is a finite set of actions that the agent can perform.
- $\mathcal{T} : \mathcal{S} \times \mathcal{A} \to \Pi(\mathcal{S})$: is a state transition function, where $\Pi(\mathcal{S})$ is a probability distribution over $\mathcal{S}$. $T(s, a, s')$ represents the probability of moving from state s to s' by performing action a.
- $\mathcal{R} : \mathcal{S} \times \mathcal{A} \to \Re$: is a scalar reward function.

The task of a RL agent is to learn an optimal policy $\pi^* : \mathcal{S} \to \mathcal{A}$ that maps the current state s into a desirable action(s) a to be performed in s. In RL, the policy π should be learned through trial-and-error interactions of the agent with its environment, that is, the RL learner must explicitly explore its environment.

The Q–learning algorithm was proposed by Watkins [11] as a strategy to learn an optimal policy π^* when the model ($\mathcal{T}$ and $\mathcal{R}$) is not known in advance. Let $Q^*(s, a)$ be the reward received upon performing action a in state s, plus the discounted value of following the optimal policy thereafter:

$$Q^*(s, a) \equiv R(s, a) + \gamma \sum_{s' \in S} T(s, a, s') V^*(s'). \tag{1}$$

The optimal policy π^* is $\pi^* \equiv \arg\max_a Q^*(s, a)$. Rewriting $Q^*(s, a)$ in a recursive form:

$$Q^*(s, a) \equiv R(s, a) + \gamma \sum_{s' \in S} T(s, a, s') \max_{a'} Q^*(s', a'). \tag{2}$$

Let $\hat{Q}$ be the learner's estimate of $Q^*(s, a)$. The Q–learning algorithm iteratively approximates $\hat{Q}$, i.e., the $\hat{Q}$ values will converge with probability 1 to Q^*, provided the system can be modeled as a MDP, the reward function is bounded $(\exists c \in \mathcal{R}; (\forall s, a), |R(s, a)| < c)$, and actions are chosen so that every state-action pair is visited an infinite number of times. The Q learning update rule is:

$$\hat{Q}(s, a) \leftarrow \hat{Q}(s, a) + \alpha \left[r + \gamma \max_{a'} \hat{Q}(s', a') - \hat{Q}(s, a) \right], \tag{3}$$

where s is the current state; a is the action performed in s; r is the reward received; s' is the new state; γ is the discount factor $(0 \leq \gamma < 1)$; $\alpha = 1/(1 + visits(s, a))$, where $visits(s, a)$ is the total number of times this state-action pair has been visited up to and including the current iteration.

An interesting property of Q–learning is that, although the exploration-exploitation tradeoff must be addressed, the $\hat{Q}$ values will converge to Q^*, independently of the exploration strategy employed (provided all state-action pairs are visited often enough) [9].

3   The Heuristically Accelerated Q–Learning Algorithm

The Heuristically Accelerated Q–Learning algorithm can be defined as a way of solving the RL problem which makes explicit use of a heuristic function $\mathcal{H} : \mathcal{S} \times \mathcal{A} \rightarrow \Re$ to influence the choice of actions during the learning process. $H_t(s_t, a_t)$ defines the heuristic, which indicates the importance of performing the action a_t when in state s_t.

The heuristic function is strongly associated with the policy: every heuristic indicates that an action must be taken regardless of others. This way, it can said that the heuristic function defines a "Heuristic Policy", that is, a tentative policy used to accelerate the learning process. It appears in the context of this paper as a way to use the knowledge about the policy of an agent to accelerate the learning process. This knowledge can be derived directly from the domain (prior knowledge) or from existing clues in the learning process itself.

The heuristic function is used only in the action choice rule, which defines which action a_t must be executed when the agent is in state s_t. The action choice rule used in the HAQL is a modification of the standard $\epsilon - Greedy$ rule used in Q–learning, but with the heuristic function included:

$$\pi(s_t) = \begin{cases} \arg\max_{a_t} \left[\hat{Q}(s_t, a_t) + \xi H_t(s_t, a_t) \right] & \text{if } q \leq p, \\ a_{random} & \text{otherwise,} \end{cases} \tag{4}$$

where:

- $\mathcal{H} : \mathcal{S} \times \mathcal{A} \rightarrow \Re$: is the heuristic function, which influences the action choice. The subscript t indicates that it can be non-stationary.
- ξ: is a real variable used to weight the influence of the heuristic function.
- q is a random value with uniform probability in [0,1] and p $(0 \leq p \leq 1)$ is the parameter which defines the exploration/exploitation trade-off: the greater the value of p, the smaller is the probability of a random choice.
- a_{random} is a random action selected among the possible actions in state s_t.

As a general rule, the value of the heuristic $H_t(s_t, a_t)$ used in the HAQL must be higher than the variation among the $\hat{Q}(s_t, a_t)$ for a similar $s_t \in S$, so it can influence the choice of actions, and it must be as low as possible in order to minimize the error. It can be defined as:

$$H(s_t, a_t) = \begin{cases} \max_a \hat{Q}(s_t, a) - \hat{Q}(s_t, a_t) + \eta & \text{if } a_t = \pi^H(s_t), \\ 0 & \text{otherwise.} \end{cases} \tag{5}$$

where η is a small real value and $\pi^H(s_t)$ is the action suggested by the heuristic.

For instance, if the agent can execute 4 different actions when in state s_t, the values of $\hat{Q}(s_t, a)$ for the actions are $[1.0 \quad 1.1 \quad 1.2 \quad 0.9]$, the action that the heuristic suggests is the first one. If $\eta = 0.01$, the values to be used are $H(s_t, 1) = 0.21$, and zero for the other actions.

As the heuristic is used only in the choice of the action to be taken, the proposed algorithm is different from the original Q–learning only in the way exploration is carried out. The RL algorithm operation is not modified (i.e., updates of the function Q are as in Q–learning), this proposal allows that many of the conclusions obtained for Q–learning to remain valid for HAQL.

Theorem 1. *Consider a HAQL agent learning in a deterministic MDP, with finite sets of states and actions, bounded rewards $(\exists c \in \mathcal{R}; (\forall s, a), |R(s, a)| < c)$, discount factor γ such that $0 \leq \gamma < 1$ and where the values used on the heuristic function are bounded by $(\forall s_t, a_t)\, h_{min} \leq H(s_t, a_t) \leq h_{max}$. For this agent, the $\hat{Q}$ values will converge to Q^*, with probability one uniformly over all the states $s \in S$, if each state-action pair is visited infinitely often (obeys the Q–learning infinite visitation condition).*

Proof: In HAQL, the update of the value function approximation does not depend explicitly on the value of the heuristic. The necessary conditions for the convergence of Q–learning that could be affected with the use of the heuristic algorithm HAQL are the ones that depend on the choice of the action. Of the conditions presented in [8,9], the only one that depends on the action choice is the necessity of infinite visitation to each pair state-action. As equation 4 considers an exploration strategy $\epsilon-$ *greedy* regardless of the fact that the value function is influenced by the heuristic $-\hat{Q} + H -$, the infinite visitation condition is guaranteed and the algorithm converges. *q.e.d.*

The condition of infinite visitation of each state-action pair can be considered valid in practice – in the same way that it is for Q–learning – also by using other visitation strategies:

– Using a Boltzmann exploration strategy [7].
– Intercalating steps where the algorithm makes alternate use of the heuristic and exploration steps.
– Using the heuristic during a period of time, smaller than the total learning time for Q–learning.

The use of a heuristic function made by HAQL explores an important characteristic of some RL algorithms: the free choice of training actions. The consequence of this is that a suitable heuristic speeds up the learning process, and if the heuristic is not suitable, the result is a delay which does not stop the system from converging to an optimal value.

The idea of using heuristics with a learning algorithm has already been considered by other authors, as in the Ant Colony Optimization presented in [5, 2]. However, the possibilities of this use were not properly explored yet. The complete HAQL algorithm is presented on table 1. It can be noticed that the only difference to the Q–learning algorithm is the action choice rule and the existence of a step for updating the function $H_t(s_t, a_t)$.

Table 1. The HAQL algorithm.

Initialize $Q(s, a)$.
Repeat:
Visit the s state.
Select an action a using the action choice rule (equation 4).
Receive the reinforcement $r(s, a)$ and observe the next state s'.
Update the values of $H_t(s, a)$.
Update the values of $Q(s, a)$ according to:
$\quad Q(s, a) \leftarrow Q(s, a) + \alpha[r(s, a) + \gamma \max_{a'} Q(s', a') - Q(s, a)]$.
Update the $s \leftarrow s'$ state.
Until some stop criteria is reached.

where: $s = s_t$, $s' = s_{t+1}$, $a = a_t$ e $a' = a_{t+1}$.

Although any function which works over real numbers and produces values belonging to an ordered set may be used in equation 4, the use of addition is particularly interesting because it allows an analysis of the influence of the values of $\mathcal{H}$ in a way similar to the one which is made in informed search algorithm (such as A^* [6]).

Finally, the function $H_t(s_t, a_t)$ can be derived by any method, but a good one increases the speedup and generality of this algorithm. In the next section, the method Heuristic from Exploration is presented.

4   The Method Heuristic from Exploration

One of the main questions addressed in this paper is how to find out, in an initial learning stage, the policy which must be used for learning speed up. For the HAQL algorithm, this question means how to define the heuristic function. The definition of an initial situation depends on the domain of the system application. For instance, in the domain of robotic navigation, we can extract an useful heuristic from the moment when the robot is receiving environment reinforcements: after hitting a wall, use as heuristic the policy which leads the robot away from it.

A method named Heuristic from Exploration is proposed in order to estimate a policy-based heuristic. This method was inspired by [3], which proposed a system that accelerates RL by composing an approximation of the value function, adapting parts of previously learned solutions. The Heuristic from Exploration is composed of two phases: the first one, which extracts information about the structure of the environment through exploration and the second one, which defines the heuristic for the policy, using the information extracted. These stages were called Structure Extraction and Heuristic Backpropagation, respectively.

Structure Extraction iteratively estimates a map sketch, keeping track of the result from all the actions executed by the agent. In the case of a mobile robot, when the agent tries to move from one position to the next, the result of the action is recorded. When an action does not result in a move, it indicates the existence of an obstacle in the environment. With the passing of time, this method generates a map sketch of the environment identified as possible actions in each state.

From the map sketch of the environment, Heuristic Backpropagation composes the heuristic, described by a sub-optimal policy, by backpropagating the possible actions over the map sketch. It propagates – from a final state – the policies which lead to that state. For instance, the heuristic of the states immediately previous to a terminal state are defined by the actions that lead to the terminal state. In a following iteration, this heuristic is propagated to the predecessors of the states which already have a defined heuristic and so on.

Theorem 2. *For a deterministic MDP whose model is known, the Heuristic Backpropagation algorithm generates an optimal policy.*

Proof Sketch: This algorithm is a simple application of the Dynamic Programming algorithm [1]. In case where the environment is completely known, both of them work the same way. In case where only part of the environment is known, the backpropagation is done only for the known states. On the example of robotic mapping, where the model of the environment is gradually built, the backpropagation can be done only on the parts of the environment which are already mapped.

Results for a complete implementation of this algorithm will be presented in the next section.

5   Experiments in the Grid-World Domain

In these experiments, a grid-world agent that can move in four directions have to find a specific state, the target. The environment is discretized in a grid with N x M positions the agent can occupy. The environment in which the agent moves can have walls (figure 1), represented by states to which the agent cannot move. The agent can execute four actions: move north, south, east or west. This domain, called *grid-world*, is well-known and was studied by several researchers [3, 4, 7, 9]. Two experiments were done using HAQL with Heuristic from Exploration in this domain: navigation with goal relocation and navigation in a new and unknown environment.

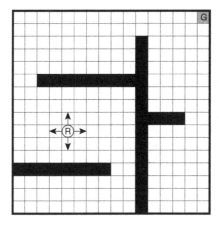

Fig. 1. Room with walls (represented by dark lines) discretized in a grid of states.

The value of the heuristic used in HAQL is defined using equation 5 as:

$$H(s_t, a_t) = \begin{cases} \max_a \hat{Q}(s_t, the) - \hat{Q}(s_t, a_t) + 1 & \text{se } a_t = \pi^H(s_t), \\ 0 & \text{otherwise.} \end{cases} \tag{6}$$

This value is computed only once, in the beginning of the acceleration. In all the following episodes, the value of the heuristic is maintained fixed, allowing the learning to overcome bad indications. If $H(s_t, a_t)$ is recalculated at each episode, a bad heuristic would be difficult to overcome.

For comparative effects, the same experiments are also executed using the Q–learning. The parameters used in Q–learning and HAQL were the same: learning rate $\alpha = 0.1$, the exploitation/exploration rate is 0.9 and the discount factor $\gamma = 0.99$. The rewards used were $+10$ when the agent arrives to the goal state and -1 when it executes any action. All the experiments presented were encoded in C++ Language and executed in a Pentium 3-500MHz, with 256MB of RAM, and Linux operating system.

The results presented in the next sub-sections show the average of 30 training sessions in nine different configurations of the navigation environment – a room with several walls – similar to the one in figure 1. The size of the environment is of 55×55 positions and the goal is initially at the right superior corner. The agent always start at a random position.

5.1   Goal Relocation During the Learning Process

In this experiment the robot must learn to reach the goal, which is initially located at the right superior corner (figure 1) and, after a certain time, is moved to the left inferior corner of the grid.

The HAQL initially only extracts the structure of the problem (using the structure extraction method described in section 4), behaving as the Q–learning.

At the end of 4999th episode the goal is relocated. With this, both algorithms must find the new position of the goal. As the algorithms are following the policies learned until then, the performance worsens and both algorithms execute a large number of steps to reach the new position of the goal.

As the robot controlled by the HAQL arrives at the new goal position (at the end of 5000th episode), the heuristic to be used is constructed using the Heuristic Backpropagation (described in section 4) with information from the structure of the environment (that was not modified) and the new position of the goal, and the values of $H(s_t, a_t)$ are defined. This heuristic then is used, resulting in a better performance in relation to Q–learning, as shown in figure 2.

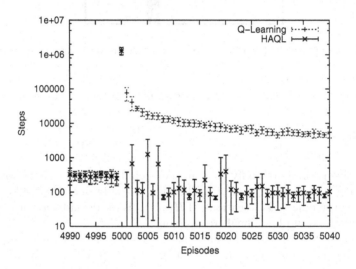

Fig. 2. Result for the goal relocation at the end of the 4999th episode (log y).

It can be observed that the HAQL has a similar performance to Q–learning until the 5000th episode. In this episode, the robot controlled by both algorithms takes more than 1 million steps to find the new position of the goal (since the known politics takes the robot to a wrong position).

After the 5001th episode, while the Q–learning needs to learn the politics from scratch, the HAQL will always execute the minimum number of steps necessary to arrive at the goal. This happens because the heuristic function allows the HAQL to use the information about the environment it already possessed.

5.2   Learning a Policy in a New Environment

In the second experiment the robot must learn to reach the goal located at the right superior corner (figure 1) when inserted in an unknown environment, at a random position.

Again, the HAQL initially only extracts the structure of the problem, without making use of the heuristic, and behaving as the Q–learning. At the end of the ninth episode, the heuristic to be used is constructed using the Heuristic Backpropagation with the information from the structure of the environment extracted during the first nine episodes, and the values of $H(s_t, a_t)$ are defined. This heuristic is then used in all the following episodes.

The result (figure 3) shows that, while the Q–learning continue to learn the action policy, the HAQL converges to the optimal policy after the speed up.

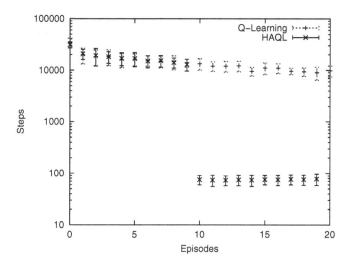

Fig. 3. Result for the acceleration at the end of the 9th episode (log y).

The 10th episode was chosen for the beginning of the acceleration because this allows to the agent to explore the environment before using the heuristic. As the robot starts every episode at a random position and the environment is small, the Heuristic from Exploration method will probably define a good heuristic.

Finally, Student's t–test [10] was used to verify the hypothesis that the use of heuristics speed up the learning process. For both experiments described in this section – goal relocation and navigation in a new environment – the value of the module of T was calculated for each episode using the same data presented in figures 2 and 3. The results confirm that after the speed up the algorithms are significantly different, with a confidence level greater than 0.01%.

6   Conclusion and Future Works

This work presented a new algorithm, called Heuristically Accelerated Q–Learning (HAQL), that allows the use of heuristics to speed up the well-known Reinforcement Learning algorithm Q–learning.

The experimental results obtained using the automatic method for the extraction of the heuristic function $\mathcal{H}$ from the learning process, called Heuristic from Exploration, showed that the HAQL attained better results than the Q-learning for the domain of mobile robots.

Heuristics allows the use of RL algorithms to solve problems where the convergence time is critic, as in real time applications. This approach can also be incorporated in other well know RL algorithms, like the SARSA, QS and Minimax-Q [8].

Among the actions that need to be taken for a better evaluation of this proposal, the more important ones are:

- Validate the HAQL, by applying it to other the domains such as the "car on the hill" [3] and the "cart-pole" [4].
- During this study several indications that there must be a large number of methods which can be used to extract the heuristic function were found. Therefore, the study of other methods for heuristic composition is needed.

References

1. D. P. Bertsekas. *Dynamic Programming: Deterministic and Stochastic Models.* Prentice-Hall, Upper Saddle River, NJ, 1987.
2. E. Bonabeau, M. Dorigo, and G. Theraulaz. Inspiration for optimization from social insect behaviour. *Nature 406 [6791]*, 2000.
3. C. Drummond. Accelerating reinforcement learning by composing solutions of automatically identified subtasks. *Journal of Artificial Intelligence Research*, 16:59–104, 2002.
4. D. Foster and P. Dayan. Structure in the space of value functions. *Machine Learning*, 49(2/3):325–346, 2002.
5. L. Gambardella and M. Dorigo. Ant–Q: A reinforcement learning approach to the traveling salesman problem. *Proceedings of the ML-95 – Twelfth International Conference on Machine Learning*, pages 252–260, 1995.
6. P. E. Hart, N. J. Nilsson, and B. Raphael. A formal basis for the heuristic determination of minimum cost paths. *IEEE Transactions on Systems Science and Cybernetics*, 4(2):100–107, 1968.
7. L. P. Kaelbling, M. L. Littman, and A. W. Moore. Reinforcement learning: A survey. *Journal of Artificial Intelligence Research*, 4:237–285, 1996.
8. M. L. Littman and C. Szepesvári. A generalized reinforcement learning model: Convergence and applications. In *Procs. of the Thirteenth International Conf. on Machine Learning (ICML'96)*, pages 310–318, 1996.
9. T. Mitchell. *Machine Learning.* McGraw Hill, New York, 1997.
10. U. Nehmzow. *Mobile Robotics: A Practical Introduction.* Springer-Verlag, Berlin, Heidelberg, 2000.
11. C. J. C. H. Watkins. *Learning from Delayed Rewards.* PhD thesis, University of Cambridge, 1989.

Using Concept Hierarchies
in Knowledge Discovery

Marco Eugênio Madeira Di Beneditto[1] and Leliane Nunes de Barros[2]

[1] Centro de Análises de Sistemas Navais - CASNAV
Pr. Barão de Ladário s/n - Ilha das Cobras - Ed 8 do AMRJ, 3° andar
Centro – 20091-000, Rio de Janeiro, RJ, Brasil
`dibeneditto@casnav.mar.mil.br`
[2] Instituto de Matemática e Estatística da Universidade de São Paulo - IME–USP
Rua do Matão, 1010, Cidade Universitária – 05508-090, São Paulo, SP, Brasil
`leliane@ime.usp.br`

Abstract. In Data Mining, one of the steps of the *Knowledge Discovery in Databases* (*KDD*) process, the use of concept hierarchies as a background knowledge allows to express the discovered knowledge in a higher abstraction level, more concise and usually in a more interesting format. However, data mining for high level concepts is more complex because the search space is generally too big. Some data mining systems require the database to be pre-generalized to reduce the space, what makes difficult to discover knowledge at arbitrary levels of abstraction. To efficiently induce high-level rules at different levels of generality, without pre-generalizing databases, fast access to concept hierarchies and fast query evaluation methods are needed.

This work presents the NETUNO-HC system that performs induction of classification rules using concept hierarchies for the attributes values of a relational database, without pre-generalizing them or even using another tool to represent the hierarchies. It is showed how the abstraction level of the discovered rules can be affected by the adopted search strategy and by the relevance measures considered during the data mining step. Moreover, it is demonstrated by a series of experiments that the NETUNO-HC system shows efficiency in the data mining process, due to the implementation of the following techniques: (i) a SQL primitive to efficient execute the databases queries using hierarchies; (ii) the construction and encoding of numerical hierarchies; (iii) the use of Beam Search strategy, and (iv) the indexing and encoding of rules in a hash table in order to avoid mining discovered rules.

Keywords: Knowledge Discovery, Data Mining, Machine Learning

1 Introduction

This paper describes a *KDD* (*Knowledge Discovery in Databases*) system named NETUNO-HC [1], that uses concept hierarchies to discover knowledge at a high abstraction level than the existing in the database (DB). The search for this kind of knowledge requires the construction of SQL queries to a Database

A.L.C. Bazzan and S. Labidi (Eds.): SBIA 2004, LNAI 3171, pp. 255–265, 2004.

Management System (DBMS), considering that the attribute values belong to a concept hierarchy, not directly represented in the DB.

We argue that this kind of task can be achieved providing fast access to concept hierarchies and fast query evaluation through: (i) an efficient search strategy, and (ii) the use of a SQL primitive to allow fast evaluation of high level hypotheses. Unlike in [2], the system proposed in this paper does not require the DB to be pre-generalized. Without pre-generalizing databases, fast access to concept hierarchies and fast query evaluation methods are needed to efficiently induce high-level rules at different levels of generality. Finally, the proposed representation of hierarchies followed by the use of SQL primitives turns NETUNO-HC independent from other inference systems [3].

2 Concept Hierarchies

The concept hierarchy can be defined as a partial order set. Given two concepts a and b belonging to a partial order relation R, i.e., $(a, b) \in R$, (described by $a \preceq b$ or a precedes b), we say that concept a is more specific than concept b, or that b is more general than a. Usually, the partial order relation in a concept hierarchy represents the *special-general* relationship between concepts, also called *subset-superset* relation. So, a concept hierarchy is defined as:

> *Definition: A* **Concept Hierarchy** $\mathcal{HC}$ *is a partial order set* $(\mathbf{HC}, \preceq)$, *where* **HC** *is a finite set of concepts, and* $\preceq$ *is a partial order relation in* **HC**.

A tree is a special type of concept hierarchy, where a concept precedes only one concept and the notion of *greatest concept* exists, i.e., a concept that does not precede anyone. The tree root will be the most general concept, called ANY, and the leaves will be the attribute values in the DB, that is, the lowest abstraction level of the hierarchy. In this work, we will use concept hierarchies that can be represented as a tree.

2.1 Representing Hierarchies

The use of concept hierarchies during the data mining to generate and evaluate hypotheses is computationally more demanding than the creation of generalized tables. The representation of a hierarchy in memory using a tree data structure gives some speed and efficiency to traverse it. Nevertheless, the number of queries necessary to verify the relationship between concepts in a hierarchy can be too high. Our approach to decrease this complexity is to encode each hierarchy concept in such a way that the code itself indicates the partial order relation between the concepts. Thus the relation verification is made by only checking the codes.

The concept encoding algorithm we propose is based on a post-fixed order traversal of the hierarchy with complexity $O(v)$, where v is the number of concepts in the hierarchy. The verification of the relationship between two concepts, is performed shifting one of the codes, in this case, the bigger one. Figure 1

Fig. 1. Two concept codes where the code 18731 represents a concept that is a descendant of the concept with code 18

shows two concept codes where the code 18731 represents a concept that is a descendant of the concept with code 18. Since the difference between the codes corresponds to ten bits, the bigger code has to be shifted to the right by this number of bits, and if this new value is equal to the smaller code, than the concepts belongs to the relation, i.e., the concept with smaller code is an ascendant of the concept with the bigger code.

In the NETUNO-HC the hierarchies are stored in relational tables in the DB and loaded before the data mining step. More than one hierarchy for each attribute can be stored leaving to the user the possibility to choose one.

2.2   Generating Numerical Hierarchies

In this work, we suppose that a concept hierarchy, related with categorical data, is a background knowledge, given by an expert in the field. However, for numerical or continuous attributes, the hierarchies can be automatically generated (from the DB) and stored in relational tables, before the data mining step. There are many ways to do this and any choice will affect the results of the data mining. In the NETUNO-HC we propose an algorithm to generate a numerical hierarchy considering the class distribution. This algorithm is based on the *InfoMerge* algorithm [4] used for discretization of continuous attributes. The idea underlying the InfoMerge algorithm is to group values in intervals which causes the smaller information loss (a dual operation of information gain in C4.5 learning algorithm [5]).

In the NETUNO-HC, the same idea is applied to the generation in a bottom-up approach of a numerical concept hierarchy, where the nodes of a hierarchy will represent numerical intervals, closed in the left. After the leaf level intervals be generated, these are merged in bigger intervals until the root is reached, which will correspond to an interval that includes all the existing values in the DB.

3   The NETUNO-HC Algorithm

The search space is organized in a general-to-specific ordering of hypotheses, beginning with the empty hypothesis. A hypothesis will be transformed (node expansion search operation) by specialization operations, i.e., by the addition of an attribute or by doing hierarchy specialization to generate more specific hypotheses. A hypothesis can be considered a discovered knowledge if it satisfies the relevance measures. The node expansion operation is made in two steps. First, an attribute is added to a hypothesis. Second, using the SQL query, the algorithm check, in a top-down fashion, which values in the hierarchy of the attribute satisfy the relevance measures.

The search strategy employed by the NETUNO-HC is Beam Search. For each level of the search space, which corresponds to hypotheses with the same number of attribute-value pairs, the algorithm selects only a fixed number of them. This number corresponds to the *beam width*, i.e., the number of hypotheses that will be specialized.

3.1   NETUNO-HC Knowledge Description Language

The power of a symbolic algorithm for data mining resides in the expressiveness of the knowledge description language used. The language specifies what the algorithm is capable of discover or learning. NETUNO-HC uses a propositional-like language extending the attribute value with concept hierarchies in order to achieve higher expressiveness.

Rules induced by NETUNO-HC take the form IF $< A >$ THEN $< class >$, where $< A >$ is a conjunction of one or more attribute-value pairs. An attribute-value pair is a condition between an attribute and a value from the concept hierarchy. For categorical attributes this condition is an equality, e.g., $(A_1 = v)$, and for continuous attributes this condition is an interval inclusion (closed on left), e.g., $A_2 \in [v, v')$, or an equality.

3.2   Specializing Hypotheses

In the progressive specialization, or top-down approach, the data mining algorithm generates hypotheses that have to be specialized. The specialization operation of hypothesis h_0 generates a new hypothesis h_1 that covers a number of tuples less or iqual the ones covered by h_0. Specialization can be realized by either adding an attribute or replacing the value of the attribute with any of its descendants according with a concept hierarchy. In NETUNO-HC, both forms of hypotheses specializations are considered.

If a hypothesis does not satisfy the relevance measures then it has to be specialized. After the addition of the attribute, the algorithm has to check which of the values forms valid hypotheses, i.e., hypotheses that satisfy the relevance measures. With the use of hierarchies, the values have to be checked in a top-down way, i.e., from the most general concept to the more specific.

3.3   Rules Subsumption

The NETUNO-HC avoids the generation of two rules, R_1 and R_2, if R_2 is subsumed by R_1, i.e., $R_2 \subseteq R_1$. This occurs when:

1. the rules have the same size and for each attribute-value pair $(A_i, v_{ij}) \in R_1$ exists a pair $(A_i, v_{ik}) \in R_2$ where $v_{ik} \preceq v_{ij}$.
2. the rules have different size and for each attribute-value pair $(A_i, v_{ij}) \in R_1$ exists a pair $(A_i, v_{ik}) \in R_2$ where $v_{ik} \preceq v_{ij}$ and R_1 is the smaller rule.

This kind of verification is done in two different phases. The first phase is done when the data mining algorithm checks for an attribute value in the hierarchy. If the value generates a rule, the descendants values that can also generate rules in the same class are not stored as valid rules, even though they satisfy the relevance measures. Second, if a discovered rule subsumes other rules previously discovered, these last ones are deleted from the *list of discovered rules*. On the contrary, if a discovered rule is subsumed by one or more previously discovered rules, this rule is not added to the list.

3.4   Relevance Measures and Selection Criteria

In NETUNO-HC system, the rule hypotheses are evaluated by two conditions: completeness and consistency. Let P denote the total number of positive examples of a given class in the training data. Let R be a rule hypothesis to cover tuples of that class; let p and n be the number of positive and negative tuples covered by R, respectively.

The completeness will be measured by the ratio $\frac{p}{P}$, which is called in this work *support* (also known in the literature as *positive coverage*). The consistency is measured by the ratio $\frac{p}{p+n}$, which is called in this work *confidence* (also known as *training accuracy*).

NETUNO-HC calculates the support and confidence values using the SQL primitive, described in Section 4.

The criteria for the selection of the best hypotheses to be expanded is based on the product *support* × *confidence*. The hypotheses in the open-list will be stored in a decreasing order according with that product, and only the k best hypotheses (the beam width) will be selected.

3.5   Interpretation of the Induced Rules

The induced rules can be interpreted as classification rules. Thus, to use the induced rules to classify new examples, NETUNO-HC employ an interpretation in which all rules are tried and only those that cover the example are collected. If a collision occurs (i.e., the example belongs to more than one class) the decision is to classify the example in the class given by the rule with the greatest value for the product *support* × *confidence*. If some example is not covered by any rule, then the number of non-classified example is incremented (as a measure of quality for the set of discovered rules). In Section 5.3, will be showed the result of applying a default rule in this case.

4   SQL Primitive for Evaluation of High Level Hypothesis

In [6] was propose a generic KDD primitive in SQL which underlies the candidate rule evaluation procedure. This primitive consists of counting the number of tuples in each partition formed by a SQL *group by* statement. The primitive has three input parameters: a tuple-set descriptor, a candidate attribute, and the class attribute. The output is a matrix $m \times n$, where m is the number of different values of the new attribute, and n is the number of different values of the class attribute.

In order to use this primitive and the output matrix for the evaluation of high level hypothesis (i.e., building a SQL primitive considering a concept hierarchy), some extensions were made to the original proposal [6]. In the primitive, the tuple-set descriptor has to be expressed by values in the DB, i.e., the leaf concepts in the hierarchy. So, for each high level value the descriptor has to be expressed by the leaf values that precedes it. This is made by NETUNO-HC, during the data mining, using the hierarchy for building the SQL primitive.

An example of the use of the extended SQL primitive is shown in Figure 2. Let {black, brown} $\preceq$ dark where {black, brown} are leaf concepts in a color domain hierarchy. If the antecedent of a hypothesis has the attribute-value pair: $spore\_print\_color = dark$, this has to be expressed in the tuple-set descriptor by leaf values, i.e., $spore\_print\_color = brown$ OR $spore\_print\_color = black$. Figure 2 shows the output matrix, where the lines are leaf concepts of the hierarchy. Adding the lines whose concepts are leaf and precedes a high level concept is equivalent to have a high level line, which can be used to evaluate the high level hypotheses (see Figure 2).

A condition between an attribute and his value may be the inequality. In this case, eg. $spore\_print\_color <> dark$, the tuple-set descriptor will be translated to $spore\_print\_color <> brown$ AND $spore\_print\_color <> black$. To calculate the relevance measures for this condition, the same matrix can be used. The line for this condition is the difference between the $Total$ line and the line that corresponds to the attribute value, i.e., $A <> a_i = line_{Total} - line_{a_i}$.

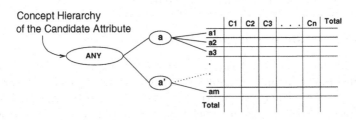

Fig. 2. The lines of the matrix represents the leaf concepts of the hierarchy

5   Experiments

In order to evaluate the NETUNO-HC algorithm we used two DBs from the UCI repository: the Mushroom and Adult. First, we tested how the size of the search space changes performing data mining with and without the use of concept hierarchies. This was done using a simplified implemented version of the NETUNO-HC algorithm that uses a complete search method.

In the rest of the experiments we analyzed the data mining process, with and without the use of concept hierarchies, with respect to the following aspects: efficiency on DB access, concept hierarchy access and rules subsumption verification; results on the accuracy of the discovered rule set; the capability of discovering high level rules and finally, the semantic evaluation of high level rules.

5.1   The Size of the Search Space

We have first analyzed how the use of concept hierarchies in data mining can affect the size of the search space considering a complete search method, such as Breadth-First Search.

Figure 3 shows, as it was expected, that the search space for high level rules increases with the size of the concept hierarchies considered in a data mining process.

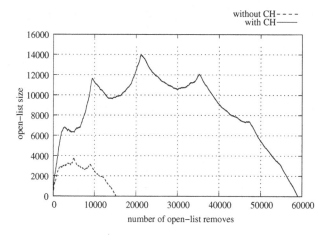

Fig. 3. Breadth-First Search algorithm execution in the Mushroom DB with and without hierarchies and sup = 20%, conf= 90%. The graphics on Figure s3 shows the open-list size (list of the candidate rules or rule hypotheses) versus the number of open-list removes (number of hypothesis specializations)

We can also see in Figure 3 that pruning techniques, based on relevance measures and rules subsumption, can eventually turn the list of open nodes (open-list) empty, i.e., end the search task. This occurs for the Mushroom DB after 15000 hypothesis specializations, in data mining WITHOUT concept hierarchies and after 59000 hypothesis specializations, in data mining WITH concept hierarchies.

Another observation we can make from Figure 3 is that the size of the open-list is approximately four times bigger when using concept hierarchies evaluation for the Mushroom DB. Therefore, it is important to improve performance on the hypotheses evaluation through efficient DB access, concept hierarchy access and rules subsumption verification.

5.2   Efficiency in High Level SQL Primitive and Hypotheses Generation

In order to evaluate the use of high level SQL primitive, it was implemented a version of the ParDRI [3]. In ParDRI, the high level queries are made in a different way: it uses the direct descendants of the hierarchy root. So, if the root concept has tree descendants, the system will issue one query for each concept, ie., three queries, while with the SQL primitive, only one query is necessary.

For the Mushroom DB, without the SQL primitive, the implemented ParDRI algorithm generated 117 queries and discovered 26 rules. By using the primitive, the same algorithm issue only 70 queries and discovered the same 26 rules, showing a reduction of 40% in the number of queries.

To evaluate the time spent on hypotheses generation, the following times were measured during the executions: (a) the time spent with DB queries, and (b) the time spent by the data mining algorithm.

The ratio between the difference of these two times and the time spent by the data mining algorithm is the percentage spent in the generation and evaluation of the hypotheses. This value is 1.87% (with $\sigma=0.15$) showing that the execution time is dominated by queries issued to the DBMS. Therefore, the use of the high level SQL primitive, combining with efficient techniques for encoding and evaluation of hypotheses in the NETUNO-HC, makes it a more efficient algorithm for high level data mining than ParDRI [3].

5.3   Accuracy

In Tab. 1, the accuracy results of the NETUNO-HC with and without hierarchies are compared with two other algorithms, C4.5 [5] and CN2 [7], which did not use concept hierarchies.

Table 1. Accuracies for the algorithms – the default class was used in NETUNO-HC

Algorithm	Mushroom	Adult
C4.5	100%	84.46%
CN2	100%	84%
NETUNO-HC without CH	99.04%	82.14%
NETUNO-HC with CH	98.45%	81.62%

In order to compare similar classification schemes, the NETUNO-HC results were obtained using a default class, the majority class in this case, to label examples not covered, similar to the two other algorithms. For the other experiments, the default class was not used.

The next experiments show the results obtained through ten-fold stratified cross validation. In Table 2 is showed the accuracy of the discovered rule set.

For both DBs we can observe that by decreasing the minimum support value, the accuracy tends to increase (in both situations: with or without hierarchies). This happens because some tuples are covered by rules with small coverage, and this rules can only be discovered defining a small support.

Table 2. Mean accuracies and standard deviations (σ) for each support and confidence value with beam width k=256

Support / Confidence	Mushroom		Adult	
	Mean accuracy without CH	Mean accuracy with CH	Mean accuracy without CH	Mean accuracy with CH
20% / 90%	0.9061 σ=0.002	0.8942 σ=0.002	0.6717 σ=0.003	0.6762 σ=0.004
20% / 94%	0.9572 σ=0.005	0.9311 σ=0.005	0.5672 σ=0.004	0.5851 σ=0.005
20% / 98%	0.9596 σ=0.004	0.9845 σ=0.002	0.3701 σ=0.002	0.5146 σ=0.004
12% / 90%	0.8991 σ=0.004	0.8931 σ=0.002	0.7048 σ=0.002	0.7031 σ=0.006
12% / 94%	0.9572 σ=0.002	0.9299 σ=0.003	0.6559 σ=0.003	0.6598 σ=0.005
12% / 98%	0.9738 σ=0.002	0.9845 σ=0.003	0.4112 σ=0.002	0.5566 σ=0.005
4% / 90%	0.8954 σ=0.003	0.8931 σ=0.004	0.7229 σ=0.004	0.7235 σ=0.003
4% / 94%	0.9524 σ=0.003	0.9275 σ=0.004	0.6797 σ=0.005	0.6646 σ=0.002
4% / 98%	0.9881 σ=0.003	0.9845 σ=0.002	0.5513 σ=0.005	0.6035 σ=0.002

As expected, the use of hierarchies does not directly affect the accuracy of the discovered rules. That can be explained by the following. On one hand, a more general concept has greater inconsistency which decreases the accuracy. On the other hand, with high support values an increase in the minimum confidence value tends to increase the accuracy. In this case, the high level concept can cover more examples (i.e., decreasing the number of non-covered examples, as can be seen in Table 3), where the number of non-classified examples is very small (considering a small beam width).

Intuitively, we can think that a larger beam width would discover a rule set with a better accuracy since the search would become closer to a complete search. However, in the Mushroom DB with hierarchies, an increase in the beam width did not result in a better accuracy as can be seen in Table 3.

Table 3. Beam Width vs Accuracy and Non-Classified examples in the Mushroom DB

Beam width	Accuracy		Non-Classified Examples	
	without CH	with CH	without CH	with CH
1	0.9501	0.9857	37	2
2	0.9501	0.9857	37	2
4	0.9501	0.9857	37	2
8	0.9548	0.9857	33	2
16	0.9845	0.9845	7	2
32	0.9845	0.9869	7	0
64	0.9881	0.9869	4	0
128	0.9881	0.9845	4	0
256	0.9881	0.9845	4	0

5.4   High Level Rules and Semantic Evaluation

The most important results we have to guarantee in this work, besides efficiency, is the discovered of high level rules at different levels of generality, without a previous choice of the abstraction level, which is the deficiency of other systems that use concept hierarchies only to pre-generalize the database like [2]. In NETUNO-HC system we found out that changes in the relevance measures affect the discovered rule set: with a confidence minimum value of 90%, in the

Table 4. Percentage of high level rules in the discovered rule set

Support	Mushroom	Adult
4%	51,8%	81,4%
20%	63,8%	85,6%

two DBs it can be seen that high support minimum values tends to discover more high level rules in the rule set (see Table 4).

The use of hierarchies introduces more general concepts and can reduce the discovered rule set. In fact, for the Mushroom DB, with support=20%, confidence=98% and beam width = 256, 66 rules were discovered without hierarchies against 58 rules discovered with hierarchies and the accuracy was 0.9596 and 0.9845, respectively.

For the Adult DB, with support=4%, confidence=98% and beam width = 256, 30 rules were discovered without hierarchies against 27 rules discovered with hierarchies and the accuracy was 0.7229 and 0.7235, respectively.

As can be seen, the discovered rule set is more concise and, sometimes, more accurate.

A more concise concept description can be explained because more general concepts can cause low level rules to be subsumed by high level ones. For example, in the Mushroom DB, given the high level concept BAD ($\{CREOSOTE, FOUL, MUSTY, FISHY, PUNGENT\} \preceq BAD$), the rule R_1 is discovered. This rule, is more general than the other following two rules, R_2 and R_3, discovered without the use of hierarchies.

- R_1: odor = BAD -> POISONOUS - Supp: 0.822 Conf: 1.0
- R_2: odor = CREOSOTE -> POISONOUS - Supp: 0.048 Conf: 1.0
- R_3: odor = FOUL -> POISONOUS - Supp: 0.549 Conf: 1.0

6   Conclusions

The use of concept hierarchies in data mining results in a trade off between the discovery of more interesting rules (expressed in high abstraction level) and, sometimes, a more concise concept description, versus a higher computational cost. In this work, we present the NETUNO-HC algorithm and its implementation to propose ways to solve the efficiency problems of the data mining with concept hierarchies, that are: the use of Beam Search strategy, the encoding and evaluation techniques of the concept hierarchies and the high level SQL primitive.

The main contribution of this work is to specify a high level SQL primitive as an efficient way to analyze rules considering concept hierarchies, and an encoding method that reduces impact of the hierarchies size during the generation and evaluation of the hypotheses. This made feasible the discovery of high level rules without pre-generalize the DB.

We also perform some experiments to show how the mining parameters affects the discovered rule set such as:

Variation of the Support Minimum Value. On one hand, a decrease in the support minimum value tends to increase the accuracy, with or without hierarchies, also increasing the rule set size. On the other hand, a high support minimum value tends to discover a more interesting rule set, i.e., a set with more high level rules.

Variation of the Confidence Minimum Value. The effect of this kind of variation depends of the DB domain. For the databases analyzed, a higher confidence value could not always result in a higher accuracy.

Alterations of the Beam Width. A higher beam width tends to increase the accuracy. However, depending on the DB domain, a better accuracy can be obtained in lower beam width, with or without hierarchies. The hierarchy also affects the discovered rule set: a higher accuracy can be obtained with a lower beam width.

References

1. Beneditto, M.E.M.D.: Descoberta de regras de classificação com hierarquias conceituais. Master's thesis, Instituto de Matemática e Estatística, Universidade de São Paulo, Brasil (2004)
2. Han, J., Fu, Y., Wang, W., Chiang, J., Gong, W., Koperski, K., Li, D., Lu, Y., Rajan, A., Stefanovic, N., Xia, B., Zaiane, O.R.: DBMiner: A system for mining knowledge in large relational databases. In Simoudis, E., Han, J.W., Fayyad, U., eds.: Proceedings of the Second International Conference on Knowledge Discovery and Data Mining (KDD-96), AAAI Press (1996) 250–263
3. Taylor, M.G.: Finding High Level Discriminant Rules in Parallel. PhD thesis, Faculty of the Graduate School of the University of Maryland, College Park, USA (1999)
4. Freitas, A., Lavington, S.: Speeding up knowledge discovery in large relational databases by means of a new discretization algorithm. In: Proc. 14th British Nat. Conf. on Databases (BNCOD-14), Edinburgh, Scotland (1996) 124–133
5. Quinlan, J.R.: C4.5: Programs for machine learning. 1 edn. Morgan Kaufmann (1993)
6. Freitas, A., Lavington, S.: Using SQL primitives and parallel DB servers to speed up knowledge discovery in large relational databases. In Trappl., R., ed.: Cybernetics and Systems'96: Proc. 13th European Meeting on Cybernetics and Systems Research, Viena, Austria (1996) 955–960
7. Clark, P., Niblett, T.: The CN2 induction algorithm. Machine Learning **3** (1989) 261–283

A Clustering Method for Symbolic Interval-Type Data Using Adaptive Chebyshev Distances

Francisco de A.T. de Carvalho, Renata M.C.R. de Souza, and Fabio C.D. Silva

Centro de Informatica - CIn / UFPE, Av. Prof. Luiz Freire, s/n
Cidade Universitaria, CEP: 50740-540, Recife-PE, Brasil
{fatc,rmcrs}@cin.ufpe.br

Abstract. This work presents a partitioning method for clustering symbolic interval-type data using a dynamic cluster algorithm with adaptive Chebyshev distances. This method furnishes a partition and a prototype for each cluster by optimizing an adequacy criterion that measures the fitting between the clusters and their representatives. To compare interval-type data, the method uses an adaptive Chebyshev distance that changes for each cluster according to its intra-class structure at each iteration of the algorithm. Experiments with real and artificial interval-type data sets demonstrate the usefulness of the proposed method.

1 Introduction

Recently, clustering has become a subject of great interest, mainly due the explosive growth in the use of databases and the huge volume of data stored in them. Due to this growth, interval data is now widely used in real applications. *Symbolic Data Analysis* (SDA) [2] is a new domain in the area of knowledge discovery and data management. It is related to multivariate analysis, pattern recognition and artificial intelligence and seeks to provide suitable methods (clustering, factorial techniques, decision tree, etc.) for managing aggregated data described by multi-valued variables, where data table cells contain sets of categories, intervals, or weight (probability) distributions (for more details on SDA, see www.jsda.unina2.it).

Concerning partitioning clustering methods, SDA has provided suitable tools for clustering symbolic interval-type data. Verde et al [10] introduced a dynamic cluster algorithm for interval-type data considering context dependent proximity functions. Chavent and Lechevalier [3] proposed a dynamic cluster algorithm for interval-type data using an adequacy criterion based on the Hausdorff distance. Souza and De Carvalho [9] presented dynamic cluster algorithms for interval-type data based on adaptive and non-adaptive City-Block distances.

The main contribution of this paper is to introduce a partitioning clustering method for interval-type data using the dynamic cluster algorithm with adaptive Chebyshev distances. The standard dynamic cluster algorithm [5] is a two-step relocation algorithm involving the construction of clusters and the identification of a representation or prototype of each cluster by locally minimizing an

A.L.C. Bazzan and S. Labidi (Eds.): SBIA 2004, LNAI 3171, pp. 266–275, 2004.

adequacy criterion between the clusters and their representatives. The adaptive version of this algorithm [4] uses a separate distance to compare each cluster with its representation. The advantage of these adaptive distances lies in the fact that the clustering algorithm is able to find clusters of different shapes and sizes for a given set of objects.

In this paper, we present a dynamic cluster method with adaptive Chebyshev distances for partitioning a set of symbolic interval-type data. This method is an extension of the use of adaptive distances of a dynamic cluster algorithm proposed in [3]. In section 2, a dynamic cluster with an adaptive Chebyshev distance for interval-type data is presented. In order to validate this new method, section 3 presents experiments with real and artificial symbolic interval-type data sets. Section 4 shows an evaluation of the clustering results based on the computation of an external cluster validity index ([7]) in the framework of the Monte Carlo experience. In section 5, the concluding remarks are given.

2   Adaptive Dynamic Cluster

Let $E = \{s_1, \ldots, s_n\}$ be a set of n symbolic objects described by p interval variables. Each object s_i $(i = 1, \ldots, n)$ is represented as a vector of intervals $\mathbf{x}_i = (x_i^1, \ldots, x_i^p)$, where $x_i^j = [a_i^j, b_i^j] \in I\{[a, b] : a, b \in \Re, a \le b\}$ $(j = 1, \ldots, p)$. Let P be a partition of E into K clusters $\{C_1, \ldots, C_K\}$, where each cluster C_k $(k = 1, \ldots, K)$ has a prototype L_k that is also represented as a vector of intervals $\mathbf{y}_k([\alpha_k^1, \beta_k^1], \ldots, [\alpha_k^p, \beta_k^p])$.

According to the standard adaptive dynamic cluster algorithm [4], at each iteration there is a different distance associated with each cluster, i.e., the distance is not determined once and for all, and is different from one class to another.

Our algorithm searches for a partition $P = (C_1, \ldots, C_K)$ of E in K classes, the corresponding set of K class prototypes $L = (L_1, \ldots, L_K)$ and a set of K different distances $d = (d_1, \ldots, d_K)$ associated with the clusters by locally minimizing an adequacy criterion, which is usually stated as:

$$W(P, L, d) = \sum_{k=1}^{K} \sum_{s_i \in C_k} d_k(\mathbf{x}_i, \mathbf{y}_k) \tag{1}$$

where $d_k(\mathbf{x}_i, \mathbf{y}_k)$ is an adaptive dissimilarity measure between an object $s_i \in C_k$ and the class prototype L_k of C_k.

2.1   Adaptive Distances Between Two Vectors of Intervals

In [4] an adaptive distance d_k is defined according to the structure of a cluster C_k and is parameterized by a vector of coefficients $\boldsymbol{\lambda}_k = (\lambda_k^1, \ldots, \lambda_k^p)$, with $\lambda_k^j > 0$ $(j = 1, \ldots, p)$ and $\prod_{j=1}^{p} \lambda_k^j = 1$. In this paper, we define the adaptive Chebyshev distance between the two vectors of intervals $\mathbf{x}_i$ and $\mathbf{y}_k$ as:

$$d_k(\mathbf{x}_i, \mathbf{y}_k) = \sum_{j=1}^{p} \lambda_k^j \phi_C(x_i^j, y_k^j) \tag{2}$$

where

$$\phi_C(x_i^j, y_k^j) = max\{|a_i^j - \alpha_k^j|, |b_i^j - \beta_k^j|\} \tag{3}$$

is the maximum between the absolute values of the differences among the lower bounds and the upper bounds of the intervals $x_i^j = [a_i^j, b_i^j]$ and $y_k^j = [\alpha_k^j, \beta_k^j]$.

The concept behind the distance function in equation (3) is to represent an interval $[a, b]$ as a point $(a, b) \in \Re^2$, where the lower bounds of the intervals are represented in the x-axis, and the upper bounds in the y-axis, and then compute the L_∞ (Chebyshev) distance between the points (a_i^j, b_i^j) and (α_k^j, β_k^j). Therefore, the distance function in equation (2) is a weighted version of the L_∞ (Chebyshev) metric for interval-type data.

2.2   The Optimization Problem

The optimizing problem is stated as follows: find the class prototype L_k of the class C_k and the adaptive Chebyshev distance d_k associated to C_k that minimizes an adequacy criterion by measuring the dissimilarity between this class prototype L_k and the class C_k according to d_k.

Therefore, the optimization problem has two stages:

a) The class C_k and the distance d_k $(k = 1, \ldots, K)$ are fixed. We look for the vector of intervals $\mathbf{y}_k$ of the prototype L_k of the class C_k which locally minimizes

$$\Delta(\mathbf{y}_k, \boldsymbol{\lambda}_k) = \sum_{i \in C_k} d_k(\mathbf{x}_i, \mathbf{y}_k) = \sum_{j=1}^{p} \lambda_k^j \sum_{i \in C_k} max\{|a_i^j - \alpha_k^j|, |b_i^j - \beta_k^j|\} \tag{4}$$

The criterion $\Delta(\mathbf{y}_k, \boldsymbol{\lambda}_k)$ being additive, the problem becomes finding the interval $y_k^j[\alpha_k^j, \beta_k^j]$ $(j = 1, \ldots, p)$ that minimizes $\sum_{i \in C_k} max\{|a_i^j - \alpha_k^j|, |b_i^j - \beta_k^j|\}$.

Proposition 1. *This problem has an analytical solution, which is* $\hat{\alpha}_k^j = \hat{\mu}_j - \hat{\gamma}_j$ *and* $\hat{\beta}_k^j = \hat{\mu}_j + \hat{\gamma}_j$, *where* $\hat{\mu}_j$ *is the median of midpoints of the intervals of the objects belonging to the cluster* C_k *and* $\hat{\gamma}_j$ *is the median of their half-lengths.*

The proof of the proposition 1 can be found in [3].

b) The class C_k and the prototype L_k $(k = 1, \ldots, K)$ are fixed. We look for the vector of weights $\boldsymbol{\lambda}_k = (\lambda_k^1, \ldots, \lambda_k^p)$, with $\lambda_k^j > 0$ $(j = 1, \ldots, p)$ and $\prod_{j=1}^{p} \lambda_k^j = 1$ that minimizes the criterion $\Delta(\mathbf{y}_k, \boldsymbol{\lambda}_k)$.

Proposition 2. *The coefficients* λ_k^j $(j = 1, \ldots, p)$ *that minimize* $\Delta(\mathbf{y}_k, \boldsymbol{\lambda}_k)$ *are:*

$$\hat{\lambda}_k^j = \frac{\left[\prod_{h=1}^{p}(\sum_{i \in C_k} max\{|a_i^h - \hat{\alpha}_k^h|, |b_i^h - \hat{\beta}_k^h|\})\right]^{\frac{1}{p}}}{\sum_{i \in C_k} max\{|a_i^j - \hat{\alpha}_k^j|, |b_i^j - \hat{\beta}_k^j|\}} \tag{5}$$

The proof of proposition 2 is based on the Lagrange multipliers method and can be found in [6].

2.3 The Adaptive Dynamic Cluster Algorithm

The adaptive dynamic cluster algorithm performs a representation step where the class prototypes and the adaptive distances are updated. This is followed by an allocation step in order to assign the individuals to the classes, until the convergence of the algorithm, when the adequacy criterion reaches a stationary value.

If a single quantitative value is considered as an interval where the lower and upper bounds are the same (i.e., when only usual data are present), this symbolic-oriented algorithm corresponds to the standard numerical one with adaptive L_1 distances introduced by Diday and Govaert [4].

The algorithm schema is the following:

1. Initialization
   To construct the initial partition $\{C_1, \ldots, C_K\}$, Choose a partition $\{C_1 \ldots, C_K\}$ of E randomly or choose K distinct objects $L_1, \ldots, L_K$ belonging to E and assign each object i to its closest prototype L_{k*}, where
   $k* = \arg \min_{k=1,\ldots,K} \sum_{j=1}^{p} max\{|a_i^j - \alpha_k^j|, |b_i^j - \beta_k^j|\}$.

2. Representation step
   a) (The partition P and the set of distances d are fixed)
      For $k = 1$ to K compute the vector of intervals (which represents the prototype L_k) $\hat{\mathbf{y}}_k^1 = [\hat{\alpha}_k^1, \hat{\beta}_k^1], \ldots, \hat{\alpha}_k^p, \hat{\beta}_k^p]$ with $\hat{\alpha}_k^j = \hat{\mu}_k^j - \hat{\gamma}_k^j$ and $\hat{\beta}_k^j = \hat{\mu}_k^j + \hat{\gamma}_k^j$, where $\hat{\mu}_k^j$ is the median of midpoints of the intervals of the objects belonging to the cluster C_k and $\hat{\gamma}_k^j$ of their half-lengths.
   b) (the partition P and the set of prototypes L are fixed)
      For $j = 1, \ldots, p$ and $k = 1, \ldots, K$, compute $\hat{\lambda}_k^j$

3. Allocation step
   $test \leftarrow 0$
   for $i = 1$ to n
      define the cluster C_{k*} such that
      $$k* = arg \min_{k=1,\ldots,K} \sum_{j=1}^{p} \hat{\lambda}_k^j max\{|a_i^j - \hat{\alpha}_k^j|, |b_i^j - \hat{\beta}_k^j|\}$$
      if $i \in C_k$ and $k* \neq k$
         $test \leftarrow 1$
         $C_{k*} \leftarrow C_{k*} \cup \{i\}$
         $C_k \leftarrow C_k \setminus \{i\}$

4. Stopping criterion
   If $test = 0$ then STOP, otherwise go to (2).

Remark: In the sub-step 2.b) (computation of $\hat{\lambda}_k^j$), if $\sum_{i \in C_k} max\{|a_i^j - \hat{\alpha}_k^j|, |b_i^j - \hat{\beta}_k^j|\} = 0$ for at least one variable j ($j = 1, \ldots, p$), stop the current iteration and re-start a new one (go to step 1).

3 Experiments

To show the usefulness of these methods, experiments with two artificial interval-type data sets with different degrees of clustering difficulty (clusters of different shapes and sizes, linearly non-separable clusters, etc) are considered in this section, along with a fish interval-type data set.

3.1   Artificial Symbolic Data Sets

Initially, we considered two standard quantitative data sets in $\Re^2$. Each data set has 450 points scattered among four clusters of unequal sizes and shapes: two clusters with ellipsis shapes and sizes 150 and two clusters with spherical shapes of sizes 50 and 100. The data points of each cluster in each data set were drawn according to a bi-variate normal distribution with non-correlated components.

Data set 1 (Fig. 1), showing well-separated clusters, is generated according to the following parameters:

a) Class 1: $\mu_1 = 28$, $\mu_2 = 22$, $\sigma_1^2 = 100$, $\sigma_{12} = 0$, $\sigma_2^2 = 9$;
b) Class 2: $\mu_1 = 65$, $\mu_2 = 30$, $\sigma_1^2 = 9$, $\sigma_{12} = 0$, $\sigma_2^2 = 144$;
c) Class 3: $\mu_1 = 45$, $\mu_2 = 42$, $\sigma_1^2 = 9$, $\sigma_{12} = 0$, $\sigma_2^2 = 9$;
d) Class 4: $\mu_1 = 38$, $\mu_2 = -1$, $\sigma_1^2 = 25$, $\sigma_{12} = 0$, $\sigma_2^2 = 25$;

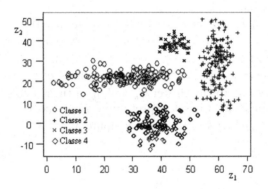

Fig. 1. Data set 1 showing well-separated classes

Data set 2 (Fig. 2), showing overlapping clusters, is generated according to the following parameters:

a) Class 1: $\mu_1 = 45$, $\mu_2 = 22$, $\sigma_1^2 = 100$, $\sigma_{12} = 0$, $\sigma_2^2 = 9$;
b) Class 2: $\mu_1 = 65$, $\mu_2 = 30$, $\sigma_1^2 = 9$, $\sigma_{12} = 0$, $\sigma_2^2 = 144$;
c) Class 3: $\mu_1 = 57$, $\mu_2 = 38$, $\sigma_1^2 = 9$, $\sigma_{12} = 0$, $\sigma_2^2 = 9$;
d) Class 4: $\mu_1 = 42$, $\mu_2 = 12$, $\sigma_1^2 = 25$, $\sigma_{12} = 0$, $\sigma_2^2 = 25$;

Each data point (z_1, z_2) of the data set 1 and 2 is a seed of a vector of intervals (rectangle): $([z_1 - \gamma_1/2, z_1 + \gamma_1/2], [z_2 - \gamma_2/2, z_2 + \gamma_2/2])$. These parameters γ_1, γ_2 are randomly selected from the same predefined interval. The intervals considered in this paper are: $[1, 8], [1, 16], [1, 24], [1, 32]$, and $[1, 40]$. Figure 3 shows artificial interval-type data set 1 (obtained from data set 1) with well separated clusters and Figure 4 shows artificial interval-type data set 2 (obtained from data set 2) with overlapping clusters.

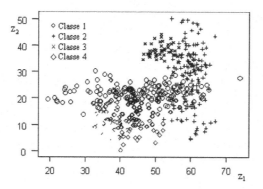

Fig. 2. Data set 2 showing overlapping classes

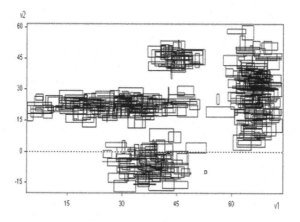

Fig. 3. Interval-type data set 1 showing well-separated classes

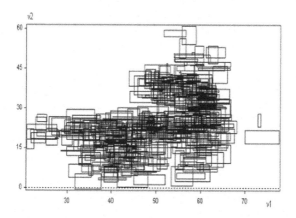

Fig. 4. Interval-type data set 2 showing overlapping classes

3.2   Eco-toxicology Data Set

A number of studies carried out in French Guyana demonstrated abnormal levels
of mercury contamination in some Amerindian populations. This contamination
has been connected to their high consumption of contaminated freshwater fish
[1]. In order to obtain better knowledge on this phenomenon, a data set was
collected by researchers from the LEESA (Laboratoire d'Ecophysi- ologie et
d'Ecotoxicologie des Systèmes Aquatiques) laboratory. This data set concerns
12 fish species, each specie being described by 13 interval variables and 1 categorical variable. These species are grouped into four a priori clusters of unequal
sizes according to the categorical variable: two clusters (Carnivorous and Detri-
tivorous) of sizes 4 and two clusters of sizes 2 (Omnivorous and Herbivorous).
Table 1 shows part of the fish data set.

Table 1. Fish Data Set described by 13 interval symbolic variables

Individuals/labels	Interval Variables				
	Length	Weight	...	Intestin/ Muscle	Stomach/ Muscle
Ageneiosusbrevifili 1	[1.8 : 7.1]	[2.1 : 7.2]	...	[7.8 : 17.9]	[4.3 : 11.8]
Cynodongibbus 1	[19 : 32]	[77 : 359]	...	[0 : 0.5]	[0.2 : 1.24]
Hopliasaïmara 1	[25.5 : 63]	[340 : 5500]	...	[0.11 : 0.49]	[0.09 : 0.4]
⋮	⋮	⋮	⋮	⋮	⋮
Semaprochilodusvari 2	[22 : 28]	[330 : 700]	...	[0.4 : 1.68]	[0 : 1.25]
Acnodonoligacanthus 4	[10 : 16.2]	[34.9 : 154.7]	...	[0 : 2.16]	[0.23 : 5.97]
Myleusrubripinis 4	[2.7 : 8.4]	[2.7 : 8.7]	...	[8.2 : 20]	[5.1 : 13.3]

4   Evaluation of Clustering Results

In order to compare the adaptive dynamic cluster algorithm proposed in the
present paper with the non-adaptive version of this algorithm, this section
presents the clustering results furnished by these methods according to artificial interval-type data sets 1 and 2 and the fish data set (see section 3).

The non-adaptive dynamic cluster algorithm uses a suitable extension of the
L_∞ (Chebyshev) metric to compare the vectors of intervals $\mathbf{x}_i$ and $\mathbf{y}_k$:

$$d(\mathbf{x}_i, \mathbf{y}_k) = \sum_{j=1}^{p} \phi_C(x_i^j, y_k^j) \tag{6}$$

where $\phi_C(x_i^j, y_k^j)$ is given by equation 3.

The evaluation of the clustering results is based on the corrected Rand (CR)
index [7]. The CR index assesses the degree of agreement (similarity) between
an a priori partition (i.e., the partition defined by the seed points of data sets 1
and 2) and a partition furnished by the clustering algorithm. We used the CR

index because it is neither sensitive to the number of classes in the partitions nor to the distributions of the items in the clusters [8].

For the artificial data sets, the CR index is estimated in the framework of a Monte Carlo experience with 100 replications for each interval-type data set, as well as for each predefined interval where the parameters γ_1 and γ_2 are selected. For each replication a clustering method is run 50 times and the best result according to the corresponding adequacy criterion is selected. The average of the corrected Rand (CR) index among these 100 replications is calculated.

Table 2 shows the values of the average CR index according to adaptive and non-adaptive methods, as well as artificial interval-type data sets 1 and 2. From these results it can be seen that the average CR indices for the adaptive method are greater than those for the non-adaptive method.

Table 2. Comparison between the clustering methods according to the average of the correct Rand index

Range of values of γ_i $i = 1, 2$	Symbolic Data Set 1		Symbolic Data Set 2	
	Non-Adaptive Method	Adaptive Method	Non-Adaptive Method	Adaptive Method
$\gamma_i \in [1, 8]$	0.800	0.942	0.436	0.492
$\gamma_i \in [1, 16]$	0.789	0.936	0.432	0.483
$\gamma_i \in [1, 24]$	0.787	0.933	0.430	0.463
$\gamma_i \in [1, 32]$	0.798	0.920	0.390	0.436
$\gamma_i \in [1, 40]$	0.769	0.904	0.329	0.340

The comparison between the proposed clustering methods is achieved by a paired Student's t-test at a significance level of 5%. Table 3 shows the suitable (null and alternative) hypothesis and the observed values of the test statistics following a Student's t distribution with 99 degrees of freedom. In this table, μ and μ_1 are, respectively, the average of the CR index for the non-adaptive and adaptive method. From these results, we can reject the hypothesis that the average performance (measured by the CR index) of the adaptive method is inferior or equal to the non-adaptive method.

Table 3. Statistics of paired Student's t-tests comparing the methods

Range of values of γ_i $i = 1, 2$	$H_0 : \mu_1 \leq \mu$			
	$H_1 : \mu_1 > \mu$			
	Symbolic data set 1	Decision	Symbolic data set 2	Decision
$\gamma \in [1, 8]$	14.00	Reject H_0	12.41	Reject H_0
$\gamma \in [1, 16]$	15.37	Reject H_0	9.08	Reject H_0
$\gamma \in [1, 24]$	15.80	Reject H_0	5.74	Reject H_0
$\gamma \in [1, 32]$	12.60	Reject H_0	6.36	Reject H_0
$\gamma \in [1, 40]$	14.65	Reject H_0	1.36	Accept H_0

Concerning the fish interval-type data set, Table 4 shows the clusters (individual labels) given by the a priori partition according to the categorical variable, as well as the clusters obtained by the non-adaptive and adaptive methods.

Table 4. Clustering results for Eco-tixicology data set

	Cluster 1	Cluster 2	Cluster 3	Cluster 4
A priori Partition	1 2 3 4	7 8 9 10	5 6	11 12
Non-Adaptive Method	5 6 9 11 12	4 8	1 10	2 3 7
Adaptive Method	1 2 3	5 6 9	4 7 8 10	11 12

The CR indices obtained from the comparison between the a priori partition and the partitions given by the adaptive and non-adaptive methods (see Table 4) are, respectively, 0.49 and -0.02. Therefore, the performance of the adaptive method is superior to the non-adaptive method for this data set also.

5   Concluding Remarks

In this paper, a clustering method for interval-type data using a dynamic cluster algorithm with adaptive Chebyshev distances was presented. The algorithm locally optimizes an adequacy criterion that measures the fitting between the classes and their representatives (prototypes). To compare classes and prototypes, adaptive distances based on a weighted version of the L_∞ (Chebyshev) metric for interval data are introduced.

With this method, the prototype of each class is represented by a vector of intervals where the lower bounds of these intervals for a variable are the difference between the median of midpoints of the intervals of the objects belonging to the class. The median of their half-lengths and the upper bounds of these intervals for a variable are the sum of the median of midpoints of the intervals of the objects belonging to the class plus the median of their half-lengths.

Experiments with real and artificial symbolic interval-type data sets showed the usefulness of this clustering method. The accuracy of the results furnished by the adaptive clustering method is assessed by the CR index and compared with results furnished by the non-adaptive version of this method. Concerning the artificial symbolic interval-type data sets, the CR index is calculated in the framework of the Monte Carlo experience with 100 replications. Statistical tests support the evidence that this index for the adaptive method is superior to the non-adaptive method. In regards to the fish interval-type data set, it is also observed that the adaptive method outperforms the non-adaptive method.

Acknowledgments

The authors would like to thank CNPq (Brazilian Agency) for its financial support.

References

1. Bobou, A. and Ribeyre, F. Mercury in the food web: accumulation and transfer mechanisms, in Sigrel A. and Sigrel H. Eds., Metal Ions in Biological Systems. M. Dekker, New York, (1988) 289–319
2. Bock, H.H. and Diday, E.: Analysis of Symbolic Data: Exploratory Methods for Extracting Statistical Information from Complex Data. Springer, Berlin Heidelberg (2000)
3. Chavent, M. and Lechevallier, Y.: Dynamical Clustering Algorithm of Interval Data: Optimization of an Adequacy Criterion Based on Hausdorff Distance. In: Sokolowsky and H.H. Bock Eds., K. Jaguja, A. (eds) Classification, Clustering and Data Analysis (IFCS2002). Springer, Berlin et al, (2002) 53–59
4. Diday, E. and Govaert, G.: Classification Automatique avec Distances Adaptatives. R.A.I.R.O. Informatique Computer Science, 11 (4) (1977) 329–349
5. Diday, E. and Simon, J.C.: Clustering analysis. In: K.S. Fu (ed) Digital Pattern Clasification. Springer, Berlin et al, (1976) 47–94
6. Govaert, G.: Classification automatique et distances adaptatives. Thèse de 3ème cycle, Mathématique appliquée, Université Paris VI (1975)
7. Hubert, L. and Arabie, P.: Comparing Partitions. Journal of Classification, 2 (1985) 193–218
8. Milligan, G. W.:Clustering Validation: results and implications for applied analysis In: Arabie, P., Hubert, L. J. and De Soete, G. (eds) Clustering and Classification, Word Scientific, Singapore, (1996) 341–375
9. Souza, R.M.C.R. and De Carvalho, F. A. T.: Clustering of interval data based on city-block distances. Pattern Recognition Letters, 25 (3) (2004) 353–365
10. Verde, R., De Carvalho, F.A.T. and Lechevallier, Y.: A dynamical clustering algorithm for symbolic data. In: Diday, E., Lechevallier, Y. (eds) Tutorial on Symbolic Data Analysis (Gfkl2001), (2001) 59–72

An Efficient Clustering Method
for High-Dimensional Data Mining

Jae-Woo Chang and Yong-Ki Kim

Dept. of Computer Engineering
Research Center for Advanced LBS Technology
Chonbuk National University, Chonju, Chonbuk 561-756, South Korea
{jwchang,ykkim}@dblab.chonbuk.ac.kr

Abstract. Most clustering methods for data mining applications do not work efficiently when dealing with large, high-dimensional data. This is caused by so-called 'curse of dimensionality' and the limitation of available memory. In this paper, we propose an efficient clustering method for handling of large amounts of high-dimensional data. Our clustering method provides both an efficient cell creation and a cell insertion algorithm. To achieve good retrieval performance on clusters, we also propose a filtering-based index structure using an approximation technique. We compare the performance of our clustering method with the CLIQUE method. The experimental results show that our clustering method achieves better performance on cluster construction time and retrieval time.

1 Introduction

Data mining is concerned with extraction of information of interest from large amounts of data, i.e. rules, regularities, patterns, constraints. Data mining is a data analysis technique that has been developed from other research areas such as Machine Learning, Statistics, and Artificial Intelligent. However, data mining has three differences from the conventional analysis techniques. First, while the existing techniques are mostly applied to a static dataset, data mining is applied to a dynamic dataset with continuous insertions and deletions. Next, the existing techniques manage only errorless data, but data mining can manage data containing some errors. Finally, unlike the conventional techniques, data mining generally deals with large amounts of data.

The typical research topics in data mining are classification, clustering, association rule, and trend analysis, etc. Among them, one of the most important topics is clustering. The conventional clustering methods have a critical drawback that they are not suitable for handling large data sets containing millions of data units because the data set is restricted to be resident in a main memory. They do not work well for clustering high-dimensional data because their retrieval performance is generally degraded as the number of dimensions increases. In this paper, we propose an efficient clustering method for dealing with a large amount of high-dimensional data. Our clustering method provides an efficient cell creation algorithm, which makes cells by splitting each dimension into a set of partitions using a split index. It also provides a cell inser-

A.L.C. Bazzan and S. Labidi (Eds.): SBIA 2004, LNAI 3171, pp. 276–285, 2004.
© Springer-Verlag Berlin Heidelberg 2004

tion algorithm to construct clusters of cells with more density than a given threshold as well as to insert the clusters into an index structure. By using an approximation technique, we also propose a new filtering-based index structure to achieve good retrieval performance on clusters.

The rest of this paper is organized as follows. The next section discusses related work on clustering methods. In Section 3, we propose an efficient clustering method to makes cells and insert them into our index structure. In Section 4, we analyze the performances of our clustering method. Finally, we draw our conclusion in Section 5.

2 Related Work

Clustering is the process of grouping data into classes or clusters, in such a way that objects within a cluster have high similarity to one another, but are very dissimilar to objects in other clusters [1]. In data mining applications, there have been several existing clustering methods, such as CLARA(Clustering LARge Applications) [2], CLARANS(Clustering Large Applications based on RANdomized Search) [3], BIRCH(Balanced Iterative Reducing and Clustering using Hierarchies) [4], DBSCAN(Density Based Spatial Clustering of Applications with Noise) [5], STING(STatistical INformation Grid) [6], and CLIQUE(CLustering In QUEst) [7]. In this section, we discuss a couple of the existing clustering methods appropriate for high dimensional data. We also examine their potential for clustering of large amounts of high dimensional data.

The first method is STING(STatistical INformation Grid)[6]. It is a method which relies on a hierarchical division of the data space into rectangular cells. Each cell is recursively partitioned into smaller cells. STING can be used to answer efficiently different kinds of region-oriented queries. The algorithm for answering such queries first determines all bottom-level cells relevant to the query, and constructs regions of those cells using statistical information. Then, the algorithm goes down the hierarchy by one level. However, when the number of bottom-level cells is very large, both the quality of cell approximations of clusters and the runtime for finding them deteriorate.

The second method is CLIQUE(CLustering In QUEst)[7]. It was proposed for high-dimensional data as a density-based clustering method. CLIQUE automatically finds subspaces(grids) with high-density clusters. CLIQUE produces identical results irrespective of the order in which input records are presented, and it does not presume any canonical distribution of input data. Input parameters are the size of the grid and a global density threshold for clusters. CLIQUE scales linearly with the number of input records, and has good scalability as the number of dimensions in the data.

3 An Efficient Clustering Method

Since the conventional clustering methods assume that a data set is resident in main memory, they are not efficient in handling large amounts of data. As the dimensionality of data is increased, the number of cells increases exponentially, thus causing the dramatic performance degradation. To remedy that effect, we propose an efficient clustering method for handling large amounts of high-dimensional data. Our clustering method uses a cell creation algorithm which makes cells by splitting each dimension into a set of partitions using a split index. It also uses a cell insertion algorithm, which constructs clusters of cells with more density than a given threshold, and stores the constructed cluster into the index structure. For fast retrieval, we propose a filtering-based index structure by applying an approximation technique to our clustering method. The figure 1 shows the overall architecture of our clustering method.

Fig. 1. Overall architecture of our clustering method.

3.1 Cell Creation Algorithm

Our cell creation algorithm makes cells by splitting each dimension into a group of sections using a split index. Density based split index is used for creating split sections and is efficient for splitting multi-group data. Our cell creation algorithm first finds the optimal split section by repeatedly examining a value between the maximum and the minimum in each dimension. That is, it finds the optimal value while the difference between the maximum and the minimum is greater than one and the value of a split index after splitting is greater than the previous value. The split index value is calculated by Eq. (1) before splitting and Eq. (2) after splitting.

$$\text{Split(S)} = 1 - \sum_{j=1}^{C} P_j^{\,2} \tag{1}$$

$$Split(S) = \frac{n_1}{n} Split(S_1) + \frac{n_2}{n} Split(S_2) \tag{2}$$

Using Eq. (1), we can determine the split index value for a data set S in three steps: i) divide S into C classes, ii) calculate the square value of the relative density of each class, and iii) subtract from one all the square values of the densities of C classes. Using Eq. (2), we compute a split index value for S after S is divided into S_1 and S_2. If the split index value is larger than the previous value before splitting, we actually divide S into S_1 and S_2. Otherwise, we stop splitting. Secondly, our cell creation algorithm creates cells being made by the optimal split sections for n-dimensional data. As a result, our cell creation algorithm creates fewer cells than the existing clustering methods using equivalent intervals. Figure 2 shows our cell creation algorithm. Here, the subprogram called 'Partition' is one that partitions input data sets according to attributes. The subprogram is omitted because it is very easy to construct it by slightly modifying the procedure 'Make_Cell'.

In Figure 3, we show an example of our cell creation algorithm. We show the process of splitting twenty records with two classes in two-dimensional data. The split index value for S before splitting is calculated as $1 - [(10/20)^2 + (10/20)^2] = 0.5$. A bold line represents a split index of twenty records in the X-axis. First, we calculate all the split index values for ten intervals. Secondly, we choose an interval with the maximum value among them. Finally, we regard the upper limit of the interval as a split axis. For example, for an interval between 0.3 and 0.4, the split index value is calculated as $(4/20)* [1 - (3/4)^2 - (1/4)^2] + (16/20)*[1 - (7/16)^2 - (9/16)^2] = 0.475$. For an interval between 0.4 and 0.5, the split index value is calculated as $(9/20)*[1 - (6/11)^2 - (5/11)^2] + (11/20)*[1 - (6/11)^2 - (5/11)^2] = 0.501$.

Procedure **Make_Cell**(attributes, input data set S)
```
Begin
   For each attribute in S do
      For each split_point in attribute do
```
Compute $\dfrac{n_1}{n}(1 - \sum P_j{}^2) + \dfrac{n_2}{n}(1 - \sum P_j{}^2)$

If $1 - \sum P_j{}^2 > MAX\ [\dfrac{n_1}{n}(1 - \sum P_j{}^2) + \dfrac{n_2}{n}(1 - \sum P_j{}^2)]$ then return
```
      Else
         Split S into S1 and S2 by max split_point
         Partition(attribute, S1)
         Partition(attribute, S2)
      Endif
      End of for
   End of for
End.
```

Fig. 2. Cell creation algorithm.

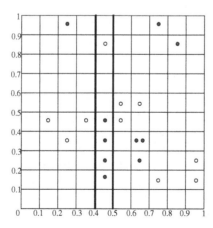

Fig. 3. Example of cell creation algorithm.

We determine the upper limit of the interval (=0.5) as the split axis, because the split index value after splitting is greater than the previous value. Thus, the X axis can be divided into two sections; the first one is from 0 and 0.5 and the second one is from 0.5 to 1.0. If a data set has n dimensions and the number of the initial split sections in each dimension is m, the conventional cell creation algorithms make m^n cells, but our cell creation algorithm makes only $K_1*K_2*...*K_n$ cells ($1 \leq K_1, K_2, .. ,K_n \leq m$).

3.2 Cell Insertion Algorithm

Using our cell creation algorithm, we obtain the cells created from the input data set. Figure 4 shows an insertion algorithm used to store the created cells. First, we construct clusters of cells with more density than a given cell threshold and store them into a cluster information file. In addition, we store all the sections with more density than a given section threshold, into an approximation information file.

```
Procedure Insert_Cell(cells)
Begin
   For each cells which is made form make cell do
      Compare the cell-threshold with cell density
      If cell_density >cell-threshold then
         Insert cell-information into cluster_info_file
      Compare section-threshold with section_density
      If secton_density > section-threshold then
         Approximation_info_file[volume] =1
      Else Approximation_info_file[volume] =0
   End of for
End.
```

Fig. 4. Cell insertion algorithm.

$$Section\ threshold = \begin{cases} \lambda = \dfrac{NR \times F}{NI} \\ NI : \text{the number of input data} \\ NR : \text{the number of sections per dimension} \\ F : \text{minimum section frequency being regarded as '1'} \end{cases} \tag{3}$$

$Cell\ threshold(\tau)$: positive integer

The insertion algorithm to store data is as follows. First, we calculate the frequency of a section in all dimensions whose frequency is greater than a given section threshold. Secondly, in an approximation information file, we set to '1' the corresponding bits to sections whose frequencies are greater than the threshold. We set other bits to '0' for the remainder sections. Thirdly, we calculate the frequency of data in a cell. Finally, we store cell id and cell frequency into the cluster information file for cells whose frequency is greater than a given cell threshold. The cell threshold and the section threshold are shown in Eq. (3).

3.3 Filtering-Based Index Scheme

In order to reduce the number of I/O accesses to a cluster information, it is possible to construct a new filtering-based index scheme using the approximation information

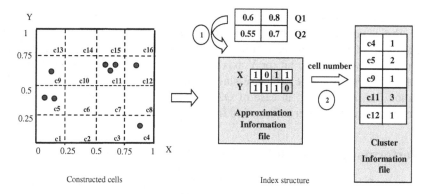

Fig. 5. Two-level filtering-based index scheme.

file. Figure 5 shows a two-level filter-based index scheme containing both the approximation information file and cluster information file.

Let assume that K clusters are created by our cell-based clustering method and the numbers of split sections in X axis and Y axis are m and n, respectively. The following equation, Eq.(4), shows the retrieval times (C) when the approximation information file is used and without the use of it. We assume that α is an average filtering ratio in the approximation information file. D is the number of dimensions of input data. P is the number of records per page. R is the average number of records in each dimension. When the approximation information file is used, the retrieval time decreases as α decreases. For high-dimension data, our two-level index scheme using the approximation information file is an efficient method because the K value increases exponentially in proportion to dimension D.

i) Retrieval time without the use of an approximation information file

$C = \lceil K/P \rceil / 2$ (Disk I/O accesses)

ii) Retrieval time with the use of an approximation information file

$$C = \lceil (D*R)/P \rceil * \alpha + (1-\alpha) \lceil K/P \rceil / 2 \text{ (Disk I/O accesses)} \qquad (4)$$

When a query is entered, we first obtain sections to be examined in all the dimensions. If all the bits corresponding to the sections in the approximation information file are set '1', we calculate a cell number and obtain its cell frequency by accessing the cluster information file. Otherwise, we can improve retrieval performance without accessing the approximation information file. Increase in dimensionality may cause high probability that a record of the approximation information file has zero in at least one dimension.

Figure 5 shows a procedure used to answer a user query in our two-level index structure when a cell threshold and a section threshold are 1, respectively. For a query Q1, we determine 0.6 in X axis as the third section and 0.8 in Y axis as the fourth section. In the approximation-information file, the value for the third section in X axis is '1' and the value for the 4-th section in Y axis is '0'. If there are one or more sections with '0' in the approximation-information file, a query is discarded without searching the corresponding cluster information file. So, Q1 is discarded in the first phase. For a query Q2, the value of 0.55 in X axis and the value of 0.7 in Y axis belong to the third section, respectively. In the approximation information file, the third bit for X axis and the third bit for Y axis have '1', so we can calculate a cell number and obtain its cell frequency by accessing the corresponding entry of the cluster information file. As a result, in case of Q2, we obtain the cell number of 11 and its frequency of 3 in the cluster information file.

4 Performance Analysis

For our performance analysis, we implemented our clustering method on Linux server with 650 MHz dual processors and 512 MB of main memory. We make use of one million 16-dimensional data created by Synthetic Data Generation Code for Classification in IBM Quest Data Mining Project [8]. A record in our experiment is composed of both numeric type attributes, like salary, commission, age, hvalue, hyears, loan, tax, interest, cyear, balance, and categorical type attributes, like level, zipcode, area, children, ctype, job. The factors of our performance analysis are cluster construction time, precision, and retrieval time. We compare our clustering method (CBCM) with the CLIQUE method, which is one of the most efficient conventional clustering method for handling high-dimensional data. For our experiment, we make use of three data sets, one with random distribution, one with standard normal distribution (variation=1), and one with normal distribution of variation 0.5. We also use 5 and 10 for the interval of numeric attributes. Table 1 shows methods used for performance comparison in our experiment.

Table 1. Methods used for performance comparison (MI:Maximal Interval).

Methods	Description
CBCM-5R	CBCM for data set with random distribution(MI = 5)
CLIQUE-5R	CLIQUE for data set with random distribution (MI=5)
CBCM-10R	CBCM for data set with random distribution (MI=10)
CLIQUE-10R	CLIQUE for data set with random distribution (MI=10)
CBCM-5SND	CBCM with standard normal distribution (MI=5)
CLIQUE-5SND	CLIQUE with standard normal distribution (MI=5)
CBCM-10SND	CBCM with standard normal distribution (MI=10)
CLIQUE-10SND	CLIQUE with standard normal distribution (MI=10)
CBCM-5ND(0.5)	CBCM with normal distribution of variation 0.5 (MI=5)
CLIQUE-5ND(0.5)	CLIQUE with normal dist. of variation 0.5 (MI=5)
CBCM-10ND(0.5)	CBCM with normal distribution of variation 0.5 (MI=10)
CLIQUE-10ND(0.5)	CLIQUE with normal dist. of variation 0.5 (MI=10)

Figure 6 shows the cluster construction time when the interval of numeric attributes equals 10. It is shown that the cluster construction time increases linearly in proportion to the amount of data. This result is applicable to large amounts of data. The experimental result shows that the CLIQUE requires about 700 seconds for one million items of data, while our CBCM needs only 100 seconds. Because our method creates smaller number of cells than the CLIQUE, our CBCM method leads to 85% decrease in cluster construction time. The experimental result with the maximal interval (MI)=5 is similar to that with MI=10.

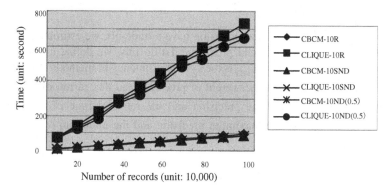

Fig. 6. Cluster Construction Time.

Figure 7 shows average retrieval time for a given user query after clusters were constructed. When the interval of numeric attributes equals 10, the CLIQUE needs about 17-32 seconds, while our CBCM needs about 2 seconds. When the interval equals 5, the CLIQUE and our CBCM need about 8-13 seconds and 1 second, respectively. It is shown that our CBCM is much better on retrieval performance than the CLIQUE. This is because our method creates a small number of cells by using our cell creation algorithm, and achieves good filtering effect by using the approximation information file. It is also shown that the CLIQUE and our CMCM require long retrieval time when using a data set with random distribution , compared with normal distribution of variation 0.5. This is because as the variation of a data set decreases, the number of clusters decreases, leading to better retrieval performance.

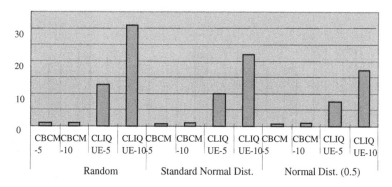

Fig. 7. Retrieval Time.

Figure 8 shows the precision of the CLIQUE and that of our CBCM, assuming that the section threshold is assumed to be 0. The result shows that the CLIQUE achieves about 95% precision when the interval equals 10, and it achieves about 92% precision when the interval equals 5. Meanwhile, our CBCM achieve over 90% precision when the interval of numeric attributes equals 10 while it achieves about 80% precision when the interval equals 5. This is because the precision decreases as the number of clusters constructed increases.

Because both retrieval time and precision have a trade-off, we estimate a measure used to combine retrieval time and precision. To do this, we define a system efficiency measure in Eq. (5). Here E_{MD} is the system efficiency of methods (MD) shown in Table 1 and W_p and W_t are the weight of precision and that of retrieval time, respectively. P_{MD} and T_{MD} are the precision and the retrieval time of the methods (MD). P_{MAX} and T_{MIN} are the maximum precision and the minimum retrieval time, respectively, for all methods.

$$E_{MD} = W_p \bullet \frac{P_{MD}}{P_{MAX}} + W_t \bullet \frac{1}{T_{MAX} / T_{MIN}} \tag{5}$$

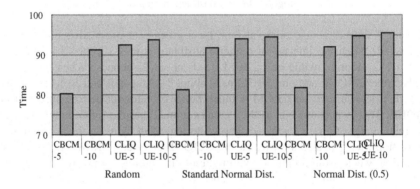

Fig. 8. Precision.

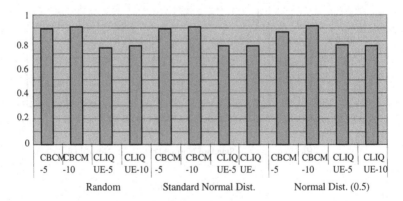

Fig. 9. System efficiency.

Figure 9 depicts the performance results of methods in terms of their system efficiency when the weight of precision are three times greater than that of retrieval time (W_p=0.75, W_t =0.25). It is shown from our performance results that our CBCM outperforms the CLIQUE with respect to the system efficiency, regardless of the data distribution of the data sets. Especially, the performance of our CBCM with MI=10 is the best.

5   Conclusion

The conventional clustering methods are not efficient for large, high-dimensional data. In order to overcome the difficulty, we proposed an efficient clustering method with two features. The first one allows us to create the small number of cells for large, high-dimensional data. To do this, we calculate a section of each dimension through split index and create cells according to the overlapped area of each fixed section. The second one allows us to apply an approximation technique to our clustering method for fast clustering. For this, we use a two-level index structure which consists of both an approximation information file and a cluster information file. For performance analysis, we compare our clustering method with the CLIQUE method. The performance analysis results show that our clustering method shows slightly lower precision, but it achieves good performance on retrieval time as well as cluster construction time. Finally, our clustering method shows a good performance on system efficiency which is a measure to combine both precision and retrieval time.

Acknowledgement

This research was supported by University IT Research Center Project.

References

1. Han, J., Kamber, M.: Data Mining: Concepts and Techniques. Morgan Kaufmann (2000)
2. Ng R.T., Han J.: Efficient and Effective Clustering Methods for Spatial Data Mining. Proc. of Int. Conf. on Very Large Data Bases (1994) 144-155
3. Kaufman L., Rousseeuw P.J.: Finding Groups in Data: An Introduction to Cluster Analysis. John Wiley & Sons (1990)
4. Zhang T., Ramakrishnan R., Linvy M.: BIRCH: An Efficient Data Clustering Method for Very Large Databases. Proc. of ACM Int. Conf. on Management of Data (1996) 103-114
5. Ester M., Kriegel H.-P., Sander J., Xu X.: A Density Based Algorithm for Discovering Clusters in Large Spatial Databases with Noise. Proc. of Int. Conf. on Knowledge Discovery and Data Mining (1996) 226-231
6. Wang W., Yang J., Muntz R.: STING: A Statistical Information Grid Approach to Spatial Data Mining. Proc. of Int. Conf. on Very Large Data Bases (1997) 186-195
7. Agrawal, R., Gehrke, J., Gunopulos, D., Raghavan, P.: Automatic Subspace Clustering of High Dimensional Data Mining Applications. Proc. of ACM Int. Conf. on Management of Data (1998) 94-105
8. http://www.almaden.ibm.com/cs/quest

Learning with Drift Detection

João Gama[1,2], Pedro Medas[1], Gladys Castillo[1,3], and Pedro Rodrigues[1]

[1] LIACC - University of Porto
Rua Campo Alegre 823, 4150 Porto, Portugal
{jgama,pmedas}@liacc.up.pt, prodrigues@dcc.fc.up.pt
[2] Fac. Economics, University of Porto
[3] University of Aveiro
gladys@mat.ua.pt

Abstract. Most of the work in machine learning assume that examples are generated at random according to some stationary probability distribution. In this work we study the problem of learning when the distribution that generate the examples changes over time. We present a method for detection of changes in the probability distribution of examples. The idea behind the drift detection method is to control the online error-rate of the algorithm. The training examples are presented in sequence. When a new training example is available, it is classified using the actual model. Statistical theory guarantees that while the distribution is stationary, the error will decrease. When the distribution changes, the error will increase. The method controls the trace of the online error of the algorithm. For the actual context we define a warning level, and a drift level. A new context is declared, if in a sequence of examples, the error increases reaching the warning level at example k_w, and the drift level at example k_d. This is an indication of a change in the distribution of the examples. The algorithm learns a new model using only the examples since k_w. The method was tested with a set of eight artificial datasets and a real world dataset. We used three learning algorithms: a *perceptron*, a *neural network* and a *decision tree*. The experimental results show a good performance detecting drift and with learning the new concept. We also observe that the method is independent of the learning algorithm.

Keywords: Concept Drift, Incremental Supervised Learning, Machine Learning

1 Introduction

In many applications, learning algorithms acts in dynamic environments where the data flows continuously. If the process is not strictly stationary (as most of real world applications), the target concept could change over time. Nevertheless, most of the work in machine learning assume that training examples are generated at random according to some stationary probability distribution. Examples of real problems where change detection is relevant include user modeling, monitoring in biomedicine and industrial processes, fault detection and diagnosis, safety of complex systems, etc [1].

A.L.C. Bazzan and S. Labidi (Eds.): SBIA 2004, LNAI 3171, pp. 286–295, 2004.
© Springer-Verlag Berlin Heidelberg 2004

In this work we present a direct method to detect changes in the distribution of the training examples. The method will be presented in the on-line learning model, where learning takes place in a sequence of trials. On each trial, the learner makes some kind of prediction and then receives some kind of feedback. A important concept through out this work is the concept of *context*. We define context as a set of examples where the function generating examples is stationary. We assume that the data stream is composed by a set of contexts. Changes between contexts can be gradual - when there is a smoothed transition between the distributions; or abrupt - when the distribution changes quickly. The aim of this work is to present a straightforward and direct method to detect the several moments when there is a change of context. If we can identify contexts, we can identify which information is outdated and re-learn the model only with relevant information to the present context.

The paper is organized as follows. The next section presents related work in detecting concept drifting. In section 3 we present the theoretical basis of the proposed method. Section 4 we evaluate the method using several algorithms on artificial and real datasets. Section 5 concludes the paper and present future work.

2   Tracking Drifting Concepts

There are several methods in machine learning to deal with changing concepts [7, 6, 5, 12]. In machine learning drifting concepts are often handled by time windows or weighted examples according to their age or utility. In general, approaches to cope with concept drift can be classified into two categories: *i*) approaches that adapt a learner at regular intervals without considering whether changes have really occurred; *ii*) approaches that first detect concept changes, and next, the learner is adapted to these changes. Examples of the former approaches are *weighted examples* and *time windows* of fixed size. Weighted examples are based on the simple idea that the importance of an example should decrease with time (references about this approach can be found in [7, 6, 9, 10, 12]). When a time window is used, at each time step the learner is induced only from the examples that are included in the window. Here, the key difficulty is how to select the appropriate window size: a small window can assure a fast adaptability in phases with concept changes but in more stable phases it can affect the learner performance, while a large window would produce good and stable learning results in stable phases but can not react quickly to concept changes. In the latter approaches,with the aim of detecting concept changes, some indicators (e.g. performance measures, properties of the data, etc.) are monitored over time (see [7] for a good classification of these indicators). If during the monitoring process a concept drift is detected, some actions to adapt the learner to these changes can be taken. When a time window of adaptive size is used these actions usually lead to adjusting the window size according to the extent of concept drift [7]. As a general rule, if a concept drift is detected the window size decreases, otherwise the window size increases. An example of work relevant to this approach is the FLORA family of algorithms developed by Widmer and Kubat [12]. For instance,

FLORA2 includes a window adjustment heuristic for a rule-based classifier. To detect concept changes the accuracy and the coverage of the current learner are monitored over time and the window size is adapted accordingly.

Other relevant works are the works of Klinkenberg and Lanquillon, both of them in information filtering. For instance, Klinkenberg [7], to detect concept drift, propose monitoring the values of three performance indicators: *accuracy*, *recall* and *precision* over time, and then, comparing it to a confidence interval of standard sample errors for a moving average value (using the last M batches) of each particular indicator. Although these heuristics seem to work well in their particular domain, they have to deal with two main problems: *i)* to compute performance measures, user feedback about the true class is required, but in some real applications only partial user feedback is available; *ii)* a considerable number of parameters are needed to be tuned. Afterwards, in [6] Klinkenberg and Joachims present a theoretically well-founded method to recognize and handle concept changes using support vector machines. The key idea is to select the window size so that the estimated generalization error on new examples is minimized. This approach uses unlabeled data to reduce the need for labeled data, it doesn't require complicated parameterization and it works effectively and efficiently in practice.

3   The Drift Detection Method

In most of real-world applications of machine learning data is collected over time. For large time periods, it is hard to assume that examples are independent and identically distributed. At least in complex environments its highly provable that class-distributions changes over time.

In this work we assume that examples arrive one at a time. The framework could be easy extended to situations where data comes on batches of examples. We consider the online learning framework. In this framework when an example becomes available, the decision model must take a decision (e.g. an action). Only after the decision has been taken the environment react providing feedback to the decision model (e.g. the class label of the example).

Suppose a sequence of examples, in the form of pairs (x_i, y_i). For each example, the actual decision model predicts $\hat{y}_i$, that can be or True ($\hat{y}_i = y_i$) or False ($\hat{y}_i \neq y_i$). For a set of examples the error is a random variable from Bernoulli trials. The Binomial distribution gives the general form of the probability for the random variable that represents the number of errors in a sample of n examples. For each point i in the sequence, the error-rate is the probability of observe False, p_i, with standard deviation given by $s_i = sqrt(p_i(1 - p_i)/i)$.

In the PAC learning model [11] it is assumed that if the distribution of the examples is stationary, the error rate of the learning algorithm (p_i) will decrease when the number of examples (i) increases[1]. A significant increase in the error of the algorithm, suggest a change in the class distribution, and that the actual decision model is not appropriate. For a sufficient large number of example, the

---

[1] For an infinite number of examples, the error rate will tend to the Bayes error.

Binomial distribution is closely approximated by a Normal distribution with the same mean and variance. Considering that the probability distribution is unchanged when the context is static, then the $1 - \alpha/2$ confidence interval for p with $n > 30$ examples is approximately $p_i \pm \alpha * s_i$. The parameter α depends on the confidence level. The drift detection method manages two registers during the training of the learning algorithm, p_{min} and s_{min}. Every time a new example i is processed those values are updated when $p_i + s_i$ is lower than $p_{min} + s_{min}$. We use a warning level to define the optimal size of the context window. The context window will contain the old examples that are on the new context and a minimal number of examples on the old context. Suppose that in the sequence of examples that traverse a node, there is an example i with correspondent p_i and s_i. In the experiments described below the confidence level for warning has been set to 95%, that is, the warning level is reached if $p_i + s_i \geq p_{min} + 2 * s_{min}$. The confidence level for drift has been set to 99%, that is, the drift level is reached if $p_i + s_i \geq p_{min} + 3 * s_{min}$. Suppose a sequence of examples where the error of the actual model increases reaching the warning level at example k_w, and the drift level at example k_d. This is an indication of a change in the distribution of the examples. A new context is declared starting in example k_w, and a new decision model is induced using only the examples starting in k_w till k_d. It is possible to observe an increase of the error reaching the warning level, followed by a decrease. We assume that such situations corresponds to a *false alarm*, without changing the context. Figure 1 details the dynamic window structure. With this method of learning and forgetting we ensure a way to continuously keep a model better adapted to the present context.

This method could be applied with any learning algorithm. It could be directly implemented inside online and incremental algorithms, and could be implemented as a wrapper to batch learners. The goal of the proposed method is to detect sequences of examples with a stationary distribution. We denote those sequences of examples as *context*. From the practical point of view, what the method does is to choose the training set more appropriate to the actual class-distribution of the examples.

4   Experimental Evaluation

In this section we describe the evaluation of the proposed method. We used three distinct learning algorithms with the drift detection algorithm: a *Perceptron*, a neural network and a decision tree [4]. These learning algorithms use different representations to generalize examples. The simpler representation is linear, the *Perceptron*. The neural networks example representation is a non linear combination of attributes. The decision tree uses DNF to represent generalization of the examples.

We have used eight artificial datasets, previously used in concept drift detection [8] and a real-world problem [3]. The artificial datasets have several different characteristics that allow us to assess the performance of the method in various conditions - abrupt and gradual drift, presence and absence of noise, presence of irrelevant and symbolic attributes, numerical and mixed data descriptions.

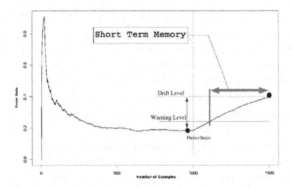

Fig. 1. Dynamically constructed Time Window. The vertical line marks the change of concept.

4.1 Artificial Datasets

The eight artificial datasets used are briefly described. All the problems have two classes. Each class is represented by 50% of the examples in each context. To ensure a stable learning environment within each context, the positive and negative examples in the training set are interchanged. Each dataset embodies at least two different versions of a target concept. Each context defines the strategy to classify the examples. Each dataset is composed of 1000 random generated examples in each context.

1. SINE1. `Abrupt concept drift, noise-free examples.` The dataset has two relevant attributes. Each attributes has values uniformly distributed in $[0,1]$. In the first context all points below the curve $y = \sin(x)$ are classified as positive. After the context change the classification is reversed.
2. SINE2. The same two relevant attributes. The classification function is $y < 0.5 + 0.3\sin(3\pi x)$. After the context change the classification is reversed.
3. SINIRREL1. `Presence of irrelevant attributes.` The same classification function of SINE1 but the examples have two more random attributes with no influence on the classification function.
4. SINIRREL2. The same classification function of SINE2 but the examples have two more random attributes with no influence on the classification function.
5. CIRCLES. `Gradual concept drift, noise-free examples.` The same relevant attributes are used with four new classification function. This dataset has four contexts defined by four circles:

center	$[0.2, 0.5]$	$[0.4, 0.5]$	$[0.6, 0.5]$	$[0.8, 0.5]$
radius	0.15	0.2	0.25	0.3

6. GAUSS. `Abrupt concept drift, noisy examples.` Positive examples with two relevant attributes from the domain $R \times R$ are normally distributed around the center $[0,0]$ with standard deviation 1. The negative examples

are normally distributed around center $[2, 0]$ with standard deviation 4. After each context change, the classification is reversed.

7. STAGGER. Abrupt concept drift,symbolic noise-free examples. The examples have three symbolic attributes - size (small, medium, large), color (red, green), shape (circular, non-circular). In the first context only the examples satisfying the description *size=small* ∧ *color=red* are classified positive. In the second context, the concept description is defined by two attributes, *color=green* ∨ *shape=circular*. With the third context, the examples are classified positive if *size=medium* ∨ *size= large*.

8. MIXED. Abrupt concept drift, boolean noise-free examples. Four relevant attributes, two boolean attributes v, w and two numeric attributes from $[0, 1]$. The examples are classified positive if two of three conditions are satisfied:$v, w, y < 0.5 + 0.3 * \sin(3\pi x)$. After each context change the classification is reversed.

4.2   Results on Artificial Domains

The propose of this experiments is to study the effect of the proposed drift detection method on the generalization capacity of each learning algorithm. We also show the method independence of the learning algorithm. The results of different learning algorithms are not comparable.

Figure 2 compare the results of the application of the drift detection method with the results without detection. These are the results for the three learning algorithms used and two artificial datasets. The use of artificial datasets allow us to control the points where the concept drift. The points where the concept drift are signaled by a vertical line. We can observe the performance curve of the learning algorithm without drift detection. During the first concept the learning algorithm error systematically decreases. After the first concept drift the error strongly increases and never drops to the level of the first concept. When the concept drift is detected the error rate grows dramatically compared to the gradual growth of the model without drift detection. But the drift detection method overcomes this and with few examples can achieve a much better performance level, as can be seen with figure 2, than the method without drift detection. While the error rate still grows with the non detection algorithm, the drift detection curve falls to a lower error rate. Both with the neural network and the decision tree it is relevant the application of the detection method over the flat application of the learning algorithm on the learning efficiency.

Table 1 shows the final values for the error rate by dataset and learning algorithm. There is a significant difference of results when the drift detection is used. We can observe that the method is effective with all learning algorithms. Nevertheless, the differences are more significant with the neural network and the decision tree.

4.3   The Electricity Market Dataset

The data used in this experiments was first described by M. Harries [3]. The data was collected from the Australian New South Wales Electricity Market. In

Decision Tree

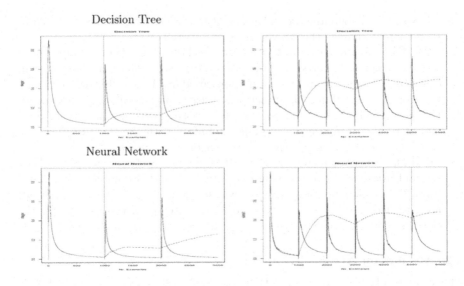

Neural Network

Fig. 2. Abrupt Concept Drift, noise-free examples. Left column: STAGGER dataset, right column: MIXED dataset.

Table 1. Error rate of the final model with and without drift detection.

Dataset	Perceptron		Neural Network		Decision Tree	
	No Detection	Detection	No Detection	Detection	No Detection	Detection
STAGGER	0.048	**0.029**	0.351	**0.002**	0.265	**0.016**
SINE1	0.126	**0.115**	0.489	**0.019**	0.490	**0.081**
SINIRREL1	0.159	**0.139**	0.479	**0.068**	0.483	**0.088**
SINE2	0.271	**0.262**	0.492	**0.118**	0.477	**0.100**
SINIRREL2	0.281	0.281	0.477	**0.059**	0.485	**0.084**
MIXED	0.100	0.111	0.240	**0.065**	0.491	**0.465**
GAUSS	0.384	0.386	0.395	**0.150**	0.380	**0.144**
CIRCLES	0.410	0.413	0.233	**0.225**	0.205	**0.109**

this market, the prices are not fixed and are affected by demand and supply of the market. The prices in this market are set every five minutes. Harries [3] shows the seasonality of the price construction and the sensitivity to short-term events such as weather fluctuations. Another factor on the price evolution was the time evolution of the electricity market. During the time period described in the data the electricity market was expanded with the inclusion of adjacent areas. This allowed for a more elaborated management of the supply. The excess production of one region could be sold on the adjacent region. A consequence of this expansion was a dampener of the extreme prices. The ELEC2 dataset contains 45312 instances dated from 7 May 1996 to 5 December 1998. Each example of the dataset refers to a period of 30 minutes, i. e. there are 48 instances for each time period of one day. Each example on the dataset has 5 fields, the day of week, the time stamp, the NSW electricity demand, the Vic electricity demand, the scheduled electricity transfer between states and the class label. The class label identifies the change of the price related to a moving average of the last 24 hours. The class level only reflect deviations of the price on a one day average and removes the impact of longer term price trends. The interest of this dataset is that it is a real-world dataset. We do not know when drift occurs or if there is drift.

Experiments with ELEC2 Data. We have considered two problems. The first problem consists in short term prediction: predict the changes in the prices relative to the last day. The other problem consists in predicting the changes in the prices relative to the last week of examples recorded. In both problems the learning algorithm, the implementation of CART available in R, learns a model from the training data. We have used the proposed method as a wrapper over the learning algorithm. After seeing all the training data, the final model classifies the test data.

As we have pointed out we don't know if and when drift occurs. In a first set of experiments we run a decision tree using two different training sets: all the available data (e.g. except the test data), and the examples relative to the last year. These choices corresponds to *ad-hoc* heuristics. Our method makes an intelligent search of the appropriate training sets. These heuristics have been used to define *upper bounds* to the generalization ability of the learning algorithm.

A second set of experiments was designed to find a *lower bound* for the predictive accuracy. We made an extensive search to look for the segment of the training dataset with the best prediction performance on the test set. There should be noted that this is not feasible in practice, because we are looking for the class in the test set. This result can only be seen as a *lower bound*. Starting with all the training data, the learning algorithm generates a model that classifies the test set. Each new experiment uses a subset of the last dataset which excludes the data of the oldest week, that is, it removes the first 336 examples of the previous experiment. In each experiment, a decision tree is generated from the training set and evaluated on the test set. The smallest test set error is chosen as a *lower bound* for comparative purposes. We made 134 experiments with the 1-day test set problem, and 133 with the 1-week test set problem, using in each a different partition of the train dataset. The figure 3 presents the trace of the error rate of the drift detection method using the full ELEC2 dataset. The figure also presents the trace of the decision tree without drift detection. The third set of experiments was the application of the drift detection method with a decision tree to the training dataset defined for each of the test datasets, 1-day and 1-week test dataset. With the 1-day dataset the trees are built using only the last 3836 examples on the training dataset. With the 1-week dataset the trees are built with the 3548 most recent examples. This is the data collected since 1998/09/16. Table 2 shows the error rate obtained with the 1-day and 1-week prediction for the three set of experiments. We can see that the 1-day prediction error rate of the Drift Detection Method is equal to the lower bound and the 1-week prediction is very close to the lower bound. This is a excellent indicator of the drift detection method performance.

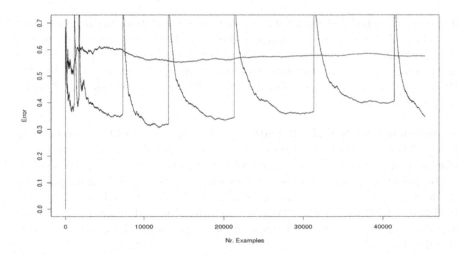

Fig. 3. Trace of the on-line error using the Drift Detection Method applied with a Decision Tree on ELEC2 dataset.

Table 2. Results of the error rate for two different Test Sets.

Test Set	Lower Bound	Upper Bound All Data	Upper Bound Last Year	Drift Detection
Last Day	0.104	0.187	0.125	0.104
Last Week	0.190	0.235	0.247	0.199

We have also tested the method using the dataset *ADULT* [2]. This dataset was created using census data in a specific point of time. The concept should be stable. Using a decision tree as inducer, the method never detects drift. This is an important aspect, because it presents evidence that the method is robust to false alarms.

5   Conclusions

We present a method for detection of concept drift in the distribution of the examples. The method is simple, with direct application and is computationally efficient. The Drift Detection Method can be applied to problems where the information is available sequentially over time. The method is independent of the learning algorithm. It is more efficient when used with learning algorithms with greater capacity to represent generalizations of the examples. This method improves the learning capability of the algorithm when modeling non-stationary problems. We intend to proceed with this research line with other learning algorithms and real world problems. We already started working to include the drift detection method in an incremental decision tree. Preliminary results are very promising. The algorithm could be applied with any loss-function given appropriate values for α. Preliminary results in regression domain using *mean-squared error* loss function confirm the results presented here.

Acknowledgments

The authors reveal its gratitude to the financial contribution of project ALES (POSI/SRI/39770/2001), RETINAE, and FEDER through the plurianual support to LIACC.

References

1. Michele Basseville and Igor Nikiforov. *Detection of Abrupt Changes: Theory and Applications*. Prentice-Hall Inc, 1993.
2. C. Blake, E. Keogh, and C.J. Merz. UCI repository of Machine Learning databases, 1999.
3. Michael Harries. Splice-2 comparative evaluation: Electricity pricing. Technical report, The University of South Wales, 1999.
4. Ross Ihaka and Robert Gentleman. R: A language for data analysis and graphics. *Journal of Computational and Graphical Statistics*, 5(3):299–314, 1996.
5. R. Klinkenberg. Learning drifting concepts: Example selection vs. example weighting. *Intelligent Data Analysis*, 2004.
6. R. Klinkenberg and T. Joachims. Detecting concept drift with support vector machines. In Pat Langley, editor, *Proceedings of ICML-00, 17th International Conference on Machine Learning*, pages 487–494, Stanford, US, 2000. Morgan Kaufmann Publishers.
7. R. Klinkenberg and I. Renz. Adaptive information filtering: Learning in the presence of concept drifts. In *Learning for Text Categorization*, pages 33–40. AAAI Press, 1998.
8. M. Kubat and G. Widmer. Adapting to drift in continuous domain. In *Proceedings of the 8th European Conference on Machine Learning*, pages 307–310. Springer Verlag, 1995.
9. C. Lanquillon. *Enhancing Text Classification to Improve Information Filtering*. PhD thesis, University of Madgdeburg, Germany, 2001.
10. M. Maloof and R. Michalski. Selecting examples for partial memory learning. *Machine Learning*, 41:27–52, 2000.
11. Tom Mitchell. *Machine Learning*. McGraw Hill, 1997.
12. Gerhard Widmer and Miroslav Kubat. Learning in the presence of concept drift and hidden contexts. *Machine Learning*, 23:69–101, 1996.

Learning with Class Skews and Small Disjuncts

Ronaldo C. Prati, Gustavo E.A.P.A. Batista, and Maria Carolina Monard

Institute of Mathematics and Computer Science at University of São Paulo
P. O. Box 668, ZIP Code 13560-970, São Carlos, SP, Brazil
{prati,gbatista,mcmonard}@icmc.usp.br

Abstract. One of the main objectives of a Machine Learning – ML – system is to induce a classifier that minimizes classification errors. Two relevant topics in ML are the understanding of which domain characteristics and inducer limitations might cause an increase in misclassification. In this sense, this work analyzes two important issues that might influence the performance of ML systems: class imbalance and error-prone small disjuncts. Our main objective is to investigate how these two important aspects are related to each other. Aiming at overcoming both problems we analyzed the behavior of two over-sampling methods we have proposed, namely Smote + Tomek links and Smote + ENN. Our results suggest that these methods are effective for dealing with class imbalance and, in some cases, might help in ruling out some undesirable disjuncts. However, in some cases a simpler method, Random over-sampling, provides compatible results requiring less computational resources.

1 Introduction

This paper aims to investigate the relationship between two important topics in recent ML research: learning with *class imbalance* (class skews) and *small disjuncts*. Symbolic ML algorithms usually express the induced concept as a set of rules. Besides a small overlap within some rules, a set of rules might be understood as a disjunctive concept definition. The size of a disjunct is defined as the number of training examples it correctly classifies. Small disjuncts are those disjuncts that correctly cover only few training cases. In addition, class imbalance occurs in domains where the number of examples belonging to some classes heavily outnumber the number of examples in the other classes. Class imbalance has often been reported in the ML literature as an obstacle for the induction of good classifiers, due to the poor representation of the minority class. On the other hand, small disjuncts have often been reported as having higher misclassification rates than large disjuncts. These problems frequently arise in applications of learning algorithms in real world data, and several research papers have been published aiming to overcome such problems. However, these efforts have produced only marginal improvements and both problems still remain open. A better understanding of how class imbalance influences small disjuncts (and of course, the inverse problem) may be required before meaningful results might be obtained.

A.L.C. Bazzan and S. Labidi (Eds.): SBIA 2004, LNAI 3171, pp. 296–306, 2004.

Weiss [1] suggests that there is a relation between the problem of small disjuncts and class imbalance, stating that one of the reasons why small disjuncts have a higher error rate than large disjuncts is due to class imbalance. Furthermore, Japkowicz [2] enhances this hypothesis stating that the problem of learning with class imbalance is potentiated when it yields small disjuncts. Even though these papers point out a connection between such problems, the true relationship between them is not yet well-established. In this work, we aim to further investigate this relationship.

This work is organized as follows: Section 2 reports some related work and points out some connections between class imbalance and small disjuncts. Section 3 describes some metrics for measuring the performance of ML algorithms regarding small disjuncts and class skews. Section 4 discusses the experimental results of our work and, finally, Section 5 presents our concluding remarks and outlines future research directions.

2   Related Work

Holt et al. [3] report two main problems when small disjuncts arise in a concept definition: (a) the difficulty in reliably eliminating the error-prone small disjuncts without producing an undesirable net effect on larger disjuncts and; (b) the algorithm maximum generality bias that tends to favor the induction of good large disjuncts and poor small disjuncts.

Several research papers have been published in the ML literature aiming to overcome such problems. Those papers often advocate the use of pruning to draw small disjuncts off the concept definition [3, 4] or the use of alternative learning bias, generally using hybrid approaches, for coping with the problem of small disjuncts [5]. Similarly, class imbalance has been often reported as an obstacle for the induction of good classifiers, and several approaches have been reported in the literature with the purpose of dealing with skewed class distributions. These papers often use sampling schemas, where examples of the majority class are removed from the training set [6] or examples of the minority class are added to the training set [7] in order to obtain a more balanced class distribution. However, in some domains standard ML algorithms induce good classifiers even using highly imbalanced training sets. This indicates that class imbalance is not solely accountable for the decrease in performance of learning algorithms. In [8] we conjecture that the problem is not only caused by class skews, but is also related to the degree of data overlapping among the classes.

A straightforward connection between both themes can be traced by observing that minority classes may lead to small disjuncts, since there are fewer examples in these classes than in the others, and the rules induced from them tend to cover fewer examples. Moreover, disjuncts induced to cover rare cases are likely to have higher error rates than disjuncts that cover common cases, as rare cases are less likely to be found in the test set. Conversely, as the algorithm tries to generalize from the data, minority classes may yield some small disjuncts to be ruled out from the set of rules. When the algorithm is generalizing, common cases can "overwhelm" a rare case, favoring the induction of larger disjuncts.

Table 1. Confusion matrix for a two-class problem.

	Positive Prediction	Negative Prediction
Positive Class	True Positive (TP)	False Negative (FN)
Negative Class	False Positive (FP)	True Negative (TN)

Nevertheless, it is worth noticing the differences between class imbalance and small disjuncts. Rare cases exist in the underlying population from which training examples are drawn, while small disjuncts might also be a consequence of the learning algorithm bias. In fact, as we stated before, rare cases might have a dual role regarding small disjuncts, either leading to undesirable small disjuncts or not allowing the formation of desirable ones, but rather small disjuncts might be formed even though the number of examples in each class is naturally equally balanced. In a nutshell, class imbalance is a characteristic of a domain while small disjuncts are not [9].

As we mentioned before, Weiss [1] and Japkowicz [2] have suggested that there is a relation between both problems. However, Japkowicz performed her analysis on artificially generated data sets and Weiss only considers one aspect of the interaction between small disjuncts and class imbalances.

3   Evaluating Classifiers with Small Disjuncts and Imbalanced Domains

From hereafter, in order to facilitate our analysis, we constrain our discussion to binary class problems where, by convention, the minority is called **positive class** and the majority is called **negative class**. The most straightforward way to evaluate the performance of classifiers is based on the confusion matrix analysis. Table 1 illustrates a confusion matrix for a two-class problem. A number of widely used metrics for measuring the performance of learning systems can be extracted from such a matrix, such as error rate and accuracy. However, when the prior class probabilities are very different, the use of such measures might produce misleading conclusions since those measures do not take into consideration misclassification costs, are strongly biased to favor the majority class and are sensitive to class skews.

Thus, it is more interesting to use a performance metric that disassociates the errors (or hits) that occur in each class. Four performance metrics that directly measure the classification performance on positive and negative classes independently can be derived from Table 1, namely true positive rate – $TP_{rate} = \frac{TP}{TP+FN}$ – (the percentage of correctly classified positive examples), false positive rate – $FP_{rate} = \frac{FP}{FP+TN}$ – (the percentage of incorrectly classified positive examples), true negative rate – $TN_{rate} = \frac{TN}{FP+TN}$ – (the percentage of correctly classified negative examples) and false negative rate – $FN_{rate} = \frac{FN}{TP+FN}$ – (the percentage of incorrectly classified negative examples). These four performance metrics have the advantage of being independent of class costs and prior probabilities. The aim of a classifier is to minimize the false positive and negative rates or, similarly, to maximize the true negative and positive rates. Unfortunately, for most real world applications there is a tradeoff between FN_{rate} and FP_{rate}, and similarly between TN_{rate} and TP_{rate}.

ROC (Receiver Operating Characteristic) analysis enables one to compare different classifiers regarding their true positive rate and false positive rate. The basic idea is to plot the classifiers performance in a two-dimensional space, one dimension for each of these two measurements. Some classifiers, such as the Naïve Bayes classifier and some Neural Networks, yield a score that represents the degree to which an example is a member of a class. For decision trees, the class distributions on each leaf can be used as a score. Such ranking can be used to produce several classifiers by varying the threshold of an example to be classified into a class. Each threshold value produces a different point in the ROC space. These points are linked by tracing straight lines through two consecutive points to produce a ROC curve. The area under the ROC curve (AUC) represents the expected performance as a single scalar. In this work, we use a decision tree inducer and the method proposed in [10] with Laplace correction for measuring the leaf accuracy to produce ROC curves.

In order to measure the degree to which errors are concentrated towards smaller disjuncts, Weiss [1] introduced the Error Concentration (EC) curve. The EC curve is plotted starting with the smallest disjunct from the classifier and progressively adding larger disjuncts. For each iteration where a larger disjunct is added, the percentage of test errors *versus* the percentage of correctly classified examples is plotted. The line $Y = X$ corresponds to classifiers having errors equally distributed towards all disjuncts. Error Concentration is defined as the percentage of the total area above the line $Y = X$ that falls under the EC curve. EC may take values from between 100%, which indicates that the smallest disjunct(s) covers all test errors before even a single correctly classified test example is covered, to -100%, which indicates that the largest disjunct(s) covers all test errors after all correctly classified test examples have been covered.

In order to illustrate these two metrics Figure 1 shows the ROC (Fig. 1(a)) and the EC (Fig. 1(b)) graphs for the pima data set and pruned trees – see Table 3. The AUC for the ROC graph is 81.53% and the EC measure from the EC graph is 42.03%. The graphs might be interpreted as follows: from the ROC graph, considering for instance a false positive rate of 20%, one might expect a true positive rate of nearly 65%; and from the EC graph, the smaller disjuncts that correctly cover 20% of the examples are responsible for more than 55% of the misclassifications.

4   Experimental Evaluation

The aim of our research is to provide some insights into the relationship between class imbalances and small disjuncts. To this end, we performed a broad experimental evaluation using ten data sets from UCI [11] having minority class distribution spanning from 46.37% to 7.94%, *i.e.*, from nearly balanced to skewed

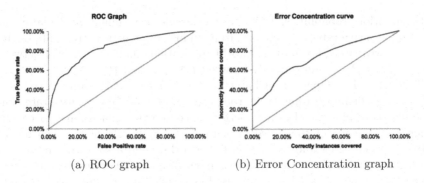

(a) ROC graph   (b) Error Concentration graph

Fig. 1. ROC and EC graphs for the pima data set and pruned trees.

distributions. Table 2 summarizes the data sets employed in this study. It shows, for each data set, the number of examples (#Examples), number of attributes (#Attributes), number of quantitative and qualitative attributes and class distribution. For data sets having more than two classes, we chose the class with fewer examples as the positive class, and collapsed the remainder classes as the negative class.

Table 2. Data sets summary descriptions.

Data sets	#Examples	#Attributes (quanti., quali.)	Classes (min., maj.)	Classes % (min., maj.)
Sonar	207	60 (60, 0)	(R, M)	(46.37%, 53.63%)
Bupa	345	6 (6, 0)	(1, 2)	(42.03%, 57.97%)
Pima	768	8 (8, 0)	(1, 0)	(34.77%, 65.23%)
German	1000	20 (7, 13)	(Bad, Good)	(30.00%, 70.00%)
Haberman	306	3 (3, 0)	(Die, Survive)	(26.47%, 73.53%)
New-thyroid	215	5 (5, 0)	(hypo, remainder)	(16.28%, 83.72%)
E-coli	336	7 (7, 0)	(iMU, remainder)	(10.42%, 89.58%)
Satimage	6435	36 (36, 0)	(4, remainder)	(9.73%, 90.27%)
Flag	194	28 (10, 18)	(white, remainder)	(8.76%, 91.24%)
Glass	214	9 (9, 0)	(Ve-win-float-proc, remainder)	(7.94%, 92.06%)

In our experiments we used the release 8 of the C4.5 symbolic learning algorithm to induce decision trees [12]. Firstly, we ran C4.5 over the data sets and calculated the AUC and EC for pruned (default parameters settings) and unpruned trees induced for each data set using 10-fold stratified cross-validation. Table 3 summarizes these results, reporting mean value results and their respective standard deviations. It should be observed that for two data sets, Sonar and Glass, C4.5 was not able to prune the induced trees. Furthermore, for data set Flag and pruned trees, the default model was induced.

We consider the results obtained for both pruned and unpruned trees because we aim to analyze whether pruning is effective for coping with small disjuncts in the presence of class skews. Pruning is often reported in the ML literature as a rule of thumb for dealing with the small disjuncts problem. The conventional wisdom beneath pruning is to perform significance and/or error rate tests aiming

Table 3. AUC and EC results for pruned and unpruned decision trees.

Data set	Pruned Trees		Unpruned Trees	
	AUC	EC	AUC	EC
Sonar	86.71(6.71)	61.51(19.03)	86.71(6.71)	61.51(19.03)
Bupa	79.44(4.51)	66.03(12.36)	79.93(5.02)	65.80(14.04)
Pima	81.53(5.11)	42.03(11.34)	82.33(5.70)	45.41(8.52)
German	78.49(7.75)	52.92(17.22)	85.67(4.37)	87.61(7.72)
Haberman	58.25(12.26)	29.33(22.51)	67.91(13.76)	36.25(20.06)
New-thyroid	94.73(9.24)	33.54(41.78)	94.98(9.38)	33.13(42.64)
E-coli	87.64(15.75)	55.13(36.68)	92.50(7.71)	71.97(26.93)
Satimage	93.73(1.91)	80.97(4.19)	94.82(1.18)	83.75(5.21)
Flag	45.00(15.81)	0.00(0.00)	76.65(27.34)	61.82(39.01)
Glass	88.16(12.28)	56.53(57.38)	88.16(12.28)	56.53(57.38)

to reliably eliminate undesirable disjuncts. The main reason for verifying the effectiveness of pruning is that several research papers indicate that pruning should be avoided when target misclassification costs or class distributions are unknown [13, 14]. One reason to avoid pruning is that most pruning schemes, including the one used by C4.5, attempt to minimize the overall error rate. These pruning schemes can be detrimental to the minority class, since reducing the error rate on the majority class, which stands for most of the examples, would result in a greater impact over the overall error rate. Another fact is that significance tests are mainly based on coverage estimation. As skewed class distributions are more likely to include rare or exceptional cases, it is desirable for the induced concepts to cover these cases, even if they can only be covered by augmenting the number of small disjuncts in a concept.

Table 3 results indicate that the decision of not pruning the decision trees systematically increases the AUC values. For all data sets in which the algorithm was able to prune the induced trees, there is an increase in the AUC values. However, the EC values also increase in almost all unpruned trees. As stated before, this increase in EC values generally means that the errors are more concentrated towards small disjuncts. Furthermore, pruning removes most branches responsible for covering the minority class, thus not pruning is beneficial for learning with imbalanced classes. However, the decision of not pruning also leaves these small disjuncts in the learned concept. As these disjuncts are error-prone, since pruning would remove them, the overall error tends to concentrate on these disjuncts, increasing the EC values. Thus, concerning the problem of pruning or not pruning, a trade-off between the increase we are looking for in the AUC values and the undesirable raise in the EC values seems to exist.

We have also investigated how sampling strategies behave with respect to small disjuncts and class imbalances. We decided to apply the sampling methods until a balanced distribution was reached. This decision is motivated by the results presented in [15], in which it is shown that when AUC is used as performance measure, the best class distribution for learning tends to be near the balanced class distribution. Moreover, Weiss [1] also investigates the relationship between sampling strategies and small disjuncts using a Random under-sampling method to artificially balance training sets. Weiss' results show that the trees

Table 4. AUC and EC results for over-sampled data and unpruned decision trees.

Data set	Random		Smote	
	AUC	EC	AUC	EC
Sonar	86.52(4.69)	47.29(27.24)	86.74(8.91)	52.07(24.63)
Bupa	80.06(3.48)	33.14(26.01)	72.81(9.13)	40.47(23.94)
Pima	86.03(4.14)	57.59(17.65)	85.97(5.82)	52.62(13.18)
German	85.03(4.91)	84.07(4.55)	84.19(5.54)	81.95(12.18)
Haberman	73.58(14.22)	54.66(22.37)	75.45(11.02)	43.15(25.55)
New-thyroid	98.89(2.68)	15.71(40.35)	98.91(1.84)	23.83(38.53)
E-coli	93.55(6.89)	81.93(13.09)	95.49(4.30)	91.48(16.12)
Satimage	95.52(1.12)	86.81(3.23)	95.69(1.28)	90.35(3.02)
Flag	79.78(28.98)	85.47(16.41)	73.87(30.34)	54.73(44.75)
Glass	92.07(12.09)	81.48(22.96)	91.27(8.38)	78.17(30.85)

induced using balanced data sets seem to systematically outperform the trees induced using the original stratified class distribution from the data sets, not only increasing the AUC values but also decreasing the EC values. In our view, the decrease in the EC values might be explained by the reduction in the number of induced disjuncts in the concept description, which is a characteristic of under-sampling methods. We believe this approach might rule out some interesting disjuncts from the concept. Moreover, in previous work [16] we showed that over-sampling methods seem to perform better than under-sampling methods, resulting in classifiers with higher AUC values. Table 4 shows the AUC and EC values for two over-sampling methods proposed in the literature: Random over-sampling and Smote [7]. Random over-sampling randomly duplicates examples from the minority class while Smote introduces artificially generated examples by interpolating two examples drawn from the minority class that lie together.

Table 4 reports results regarding unpruned trees. Besides our previous comments concerning pruning and class imbalance, whether pruning can lead to a performance improvement for decision trees grown over artificially balanced data sets still seems to be an open question. Another argument against pruning is that if pruning is allowed to execute under such conditions, the learning system would prune based on false assumption, *i.e.*, that the test set distribution matches the training set distribution.

The results in Table 4 show that, in general, the best AUC result obtained by an unpruned over-sampled data set is similar (less than 1% difference) or higher than those obtained by pruned and unpruned trees grown over the original data sets. Moreover, unpruned over-sampled data sets also tend to produce higher EC values than pruned and unpruned trees grown over the original data sets. It is also worth noticing that Random over-sampling, which can be considered the simplest method, produced similar results to Smote (with a difference of less than 1% in AUC) in six data sets (Sonar, Pima German, New-thyroid, Satimage and Glass); Random over-sampling beats Smote (with a difference greater than 1%) in two data sets (Bupa and Flag) and Smote beats Random over-sampling in the other two (Haberman and E-coli). Another interesting point is that both over-sampling methods produced lower EC values than unpruned trees grown over the original data for four data sets (Sonar, Bupa, German and New-thyroid),

Table 5. AUC and EC results for over-sampled data: Smote + ENN and Smote + Tomek links and unpruned decision trees.

Data set	Smote + ENN		Smote + Tomek	
	AUC	EC	AUC	EC
Sonar	85.31(11.09)	52.56(28.21)	86.90(9.62)	49.77(17.24)
Bupa	78.84(5.37)	41.72(14.68)	75.35(10.65)	38.39(18.71)
Pima	83.64(5.35)	54.07(19.65)	85.56(6.02)	47.54(21.06)
German	82.76(5.93)	82.21(10.52)	84.40(6.39)	88.53(6.54)
Haberman	77.01(5.10)	62.18(19.08)	78.41(7.11)	43.26(29.39)
New-thyroid	99.22(1.72)	27.39(44.34)	98.91(1.84)	23.83(38.53)
E-coli	95.29(3.79)	87.58(18.36)	95.98(4.21)	90.92(16.17)
Satimage	96.06(1.20)	88.56(3.31)	95.69(1.28)	90.35(3.02)
Flag	78.56(28.79)	78.78(20.59)	82.06(29.52)	70.55(38.54)
Glass	93.40(7.61)	80.14(30.72)	91.27(8.38)	78.17(30.85)

and Smote itself produced lower EC values for another one (Flag). Moreover, in three data sets (Sonar, Bupa and New-thyroid) Smote produced lower EC values even if compared with pruned trees grown over the original data.

These results might be explained observing that by using an interpolation method, Smote might help in the definition of the decision border of each class. However, as a side effect, by introducing artificially generated examples Smote might introduce noise in the training set. Although Smote might help in overcoming the class imbalance problem, in some cases it might be detrimental regarding the problem of small disjuncts. This observation, allied to the results we obtained in a previous study that poses class overlapping as a complicating factor for dealing with class imbalance [8] motivated us to propose two new methods to deal with the problem of learning in the presence of class imbalance [16]. These methods ally Smote [7] with two data cleaning methods: Tomek links [17] and Wilson's Edited Nearest Neighbor Rule (ENN) [18]. The main motivation behind these methods is to pick up the best of the two worlds. We not only balance the training data aiming at increasing the AUC values, but also remove noisy examples lying in the wrong side of the decision border. The removal of noisy examples might aid in finding better-defined class clusters, allowing the creation of simpler models with better generalization capabilities. As a net effect, these methods might also remove some undesirable small disjuncts, improving the classifier performance. In this matter, these data cleaning methods might be understood as an alternative for pruning.

Table 5 shows the results of our proposed methods on the same data sets. Comparing these two methods it can be observed that Smote + Tomek produced the higher AUC values for four data sets (Sonar, Pima, German and Haberman) while Smote+ENN is better in two data sets (Bupa and Glass). For the other four data sets they produced compatible AUC results (with a difference lower than 1%). However, it should be observed that for three data sets (New-thyroid, Satimage and Glass) Smote+Tomek obtained results identical to Smote – Table 4. This occurs when no Tomek links or just a few of them are found in the data sets.

Table 6 shows a ranking of the AUC and EC results obtained in all experiments for unpruned decision trees, where: O indicates the original data set

Table 6. AUC and EC ranking results for unpruned decision trees.

Data sets	AUC					EC				
	O	R	S	S+E	S+T	O	R	S	S+E	S+T
Sonar	$\surd_1$	$\surd_1$	$\surd_1$	$\surd_2$	$\surd_1$		$\surd_1$			$\surd_2$
Bupa	$\surd_1$	$\surd_1$	$\surd_2$				$\surd_1$			$\surd_2$
Pima		$\surd_1$	$\surd_1$	$\surd_2$	$\surd_1$	$\surd_1$				$\surd_2$
German	$\surd_1$	$\surd_1$		$\surd_2$	$\surd_2$	$\surd_2$	$\surd_1$		$\surd_1$	
Haberman			$\surd_2$	$\surd_1$		$\surd_1$		$\surd_2$		$\surd_2$
New-thyroid	$\surd_2$	$\surd_1$	$\surd_1$	$\surd_1$	$\surd_1$		$\surd_1$	$\surd_2$		$\surd_2$
E-coli		$\surd_2$	$\surd_1$	$\surd_1$	$\surd_1$	$\surd_1$	$\surd_2$			
Satimage	$\surd_2$	$\surd_1$	$\surd_1$	$\surd_1$	$\surd_1$	$\surd_1$	$\surd_2$			
Flag		$\surd_2$		$\surd_1$		$\surd_2$		$\surd_1$		
Glass		$\surd_2$	$\surd_2$	$\surd_1$	$\surd_2$	$\surd_1$		$\surd_2$		$\surd_2$

(Table 3) R and S stand respectively for Random and Smote over-sampling (Table 4) while S+E and S+T stand for Smote + ENN and Smote + Tomek (Table 5). $\surd_1$ indicates that the method is ranked among the best and $\surd_2$ among the second best for the corresponding data set. Observe that results having a difference lower than 1% are ranked together. Although the proposed conjugated over-sampling methods obtained just one EC value ranked in the first place (Smote + ENN on data set German) these methods provided the highest AUC values in seven data sets. Smote + Tomek produced the highest AUC values in four data sets (Sonar, Haberman, Ecoli and Flag), and the Smote + ENN method produced the highest AUC values in another three data sets (Satimage, New-thyroid and Glass). If we analyze both measures together, in four data sets where Smote + Tomek produced results among the top ranked AUC values, it is also in second place with regard to lower EC values (Sonar, Pima, Haberman and New-thyroid). However, it is worth noticing in Table 6 that simpler methods, such as the Random over-sampling approach (R) or taking only the unpruned tree (O), have also produced interesting results in some data sets. In the New-thyroid data set, Random over-sampling produced one of the highest AUC values and the lowest EC value. In the German data set, the unpruned tree produced the highest AUC value, and the EC value is almost the same as in the other methods that produced high AUC values. Nevertheless, the results we report suggest that the methods we propose in [16] might be useful, specially if we aim to further analyze the induced disjuncts that compound the concept description.

5 Conclusion

In this work we discuss results related to some aspects of the interaction between learning with class imbalances and small disjuncts. Our results suggest that pruning might not be effective for dealing with small disjuncts in the presence of class skews. Moreover, artificially balancing class distributions with over-sampling methods seems to increase the number of error-prone small disjuncts. Our proposed methods, which ally over sampling with data cleaning methods produced meaningful results in some cases. Conversely, in some cases, Random over-sampling, a very simple over-sampling method, also achieved compatible results. Although our results are not conclusive with respect to a general approach for dealing with both problems, further investigation into this relationship might help to produce insights on how ML algorithms behave in the presence of such conditions. In order to investigate this relationship in more depth, several further approaches might be taken. A natural extension of this work is to individually analyze the disjuncts that compound each description assessing their quality concerning some objective or subjective criterium. Another interesting topic is to analyze the ROC and EC graphs obtained for each data set and method. This might provide us with a more in depth understanding of the behavior of pruning and balancing methods. Last but not least, another interesting point to investigate is how alternative learning bias behaves in the presence of class skews.

Acknowledgements

We wish to thank the anonymous reviewers for their helpful comments. This research was partially supported by the Brazilian Research Councils CAPES and FAPESP.

References

1. Weiss, G.M.: The Effect of Small Disjuncts and Class Distribution on Decision Tree Learning. PhD thesis, Rutgers University (2003)
2. Japkowicz, N.: Class Imbalances: Are we Focusing on the Right Issue? In: ICML Workshop on Learning from Imbalanced Data Sets. (2003)
3. Holte, R.C., Acker, L.E., Porter, B.W.: Concept Learning and the Problem of Small Disjuncts. In: IJCAI. (1989) 813–818
4. Weiss, G.M.: The problem with Noise and Small Disjuncts. In: ICML. (1988) 574–578
5. Carvalho, D.R., Freitas, A.A.: A Hybrid Decision Tree/Genetic Algorithm for Coping with the Problem of Small Disjuncts in Data Mining. In: Genetic and Evolutionary Computation Conference. (2000) 1061–1068
6. Kubat, M., Matwin, S.: Addressing the Course of Imbalanced Training Sets: One-Sided Selection. In: ICML. (1997) 179–186
7. Chawla, N.V., Bowyer, K.W., Hall, L.O., Kegelmeyer, W.P.: SMOTE: Synthetic Minority Over-sampling Technique. JAIR 16 (2002) 321–357
8. Prati, R.C., Batista, G.E.A.P.A., Monard, M.C.: Class Imbalances *versus* Class Overlapping: an Analysis of a Learning System Behavior. In: MICAI. (2004) 312–321 Springer-Verlag, LNAI 2972.
9. Weiss, G.M.: Learning with Rare Cases and Small Disjucts. In: ICML. (1995) 558–565
10. Ferri, C., Flach, P., Hernández-Orallo, J.: Learning Decision Trees Using the Area Under the ROC Curve. In: ICML. (2002) 139–146
11. Blake, C., Merz, C.: UCI Repository of Machine Learning Databases (1998) http://www.ics.uci.edu/~mlearn/MLRepository.html.
12. Quinlan, J.R.: C4.5 Programs for Machine Learning. Morgan Kaufmann (1993)

13. Zadrozny, B., Elkan, C.: Learning and Making Decisions When Costs and Probabilities are Both Unknown. In: KDD. (2001) 204–213
14. Bauer, E., Kohavi, R.: An Empirical Comparison of Voting Classification Algorithms: Bagging, Boosting, and Variants. Machine Learning **36** (1999) 105–139
15. Weiss, G.M., Provost, F.: Learning When Training Data are Costly: The Effect of Class Distribution on Tree Induction. JAIR **19** (2003) 315–354
16. Batista, G.E.A.P.A., Prati, R.C., Monard, M.C.: A Study of the Behavior of Several Methods for Balancing Machine Learning Training Data. SIGKDD Explorations **6** (2004) (to appear).
17. Tomek, I.: Two Modifications of CNN. IEEE Transactions on Systems Man and Communications **SMC-6** (1976) 769–772
18. Wilson, D.L.: Asymptotic Properties of Nearest Neighbor Rules Using Edited Data. IEEE Transactions on Systems, Man, and Communications **2** (1972) 408–421

Making Collaborative Group Recommendations Based on Modal Symbolic Data*

Sérgio R. de M. Queiroz and Francisco de A.T. de Carvalho

Centro de Informática (CIn/UFPE) Cx. Postal 7851, CEP 50732-970, Recife, Brazil
{srmq,fatc}@cin.ufpe.br

Abstract. In recent years, recommender systems have achieved great success. Popular sites give thousands of recommendations every day. However, despite the fact that many activities are carried out in groups, like going to the theater with friends, these systems are focused on recommending items for sole users. This brings out the need of systems capable of performing recommendations for groups of people, a domain that has received little attention in the literature. In this article we introduce a novel method of making collaborative recommendations for groups, based on models built using techniques from symbolic data analysis. After, we empirically evaluate the proposed method to see its behaviour for groups of different sizes and degrees of homogeneity, and compare the achieved results with both an aggregation-based methodology previously proposed and a baseline methodology.

1 Introduction

You arrive at home and turn on your cable TV. There are 150 channels to choose from. How can you quickly find a program that will likely interest you? When one has to make a choice without full knowledge of the alternatives, a common approach is to rely on the recommendations of trusted individuals: a TV guide, a friend, a consulting agency. In the 1990s, computational *recommender systems* appeared to automatize the recommendation process. Nowadays, we have (mostly in the Web) various recommender systems. Popular sites, like *Amazon.com*, have recommendation areas where users can see which items would be of their interest.

One of the most successfully technologies used by these systems has been *collaborative filtering* (CF) (see e.g. [1]). The CF technique is based on the assumption that the best recommendations for an individual are those given by people with preferences similar to his/her preferences.

However, until now, these systems have focused only on making recommendations for individuals, despite the fact that many day-to-day activities are performed in groups (e.g. watching TV at home). This highlights the need of developing recommender systems for groups, that are able to capture the preferences of whole groups and make recommendations for them.

---

* The authors would like to thank CNPq and CAPES (Brazilian Agencies) for their financial support.

A.L.C. Bazzan and S. Labidi (Eds.): SBIA 2004, LNAI 3171, pp. 307–316, 2004.

When recommending for groups, the utmost goal is that the recommendations should be the best possible for the group. Thus, two prime questions are raised: *What is the best suggestion for a group? How to reach this suggestion?*

The concept of making recommendations for groups has received little attention in the literature of recommender systems. A few works have developed recommender systems capable of recommending for groups ([2–4]), but none of them have delved into the difficulties involving the achievement of good recommendation for groups (i.e., the two fundamental questions previously cited).

Although little about this topic has been studied in the literature of recommender systems, how to achieve good group results from individual preferences is an important topic in many research areas, with different roots. Beginning in the XVIII century motivated by the problem of voting, to modern research areas like operational research, social choice, multicriteria decision making and social psychology, this topic has been treated by diverse research communities.

Developments in these research fields are important for a better understanding of the problem and the identification of the limitations of proposed solutions; as well as to the development of recommender systems that achieve similar results to the ones groups of people would achieve during a discussion.

A conclusion that can be drawn from these areas is that there is no "perfect" way to aggregate individual preferences in order to achieve a group result. Arrow's impossibility theorem [5] which showed that it is impossible for any procedure (termed a social function in social choice parlance) to achieve at the same time a set of simple desirable properties is but one of the most known results in social choice to show that an ideal social function is unattainable. Furthermore, many empirical studies in social psychology have noted that the adequacy of a decision scheme (the mechanism used by a group of people to combine the individual preferences of its members into the group result) to the group decision process is very dependent to the group's intrinsic characteristics and the problem's nature (see e.g. [6]). Multi-criteria decision making strengthens the view that the achievement of an "ideal configuration" is not the most important feature when working with decisions (in fact, this ideal may not exist in most of the times) and highlights the importance of giving the users interactivity and permit the analysis of different possibilities.

However, the nonexistence of an ideal does not mean that we cannot compare different possibilities. Based on good properties that a preference aggregation scheme should have, we can define meaningful metrics to quantify the goodness of group recommendations. They will not be completely free of value judgments, but these will reflect desirable properties.

In this article we introduce a novel method of making recommendations for groups, based on the ideas of collaborative filtering and symbolic data analysis [7]. To be used to recommend for groups, the CF methodology has to be adapted. We can think of two different ways to modify it with this goal. The first is to use CF to recommend to the individual members of the group, and then aggregate the recommendations in order to achieve the recommendation for the group as a whole (we will call this approaches "aggregation-based methodologies"). The second is to modify the CF process so that it directly generates a recommendation for the group. This involves the modeling of the group as a single entity, a meta-user (we will call this approaches "model-based methodologies"). Here we take the second approach, using techniques from symbolic data analysis to model the users. After, we experimentally evaluate the proposed method to see its behaviour under groups of different sizes and degrees of homogeneity. For each group configuration the behaviour of the proposed method is compared with both an aggregation-based methodology we have previously proposed (see [8]) and a baseline methodology. The metric used reflects good social characteristics for the group recommendations.

2   Recommending for Groups

2.1   The Problem

The problem of recommendations for groups can be posed as follows: *how to suggest (new) items that will be liked by the group as a whole, given that we have a set of historical individual preferences from the members of this group as well as preferences from other individuals (who are not in the group).*

Thinking collaboratively, we want to know how to use the preferences (evaluations over items) of the individuals in the system to predict how one group of individuals (a subset of the community) will like the items available. Thence, we would be able to suggest items that will be valuable for this group.

2.2   Symbolic Model-Based Approach

In this section we develop a model-based recommendation strategy for groups. During the recommendation process, it uses models for the items – which can be pre-computed – and does not require the computation of on-line user neighborhoods, not having this scalability problem present in many collaborative filtering algorithms (for individuals). To create the models and compare them techniques from symbolic data analysis are used.

The intuition behind our approach is that for each item we can identify the group of people who like it and the group of people that do not like it. We assume that the group for which we will make a recommendation will appreciate an item if the group has similar preferences to the group of people who like the item and is dissimilar to the group of people who do not like it.

To implement this, first the group of users for whom the recommendations will be computed is represented by a prototype that contains the histogram of rates for each item evaluated by the group. The target items (items that can be recommended) are also represented in a similar way, but now we create two prototypes for each target item: a positive prototype, that contains the histogram of rates for (other) items evaluated by individuals who liked the target item; and a negative prototype that is analogous to the positive one, but the individuals chosen are those who did not like the target item. Next we compute the similarity between the group prototype and the two prototypes of each target item. The final similarity between a target item and a group is given by a simple linear combination of the similarities between the group prototype and both item prototypes using the formula: $sim_f = \frac{sim_{pos}+1-sim_{neg}}{2}$, where sim_f is the final similarity value, sim_{pos} is the similarity between the group prototype and the positive item prototype and sim_{neg} analogously for the negative one. Finally, we order the target items by decreasing order of similarity values. If we want to recommend k items to the users, we can take the first k items of this ordering. Figure 1 depicts the recommendation process. Its two main aspects, the creation of prototypes and the similarity computation will be described in the following subsections.

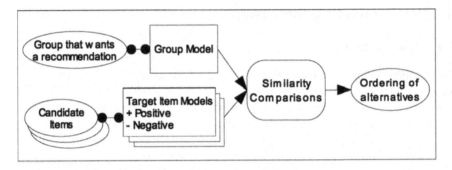

Fig. 1. The recommendation process

Prototype Generation. A fundamental step of this method is the prototype generation. The group and the target items are represented by the histograms of rates for items. Different weights can be attributed to each histogram that make up the prototypes. In other words, each prototype is described by a set of p symbolic variables Y_j. Each item corresponds to a categorical modal variable Y_j that may also have an associated weight. The modalities of Y_j are the different rates that can be given to items. In our case, we have six modalities.

Group Prototype. In the group prototype we have the rate histograms for every item that has been evaluated by at least one member of the group. The rate histogram is built by computing the frequency of each modality in the ratings of the group members for the item being considered. The used data has a discrete set of 6 rates: $\{0.0, 0.2, 0.4, 0.6, 0.8, 1.0\}$, where 0.0 is the worst and 1.0 is the best rate. For example, if an item i_1 was evaluated by 2 users in a group of 3 individuals and they gave the ratings 0.4 and 0.6 for the item, the row in the symbolic data table corresponding to the item would be: $\{i_1, \{0.0,0.0,0.5,0.5,0.0,0.0\}, 0.667\}$, assuming the weight as the fraction of the group that has evaluated the item.

Item Prototypes. To build a prototype for a target item, the first step is to decide which users will be selected to have their evaluations in the prototype. This users have the role of characterizing the profile of those who like the target item, for the positive profile; and of characterizing the profile of those who do not like the target item, for the negative profile. Therefrom, for the positive prototype only the users that evaluated the target item highly are chosen. Users that have given rates 0.8 or 1.0 were chosen as the "positive representatives" for the group. For the negative prototype the users that have given 0.0 or 0.2 for the target item were chosen. One parameter for the building of the models is how many users will be chosen for each target item. We have chosen 300 users for each prototype, after experimenting with 30, 50, 100, 200 and 300 users.

Similarity Calculation. To compute the similarity between the prototype of a group and the prototype of a target item, we only consider the items that are in both prototypes. As similarity measure we tried Bacelar-Nicolau's weighted affinity coefficient (presented in [7]) and two measures based on the Euclidean distance and the Pearson correlation, respectively. At the end we used the affinity coefficient, as it achieved slightly better results. The similarity between two prototypes k and k' based on the affinity coefficient is given by:

$$\text{protsim}(k, k') = \sum_{j=1}^{p} w_j \times \sum_{l=1}^{m_j} \sqrt{n_{kjl} \times n_{k'jl}} \tag{1}$$

where:

- p is the number of items present in both prototypes;
- w_j is the weight attributed to item j;
- m_j is the number of modalities (six, for the six different rates);
- n_{kjl} and $n_{k'jl}$ are the relative frequencies obtained by rate l in the prototypes k and k' for the item j, respectively.

3 Experimental Evaluation

We carried on the experiments with the same groups that were used in [8]. To make this article more self-contained, we describe in the next subsections how these groups were generated.

3.1 The EachMovie Dataset

To run our experiments, we used the Eachmovie dataset. Eachmovie was a recommender service that run as part of a research project at the Compaq Systems Research Center. During that period, 72,916 users gave 2,811,983 evaluations to 1,628 different movies. Users' evaluations were registered using a 6-level numerical scale (0.0, 0.2, 0.4, 0.6, 0.8, 1.0). The dataset can be obtained from Compaq Computer Corporation[1]. The Eachmovie dataset has been used in various experiments involving recommender systems.

We restricted our experiments to users that have evaluated at least 150 movies (2,551 users). This was adopted to allow an intersection (of evaluated movies) of reasonable size between each pair of users, so that more credit can be given to the comparisons related to the homogeneity degree of a group.

---

[1] Available at the URL: http://www.research.compaq.com/SRC/eachmovie/

3.2   Data Preparation: The Creation of Groups

To conduct the experiments, groups of users with varying sizes and homogeneity degrees were needed. The EachMovie dataset is only about individuals, therefore it was needed to build the groups first.

Four group sizes were defined: 3, 6, 12 and 24 individuals. We believe that this range of sizes includes the majority of scenarios where recommendation for groups can be used. For the degree of homogeneity factor, 3 levels were used: high, medium and low homogeneity. The groups don't need to be a partition of the set of users, i.e. the same user can be in more than one different group. The next subsections describe the methodology used to build the groups.

Obtaining a Dissimilarity Matrix. The first step in the group definition was to build a dissimilarity matrix for the users. That is, a matrix m of size $n \times n$ (n is the number of users) where each m_{ij} contains the dissimilarity value between users i and j. To obtain this matrix, the dissimilarity of each user against all the others was calculated.

The dissimilarities between users will be subsequently used to construct the groups with the three desired homogeneity degrees. To obtain the dissimilarity between two users i and j, we calculated the Pearson correlation coefficient ρ_{ij} between them (which is in the interval $[-1, 1]$) and transformed this value into a dissimilarity using the formula: $\operatorname{dissim}(i, j) = 1 - (\rho_{ij} + 1)/2$. The Pearson correlation coefficient is the most common measure of similarity between users used in collaborative filtering algorithms (see e.g. [1]). To compute ρ_{ij} between two users we consider only the items x that both users have rated and use the formula: $\rho_{ij} = \dfrac{\sum_x (i_x - \bar{i})(j_x - \bar{j})}{\sqrt{\sum_x (i_x - \bar{i})^2}\sqrt{\sum_x (j_x - \bar{j})^2}}$, where i_x is the rate that user i has given for item x and $\bar{i}$ is the average rate (over the items x) for user i (analogously for user j).

For our experiments, the movies were randomly separated in three sets: a profile set with 50% of the movies, a training set with 25% and a test set with 25% of the movies. Only the user's evaluations which refer to elements of the first set were used to obtain the dissimilarity matrix. The evaluations that refer to movies of the other sets were not used at this stage. The rationale behind this procedure is that the movies from the test set will be the ones used to evaluate the behavior of the model (Section 3.3). That is, it will be assumed that the members of the group did not know them previously. The movies from the training set were used to adjust the model parameters.

Group Formation

High Homogeneity Groups. We wanted to obtain 100 groups with high homogeneity degree for each of the desired sizes. To this end, we first randomly generated 100 groups of 200 users each. Then the hierarchical clustering algorithm divisive analysis (diana) was run for each of these 100 groups. To extract a high homogeneity group of size n from each tree, we took the "lowest" branch with at least n elements. If the number of elements of this branch was larger than

n we tested all combinations of size n and selected the one with lowest total dissimilarity (sum of all dissimilarities between the n users). For groups of size 24, the number of combinations was too big. In this case we used a heuristic method, selecting the n users which have the lowest sum of dissimilarities in the branch (sum of dissimilarities between the user in consideration and all others in the branch).

Low Homogeneity Groups. To select a group of size n with low homogeneity from one of the groups with 200 users, we first calculated for each user its sum of dissimilarities (between this user and all the other 199). The n elements selected were the ones with the n largest sum of dissimilarities.

Medium Homogeneity Groups. To select a group of size n with medium homogeneity degree, n elements were randomly selected from the total population of users. To avoid surprises due to randomness, after a group was generated, a test to compare a single mean (the one of the extracted group) to a specified value (the mean of the population) was done (using $\alpha = 0.05$).

3.3   Experimental Methodology

For each of the 1200 generated groups (4 sizes $\times$ 3 homogeneities $\times$ 100 repetitions) recommendations for items from the test set were generated. We also generated recommendations using two other strategies: a baseline model, inspired by a "null model" used in group experiments in social psychology (e.g. [6]); and an aggregation-based method using fuzzy majority we have previously proposed in [8].

Null Model. The null model takes the opinion of one randomly chosen group member as the group decision (random dictator). Taking this to the domain of recommender systems, we randomly selected one group member and make recommendations for this individual (using traditional neighbourhood-based collaborative filtering). These recommendations are taken as the group recommendations.

Aggregation-Based Method Using Fuzzy Majority. This method works in two steps: first individual recommendations are generated for the members of the group, and after the individual recommendations are aggregated to make the group recommendation.

For the first step, a traditional neighborhood-based collaborative filtering algorithm was used (see [8] for the details). For the second one, a classification method of alternatives using fuzzy majority (introduced in [9]) was adopted. The rationale for using a method based on fuzzy majority for the aggregation of recommendations was that given the impossibility of having an ideal method for the aggregation, one that offered some degree of "human meaning" was a good choice. The kind of human meaning of the fuzzy majority aggregation is provided by the use of fuzzy linguistic operators that model the human discourse (like *as many as possible*, *most* and *at least half*). This could make possible to the users specify in what general terms they would like the aggregation, for example: "show me the alternatives that are 'better' than *most* of the others according to the recommendations for *as many as possible* persons in the group".

The fuzzy majority procedure follows two phases to achieve the classification of alternatives: *aggregation* and *exploitation*. The aggregation phase defines an outranking relation which indicates the global preference (in a fuzzy majority sense) between every pair of alternatives, taking into consideration different points of view. Exploitation compares the alternatives, transforming the global preference information into a global ranking, thus supplying a selection set of alternatives. Each phase uses a fuzzy linguistic operator, resulting in a classification of alternatives with an interpretation like the one cited in the previous paragraph (assuming that the operator *as many as possible* was used in the aggregation phase and the operator *most* in the exploitation phase).

Evaluating the Strategies. To evaluate the behaviour of the strategies for the various sizes and degrees of homogeneity of the groups, a metric is needed. As we have a set of rankings as the input and a ranking as the output, a ranking correlation method was considered a good candidate. We used the Kendall's rank correlation coefficient (τ) with ties (see [10]). For each generated recommendation, we calculated τ between the final ranking generated for the group and the users' individual rankings (obtained from the users' rates available in the test set). Then we calculated the average τ, for the recommendation. The $\bar{\tau}$ has a good social characteristic. One ranking with largest $\bar{\tau}$ is a Kemeny optimal aggregation (it is not necessarily unique). Kemeny optimal aggregations are the only ones that fulfill at the same time the principles of neutrality and consistency of the social choice literature and the extended Condorcet criterion [11], which is: if a majority of the individuals prefer alternative a to b, then a should have a higher ranking than b in the aggregation. Kemeny optimal aggregations are NP-hard to obtain when the number of rankings to aggregate is ≥ 4 [11]. Therefore, it is not possible to implement an optimal strategy in regard of the $\bar{\tau}$, making it a good reference for comparison.

The goal of the experiment was to evaluate how $\bar{\tau}$ is affected by the variation on the size and homogeneity of the groups, as well as by the strategy used (symbolic approach *versus* null model *versus* fuzzy aggregation-based approach). To verify the influence of each factor, we did a three-way (as we have 3 factors) analysis of variance (ANOVA). After the verification of significant relevance, a comparison of means for the levels of each factor was done. To this end we used Tukey Honest Significant Differences test at the 95% confidence level.

4   Results and Discussion

Figure 2 shows the observed $\bar{\tau}$'s for the three approaches.

For low homogeneity groups, the symbolic approach outperformed by a large difference the other two in groups of 3 and 6 people (in these configurations

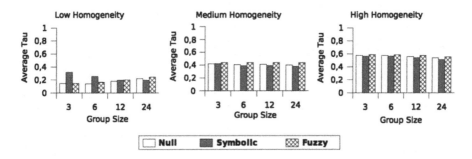

Fig. 2. Observed $\bar{\tau}$'s by homogeneity degree for the null, symbolic and fuzzy approaches. Fuzzy results refer to the use of the linguistic quantifiers *as many as possible* followed by *most*. Other combinations of quantifiers achieved similar results.

the null model was statistically equivalent to the fuzzy approach). This shows that for highly heterogeneous groups, trying to aggregate individual preferences is not a good approach. All results were statistically equivalent for groups of 12 people, and the fuzzy approach had a better result for groups of 24 people, followed by the null model and the symbolic approach. It is not clear if the symbolic model is inadequate for larger heterogeneous groups, or if this result is due to the biases present in the data used. Due to the process of group formation, larger heterogeneous groups (even in the same homogeneity degree) are more homogeneous than smaller groups, as it is much more difficult to find a large strongly heterogeneous group than it is to find a smaller one. Experiments using synthetic data where the homogeneity degree was more carefully controlled would be more useful to do this comparisons.

Under medium and high homogeneity levels, the null model shows that for more homogeneous groups it may be a good alternative. Under medium homogeneity, it was statistically equivalent to the other two for groups of 3 people and second-placed after the fuzzy approach for the other group sizes. Under high homogeneity, the null model was statistically equivalent to the fuzzy approach for all group sizes (indicating that taking the opinion of just one member of a highly homogeneous group is good enough) and the symbolic approach lagged behind (by a small margin) in these cases. This suggests that the symbolic strategy should be improved to better accommodate these cases, as well that aggregation-based approaches have a good performance for more homogeneous groups.

Making comparisons for the factor homogeneity, in all cases the averages of the levels differed significantly. Besides, we had: average tau under high homogeneity > avg. tau under medium homogeneity > avg. tau under low homogeneity, i.e. the compatibility degree between the group recommendation and the individual preferences was proportional to the group's homogeneity degree. These facts were to be expected if the strategies were coherent.

For the group size, in many cases the differences between its levels were not significant, indicating that the size of a group is less important than its homogeneity degree for the performance of recommendations.

References

1. Herlocker, J., Konstan, J., Borchers, A., Riedl, J.: An algorithm framework for performing collaborative filtering. In: Proc. of the 22nd ACM SIGIR Conference, Berkley (1999) 230–237
2. Hill, W., Stead, L., Rosenstein, M., Furnas, G.: Recommending and evaluating choices in a virtual community of use. In: Proc. of the ACM CHI'95 Conference, Denver (1995) 194–201
3. Lieberman, H., Van Dyke, N., Vivacqua, A.: Let's browse: A collaborative web browsing agent. In: Proc. of the IUI-99, L.A. (1999) 65–68
4. O'Connor, M., Cosley, D., Konstan, J., Riedl, J.: Polylens: A recommender system for groups of users. In: Proc. of the 7th ECSCW conference, Bonn (2001) 199–218
5. Arrow, K.J.: Social Choice and Individual Values. Wiley, New York (1963)
6. Hinsz, V.: Group decision making with responses of a quantitative nature: The theory of social schemes for quantities. Organizational Behavior and Human Decision Processes **80** (1999) 28–49
7. Bock, H., Diday, E.: Analysis of Symbolic Data: Exploratory Methods for Extracting Statistical Information from Complex Data. Springer, Berlin Heidelberg (2000)
8. Queiroz, S., De Carvalho, F., Ramalho, G., Corruble, V.: Making recommendations for groups using collaborative filtering and fuzzy majority. In: Proc. of the 16th Brazilian Symposium on Artificial Intelligence (SBIA), LNAI 2507, Recife (2002) 248–258
9. Chiclana, F., Herrera, F., Herrera-Viedma, E., Poyatos, M.: A classification method of alternatives for multiple preference ordering criteria based on fuzzy majority. Journal of Fuzzy Mathematics **4** (1996) 801–813
10. Kendall, M.: Rank Correlation Methods. 4th edn. Charles Griffin & Company, London (1975)
11. Dwork, C., Kumar, R., Moni, N., Sivakumar, D.: Rank aggregation methods for the web. In: Proc. of the WWW10 Conference, Hong Kong (2001) 613–622

Search-Based Class Discretization for Hidden Markov Model for Regression

Kate Revoredo and Gerson Zaverucha

Programa de Engenharia de Sistemas e Computação(COPPE)
Universidade Federal do Rio de Janeiro
Caixa Postal 68511, 21945-970, Rio de Janeiro, RJ, Brasil
{kate,gerson}@cos.ufrj.br

Abstract. The regression-by-discretization approach allows the use of classification algorithm in a regression task. It works as a pre-processing step in which the numeric target value is discretized into a set of intervals. We had applied this approach to the Hidden Markov Model for Regression (HMMR) which was successfully compared to the Naive Bayes for Regression and two traditional forecasting methods, Box-Jenkins and Winters. In this work, to further improve these results, we apply three discretization methods to HMMR using ten time series data sets. The experimental results showed that one of the discretization methods improved the results in most of the data sets, although each method improved the results in at least one data set. Therefore, it would be better to have a search algorithm to automatically find the optimal number and width of the intervals.

Keyword: Hidden Markov Models, regression-by-discretization, time-series forecasting, machine learning

1 Introduction

As discussed in [5], the effective handling of continuous variables is a central problem in machine learning and pattern recognition. In statistics and pattern recognition the typical approach is to use a parametric family of distributions, which makes strong assumptions about the nature of the data; the induced model can be a good approximation of the data, if these assumptions are warranted. Machine learning, on the other hand, deal with continuous variables by discretizing them, which can lead to information loss. When the continuous variable is the target this approach is known as regression-by-discretization [13, 4, 15, 14], which allows the use of more comprehensible models.

Naive Bayes for Regression (NBR) [4] uses the regression-by-discretization approach in order to apply Naive Bayes Classifier (NBC) [3] to predict numerical values. In [4], it was pointed out that NBR "...performed comparably to well known methods for time series predictions and sometime even slightly better.". In [2], it was argued that although in the theory of supervised learning the training examples are assumed independent and identically distributed (i.i.d), this is not the case in applications where a temporal dependence among the examples

A.L.C. Bazzan and S. Labidi (Eds.): SBIA 2004, LNAI 3171, pp. 317–325, 2004.

exists. An example was given in [2] for a classification task comparing NBC and Hidden Markov Model (HMM). While NBC ignored temporal dependence HMM took it into account. Consequently, HMM performed better than NBC. Similar results were found in [10] when Hidden Markov Model for Regression (HMMR), using the regression-by-discretization approach, was applied to the task of monthly electric load forecasting of real world data from Brazilian utilities and successfully compared to NBR and two traditional forecasting methods, Box-Jenkins[1] and Winters [7].

In this work, to further improve these results we apply to HMMR the three alternative ways of transforming a set of continuous values into a set of intervals described in [13] using ten time series data sets.

The paper is organized as follows. In section 2 HMM, HMMR and misclassification cost are reviewed and the methods used for discretizing the numeric target value are described. In section 3 the experimental results are presented. Finally, in section 4 our work is concluded.

2   Background Knowledge

Throughout this paper, we use capital letters, such as Y and Z, for random variables names and lowercase letters such as y and z to denote specific values assumed by them. Sets of variables are denoted by boldface capital letters such as $\mathbf{Y}$ and $\mathbf{Z}$, and assignments of values to the variables in these sets are denoted by boldface lowercase letters such as $\mathbf{y}$ and $\mathbf{z}$. The probability of a possible value of a random variable is denoted by $p(.)$, and the probability distribution of a random variable is denoted by $\mathbf{p}(.)$; this can be generalized for sets of variables.

2.1   Discretization Methods

A discretization method divides a set of numerical values into a set of intervals. Three discretization methods are described as follows:

- Equal width intervals (EW): the set of numerical values is divided into equal width intervals.
- Equal probable intervals (EP): the set of intervals is created with the same number of elements. It can be said that this method has the focus on class frequencies and that it makes the assumption that equal class frequencies is best for a classification problem.
- K-means clustering (KM): this method starts with the EW approximation and then moves the elements of each interval to contiguous intervals if these changes reduce the sum of the distances of each element of an interval to its gravity center[1]. Each interval must have at least one element.

Table 1 shows the intervals found for these three methods considering that the best number of intervals is 5 when applied to the task of monthly electric load forecasting using real world data from Brazilian utilities (Serie 1).

---

[1] We used the median of the elements in each interval as the gravity center.

Table 1. Intervals found by the three discretization methods

Method	Intervals
EW	[0.0...0.2) [0.2...0.4) [0.4...0.6) [0.6...0.8) [0.8...1.0]
EP	[0.0...0.44) [0.44...0.53) [0.53...0.59) [0.59...0.65) [0.65...1.0]
KM	[0.0...0.40) [0.40...0.49) [0.49...0.57) [0.57...0.65) [0.65...1.0]

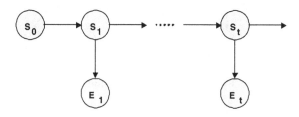

Fig. 1. First-order Dynamic Bayesian Network

2.2   Hidden Markov Model

For a classification task, as discussed in section 1, if the training examples have a temporal dependence then HMM performs better than NBC. HMM is a particular Dynamic Bayesian Network (DBN) [6, 8, 9]. A DBN is a Bayesian Network (BN) that represents a temporal probability model like the one seen in figure 1: in each slice, $\mathbf{S_t}$ is a set of hidden state variables (discrete or continuous) and $\mathbf{E_t}$ is a set of evidence variables (discrete or continuous). Two important inference tasks in a DBN are: filtering (computes $\mathbf{p(S_t|e_{1:t})}$, where $\mathbf{p}(.)$ is a probability distribution of the random variables and $\mathbf{e}_{1:t}$ denotes $(\mathbf{e}_1, ..., \mathbf{e}_t)$) and smoothing (computes $\mathbf{p(S_k|e_{1:t})}$, for $1 < k < t$). Normally, it is assumed that the parameters do not change, that is, the model is time-invariant (stationary): $\mathbf{p(S_t|S_{t-1})}$ and $\mathbf{p(E_t|S_t)}$ are the same for all t. In the HMM, each $\mathbf{S}_t$ is a single discrete random variable.

For a classification task if the training examples are fully observable, have a temporal dependence such that each $\mathbf{S}_t$ is observed in the training data and hidden (and hence predicted) in the test data and the model structure is known we can use Maximum Likelihood (ML) Estimation (we do not need to use EM [6]) for learning.

In order to use this approach in HMM, each example is given by a class v_t (representing S_t) and a conjunction of attributes $[a_{t,1}, a_{t,2}, ..., a_{t,m}] = \mathbf{a_t}$ (representing $\mathbf{e}_t$) (see figure 2). Additionally, it is also assumed that the attributes are conditionally independent given the class. The ML estimation for the HMM must compute the probabilities, using the formulas showed in 1, by counting the discrete values from the training examples. For each $v_{t-1} \in dom(V)$, $v_t \in dom(V)$ and $a_{t,j} \in dom(A_j)(j = 1, ..., m)$ we compute

$$p(v_t) = \frac{N(v_t)}{N} \quad p(a_{t,j}|v_t) = \frac{N(a_{t,j}, v_t)}{N(v_t)} \quad p(v_t|v_{t-1}) = \frac{N(v_t, v_{t-1})}{N(v_{t-1})} \quad (1)$$

where N is the total number of training examples, $N(v_t)$ is the number of training examples with the class "v_t", and $N(a_{t,j}, v_t)$ is the number of training examples with the attribute "$a_{t,j}$" and the class "v_t".

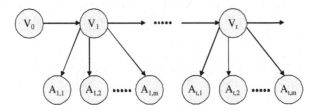

Fig. 2. Hidden Markov Model

Let $\mathbf{a_{1:t}}$ be the representation of $a_1, a_2, ..., a_t$. At any time t the HMM can choose a class v_{HMM_t} by

$$v_{HMM_t} = argmax_{v_t \in dom(V)} p(v_t|\mathbf{a_{1:t}}) \tag{2}$$

where (filtering - computing $p(v_t|\mathbf{a_{1:t}})$)
  if $t = 0$ then $p(v_t|\mathbf{a_{1:t}}) = p(v_t)$;
  if $t > 0$ then $p(v_t|\mathbf{a_{1:t}}) = \alpha\{\prod_j p(a_{t,j}|v_t)\}.\sum_{v_{t-1}}\{p(v_t|v_{t-1})p(v_{t-1}|\mathbf{a_{1:t-1}})\}$
  where α is a normalization constant.

2.3   Hidden Markov Model for Regression

Hidden Markov Model for Regression (HMMR) [10] uses the regression-by-discretization approach in order to apply HMM (see figure 2) to predict a numerical value (o_t) given a conjunction of attributes $[i_{t,1}, i_{t,2}, ..., i_{t,m}] = \mathbf{i_t}$, which can also be numerical.

In this approach, for each target ((o_t)/attribute $(i_{t,j})$) there is a corresponding discrete value (pseudo-class v_t/attribute $a_{t,j}$) representing the interval that contains the numerical value. In this way the HMM can be applied to the discretized data. The predicted numerical value by HMMR is the sum of the means of each of the pseudo-classes that were output by HMM, weighted according to the pseudo-class probabilities assigned by HMM:

$$o_{HMMR \ \ t} = \frac{\sum_{v_t \in dom(V)} m(v_t)p(v_t|\mathbf{a_{1:t}})}{\sum_{v_t \in dom(V)} p(v_t|\mathbf{a_{1:t}})} \tag{3}$$

where $m(v_t)$ is the mean of the pseudo-class v_t.

Figure 3 sketches the HMMR's forecasting of a numerical value, where $v^1, ...,$ $v^p \in Dom(V_t)$. First, the discretization of a new input is done producing a conjunction of discrete attributes, $[a_{t,1}, a_{t,2}, ..., a_{t,m}] = \mathbf{a_t}$. Then this conjunction uses the prior distribution $\mathbf{p}(V_{t-1}|\mathbf{a_{1:t-1}})$ of the pseudo-classes to produce a posterior distribution $\mathbf{p}(V_t|\mathbf{a_{1:t-1}}, \mathbf{a_t})$ of pseudo-classes. Finally, the prediction of

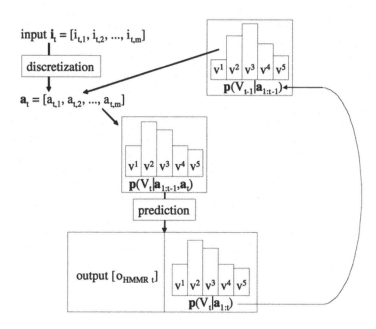

Fig. 3. HMMR's prediction of a numerical value

the numerical value is calculated by the weighted average of the means of pseudo-classes, where the weights are the probabilities from the posterior distribution. This posterior distribution will be the prior distribution for the next input.

2.4 Misclassification Costs

Decreasing the classification error does not necessarily decreases the regression error [13]. In order to ensure that, the absolute difference between the pseudo-class that was output by NBC and the true pseudo-class should be minimized. Towards this objective, [13] has shown the accuracy benefits of using misclassification costs. Considering m(.) as the median of the values that were discretized into the interval w, the cost of classifying a pseudo-class v instance as pseudo-class w is defined by

$$c_{w,v} = |m(w) - m(v)| \tag{4}$$

Using this approach, the predicted numerical value by a classifier (C) is:

$$o_C = m(\min_{w \in dom(W)} \sum_{v \in dom(V)} c_{w,v} p(v|a_1, ..., a_m)) \tag{5}$$

3 Experimental Results

For each discretization method HMMR is applied to ten time series data sets, including two well-known benchmarks, the Wölfer sunspot number and the

Mackey-Glass chaotic time series, and two real world data of monthly electric load forecasting from Brazilian utilities (Serie 1 and Serie 2). These series are differentiated and then the values are rescaled linearly to between 0.1 and 0.9. Using measurements of these time series $[y_1, y_2, ..., y_m]$, a forecast model needs to be constructed in order to predict the value immediately posterior $[y_{m+1}]$.

For HMMR, the target and attribute values are set to y_{m+1} and $[y_1, y_2, ..., y_m]$, respectively. A different version of HMMR, considering misclassification costs with m(.) as a median of each of the pseudo-classes, is also used (HMMR-mc). To select the best model, forward validation [16] is applied considering as parameters (p), p_1 the number of discretized regions and p_2 the number of atributes considered.

Forward validation begins with $r - 1$ training examples (r is considered as a sufficient number of training examples) and as the validation set the example y_s, where $s = r$. In the next step, y_s is included in the training set and the validation set is the example y_{s+1}. This procedure continues until s is equal to N. The decision measure $(C(p))$ is defined as a weighted average of the losses for p:

$$C(p) = \sum_{s=r}^{N} \gamma_s Loss(actual_s, forecast_s) \qquad (6)$$

The chosen model will be the one that minimizes $C(p)$.

This paper has considered as the loss function:

$$Loss(actual_s, forecast_s) = \frac{actual_s - forecast_s}{actual_s} \qquad (7)$$

The weights γ_s are defined as:

$$\gamma_s = \frac{\frac{1}{1+\frac{N_p}{s-1}}}{\sum_{i=r}^{N} \frac{1}{1+\frac{N_p}{i-1}}} \qquad (8)$$

where N_p is the number of parameters used for the model associated with p.

The error metric used is MAPE (Mean Absolute Percentage Deviation):

$$MAPE = \frac{\sum_{i=1}^{N} |\frac{actual_i - forecast_i}{actual_i} * 100\%|}{N} \qquad (9)$$

where N in this case is the number of examples in the test set.

For the two time series data of monthly electric load forecasting (Serie 1 and Serie 2) we consider 12 months in the test set, the measured load values of the previous 10 years for the training set ($N = 10 * 12$) and $r = 61$.

In the Wölfer sunspot time series, the values for the years 1770-1869 are used as the training set with $r = 31$ and the years 1870-1889 as the test set.

The data set for the Mackey-Glass chaotic time series is a solution of the Mackey-Glass delay-differential equation

$$\dot{x}(t) = -bx(t) + \frac{ax(t - \Delta)}{1 + x(t - \Delta)^c} \qquad (10)$$

where $\Delta = 30, a = 0.2, b = 0.1, c = 10$, initial conditions $x(t) = 0.9$ for $0 \le t \le \Delta$ and sampling rate $\tau = 6$. This series is obtained by integrating the equation (10) with the 4th order Runge-Kutta method at a step size of 1, and then downsampling by 6. The training set consists of the first 500 samples with $r = 100$ and as the test set the next 100 samples.

The others time series were mentioned in [17] except the last two which were used in a competition sponsored by the Santa Fe institute (time series A [18]) and in the K.U. Leuven competition (time series Leuven [19]). For all these time series the training set consists of the first 600 samples with $r = 180$ and the test set the next 200 samples.

Table 2 indicates the MAPE for the 3 discretization methods when applying HMMR and HMMR_mc to the ten time series. The boldface numbers indicate the discretization method that provides the lowest error and the italic numbers indicate that the difference between each of them and the correspond lowest error is statistically significant (paired t-test at 95% confidence level). The table 3 shows the parameters chosen (p_1/p_2).

Table 2. Experimental Results

	HMMR			HMMR_mc		
	EW	EP	KM	EW	EP	KM
Series 1	2,05	2,23	**1,97**	**2,10**	2,57	2,31
Series 2	1,84	1,75	**1,72**	1,81	*1,96*	**1,50**
Sunspot	**56,50**	57,21	71,44	78,91	103,54	**51,29**
Mackey-Glass	**7,72**	*10,77*	8,60	9,77	**9,50**	10,06
darwin	10,57	10,67	**10,48**	*12,18*	**11,06**	*11,85*
powerplant	**2,71**	*4,10*	*3,48*	**2,72**	*3,66*	*3,08*
soiltemp	13,39	13,00	**12,95**	*14,63*	*13,28*	**12,75**
speech	*5,02*	4,93	**4,43**	*5,54*	*5,44*	**4,67**
A	67,35	**52,20**	*61,85*	**46,31**	46,82	49,77
Leuven	*18,40*	*17,39*	**16,43**	19,50	**16,47**	17,87

4   Conclusion and Future Work

To further improve the successful results already obtained with the Hidden Markov Model for Regression [10] we applied the three discretization methods described in [13] to it and to a version of HMMR considering misclassification costs using ten time series data sets. A summary of the wins and losses of the three methods can be seen in table 4.

The experimental results (see table 2) showed that the KM discretization method improved the results in most of the data sets considered confirming our expectation that better results can be found when a better discretization method is used.

Table 3. Number of parameters

	HMMR			HMMR_mc		
	EW	EP	KM	EW	EP	KM
Serie 1	5/7	3/12	3/12	7/20	3/11	3/12
Serie 2	4/18	3/12	3/12	4/18	12/1	3/1
Sunspot	5/7	7/7	5/6	5/8	4/14	4/12
Mackey-Glass	15/10	11/10	9/12	13/9	8/12	9/12
darwin	13/12	7/11	3/11	7/18	7/18	7/16
powerplant	6/9	14/14	15/16	6/17	9/1	8/1
soiltemp	15/2	10/2	7/2	8/4	10/2	7/2
speech	13/13	10/14	11/14	13/15	12/15	11/14
A	11/5	14/3	15/6	11/9	14/4	15/4
Leuven	4/2	11/3	15/3	12/17	11/3	8/16

Table 4. Results of the discretization methods

	HMMR	HMMR_mc
EW	3	3
EP	1	3
KM	6	4

Since each discretization method improved the results in at least on data set, if time allows, it is better to have a search based system to automatically find the optimal number and width of the intervals.

As future work, we intend to extend this experiments to the Fuzzy Bayes and Fuzzy Markov Predictors [11], since they used the EW discretization method. Furthermore, HMMR will be applied to multi-step forecasting [12].

Acknowledgments

The authors would like to thank João Gama and Luis Torgo for giving us the Recla code, Marcelo Andrade Teixeira for useful discussions and Ana Luisa de Cerqueira Leite Duboc for her help in the implementation. We are all partially financially supported by the Brazilian Research Council CNPq.

References

1. Box G.E.P. , Jenkins G.M. and Reinsel G.C.. Time Series Analysis: Forecasting & Control. Prentice Hall, 1994.
2. Dietterich T.G.. The Divide-and-Conquer Manifesto. Proceedings of the Eleventh International Conference on Algorithmic Learning Theory. pp. 13-26, 2000.
3. Domingos P. and Pazzani M.. On the Optimality of the Simple Bayesian Classifier under Zero-One Loss. Machine Learning Vol.29(2/3), pp.103-130, November 1997.

4. Frank E., Trigg L., Holmes G. and Witten I.H.. Naive Bayes for Regression. Machine Learning. Vol.41, No.1, pp.5-25, 1999.
5. Friedman N., Goldszmidt M. and Lee T.J.. Bayesian network classification with continuous attributes: Getting the best of both discretization and parametric fitting. In 15th Inter. Conf. on Machine Learning (ICML), pp.179-187, 1998.
6. Ghahramani Z.. Learning Dynamic Bayesian Networks. In C.L.Giles and M.Gori (eds.). Adaptive Processing of Sequences and Data Structures, Lecture Notes in Artificial Intelligence. pp.168-197, Berlin, Springer-Verlag, 1998.
7. Montgomery D.C., Johnson L.A. and Gardiner J.S.. Forecasting and Time Series Analysis. McGraw-Hill Companies, 1990.
8. Roweis S. and Ghahramani Z.. A Unifying Review of Linear Gaussian Models. Neural Computation Vol.11, No.2, pp.305-345, 1999.
9. Russell S. and Norvig P.. Artificial Intelligence: A Modern Approach, Prentice Hall, 2nd edition, 2002.
10. Teixeira M.A. and Revoredo K. and Zaverucha G.. Hidden Markov Model for Regression in Electric Load Forecasting. In Proceedings of the ICANN/ICONIP-2003, Turkey, v.1, pp.374-377.
11. Teixeira M.A. and Zaverucha G.. Fuzzy Bayes and Fuzzy Markov Predictors. Journal of Intelligent and Fuzzy Systems, Amsterdam, The Netherlands, V.13, n.2-4,pp. 155-165, 2003.
12. Teixeira M.A. and Zaverucha G.. Fuzzy Markov Predictor in Multi-Step Electric Load Forecasting. In the Proceedings of the IEEE/INSS International Joint Conference on Neural Networks (IJCNN'2003), Portland, Oregon, v.1 pp.3065-3070.
13. Torgo L., Gama J.. Regression Using Classification Algorithms. Intelligent Data Analysis. Vol.1, pp. 275-292, 1997.
14. Weiss S. and Indurkhya N.. Rule-base Regression. In Proceedings of the 13th Internationa Joing Conference on Artificial Intelligence. pp. 1072-1078. 1993.
15. Weiss S. and Indurkhya N.. Rule-base Machine Learning Methods for Functional Prediction. Journal of Artificial Intelligence Research (JAIR). Vol. 3, pp. 383-403. 1995.
16. Urban Hjorth J.S.. Computer Intensive Statistical Methods. Validation Model Selection and Bootstrap. Chapman & Hall. 1994.
17. Keogh E. and Kasetty S.. On the Need for Time Series Data Mining Benchmarks: A Survey and Empirical Demonstration. Data Mining and Knowledge Discovery,7, 349-371,2003.
18. http://www-psych.stanford.edu/%7Eandreas/Time-Series/SantaFe
19. ftp://ftp.esat.kuleuven.ac.be/pub/sista/suykens/workshop/datacomp.dat

SKDQL: A Structured Language
to Specify Knowledge Discovery Processes and Queries

Marcelino Pereira dos Santos Silva[1] and Jacques Robin[2]

[1] Universidade do Estado do Rio Grande do Norte
BR 110, Km 48, 59610-090, Mossoró, RN, Brasil
mpss@dpi.inpe.br
[2] Universidade Federal de Pernambuco, Centro de Informática, 50670-901, Recife, PE, Brasil
jr@cin.ufpe.br

Abstract. Tools and techniques used for automatic and smart analysis of huge data repositories of industries, governments, corporations and scientific institutes are the subjects dealt by the field of Knowledge Discovery in Databases (KDD). In MATRIKS context, a framework for KDD, SKDQL (Structured Knowledge Discovery Query Language) is the proposal of a structured language for KDD specification, following SQL patterns within an open and extensible architecture, supporting heterogeneity, interaction and increment of KDD process, with resources for accessing, cleaning, transforming, deriving and mining data, beyond knowledge manipulation.

1 Introduction

The high availability of huge databases, and the eminent necessity of transforming such data in information and knowledge, have demanded valuable efforts from the scientific community and software industry. The tools and techniques used for smart analysis of large repositories are the subjects dealt by Knowledge Discovery in Databases (KDD). However, the KDD process has challenges related to the specification of queries and processes, once several tools are often used to extract knowledge. It is generally a problem, because the complexity of the process itself is augmented by the heterogeneity of tools employed.

An approach to face the problems that arise in such context must provide resources to specify queries and processes, avoiding common bottlenecks and respecting KDD requirements. This article presents as contribution SKDQL (Structured Knowledge Discovery Query Language) [12], which contains specific clauses for KDD tasks. In order to use the language and validate the concepts of this work, part of the SKDQL specification was implemented. This prototype of SKDQL was effectively tested on the log database of the RoboCup domain. Such domain contains the real problems that arise in KDD tasks, once its logs offer a wide and detailed data repository about the teams behavior.

The paper is organized as follows: the next section presents the KDD process and its bottlenecks; the third topic is about a case study of SKQL; the next section describes SKDQL specification; in the fifth part a prototype of the language is presented; the following section brings related work, finishing with conclusions.

A.L.C. Bazzan and S. Labidi (Eds.): SBIA 2004, LNAI 3171, pp. 326–335, 2004.

2 Knowledge Discovery in Databases

Knowledge Discovery in Databases is the nontrivial process of identifying valid, novel, potentially useful and ultimately understandable patterns in data, aiming to improve the understanding of a problem or a procedure of decision-making. The KDD process is interactive, iterative, cognitive and exploratory, involving many steps (Figure 1) with many decisions being taken by the analyst, according to the following description [3]:

1. Definition of the kind of knowledge to be discovered, what demands a good comprehension of the domain and the kind of decision such knowledge can improve.
2. Selection - in order to create a target dataset where discovery will be performed.
3. Preprocessing - including noise removal, manipulation of null/absent data fields, data formatting.
4. Transformation – data reduction and projection, aiming to find useful features to represent data and reduce variables or instances considered in the process.
5. Data Mining – selection of methods that will be used to find patterns in data, followed by the effective search for patterns of interest, in a particular representation or set of representations.
6. Interpretation/Evaluation of the mined patterns, with possible returns to steps 2-6.
7. Implantation of the discovered knowledge, incorporating it to the system performance or reporting it to interested parts.

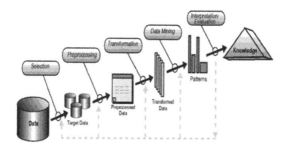

Fig. 1. KDD steps [3].

2.1 Bottlenecks in KDD Process

In KDD systems, bottlenecks are generally characterized by the absence of:

- Support for heterogeneous platforms: wrappers to integrate legacy systems, implemented in platform independent language; the lack of this resource hinders the reuse of the components.
- Efficiency and performance: basic requirements, once KDD deals with huge amounts of data for pattern extraction.
- Modularity and integration: KDD systems must present modularity in its components, in order to facilitate the resources addition, removal or update.

This way, an interesting feature in KDD systems is the interactive and ad hoc support of data mining tasks, providing flexibility and efficiency in knowledge discovery, through an open and extensible environment. An intuitive and declarative query and process definition language comes to this direction, which is the SKDQL proposal.

3 Case Study

The Robot World Cup Soccer (RoboCup) [10] is an international initiative to stimulate research in artificial intelligence, robotics and multi agents systems. The environment models a hypothetic robot system, combining features of different systems and simulating human soccer players. This simulator, acting like a server, provides a domain and supports users that want to construct their own agents/players.

In order to get relevant knowledge related to the behavior (play, attitude and peculiarity of the players and the teams), logs were extracted from RoboCup games, through Soccer Monitor, a software that using binary logs presents the matches in its simulated environment, allowing to visualize the context of the players and its movements. This software also converts binary logs into ASCII code. Processed logs of the Soccer Server originated two important behavior data tables (Figure 2).

- Primitive flat table – constituted by minimal granularity statistics, information about each player's action and position at each cycle of the simulator.
- Derived flat table – constituted by higher granularity statistics, demonstrating different actions (pass, goal, kickoff, offside, and so on), and relevant data about them (the moment it started and finished, players involved, relative positions, and so on).

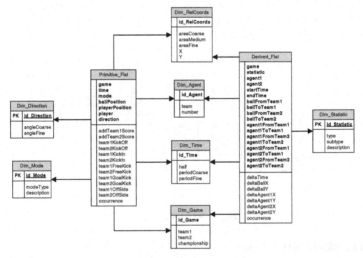

Fig. 2. RoboCup data model.

Among the performed experiments, it was verified that in classification cases with Id3 and J48, algorithms confirm in a reciprocal way their results, presenting a game tendency in specific areas of the game field for continuous activity. It was also observed that the filtering of attribute relevance improves the information quality, avoiding mistakes related, for example, to area hierarchy. It was verified that in many cases it's not generated an immediately comprehensible pattern, what indicates that data, its format or mining algorithm must be modified in the KDD task. Further results and experiments may be found in [13].

This RoboCup case study provided relevant experience in the use of different tools and paradigms for data mining, and outlined the need of open and integrated KDD environments with languages for a set of integrated resources and functionalities.

4 SKDQL Specification

The MATRIKS project (Multidimensional Analysis and Textual Summarizing for Insight Knowledge Search) [2, 4, 6] aims the creation of an open and integrated environment for decision support and KDD. This project intends to fill KDD environment lacks, related to tools integration, knowledge management of the mined model, language for query/process specification, and to the variety of input data, models and mining algorithms.

In MATRIKS environment, a set of resources will be accessed through a declarative language of KDD queries and processes specification which, in a transparent way, will provide all the tools in an integrated manner, using the open, multi platform and distributed power of this KDSE (Knowledge Discovery Support Environment) proposal. Based on the natural flow of data and results manipulation, SKDQL (Structured Knowledge Discovery Query Language) is the language proposal for KDD with clauses that access in an integrated and transparent way the resources in MATRIKS.

The knowledge discovery in databases demands tasks for data manipulation and analysis. Each task includes sequences of steps to perform selection, cleaning, transformation and mining, beyond presentation and storage of results and knowledge. Considering the manipulation of data and results, SKDQL has four kinds of clauses:

- Resources to access, load and store data during the knowledge discovery process.
- Clauses to preprocess the selected data, including cleaning, transformation, deduction and enrichment of these data.
- Commands to visualize, store and present the knowledge.
- Data mining algorithms for classification, association, clustering.

4.1 SKDQL High Level Grammar

The initial symbol of the language is the non-terminal `<SKDQLtask>`, which defines recursively a task as a sequence of data treatment steps (SKDQLstep):

```
<SKDQLtask> ::= <SKDQLstep> {<Conj> <SKDQLtask>}
```

where `<Conj>` is the terminal "and" or "then", depending on the semantics that must be represented between the proposed tasks (serial or parallel).

`<SKDQLstep>` is defined as a step of data preparation (Prepare), followed by an optional activity of previous knowledge (PriorKnowledge). A data mining step follow it, with a subsequent result presentation (Present) for interpretation and evaluation:

```
<SKDQLstep> ::= <Prepare> <Conj> [<PriorKnowledge> <Conj>] <Mine>
               [<Conj> <Present>]  | <Prepare>            |
               <Preprocess>        | <PriorKnowledge>     |
               <Mine>              | <Present>
```

`<Present>` allows information visualization (previously stored) through the clause `<Display>`. The junction of different files of this type can be performed with `<JoinDisplay>`.

```
<Present> ::= <Display>     |    <JoinDisplay>
```

4.1.1 Clause for Data Access and Storage Task Specification

The clause <Prepare> has two clauses to be considered, <Pick> and <Pre-process>:

```
<Prepare> ::= <Pick> {<Conj> <Preprocess>}
```

The initial step in a KDD task is the specification of the dataset to be explored during the whole process. This step demands the indication of data source (servers, database, and so on). An example follows:

```
connectTo relationalDB at Server03, Robocup, robo_login, robo_passwd
```

It can also perform a peculiar data selection (with sampling, for example):

```
sample % 50 from alldata using randomWithoutReplacement
```

4.1.2 Clause for Data Preprocessing Task Specification

In the clause <Prepare>, right after <Pick>, follows <Preprocess> which deals with cleaning, transformation, derivation, randomization and data recovery:

```
<Preprocess> ::=    <Clean>          |        <Transform>    |
                    <Derive>         |        <Randomize>    |
                    <RestoreDataSet>
```

For example ("4" is the position of the attribute in the dataset):

```
from dataset area.dat clean 4 using removeWithMissingValues
```

4.1.3 Clause for Knowledge Presentation Task Specification

The previous knowledge of a domain may indicate good ways and solutions that effectively improve the KDD process in terms of quality and speed. It can modify completely the chosen approach over a dataset. Therefore, SKDQL has clauses to specify the previous knowledge, and present knowledge discovered in the task.

<PriorKnowledge> has resources to access a database, to verify a dataset sampling, and to previously define the layout of association rules, according to its syntax:

```
<PriorKnowledge> ::=    <ConnectTo> <Conj> <BDQuery>    |
                        <ViewSampleOfDataset>           |
                        <AssociationPriorKnowledge>     |
                        <Present>
```

<AssociationPriorKnowledge> allows the definition of a meta-rule that will determine the layout of the association rules that will be created.

<PriorKnowledge> uses the structure previously described to connect a database and query it. Moreover, it is also possible to visualize a dataset sampling previously stored using the clause <ViewSampleOfDataset>, when it is informed the percentage of the sample to be visualized. For example:

```
viewSampleOf % 30 dataset area.dat
```

4.1.4 Clause for Data Mining Task Specification

SKDQL has resources to mine many kinds of knowledge (or models) through different methods and algorithms using validation, testing and other options. The relevant attributes, classification models, association rules and clustering mining tasks are present in this specification [17]. <Mine> is defined according to the following syntax:

```
<Mine> ::= <MineRelevantAttributes>    |    <MineClassification>|
           <MineAssociations>          |    <MineClusters>
```

In a dataset, there are attributes that has a higher influence in data mining tasks. For example: to classify a good or bad loan client, certainly his income will be much more relevant than his birthplace. The income and other attributes with highly influence in the task are called relevant attributes, which can be mined through the <MineRelevantAttributes> clause.

Classification methods in data mining are used to determine and evaluate models that classify or foresee an object or event. The syntax of the classification task is specified in <MineClassification>.

The classification, as well as the relevance attribute, must be performed according to an attribute called class, where the prototype default is the last attribute of the dataset. An example of this task follows:

```
mineClassification
present model
store in naive.skdql
classifier naiveBayes
```

Association rules are similar to classification rules, except that the former can foresee any attribute, not only the one that must be previously determined (class), allowing this way that different combinations of attributes occur in the rules through <MineAssociations>.

Clusters mining (<MineClusters>) presents, following criterions, the format of a diagram, which reveals how instances of a dataset are distributed in groups/clusters.

The entire specification of the language is available at [13]. The example below gives an idea of the usage of SKDQL:

- After connecting the RoboCup database through a SQL query, a dataset is selected. Right after, a sampling task of 50% is performed on this dataset, with a subsequent application of Naïve Bayes classification algorithm. This task aims to acquire general knowledge about the context of the dataset using a basic classifier:

```
connectTo relationalDB at Server03, Robocup, robo_login, robo_passwd
then sqlQuery
        select T.periodFine, C.areaFine, C.areaMedium, A.number,
               M.description
        from   Primitive_Flat F, Dim_Time T, Dim_Mode M,
               Dim_RelCoords C, Dim_Agent A
        where  F.time = T.id_Time  and
               F.mode = M.id_Mode  and
               F.ballPosition = C.id_RelCoords and
               F.playerPosition = C.id_RelCoords and
               F.player = A.id_Agent and
               F.game = 1 and F.time < 200
        sqlQuery
then sample % 50 from alldata using randomWithoutReplacement
then mineClassification
        present model
        store in naive.skdql
        classifier naiveBayes
```

5 SKDQL Implementation

SKDQL was implemented through a prototype that has the main functionalities of the language. In this implementation, Java [14] was chosen because MATRIKS already adopts Java as a pattern development platform. Moreover, the developed interfaces support heterogeneous platforms, very common in KDD. This way, distribution, extensibility, interoperability and modularity adopted for MATRIKS are supported via Java. Different software, components and API's were used for the implementation of SKDQL functionalities (Figure 3 and Table 1).

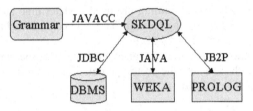

Fig. 3. System Architecture.

To access relational databases, JDBC [15] was used, an API that supports connection to tables of datasets from Java programs. In this implementation, the DBMS (Database Management System) Microsoft SQL Server [8] was used.

For preprocessing and data mining functionalities, WEKA [17] components were used, a collection of algorithms for data manipulation and data mining (filtering, normalization, classification, association, clustering, and others), which were written in Java and modularized in components called by SKDQL.

The XSB Prolog [19] is a programming language and a deductive database used in derivation tasks of SKDQL, once WEKA has many resources for preprocessing and mining, while nothing for deduction. It is accessed through JB2P [11], an API that allows Java programs make calls and receive results from XSB.

For code generation of SKDQL, functionalities of access, preprocessing, data mining and data presentation were selected. Via JDBC, the SKDQL code generated by JavaCC [18] performs the relational data access, when it requires URL, database, login and password. The preprocessing and data mining tasks are performed via calls to Prolog and WEKA components, which are also implemented in Java.

Table 1. Steps, clauses and components used in SKDQL implementation.

KDD Steps	SKDQL Clauses	Software Components
Selection	Prepare (Pick)	SQL Server, JDBC
Preprocessing	Preprocess (Clean)	Weka
Transformation	Transform, Randomize, Derive	Weka, Prolog, JB2P
Data Mining	Mine (Attrib., Classif., Assoc., Clusters)	Weka
Interpretation/Evaluation	Present, Display, JoinDisplay	OS file manipulation

6 Related Work

6.1 DMQL

In Simon Fraser University (Canada) DMQL (Data Mining Query Language) [5] was developed with clauses for relevant dataset, kind of knowledge to be mined, prior knowledge used in the KDD process, interest measures, limits to evaluate patterns, and visualization representation of the discovered patterns.

However, the language does not have resources for data preprocessing. The specification presents a limited and invariable set of mining algorithms. DMQL isn't implemented, once its single practical application is found in DBMiner [1], where it is used as a task description resource.

6.2 OLE DB for DM

OLE DB for Data Mining (OLE DB for DM) [7] is an extension of Microsoft OLE DB, which supports data mining operations on OLE DB providers. As an OLE DB extension, it introduces a new virtual object called Data Mining Model (DMM), as well commands to manipulate this virtual object. DMM is like a relational table, except that it contains special columns that can be used for pattern training and discovery allowing, for example, the creation of a prediction model and the generation of predictions.

While a relational table stores data, DMM stores the patterns discovered by the mining algorithm. The manipulation of a DMM is similar to the manipulation of a table. However, this approach is not adequate, once tables are not flexible enough to represent data mining models (for example, decision tables or bayesian networks).

6.3 CWM

Common Warehouse Metamodel (CWM) [9] is a recent pattern defined by the Object Management Group (OMG) for data interchange in different environments: data warehousing, KDD and business analysis. CWM provides a common language to describe metadata (based on a generic metamodel, but semantically complete) and facilities data interchange and specification of KDD classes and processes.

The scope of CWM specification includes metamodels definitions of different domains, what imposes CWM a high complexity, demanding knowledge of its principles. Moreover, there is a lack of tutorials, documents and cases enough for a wide comprehension of the specification and techniques to use it in practical problems.

6.4 KDDML-MQL

KDDML-MQL [16] is an environment that supports the specification and execution of complex KDD processes in the form of high-level queries.

KDDML (KDD Markup Language) is XML-based, i.e. both data, meta-data, mining models and queries are represented as XML documents. Query tags specify data acquisition, preprocessing, mining and post-processing algorithms taken from possibly distinct suites of tools. MQL (Mining Query Language) is an algebraic language, in the style of SQL. The MQL system compiles an MQL query into KDDML queries.

7   Conclusions

The SKDQL proposal provides a specification language and its prototype for the application of different tasks of knowledge discovery in databases, taking into account features of the KDD process, overcoming most of the KDD bottlenecks and limitations of alternative approaches. This work contributes in the following points:

- Iteration – application and reapplication of resources and tools in the process.
- Interaction – SKDQL allows the analyst perform tasks in an interactive manner, requesting tasks and chaining operations to results previously reached.
- Systematization of KDD tasks – resources are available to users in a style very similar to SQL, with specific clauses for each task, freeing the "miner" of implementation details of the tools.
- Support to heterogeneous resources – SKDQL proposal supports the access to different data models widely used, increasing the user autonomy regarding to the manipulation of different databases in the same environment.
- Integration – due to KDD requirement in the points above, the language integrates resources of different tools.

Considering the wide scope, evolution and dynamics of KDD, the extension of the language is a consequence of the continuity of this work, once the present specification supports resources for a limited and open set of steps in a knowledge discovery process. Although sequences of tests have been performed, it is necessary to apply SKDQL to a wider set of tasks to improve resources and validate functionalities.

Acknowledgments

The supports of UERN and CAPES are gratefully acknowledged. We also thank Alexandre Luiz, João Batista and Rodrigo Galvão for their valuable contributions.

References

1. Dbminer Technology Inc. *DBMiner Enterprise 2.0*. Available at DBMiner Technology site (2000). URL: http://www.dbminer.com/
2. Favero, E. *HYSSOP - Hypertext Summary System for Olap*. Doctorate Thesis. UFPE, 2000.
3. Fayyad, U. M.; Piatesky-Shapiro, G.; Smyth, P. *From Data Mining to Knowledge Discovery: An Overview*. Advances in KDD and Data Mining, AAAI, 1996.
4. Fidalgo, R. N. *JODI: A Java API for OLAP Systems and OLE DB for OLAP Interoperability*. Master Thesis. UFPE, 2000.
5. Han, J. et al. DMQL: A Data Mining Query Language for Relational Databases. Simon Fraser University, 1996.
6. Lino, N. C. Q. *DOODCI: An API for Multidimensional Databases and Deductive Systems Integration*. Master Thesis. UFPE, 2000.
7. Microsoft Corporation. *OLE DB for Data Mining*. Available at Microsoft Corporation site (2000). URL: http://www.microsoft.com/data/oledb/dm.htm
8. Microsoft Corporation. *Microsoft SQL Server*. Available at Microsoft Corporation site (2002). URL: http://www.microsoft.com/sql/default.asp
9. Poole, J. et al. *Common Warehouse Metamodel – An Introduction to the Standard for Data Warehouse Integration*. OMG Press, 2002.

10. The RoboCup Federation. *The Robot World Cup Initiative (RoboCup).* Available at RoboCup site (2002). URL: http://www.robocup.org
11. Rocha, J.B. *Java Bridge to Prolog – JB2P (2001).* Available at Rocha site (2001). URL: http://www.cin.ufpe.br/~jbrj/msc/courses/taias/jb2p
12. Silva, M. P. S.; Robin, J. R. *SKDQL – A Declarative Language for Queries and Process Specification for KDD and its Implementation (2002).* Master Thesis. UFPE, 2002.
13. Silva, M. P. S.; Robin, J. R. *SKDQL Grammar Specification.* Available at Silva site (2002). URL: http://www.dpi.inpe.br/~mpss/skdql
14. Sun Microsystems, Inc. *Java Developer Connection: Documentation and Training.* Available at Sun Microsystems site (2001). URL: http://developer.java.sun.com
15. Sun Microsystems Inc. *Java Database Connection - JDBC.* Available at Sun Microsystems site (2002). URL: http://java.sun.com/products/jdbc
16. Turini, F. et al. *KDD Markup Language (2003).* Available at Universita' di Pisa site (2003). URL: http://kdd.di.unipi.it/kddml/
17. University of Waikato. *Weka 3 – Machine Learning Software in Java.* Available at University of Waikato site (2001). URL: http://www.cs.waikato.ac.nz/ml/weka
18. Webgain Inc. *Java Compiler Compiler – JavaCC.* Available at WebGain Inc. site (2002). URL: http://www.webgain.com/products/java_cc/
19. The XSB Research Group. *XSB Prolog.* Available at XSB Research Group site (2001). URL: http://xsb.sourceforge.net/

Symbolic Communication in Artificial Creatures: An Experiment in Artificial Life

Angelo Loula, Ricardo Gudwin, and João Queiroz

Dept. Computer Engineering and Industrial Automation
School of Electrical and Computer Engineering, State University of Campinas, Brasil
{angelocl,gudwin,queirozj}@dca.fee.unicamp.br

Abstract. This is a project on Artificial Life where we simulate an ecosystem that allows cooperative interaction between agents, including intra-specific predator-warning communication in a virtual environment of predatory events. We propose, based on Peircean semiotics and informed by neuroethological constraints, an experiment to simulate the emergence of *symbolic* communication among artificial creatures. Here we describe the simulation environment and the creatures' control architectures, and briefly present obtained results.

Keywords: symbol, communication, artificial life, semiotics, C.S.Peirce

1 Introduction

According to the semiotics of C.S.Peirce, there are three fundamental kinds of signs underlying meaning processes: icons, indexes and symbols (CP 2.275[1]). Icons are signs that stand for their objects through similarity or resemblance (CP 2.276, 2.247, 8.335, 5.73); indexes are signs that have a spatio-temporal physical correlation with its object (CP 2.248, see 2.304); symbols are signs connected to O by the mediation of I. For Peirce (CP 2.307), a symbol is "A Sign which is constituted a sign merely or mainly by the fact that it is used and understood as such, whether the habit is natural or conventional, and without regard to the motives which originally governed its selection."

Based on this framework, Queiroz and Ribeiro [2] performed a neurosemiotic analysis of vervet monkeys' intra-specific communication. These primates use vocal signs for intra-specific social interactions, as well as for general alarm purposes regarding imminent predation on the group [3]. They vocalize basically three predator-specific alarm calls which produce specific escape responses: alarm calls for terrestrial predators (such as leopards) are followed by a escape to the top of trees, alarm calls for aerial raptors (such as eagles) cause vervets to hide under bushes, and alarm calls for ground predators (such as snakes) elicit careful scrutiny of the surrounding terrain. Queiroz and Ribeiro[2] identified the different signs and the possible neuroanatomical substrates involved. Icons correspond to neural responses to the physical properties of the visual image of the predator

---

[1] The work of C.S.Peirce[1] is quoted as CP, followed by the volume and paragraph.

A.L.C. Bazzan and S. Labidi (Eds.): SBIA 2004, LNAI 3171, pp. 336–345, 2004.
© Springer-Verlag Berlin Heidelberg 2004

and the alarm-call, and exist within two independent primary representational domains (visual and auditory). Indexes occur in the absence of a previously established relationship between call and predator, when the call simply arouses the receiver's attention to any concomitant event of interest, generating a sensory scan response. If the alarm-call operates in a sign-specific way in the absence of an external referent, then it is a symbol of a specific predator class. This symbolic relationship implies the association of at least two representations of a lower order in a higher-order representation domain.

2   Simulating Artificial Semiotic Creatures

The framework (above) guided our experiments of simulating the emergence of symbolic alarm calls[2]. The environment is bi-dimensional having approximately 1000 by 1300 positions. The creatures are autonomous agents, divided into *preys* and *predators*. There are objects such as *trees* (climbable objects) and *bushes* (used to hide), and three types of predators: *terrestrial predator*, *aerial predator* and *ground predator*. Predators differentiate by their visual limitations: terrestrial predators can't see preys over trees, aerial predators can't see preys under bushes, but ground predators don't have these limitations. The preys can be *teachers*, which vocalizes pre-defined alarms to predators, or *learners*, which try to learn these associations. There is also the *self-organizer prey*, which is a teacher and a learner at the same time, able to create, vocalize and learn alarms, simultaneously.

The sensory apparatus of the preys include *hearing* and *vision*; predators have only a visual sensor. The sensors have parameters that define sensory areas in the environment, used to determine the stimuli the creatures receive. Vision has a range, a direction and an aperture defining a circular section, and hearing has just a range defining a circular area. These parameters are fixed, with exception to visual direction, changed by the creature, and visual range increased during scanning. The received stimuli correspond to a number, which identifies the creature or object seen associated with the direction and distance from the stimulus' receiver.

The creatures have interactive abilities, high-level motor actions: *adjust visual sensor, move, attack, climb tree, hide on bush*, and *vocalize*. These last three actions are specific to preys, while attacks are only done by predators. The creatures can perform actions concomitantly, except for displacement actions (move, attack, climb and hide) which are mutually exclusive. The move action changes the creature position in the environment and takes two parameters velocity (in positions/interaction, limited to a maximum velocity) and a direction (0-360 degrees). The visual sensor adjustment modifies the direction of the visual sensor (and during scanning, doubles the range), and takes one parameter, the new direction (0-360 degrees). The attack action has one parameter that indicates the creature to be attacked, that must be within action range. If successful the

---

[2] The simulator is called *Symbolic Creatures Simulation*. For more technical details, see http://www.dca.fee.unicamp.br/projects/artcog/symbcreatures

attack increases an internal variable, number of attacks suffered, from the attacked creature. The climb action takes as a parameter the tree to be climbed, that must be within the action range. When up in a tree, an internal variable called 'climbed' is set to true; when the creature moves it is turned to false and it goes down the tree. Analogously, the hide action has the bush to be used to hide as a parameter, and it uses an internal variable called 'hidden'. The vocalize action has one parameter the alarm to be emitted, a number between 0 and 99, and it creates a new element in the environment that lasts just one interaction, and is sensible by creatures having hearing sensors.

To control their actions after receiving the sensory input, the creatures have a behavior-based architecture [4], dedicated to action selection [5]. Our control mechanism is composed of various behaviors and drives. Behaviors are independent and parallel modules that are activated at different moments depending on the sensorial input and the creature's internal state. At each iteration, behaviors provide their motivation value (between 0 and 1), and the one with highest value is activated and provides the creature actions at that instant. Drives define basic needs, or 'instincts', such as 'fear' or 'hunger', and they are represented by numeric values between 0 and 1, updated based on the sensorial input or time flow. This mechanism is not learned by the creature, but rather designed, providing basic responses to general situations.

Predators' Cognitive Architecture

The predators have a simple control architecture with basic behaviors and drives. The drives are hunger and tiredness, and the behaviors are wandering, rest and prey chasing. The drives are implemented as follows:

$$hunger(0) = 1$$

$$hunger(t+1) = \begin{cases} 0.01, \text{ if it attacked a prey} \\ ramp_1(hunger(t) + 0.01.hunger(t)), \text{ otherwise} \end{cases}$$

$$\text{where } ramp_1(x) = \begin{cases} 0, x < 0 \\ x, 0 \leq x \leq 1 \\ 1, x > 1 \end{cases}$$

$$tiredness(t+1) = \begin{cases} ramp_1(tiredness(t) - 0.1), \\ \qquad velocity(t) = 0 \\ ramp_1\left(tiredness(t) + 0.05.\frac{velocity(t)}{maximum\_velocity}\right), \\ \qquad velocity(t) > maximum\_velocity/2 \end{cases}$$

where $velocity(t)$ is the creature's velocity at the current instant (t).

The wandering behavior has a constant motivation value of 0.4, and makes the creature basically move at random direction and velocity, directing its vision toward movement direction. The resting behavior makes the creature stop moving and its motivation is given by

$$rest\_motivation(t) = \begin{cases} tiredness(t), \; tiredness(t) > 0.5 \\ 0.5, \; velocity(t) = 0 \; and \; tiredness(t) > 0 \\ 0, \; otherwise \end{cases}$$

The behavior chasing makes the predator move towards the prey, if its out of range, or attack it, otherwise. The motivation of this behavior is given by

$$chasing\_motivation(t) = \begin{cases} hunger(t), \; hunger(t) > 0.5 \text{ and a prey is seen} \\ 0, \; otherwise \end{cases}$$

Preys' Cognitive Architecture

Preys have two sets of behavior: communication related behaviors and general behaviors. The communication related behaviors are vocalizing, scanning, associative learning and following, the general ones are wandering, resting and fleeing. Associated with these behaviors, there are different drives: boredom, tiredness, solitude, fear and curiosity. The learner and the teacher don't have the same architecture, only teachers have the vocalize behavior and only learners have the associative learning behavior, the scanning behavior and the curiosity drive (figure 1). On the other hand, the self-organizer prey has all behaviors and drives.

The prey's drives are specified by the expressions

$$boredom(t + 1) = \begin{cases} ramp_2(boredom(t) + rate \cdot boredom(t)), \; velocity(t) = 0 \\ ramp_2(boredom(t) - 0.1), \; otherwise \end{cases}$$

$$\text{where } rate = \begin{cases} 0.05, \text{ hidden on bush or climbed on tree} \\ 0.1, \; otherwise \end{cases} \text{ and}$$

$$ramp_2(x) = \begin{cases} 0.01, \; x < 0.01 \\ x, \; 0.01 \le x \le 0.99 \\ 0.99, \; x > 0.99 \end{cases}$$

$$fear(t + 1) = \begin{cases} ramp_2(1.0), \text{ if predator was seen} \\ ramp_2(fear(t) - 0.05(1.0 - fear(t))), \; otherwise \end{cases}$$

$$solitude(t + 1) = \begin{cases} rampa_2(solitude(t) + 0.1.solitude(t)), \text{ no prey is seen} \\ rampa_2(solitude(t) - 0.1(1.0 - solitude(t))), \; otherwise \end{cases}$$

$$curiosity(t) = ramp_2(max_i \, strengthWM_i(t)), \text{ where } i \in WMAud$$

The tiredness drive is computed by the same expression used by predators.

The vocalize behavior and associative learning behavior can run in parallel with all other behaviors, so it does not undergo behavior selection. The vocalize behavior makes the prey emit an alarm when a predator is seen. The teacher has a fixed alarm set, using alarm number 1 for terrestrial predator, 2 for aerial predator and 3 for ground predator. The self-organizer uses the alarm with the highest association value in the associative memory (next section), or chooses randomly an alarm from 0 to 99 and places it in the associative memory, if none is known. (The associative learning behavior is described in the next section.)

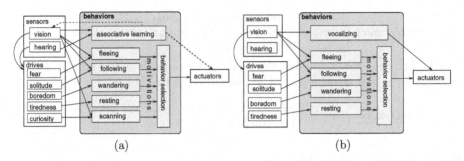

Fig. 1. Preys' cognitive architecture: (a) learners have scanning and associative learning capabilities and (b) teachers have vocalizing capability. The self-organizer prey is a teacher and a learner at the same time and has all these behaviors.

The scanning behavior makes the prey turn towards the alarm emitter direction and move at this direction, if an alarm is heard, turn to the same vision direction of the emitter, but still moving towards the emitter, if the emitter is seen, or keep the same vision and movement direction, if the alarm is not heard anymore. The motivation is given by *curiosity(t)*, if an alarm is heard or if *curiosity(t)¿0.2*. This behavior also makes the vision range double, simulating a wide sensory scanning process.

To keep preys near each other and not spread out in the environment, the following behavior makes the prey keep itself between a maximum and a minimum distance of another prey, by moving towards or away from it. This was inspired by experiments in simulation of flocks, schools and herds. The motivation for following is equal to *solitude(t)*, if another prey is seen.

The fleeing behavior has its motivation given by *fear(t)*. It makes the prey move away from the predator with maximum velocity, or in some situations, perform specific actions depending upon the type of prey. If a terrestrial predator is or was just seen and there's a tree not near the predator (the difference between predator direction and tree direction is more than 60 degrees), the prey moves toward the tree and climbs it. If it is an aerial predator and there's a bush not near it, the prey moves toward the bush and hides under it. If the predator is not seen anymore, and the prey is not up on a tree or under a bush, it keeps moving in the same direction it was before, slightly changing its direction at random.

The wandering behavior makes the prey move at a random direction and velocity, slightly changing it at random. The vision direction is alternately turn left, forward and right. The motivation is given by *boredom(t)*, if the prey is not moving and *boredom(t)¿0.2*, or zero, otherwise. The rest behavior makes the prey stop moving, with a motivation as for predators.

Associative Learning

The associative learning allows the prey to generalize spatial-temporal relations between external stimuli from particular instances. The mechanism is inspired on the neuroethological and semiotic constraints described previously, implementing

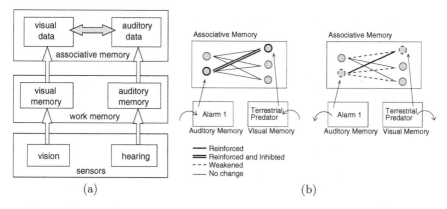

Fig. 2. (a) Associative learning architecture. (b) Association adjustment rules.

a lower-order sensory domain through work memories and a higher order multi-modal domain by a associative memory (figure 2a).

The work memories are temporary repositories of stimuli: when a sensorial stimulus is received from either sensor (auditory or visual), it is placed on the respective work memory with maximum strength, at every subsequent iteration it is lowered and when its strength gets to zero it is removed. The strength of stimuli in the work memory (WM) varies according to the expression

$$strengthWM_i(t+1) = \begin{cases} 1.0, & \text{if stimulus } i \text{ arrived at sensors} \\ & \text{and it isn't already} \\ & \text{in the work memory} \\ strengthWM_i(t) - 0.2, & \text{if stimulus } i \text{ is in the work memory} \end{cases}$$

The items in the work memory are used by the associative memory to produce and update association between stimuli, following basic Hebbian learning (figure 2b). When an item is received in the visual WM and in the auditory WM, an association is created or reinforced in the associative memory, and changes in its associative strength are inhibited. Inhibition avoids multiple adjustments in the same association caused by persisting items in the work memory. When an item is dropped from the work memory, its associations not inhibited, i.e. not already reinforced, are weakened, and the inhibited associations have their inhibition partially removed. When the two items of an inhibited association are removed, the association ends its inhibition, being subject again to changes in its strength. The reinforcement and weakening adjustments for non-inhibited associations, with strengths limited to the interval $[0.0; 1.0]$, are done as follows:

– reinforcement, given a visual stimulus i and a hearing stimulus j present in the work memories

$$strength_{ij}(k+1) = strength_{ij}(k) + 0.1(1.0 - (maxstrength_j(k) - strength_{ij}(k)))$$
$$+0.01$$
where $maxstrength_j(k) = max_i \, strength_{ij}(k)$

– weakening, for every association related to the dropped visual stimuli i

$\forall j$ associated with i,
$$strength_{ij}(k + 1) = strength_{ij}(k) - 0.1(maxstrength_j(k) - strength_{ij}(k)))$$
$$+0.01$$

– weakening, for every association related to the dropped hearing stimuli j

$\forall i$ associated with j,
$$strength_{ij}(k + 1) = strength_{ij}(k) - 0.1(maxstrength_j(k) - strength_{ij}(k)))$$
$$+0.01$$

As shown in figure 1, the associative learning can produce a feedback that indirectly affects drives and other behaviors. When an alarm is heard and it is associated with a predator, a new internal stimulus is created composed of the associated predator, the association strength, and the direction and distance of the alarm, which is used as an approximately location of the predator. This new stimulus will affect the fear drive and fleeing behavior. The fear drive is changed to account for this new information, which gradually changes fear value:

$$fear(t + 1) = \begin{cases} ramp_2(1.0), & \text{predator is seen} \\ ramp_2(strength_{ij}(t)), & \text{predator is not seen, but an alarm } i \text{ is heard} \\ & \text{and the strongest association is related to a predator } j \\ ramp_2(fear(t) - 0.05(1.0 - fear(t))), & \text{otherwise} \end{cases}$$

This allows the associative learning to produce an escape response, even if the predator is not seen. This response is gradually learned and it describes a new action rule associating alarm with predator and subsequent fleeing behavior. The initial response to an alarm is a scanning behavior, typically indexical. If the alarm produces an escape response due to its mental association with a predator, our creature is using a symbol.

3   Creatures in Operation

The virtual environment inhabited by creatures works as a laboratory to study the conditions for symbol emergence. In order to evaluate our simulation architecture, we performed different experiments to observe the creatures during associative learning of stimuli. We simulate the communicative interactions between preys in an environment with the different predators and objects, varying the quantity of creatures present in the environment.

Initially, we used teacher and learner preys and change the number of teachers, predators and learners (figure 3). Results show that learners are always able to establish the correct associations between alarms and predators (alarm 1 - terrestrial predator, alarm 2 - aerial predator, alarm 3 - ground predator). The number of interactions decreased whereas the amount of competition among associations increased, as the number of teachers or predators increased. This is due to an increase in the numbers of vocalizing events from teachers, what corresponds to more events of reinforcement and less of weakening. Placing two learners in the environment, we could also notice that the trajectories described by the association values in each prey are quite different, partially because of random properties in their behavior.

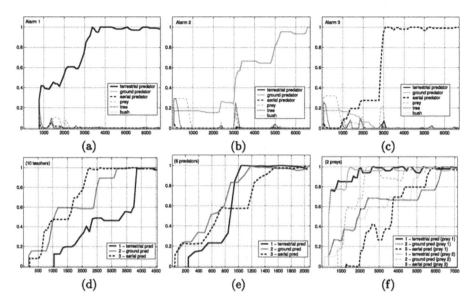

Fig. 3. Evolution of association strength values using Teachers and Learners (association value x iteration). Exp. A (1 learner (L), 5 teachers (T) and 3 predators (P)): associations with (a) alarm 1, (b) alarm 2 and (c) alarm 3. Exp. B (1 L, 5 T, 6 P): (d) winning associations for alarms. Exp. C (1 L, 10 T, 3 P): (e) winning assoc. for alarms. Exp. D (2 L, 5 T, 3 P): (d) winning associations in each creature.

Using self-organizers, all preys can vocalize and learn alarms. Therefore, the number of alarms present in the simulations is not limited to three as before. Each prey can create a different alarm to the same predator and the one mostly used tends to dominate the preys' repertoire at the end (figure 4). Increasing the number of preys, tends to increase the number of alarms, the number of interactions and also the amount of competition, since there are more preys creating alarms and also alarms have to disseminate among more preys.

In a final experiment, we wanted to evaluate the adaptive advantage of using symbols instead of just indexes (figure 5). We adjusted our simulations by modelling an environment where visual cues are not always available, as predators, for instance, can hide themselves in the vegetation to approach preys unseen. This was done by including a probability of predators been actually seen even if they are in the sensory area. We then placed learner preys that responded to alarms by just performing scanning (indexical response) and preys that could respond to alarms using their learned associations (symbolic response). Results show that the symbolic response to alarm provides adaptive advantage, as the number of attacks suffered is consistently lower than otherwise.

4   Conclusion

Here we presented a methodology to simulate the emergence of symbols through communicative interactions among artificial creatures. We propose that symbols

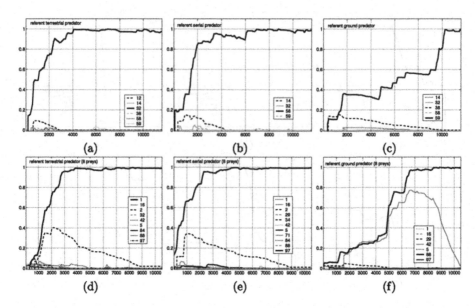

Fig. 4. Evolution of association strength values for Self Organizers (mean value in the preys population). Exp. A (4 self-organizers (S) and 3 predators (P)): associations with (a) terrestrial predator, (b) aerial predator and (c) ground predator. Exp. B (8 S, 3 Ppredators): associations with (d) terrestrial pred., (e) aerial pred. and (f) ground pred.

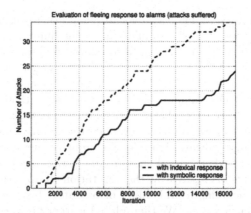

Fig. 5. Number of attacks suffered by preys responding indexically or symbolically to alarms. We simulated an environment where preys can't easily see predators, introducing a 25% probability of a predator being seen, even if it is within sensorial area.

can result from the operation of simple associative learning mechanisms between external stimuli. Experiments show that learner preys are able to establish the correct associations between alarms and predators, after exposed to vocalization events. Self-organizers are also able to converge to a common repertoire, even though there were no pre-defined alarm associations to be learned. Symbols learning and use also provide adaptive advantage to creatures when compared to indexical use of alarm calls.

Although there have been other synthetic experiments simulating the development and evolution of sign systems, e.g. [4,6], this work is the first to deal with multiple distributed agents performing autonomous (self-controlled) communicative interactions. Different from others, we don't establish a pre-defined 'script' of what happens in communicative acts, stating a sequence of fixed task to be performed by one speaker and one hearer. In our work, creatures can be speakers and/or hearers, vocalizing and hearing from many others at the same time, in various situations.

Acknowledgments

A.L. was funded by CAPES; J.Q. is funded by FAPESP.

References

1. Peirce, C.S.: The Collected Papers of Charles Sanders Peirce. Harvard University Press (1931-1958) vols.I-VI. Hartshorne, C., Weiss, P., eds. vols.VII-VIII. Burks, A.W., ed.
2. Queiroz, J., Ribeiro, S.: The biological substrate of icons, indexes, and symbols in animal communication: A neurosemiotic analysis of vervet monkey alarm calls. In Shapiro, M., ed.: The Peirce Seminar Papers 5. Berghahn Books, New York (2002) 69–78
3. Seyfarth, R., Cheney, D., Marler, P.: Monkey responses to three different alarm calls: Evidence of predator classification and semantic communication. Science **210** (1980) 801–803
4. Cangelosi, A., Greco, A., Harnad, S.: Symbol grounding and the symbolic theft hypothesis. In Cangelosi, A., Parisi, D., eds.: Simulating the Evolution of Language. Springer, London (2002)
5. Franklin, S.: Autonomous agents as embodied ai. Cybernetics and Systems **28(6)** (1997) 499–520
6. Steels, L.: The Talking Heads Experiment: Volume I. Words and Meanings. VUB Artificial Intelligence Laboratory, Brussels, Belgium (1999) Special pre-edition.

What Makes a Successful Society?

Experiments with Population Topologies in Particle Swarms

Rui Mendes[*] and José Neves

Departamento de Informática, Universidade do Minho, Portugal

Abstract. Previous studies in Particle Swarm Optimization (PSO) have emphasized the role of population topologies in particle swarms. These studies have shown that a relationship between the way individuals in a population are organized and their aptitude to find global optima exists. A study of what graph statistics are relevant is of paramount importance. This work presents such a study, which will provide guidelines that can be used by researchers in the field of PSO in particular and in the Evolutionary Computation arena in general.

Keywords: Particle Swarm Optimization, Swarm Intelligence, Evolutionary Computation

1 Introduction

The field of Particle Swarm Optimization (PSO) is evolving fast. Since its creation in 1995 [1,2], researchers have proposed important contributions to the paradigm in the field of parameter selection [3,4]. Lately, the field of population topologies has also been object of study, as its importance has been demonstrated [5,6]. The study of topologies has also triggered the development of a very successful algorithm, Fully Informed Particle Swarm (FIPS), that has demonstrated to perform better than the canonical particle swarm, widely accepted by researchers as the state-of-the-art algorithm, in a well-known benchmark of hard functions [7,8].

Due to the fact that FIPS has demonstrated superior results and its close relationship to the structure of the population, a study to understand the relationship between the population structure and the algorithm was conducted.

2 Canonical Particle Swarm

The standard algorithm is given in some form resembling the following:

$$v_{t+1} = \alpha \, v_t + \mathbf{U}[0, \varphi_1] \otimes (\boldsymbol{P}_i - \boldsymbol{X}_t)$$
$$+ \mathbf{U}[0, \varphi_2] \otimes (\boldsymbol{P}_g - \boldsymbol{X}_t) \tag{1}$$
$$\boldsymbol{X}_{t+1} = \boldsymbol{X}_t + v_{t+1} \tag{2}$$

[*] The work of Rui Mendes is sponsored by the grant POSI/ROBO/43904/2002.

A.L.C. Bazzan and S. Labidi (Eds.): SBIA 2004, LNAI 3171, pp. 346–355, 2004.

where $\otimes$ denotes point-wise vector multiplication, $\mathbf{U}[min, max]$ is a function that returns a vector whose positions are randomly generated, following the uniform distribution between min and max, α is called the inertia weight and is less than 1, $\boldsymbol{v}_t$ and $\boldsymbol{X}_t$ represent the speed and position of the particle at time t, $\boldsymbol{P}_i$ refers to the best position found by the particle, and $\boldsymbol{P}_g$ refers to the position found by the member of its neighborhood that has had the best performance so far. The Type $1''$ constriction coefficient is often used [4]:

$$\boldsymbol{v}_{t+1} = \chi \left(\boldsymbol{v}_t + \mathbf{U}[0, \varphi_1] \otimes (\boldsymbol{P}_i - \boldsymbol{X}_t) \right.$$
$$\left. + \mathbf{U}[0, \varphi_2] \otimes (\boldsymbol{P}_g - \boldsymbol{X}_t) \right) \tag{3}$$
$$\boldsymbol{X}_{t+1} = \boldsymbol{X}_t + \boldsymbol{v}_{t+1} \tag{4}$$

The two versions are equivalent, but are simply implemented differently. The second form is used in the present investigations. Other versions exist, but all are fairly close to the models given above.

A particle searches through its neighbors in order to identify the one with the best result so far, and uses information from that source to bias its search in a promising direction. There is no assumption, however, that the best neighbor at time t actually found a better region than the second or third-best neighbors. Important information about the search space may be neglected through overemphasis on the single best neighbor.

When constriction is implemented as in the second version above, lightening the right-hand side of the velocity formula, the constriction coefficient χ is calculated from the values of the acceleration coefficient limits, φ_1 and φ_2; importantly, it is the sum of these two coefficients that determines what χ to use. This fact implies that the particle's velocity can be adjusted by any number of terms, as long as the acceleration coefficients sum to an appropriate value. For instance, the algorithm given above is often used with $\chi = 0.7298$ and $\varphi_1 = \varphi_2 = 2.05$. The φ coefficients must sum, for that value of χ, to 4.1.

3   Fully Informed Particle Swarm

The idea behind FIPS is that social influence comes from the group norm, i.e., the center of gravity of the individual's neighborhood. Contrary to canonical particle swarm, there is no individualism. That is, the particle's previous best position takes no part in the velocity update.

In the canonical particle swarm, each particle explores around a region defined by its previous best success and the success of the best particle in its neighborhood. The difference in FIPS is that the individual should gather information about the whole neighborhood. For that, let us define $\mathcal{N}$ as the set of neighbors of i and p_k as the best position found by individual k.

$$v_{t+1} = \chi \left(v_t + \frac{\sum_{k \in \mathcal{N}} \mathbf{U}[0, \varphi_{max}](p_k - x_t)}{|\mathcal{N}|} \right) \tag{5}$$
$$x_{t+1} = \qquad\qquad x_t + v_{t+1}$$

This formula is a generalization of the canonical version. In fact, if $\mathcal{N}$ is defined to contain only i itself and its best neighbor, this formula is equivalent to the one presented in equation 4. Thus, in FIPS the velocity update is performed according to a stochastically weighted average of the difference between the particle's current position and each of its neighbors' previous best.

As can be concluded from equation 5, the algorithm uses neither information about the relative quality of each of the solutions found by its neighbors nor about the particle's previous best position. The particle simply oscillates around the stochastic center of gravity of its neighbors' previous findings.

4   Population Structures and Graph Statistics

In particle swarms, individuals strive to improve themselves by imitating traits found in their successful peers. Thus, "social norms" emerge because individuals are influenced by their neighbors. The definition of the social neighborhood of an individual, i.e., which individuals influence it, is very important. As practice demonstrates, the topology that is most widely used – *gbest*, where all individuals influence one another – is vulnerable to local optima.

Social influence is dictated by the information found in the neighborhood of each individual, which is only a subset of the population. The relationship of influence is defined by a social network – represented as a graph – that we call *population topology* or *sociometry*.

The goal of sociometries is to control how soon the algorithm converges. The goal is find which aspects of the graph structure are responsible for the information "spread". It does not make sense to study topologies where there are isolated subgroups, as they would not communicate among themselves. Therefore, all graphs studied are connected, i.e., there is a path between any two vertices. Results reported by researchers confirm that PSO performs well with small populations of 20 individuals.

4.1   Degree and Distribution Sequence

Degree determines the scale of socialization: An individual without neighbors is an outsider; an individual with few neighbors cannot gather information from nor influence others in the population; an individual with many neighbors is both well informed and i possesses a large sphere of influence.

One of the most interesting measures of the spread of information seems to be the distribution sequence. In fact it can be seen as an extension of the degree. In short, this sequence, named Λ_l, gives the number of individuals that can only be reached through a path of l edges.

$\Lambda_1(\mathbf{v})$ This is the degree of vertex v. It represents the number of individuals immediately influenced by v.

$\Lambda_2(\mathbf{v})$ This is the number of v's neighbor's neighbors. To influence these individuals, v must influence its neighbors for a sufficiently long period of time.

$\Lambda_3(\mathbf{v})$ This is the number of individuals three steps away from v. To influence these individuals, v has to transitively influence its neighbors and its neighbors' neighbors.

Besides the degree, this study also investigates the effects of Λ_2. Λ_3 is not used because it is not defined on most of the graphs used.

4.2   Average Distance, Radius and Diameter

In a sparsely connected population, information takes a long time to travel. The spreading of information is an important object of study. Scientists study this effect in many different fields, from social sciences to epidemiology. A measure of this is path length. Path length presents a compromise between exploration and exploitation: If it is too small, it means that information spreads too fast, which implies a higher probability of premature convergence. If it is large, it means that information takes a long time to travel through the graph and thus the population is more resilient and not so eager to exploit earlier on.

However, robustness comes at a price: speed of convergence. It seems important to find an equilibrium. This statistic correlates highly with degree: a high degree means a low path length and vice-versa. The radius of a graph is the smallest maximal difference of a vertex to any other. The diameter of a graph is the largest distance between any two vertices.

4.3   Clustering

Clustering measures the percentage of a vertex's neighbors that are neighbors to one another. It measures the degree of "cliquishness" of a graph. Overlapping plays an important part in social networks. We move in several circles of friends. In these, almost everyone knows each other. In fact we act as bridges or shortcuts between the various circles we frequent. Clustering influences the information spread in a graph. However, its influence is more subtle. The degree of homogenization forces the cluster to follow a social norm. If most of the connections are inside the cluster; all individuals in it will tend to share their knowledge fairly quickly. Good regions discovered by one of them are quickly passed on to the other members of the group. Even a partial degree of clustering helps to disseminate information. It is easier to influence an individual if we influence most of its neighbors.

5   Parallel Coordinates and Visual Data Analysis

Parallel coordinates provide an effective representation tool to perform hyperdimensional data analysis [9]. Parallel coordinates were proposed by Inselberg [10] as a new way to represent multi-dimensional information. Since the original proposal, much subsequent work has been accomplished, e.g., [11]. In traditional Cartesian coordinates, all axes are mutually perpendicular. In parallel coordinates, all axes are parallel to one another and equally spaced. By drawing the axes parallel to one another, one can represent points, lines and planes in hyper-dimensional spaces. Points are represented by connecting the coordinates on each of the axes by a line.

Parallel coordinates are a very useful tool in visual analysis. It is very easy to identify clusters visually in high dimensional data by using color transparency. Color transparency is used to darken less clustered areas and brighten highly clustered ones. By using brushing techniques, it is possible to examine subsets of the data and to identify relationships between variables.

In this study, parallel coordinates were used to identify the graph statistics present in all highly successful population topologies. By using brushing, it is possible to identify highly successful groups and identify what characteristics are shared by all topologies belonging to them.

6 Parameter Selection and Test Procedure

The present experiments extracted two kinds of measures of performance on a standard suite of test functions. The functions were the sphere or parabolic function in 30 dimensions, Rastrigin's function in 30 dimensions, Griewank's function in 10 and 30 dimensions (the importance of the local minima is much higher in 10 dimensions, due to the product of co-sinuses, making it much harder to find the global minimum), Rosenbrock's function in 30 dimensions, Ackley's function in 30 dimensions, and Schaffer's f6, which is in 2 dimensions. Formulas can be found in the literature (e.g., in [12]).

The experiments conducted compare several conditions among themselves. A condition is an algorithm paired with a topology. To have a certain degree of precision as to the value of a certain measure pertaining to a given condition, 50 runs were performed per condition.

6.1 Mean Performance

One of the measures used is the best function result attained after a fixed number of function evaluations. This measure reports the expected performance an algorithm will have on a specific function. The mean performance is a measure of sloppy speed. It does not necessarily indicate whether the algorithm is close to the global optimum. A relatively high score can be obtained on some of these multi-modal functions simply by finding the best part of a locally optimal region.

When using many functions, results are usually presented independently on each of the functions used and there is no methodology to conclude which of the approaches has a good performance over all the functions. However, this considerably complicates the task of evaluating which approach is the best. It is not possible to combine raw results from different functions, as they are all scaled differently. To provide an easier way of combining the results from different functions, uniform fitness is used, instead of raw fitness. A uniform fitness can simply be regarded as a proportion: a uniform fitness of less than 0.1 can be interpreted as being one of the top 10% solutions. In this study, the number of iterations elapsed before performance is recorded is of 1,000.

6.2   Proportion of Successes

While the measure of mean performance gives an indication of the quality of the solution found, an algorithm can achieve a good result while getting stuck in a local optimum. The proportion of successes shows the percentage of times that the algorithm was able to reach the globally optimal region. The proportion of successes validates the results of the average performance. It may be possible for good results to be achieved by combining an extremely good result in a function (e.g. the Sphere, with an average result in a more difficult function). The algorithm is left to run until 3,000 iterations have elapsed and then its success is recorded.

6.3   Parameter Selection

As the goal of this study is to verify the impact of the choice of social topologies in the behavior of the algorithm, the tuning parameters are fixed. They are set to the values that are widely used by the community and that are deemed to be the most appropriate ones, as demonstrated in [4]. The value of φ was set to 4.1, which is one of the most used in the community of particle swarms. This value is split equally between φ_1 and φ_2. The value of χ was set to 0.729. All the population topologies used in this study comprise 20 individuals.

6.4   Topology Generation

The graphs representing the social topologies were generated according to a given set of constraints. These were representative of several parameters deemed important in the graph structure. Preliminary studies of the graph statistics indicated that by manipulating the average degree and average clustering, along with the corresponding standard deviations, it was possible to manipulate the other statistics over the entire range of possible values. These parameters were used to create a database of graphs with average degrees ranging from 3 to 10 and clustering from 0 to 1. A database of graph statistics of these topologies was collected, to be used in the analysis. The total number of population topologies used amounts to 3,289.

7   Analysis of the Results

The results obtained are analyzed visually using Parvis, a tool for parallel coordinates visualization of multidimensional data sets. To allow for an easier interpretation of the figures, the name of each of the axes is explained:

Alg 1 for Canonical Particle Swarm, 2 for FIPS.
Prop Proportion of successes.
Perf Average performance.
Degree Average degree of the population topology.
ClusteringCoefficient Clustering coefficient of the population topology.

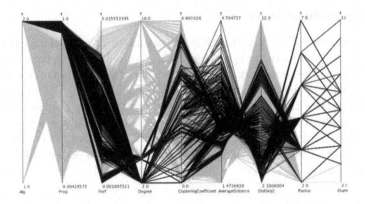

Fig. 1. Experiments with a proportion of successes higher than 93%. All the experiments belong to the FIPS algorithm.

AverageDistance Average distance between two nodes in the graph.
DistSeq2 The distribution sequence of order 2.
Radius The radius of the graph.
Diameter The diameter of the graph.

First, the experiments responsible for a proportion of successes higher than 93% are isolated (Figure 1). All the results belong to the FIPS algorithm. None of the canonical experiments was this successful. However, some of the experiments have low quality average performance. The next step is to isolate the topologies with both a high proportion of successes and a high quality average performance (Figure 2). Fortunately, all of these have some characteristics in common:

- the average degree is always 4;
- the clustering coefficient is low;
- the average distance is always similar.

As most of the graph statistics are related to some degree, it seems interesting to display the graph statistics of all graphs with degree 4 (Figure 3). This shows that the average distance is similar for graphs with a somewhat low clustering coefficient. Thus, it makes sense to concentrate the efforts in just the average degree and clustering coefficient.

Figure 4 shows the experiments of FIPS, using topologies with average degree 4 and clustering lower than 0, 5. This figure is similar to Figure 2. As a further exercise, Figure 5 shows what happens when the clustering is restricted to values lower than 0, 0075. This set identifies very high quality solutions, according to both measures.

8   Conclusions and Further Work

This study corroborates the results reported in [7, 8] that FIPS shows superior results to the ones of the canonical particle swarm. It showed that the successful

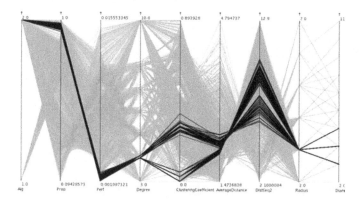

Fig. 2. Experiments with a high proportion of successes and a high quality average performance. The following conclusions can be drawn: the average degree is always 4; the clustering coefficient is low; the average distance is always similar.

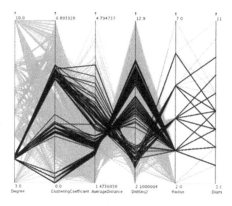

Fig. 3. Graph statistics of all topologies with average degree 4.

topologies had an average of four neighbors. This result can be easily rationalized: The use of more particles triggers the possibility of crosstalk effects encountered in neural network learning algorithms. In other words, the pulls experienced in the directions of multiple particles will mostly cancel each other and reduce the possible benefits of considering their knowledge.

Parallel coordinates proved to be a powerful tool to analyze the results. The capabilities of the tool used allowed for a very straightforward test of different hypothesis. The visual analysis of the results was able to find a set of graph statistics that explains what makes a good social topology.

To validate the conjectures concluded by this work, a large number of graphs with the characteristics found should be generated and tested to see if all the graphs in the set have similar characteristics when interpreted as a population topology. Further tests with other problems should also be performed, especially with real-life problems, to validate the results found.

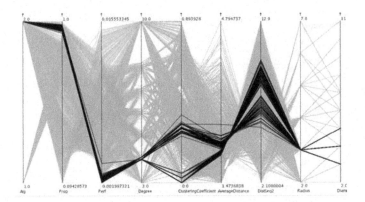

Fig. 4. Experiments of FIPS with topologies with average degree 4 and clustering lower than 0, 5.

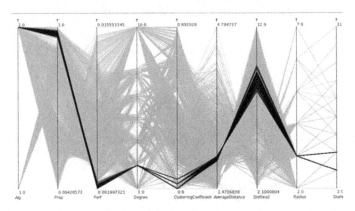

Fig. 5. Experiments of FIPS with topologies with average degree 4 and clustering lower than 0, 0075.

References

1. Eberhart, R., Kennedy, J.: A new optimizer using particle swarm theory. In: Proceedings of the Sixth International Symposium on Micro Machine and Human Science, Nagoya, Japan, IEEE Service Center (1995) 39–43
2. Kennedy, J., Eberhart, R.: Particle swarm optimization. In: Proceedings of ICNN'95 - International Conference on Neural Networks. Volume 4., Perth, Western Australia (1995) 1942–1948
3. Shi, Y., Eberhart, R.C.: Parameter selection in particle swarm optimization. In Porto, V.W., Saravanan, N., Waagen, D., Eiben, A.E., eds.: Evolutionary Programming VII, Berlin, Springer (1998) 591–600 Lecture Notes in Computer Science 1447.
4. Clerc, M., Kennedy, J.: The particle swarm: Explosion, stability, and convergence in a multi-dimensional complex space. IEEE Transactions on Evolutionary Computation **6** (2002) 58–73

5. Kennedy, J.: Small worlds and mega-minds: Effects of neighborhood topology on particle swarm performance. In: Proceedings of the 1999 Conference on Evolutionary Computation, IEEE Computer Society (1999) 1931–1938

6. Kennedy, J., Mendes, R.: Topological structure and particle swarm performance. In Fogel, D.B., Yao, X., Greenwood, G., Iba, H., Marrow, P., Shackleton, M., eds.: Proceedings of the Fourth Congress on Evolutionary Computation (CEC-2002), Honolulu, Hawaii, IEEE Computer Society (2002)

7. Mendes, R., Kennedy, J., Neves, J.: Watch thy neighbor or how the swarm can learn from its environment. In: Proceedings of the Swarm Intelligence Symposium (SIS-2003), Indianapolis, IN, Purdue School of Engineering and Technology, IUPUI, IEEE Computer Society (2003)

8. Mendes, R., Kennedy, J., Neves, J.: The fully informed particle swarm: Simpler, maybe better. IEEE Transactions of Evolutionary Computation (in press 2004)

9. Wegman, E.: Hyperdimensional data analysis using parallel coordinates. Journal of the American Statistical Association **85** (1990) 664–675

10. Inselberg, A.: n-dimensional graphics, part I–lines and hyperplanes. Technical Report G320-2711, IBM Los Angeles Scientific Center, IBM Scientific Center, 9045 Lincoln Boulevard, Los Angeles (CA), 900435 (1981)

11. Inselberg, A.: The plane with parallel coordinates. The Visual Computer **1** (1985) 69–91

12. Reynolds, R.G., Chung, C.: Knowledge-based self-adaptation in evolutionary programming using cultural algorithms. In: Proceedings of IEEE International Conference on Evolutionary Computation (ICEC'97). (1997) 71–76

Splinter: A Generic Framework
for Evolving Modular Finite State Machines

Ricardo Nastas Acras and Silvia Regina Vergilio

Federal University of Parana (UFPR), CP: 19081
CEP: 81531-970, Curitiba, Brazil
ricardo@acras.net, silvia@inf.ufpr.br

Abstract. Evolutionary Programming (EP) has been used to solve a
large variety of problems. This technique uses concepts of Darwin's theory to evolve finite state machines (FSMs). However, most works develop
tailor-made EP frameworks to solve specific problems. These frameworks
generally require significant modifications in their kernel to be adapted
to other domains. To easy reuse and to allow modularity, modular FSMs
were introduced. They are fundamental to get more generic EP frameworks. In this paper, we introduce the framework Splinter, capable of
evolving modular FSMs. It can be easily configured to solve different
problems. We illustrate this by presenting results from the use of Splinter
for two problems: the artificial ant problem and the sequence of characters. The results validate the Splinter implementation and show that the
modularity benefits do not decrease the performance.

Keywords: evolutionary programming, modularity

1   Introduction

Evolutionary Computation (CE) techniques have been gained attention in last
years mainly due to the fact that they are able to solve a great number of complex
problems [7, 11]. These techniques are based on Darwin's theory [4]: The individuals that better adapt to the environment that surrounds them have a greater
chance to survive. They pass their genetic characteristics to their descendents
and consequently, after several generations, this process tends to naturally select
individuals, eliminating the ones that do not fit the environment. The concepts
are usually applied by genetic operators, such as: selection, crossover, mutation
and reproduction. CE techniques are: Genetic Algorithms, Genetic Programming, Evolution Strategies and Evolutionary Programming. This last one is the
focus of this paper. In Evolutionary Programming (EP) the individuals, that
represent the solutions for a given problem, are finite state machines (FSMs).

   EP is not a new field. It was first proposed by Fogel for evolving artificial
intelligence in the early 1960's [6]. Since then, it has been used for the evolution
and optimization of a wide variety of architectures and parameters. According
to Chellapilla and Czarnechi [3] such applications include linear and bilinear
models, neural networks, fuzzy systems, lists, etc. However, most works and EP

A.L.C. Bazzan and S. Labidi (Eds.): SBIA 2004, LNAI 3171, pp. 356–365, 2004.
© Springer-Verlag Berlin Heidelberg 2004

frameworks found in the literature deal with problem-specific representations [2, 11]. EP frameworks need significant modifications in their kernel to be adapted to other domains. In this sense, an evolutionary framework capable of implementing different problem representations is necessary. This generic framework should be easily configurable and scalable to problems of practical value.

Chellapilla and Czarnechi [3] points that such framework should support automatic discovery of problem representations. To allow this feature it should use modular FSMs (MFSMs). The use of MFSMs favors the generation of hierarchical, modular structures that can decompose a difficult task into simpler subtasks. These subtasks may then be solved with lower computational effort and they solutions combined to give the general solution. This also allow reuse to solve similar sub-problems and easy comprehension.

The modularity is an important concept to reach generic solutions. Because of this, we find in CE some works focusing modularity, such as the evolution of modules using Genetic Programming [1, 9, 12, 13], and using EP [3]. In this last work, the authors propose a procedure to evolve MFSMs and present results showing that the evolution of MFSMs is statistically significant faster. However, the authors do not implement a generic framework. In [10] a generic EP framework is described. It offers a set of C++ classes to be configured to evolve FSMs but, it does not allow the evolution of MFSMs.

We introduce Splinter, a generic EP framework, capable of evolving MFSMs. Splinter implements the procedure described in [3]. Because of this, it supports modularity and reuse. It can be easily configured to solve different problems and allows non-expert people to use EP for solving their specific problems, reducing effort and time.

To illustrate this, we describe two examples of problems solved with Splinter. The obtained results allow the validation of the Splinter implementation and the performance evaluation of MFSMs.

The paper is organized as follows. Section 2 presents an overview of MSFMs and of the evolution process for this kind of machines. Section 3 describes the framework Splinter. Section 4 shows use examples and results obtained with Splinter. Section 5 concludes the paper.

2   MFSMs

A finite state machine M is represented as $M = (I, O, S, \gamma, \lambda)$, where:

I, O, and S are finite sets of input symbols, output symbols and states respectively.

$\gamma : S \times I \to S$ is the state transition function, it can be null.

$\lambda : S \times I \to O$ is the output function.

When the machine is in a current state s in S and receives an input a from I, it moves to the next state specified by $\gamma(s, a)$ and produces an output given by $\lambda(s, a)$. S includes a special state S_0 called the initial state.

A FSM can be represented by a state transition diagram, a directed graph whose vertices correspond to the states of the machine and whose edges correspond to the state transitions; each edge is labeled with the input an output

symbols associated with the transition. For example, consider the diagram of
Figure 1 and the machine in state S_0 (initial state with an extra arrow), upon
input b, the machine moves to state S_2 and outputs c. Equivalently, a FSM can
be represented by a state table[1] as given in Table 1. Observe that the initial
state is marked with a $*$ and null transitions are represented by $-$.

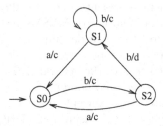

Fig. 1. An Example of State Transition Diagram

Table 1. State Table of the FSM in Figure 1

Current State	$S_0{}^*$		S_1		S_2	
Input	a	b	a	b	a	b
Output	-	c	c	c	c	d
Next State	-	S_2	S_0	S_1	S_0	S_1

There are in the literature many extensions to FSM, some of them allow representation of guards and actions [15] and of data-flow information [14]. To allow
modularity and reuse a FSM can be extended and have one or more modules.
A modular FSM consists of one main FSM and k sub-modules (which are also
FSMs, that is, are sub-FSMs). In a MFSM transitions between the main FSM
and the sub-FSM are possible. They are represented by hexagons in the state
diagram and by other row in the state table (Control).

For example, Figure 2 represents a MFSM whit one sub-FSM, Sub_1 and the
Main FSM. S_0 is the initial state, upon input symbol a, the machine moves to
state S_1 and outputs c. Currently in state S_1 and upon the input b, the machine
moves to initial state S_0 in sub-machine Sub_1 and outputs d. According to the
input received, the sub-machine retains control until the one of the transitions
represented by the hexagon *Main* is reached. In this case, the control returns to
the Main-FSM in the state S_2.

Observe that when control is transferred to a sub-FSM, the processing of the
input symbol always starts in the sub-FSM initial state. However, when control
returns to the main-FSM or to any other sub-FSM, processing continues from
the last state, during a transition to which control was transferred. The control

---

[1] We will consider only deterministic machines. These machines do not have more
than one transition for each input symbol.

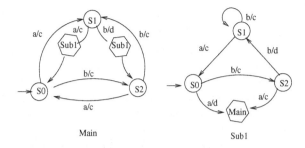

Fig. 2. An Example of State Transition Diagram for a MFSM

Table 2. State Table of the MFSM in Figure 2

State table of the Main-FSM							State table of the sub-FSM Sub_1						
Current State	$S_0{}^*$		S_1		S_2		Current State	$S_0{}^*$		S_1		S_2	
Input	a	b	a	b	a	b	Input	a	b	a	b	a	b
Output	c	c	c	d	c	c	Output	d	c	c	c	c	d
Next State	S_1	S_2	S_0	S_2	S_0	S_1	Next State	-	S_2	S_0	S_1	-	S_1
Control	0	0	1	1	0	0	Control	0	1	1	1	0	1

transfer is represented in the state table by the number of the sub-FSM, the main FSM has number 0.

The evolution process for MFSMs is based on the evolutionary procedure of Fogel [5] and of Chellapila and Czarnecki [3]. This procedure includes the following steps.

1. Initialization: a population is randomly created and consists on n MFSMs. Each sub-FSM is initialized at random in a identical manner. First the number n of states is initialized and the initial state is selected. The transitions are created and after this, based on the provided input and output alphabets, the symbols are assigned to each transition.
2. Application of the mutation operators: when the individuals are FSMs only mutation operators are applied. An individual P is modified to produce one offspring P'. The mutation operations are:
    - delete states: one or more states are randomly selected for deletion. The links in the machine are reassigned randomly to other states. If the initial state was deleted, a new one is selected.
    - reassign the initial state: a new initial state is chosen at random.
    - reassign transitions: n randomly selected links in m states are randomly reassigned to different states.
    - reassign output symbols: n output symbols are randomly chosen and reassigned to different symbols randomly chosen from the alphabet.
    - change control: n control entries in the state table are randomly chosen and reassigned to different machines.

- add states: a new state is created and its transitions are randomly generated. This new state will be really connected to the machine if another mutation occurs, such as, reassign transitions.
3. Fitness Evaluation: the fitness of each individual is evaluated according to the objective function for the task.
4. Selection: to determine the individuals to be modified by the mutation operators the tournament selection [5] is used. For a machine M, a number q of opponents is randomly chosen. If the machine's fitness is no lesser than the opponent's fitness, it receives a win. The k individuals with the most wins are selected to be mutated for the next generation.
5. The procedure ends if the halting criterion is satisfied; otherwise, the maximum number of generations is reached.

Chellapila and Czarnecki [3] used the above procedure to the artificial ant problem. The results indicate that the proposed EP procedure can rapidly evolve optimal modular machines in comparison with the evolution of non-modular FSMs. In 48 of the 50 MFSMs, the perfect machines were found. In 44 of the 50 non-modular FSM evolution trials, the perfect machines were found.

3   The Framework Splinter

The framework Splinter supports the evolution of MFSM. It was implemented in C++. This language allows the use of containers besides of the object-oriented concepts, such as: polymorphism, overloading and inheritance. They simplify the framework implementation.

Fig. 3 shows diagrams illustrating the main modules and classes of Splinter. They are described as follows.

1. Population: responsible for maintaining the population during the evolution process. It is implemented by the class *CPopulation* that is associated to several MFSMs, that are the individuals in the population. Each individual is represented by the class *CMFSM*, according to the tables presented in Section 2. This class is composed by a set of n instances of *CModule*, where n is the number of modules of the modular machine. Each class *CModule* by its turn is composed by a set of states and transitions, implemented respectively by the classes *CState* and *CTransition*.
2. Fitness: this module is implemented by the class *CFitness* associated to *CPopulation*. This class has a method *evaluate* that is related to the fitness function and is dependent on the problem.
3. Evolver: module responsible for the evolution process and the application of the genetic operators. The evolution procedure and operators used by Evolver were described in Section 2.
4. Creator: creates the initial population. It is implemented by the class *CCreator*. There are two special class *CUtilsRandom* and *CUtilsSymbols* responsible by the random generation of the individuals, which are randomly created, according to the initial configuration file.

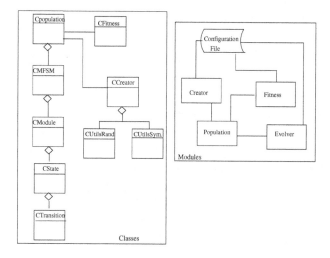

Fig. 3. Splinter Diagrams

The configuration file is organized in related sections, delimited by "[". Each section defines several parameters. An example of configuration file is presented in Fig. 4. This figure is explained below.

- population and individuals: this section contains information for the random generation of the individuals. The number of individuals in the initial population, the maximum and minimum numbers of individuals during the process, the maximum and minimum numbers of modules for an individual, the maximum and minimum numbers of states and transitions. If the maximum number of modules is 1, non-modular FSMs are evolved.
- evolution: this section contains information necessary to the evolution process. The maximum number of generations and better fitness are possible termination criteria. The second one depends on the fitness function implemented. The number of opponents used to select an individual to be mutated, the maximum and minimum numbers of children and of mutations to generate a child.
- mutation: this section contains information necessary for the mutation operators application. The mutation rate defines the probability of a mutation occurs. In a population of 100 individuals a mutation rate of 0.7 means that 70 of the parents will be mutated to compose the next generation. A probability is also given for each mutation operator.
- symbols: this section defines the input and output alphabets.
- recursion: this section contains only a boolean information to indicate that recursion is or not allowed.

To configure Splinter ,it is necessary to define the fitness function adequate to the problem to be solved. The user should overwrite the method *evaluate* of *CPopulation*. Beside of this, he or she needs to write the configuration file. When necessary, all the evolution procedure can be changed. In such case, the method *evolver* of *CPopulation* needs to be overwritten. But this last modification requires more knowledge about CE evolution strategies.

```
[population]
numInitial     = 100 #inicial number of individuals in the initial population
numMaxIndiv    = 200 #maximum number of individuals in the population
numMinIndiv    = 50  #minimum number of individuals in the population
[evolution]
numMaxGer      = 300 #maximum number of generations
betterfitness  = 1.0 #better fitness
numOponent     = 3   #number of oponents in the competition
numMaxChildren = 3   #maximum number of children of an individual
numMinChildren = 1   #minimum number of children of an individual
numMinMut      = 1   #minimum number of mutations to generate a child
numMaxMut      = 5   #maximum number of mutations to generate a child
[mutation]
mutationRate   = 0.7
probMut        = ADD_STATE,0.1
probMut        = DELETE_STATE,0.1
probMut        = CHANGE_INITIAL_STATE,0.1
probMut        = CHANGE_TRANSITION,0.1
probMut        = CHANGE_OUTPUT_SYMBOL,0.1
probMut        = CHANGE_CONTROL,0.1
[individuals]
numMinModules  = 1   #minimum number of modules of an individual
numMaxModules  = 1   #maximum number of modules of an individual
numMinStates   = 1   #minimum number of states of an individual
numMaxStates   = 5   #maximum number of states of an individual
numMinTransit  = 1   #minimum number of transitions of an individual
numMaxTransit  = 3   #maximum number of transitions of an individual
[symbols]
input= a,e,i,o,u    #input alphabet
output= x           #output alphabet
[transition]
recursion=N         #Is recursion allowed?
```

Fig. 4. Splinter Configuration File

4   Using Splinter

This section presents how Splinter was configured to solve two different problems and shows some preliminary results.

4.1   The Tracker Task

This problem was introduced in [8] and is also known as the artificial ant problem. The problem consists of an ant placed on a 32x32 toroidal grid. Food packets are scattered along a trail on the grid. The trail begins on the second square in the first row near the left top corner. It is 127 squares long, and contains 20 turns and 89 squares with food packets. The ant can sense the presence of a food packed in the square directly ahead and can take three decisions: turn left or right or, move forward one square. The goal of the machine is to guide the ant to collect all 89 food packets. The ant starts out facing East on the second square in the first row.

The objective function for evaluation a FSM is the total number of food packets collected within the allotted time. Each of the ant's actions cost one time step. A maximum of 600 time steps were allowed.

As mentioned in Section 2, Chellapilla and Czarnecki [3] used this problem to evaluate their EP procedure. As Splinter implements that procedure, we used Splinter to solve this problem too. The goal is to validate our implementation.

To configure Splinter, the input alphabet used is {F,N}, representing respectively that are or not food ahead. The output alphabet consists on {L, R, M}, representing the three movements mentioned above.

We started with a configuration file similar to the one presented in Fig. 4. After an amount of experimentation, we used the following main parameters: number of opponents is 10; number of children varying between [1..4]; in each children was applied [1..6] mutations; number of states in [3..6] and number of modules in [2..5]. Splinter was run 4 times and 50 trials were obtained in each run, in a total of 200. Only three of them were not successful. This result is very similar to the obtained by Chellapilla and Czarnecki, described in Section 2. They obtained two not successful modular machines and six non-modular ones.

4.2   Sequence of Characters

This is a very common problem on the programming language area. The machine has to identify a specific sequence of characters; in our example, the sequence of vowels: (a, e, i, o, u). The idea of this second experiment is to evaluate the implementation of Splinter in another context. Beside of this, we run Splinter with several configuration files to investigate the influence of its different parameters.

The fitness function for evaluating a FSM is given by the number of identified vowels. The best fitness (of 100%) means that all the sequence was identified. The input alphabet for this problem is {a, e, i, o, u}. The output alphabet is {x}, because the output is not significant in this case.

The different configurations are modifications of the file presented in Fig. 4. These modifications are described below.

1. configuration of Fig. 4, this configuration does not include modules.
2. changing the number of modules for the interval [2..4] with [2..5] states.
3. changing the size of population to 1000
4. changing the maximum number of transitions for 5 (the same number of input symbols)
5. changing the number of opponents to 7 and the number of children to [5..10]
6. combination of the above modifications.

Splinter was run 10 times for each configuration. Table 3 presents the results obtained for each run. For example, using Configuration 1 the solution with best fitness was found in the 14th generation in the first run. This configuration presents the worst result, that is to find the solution in the 275th run, however it always find the best solution. Configuration 2, that includes modules, does not find the solution in two runs (marked with a '-' in the table). The zero indicates that the initial population presented the best fitness. Better solutions were found by increasing the number of transitions and the number of opponents, represented in the last rows of the table. These parameters really influence on the result. The best result is found by introducing all the modifications together. This configuration includes modules. The modularity does not seem to influence the evolution process in such case.

Table 3. Results Obtained for Each Configuration

Config.					Run					
Number	1	2	3	4	5	6	7	8	9	10
1	14	28	275	4	6	3	14	7	5	6
2	3	9	-	224	5	3	-	11	9	183
3	55	5	4	2	4	8	4	4	4	6
4	0	2	3	0	2	1	1	2	2	3
5	3	5	3	4	3	3	6	3	3	4
6	1	1	1	1	1	0	0	0	0	0

5   Conclusions

EP is a CE technique that can be used to solve different problems in several domains. However, for its large application, many in industrial environments a generic framework is necessary. This work contributes in this direction by describing Splinter, a generic EP framework, that is capable of evolving MFSMs.

Splinter supports modularity and all its benefits: decomposition of problems, reduction of complexity and reuse. Beside of this, the structure of Splinter allows easy and quick configuration for diverse kinds of problems. The evolution kernel, responsible for the genetic operations, is totally independent on the domain. The user needs only to provide the configuration file and to write the method responsible for the fitness function. More expert users can easily overwritten other methods and even modify the evolution process, if desired.

To validate the implementation of Splinter, we explore its use in two problems. The tracker task problem, used by other authors and by Chellapila and Czarnecki to investigate MFSMs and the sequence of characters problem.

To the first problem a very good result was obtained with MFSMs: only three of the modular machines were not successful. This result are very similar to the results found in the literature. MFSMs get a better performance.

In the second problem, we compare modular and non-modular machines and investigate the influence of the configuration parameters of Splinter. We obtained better solutions by increasing the number of transitions and opponents. The results show that the use of modularity does not seem to influence the evolution process and does not imply a lower performance. However, new experiments should be conducted to better evaluate MFSMs.

The preliminary experience with Splinter is very encouraging. Due this easy configuration, we are now exploring Splinter in the context of software engineering to select and evaluate test data for specifications models. We also intend to conduct other experiments with Splinter. These new studies should explore explore other contexts and the performance of MFSMs.

References

1. Angeline, P.J. and Pollack, J. Evolutionary module acquisition. Proceedings of the Sec. Annual Conference on Evolutionary Programming. pp 154-163, 1993.
2. Báck, T. and Urich, H. and Schwefel, H.P. Evolutionary Computation: Comments on the History and Current State IEEE Trans. on Software Engineering Vol 17(6), pp 3-17, June, 1991
3. Chellapila K. and Czarnecki, D. A Preliminary Investigation into Evolving Modular Finite States Machines. Proceedings of the Congress on Evolutionary Computation- CEC 99. IEEE Press. Vol 2, pp 1349-1356, 6-9 July 1999.
4. Darwin, C. On the Origin of Species by Means of Natural Selection or the Preservation of Favored Races in the Struggle for Life, Murray, London-UK", 1859.
5. Fogel, D.B. Evolutionary Computation - Toward a New Philosophy of Machine Intelligence", IEEE Press, Piscataway, NJ, 1995.
6. Fogel, L.J. On the Organization of Intellect, Ph.D. Dissertation, UCLA-USA 1964.
7. Proceedings of Genetic and Evolutionary Computation Conference, New York-USA 2002, Chicago-USA 2003.
8. Jefferson, D. and et al. Evolution of a Theme in Artificial Life: The Genesys: Tracker System, Tech. Report, Univ. California, Los Angeles, CA, 1991.
9. Koza, J.R. Genetic Programming II: Automatic Discovery of Reusable Programs MIT Press, 1994.
10. Ladd, S.R. libevocosm - C++ Tools for Evolutionary Software http://www.coyotegulch.com/docs/evocosm, February, 2004.
11. Michalewicz, Z. and Michalewicz, M. Evolutionary Computation Techniques and Their Applications. IEEE International Conf. on Intelligent Processing Systems, 1997.
12. Rodrigues, E. and Pozo, A.R.T. Grammar-Guided Genetic Programming and Automatically Defined Functions. Brazilian Symposium on Artificial Intelligence, SBIA-2002, Porto de Galinhas, Recife.
13. Rosca, J.P. and Ballard, D.H. Discovery of Sub-routines in Genetic Programming. Advances in Genetic Programming. pp 177-201. MIT Press, 1996.
14. Shehady, R.K. and Siewiorek, D.P. A Method to Automate User Interface Testing Using Variable Finite State Machines. Proc. of International Symposium on Fault-Tolerant Computing -FTCS'97. 25-27, June, Seattle, Washington, USA.
15. Wang, C-J. and Liu, M.T. Axiomatic Test Sequence Generation for Extended Finite State Machines Proc. International Conference on Distributed Computing Systems. 9-12, June, 1992 pp:252-259.

An Hybrid GA/SVM Approach for Multiclass Classification with Directed Acyclic Graphs

Ana Carolina Lorena and André C. Ponce de Leon F. de Carvalho

Instituto de Ciências Matemáticas e de Computação (ICMC)
Universidade de São Paulo (USP)
Av. do Trabalhador São-Carlense, 400 - Centro - Cx. Postal 668
São Carlos, São Paulo, Brasil
{aclorena,andre}@icmc.usp.br

Abstract. Support Vector Machines constitute a powerful Machine Learning technique originally proposed for the solution of 2-class problems. In the multiclass context, many works divide the whole problem in multiple binary subtasks, whose results are then combined. Following this approach, one efficient strategy employs a Directed Acyclic Graph in the combination of pairwise predictors in the multiclass solution. However, its generalization depends on the graph formation, that is, on its sequence of nodes. This paper introduces the use of Genetic Algorithms in intelligently searching permutations of nodes in a DAG. The technique proposed is especially useful in problems with relatively high number of classes, where the investigation of all possible combinations would be extremely costly or even impossible.

Keywords: Support Vector Machines, Directed Acyclic Graphs, Genetic Algorithms, multiclass classification

1 Introduction

Multiclass classification using Machine Learning (ML) techniques consists of inducing a function $f(\mathbf{x})$ from a dataset composed of pairs $(\mathbf{x}_i, y_i)$ where $y_i \in \{1, \ldots, k\}$. Some learning methods are originally binary, being able to carry out classifications where $k = 2$. Among these one can mention Support Vector Machines (SVMs) [2].

To generalize a SVM to multiclass problems, several strategies may be employed [3, 9, 10, 15]. One common extension consists in generating $k(k-1)/2$ classifiers, one for each pair of classes (c_i, c_j), with $i < j$. For combining these predictors, Platt et al. [15] suggested the use of a Decision Directed Acyclic Graph (DDAG). Each node of the graph corresponds to one binary classifier, which decides for a class c_i or c_j. Based on this decision, a new node is visited. In each prediction, $k-1$ nodes are visited, so that the final classification is given by the $(k-1)$th node. This technique presents in general fast prediction times and high accuracies. However, its results depends on the sequence of nodes chosen to compose the graph. Kijsirikul and Ussivakul [9] point out that this causes high variances in classification results, affecting the reliability of the algorithm.

A.L.C. Bazzan and S. Labidi (Eds.): SBIA 2004, LNAI 3171, pp. 366–375, 2004.

Based on this observation and also in the fact that the DDAG architecture requires an unnecessary number of node evaluations for the correct class, these authors presented a new graph based structure for multiclass prediction with pairwise SVM classifies, the Adaptive Directed Acyclic Graph (ADAG) [9]. In the ADAG the graph structure is adaptive, depending on the predictions made by previous layers of nodes. Although this new approach showed less variance on results, there were still differences of accuracy between distinct node configurations in the graph.

The present paper introduces then the use of Genetic Algorithms (GAs), an intelligent search technique found on principles of genetics and evolution [12], in finding the ordering of nodes in a DAG (DDAG or ADAG) based on its accuracy in solving the overall multiclass problem. The coding scheme and genetic operators definition were adapted from evolutionary strategies commonly used in the traveling salesman problem solution, in which one wishes to find an order of cities to be visited at lower cost. Initial experimental results indicate that the GA approach can be efficient in finding good class permutations for both DDAG and ADAG structures.

This paper is organized as follows: Section 2 briefly describes the Support Vector Machine technique. Section 3 presents the graph based extensions of SVMs to multiclass problems. Section 4 introduces the genetic algorithm approach for finding the sequence of nodes in a DAG. Section 5 presents some experimental results. Section 6 concludes this paper.

2   Support Vector Machines

Support Vector Machines (SVMs) represent a learning technique based on the Statistical Learning Theory [17]. Given a dataset with n samples $(\mathbf{x}_i, y_i)$, where each $\mathbf{x}_i \in \Re^m$ is a data sample and $y_i \in \{-1, +1\}$ corresponds to $\mathbf{x}_i$'s label, this technique seeks an hyperplane $(\mathbf{w} \cdot \mathbf{x} + b = 0)$ able of separating data with a maximal margin. For performing this task, it solves the following optimization problem:

$$\text{Minimize: } \|\mathbf{w}\|^2 + C \sum_{i=1}^{n} \xi_i$$

$$\text{Restrictions: } \begin{cases} \xi_i \geq 0 \\ y_i \left(\mathbf{w} \cdot \mathbf{x_i} + b\right) \geq 1 - \xi_i \end{cases}$$

where C is a constant that imposes a tradeoff between training error and generalization and the ξ_i are slack variables. The former variables relax the restrictions imposed to the optimization problem, allowing some patterns to be within the margins and also some training errors.

In the case a non-linear separation of the dataset is needed, its data samples are mapped to a high-dimensional space. In this space, also named feature space, the dataset can be separated by a linear SVM with a low training error. This mapping process is performed with the use of Kernel functions, which compute dot products between any pair of patterns in the feature space in a simple way.

Thus, the only modification necessary to deal with non-linearity with SVMs is to substitute any dot product among patterns by a Kernel function. In this work, the Kernel function used was a Gaussian, illustrated in Equation 1.

$$K(\mathbf{x}_i, \mathbf{x}_j) = \exp(-\frac{1}{\sigma^2}\|\mathbf{x}_i - \mathbf{x}_j\|^2) \tag{1}$$

3   Multiclass SVMs with Graphs

As described in the previous section, SVMs are originally formulated for the solution of problems with two classes (+1 and -1, respectively). For extending this learning technique to multiclass solutions, one common approach consists of combining the predictions obtained in multiple binary subproblems [8].

One standard method to do so, called *all-against-all* (AAA), consists of building $k(k-1)/2$ predictors, each differentiating a pair of classes c_i and c_j, with $i < j$. For combining these classifiers, Platt et al. [15] suggested the use of Decision Directed Acyclic Graphs (DDAG).

A Directed Acyclic Graph (DAG) is a graph with oriented edges and no cycles. The DDAG approach uses the classifiers generated in an AAA manner in each node of a DAG. Computing the prediction of a pattern using the DDAG is equivalent to operating a list of classes. Starting from the root node, the sample is tested against the first and last elements of the list. If the predicted value is +1, the first class is maintained in the list, while the second class is eliminated. If the output is -1, the opposite happens. The node equivalent to the first and last elements of the new list obtained is then consulted. This process continues until one unique class remains. For k classes, $k-1$ SVMs are evaluated on test.

Figure 1 illustrates an example of DDAG where four classes are present. It also shows how this DDAG can be implemented with the use of a list, as described above.

Kijsirikul and Ussivakul [9] observed that the DDAG results have dependency on its sequence of nodes, adversely affecting its reliability. They also pointed out that, depending on the position of the correct class on the graph, the number of node evaluations with it is unnecessarily high, resulting in a large cumulative error. For instance, if the correct class is evaluated at the root node, it will be tested against the others $k-1$ classes before generating a response. If there is a probability of 1% of misclassification in each node, this will cause a $1 - (0.99)^{k-1}$ rate of cumulative error.

Based on these observations, these authors proposed a new graph architecture, the Adaptive DAG (ADAG) [9]. An ADAG is a DDAG with a reversed structure. The first layer has $k/2$ nodes, followed by $k/2^2$ nodes on the second layer, and so on, until a layer with one unique node is reached, which outputs the final class.

In the prediction phase, a pattern is submitted to all binary nodes in the first layer. These nodes give then outputs of their preferred classes, composing the next layer. In each round, the number of classes is reduced by half. Like in DDAG, $k-1$ nodes are evaluated in each prediction. However, the correct class

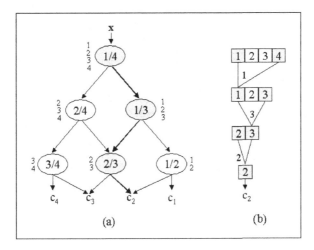

Fig. 1. (a) Example of DDAG for a problem with four classes; (b) Implementation of this DDAG with a list [15]

is tested against others $\log_2 k$ times or less, lower than in DDAG, where this number is (at most) $k - 1$ times.

Figure 2 illustrates an example of ADAG for eight classes. It also shows how this structure can be implemented with a list. The list is initialized with a permutation of all classes. A test pattern is evaluated against the first and last elements of the list. The node's preferred class is kept in the left element's position. The ADAG then tests against the second class and the class before the last in the list. This process is repeated until one or no class remains untested in the list. A new round is then initiated, with the list reduced to $k/2$ elements. A total of $k - 1$ rounds are made, when an unique class remains on the list.

Empirically, [9] verified that the ADAG was more advantageous especially for problems with a relatively large number of classes. However, they also pointed that, although the ADAG was less dependent on the sequence of nodes in the graph, its accuracy was also affected by this selection, arising in differences for distinct combinations of classes.

4   GA-Based Approach for Fiding Node Sequences

Genetic Algorithms (GAs) are search and optimization techniques based on the mechanisms of genetics and evolution [14]. They aim to solve a particular problem by investigating populations of possible solutions (also named individuals). Through several generations, population's individuals suffer constant evolutions based on their fitness to solve the problem. In each generation, a new population of individuals is produced by genetic operators. The most common genetic operators are elitism, that maintains copies of the best individuals in the next generation, cross-over, which combines the structures of pairs of individuals, and

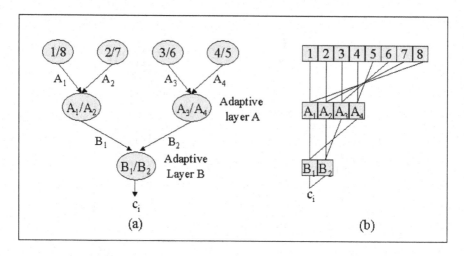

Fig. 2. (a) Example of ADAG for a problem with eight classes; (b) Implementation of this ADAG with a list [9]

mutation, that changes the features of selected individuals. The principle of using various individuals representing possible solutions, allied to the process of cross-over and mutation, allows a large search space to be swept in multiple directions, making GAs a global search technique.

Next, the authors show how GAs were applied in finding node orderings in a DDAG/ADAG.

Individuals Representation. Since the DDAG and ADAG approaches can be implemented by operating a list of classes, a vector representation was chosen. Each individual consists of a list (vector) of integers, representing the classes. Every class has to be present on the list and no repetitions of classes are allowed. The task is to find the ordering of these classes that leads to higher accuracies in the multiclass graph operation.

The adopted representation is similar to the path representation commonly employed in the solution of the traveling salesman problem (TSP), in which one wants to find the ordering of cities that have minimum traveling cost [12].

However, it should be noticed that, in the present application, a pair of classes (c_i, c_j) with $i > j$ is equivalent to the pair (c_j, c_i). This leads to a search space of size $k!/2^{\lfloor k/2 \rfloor}$ for ADAGs and $k!/2$ for DDAGs (against a size of $k!$ for an ordering problem without the previous restriction), which becomes especially critical for problems with relatively high number of classes.

Fitness Function. The fitness of each individual was given by its mean accuracy in the multiclass solution through cross-validation. The datasets used in the experiments conduction were then divided following the r-fold cross-validation methodology [13]. According to this method, the dataset is divided in r disjoint subsets of approximately equal size. In each train/validation round, $r-1$ subsets are used for training and the remaining is left for validation. This makes a total of r pairs of training and validation sets. The accuracy (error) of a classifier on the total dataset is then given by the average of the accuracies (errors) observed in each validation partition.

The standard deviation of accuracies in cross-validation was also considered, so that among two individuals with the same mean accuracy, the one with lower standard deviation was considered better. This was accomplished by subtracting from each individual mean accuracy its standard deviation.

Elistism. The elitism operator was applied, selecting in each next generation a fraction of the best individuals of the current population.

Cross-over. Given the similarity between the present GA application and the travelling salesman one, the partially-mapped cross-over (PMX) operator [7] from the TSP literature was considered. This operator is able of preserving more the order and position of the parents classes during recombination, and thus good parent's graph orderings. For such, in obtaining an offspring it chooses a subsequence of classes from one parent and maintains the order and position of as many classes as possible from the other parent [12]. The subsequence is obtained by choosing at random two cut points.

Since in the ADAG implementation a class in position i of the list pairs with the class in position $k-i$, only a random point was generated. The second point was given by its pair following the above rule, so that pairs of classes (the graph nodes) of the parents could be further preserved.

For selection of parents in the cross-over process a tournament matching mechanism was employed [14]. In selecting a parent through the tournament procedure, initially two individuals of the population are randomly chosen. A random number in $[0, 1]$ is then generated. If this number is less than a constant, for example 0.75, the individual with highest fitness is selected. Otherwise, the one with lowest fitness is chosen.

Mutation. The mutation operator applied was the insertion, also borrowed from the TSP literature. It consists of selecting a class and inserting it in a random place in the individual [12]. This operator allows large changes in the graphs nodes configuration.

For each individual suffering mutation, this operator was applied a fixed number of times (equal to the individuals size) and the best mutation product was then chosen, constituting a kind of local search procedure.

5   Experiments

Experiments were conducted with the aim of evaluating the GA based approach performance in obtaining DDAG and ADAG structures. Three datasets were employed in these experiments: the UCI dataset for optical recognition of hand-written digits [16], the UCI letter image recognition dataset [16] and a protein fold recognition dataset [5]. These datasets are described in Table 1. This table shows, for each dataset, the number of training and test examples, the number of attributes and the number of classes.

Table 1. Datasets summary description

Dataset	♯training data	♯test data	♯attributes	♯classes
optical	3823	1797	64	10
letter	16000	4000	16	26
protein	313	385	126	27

A scaling step was applied to all training datasets, consisting of a normalization of attributes to mean zero and unit variance. The independent test datasets were also pre-processed according to the normalization factors extracted from training data.

All experiments with SVMs were conducted with the SVMTorch II tool [1]. The Gaussian Kernel standard deviation parameter was set to 10. Other parameters were kept with default values. Although the best values for the SVM parameters may differ for each multiclass strategy, they were kept the same to allow a fair evaluation of the differences between the techniques considered. The GA and DDAG/ADAG codes were implemented in the Perl language.

For the GA fitness evaluation, the training datasets were divided according to the r-fold cross validation methodology. For speeding the GA processing, a number of $r = 5$ folds was employed. This procedure was adopted in a stratified manner, in which each validation partition must have the same class distribution as the original dataset. In the letter dataset, as such a huge number of examples would slow the GA processing, only a fraction of it was used in the GA training. For such, 25 elements of every class were randomly selected to compose each validation dataset.

Table 2 shows the GA parameters employed in each dataset. It shows the individuals size (Ind size), the population size (Pop size), elitism rate (Elitism), cross-over rate (Cross-over), mutation rate (Mutation) and the maximum number of generations the GA is run (♯generations). If no improvement could be observed in the best fitness for 10 generations, the GA was also stopped. To prevent early stop, this criterion begun to be evaluated only after 20 generations.

After the GA training process (in which the permutation is search), the best individual obtained in each case was trained on the whole original dataset and tested on the independent test dataset. As GAs solutions depend on the initial population provided, a total of 5 runs of the GA were performed and the final accuracy was then averaged over these runs. In each of these rounds, the same initial random population was provided for both DDAG and ADAG GA search.

Table 3 presents the results achieved. Best results are detached in boldface. This table also shows the results of a majority voting (MV) of the pairwise clas-

Table 2. GA parameters

Dataset	Ind size	Pop size	Elistism	Cross-over	Mutation	♯generations
optical	10	20	20%	80%	5%	100
letter	26	52	20%	80%	2%	200
protein	27	54	20%	80%	2%	200

sifiers outputs. Following this technique, described in [10], each classifier gives one vote for its preferred class. The final result is given by the class with most votes. This method is largely employed in the combination of pairwise classifiers. Nevertheless, it has a drawback. If more than one class receives the same number of votes, the pattern cannot be classified. The graph integration does not suffer from this problem and has also the advantage of speeding prediction time. The numbers of unclassified patterns by MV in each dataset are indicated in parentheses. The best solutions produced in the GA rounds for ADAG and DDAG are also shown (B-GA-ADAG and B-GA-DDAG, respectively).

Table 3. Mean accuracies

Technique	Optical dataset	Letter dataset	Protein dataset
GA-DDAG	97.07 ± 0.09	95.16 ± 0.11	55.58 ± 0.18
B-GA-DDAG	**97.22**	95.28	55.84
GA-ADAG	97.11 ± 0.04	95.44 ± 0.12	55.84 ± 0.37
B-GA-ADAG	97.16	**95.53**	**56.10**
MV	96.88 (0.67)	94.93 (1.56)	55.32 (3.38)

Analyzing the results of Table 3, it can be verified that, although the GA-ADAG showed slightly better mean accuracies, the results of GA-ADAG and GA-DDAG were similar in all cases. Comparing the performance of the best GA solutions obtained by GA-ADAG and GA-DDAG in each case with the McNemar statistical test [4], it is not possible to detect a significant difference between the results achieved, at 95% of confidence level.

Besides that, the accuracies of the MV approach were inferior to the GA ones in all datasets. In the optical dataset, the difference of performance between MV and the B-GA-ADAG solution can be considered statistically significant, at 95% of confidence. In the letter dataset, the difference of performance among MV and both B-GA-ADAG and B-GA-DDAG was significant, at 95% of confidence. In the protein dataset, no statistical significance (at 95% of confidence) was found among the mean accuracies of these techniques, which showed then similar results. In all tests conducted, unknown classifications were considered errors in the computation of the statistics. This represents a deficiency of MV over DDAGs and ADAGs, which was reflected on the results verified. Anyway, the analysis presented indicate that the GA-based strategy was able of finding good and plausible multiclass solutions.

In the optical dataset, the GA-ADAG results were more stable than of the GA-DDAG, showing a lower standard deviation. This situation was opposite in the letter and protein datasets. In general, however, the GA found similar results in the distinct rounds, what was reflected in the low standard deviation rates obtained in the experiments. This suggests a robustness of the proposed approach.

It was also observed that the graphs generated by the GAs showed good performance in the distinction of each class composing the multiclass datasets investigated.

6   Conclusion

This paper presented a novel approach to determine the graph structure in a Decision Directed Acyclic Graph (DDAG) and an Adaptive Directed Acyclic Graph (ADAG) for multiclass classification with pairwise SVM predictors. This can be considered an important task, since the results of these strategies depend on the sequence of classes in the nodes of the graph. It becomes specially critical for relatively large numbers of classes. The proposed approach offers an automatic and structured mean of searching good node permutations in these sets. Besides that, the proposed approach is general and can also employ other base learning techniques generating binary classifiers.

Future experiments succeeding this work should consider modifying the GAs and (also) the SVMs parameters, since this procedure can improve the results obtained in the experiments conducted. The GA algorithm can also be further improved with the definition and introduction of new genetic operators. In a recent work, Martí et al. [11] analyzed the performance of GAs in the solution of various permutation problems and suggested that the combination of GAs with a local search procedure can improve the results achieved by this technique. Since a simple GA algorithm implementation was able of finding good class permutations in this work, its modification with the introduction of a more sophisticated local search strategy can improve the results verified.

Others modifications being considered include using leave-one-out bounds of the SVM literature [18] in the GA's fitness evaluation. Others works using GAs in conjunction with SVMs have proved that these bounds can be more effective in evaluating the SVMs fitness than a cross-validation methodology (ex.: [6]).

The GA approach proposed could also be extended to provide a model selection mechanism for SVMs, by incorporating the parameters of this technique in the GA search process.

Acknowledgements

The authors would like to thank the financial support provided by the Brazilian research councils FAPESP and CNPq.

References

1. Collobert, R., Bengio, S.: SVMTorch: Support Vector Machines for Large Scale Regression Problems. Journal of Machine Learning Research, Vol. 1 (2001) 143–160
2. Cristianini, N., Taylor, J. S.: An Introduction to Support Vector Machines. Cambridge University Press (2000)
3. Dieterich, T. G., Bariki, G.: Solving Multiclass Learning Problems via Error-Correcting Output Codes. Journal of Artificial Intelligence Research, Vol. 2 (1995) 263–286
4. Dietterich, T. G.: Approximate Statistical Tests for Comparing Supervised Classification Learning Algorithms. Neural Computation, Vol. 10, N. 7 (1998) 1895–1924
5. Ding, C. H. Q., Dubchak, I.: Multi-class Protein Fold Recognition using Support Vector Machines and Neural Networks. Bioinformatics, Vol. 4, N. 17 (2001) 349–358
6. Fröhlich, H., Chapelle, O., Schölkopf, B.: Feature Selection for Support Vector Machines by Means of Genetic Algorithms. Proceedings of 15th IEEE International Conference on Tools with AI (2003) 142–148
7. Goldberg, D. E., Lingle, R.: Alleles, Loci, and the TSP. Proceedings of the 1st International Conference on Genetic Algorithms, Lawrence Erlbaum Associates (1985) 154–159
8. Hsu, C.-W., Lin, C.-J.: A Comparison of Methods for Multi-class Support Vector Machines. IEEE Transactions on Neural Networks, Vol. 13 (2002) 415–425
9. Kijsirikul,B., Ussivakul,N.: Multiclass Support Vector Machines using Adaptive Directed Acyclic Graph. Proceedings of International Joint Conference on Neural Networks (IJCNN 2002) (2002) 980–985
10. Kreßel, U.: Pairwise Classification and Support Vector Machines. In Scholkopf, B., Burges, C. J. C., Smola, A. J. (eds.), Advances in Kernel Methods - Support Vector Learning, MIT Press (1999) 185–208
11. Martí, R., Laguna, M., Campos, V.: Scatter Search vs. Genetic Algorithms: An Experimental Evaluation with Permutation Problems. To appear in Rego, C., Alidaee, B. (eds.), Adaptive Memory and Evolution: Tabu Search and Scatter Search (2004)
12. Michaelewicz, Z.: Genetic Algorithms + Data Structures = Evolution Programs. Springer-Verlag (1996)
13. Mitchell, T.: Machine Learning. McGraw Hill (1997)
14. Mitchell, M.: An Introduction to Genetic Algorithms. MIT Press (1998)
15. Platt, J. C., Cristianini, N., Shawe-Taylor, J.: Large Margin DAGs for Multiclass Classification. In: Solla, S. A., Leen, T. K., Müller, K.-R. (eds.), Advances in Neural Information Processing Systems, Vol. 12. MIT Press (2000) 547–553
16. University of California Irvine: UCI benchmark repository - a huge collection of artificial and real-world datasets. http://www.ics.uci.edu/~mlearn
17. Vapnik, V. N.: Statistical Learning Theory. John Wiley and Sons, New York (1998)
18. Vapnik, V. N., Chapelle, O.: Bounds on Error Expectation for Support Vector Machines. Neural Computation, Vol. 12, N. 9 (2000)

Dynamic Allocation of Data-Objects in the Web, Using Self-tuning Genetic Algorithms⋆

Joaquín Pérez O.[1], Rodolfo A. Pazos R.[1], Graciela Mora O.[2],
Guadalupe Castilla V.[2], José A. Martínez.[2], Vanesa Landero N.[2],
Héctor Fraire H.[2], and Juan J. González B.[2]

[1] Centro Nacional de Investigación y Desarrollo Tecnológico (CENIDET)
AP 5-164, Cuernavaca, Mor. 62490, México
{jperez,pazos}@sd-cenidet.com.mx
[2] Instituto Tecnológico de Ciudad Madero, México
hfraire@prodigy.net.mx

Abstract. In this paper, a new mechanism for automatically obtaining some control parameter values for Genetic Algorithms is presented, which is independent of problem domain and size. This approach differs from the traditional methods which require knowing the problem domain first, and then knowing how to select the parameter values for solving specific problem instances. The proposed method uses a sample of problem instances, whose solution allows to characterize the problem and to obtain the parameter values. To test the method, a combinatorial optimization model for data-object allocation in the Web (known as DFAR) was solved using Genetic Algorithms. We show how the proposed mechanism allows to develop a set of mathematical expressions that relates the problem instance size to the control parameters of the algorithm. The expressions are then used, in on-line process, to control the parameter values. We show the last experimental results with the self-tuning mechanism applied to solve a sample of random instances that simulates a typical Web workload. We consider that the proposed method principles must be extended to the self-tuning of control parameters for other heuristic algorithms.

1 Introduction

A large number of real problems are NP-hard combinatorial optimization problems. These problems require the use of heuristic methods for solving large size instances. Genetic Algorithms (GA) constitute an alternative that has been used for solving this kind of problems [1].

A framework used frequently for the study of evolutionary algorithms includes: the population, the selection operator, the reproduction operators, and the generation overlap. The GA's components have control parameters associated. The choice of appropriate parameters setting is one of the most important factors that affect the algorithms efficiency. Nevertheless, it is a difficult task to

---

⋆ This research was supported in part by CONACYT and COSNET.

A.L.C. Bazzan and S. Labidi (Eds.): SBIA 2004, LNAI 3171, pp. 376–384, 2004.

devise an effective control parameter mechanism that obtains an adequate balance between quality and processing time. It requires having a deep knowledge of the nature of the problem to be solved, which is not usually trivial.

For several years we have been working on the distribution design problem and the design of solution algorithms. We have carried out a large number of experiments with different solution algorithms, and a recurrent problem is the tuning of the algorithm control parameters; hence our interest in incorporating self-tuning mechanisms for parameter adjustment. In [2], we proposed an on-line method to set the control parameters of the Threshold Accepting algorithm. However, in that method we cannot relate algorithm parameters to the problem size. Now, we want to explore, with genetic algorithms, the off-line automatic configuration of parameters.

2   Related Work

Diverse works try to establish the relationship between the values of the genetic algorithm control parameters and the algorithm performance.

The following are some of the most important research works on the application of the theoretical results in practical methodologies.

Back uses an evolutionary on-line strategy to adjust the parameter values [3]. Mercer and Grefenstette use a genetic meta-algorithm to evolve the control parameter values of another genetic algorithm [4,5]. Smith uses an equation derived from the theoretical model proposed by Goldberg [6]. Harik uses a technique prospection based [7], for tuning the population size using an on-line process.

Table 1 summarizes research works on parameter adaptation. It shows the work reference, applied technique and on-line controlled parameters (population size P, crossover rate C and mutation rate M).

Table 1. Parameter adaptation work summary

Ref.	Tech.	P	C	M
[3]	Evolution		√	√
[4]	Meta-algorithm		√	√
[5]	Meta-algorithm		√	√
[6]	Theoretical model	√		
[7]	Prospection	√		

We propose a new method to obtain relationships between the problem size and the population size, generation number, and the mutation rate. The process consists of applying off-line statistical techniques to determine mathematical expressions for the relationships between the problem size and the parameter values. With this approach it is possible to tune a genetic algorithm to solve many instances at a lower cost than using the prospection approach.

3   Proposed Method for Self-tuning GA Parameters

In this work we propose the use of off-line sampling to get the relationship between the problem size and the control parameters of a Genetic Algorithm. The self-tuning mechanism is constructed iteratively by solving a set of problem instances and gathering statistics of algorithm performance to obtain the relationship sought. With this approach it is possible to tune a genetic algorithm for solving many problem instances at a low cost. To automate the configuration of the algorithm control parameters the following procedure was applied:

Iteratively execute next steps:

Step 1. Record instances. Keep a record of all the instances currently solved with the GA configured manually. For each instance, its size, configuration used and the corresponding performance are recorded.

Step 2. Select a representative sample. Get a representative sample of recorded instances, each one of different size. The sample is built considering only the best configuration for each selected instance.

Step 3. Determine correlation functions. Get the relationship between the problem size and the algorithm parameters.

Step 4. Feedback. The established relationships reflect the behavior of the recorded instances. When new instances with a different structure occur, the adjustment mechanism can lose effectiveness.

The proposed method allows advancing toward an optimal parameter configuration with an iterative and systematic approach. An important advantage of this method is that the experimental costs are reduced gradually. We can start using an initial solved instance set and continue adding new solved instances. In the next section we describe an application problem to explain some method details.

4   Application Problem

To test the method, a combinatorial optimization model for data-objects allocation in the Web (known as DFAR) was solved using Genetic Algorithms. We show how the proposed method allows to develop a set of mathematical expressions that relates the problem instance size to the control parameters of the algorithm. In this section we describe the distribution design problem and the DFAR mathematical model.

4.1   Problem Description

Traditionally it has been considered that the distributed database (DDB) distribution consists of two sequential phases. Contrary to this widespread belief, it has been shown that it is simpler to solve the problem using our approach which combines both phases [8]. In order to describe the model and its properties, the following definition is introduced:

$DB - object$: Entity of a database that requires to be allocated, which can be an attribute, a relation or a file. They are independent units that must be allocated in the sites of a network.

The DDB distribution design problem consists of allocating DB-objects, such that the total cost of data transmission for processing all the applications is minimized. New allocation schemas should be generated that adapt to changes in a dynamic query processing environment, which prevent the system degradation. A formal definition of the problem is the following:

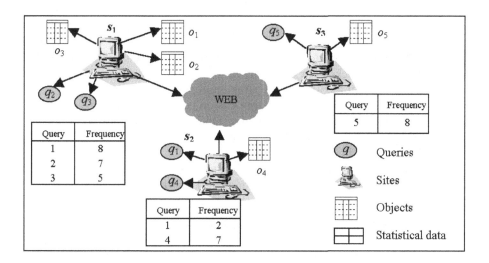

Fig. 1. Distribution Design Problem

Assuming there are a set of DB-objects $O = \{o_1, o_2, ..., o_n\}$, a computer communication network that consists of a set of sites $S = \{s_1, s_2, ..., s_n\}$, where a set of queries $Q = \{q_1, q_2, ..., q_n\}$ are executed, the DB-objects required by each query, an initial DB-object allocation schema, and the access frequencies of each query from each site in a time period. The problem consists of obtaining a new allocation schema that adapts to a new database usage pattern and minimizes transmission costs. Figure 1 shows the main elements related with this problem.

4.2   Objective Function

The integer (binary) programming model consists of an objective function and four intrinsic constraints. The decision about storing a DB-object m in site j is represented by a binary variable x_{mj}. Thus, $x_{mj} = 1$ if m is stored in j, and $x_{mj} = 0$ otherwise.

The objective function below (1) models costs using four terms: 1) the transmission cost incurred for processing all the queries, 2) the cost for accessing multiple remote DB-objects required for query processing, 3) the cost for DB-object storage in network sites, and 4) the transmission cost for migrating DB-objects between nodes.

$$\min z = \sum_k \sum_i f_{ki} \sum_m \sum_j q_{km} l_{km} c_{ij} x_{mj} + \sum_i \sum_k \sum_j c1 f_{ki} y_{kj}$$

$$+ \sum_j c2 w_j + \sum_m \sum_i \sum_j a_{mi} c_{ij} d_m x_{mj}. \tag{1}$$

where
f_{ki} = emission frequency of query k from site i, during a given period of time;
q_{km} = usage parameter, $q_{km} = 1$ if query k uses DB-object m, else $q_{km} = 0$;
l_{km} = number of packets for transporting DB-object m for query k;
c_{ij} = communication cost between sites i and j;
$c1$ = cost for accessing several remote DB-objects for processing a query;
y_{kj} = indicates if query k accesses one or more DB-objects located at site j;
$c2$ = cost for allocating DB-objects in a site;
w_j = indicates if there exist DB-objects at site j;
a_{mi} = indicates if DB-object m was previously located in site i;
d_m = number of packets required for moving DB-object m to another site.

4.3   Intrinsic Constraints of the Problem

The model solutions are subject to four constraints: each DB-object must be stored in one site only, each DB-object must be stored in a site that executes at least one query that uses it, a constraint to determinate for each query where is the DB-objects required, and a constraint to determinate if the sites contains DB-objects. The detailed formulation of the constraints can be found in [2, 8].

5   Implementation

In this section we present some application examples of the proposed method, using the DDB design problem.

5.1   Record Instances

Table 2 shows four entries of the historical record. These correspond to an instance solved using a manually configured GA. Columns 1 and 2 contain the instance identifier I and the instance size S in bytes. Columns 3-6 show the configuration of four GA parameters (population size P, generation number G, crossover rate C, and mutation rate M). Columns 7 and 8, present the algorithm

Table 2. Four entries of the P8 instance on the historical file

I	S	P	G	C	M	B	T
P8	921620	30	300	1	0	415899.7	2.81
P8	921620	30	300	0.9	0.1	408754.9	2.61
P8	921620	30	300	0.9	0.01	385483.3	2.62
P8	921620	375	19200	0.9	0.01	61188.0	128.52

performance (the best solution B found by the GA, and the execution time T in seconds).

Table 2 shows the best solutions that were obtaining with the specified configurations.

5.2 Select a Representative Sample

Table 3 presents an example of a sample of instances of different size extracted from the record, where column headings have the same meaning as those of Table 2. For each selected instance only its best configuration is included in the sample.

Table 3. Instances representative sample

I	S	P	G	M	B	T
P1	108	30	300	0	302.2	0.015
P2	308	30	300	0	604.4	0.017
P3	1044	30	300	0	1208.8	0.021
P4	3860	30	300	0	2417.6	0.032
P5	14868	30	300	1	4835.2	0.085
P6	58388	60	1200	1	9670.4	0.467
P7	231444	150	4800	1	19340.8	8.137
P8	921620	375	19200	1	61188.0	128.5
P9	3678228	750	96000	1	185679.0	1543.5

5.3 Determine Correlation Functions

Population Correlation Functions. To find the relationship between the problem size and the population size we used two techniques: statistical regression and estimate based on proportions. Three mathematical expressions (2,3,4) were constructed to determinate the population P size in function of the problem size x. The expressions contain derived coefficients of the lineal and logarithmic statistical estimates and a constant of proportionality.

$$Linear\ estimate: \qquad P(x) = 0.00019843x + 56.7506298. \qquad (2)$$

$$Logarithmic\ estimate: \qquad P(x) = 45.7182388\,(1.00000087)^x. \qquad (3)$$

$$Proportional\ estimate: \qquad P(x) = 2^{(\log_4 x)\,0.938523962}. \qquad (4)$$

The proportional estimate was adjusted to get the best estimation. As a result of the fine adjustment the following factors were defined: $\alpha = 14868, \beta = 309$.

$$p(x) = \begin{cases} 30 & if \quad x \leq \alpha \\ \frac{x}{\lfloor \beta * 2^{\lceil \log_4(x/\alpha) \rceil} \rfloor} & if \quad x > \alpha. \end{cases} \tag{5}$$

Figure 2 shows the graphs of the real data and the adjusted proportional estimate.

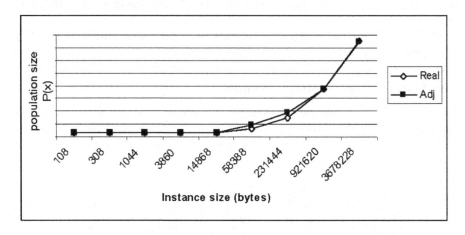

Fig. 2. Correlation functions graphs

Correlation Functions for the Generation Number and Mutation Rate.
Similarly the relationships between the size of the problem, and the number of generations and the mutation rate were determined. Expressions (6,7) specify the relationship between the instance size and these algorithm parameters. In these expressions, G is the number of generations, and M is the mutation rate and $\delta = 4.8$, is an adjust factor.

$$G(x) = \begin{cases} 300 & if \quad x \leq \alpha \\ \frac{[P(x)]^2}{\delta} & if \quad x > \alpha. \end{cases} \tag{6}$$

$$M(x) = \begin{cases} 0 & if \quad x \leq \alpha \\ 1 & if \quad x > \alpha. \end{cases} \tag{7}$$

As observed, the parameter tuning mechanism is defined using an offline procedure. The evaluation and subsequent use of this mechanism should be carried out online. In this example, for the evaluation of the mechanism a comparative experiment was carried out using a GA configured manually, according to the recommendations proposed in the literature, and our self-tuning GA. To carry out the evaluation, a sample of 14 random instances was solved using both algorithms. The instances were created in order to simulate a typical Web workload. In that environment 20% of the queries access 80% of the data-objects and 80% of the queries only access 20% of the data-objects. The improvement of the quality solution percentage is calculated, getting the objective value diminution with respect to the solution with the GA configured using the literature recommendations. In Figure 3 the graph of the improve solution percentage is showed, for the 14 random instances ordered by size. The graph shows that the self-tuning mechanism exhibits a tendency to get better results in the large scale instances range.

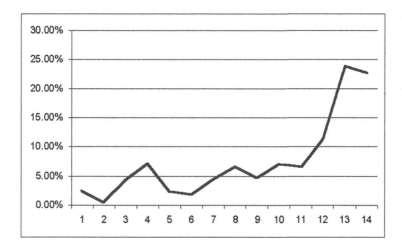

Fig. 3. Improvement of quality solution percentage

5.4   Feedback

Since the tuning mechanism requires a periodic refinement, the performance of the GA configured automatically can be compared versus other algorithms when solving new instances. If for some instance another algorithm is superior, the GA will be configured manually to equal or surpass the performance of that algorithm. The instance and their different configurations must be recorded in the historical record and the process is repeated from step 2 through step 4. Hence the experimental cost it is relatively low, because it takes advantage of all the experimental results stored in the historical record.

6   Conclusions and Future Work

In this work, we propose a new method to obtain relationships between the problem size and the population size, generation number, and the mutation rate. The process consists of applying off-line statistical techniques to determine mathematical expressions for these relationships. The mathematical expressions are used on-line to control the values of the algorithm parameters. With this approach it is possible to tune a genetic algorithm to solve many problem instances at a lower cost than other approaches.

We present a genetic algorithm configured with mathematical expressions, designed with the proposed method, which was able to obtain a better solution than the algorithm configured according to the literature.The self-tuning mechanism exhibits a tendency to get better results in the large scale instances range. To test the method, a mathematical model for dynamic allocation of data-objects in the Web (known as DFAR) was solved using both algorithms with typical Web workloads.

Currently the self-tuning GA is being tested for solving a new model of the DDB design problem that incorporates data replication, and the preliminary results are encouraging.

References

1. Fogel, D., Ghozeil, A.: Using Fitness Distributions to Design More Efficient Evolutionary Computations. Proceedings of the 1996 IEEE Conference on Evolutionary Computation, Nagoya, Japan. IEEE Press, Piscataway N.J. (1996) 11-19
2. Pérez, J., Pazos, R.A., Velez, L. Rodriguez, G.: Automatic Generation of Control Parameters for the Threshold Accepting Algorithm, Lectures Notes in Computer Science, Vol. 2313. Springer-Verlag, Berlin Heidelberg New York (2002) 119-127.
3. Back, T., Schwefel, H.P.: Evolution Strategies I: Variants and their computational implementation. In: Winter, G., Périaux, J, Galán, M., Cuesta, P. (eds.): Genetic Algorithms in Engineering and Computer Science. Chichester: John Wiley and Sons. (1995) Chapter 6, 111-126
4. Mercer, R.E., Sampson, J.R.: Adaptive Search Using a Reproductive Meta-plan. Kybernets 7 (1978) 215-228
5. Grefenstette, J.J.: Optimization of Control Parameters for Genetic Algorithms. In: Sage, A.P. (ed.): IEEE Transactions on Systems, Man and Cybernetics, Volume SMC-16(1). New York: IEEE (1986) 122-128
6. Smith, R.E., Smuda, E.: Adaptively Resizing Population: Algorithm Analysis and First Results. Complex Systems 9 (1995) 47-72
7. Harik, G.R., Lobo, F.G.: A parameter-less Genetic Algorithm. In: Banzhaf, W., Daida, J., Eiben, A.E., Garzon, M.H., Honavar, V., Jakiela. M., Smith, R.E. (eds.): Proceedings of the Genetic and Evolutionary Computation Conference GECCO-99. San Francisco, CA: Morgan Kaufmann (1999) 258-267
8. Pérez, J., Pazos, R.A., Romero, D., Santaolaya, R., Rodríguez, G., Sosa, V.: Adaptive and Scalable Allocation of Data-Objects in the Web. Lectures Notes in Computer Science, Vol. 2667. Springer-Verlag, Berlin Heidelberg New York (2003) 134-143

Detecting Promising Areas
by Evolutionary Clustering Search

Alexandre C.M. Oliveira[1,2] and Luiz A.N. Lorena[2]

[1] Universidade Federal do Maranhão - UFMA, Departamento de Informática
S. Luís MA, Brasil
acmo@deinf.ufma.br
[2] Instituto Nacional de Pesquisas Espaciais - INPE
Laboratório Associado de Computação e Matemática Aplicada
S. José dos Campos SP, Brasil
lorena@lac.inpe.br

Abstract. A challenge in hybrid evolutionary algorithms is to define efficient strategies to cover all search space, applying local search only in actually promising search areas. This paper proposes a way of detecting promising search areas based on clustering. In this approach, an iterative clustering works simultaneously to an evolutionary algorithm accounting the activity (selections or updatings) in search areas and identifying which of them deserves a special interest. The search strategy becomes more aggressive in such detected areas by applying local search. A first application to unconstrained numerical optimization is developed, showing the competitiveness of the method.

Keywords: Hybrid evolutionary algorithms; unconstrained numerical optimization

1 Introduction

In the hybrid evolutionary algorithm scenario, the inspiration in nature have been pursued to design flexible, coherent and efficient computational models. The main focus of such models are real-world problems, considering the known little effectiveness of canonical genetic algorithms (GAs) in dealing with them. Investments have been made in new methods, which the evolutionary process is only part of the whole search process. Due to their intrinsic features, GAs are employed as a generator of promising search areas (search subspaces), which are more intensively inspected by a heuristic component. This scenario comes to reinforce the parallelism of evolutionary algorithms.

Promising search areas can be detected by fit or frequency merits. By fit merits, the fitness of the solutions can be used to say how good their neighborhood are. On other hand, in frequency merits, the evolutionary process naturally privileges the good search areas by a more intensive sampling in them. Figure 1 shows the 2-dimensional contour map of a test function known as *Langerman*. The points are candidate solutions over fitness surface in a typical simulation. One can note their agglomeration over the promising search areas.

A.L.C. Bazzan and S. Labidi (Eds.): SBIA 2004, LNAI 3171, pp. 385–394, 2004.

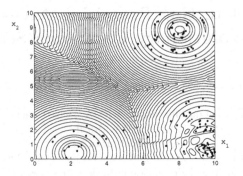

Fig. 1. Convergence of typical GA into fitter areas

The main difficulty of GAs is a lack of exploitation moves. Some promising search areas are not found, or even being found, such areas are not consistently exploited. The natural convergence of GAs also contributes for losing the reference to all promising search areas, implicating in poor performance.

Local search methods have been combined with GAs in different ways to solve multimodal numerical functions more efficiently. Gradient as well as direct search methods have been employed as exploitation tool. In the Simplex Genetic Algorithm Hybrid [1], a probabilistic version of Nelder and Mead Simplex [2] is applied in the elite of population. In [3], good results are obtained just by applying a conjugate gradient method as mutation operator, with certain probability. In the Population-Training Algorithm [4], improvement heuristics are employed in fitness definition, guiding the population to settle down in search areas where the individuals can not be improved by such heuristics. All those approaches report an increase in function calls that can be prohibitive in optimization of complex computational functions.

The main challenge in such hybrid methods is the definition of efficient strategies to cover all search space, applying local search only in actually promising areas. Elitism plays an important role towards achieving this goal, once the best individuals represent such promising search area, *a priori*. But the elite of population can be concentrated in few areas and thus the exploitation moves are not rationally applied.

More recently, a different strategy was proposed to employ local search more rationally: the Continuous Hybrid Algorithm (CHA) [5]. The evolutionary process run normally until be detected a promising search area. The promising area is detected when the highest distance between the best individual and other individuals of the population is smaller than a given radius, i.e., when population diversity is lost. Thereafter, the search domain is reduced, an initial simplex is built inside the area around the best found individual, and a local search based upon Nelder and Mead Simplex is started. With respect to detection of promising areas, the CHA has a limitation. The exploitation is started once, after diversity loss, and the evolutionary process can not be continued afterwards, unless a new population takes place.

Another approach attempting to find out relevant areas for numerical optimization is called UEGO by its authors. UEGO is a parallel hill climber, not an evolutionary algorithm. The separated hill climbers work in restricted search areas (or clusters) of the search space. The volume of the clusters decreases as the search proceeds, which results in a cooling effect similar to simulated annealing [6]. UEGO do not work so well as CHA for high dimensional functions.

Several evolutionary approaches have evoked the concept of species, when dealing with optimization of multimodal and multiobjective functions [6],[7]. The basic idea is to divide the population into several species according to their similarity. Each species is built around a dominating individual, staying in a delimited area.

This paper proposes an alternative way of detecting promising search areas based on clustering. This approach is called Evolutionary Clustering Search (ECS). In this scenario, groups of individuals (clusters) with some similarities (for example, individuals inside a neighborhood) are represented by a dominating individual. The interaction between inner individuals determines some kind of exploitation moves in the cluster. The clusters work as sliding windows, framing the search areas. Groups of mutually close points hopefully can correspond to relevant areas of attraction. Such areas are exploited as soon as they are discovered, not at the end the process. An improvement in convergence speed is expected, as well as a decrease in computational efforts, by applying local optimizers rationally.

The remainder of this paper is organized as follows. Section 2 describes the basic ideas and conceptual components of ECS. An application to unconstrained numerical optimization is presented in section 3, as well as the experiments performed to show the effectiveness of the method. The findings and conclusions are summarized in section 4.

2   Evolutionary Clustering Search

The Evolutionary Clustering Search (ECS) employs clustering for detecting promising areas of the search space. It is particularly interesting to find out such areas as soon as possible to change the search strategy over them. An area can be seen as an abstract search subspace defined by a neighborhood relationship in genotype space.

The ECS attempts to locate promising search areas by framing them by clusters. A cluster can be defined as a tuple $\mathcal{G} = \{c, r, s\}$, where c and r are the *center* and the *radius* of the area, respectively. There also exists a *search strategy* s associated to the cluster. The radius of a search area is the distance from its center to the edge.

Initially, the center c is obtained randomly and progressively it tends to slip along really promising points in the close subspace. The total cluster volume is defined by the radius r and can be calculated, considering the problem nature. The important is that r must define a search subspace suitable to be exploited by aggressive search strategies.

In numerical optimization, it is possible to define r in a way that all search space is covered depending on the maximum number of clusters. In combinatorial optimization, r can be defined as a function of some distance metric, such as the number of movements needed to change a solution inside a neighborhood. Note that neighborhood, in this case, must also be related with the search strategy s of the cluster. The search strategy s is a kind of local search to be employed into the clusters and considering the parameters c and r. The appropriated conditions are related with the search area becoming promising.

2.1   Components

The main ECS components are conceptually described here. Details of implementation are left to be explained later. The ECS consist of four conceptually independent parts: (a) an evolutionary algorithm (EA); (b) an iterative clustering (IC); (c) an analyzer module (AM); and (d) a local searcher (LS). Figure 2 brings the ECS conceptual design.

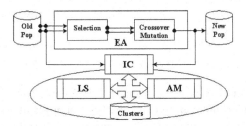

Fig. 2. ECS components

The EA works as a full-time solution generator. The population evolves independently of the remaining parts. Individuals are selected, crossed over, and updated for the next generations. This entire process works like an infinite loop, where the population is going to be modified along the generations.

The IC aims to gather similar *information* (solutions represented by individuals) into groups, maintaining a representative solution associated to this information, named the center of cluster. The term *information* is used here because the individuals are not directly grouped, but the similar information they represent. Any candidate solution that is not part of the population is called information. To avoid extra computational effort, IC is designed as an iterative process that forms groups by reading the individuals being selected or updated by EA. A similarity degree, based upon some distance metric, must be defined, *a priori*, to allow the clustering process.

The AM provides an analysis of each cluster, in regular intervals of generations, indicating a probable promising cluster. Typically, the *density* of the cluster is used in this analysis, that is, the number of selections or updatings recently happened. The AM is also responsible by eliminating the clusters with lower densities.

At last, the LS is an internal searcher module that provides the exploitation of a supposed promising search area, framed by cluster. This process can happen after AM having discovered a target cluster or it can be a continuous process, inherent to the IC, being performed whenever a new point is grouped.

2.2   The Clustering Process

The clustering process described here is based upon Yager's work, which says that a system can learn about an external environment with the participation of previously learned beliefs of the own system [8],[9]. The IC is the ECS's core, working as an information classifier, keeping in the system only relevant information, and driving a search intensification in the promising search areas. To avoid propagation of unnecessary information, the local search is performed without generating other points, keeping the population diversified. In other words, clusters concentrate all information necessary to exploit framed search areas.

All information generated by EA (individuals) passes by IC that attempts to group as known information, according to a distance metric. If the information is considered sufficiently new, it is kept as a center in a new cluster. Otherwise, redundant information activates a cluster, causing some kind of perturbation in it. This perturbation means an assimilation process, where the knowledge (center of the cluster) is updated by the innovative received information.

The assimilation process is applied over the center c, considering the new generated individual p. It can be done by: (a) a random recombination process between c and p, (b) deterministic move of c in the direction of p, or (c) samples taken between c and p. Assimilation types (a) and (b) generate only one internal point to be evaluated afterwards. Assimilation type (c), instead, can generate several internal points or even external ones, holding the best evaluated one to be the new center, for example. It seems to be advantageous, but clearly costly. These exploratory moves are commonly referred in path relinking theory [10].

Whenever a cluster reaches a certain density, meaning that some information template becomes predominantly generated by the evolutionary process, such information cluster must be better investigated to accelerate the convergence process in it. The cluster activity is measured in regular intervals of generations. Clusters with lower density are eliminated, as part of a mechanism that will allow to create other centers of information, keeping framed the most active of them. The cluster elimination does not affect the population. Only the center of information is considered irrelevant for the process.

3   ECS for Unconstrained Numerical Optimization

A real-coded version of ECS for unconstrained numerical optimization is presented in this section. Several test functions can be found in literature related to such problems. Their general presentation is:

$$\text{min / max}\ \ f(x), x = (x_1, x_2, x_3, \ldots, x_n)^T \in R^n \text{ where } L_i < x_i < U_i \qquad (1)$$

In test functions, the upper U_i and lower L_i bounds are defined *a priori* and they are part of the problem, bounding the search space over the challenger areas in function surface. This work uses some of well-known test functions, such as *Michalewicz, Langerman, Shekel* [11], *Rosenbrock, Sphere* [12], *Schwefel, Griewank,* and *Rastrigin* [13]. Table 1 shows all test functions, their respective known optimal solution and bounds.

Table 1. Test functions

Function	var	opt	$L_i; U_i$	Function	var	opt	$L_i; U_i$	Function	var	opt	$L_i; U_i$
Ackley	n	0	-15 ; 30	Goldstein	2	3	-2 ; 2	Zakharov	n	0	-5 ; 10
Sphere	n	0	-5.12;5.12	Griewank	n	0	-600; 600	Rastrigin	n	0	-5.12;5.12
Easom	2	-1	-100;100	Hartman	6	-3.322	0 ; 1	Rosenbrock	n	0	-5.12;5.12
Michalewicz	5	-4.687	0; π	Langerman	5	-1.4	0;10	Schwefel	n	0	-500;500
Michalewicz	10	-9,66	0; π	Langerman	10	-1.4	0;10	Shekel 10	4	-10.536	-10 ; 10

3.1   Implementation

The application details are now described, clarifying the approach. The component EA is a steady-state real-coded GA employing well-known genetic operators as roulette wheel selection [14], blend crossover ($BLX0.25$) [15], and non-uniform mutation [16]. Briefly explaining, in each generation, a fixed number of individuals NS are selected, crossed over, mutated and updated in the same original population, replacing the worst individual (steady-state updating). Parents and offspring are always competing against each other and the entire population tends to converge quickly.

The component IC performs an iterative clustering of each selected individual. A maximum number of clusters, MC, must be defined *a priori*. The ith cluster has its own center c_i, but a common radius r_t, in each generation t, is calculated for all clusters by:

$$r_t = \frac{x_{sup} - x_{inf}}{2 \cdot \sqrt[n]{|C_t|}} \qquad (2)$$

where $|C_t|$ is the current number of clusters (initially, $|C_t| = MC$), x_{sup} and x_{inf} are, respectively, the known upper and lower bounds of the domain of variable x, considering that all variables x_i have the same domain.

Whenever a selected individual p_k is *far away* from all centers (a distance above r_t), then a new cluster must be created. Evidently, MC is a bound value that prevents a unlimited cluster creation, but this is not a problem because the clusters can slip along the search space.

The cluster assimilation is a foreseen step that can be implemented by different techniques. The selected individual p_k and the center c_i, which it belongs to, are participants of the assimilation process by some operation that uses new information to cause some changing in the cluster location. In this work, the cluster assimilation is given by:

$$c_i' = c_i + \alpha \cdot (p_k - c_i) \qquad (3)$$

where α is called disorder degree associated with assimilation process. In this application, the center are kept more conservative to new information ($\alpha = 0.05$).

These choices are due to computational requests. Complex clustering algorithms could make ECS a slow solver for high dimensional problems. Considering the euclidean distance calculated for each cluster, for a n-dimensional problem, the IC complexity is about $O(\mathcal{MC} \cdot n)$.

At the end of each generation, the component AM performs the *cooling* of all clusters, i.e., they have their accounting of density, δ_i, reset. Eventually some (or all) clusters can be *re-heated* by selections or become inactive, being eliminated thereafter by AM. A cluster is considered inactive when no selection has occurred in the last generation. This mechanism is used to eliminate clusters that have lost the importance along the generations, allowing that other search areas can be framed. The AM is also evoked whenever a cluster is activated. It starts the component LS, at once, if

$$\delta_i \geq \mathcal{PD} \cdot \frac{\mathcal{NS}}{|C_t|} \tag{4}$$

The pressure of density, $\mathcal{PD}$, allows to control the sensibility of the component AM. The meaning of $\mathcal{PD}$ is the desirable cluster density beyond the normal density, obtained if $\mathcal{NS}$ was equally divided to all clusters. In this application, satisfactory behavior has been obtained setting $\mathcal{NS} = 200$ and $\mathcal{PD} = 2.5$.

The component LS was implemented by a Hooke and Jeeves direct search (HJD) [17]. The HJD is an early 60's method that presents some interesting features: excellent convergence characteristics, low memory storage, and requiring only basic mathematical calculations. The method works by two types of move. At each iteration there is an exploratory move with one discrete step size per coordinate direction. Supposing that the line gathering the first and last points of the exploratory move represents an especially favorable direction, an extrapolation is made along it before the variables are varied again individually. Its efficiency decisively depends on the choice of the initial step sizes $\mathcal{SS}$. In this application, $\mathcal{SS}$ was set to 5% of initial radius.

The Nelder and Mead Simplex (NMS) has been more widely used as a numerical parameter optimization procedure. For few variables the simplex method is known to be robust and reliable. But the main drawback is its cost. Moreover, there are n parameter vectors to be stored. According to the authors, the number of function calls increases approximately as $O(n^{2.11})$, but these numbers were obtained only for few variables ($n \leq 10$) [2]. On the other hand, the HJD is less expensive. Hooke and Jeeves found empirically that the number of function evaluations increase only linearly, i.e., $O(n)$ [17].

3.2   Computational Experiments

The ECS was coded in ANSI C and it was run on Intel AMD (1.33 GHz) platform. The population size was varied in $\{10, 30, 100\}$, depending upon the problem size. The parameter $\mathcal{NC}$ was set to 20 for all test functions. In the first experiment, ECS is compared against two other approaches well-known in the literature: Genocop III [16] and the OptQuest Callable Library (OCL) [18]. Genocop III is the third version of a genetic algorithm designed to search for optimal solutions in optimization problems with real-coded variables and linear and nonlinear constraints. The OCL is a commercial software designed for optimizing complex systems based upon metaheuristic framework known as scatter search [10]. Both approaches were run using the default values that the systems recommend and the results showed in this work were taken from [18].

The results in Table 2 were obtained, in 20 trials, allowing ECS to perform 10,000 function evaluations, at the same way that Genocop III and OCL are tested. The average of the best solutions found (FS) and the average of function calls (FC) were considered to compare the algorithm performances. The average of execution time in seconds (ET) is only illustrative, since the used platforms are not the same. The values in bold indicate which procedure yields the solution with better objective function value for each problem. Note that ECS has found better solutions in two test functions, while both OCL and Genocop III have better results in one function.

Table 2. Comparison against OCL and GENOCOP-3

Function	var	ECS FS	ET	OCL FS	ET	GENOCOP III FS	ET
Ackley	50	0.000	0.181	0.000	16.800	0.000	13.400
Ackley	100	0.000	0.374	0.000	103.600	0.000	46.600
Sphere	100	**0.000**	0.128	2.419	60.300	1114.451	43.700
Griewank	20	0.000	0.123	0.000	3.800	1.076	2.600
Rastrigin	10	1.087	0.036	**0.000**	4.500	1.026	0.900
Rastrigin	20	10.129	0.063	**0.000**	6.300	10.508	2.500
Rosenbrock	6	**0.002**	0.065	5.950	6.300	273.309	0.800
Rosenbrock	8	**0.000**	0.077	0.484	3.200	5.601	0.800
Rosenbrock	20	**0.003**	0.022	5.600	6.900	7.685	2.800
Schwefel	10	118.160	0.042	844.069	1.800	**1.387**	0.800
Schwefel	20	1360.397	0.047	1506.067	2.400	**134.491**	2.100

In the second experiment, ECS is compared against other approach found in literature that works with the same idea of detecting promising search areas: the Continuous Hybrid Algorithm (CHA), briefly described in the introduction. The CHA results were taken from [5], where the authors worked with several n dimensional test functions. The most challenging of them are used for comparison in this work. The results in Table 3 were obtained allowing ECS to perform up to 100,000 function evaluations in each one of the 20 trials. There is no information about the corresponding CHA bound. The average of the gaps between the solution found and the best known one (GAP) and the average of function calls (FC) were considered to compare the algorithm performances, besides the success rate (SR) obtained. In the **ECS** experiments, the SR reflects the percentage of trials that have reached at least a gap of 0.001. The SR obtained in CHA experiments is not a classical one, according the authors, because it considers the actual landscape of the function at hand [5].

One can observe that ECS seems to be better than CHA in all test functions showed in Table 3, except for the *Zakharov*, which ECS has not found the best known solution. It is known that the 2-dimensional *Zakharov*'s function is a monomodal one with the minimum lying at a corner of a wide plain. Nevertheless,

Table 3. Comparison against CHA

Function	var	ET	GAP	ECS FC	ECS SR	ECS GAP	CHA FC	CHA SR
Eason	2	0.002	0.00060	593.5	100	0.001	952.0	100
Goldstein	2	0.001	0.00060	**345.4**	100	0.001	259.0	100
Hartman	6	0.003	0.00000	633.9	100	0.008	930.0	100
Rosenbrock	5	0.007	0.00040	2561.7	100	0.018	3290.0	100
Rosenbrock	10	0.023	0.00005	8979.5	100	0.008	14563.0	83
Rosenbrock	50	0.049	0.00015	32780.6	100	0.005	55356.0	79
Rosenbrock	100	0.286	0.00444	85821.0	80	0.008	124302.0	72
Shekel	4	0.003	0.00007	506.8	75	0.015	635.0	**85**
Zakharov	10	0.004	0.00050	2328.6	100	**1e-6**	4291.0	100
Zakharov	50	0.153	33.75020	100040.6	0	**1e-5**	75520.0	100

Table 4. ECS results for other test functions

Function	var	ET	GAP	FC	SR	Function	var	ET	GAP	FC	SR
Griewank	50	0.053	0.00010	5024.550	100.00	Rastrigin	10	0.100	0.00060	26379.950	100.00
Griewank	100	0.432	0.00000	24344.450	100.00	Rastrigin	20	0.339	0.00078	71952.667	90.00
Langerman	5	0.023	0.00000	5047.684	95.00	Schwefel	20	0.211	0.00035	39987.950	100.00
Langerman	10	0.075	0.00000	17686.692	65.00	Schwefel	30	0.591	0.00029	90853.429	70.00
Michalewicz	5	0.054	0.00035	12869.550	100.00	Michalewicz	10	0.222	0.00038	37671.923	65.00

there was not found any reason for such poor performance. In function *Shekel*, although ECS have found better gaps, the success rate is not as good as CHA. The values in bold indicate in which aspects ECS was worse than CHA.

Other results obtained by ECS are showed in Table 4. The gap of 0.001 was reached a certain number of times for all these functions. The worst performance was in *Michalewicz* and *Langerman*'s functions (SR about 65%).

4   Conclusion

This paper proposes a new way of detecting promising search areas based upon clustering. The approach is called Evolutionary Clustering Search (ECS). The ECS attempts to locate promising search areas by framing them by clusters. Whenever a cluster reaches a certain density, its center is used as start point of some aggressive search strategy.

An ECS application to unconstrained numerical optimization is presented employing a steady-state genetic algorithm, an iterative clustering algorithm and a local search based upon Hooke and Jeeves direct search. Some experiments are presented, showing the competitiveness of the method. The ECS was compared with other approaches, taken from the literature, including the well-known Genocop III and the OptQuest Callable Library.

For further work, it is intended to perform more tests on other bench-mark functions. Moreover, heuristics and distance metrics for discrete search spaces are being studied aiming to build applications in combinatorial optimization.

References

1. Yen, J., Lee, B.: A Simplex Genetic Algorithm Hybrid, In: IEEE International Conference on Evolutionary Computation -ICEC97, (1997)175-180.

2. Nelder, J.A., Mead, R.: A simplex method for function minimization. Computer Journal. (1956) 7(23):308-313.
3. Birru, H.K., Chellapilla, K., Rao, S.S.: Local search operators in fast evolutionary programming. Congress on Evolutionary Computation,(1999)2:1506-1513.
4. Oliveira A.C.M.; Lorena L.A.N. Real-Coded Evolutionary Approaches to Unconstrained Numerical Optimization. Advances in Logic, Artificial Intelligence and Robotics. Jair Minoro Abe and João I. da Silva Filho (Eds). Plêiade, ISBN: 8585795778. (2002)2.
5. Chelouah, R., Siarry, P.: Genetic and Nelder-Mead algorithms hybridized for a more accurate global optimization of continuous multiminima functions. Euro. Journal of Operational Research, (2003)148(2):335-348.
6. Jelasity, M., Ortigosa, P., García, I.: UEGO, an Abstract Clustering Technique for Multimodal Global Optimization, Journal of Heuristics (2001)7(3):215-233.
7. Li, J.P., Balazs, M.E., Parks, G.T., Clarkson, P.J.: A species conserving genetic algorithm for multimodal function optimization, Evolutionary Computation, (2002)10(3):207-234.
8. Yager, R.R.: A model of participatory learning. IEEE Trans. on Systems, Man and Cybernetics, (1990)20(5)1229-1234.
9. Silva, L.R.S. Aprendizagem Participativa em Agrupamento Nebuloso de Dados, Dissertation, Faculdade de Engenharia Elétrica e de Computação, Unicamp, Campinas SP, Brasil (2003).
10. Glover, F., Laguna, M., Martí, R.: Fundamentals of scatter search and path relinking. Control and Cybernetics, (2000) 39:653-684.
11. Bersini, H., Dorigo, M., Langerman, S., Seront G., Gambardella, L.M.: Results of the first international contest on evolutionary optimisation - 1st ICEO. In: Proc. IEEE-EC96. (1996)611-615.
12. De Jong, K.A.: An analysis of the behavior of a class of genetic adaptive systems, Ph.D. dissertation, *University of Michigan Press*, Ann Arbor, 1975.
13. Digalakis, J., Margaritis, K.: An experimental study of benchmarking functions for Genetic Algorithms. IEEE Systems Transactions,(2000)3810-3815.
14. Goldberg, D.E.: Genetic algorithms in search, optimisation and machine learning. Addison-Wesley, (1989).
15. Eshelman, L.J., Schawer, J.D.: Real-coded genetic algorithms and interval-schemata, In: Foundation of Genetic Algorithms-2, L. Darrell Whitley (Eds.), Morgan Kaufmann Pub. San Mateo (1993) 187-202.
16. Michalewicz, Z.: *GeneticAlgorithms + DataStructures = EvolutionPrograms*. Springer-Verlag, New York (1996).
17. Hooke, R., Jeeves, T.A.: "Direct search" solution of numerical and statistical problems. Journal of the ACM, (1961)8(2):212-229.
18. Laguna, M., Martí, R.: The OptQuest Callable Library In Optimization Software Class Libraries, Stefan Voss and David L. Woodruff (Eds.), Kluwer Academic Pub., (2002)193-218.

A Fractal Fuzzy Approach
to Clustering Tendency Analysis

Sarajane Marques Peres[1,2] and Márcio Luiz de Andrade Netto[1]

[1] Unicamp - State University of Campinas
School of Electrical and Computer Engineering
Department of Computer Engineering and Industrial Automation
Campinas SP 13083-970, Brazil
{smperes,marcio}@dca.fee.unicamp.br
[2] Unioeste - State University of Western of Paraná
Department of Computer Science
Campus Cascavel, Cascavel PR 85814-110, Brazil

Abstract. A hybrid system was implemented with the combination of Fractal Dimension Theory and Fuzzy Approximate Reasoning, in order to analyze datasets. In this paper, we describe its application in the initial phase of clustering methodology: the clustering tendency analysis. The Box-Counting Algorithm is carried out on a dataset, and with its resultant curve one obtains numeric indications related to the features of the dataset. Then, a fuzzy inference system acts upon these indications and produces information which enable the analysis mentioned above.

Keywords: Clustering Tendency Analysis, Fractal Dimension Theory, Fuzzy Approximate Reasoning

1 Introduction

The treatment of high-dimension and large datasets is a critical issue for data analysis, and necessary for most of the problems in this area. The computational complexity of the used methods plays an important role when they are applied to datasets with a high number of descriptive attributes and a high number of data points. Efforts to find simpler and more efficient alternatives have grown in recent years. In this paper, we present a new approach (described with details in [13]), implemented with the aid of the Fractal Dimension Theory (FDT) and Fuzzy Approximate Reasoning (FAR), to analyze the clustering tendency (CT) of a dataset. This task, also known as the Clustering Tendency Problem, helps make decisions about "applying or not applying" a clustering process to a dataset. The main objective is to avoid excessive computational time and resources in a poor and more complex data analysis process, as in [3] e [9].

In fact, this hybrid system classifies, in a heuristic way, the "spatial distribution" of the data points in the dataset[1] space by: uniform, normal and clustered.

---

[1] In this context, the dataset is a stochastic fractal.

A.L.C. Bazzan and S. Labidi (Eds.): SBIA 2004, LNAI 3171, pp. 395–404, 2004.
© Springer-Verlag Berlin Heidelberg 2004

This discovery is made by the fuzzy analysis of the information obtained from the measuring process of the dataset's fractal dimension.

This paper is organized as follows: Section 2 describes the CT analysis and a classical approach to solve it - the Hopkins approach; the motivation to use FDT and FAR[2] in the conception of our system is discussed in Section 3; in Sections 4 and 5 we describe our hybrid system and compare the complexity of the two approaches; the tests and results are shown in Section 6. The considerations about the limitations of our approach and future works are discussed in Section 7 and, finally, the references are listed.

2   Clustering Tendency Analysis

Some methodologies are defined, with different phases and taxonomy, to guide the clustering process [6]. One of these phases is the CT analysis, which is defined as a problem of deciding whether the dataset exhibits a "predisposition" to cluster in natural groups. The information acquired from this phase can avoid the inappropriate application of clustering algorithms, which could find clusters where they do not exist. The most common approach to solve it is the Hopkins approach [6].

The Hopkins approach provides a numeric indicator useful to discover the CT. It examines if the data points contradict the assertion that they are distributed uniformly. If the disposition is not similar to a uniform distribution, the CT is certified. According to [6], the Hopkins index to multi-dimensional datasets is determined by (1), where: y_j is the set of m-points uniformly spread on the d-dimensional space of the dataset; x_i is the set of n-points randomly chosen from the dataset with $m <= n$; U_j is the set of minimal distances between each point of y_j and its nearest neighbor from x_i; and W_j is the set of distances between each point of x_i and its nearest neighbor.

$$H_{hpk} = \frac{\sum_{j=1}^{m} U_j^d}{\sum_{j=1}^{m} U_j^d + \sum_{j=1}^{m} W_j^d} \qquad (1)$$

Generally, in clusters, neighbors are closer than the samples of a uniformly distributed set of points. Thus, if H_{hpk} is close to 1, clusters are suggested. Similarly, values near 0 suggest uniform scattering.

3   Motivation: FDT and FAR

Fractal Theory studies "complex" subsets located inside simple metric space (like Euclidean space) and generated by simple self-transformations of this space. The Fractal Dimension of a dataset is the real dimension represented by its data points, i.e. a dataset can represent an object, which has lower dimensions

---

[2] We presumed that the reader is familiar with FDT and FAR. [1] and [7] has specific information about them.

than the dimensions of the space where it is located. One of the ways to obtain this measure is through the BC algorithm. A classical implementation of this algorithm is described in [10].

The BC algorithm analyzes the distribution of the data points through successive hypercube grid coverings of the dataset space. Every iterations realize a finer covering than the previous one, by shrinking the sides of all hypercubes needed to cover all the space. Thus, it is possible to observe the distribution behavior of the data points under the successive coverings. For datasets with uniform distributions, this behavior must be uniform, i.e. the number of occupied hypercubes must increase uniformly. Datasets with clusters cause stronger or weaker changes in the number of occupied hypercubes. This behavior of distribution is reflected on a log/log curve, which is formed by a sequence of straightlines, with different slopes, limited by the points that represent the relationship between the shrinking of the hypercubes and their occupation rates.

The difference of the slopes between successive straight-line segments on the curve represents the changes in the number of occupied hypercubes in successive coverings. Bigger or smaller slopes represent the dataset structure, or its spatial styles of distribution. Thus, it is needed to know how big or how small the variation must be to indicate a specific spatial distribution. The FAR, which allows working with linguistic variables and fuzzy values modeled by fuzzy sets (see some examples in [11]), can make it possible to answer this question.

4   The Fractal Fuzzy Approach – FFA

The FFA is composed of two modules: the former carries out the classical BC algorithm and the latter makes the fuzzy analysis of the resultant curve. The output of this system enables the decision about the distribution's style observed in the analyzed dataset, and the possible conclusions are: uniform, normal and clustered distribution. The first option means that the CT is not verified and the others mean that it is verified. The "normal distribution" can characterise the presence of clusters or not. This case demands an analysis more specific and the CT must be considered. However, the conclusion "normal distribution" is weaker than the conclusion clustered distribution, in relation to the CT. The outputs are followed by a membership degree (a confidence value between [0,1]), which allows an evaluation of the strength of each answer.

The curve resultant from the BC module is described by the coordinates[3] $ln(1/2^n)$ and $ln(Nn(A))$. The fuzzy module analyzes the information obtained from this curve (normalized): the difference of slope between each pair of consecutive segments and the slope of the second segment of each pair. These values are mapped to linguistic variables through the fuzzy sets and the *Mamdami* fuzzy inference (with the operators *mim* for implications and *max* for aggregations) is triggered (Figure 1). The parameters of the fuzzy system are listed in Tables 1 and 2. They were obtained through a supervised procedure of adjustment, which

---

[3] $1/2^n$ is used as a precision measurement and n is the current iteration of the algorithm.

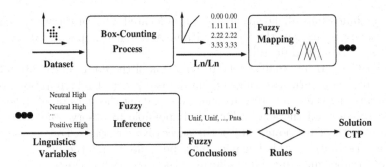

Fig. 1. Fractal Fuzzy Approach process. The parameters in this figure are only illustrative.

Table 1. Parameters of the system: fuzzy sets.

Var.[a] Type	Var. Name	Range	MF Type	MF Label	MF Parameters
Input	Slope-Diff	[-3 3]	zmf	Negative	[-2.5 1e-006]
			trapmf	Neutral	[-0.077 0.051 0.39 0.628]
			smf	Positive	[0.0769 2.5]
	Slope-2$^{\underline{o}}$	[0 3]	zmf	Low	[0.2 0.8]
	Segment		gaussmf	Mean	[0.0765 0.808]
			smf	High	[0.8 1.5]
Output	Conclusion	[0 1]	trapmf	Pnts	[0.19 0.284]
			trapmf	Norm	[0.192 0.252 0.299 0.357]
			zmf	Clus	[0.327 0.37 0.421 0.481]
			smf	Unif	[0.342 0.557]

[a] Var = variable; MF = Membership Function; Range = Suport of the fuzzy set.

relates the spatial distribution of known datasets to features of their BC curves. Changes in these parameters can make the system more sensitive or less sensitive to anomalies in the curve.

The fuzzy rules are based on the relationship between the behavior of occupation of the hypercube and the number of hypercubes on the grid. For example, the third rule in Table 2 infers the existence of a clustered spatial distribution (this situation can be observed in Figure 2). The two straight-line segments created by the second, third and fourth iterations of the BC process have a negative difference of slope. The existence of a change in the features of the curve can be inferred. It specifies an increase of the relative hypercube occupation rate. The high value of this difference, indicated by the slope of the second segment, reveals the existence of very close data points[4]. This situation explains that the hypercube grid was not able to separate some subsets of data points, on second and third iteration. So, these subsets form clusters with some degree of granularity.

---

[4] There are justifications for the establishment of all the rules. We mentioned just one as an example, due to space restrictions.

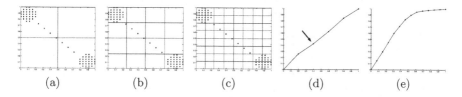

Fig. 2. Didactal example. (a) second BC iteration; (b) third BC iteration; (c) fourth BC iteration; (d) resultant curve from a clustered distribution; (e) resultant curve from a normal distribution. All graphs have the axes normalized in [0,1].

The sequence of conclusions represents the behavior of the BC curve and to analyse it means to discover the style of the spatial distribution of the datasets and, consequently, to analyse the CT. For example: if most of the conclusions in the sequence is *"Uniformity"*; it means that the curve has a behavior as a "straight-line", i.e. the data points are uniformly distributed in the space and the CT does not exist. We defined some *rules of thumb*, in order to analyse the sequence. The algorithm below describes these rules[5].

```
if "Clusters" appears in the sequence of conclusion then CT exists
  else
    if most of the conclusions in the sequence are "Uniformity" then
      if "Points" appears after the first conclusion of the sequence
      then the CT exists with tendencies of uniform distribution
                        % indicates the start of a negative influence
                        % of very closed data points
      else uniform distribution exists
    else
      if half or most of the conclusions in the sequence are
        "Normality" then
          if "Points" appears after the first conclusion of
            the sequence
          then the CT exists with tendencies of normal distribution
                        % indicates the start of a negative influence
                        % of very closed data points
          else normal distribution exists
      else CT exists    % because "Points" appears as the first
                        % conclusion of the sequence
```

In this context, the sequence of straight-line segments, which determine the result supplied by the system (for example, the most of the sequence of conclusions that is composed by *"Uniformity"*), is called "meaningful part".

---

[5] All possibilities of arrangement for the sequence of conclusions are covered by these rules

Table 2. Parameters of the system: fuzzy rules.

Rules Id	Premise 1	Premise 2	Connector	Conclusion[a]	Weight
1	Negative	Low	And	Norm	1
2	Negative	Mean	And	Norm	1
3	Negative	High	And	Clus	1
4	Neutral	Low	And	Norm	1
5	Neutral	Mean	And	Norm	1
6	Neutral	High	And	Unif	1
7	Positive	Low	And	Pnts	1
8	Positive	Mean	And	Unif	0.5
9	Positive	High	And	Unif	0.6

[a] Norm = Normality; Clus = Clusters; Unif = Uniformity; Pnts = Close Points.

5   Complexity Analysis

The computational complexity of the Hopkins approach is $nSS*mUD*d$, where: nSS is the number of data points on the sample set; and mUD is the number of samples on the uniform distribution[6]; and d is the dimensionality of the space where the dataset is located. Thus, the upper limit of the complexity function is summarized to $\theta(n^2 * d)$.

The computational complexity of the FFA approach is determined by the BC algorithm which is the only process carried out with the data points. Fuzzy mappings and fuzzy inferences are carried out with a very short sequence of numbers, and their running times are not expressive for the whole process. There are several implementations of the BC algorithm with different upper limit functions, as in: [14] with complexity $\theta(N*D*I)$; [5], a recursive algorithm with complexity $\theta(2^D)$ plus the running time of each iteration $(O(N))$; and [8] with complexity $D * N * log(N)$; where N is the number of data points, D is the dimension of the dataset space and I is the number of points on the resultant curve. The algorithm presented by [14] constitutes the best solution for high-dimensional and large datasets.

6   Test and Results

The tests were done using numerical[7] datasets with several characteristics referring to the spatial distributions, number of instances and dimensionality of the space[8].

---

[6] I.e.: nSS is equal to mUD.

[7] No numerical datasets must be changed to numerical datasets.

[8] We shown some datasets used on the tests, as a representative set. The others datasets and the respective results can be obtained with the authors.

In order to analyze the performance of the Hopkins approach, the tests were done with different configurations for two parameters: the number of the iterations and the size of the sample set. There were variations in the results obtained due to the random features of this approach. The tests which presented an average result had 50 iterations and a sample set with half of the analyzed dataset.

The "uniform spatial distribution" was detected by the FFA when the resultant curve, or its meaningful part, was like an "inclined straight-line". This fact was observed with datasets whose distribution occupied all the space, with few or many data points, without concentrations. Table 3[9] lists three examples where the conclusion "uniform distribution" was obtained. It shows the comparisons with the Hopkins index and with the expected result[10]. The dataset "Space Clusters" is a difficult example for our approach (due to the sparcity of the data points)and the Hopkins index obtained a low indication of CT. The conclusion obtained by the FFA for the dataset "Normal Distribution 1" (a normal distribution with 3000 data points in a 5-dimensional space - mean 0 and variance 1) showed a weak TC, which was revealed by a decision limit situation.

Table 3. Identification of the "uniform spatial distribution".

Dataset	Result of FFA[11]	Member-ship Grade	Result of Hopkins	Hopkins Index	Expected Result
Uniform Dist.	Uniform (Ok)	1.0	Uniform (Ok)	0.2864	Uniform
Spaced Clus.	Uniform (Not)	1.0	Cluster (Ok)	0.5600	Cluster
Normal Dist.1	Uniform* (Ok)	1.0	Cluster (Ok)	0.8585	Normal

Table 4 shows the datasets for which the FFA observed the "normal spatial distribution". In these cases, the resultant curve was like a "simple curve" (see Figure 2(e)). This distribution was found in two situations: when the data points were strongly concentrated in one region of the distribution, with some dispersion around it[12]; or when the data points presented ill-defined concentrations.

The datasets Normal Distribution[13] 2 and 3 (located in a 1-dimensional and 3-dimensional space, respectively, with 100 data points), 4 (located in a 1-dimensional space, 3000 data points) were classified by the Hopkins Index as clustered datasets. Our approach was able to identify them as a normal set (with CT). The dataset Random Distribution has short clusters scattered in the space. The dataset Spiral has two spirals [4].

---

[9] For all tables like this, the marks (Ok) and (Not) assign our evaluation about the results obtained as the solution to the CT analisys: (Ok) correct result; (Not) not correct result.

[10] The expected result is determined by the feature of the distribuition used to create the datasets or by information found on the reference where the dataset was obtained.

[11] The symbol * specifies a conclusion obtained on a decision limit region.

[12] Like a cloud of data points.

[13] All uniform distributions were generated with: mean 0 and variance 1.

Table 4. Identification of the "normal spatial distribution".

Dataset	Result of FFA	Member- ship Grade	Result of Hopkins	Hopkins Index	Expected Result
Spirals	Normal (Ok)	0.9	Cluster (Ok)	0.7149	Cluster
Normal Dist.2	Normal (Ok)	0.8	Regular (Not)	0.3806	Normal
Normal Dist.3	Normal (Ok)	1.0	Cluster (Ok)	0.6334	Normal
Normal Dist.4	Normal (Ok)	0.6	Cluster (Ok)	0.9086	Normal
Randon Dist.	Normal (Ok)	0.9	Cluster (Ok)	0.7540	Random

Table 5. Identification of the "normal spatial distribution" in a decision limit situation.

Dataset	Result of FFA	Member- ship Grade	Result of Hopkins	Hopkins Index	Expected Result
Normal Dist.4	Normal* (Ok)	1.0	Cluster (Ok)	0.9790	Normal
Normal Dist.5	Normal* (Ok)	1.0	Cluster (Ok)	0.5545	Normal
Normal Dist.6	Normal* (Ok)	1.0	Cluster (Ok)	0.6033	Normal
Normal Dist.7	Normal* (Ok)	1.0	Cluster (Ok)	0.7872	Normal
Normal Dist.8	Normal* (Ok)	1.0	Cluster (Ok)	0.7678	Normal
Iris4d	Normal* (Ok)	1.0	Cluster (Ok)	0.8391	Cluster
Abalone	Normal* (Ok)	0.5	Cluster (Ok)	0.9580	Cluster
Hungary	Normal* (Ok)	1.0	Cluster (Ok)	0.8535	Cluster

The results shown in Table 5 refer to decision limit situations. The datasets have high dimension, with the exception of the dataset Normal Distribution 4, that is located in 1-dimensional space (5000 data points). The Hopkins index was very high for this dataset. The next four datasets are normal distributions with: 100 points in 4-dimensional space; 100 points in 5-dimensional space; 3000 points in 4-dimensional space; and 3000 points in 5-dimensional space. The others datasets [2] are: Iris (4-dimensional space), Abalone (8-dimensional space) and Hungary Heart Diseases (13-dimensional space).

The "clustered spatial distribution" was observed when the resultant curve presented some style of anomaly (as shown on Figure 2(d)). Table 6 shows the datasets where this situation was observed. The first four datasets are located in 2-dimensional space and have groups: well separated, with partial overlap, stronger overlap forming two groups. The other datasets are located, respectively, in: 34, 7, 13, 13-dimensional space, and they are available in [2].

In relation to the solutions for the CT, the FFA approach presented 96% of the correct answers. The same percentual result was obtained by the Hopkins index. The FFA obtained 76% of the correct results referent to expected answers. The datasets with "normal spatial distribution" were not considered in evaluating the Hopkins approach, in relation to this resquisite (because answer "normality" could not be obtained). So, its performance was 100%, under these restrictive conditions (on 16 datasets, including the random dataset). Others considerations about the Hopkins index could be made, and these results could be changed, for example: a more restrictive, however common, index threshold to determine the CT is 0.75. Thus, under this condition, the performance of this approach was: 43.75% in relation to expected answers and 52% in relation to CT; other possibility (less common) is determine using three indexes (as a politic of intervals): $[0, 0.3]$ - regularity; $(0.3, 0.75)$ - normality; $[0.75, 1]$ - clustered. For this condition, the performance of the approach was: 48% in relation to expected answers (now, considering all datasets) and 100% in relation to CT.

Table 6. Identification of the "clustered spatial distribution".

Dataset	Result of FFA	Member- ship Grade	Result of Hopkins	Hopkins Index	Expected Result
Four Groups 1	Cluster (Ok)	1.0	Cluster (Ok)	0.9157	Cluster
Four Groups 2	Cluster (Ok)	0.3	Cluster (Ok)	0.6889	Cluster
Four Groups 3	Cluster (Ok)	1.0	Cluster (Ok)	0.6497	Cluster
Iris2d	Cluster (Ok)	1.0	Cluster (Ok)	0.8771	Cluster
Dermato	Cluster (Ok)	1.0	Cluster (Ok)	0.7333	Cluster
Auto-mpg	Cluster (Ok)	1.0	Cluster (Ok)	0.8482	Cluster
Va	Cluster (Ok)	1.0	Cluster (Ok)	0.7205	Cluster
Cleveland	Cluster (Ok)	1.0	Cluster (Ok)	0.7020	Cluster
Switzerland	Cluster (Ok)	1.0	Cluster (Ok)	0.7281	Cluster

7   Conclusions and Trends

In this paper we demonstrated how to solve the preliminary phase of a clustering methodology - the CT analysis - using a new approach. We implemented a hybrid system combining FDT and FAR to enable the analysis of the relationship between the data points and the dataset space. The efficiency of this system was evaluated in relation to the algorithmic complexity and the quality of the analysis (with test on synthetic and real datasets). We compared the efficiency of our approach with the efficiency of the classical Hopkins approach.

The capacity of the FFA, to detect the CT, is similar to the capacity of the Hopkins approach with the classical parameters. In this question, the FFA presented 96% of correct answers and the Hopkins approach reached: 96% with the common index threshold (0.5); 52% with a more restrictive index threshold (0.75); and 100% with a relaxed index threshold (the politics of intervals). The FFA is able to supply discriminatory information of the dataset structure, with more efficiency than the Hopkins approach. The percent of correct answers, in relation to expected result - uniform, normal and clustered - was better to our approach (76% against 48%). Moreover, the Hopkins approach is able to supply these three styles of information only with the use of the politics of intervals. The upper limit of the complexity function for the Hopkins approach indicates that it can be slower than some implementations of the BC algorithm (which determines the complexity of our approach). For large datasets, the implementations for the

BC algorithms developed by [14] or [8] are good alternatives to implement our approach, because the upper limit of the complexity function are not dependent on a quadratic function of the number of used data points.

The studies about FAR are not finished. There are problems in relation to sparse datasets and we are exploring this problem now. The use of this system to determine a style of "accurate fractal dimension measure", and the application of this measure in others problems of clustering processing also is being explored. We have reached some interesting preliminary results with the combination of FAR with Neural Networks [12].

References

1. M. Barnsley. *Fractals Everywhere*. Academic Press Inc, San Diego, California, USA, 1988.
2. C.L. Blake and C.J. Merz. UCI repository of machine learning databases, 1998.
3. F. Can, Altingovde, and E. I. S., Demir. Efficiency and effectiveness of query processing in cluster-based retrieval. *Information Systems*, 2003. to appear.
4. L. N. Castro and F. J. Voz Zuben. *Data Mining: A Heuristic Approach*, chapter aiNet: an artificial immune network for data analysis, pages 231–259. Idea Group Publishing, USA, 2001.
5. B.F. Feeny. Fast multifractal analysis by recursive box covering. *International Journal of Bifurcation and Chaos*, 10(9):2277–2287, 2000.
6. K. J. Jain and R. C. Dubes. *Algorithms for Clustering Data*. Prentice-Hall, Inc., New Jersey, USA, 1988.
7. G. J. Klir and B. Yuan. *Fuzzy Sets and Fuzzy Logic: Theory and Applications*. Prentice-Hall, 1995.
8. A. Kruger. Implementation of a fast box-counting algorithm. *Computer Physics Communications*, 98:224–234, 1996.
9. Massey L. *Using ART1 Neural Networks to Determine Clustering Tendency*, chapter Applications and Science in Soft Computing. Springer-Verlag, 2003.
10. H. O. Peitgen, H. Jurgens, and D. Saupe. *Chaos and Fractals: New Frontiers of Science*. Springer-Verlag New York Inc., New York, USA, 1992.
11. S.M. Peres and M.L.A. Netto. Using fractal dimension to fuzzy pre-processing of n-dimensional datasets. In *ICSE 2003 - Sixteenth International Conference on System Engineering*, Conventry, United Kingdom, 2003. (Accepted to).
12. S.M. Peres and M.L.A. Netto. Fractal fuzzy decision making: What is the adequate dimension for self-organizing maps. In *NAFIPS 2004 - North American Fuzzy Information Processing Society*, Banff, Canada, 2004. to appear.
13. S.M. Peres and M.L.A. Netto. Um sistema hibrido para analise heuristica de dados utilizando teoria de fractais e raciocinio aproximado. Technical report, Universidade Estadual de Campinas, Campinas, Sao Paulo, Brasil, 2004.
14. C. Jr. Traina, A. Traina, Wu L., and C. Faloutsos. Fast feature selection using fractal dimension. In *XV Brazilian Database Symposium*, pages 158–171, João Pessoa, PA, Brazil, 2002.

On Stopping Criteria for Genetic Algorithms

Martín Safe[1], Jessica Carballido[1,2], Ignacio Ponzoni[1,2], and Nélida Brignole[1,2]

[1] Grupo de Investigación y Desarrollo en Computación Científica (GIDeCC)
Departamento de Ciencias e Ingeniería de la Computación
Universidad Nacional del Sur, Av. Alem 1253, 8000, Bahía Blanca, Argentina
msafe@uns.edu.ar, {jac,ip@cs.uns.edu.ar}, dybrigno@criba.edu.ar
[2] Planta Piloto de Ingeniería Química - CONICET
Complejo CRIBABB, Camino La Carrindanga km.7
CC 717, Bahía Blanca, Argentina

Abstract. In this work we present a critical analysis of various aspects associated with the specification of termination conditions for simple genetic algorithms. The study, which is based on the use of Markov chains, identifies the main difficulties that arise when one wishes to set meaningful upper bounds for the number of iterations required to guarantee the convergence of such algorithms with a given confidence level. The latest trends in the design of stopping rules for evolutionary algorithms in general are also put forward and some proposals to overcome existing limitations in this respect are suggested.

Keywords: stopping rule, genetic algorithm, Markov chains, convergence analysis

1 Introduction

During the last few decades genetic algorithms (GAs) have been widely employed as effective search methods in numerous fields of application. They are typically used in problems with huge search spaces, where no efficient algorithms with low polynomial times are available, such as NP-complete problems [1].

Although in practice GAs have clearly proved to be efficacious and robust tools for the treatment of hard problems, the theoretical fundamentals behind their success have not been well-established yet [2]. There are very few studies on key aspects associated with how a GA works, such as parameter control and convergence analysis [3]. More specifically, the answers to the following questions concerning GA design remain open and constitute subjects of current interest. How can we define an adequate termination condition for an evolutionary process? [4–6]. Given a desired confidence level, how can we estimate an upper bound for the number of iterations required to ensure convergence? [7–9].

In this work we present a critical review of the state-of-the-art in the design of termination conditions and convergence analysis for canonical GAs. The main contributions in the field are discussed, as well as some existing limitations. On the basis of this analysis, future research lines are put forward. The article has been organized as follows. In section 2 the traditional criteria typically employed

A.L.C. Bazzan and S. Labidi (Eds.): SBIA 2004, LNAI 3171, pp. 405–413, 2004.
© Springer-Verlag Berlin Heidelberg 2004

to express GA termination conditions are presented. Then, basic concepts on the use of Markov chain models for GA convergence analysis are summed up. Section 4 contains a discussion of the results obtained in the estimation of upper bounds for the number of iterations required for GA convergence. A description of the present trends as regards termination conditions for evolutionary algorithms in general is given next. Finally, some conclusive remarks and proposals for further work are stated in section 6.

2   Termination Conditions for the sGA

A simple Genetic Algorithm (sGA) exhibits the following features: finite population, bit representation, one-point crossover, bit-flip mutation and roulette wheel selection. The sGA and its elitist variation are the most widely employed kinds of GA. Consequently, this variety has been studied quite extensively. In particular, most of the scarce theoretical formalizations of GAs available in the literature are focused on sGAs. The following three kinds of termination conditions have been traditionally employed for sGAs [10, p. 67]:

- An upper limit on the number of generations is reached,
- An upper limit on the number of evaluations of the fitness function is reached, or
- The chance of achieving significant changes in the next generations is excessively low.

The choice of sensible settings for the first two alternatives requires some knowledge about the problem to allow the estimation of a reasonable maximum search length. In contrast, the third alternative, whose nature is adaptive, does not require such knowledge. In this case, there are two variants, namely genotypical and phenotypical termination criteria. The former end when the population reaches certain convergence levels with respect to the chromosomes in the population. In short, the number of genes that have converged to a certain value of the allele is checked. The convergence or divergence of a gene to a certain allele is established by the GA designer through the definition of a preset percentage, which is a threshold that should be reached. For example, when 90% of the population in a GA has a 1 in a given gene, it is said that that gene has converged to the allele 1. Then, when a certain percentage of the genes in the population (e.g. 80%) has converged, the GA ends. Unlike the genotypical approach, phenotypical termination criteria measure the progress achieved by the algorithm in the last n generations, where n is a value preset by the GA designer. When this measurement, which may be expressed in terms of the average fitness value for the population, yields a value beyond a certain limit ϵ, it is said that the algorithm has converged and the evolution is immediately interrupted.

The main difficulty that arises in the design of adaptive termination policies concerns the establishment of appropriate values for their associated parameters (such as ϵ in phenotypical rules), while for the criteria that set a fixed amount of iterations, the fundamental problem is how to determine a reasonable value for that number, so that sGA convergence is guaranteed with a certain confidence level. In this case, the values not only depend on the dimension of the search space, but also on the rest of the parameters involved in the sGA, which include the crossover and mutation probabilities as well as the population size.

The minimum number of iterations required in a GA can be found by means of a convergence analysis. This study may be carried out from different approaches, such as the scheme theory [11, Chap. 2] or Markov chains [12–14]. The usefulness of the schema theorem has been widely criticised [15]. As it gives a lower bound for the expectation for one generation, it is very difficult to extrapolate its conclusions to multiple generations accurately. In this article we have concentrated on Markov chains because, as pointed out by Bäck et al. [2], this approach has already provided remarkable insight into convergence properties and dynamic behaviour.

3   Markov Chains and Convergence Analysis of the sGA

A *Markov chain* may be viewed as a stochastic process that traverses a sequence of states $\sigma_0, \sigma_1, \sigma_2, \ldots$ through time. The passage from state σ_i to state σ_{i+1} is called a transition. A distinguishing feature that characterizes Markov chains is the fact that, given the present state, future states are independent from past states, though they may depend on time. For a formal definition see, for example, [16, pp. 106–107].

Nix and Vose [12] showed how the sGA can be modelled exactly as a finite Markov chain, i.e. a Markov chain with a finite set of states. In their model, each state represents a population and each transition corresponds to the application of the three genetic operators. They found exact formulas for the transition probabilities to go from one population to another in one GA iteration as functions of the mutation and crossover rates. By forming a matrix with these transition probabilities and computing its powers, one can predict precisely the behaviour of the sGA in terms of probability, for fixed genetic rates and fitness function. This approach was taken up by De Jong et al. [17]. Unfortunately, the number of rows and columns of the corresponding matrices is equal to the number of all possible populations, which, according to [12], amounts to

$$\binom{2^\ell + n - 1}{n} . \tag{1}$$

This quantity becomes extremely large as the population size n or the strings length ℓ grows. Also notice that these matrices are not sparse because their entries are all non-zero probabilities. Therefore, this method can only be applied for small values of n and ℓ.

Nevertheless, Nix and Vose's formulation can lead to an analysis of the sGA convergence behaviour. For instance, they confirm the intuitive fact that, unless mutation rate is zero, each population is reachable from any other in one transition, i.e. the transition probability is non-zero for any pair of populations.

According to the theory about finite Markov chains, this simple fact has immediate consequences in the sGA behaviour as the number of iterations grows indefinitely. More specifically, whatever the initial population σ, the probability to reach any other population σ' after t iterations does not approach 0 as t tends to infinity. It tends to a positive limit probability instead. This limit depends on σ', but is independent from σ. Then, although the selection process tends to favour populations that contain high-fitness individuals by making them more probable, the constant-rate mutation introduces enough diversity to ensure that all populations are visited again and again. Thus, the sGA fails to converge to a population subset, no matter how much time has elapsed.

Moreover, Rudolph [14] showed that the same holds for more general crossover and selection operators, if a constant-rate mutation is kept. Nevertheless, reducing mutation rates progressively does not seem to be enough. Davis and Príncipe [13] presented a variation of the sGA that uses the mutation rate as a control parameter analogous to temperature in simulated annealing. They show how the mutation rate can be reduced during execution in order to ensure that the limiting distribution focuses only on populations consisting of replicas of the same individual, which is however, not necessarily a globally optimal one.

In contrast, the elitist version of the sGA, which always remembers the best individual found so far, does converge in a probabilistic sense. In this respect, Rudolph [14] shows that the probability of having found the best individual sometime during the process approaches 1 when the number of iterations tends to infinity, and he points out that this property does not mean that genetic algorithms have special capabilities to find the best individual. In fact, since any population has nonzero probability of being visited and there is a finite number of populations, then each of them will eventually be visited with probability 1 as the number of iterations grows indefinitely. Then, this observation lacks significance in practice because, for example, the direct enumeration of all the individuals guarantees the discovery of the global optimum in a finite time.

4   Stopping Criteria for the sGA with Elitism

Aytug and Koehler [7, 8] formulated a stopping criterion for the elitist sGA from the fact that all populations are visited with probability 1. Given a threshold α, they aimed at finding an upper bound for the number of iterations t required to guarantee that the global optimum has been visited with probability at least α in one of these iterations. Using Nix and Vose's model [12], they showed [7] that it is enough to have

$$t \geq \left\lceil \frac{\ln(1-\alpha)}{\ln(1 - \min\{\mu^{\ell n}, (1-\mu)^{\ell n}\})} \right\rceil \qquad (2)$$

to ensure that all the populations, and consequently all the individuals, have been visited with probability greater or equal to α. In equation 2, $\mu \in (0,1)$ is the mutation rate, ℓ is the length of the chains that represent the individuals, and n is the population size. Later, Aytug and Koehler [8] determined an upper bound for the number of iterations required to guarantee, with probability at least α, that all possible individuals have been inspected, instead of imposing the condition on all the populations. In this way, they managed to improve the bound in (2) significantly, proving that a number of iterations t that satisfies

$$t \geq \left\lceil \frac{\ln(1 - \alpha)}{n \ln(1 - \min\{\mu^\ell, (1 - \mu)^\ell\})} \right\rceil \qquad (3)$$

is enough to achieve this objective. Greenhalgh and Marshall [9] obtained similar results independently on the basis of simpler arguments. In the rest of this section, we will show that, in spite of being theoretically correct, these criteria are of little practical interest.

Let us consider a random algorithm (RA) that generates in each iteration a population of n individuals, not necessarily different from each other, chosen at random and independently. Just like Aytug and Koehler [7, 8] did for the elitist sGA, we shall determine the lowest number of iterations required to guarantee with probability at least α that the RA has generated all the possible individuals in the course of the procedure. Let us consider the populations $\sigma_1, \sigma_2, \sigma_3 \ldots$ generated by the RA and an element ω from the space of individuals (for example, a global optimum). Our objective is to find the lowest value for t so that $\Pr(\omega \in \sigma_1 \cup \cdots \cup \sigma_t) \geq \alpha$. Since the populations are generated independently from each other, then

$$\Pr(\omega \in \sigma_1 \cup \cdots \cup \sigma_t)$$

$$= 1 - \Pr(\omega \notin \sigma_1) \times \cdots \times \Pr(\omega \notin \sigma_t) = 1 - \left[1 - \left(\frac{1}{2} \right)^\ell \right]^{nt} . \qquad (4)$$

The expression in brackets is lower than 1, so the whole expression approaches 1 as t tends to infinity. Since ω is an arbitrary individual, (4) shows that the RA will visit all individuals with probability 1 if it is allowed to iterate indefinitely. Moreover, by applying logarithms to (4), we get

$$\Pr(\omega \in \sigma_1 \cup \cdots \cup \sigma_t) \geq \alpha \quad \text{if and only if} \quad t \geq \left\lceil \frac{\ln(1 - \alpha)}{n \ln(1 - (1/2)^\ell)} \right\rceil . \qquad (5)$$

This is an upper bound for the number of iterations required to ensure with probability at least α that the RA has examined all the individuals, and consequently discovered the global optimum.

Since (3) reaches its minimum for $\mu = 1/2$, then the bound for RAs given in (5) is always at least as good as the bound for GAs presented in (3). Then, the latter does *not* provide a stopping criterion in practice because it always suggests waiting for the execution of at least as many iterations as the amount that an RA without heuristics of any kind would require. Moreover, when μ tends to 0, which constitutes the situation of practical interest, the amount of iterations required by (3) grows to infinity. Figure 1 depicts the behaviour of (3) and its relation to (5).

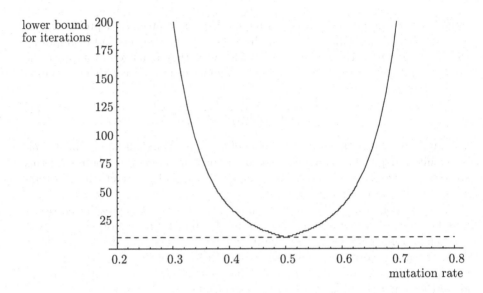

Fig. 1. This graph illustrates how the lower bound for GA iterations (3) (*continuous line*) grows quickly to infinity as mutation rate μ moves away from 1/2. In this case $\ell = 6$, $n = 20$ and $\alpha = 0.95$. The lower bound for RA iterations (5) for the same ℓ, n and α is also indicated (*dashed line*) and coincides with the minimum attained by (3)

Due to the way Aytug and Koehler posed their problem, they were theoretically impeded to go beyond the bound for RAs given in (5). In fact, since they make no hypotheses on the fitness function, they implicitly include the possibility of dealing with a fitness function that assigns a randomly-chosen value to each individual. When this is the case, only exploration is required and no exploitation should be carried out. Therefore, the RA exhibits better performance than the sGA.

5   Present Trends in Stopping Rules for Evolutionary Algorithms

Whatever the problem, it is nowadays considered inappropriate to employ sets of fixed values for the parameters in an evolutionary algorithm [3]. Therefore, it would be unadvisable to choose a termination condition based on a preestablished number of iterations. Some adaptive alternatives have been explored in the last decade.

Among them we can cite Meyer and Feng [4], who suggested using fuzzy logic to establish the termination condition, and Howell et al. [5], who designed a new variant of the evolutionary algorithms called Genetic Learning Automata (GLA). This algorithm uses a peculiar representation of the chromosomes, where each gene is a probability. On this basis, a novel genotypical stopping rule is defined. The execution stops when the alleles reach values close to 0 or 1.

In turn, Carballido et al. [6] present a representative example of a stopping criterion designed ad hoc for a specific application, namely the traveling salesman problem (TSP). In that work, a genotypical termination criterion defined for both ordinal and path representations is proposed.

Finally, it is important to remark the possibility of increasing efficiency by using parallel genetic algorithms (pGAs) in particular. As stated in Hart et al. [18], the performance measurements employed in parallel algorithms, such as the speed-up, are usually defined in terms of the cost required to reach a solution with a pre-established precision. For this reason, when you wish to calculate metrics of parallel performance, it is incorrect to stop a pGA either after a fixed number of iterations or when the average fitness exhibits little variation. This constitutes a motivation for the definition of stopping rules based on the attainment of thresholds. The central idea is to stop the execution of the pGA when a solution that reaches this threshold is found. For instance, Sena et al. [19] present a parallel distributed GA (pdGA) based on the master-worker paradigm. The authors illustrate how this algorithm works by applying it to the TSP, using a lower bound estimated for the minimum-cost tour as threshold for the termination condition.

Nevertheless, threshold definition requires a good estimation of the optimum of the problem under study, which is unavailable in many cases. Unfortunately, the most recent reviews on pGAs ([20, 21]) fail to provide effective strategies to overcome these limitations.

6   Conclusions

Research work in this field shows that the sGA does not necessarily lead to better and better populations. Although its elitist version converges probabilistically to the global optimum, this is due to the fact that the sGA tends to explore the whole space, rather than to the existence of any special capability in its exploitation mechanism. This is not, indeed, in contradiction to the interpretation of sGAs as evolutionary mechanisms because the introduction of a fixed fitness function implies an assumption that may not be in exact correspondence with natural environments, whose character is inherently dynamic. As pointed out by De Jong [22], Holland's initial motivation for introducing the concept of GAs was to devise an implementation for robust adaptive systems, without focusing on the optimization of functions. Furthermore, De Jong makes a clear distinction between sGA and GA-based function optimizers. The successful results achieved through the use of the latter for the solution of hard problems often blurs this distinction.

Until recently, this trend has led researchers to look for a general measure of elitist sGA efficiency from a theoretical viewpoint, applicable when finding the solution of *any* optimization problem on binary strings of length ℓ [8,9]. The smoothness of the fitness function is extremely important when choosing the most convenient kind of heuristic strategy to adopt when facing a given problem. The higher the smoothness, the higher the exploitation level and conversely, as the function is less smooth, more exploration is required. This fact is so clear that it should not be overlooked. Since no hypotheses on the fitness function have been made, and also considering that no measure of its smoothness has been included in its formula, this approach is overestimating exploration to the detriment of exploitation, this being just the opposite of what one really wishes in practice when implementing a heuristic search.

In view of the fact that the sGA is not an optimizer of functions, efforts should be directed to the devise of adequate modifications to tackle each specific problem in order to design an optimizer that is really efficient for a determinate family of functions. Besides, it is important to remark that current trends are towards the employment of adaptive termination conditions, either genotypical or phenotypical, instead of using a fixed number of iterations, because for most applications in the real world the mere estimation of the size of the search space constitutes in itself an extremely complex problem.

Acknowledgments

The authors would like to express their acknowledgment to the "Agencia Nacional de Promoción Científica y Tecnológica" from Argentina, for their economic support given through Grant N°11-12778. It was awarded to the research project entitled "Procesamiento paralelo distribuido aplicado a ingeniería de procesos" (ANPCYT Res N°117/2003) as part of the "Programa de Modernización Tecnológica, Contrato de Préstamo BID 1201/OC-AR".

References

1. Brassard, G., Bratley, P.: Algorithmics: Theory and Practice. Prentice-Hall, Inc., New Jersey (1988)
2. Bäck, T., Hammel, U., Schwefel, H.P.: Evolutionary computation: Comments on the history and current state. IEEE Transactions on Evolutionary Computation 1 (1997) 3–17
3. Eiben, Á.E., Hinterding, R., Michalewicz, Z.: Parameter control in evolutionary algorithms. IEEE Transactions on Evolutionary Computation 3 (1999) 124–141
4. Meyer, L., Feng, X.: A fuzzy stop criterion for genetic algorithms using performance estimation. In: Proceedings of the Third IEEE Conference on Fuzzy Systems. (1994) 1990–1995
5. Howell, M., Gordon, T., Brandao, F.: Genetic learning automata for function optimization. IEEE Transactions on Systems, Man, and Cybernetics-Part B: Cybernetics 32 (2002) 804–815
6. Carballido, J.A., Ponzoni, I., Brignole, N.B.: Evolutionary techniques for the travelling salesman problem. In Rosales, M.B., Cortínez, V.H., Bambill, D.V., eds.: Mecánica Computacional. Volume XXII. Asociación Argentina de Mecánica Computacional (2003) 1286–1294
7. Aytug, H., Koehler, G.J.: Stopping criterion for finite length genetic algorithms. INFORMS Journal on Computing 8 (1996) 183–191
8. Aytug, H., Koehler, G.J.: New stopping criterion for genetic algorithms. European Journal of Operational Research 126 (2000) 662–674

9. Greenhalgh, D., Marshall, S.: Convergence criteria for genetic algorithms. SIAM Journal on Computing **20** (2000) 269–282
10. Michalewicz, Z.: Genetic Algorithms + Data Structures = Evolution Programs. Springer, New York (1996)
11. Goldberg, D.E.: Genetic Algorithms in Search, Optimization, and Machine Learning. Addison-Wesley Longman, Inc., Reading, Massachusetts (1989)
12. Nix, A.E., Vose, M.D.: Modeling genetic algorithms with Markov chains. Annals of Mathematics and Artificial Intelligence **5** (1992) 79–88
13. Davis, T.E., Príncipe, J.C.: A Markov chain framework for the simple genetic algorithm. Evolutionary Computation **1** (1993) 269–288
14. Rudolph, G.: Convergence analysis of canonical genetic algorithms. IEEE Transactions on Neural Networks **5** (1994) 96–101
15. Poli, R.: Exact schema theorem and effective fitness for GP with one-point crossover. In Whitley, L.D., Goldberg, D.E., Cantú-Paz, E., Spector, L., Parmee, I.C., Beyer, H.G., eds.: Proceedings of the Genetic and Evolutionary Computation Conference, Morgan Kaufmann (2000) 469–476
16. Çinlar, E.: Introduction to Stochastic Processes. Prentice-Hall, Inc., Englewood Cliffs, New Jersey (1975)
17. De Jong, K.A., Spears, W.M., Gordon, D.F.: Using Markov chains to analyze GAFOs. In Whitley, L.D., Vose, M.D., eds.: Proceedings of the Third Workshop on Foundations of Genetic Algorithms, Morgan Kaufmann (1995) 115–137
18. Hart, W.E., Baden, S., Belew, R.K., Kohn, S.: Analysis of the numerical effects of parallelism on a parallel genetic algorithm. In: Proceedings of the 10th International Parallel Processing Symposium, IEEE Computer Society (1996) 606–612
19. Sena, G.A., Megherbi, D., Isern, G.: Implementation of a parallel genetic algorithm on a cluster of workstations: travelling salesman problem, a case study. Future Generation Computer Systems **17** (2001) 477–488
20. Alba, E., Tomassini, M.: Parallelism and evolutionary algorithms. IEEE Transactions on Evolutionary Computation **6** (2002) 443–462
21. Veldhuizen, D.A.V., Zydallis, J.B., Lamont, G.B.: Considerations in engineering parallel multiobjetive evolutionary algorithms. IEEE Transactions on Evolutionary Computation **7** (2003) 144–173
22. De Jong, K.A.: Genetic algorithms are NOT function optimizers. In Whitley, L.D., ed.: Proceedings of the Second Workshop on Foundations of Genetic Algorithms, Morgan Kaufmann (1993) 5–17

A Study of the Reasoning Methods Impact on Genetic Learning and Optimization of Fuzzy Rules

Pablo Alberto de Castro and Heloisa A. Camargo

Federal University of São Carlos
São Carlos SP 13565-905, Brazil
{pablo,heloisa}@dc.ufscar.br

Abstract. A Genetic Algorithm based learning procedure was proposed earlier by the authors and the results, advantages and usefulness of the proposal have been reported in the literature. The procedure is based on the Pittsburgh approach and is divided in two separate phases: learning of candidate rules and selection of relevant rules. The learning and the optimization processes involve an evaluation function that considers the performance of the candidate rule base, requiring the selection and use of a particular reasoning method. With the objective of investigating further the robustness and usefulness of the previous approach, the authors developed a comparative study of the GA learning algorithm focusing on the impact of the reasoning method used. Two different methods were used: the one based on a single winner rule, and the one based on the combination of all rules. Following the description of the rules format and reasoning methods used, the GA learning and optimization approach proposed before is also reviewed. The comparison of simulation results is presented based on the criteria of correct classification rates and number of rules in the rule base. The results demonstrate that the knowledge base performance is similar in both cases, suggesting that the GA learning procedure derives good rule bases despite the reasoning method used.

Keywords: Genetic Fuzzy Rule-Based Systems, Pattern Classification, Learning, Fuzzy Reasoning Methods.

1   Introduction

One of the most important tasks in the development of fuzzy systems is the design of its knowledge base. An expressive effort has been devised in the recent past to develop or adapt methodologies that are capable of automatically extracting knowledge from numerical data to generate it: clustering algorithms [7], gradient-based methods [8], neural networks [6] and genetic algorithms (GA) [9].

Particularly in the framework of soft computing, significant research work has been carried out with the objective of developing hybrid or cooperating

A.L.C. Bazzan and S. Labidi (Eds.): SBIA 2004, LNAI 3171, pp. 414–423, 2004.

systems involving different methodologies that provide learning capabilities to fuzzy systems. In this direction, two successful approaches emerged: the one combining neural networks and fuzzy systems and the one combining genetic algorithms and fuzzy systems.

Genetic Algorithms have demonstrated to be a powerful tool to perform tasks such as [10]: generation of fuzzy rule base, optimization of fuzzy rule bases, generation of membership functions and tuning of membership functions. All theses tasks can be considered as optimization or search processes. The combination Fuzzy Systems + Genetic Algorithms have great acceptance in the scientific community, once these algorithms are robust and capable of performing a global search in wide and irregular spaces, finding a good solution [12]. Some examples of very good results among the ones reported in the literature can be found in [13] [14].

Genetic-based learning methods when used for rule generation fall into three categories: Michigan approach, Pittsburgh approach and Iterative approach. In the first one, each chromosome correspond to a single rule, while in the Pittsburgh approach each chromosome encodes a complete set of rules. In the Iterative approach, like Michigan, each chromosome encodes only one rule, but only the best rule of the population is returned as solution, discarding the remaining chromosomes.

In our previous work [15], we investigated the genetic fuzzy rule learning process based on the Pittsburgh approach and genetic optimization of the fuzzy rule base. The objective was to demonstrate that, although the Pittsburgh representation can make the chromosomes very extensive, increasing the complexity of the search process and consequently imposing a heavier computational effort, an advantage compensates and justifies its use: the fact that the complete rules set is coded in each chromosome, what allows to evaluate the entire rules set in the fitness function and not only isolated rules. Besides that, the approach used avoids the problem of competition among individual rules, as occurs in the Michigan and Iterative approaches. A self-adaptive version of the same algorithm has also been developed and analyzed by the authors, leading to some important improvements concerning both the classification ability and number of rules. The obtained results have been reported in [2]. A comparative study between the described approach and another one that focuses on the genetic learning of the knowledge database can be found in [3].

The learning process proposed in [15] is divided in 2 stages: The first one is the Genetic Learning Process for obtaining a set of candidate fuzzy rules. The other stage is the Genetic Optimization Process for excluding the unnecessary and redundant rules. In both stages, the fitness function involves an evaluation of rule base performance with respect to correct classification rate, where a particular reasoning method has to be selected and plays a relevant role. Aiming at investigating the impact of the reasoning method adopted during the learning process in the knowledge base performance, this work describes an study developed to compare the results of the GA learning algorithm using two different reasoning methods. The two reasoning methods considered in the present investigation were the one based on a single winner rule, also used in the authors previous works, and the fuzzy reasoning method based on the combination of all rules.

As before, the application domain is multidimensional fuzzy pattern classification, where the class also is fuzzy. The membership functions were defined by means of fuzzy clustering algorithm FC-Means.

This paper is organized as follows. Section 2 shows the fuzzy classification rule format and the two fuzzy reasoning methods employed in the comparisons. Section 3 describes the genetic learning process for fuzzy classification rules proposed earlier, while section 4 describes the optimization phase. The analyses of learning algorithm behavior under the assumption of different reasoning methods is presented in section 5 through the description of the computational simulations developed. The conclusions are discussed in section 6.

2   Fuzzy Classification Rule Format and Fuzzy Reasoning Methods

Classification is an important task encountered in various fields such as pattern recognition, decision making, data mining and modeling [16]. The goal of classification is to assign classes to a set of data instances, called patterns, that are described by multiple attributes.

In this work, the attributes as well the classes are described by linguistic terms defined by fuzzy sets. We use fuzzy rules for pattern classification problems of the following type:

$$R_k: \text{IF } x_1 \text{ is } A_{i_1} \text{ and } \ldots \text{and } x_n \text{ is } A_{i_n}, \text{ THEN Class} = C_j$$

where R_k is the rule identifier , $x_1, \ldots, x_n$ are attributes of the pattern, $A_{i_1}, \ldots,$ A_{i_n} are linguistic terms defined by fuzzy sets used to represent the attributes and C_j is also a linguistic term defined by fuzzy set to represent the class.

In a Fuzzy Classification System, the reasoning method is based on fuzzy logic. It derives conclusions from a set of fuzzy rules and a pattern. This section presents two fuzzy reasoning methods: the *fuzzy reasoning method based on a single winner rule* and the *fuzzy reasoning based on the combination of all rules*.

Let $e_p = \{a_{p_1}, a_{p_2}, \ldots, a_{p_n}\}$ be the pattern to be classified, $a_{p_1}, \ldots, a_{p_n}$ the attributes of the pattern and R=$\{R_1, R_2, \ldots, R_S\}$ the fuzzy rule set. The **reasoning method based on a single winner rule** is performed by the follows steps, adapted from [17]:

Step 1: Calculate the compatibility degree, $Compat(R_k, e_p)$, between the pattern e_p and each rule R_k, k=1...S, applying a T-norm [18] to the membership degree of the pattern attribute values, a_{p_j}, in the corresponding fuzzy sets that appear in the antecedent part of the rule, A_{i_j}, j=1...n.

$$Compat(R_k, e_p) = T(\mu_{A_{i_1}}(a_{p_1}), \ldots, \mu_{A_{i_n}}(a_{p_n})) \tag{1}$$

Step 2: Find the rule with higher compatibility degree with the given pattern,

$$\text{Max } \{Compat(R_k, e_p)\} , \quad k=1...S \qquad (2)$$

Step 3: The pattern e_p will be classified in the class C_j, such that C_j is the class of the rule R_k that possess the higher compatibility degree with the pattern.

This reasoning method uses only one rule to classify the pattern and wastes the information associated with the other rules whose the compatibility degree is lower than the selected rule. On the other hand, there is another reasoning method that combines informations provided by all rules to classify the pattern. The **reasoning method which combines all rules** is performed by the follows steps, adapted from [13]:

Step 1: Calculate the compatibility degree, $Compat(R_k, e_p)$, between the pattern e_p and each rule R_k, $k=1...$S, applying a T-norm to the membership degree of the pattern attribute values, a_{p_j}, in the corresponding fuzzy sets that appear in the antecedent part of the rule, A_{i_j}, $j=1...$n.

$$Compat(R_k, e_p) = T(\mu_{A_{i_1}}(a_{p_1}), ..., \mu_{A_{i_n}}(a_{p_n})) \qquad (3)$$

Step 2: Calculate for each class C, C=1...M, the $Class_C$ as follows:

$$Class_C = \Sigma \{Compat(R_k, e_p) \mid C \text{ is the class of the rule } R_k\} \qquad (4)$$

Step 3: The pattern e_p will be classified in the class C_j, such that C_j is the class of $Class_C$ that possess the higher value.

For both reasoning methods, if two or more rules present the same compatibility degree with the pattern but different consequent, then the rule that first appear will be fired. The pattern is considered correctly classified if the class wich was assigned to it is the class such that the pattern has the highest membership degree.

3   Genetic Learning Process

This section attempts to describe the genetic fuzzy rule base generating process used here. Starting from a data set that represents samples or examples of the problem and with membership functions previously defined, the proposed method uses GA to generate a suitable fuzzy rule base that correctly classify these examples. We present in the sequel the basic mechanisms of GA (coding, initial population creation, fitness function, genetic operators and stopping condition), adopted in the present work.

Coding of Fuzzy Rule Base
The rules are coded by integer numbers that represent the index of fuzzy sets that appear in the antecedent and consequent part of the rule. The number 0 is utilized to represent the *"don't care"* condition.

Once the learning approach utilized is the Pittsburgh approach, each chromosome encodes a entire fuzzy rule base. For instance, suppose a classification problem where the patterns have 3 attributes - X_1, X_2 e X_3 - and 1 class - C_j. The attributes are associated with the domains $D_1 = \{A_{1_1}, A_{2_1}, A_{3_1}\}$, $D_2 = \{A_{1_2}, A_{2_2}, A_{3_2}\}$ and $D_3 = \{A_{1_3}, A_{2_3}, A_{3_3}\}$, respectively and the class is associated with the domain $D_C = \{C_1, C_2, C_3\}$.

The chromosome Cr_i of Figure 1 is coded with k rules and each one is represented by 4 genes, where the 3 first genes indicate the index of the fuzzy sets of the attributes X_1, X_2 e X_3 and the 4th gene represents the index of the fuzzy set of the class.

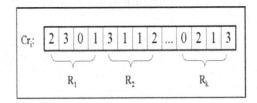

Fig. 1. Coding of Fuzzy Rule Bases

The rule base coded by the chromosome of the Figure 1 is as follow:

R_1: IF X_1 is A_{2_1} and X_2 is A_{3_2} and X_3 is *"don't care"*, THEN Class $= C_1$
R_2: IF X_1 is A_{3_1} and X_2 is A_{1_2} and X_3 is A_{1_3}, THEN Class $= C_2$

$\vdots$

R_k: IF X_1 is *"don't care"* and X_2 is A_{2_2} and X_3 is A_{1_3}, THEN Class $= C_3$

The use of *"don't care"* condition provides better fuzzy rule base generalization capacity to classify new patterns correctly. Besides that, the introduction of *"don't care"* has also an important effect on the rules comprehensibility, once these rules have fewer attributes on antecedent part. Short rules can be more easily understood by human that long rules with many attributes.

It is necessary to define previously the number of fuzzy rules to be coded in the chromosomes.

Initial Population
The initial population is randomly generated. It is formed by random numbers that can assume values from 0 to q_i, where q_i is the number of fuzzy sets utilized to represent the attribute a_i.

Fitness Function
The fitness function is defined based on performance of the fuzzy rule base, calculated by the number of training patterns correctly classified, using some fuzzy reasoning method presented in section 2. The fitness function is expressed by:

$$\text{fitness\_value } (Cr_i) = \text{NPC}(Cr_i) \tag{5}$$

where $NPC(Cr_i)$ is the Number of Patterns Correctly Classified by the fuzzy rule base coded in the chromosome Cr_i.

Genetic Operators

The genetic operators utilized in this work are one point crossover, standard mutation and the stochastic universal sampling selection, together with the elitist strategy.

Stopping Condition

In computer simulations of this work, we used the maximum number of generations as the stopping condition. The solution returned is the chromosome with better fitness value in the last generation.

4 Genetic Optimization Process

As soon as the fuzzy rule base generation process terminates, the rule base contain some redundant and unnecessary rules. So, a process to eliminate them is required.

This section describes the genetic process to simplify the fuzzy rule base, selecting a small number of effective rules from the previous rules obtained. The final rule base must have a high classification power.

The genetic operators and stopping condition are the same that used in the previous algorithm. Coding, initial population creation and fitness function are presented below:

Coding

In this stage the chromosomes $Cr_i = (c_{i1}, c_{i2}, ..., c_{im})$ are coded with sequence of binary digits with length m, where m is the number of rules generated in the previous stage. Each gene c_{ij} (a binary digit) is associated with one rule. If $c_{ij}=1$ (rule active), then the rule associated with this gene will be in the final rule base, otherwise will not.

Initial Population

The initial population is generated by introducing a chromosome that represent all rules previously obtained, that is, all genes of the chromosome will receive value 1. The remaining chromosomes are generated at random.

Fitness Function

The fitness function evaluates each chromosome, that is, each sub-set of candidate rules based on 2 criteria: Number of Patterns Correctly Classified – $NPC(Cr_i)$ – and Number of active rules contained in this sub-set – $NR(Cr_i)$. The fitness function is expressed by:

$$\text{fitness\_value } (Cr_i) = \text{NPC}(Cr_i) * (\text{S} - \text{NR}(Cr_i)) \tag{6}$$

where S is the number of total candidate rules.

When the fitness value of a chromosome Cr_i is calculated, all given training patterns are classified by the sub rule set coded in Cr_i. The number of patterns correctly classified are stored in $\text{NPC}(Cr_i)$. If a fuzzy rule in Cr_i not classify any pattern, then this rule can be removed from the sub rule set by assigning value 0 to its associated gene. Thus, we remove all rules that not classify any pattern. The number of active rules is stored in $NR(Cr_i)$.

5   Experiments

In order to evaluate the presented methodology to automatic generation of fuzzy rules for pattern classification problems under different fuzzy reasoning methods, some tests were realized using two data sets obtained from UCI Repository of Machine Learning Databases [1].

The used data sets are Auto_mpg and Boston Housing. The first one contains 392 examples reporting automobiles fuel consumption in miles per gallon, in terms of 07 attributes The Boston Housing data set comprises 506 examples about the price of houses in suburbs of Boston described by 13 attributes.

The domain of each attribute of the data sets are represented by continuous values and it is necessary to granularize them in a number of fuzzy sets that represent the linguistic values that each attribute can assume, in order to generalize the knowledge. The output variables of both data sets, automobile consumption and house price, also have continuous values. So, it is necessary to granularize them too.

The membership functions associated to fuzzy sets were defined by fuzzy clustering algorithm FC-Means [21] [22]. Clustering is a technique to group in clusters data or objects that have some similarity. The classical clustering algorithm generate partitions such that each object belongs only to one cluster. Fuzzy clustering allows that an object belongs to many groups simultaneously, with different membership degree.

The generation of membership functions process using FC-Means was applied to each attribute as follows: suppose a set of L training examples $E = \{e_1, e_2, ..., e_L\}$ is given and each example $e_p = \{a_{p_1}, a_{p_2}, ..., a_{p_n}\}$ is composed by n attributes. For each attribute the number of fuzzy sets to be generated is defined. The FC-Means algorithm is then applied over each attribute domain separately, generating the fuzzy sets and respective membership functions used in the algorithm.

Both data sets were partitioned at random in 2 groups: 70% to training and 30% to test. This partitioning was done 5 times, generating 5 pairs of training-test data. The genetic algorithm is applied to the training data in order to generate the fuzzy rules. The test data are used to evaluate the performance of the obtained rule base to classify new patterns.

The genetic algorithm parameters values utilized are as follows. Maximum number of generations: 1000; Population size: 100; Crossover rate: 0.7 and Mutation rate: 0.015.

We examined the algorithm performance for both data sets using the fuzzy reasoning method based on a single winner rule, denoted here by FRM1 and using the fuzzy reasoning method which combines all rules, denoted by FRM2.

It was established that each chromosome will codify a high number of rules in order to offer a wide covering of the search space. Thus, each chromosome represents a fuzzy rule base composed by 50 fuzzy rules but most of them will be eliminated in the optimization stage.

Table 1 shows the results obtained for Auto_mpg test data set with different granularization level. We used 3, 4 and 5 fuzzy sets for all variables. The same test was applied to Boston Housing test data set and the results can be seen in Table 2.

The results presented in both tables are the average of the results under 5 executions of the algorithm and the number of rules is the average of the number of rules obtained after the rule base optimization process.

Table 1. Results for Auto_mpg test data set

Number of fuzzy sets:	3		4		5	
Resoning Method:	FRM1	FRM2	FRM1	FRM2	FRM1	FRM2
Classification rate (%)	96.4	96.2	96.6	96.8	96.4	96.8
Standard deviation	0.549363	0.487324	0.549786	0.5002367	0.549363	0.496721
Number of rules	13	12	14	14	13	14

Table 2. Results for Boston Housing test data set

Number of fuzzy sets:	3		4		5	
Resoning Method:	FRM1	FRM2	FRM1	FRM2	FRM1	FRM2
Classification rate (%)	91.2	92.4	90.8	92.7	91.8	91.6
Standard deviation	0.574381	0.647980	0.572006	0.661325	0.580119	0.569867
Number of rules	14	11	13	11	12	15

From Table 1 and Table 2 we can see that the algorithm presented good performance under both reasoning methods. The accuracy of the rule bases and the number of fuzzy rules did not vary so much for both reasoning method. Besides that, we can see also that the algorithm is not very sensitive to choice of data granularization. For 3, 4 or 5 fuzzy sets, the results did not change significantly in FRM1 neither in FRM2.

6 Conclusions

This paper presented a comparative investigation of a GA learning and optimization procedure presented by the authors in a previous work, which reinforced, from a different point of view, the robustness and usefulness of the learning method. The learning process is divided into 2 stages. The first one is the genetic learning process based on Pittsburgh approach for obtaining desirable fuzzy rules that cover a high number of examples. Although this representation form increases the complexity of the search process, two advantages justify and viabilize its use: 1) the possibility of evaluating the complete rule base in the fitness function and 2) avoiding the problem of competition among rules. The other stage is the genetic optimization process for excluding the unnecessary and redundant fuzzy rules. By computational experiments in some data sets, we demonstrated that the performance of proposed methodology under two different fuzzy reasoning methods is very good. The results showed the algorithm ability to find a compact set of fuzzy rules with high classification rates for both reasoning methods.

Acknowledgment

Pablo A. D. Castro would like to thank CAPES for financial support.

References

1. C. L. Blake and C. J. Merz. UCI Repository of machine learning databases [http://www.ics.uci.edu/m̃learn/MLRepository.html], Irvine, CA: University of California, Department of Information and Computer Science", 1998.
2. P. A. D. Castro and H. A. Camargo. "Learning and Optimization of Fuzzy Rule Base by Means of Self Adaptive Genetic Algorithms". IEEE International Conference on Fuzzy Systems, 2004.
3. H. A. Camargo, M. G. Pires and P. A. D. Castro. "Genetic Design of Fuzzy Knowledge Bases - a study of different approaches". 23rd IEEE International Conference of NAFIPS, Alberta, Canadá, 2004.
4. O. Cordón, F. Herrera, F. Gomide, F. Hoffmann and L. Magdalena, "Ten years of genetic-fuzzy systems: a current framework and new trends", *Proceedings of Joint 9th IFSA World Congress and 20th NAFIPS Internation Conference*, pp. 1241-1246, Vancouver - Canada, 2001.
5. O. Cordón and F. Herrera, "Hybridizing genetic algorithms with sharing scheme and evolution strategies for designing approximate fuzzy rule-based systems", *Fuzzy Sets and Systems,* vol. 118, pp. 235-255, 2001.
6. D. Nauck and R. Cruse, "A neuro-fuzzy method to learn fuzzy classification rules from data", *Fuzzy Sets and Systems*, vol. 89, pp. 277-288, 1997.
7. T. W. Liao, Aivars K. Celmins and Robert J. Hammell, "A fuzzy c-means variant for the generation of fuzzy term sets", *Fuzzy Sets and Systems*, vol. 135, pp. 241-257, 1997.
8. H. Nomura , L. Hayashi and N. Wakami, "A learning method of fuzzy inference rules by descent method", *Proceedings of the 1st IEEE International Conference on Fuzzy Systems*, pp. 203-210, San Diego - USA, 1992.
9. O. Cordón, F. Herrera, F. Hoffmann and L. Magdalena", "Recent Advances in Genetic Fuzzy Systems", *Journal of Information Sciences,* vol. 136, pp. 1-5, 2001.
10. H. Ishibuchi, T. Murata and I. B. Turksen", "Single-objective and two-objective genetic algorithms for selecting linguistic rules for pattern classification problems", *Fuzzy Sets and Systems,* vol. 89, pp. 134-150, 1997.
11. H. Ishibuchi, T. Nakashima and T. Morisawa", "Voting fuzzy rule-based systems for pattern classification problems", *Fuzzy Sets and Systems,* vol. 103, pp. 223-238, 1999.

12. Y. Yuan and H. Zhuang, "A genetic algorithm for generating fuzzy classification rules", *Fuzzy Sets and Systems*, vol. 84, no. 4, pp. 1-19, 1996.
13. H. Ishibuchi, T. Nakashima and T. Murata, "Performance evaluation of fuzzy classifier systems of multidimensional Pattern Classification Problems", *IEEE Transactions on Fuzzy Systems,* vol. 29, pp. 601-618, 1999.
14. F. Hoffman, B. Baesens, J. Martens, F. Put and J. Vanthienen", "Comparing a genetic fuzzy and a neurofuzzy classifier for credit scoring", *International Journal of Intelligent Systems,* vol. 17, no. 11, pp. 1067-1083, 2002.
15. P. A. D. Castro, M. G. Pires and H. A. Camargo, "Aprendizado e seleção de regras nebulosas usando algoritmos genéticos", *VI Simpósio Brasileiro de Automação Inteligente*, pp. 970-975, 2003.
16. Jan van den Berg, Uzay Kaymak and Willem-Max van den Bergh", "Fuzzy Classification using Probability-based Rule Weighting", *Proceedings of the 11th IEEE International Conference on Fuzzy Systems*, Hawaii - USA, 2002.
17. O. Cordón, M. J. del Jesus and F. Herrera, "A proposal on reasoning methods in fuzzy rule-based classification systems", *International Journal of Approximate Reasoning,* vol. 20, pp. 21-45, 2001.
18. G. Klir and B. Yuan, *Fuzzy sets and Fuzzy Logic - Theory and Applications,* Prentice-Hall, 1995.
19. J. J. Grefenstette, "Optimization of Control Parameters for Genetic Algorithms", *IEEE Trans. Systems, Man, and Cybernetics*, vol. 16, no. 1, pp. 122–128, 1986.
20. J. A. Vasconcelos, J. A. Ramirez, R. H. C. Takahashi and R. R. Saldanha, "Improvements in Genetic Algorithms", *IEEE Trans. on Magnetics*, vol. 37, no. 5 pp. 3414-3417, 2001.
21. A. Baraldi and P. Blonda, "A survey of fuzzy clustering algorithms for patterns recognition - Part I", *IEEE Trans. Systems, Man,* and *Cybernetics*Part B: Cybernetics, vol. 29, pp. 778-785, 1999.
22. A. Baraldi and P. Blonda, "A survey of fuzzy clustering algorithms for patterns recognition - Part II", *IEEE Trans. Systems, Man,* and *Cybernetics*Part B: Cybernetics, vol. 29, pp. 786-801, 1999.

Using Rough Sets Theory and Minimum Description Length Principle to Improve a β-TSK Fuzzy Revision Method for CBR Systems

Florentino Fdez-Riverola[1], Fernando Díaz[1], and Juan M. Corchado[2]

[1] Dept. Informática, University of Vigo, Escuela Superior de Ingeniería Informática
Edificio Politécnico, 32004, Ourense, Spain
{riverola,fdiaz}@uvigo.es
[2] Dept. de Informática y Automática, University of Salamanca
Plaza de la Merced s/n, 37008, Salamanca, Spain
corchado@usal.es

Abstract. This paper examines a fuzzy logic based method that automates the review stage of a 4-step Case Based Reasoning system and aids in the process of obtaining an accurate solution. The proposed method has been derived as an extension of the Sugeno Fuzzy model, and evaluates different solutions by reviewing their score in an unsupervised mode. In addition, this paper proposes an improvement of the original fuzzy revision method based on the reduction of the original set of attributes that define a case. This task is performed by a feature subset selection algorithm based on the Rough Set theory and the minimum description length principle.

Keywords: CBR, TSK fuzzy models, rough sets, minimum description length, automated revision stage.

1 Introduction

Case Based Reasoning (CBR) systems have been successfully used in several domains such as diagnosis, prediction, control and planning [1,2]. However, a major problem of these systems is their difficulty to evaluate the proposed solution and, if it is necessary, repairing it using domain-specific knowledge [3]. This is usually done by means of interacting with a human expert and it is highly dependent of the problem domain. Also there are very few standard techniques to automate their construction, since each problem may be represented by a different data set and requires a customised solution [4]. This is a current weakness of CBR systems and one of their major challenges. For several years we have been working in the identification of techniques to automate the reasoning cycle of CBR systems [5,6,7]. This paper presents an improved Takagi Sugeno Kang (TSK) fuzzy based model able to automate the process of case revision of CBR systems.

First we summarize the automated fuzzy revision method, showing the phases that need to be executed in order to set up the proposed algorithm. Then we explore the possibility of improving the method with the use of rough sets as a pre-processing

A.L.C. Bazzan and S. Labidi (Eds.): SBIA 2004, LNAI 3171, pp. 424–433, 2004.

feature subset selection step. Results from a real biological forecasting problem are shown and finally, we remark the conclusions and specify the future work.

2 β-TSK Fuzzy Revision Method

For the last few years, there has been a lot of work employing fuzzy-based methods to improve CBR systems [2]. The theories of fuzzy sets, neural networks and neuro-fuzzy techniques are tools of what is known as *soft computing*. The main application areas of fuzzy set theory in case based reasoning are (*i*) maintenance of the case base (with concepts like competence and coverage) [8,9,10,11] and (*ii*) fuzzy indexing and retrieval [12,13], where several real CBR applications have been successfully developed [14,2].

The use of fuzzy modelling proposed in this paper for the revision stage of CBR systems, is based on the demonstrated accuracy of fuzzy set theory for dealing with uncertainties, arising from deficiency in information, in an efficient manner. Apart from the accuracy of this technique itself, one of the aspects that distinguishes fuzzy modelling from other black-box approaches like neural networks, is that fuzzy models are transparent to interpretation and analysis (to some extent). This characteristic can be used, as we will see later, as a mechanism able to produce an explanation of the solution generated by the CBR system.

The purpose of the new approach introduced in this paper is twofold. On the one hand, we try to develop an automated fuzzy revision model with a high degree of accuracy. On the other hand, we intend that the resulting fuzzy rule system may improve the knowledge that the user has over the problem domain.

2.1 Obtaining the Fuzzy Model and Constructing the Revision Subsystem

The first step in the generation of the β-TSK fuzzy model is the construction of an initial fuzzy system [15] able to model the knowledge represented by the case base of the CBR system. This can be done following the advice of human experts, learning symbolic rules from artificial neural networks [16], using evolutionary strategies [17], applying fuzzy clustering to the data or using a hybrid approach.

A novel method of fuzzy clustering able to extract interpretable fuzzy rules from a Radial Basis Function (RBF) neural network [18] is proposed in [19], and applied successfully in the work of [20]. Starting from the TSK fuzzy rule base obtained in the previous step, a measure of similarity is applied with the purpose of reducing the number of fuzzy sets describing each variable. We use a similarity measure for identifying similar fuzzy sets and replace these by a common fuzzy set representative for the original ones. If the redundancy in the model is high, merging similar fuzzy sets for each variable might result in equal rules that also can be merged, thereby reducing the number of rules as well [21]. As a result, the new fuzzy rule base increments the capacity of generalisation of the original TSK fuzzy system.

In order to generate several fuzzy rule bases with different generalization degrees, it is necessary to set up a λ-limit from which two membership functions can be considered analogous and therefore can be joined [22]. In our revision method, the parameter λ goes from 0.9 to 0.6 with decrements of 0.1 [23], generating four fuzzy rule bases corresponding with the TSK fuzzy systems (in this case, β is equal to 4).

The algorithm starts in an iterative way grouping membership functions attribute by attribute. In each iteration, the similarity S between all the membership functions for a given attribute is calculated, selecting the pair of functions that holds a higher degree of similarity providing that $S > \lambda$. The selected pair of functions are joined and the rule base is brought up to date with the new membership function. The algorithm continues until the maximum similarity between two memberships functions belonging to any attribute is less or equal to λ. Finally, the fuzzy rules with similar antecedent part are merged, and the consequent of the new rule is recalculated.

2.2   Training the Fuzzy Revision Subsystem

The process of training the fuzzy revision subsystem can be viewed as a wrapper algorithm that envelops the whole CBR cycle. We propose the use of a clustering retrieval method, in order to maintain a local adaptation (*importance vector*) of each fuzzy system for each class of identified problems [23].

In this model, the β-fuzzy systems are associated with each class identified by the retrieval stage, mapping each one with its corresponding score in the importance vector as said before. There is one importance vector for each class or "prototype". These fuzzy systems are used to validate and refine the proposed solution. Given a new problem and a proposed solution for it, each of the fuzzy systems that compose the revision subsystem generates a solution that is pondered according to the importance vector associated to the class to which the problem belongs. The importance value of the fuzzy system that best suits a particular class is increased, whilst the others are proportionally decreased based on the error percentage with respect to the real value.

The continuous adaptation of the importance vector belonging to the problem prototype, guarantees that the most accurate fuzzy system will have a higher weight for each class of problems [21].

2.3   Working Mode: Reviewing the Solution and Generating an Explanation

When a new problem arise, its class and the importance vector for the β-fuzzy systems are identified by the clustering retrieval method. Then the reuse stage of the CBR proposes a solution for the problem. The parallel solution calculated by the TSK fuzzy revision method is computed and its difference (in percentage) is calculated. The proposed revision schema is based on the definition of two revision limits: *acceptance_limit* and *reject_limit*. Although the precise values of these parameters depend on the problem domain, we have identified after carrying out several experiments that a correct initial approximation is to assign values of 10% and 30% respectively [23].

Both limits refer to the variation rate between the initial proposed solution and the solution obtained from the TSK fuzzy system. The adoption of this schema leads to the definition of three possible behaviors and explanations adopted by the system:

- If the variation rate is less or equal than the acceptance_limit, the initial solution is endorsed by the fuzzy revision subsystem and it is presented as the final solution for the new problem. The justification is based on the fuzzy rules that belong to the initial TSK fuzzy system.
- If the variation rate is greater or equal than the reject_limit, it means that the fuzzy revision subsystem contradicts the initial solution, so the CBR system is unable to solve the problem. The justification is based on the fuzzy rules from the previous item plus those belonging to the fuzzy system that produced the most distant solution.
- If the variation rate is in the open interval defined by the two limits, then the fuzzy revision subsystem adapts the initial solution weighting by 50% each possible solution (the initial one and the solution obtained from the TSK fuzzy system). The output of the CBR system is the modified solution. The justification is based on the fuzzy rules from the first item plus those fuzzy rules belonging to the fuzzy system with a high degree of importance for the prototype to which the problem belongs.

The explanation of the adopted decision is generated keeping in mind the behavior of the revision subsystem. The justification is based on the evaluated fuzzy rules that take part on the final decision. An important point in the previous explained operation, is that the fuzzy revision method is able to identify those situations in which the CBR system is unable to provide a correct solution for a given problem (cases with similar features and different answer).

3 Improving the β-Fuzzy Revision Method with Rough Set Theory

As we show in [21], the method exposed is able to produce accurate results, but the time needed for generating the fuzzy revision subsystem is high and the explanatory strength of the fuzzy rule bases is not clear enough.

We propose the use of a feature subset selection algorithm based on the Rough Set theory in order to improve the construction of the different fuzzy models used by the β-TSK fuzzy revision method.

Rough set theory, proposed by Pawlak [24,25], is an attempt to provide a formal framework for the automated transformation of data into knowledge. It is based on the idea that any inexact concept (for example, a class label) can be approximated from below and from above using an indiscernibility relationship. Pawlak [26] points out that one of the most important and fundamental notions to the rough sets philosophy is the need to discover redundancy and dependencies between features. Briefly, the relevant rough set terminology is stated below. An information system is a pair $S = \langle U, A \rangle$, where U is a non-empty, finite set called the universe, and A is a non-empty, finite set of attributes (or features). An equivalence relation, referred to as indiscernibility relation, is associated with every subset of attributes $P \subseteq A$. This relation is defined as:

$$IND(P) = \{(x, y) \in UxU : \text{for every } a \in P, \ a(x) = a(y)\}. \tag{1}$$

Given any subset of features P, any concept $X \subseteq U$ can be defined approximately by the employment of two sets, called lower and upper approximations. The lower approximation, denoted by $\underline{P}X$, is the set of objects in U which can be certainty classified as elements in the concept X using the set of attributes P, and is defined as:

$$\underline{P}X = \cup\{Y \in U / IND(P) : Y \subseteq X\}. \tag{2}$$

The upper approximation, denoted by $\overline{P}X$, is the set of elements in U that can be possibly classified as elements in X, formally:

$$\overline{P}X = \cup\{Y \in U / IND(P) : Y \cap X \neq \varnothing\}. \tag{3}$$

The degree of dependency of a set of features P on a set of features R is denoted by $\gamma_R(P)$, $0 \leq \gamma_R(P) \leq 1$, and is defined as:

$$\gamma_R(P) = \frac{card(POS_R(P))}{card(U)} \quad \text{where } POS_R(P) = \bigcup_{X \in U / IND(P)} \underline{R}X. \tag{4}$$

$POS_R(P)$ contains the objects of U which can be classified as belonging to one of the equivalence classes of $IND(P)$, using only features from the set R. If $\gamma_R(P) = 1$, then R functionally determines P.

P is an independent set of features if there does not exist a strict subset P' of P such that $IND(P) = IND(P')$. A set $R \subseteq P$ is a reduct of P if it is independent and $IND(R) = IND(P)$. Each reduct has the property that a feature can not be removed from it without changing the indiscernibility relation. Many reducts for a given set of features P may exists. The set of attributes belonging to the intersection of all reducts of P is called the core of P:

$$core(P) = \bigcap_{R \in Re\,duct(P)} R. \tag{5}$$

An attribute $a \in P$ is indispensable if $IND(P) \neq IND(P \setminus \{a\})$. The core of P is the union of all the indispensable features in P. The indispensable attributes, reducts, and core can be similarly defined relative to a decision attribute or output feature. The precise definitions of these concepts can be fount in Pawlak's book on Rough Sets [25]. Various extensions have been defined from the basic model proposed by Pawlak. Among these extensions stands out the Variable Precision Rough Set model (VPRS) [27] which is a generalisation that introduces a controlled degree of uncertainty within its formalism, which is established by an additional parameter ϕ.

This paper proposes a process of feature subset selection before the induction process carried out by the β-TSK fuzzy revision method. The aim of this proposal is to reduce the original set of attributes and therefore decrease the computational effort for the generation of the different fuzzy models. At the same time the understanding and interpretation of the models will increase, since they will be less complex than the models generated without the feature selection step. This pre-processing step is fitted in the filter approach to the feature subset selection. Filter methods select features based on properties of the data itself and are independent of the method used to construct the models.

In the rough set framework, the natural way to measure the prediction success is the degree of dependency defined above. However, [28] have shown the weakness of this measure in order to assess an estimation of the predictive accuracy of a set of condition attributes Q with regard to a class attribute d. To overcome this deficiencies, [29] define the notion of rough entropy. Based on this notion and its adaptation to the VPRS model (in order to exploit more efficiently the knowledge that is provided for the observations in the boundary region or the uncertain area of the universe), we have defined a coefficient that allows to asses the significance of an attribute within a set of attributes [30]. The significance of an attribute $a \in Q$ is defined in a way that its value is greater when the removal of this attribute leads to a greater diminution of the complexity of the hypothesis $Q \setminus \{a\}$, and simultaneously, to a lesser loss of accuracy of the hypothesis. Implicitly, the underlying principle used to evaluate the relevance of an attribute in this way is the Minimum Description Length principle (MDLP) [31].

The associated complexity of a given set of condition attributes Q can be evaluated through the entropy of the partition $U / IND(Q)$, which will be denoted by $H(Q)$. On the other hand, the conditional rough entropy $H_\phi (d \mid Q)$ can be used to evaluate the accuracy that is achieved when the condition attributes Q are used to predict the value of the condition attribute d. Therefore, the formal definition of the ϕ-rough entropy, denoted by $RH_\phi (d \mid Q)$, is given by the following expression:

$$RH_\phi (Q,d) = H(Q) + H_\phi (d \mid Q) = H(Q) +$$

$$\left[\{1 - \gamma_{Q,\phi}(d)\} \log_2 |U| + \sum_{x_i \subseteq U \setminus POS_{Q,\phi}(d)} \frac{|x_i|}{|U|} \log_2 \frac{|x_i|}{|U|} \right].$$

$$= \{1 - \gamma_{Q,\phi}(d)\} \log_2 |U| - \sum_{x_i \subseteq POS_{Q,\phi}(d)} \frac{|x_i|}{|U|} \log_2 \frac{|x_i|}{|U|} \tag{6}$$

where X_i represents each one of the classes of the partition $U / IND(Q)$, the set $POS_{Q,\phi}(d)$ is the positive region of Q with regard to the decision attribute d, and $\gamma_{Q,\phi}(d)$ is the degree of dependence of attribute d on the set of attributes Q.

Then, the ϕ-significance of a condition attribute, $a \in Q$, with regard to the decision attribute d, denoted by $\sigma_{a,\phi}(Q,d)$, is defined as the variation that the ϕ-rough entropy suffers when the considered attribute is discarded from Q. Namely, it is computed the term $\Delta_a RH_\phi(Q,d)$, given by the difference between $RH_\phi(Q,d)$ and $RH_\phi(Q \setminus \{a\}, d)$:

$$\sigma_{a,\phi}(Q,d) = \Delta_a RH_\phi(Q,d) = RH_\phi(Q,d) - RH_\phi(Q \setminus \{a\}, d)$$
$$= \{H(Q) - H(Q \setminus \{a\})\} - \{H_\phi(d \mid Q \setminus \{a\}) - H_\phi(d \mid Q)\} \tag{7}$$

Once is defined the metric that is used to evaluate the significance of an attribute (ϕ-rough coefficient), the proposed algorithm for selecting relevant features is described according to the view proposed by [32]. These authors state that a convenient paradigm for viewing feature selection methods is that of heuristic search, with each state in the search space specifying a subset of the possible features. Following Blum and Langley viewpoint the four basic issues that characterise this method are:

- The starting point in the space, which in turn influences the direction of search and the operators used to generate successor states. The proposed algorithm starts with all attributes and successively removes them (backward elimination).
- The organisation of the search. Any realistic approach relies on a greedy method to traverse the space considering that an exhaustive search is impractical. At each point in the search, the proposed algorithm considers all local changes, namely, it evaluates the significance of each attribute of the current set of attributes.
- The strategy used to evaluate alternative subsets of attributes. In this paper, the variation of the normalised ϕ-rough entropy has been chosen for this purpose. Specifically, at each decision point the next state that is selected is that one which results from removing the attribute with the least significant ϕ-rough coefficient.
- A criterion for halting the search. In the algorithm, the criterion for halting is that the difference between the degree of dependency at initial state and the current state (both with respect to the decision) does not go beyond a predefined threshold.

4   Applying the Method: IBR System for Biological Forecasting

Applying the initial revision method summarized in this paper, a forecasting biological IBR system capable of predicting, in different water masses and to different depths, the concentration of diatoms (a type of single-celled algae) has been successfully developed [21]. The instance base of the system consists on approximately 6.300 instances, each one represented as a feature vector that holds 56 physical measures (temperature, PH, oxygen, etc.) and complemented with several indexes derived from satellite images (cloud and superficial temperature, etc).

Although the experiments carried out showed the effectiveness and the straightforward improvement of the upgraded β-fuzzy revision IBR system over other approaches, some issues remained unsolved in order to deploy the application for real use. The main drawbacks of the proposed system were (i) the time needed for generating each one of the β-TSK fuzzy systems and (ii) the explanatory complexity of the fuzzy rules used for the final solution proposed by the IBR system.

In order to simplify the rule base of the initial fuzzy system maintaining the accuracy level, we have applied the feature subset selection algorithm previous to the construction of the β-fuzzy systems. Fig. 1 shows the core of the proposed method.

As we can see in Fig. 1, several ϕ values have been tested in order to obtain the most accurate set of representative features defining each problem case. For the current problem of diatoms forecasting, the optimal number of features was 12 (ϕ = 0.01), corresponding to the physical magnitudes measured with a smaller level of depth and those generated from satellite images.

A critical aspect here is the accuracy level of the new revision subsystem and its comparison with the initial one. Starting from the error series generated by the different models, the Kruskall-Wallis test has been carried out. Since the P-value is less than 0.01, there is a statistically significant difference among the models at the 99.0% confidence level.

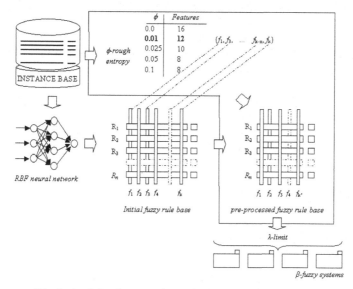

Fig. 1. Applying feature subset selection based on rough sets.

	IBR $\phi(\beta)$ TKS	IBR β- TKS	RBF	RBF + GCS	ARIMA	Quadratic Trend	Moving Average	Simp. Exp. Smooth	Lin. Exp. Smooth
IBR $\phi(\beta)$ TKS									
IBR β-TKS	=								
RBF	*	*							
RBF+GCS	*	*	=						
ARIMA	*	*	*	*					
Quadratic Trend	*	*	*	*	*				
Moving Average	*	*	*	*	*	*			
Simp. Exp. Smooth.	*	*	=	=	*	*	=		
Lin. Exp. Smooth.	*	*	=	=	*	*	=	=	

Fig. 2. Mann-Withney test among the models.

Based on the results provided by the Kruskall-Wallis test, Fig. 2 shows a multiple comparison procedure (Mann-Withney test) used to determine which models are significantly different from the others. The experiments were made with a data set of 448 instances randomly taken from the instance base. It can be seen that the IBR with β-TSK fuzzy revision subsystem presents statistically significant differences with the rest of the models whilst it is as accurate as the improved method presented here (no differences are shown).

5 Conclusion

We have proposed a new technique to improve case revision, which could be used to automate the revision stage of case/instance based reasoning systems. The basis of the method is a set of TSK fuzzy models that employs a pre-processed feature subset selection created by the rough set algorithm.

The simplified fuzzy rule bases allow us to obtain a more general knowledge of the system and gain a deeper insight into the logical structure of the system to be approximated. Employing the pre-processed fuzzy rule base as the starting point to generate the β-fuzzy systems (ϕ (β)TSK) leads to a dramatic decrease of the time needed for this task. The reviewing and adaptation of the initial solutions is a very simple operation using the proposed method and presents no major computational obstacles, moreover it can be done in parallel. These benefits are augmented with the simplicity of the new fuzzy rules used by the IBR as explanation of the final adopted solution.

An area of ongoing research for us is the automatic identification of the optimal value for the β parameter, as well as the application of the rough set theory in conjunction with the retrieval phase in order to propose a correct value for ϕ in advance.

References

1. Watson, I.: Applying Case-based Reasoning: Techniques for Enterprise Systems, Morgan Kaufmann, San Mateo, CA (1997)
2. Pal, S.K., Dilon, T.S., Yeung, D.S.: Soft Computing in Case Based Reasoning, Springer Verlag, London (2000)
3. Lenz, M., Bartsch-Sprl, B., Burkhard, H.-D., Wess, S. (eds.): Case Based Reasoning Technology - From Foundations to Applications. Springer Verlag, LNAI 1400 (1998)
4. Bergmann, R., Breen, S., Göker, M., Manago, M., Wess, S.: Developing Industrial Case-Based Reasoning Applications - The INRECA Methodology. Springer Verlag, LNAI 1612 (1998)
5. Fyfe, C., Corchado, J.M.: Automating the construction of CBR Systems using Kernel Methods'. International Journal of Intelligent Systems, Vol. 16 (4). (2001) 574–586
6. Corchado, J.M., Aiken, J., Corchado, E.S., Fyfe, C., Fdez-Riverola, F., González, M.: Maximum Likelihood Hebbian Learning Based Retrieval Method for CBR Systems. Proc. of the Fifth International Conference on Case-Based Reasoning, (2003) 107–121
7. Corchado, J.M., Aiken, J.: Hybrid Artificial Intelligence Methods in Oceanographic Forecasting Models. IEEE SMC Transac. Part C, (2003)
8. Smyth, B., McKenna, E.: Modelling the Competence of Case-Bases. Proc. of Fourth European Workshop on Case-Based Reasoning, (1998) 221–232
9. De, R.K., Pal, S.K.: Case Based Systems: A Neuro-Fuzzy Method for Selecting Cases. In Sankar K. Pal, Tharam S. Dillon and Daniel S. Yeung (eds.). Soft computing in Case Based Reasoning. Springer Verlag, London (2000) 241–257
10. Shiu, S.C.K., Wang, X.Z., Yeung, D.S.: Neuro-Fuzzy Approach for Maintanining Case Bases. In Sankar K. Pal, Tharam S. Dillon and Daniel S. Yeung (eds.). Soft computing in Case Based Reasoning. Springer Verlag, London (2000) 259–273
11. Leake, D.B., Wilson, D.C.: Categorizing Case-Base Maintenance: Dimensions and Directions. Proc. of the Fourth European Workshop on Case-Based Reasoning, (1998) 196–207

12. Main, J. Dillon, T.S.: A Neuro-Fuzzy Methodology for Case Retrieval and an Object-Oriented Case Schema for Structuring Case Bases and their Application to Fashion Footwear Design. In Sankar K. Pal, Tharam S. Dillon and Daniel S. Yeung (eds.). Soft computing in Case Based Reasoning. Springer Verlag, London (2000) 276–291

13. Jeng, B.C., Liang, T.P.: Fuzzy Indexing and Retrieval in Case-Based Systems. Expert Systems with Applications, Vol. 8 (1). (1995) 135–142

14. Cheetham, B., Cuddihy, P., Goebel, K.: Applications of Soft CBR al General Electric. In Sankar K. Pal, Tharam S. Dillon and Daniel S. Yeung (eds.). Soft computing in Case Based Reasoning. Springer Verlag, London (2000) 335–365

15. Takagi, T., Sugeno, M.: Fuzzy identification of systems and its applications to modeling and control. IEEE Transac. on Systems, Man and Cybernetics, Vol. 15. (1985) 116–132

16. Towell, G., Shavlik, J.: Extracting refined fuzzy rules from knowledge-based neural networks. Machine Learning, Vol. 13. (1993) 71–101

17. Jin, Y., von Seelen, W., Sendhoff, B.: On generating FC3 fuzzy rule systems from data using evolution strategies. IEEE Transac. on Systems, Man and Cybernetics, Vol. 29 (6). (1999) 829–845

18. Fritzke, B.: Fast learning with incremental RBF Networks. Neural Processing Letters, Vol. 1 (1). (1994) 2–5

19. Jin, Y., von Seelen, W., Sendhoff, B.: Extracting Interpretable Fuzzy Rules from RBF Neural Networks, Technical Institut für Neuroinformatik, Ruhr-Universität Bochum, January (2000)

20. Fdez-Riverola, F., Corchado, J.M.: CBR based system for forecasting red tides. Knowledge-Based Systems, Vol. 16 (5-6). (2003) 321–328

21. Fdez-Riverola, F., Corchado, J.M.: An automated CBR Revision method based on a set of β-TSK Fuzzy models. Proc. of the X CAEPIA - V TTIA, Vol. 1. (2003) 395–404

22. Setnes, M., Babuška, R., Kaymak, U., Lemke, R.: Similarity measures in fuzzy rule base simplification. IEEE Transac. on Systems, Man and Cybernetics, Vol. 28. (1998) 376–386

23. Fdez-Riverola, F.: Neuro-symbolic model for unsupervised forecasting of changing environments. Ph.D. diss., Dept. of Computer Science, Vigo University, Spain (2002)

24. Pawlak, Z.: Rough Sets. International Journal of Computer and Information Sciences, Vol. 11. (1982) 341–356

25. Pawlak, Z.: Rough Sets: Theoretical Aspects of Reasoning about Data. Kluwer Academic Publishers, Dordrecht (1991)

26. Pawlak, Z.: Rough sets: present state and the future. Foundations of Computing and Decision Sciences, Vol. 11 (3-4). (1993) 157–166

27. Ziarko, W.: Variable Precision Rough Set Model. Journal of Computer and System Sciences, Vol. 46. (1993) 39–59

28. Düntsch, I., Gediga, G.: Statistical evaluation of rough set dependency analysis. International Journal of Human-Computer Studies, Vol. 46. (1997) 589–604

29. Düntsch, I., Gediga, G.: Uncertainty measures of rough set prediction. Artificial Intelligence, Vol. 106. (1998) 77–107

30. Díaz, F., Corchado, J.M.: A method based on the Rough Set theory and the MDL principle to select relevant features. Proc. of the X CAEPIA - V TTIA, Vol. 1. (2003) 101–104

31. Rissanen, J.: Minimum description length principle. In Kotz, S. and Johnson, N. L. (eds.). Encyclopedia of Statistical Sciences. John Wiley and Sons, New York (1985) 523–527

32. Blum, A.L., Langley, P.: Selection of relevant features and examples in machine learning. Artificial Intelligence, Vol. 97. (1997) 245–271

Forgetting and Fatigue
in Mobile Robot Navigation

Luís Correia[1] and António Abreu[2]

[1] Universidade de Lisboa, FC-DI, Campo Grande, 1749-016 Lisboa, Portugal
Luis.Correia@di.fc.ul.pt
[2] Instituto Politécnico de Setúbal, ESTS-DEE
Campus do IPS, 2910-761, Setúbal, Portugal
abreu@est.ips.pt

Abstract. This paper presents an enhancement of autonomous robot navigation behaviour by incorporating models of fatigue and forgetting. These models are inspired in ethology concepts. The robot maintains itself in a limited range of safe landmarks and sets out to explore new areas or to revisit places in the map where it has not been for some time. Places not visited for too long are forgotten. With this model, navigation is possible in dynamic environments and even when the robot is displaced by external means. Experimental results in a simulated robot support the proposed model.

Keywords: Autonomous Mobile Robots, Navigation, Biologically inspired models

1   Introduction

Navigation in autonomous mobile robots has several aspects that may be solved in different ways by a robot [11], [18], [20], [7] and [17]. First we may consider map learning. The robot may have a map of the environment loaded or it may learn it from scratch. Mixed forms may also be used, e.g. a supplied partial map is completed by learning. And if the robot learns a map, when and for how long should it engage itself in exploring behaviours? A second issue is the dynamics of map representation. Once a map is known, the robot may consider it as a static data structure, or may modify it according to its interaction with the environment. Further features can be considered, such as how to handle porting the robot from one environment to another. Should it maintain representations of both or should it be reinitialized in each environment?

It seems natural that we would prefer to build robots as intelligent as possible, therefore with the capability of learning maps, updating them and identifying environments. However this poses not only a problem of difficulty in learning maps from sensory input, but also a problem of memory management. The robot may not indefinitely keep track of environment changes while maintaining all the map knowledge previously stored. Moreover, if enough time is elapsed, previous information is bound to get outdated and may turn out to be useless.

A.L.C. Bazzan and S. Labidi (Eds.): SBIA 2004, LNAI 3171, pp. 434–443, 2004.

In this paper we present a combination of two behaviour properties - forgetting and fatigue - as a useful approach to help in solving the problem of autonomous robot navigation. This solution may handle the somehow delicate balance between exploring and learning new places, on one hand, and dealing with outdated information, on the other hand. In particular, we will show that autonomous exploration and maintenance of a map representation can be easily achieved in this way. This allows the robot to live in dynamic environments and to adapt itself easily to new environments altogether, in the case it is ported by external means. We applied this solution to a behaviour based control architecture, but it could as well be used in neural network based architectures, for instance. Actually, the concept of forgetting is common in some types of neural networks [8] and [15].

The use of fatigue in robot behaviours has been explored as a way to avoid deadlocks in behaviour based control architectures [6] but, to our knowledge, is here originally applied to map based navigation. A similar concept, habituation, was used not for navigation but to obtain a kind of map signature, allowing detection of new features in a map [10]. The idea of forgetting map locations has been proposed in [4] for a neural network support and has been also used in [3] for a behaviour based model, with a primary focus on forgetting as a function of time. In [14] and [19] two approaches are presented to explore maps, the former with neural networks and the later with a behaviour based architecture. However maps are considered static in both cases. They do not change nor are forgotten. Exploration is not faced as an internal autonomous behaviour of the robot but only to the extent of reaching a goal. The concept of eligibility trace, similar to forgetting, is used in reinforcement learning for mobile robots in [13], though it is not related to map maintenance. Instead, the robot has to learn which actions take it to a goal in a grid world. Another approach uses forgetting, [9], but, in that work, behaviour cases used for navigation are forgotten to give space to newly generated behaviours. It is not a part of the map itself that is forgotten. The integration of map forgetting with dynamic map exploration, using fatigue, and active place re-visiting is approached in our work for the first time.

This paper is organized in four more sections besides this one. In Section 2 we describe the fatigue model used, which is based on animal behaviour features, and its application to map exploration and maintenance. In Section 3 the forgetting model is detailed. We also analyse the way outdated map information is deleted by using the forgetting model. Section 4 is devoted to the presentation of results of integrating fatigue and forgetting in experiments done with a simulated robot. Section 5 finishes the paper with comments and a set of ideas on how to proceed with research in this line of work.

2   Exploring Fatigue

Fatigue is found in animal behaviour as one of the common forms of loosing capability to respond to a stimulus. Habituation is another form [16] but we are not too concerned with the specificities. The basic idea we want to retain for autonomous robots is to use fatigue as the umbrella concept of loosing capability to react to a stimulus and regaining that capability again after a recovery period in the absence of stimulus.

In animal behaviour, when a stimulus appears, the response takes some time to start (*latency*) and then to reach its maximum level (*warm-up period*). Afterwards it maintains this level. However, past some time of continued stimulus presence (*fatigue time*) the response starts to decrease until it eventually ceases, (*after-discharge period*). If that happens, the behaviour is inhibited from further response, until the stimulus is removed. It stays in a fatigued state. In that mode, and only after stimulus removal, the behaviour takes some time (*recovery time*) to be able to respond normally to a new stimulus. In fig.1 we depict this model. It should be noticed that, if the stimulus disappears before fatigue time, the behaviour is still able to respond to a new stimulus. The response, quantitatively may not be exactly the same though.

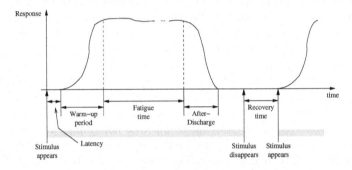

Fig. 1. Animal behaviour fatigue model.

2.1 The Fatigue Model

For the purpose of incorporating fatigue in autonomous robot behaviour, we use a simplified model with the basic concepts we are interested in.

In the simplified model, we consider latency, warm-up and after-discharge periods to have duration zero. Therefore, fatigue is defined simply by two parameters: *fatigue time* - time from beginning of action in response to a stimulus till end of action due to fatigue (entering fatigued state) - and *recovery time* - taken from stimulus ceasing till action allowed again. This model is depicted in fig.2.

We also consider that if stimulus is removed before reaching *fatigue time* the behaviour resets instantaneously its fatigue state. This model, however simple it is, is quite useful in avoiding deadlocks in behaviour based control architectures [6] and, as we will see in the next subsection, in controlling map exploration behaviour.

2.2 Applying Fatigue in Map Navigation

The work here presented uses a behaviour based control architecture [1] in an autonomous indoor robot. The type of architecture is not mandatory for this purpose but we think it turns out easier to apply the idea.

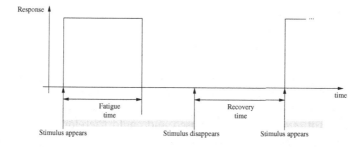

Fig. 2. Simplified fatigue model used.

The robot has a behaviour dedicated to exploring the environment, *Explore* behaviour. It discovers and maintains a map. The map is a global data structure which can be consulted and modified by other modules. A map is represented by a graph, where nodes mean salient places found by the robot and arcs mean direct connections between those places. Further details about the map representation used can be found in [2]. It should be pointed out that the robot doesn't have specific external navigation aids and must determine its position by its own sensors and odometry.

In our approach we consider a distinct location in the environment, called *home*, where the robot is initially placed. The robot is programmed to recognize *home*, but doesn't have any further knowledge of the environment.

The *Explore* behaviour is triggered by map depletion. This means that when it detects less then some number of places in the map or when any places are on the verge of being forgotten (more on this in next section), the behaviour is activated. As a result of the *Explore* behaviour the robot explores unknown regions of the environment in order to find salient places or it tries to get back to known places not visited for a long time. The idea is twofold: to explore unknown places and to maintain a representation of a known map as updated as possible.

If the proprioceptive stimulus (few known places, or long-ago-visited places) disappears along the exploration process, the *Explore* behaviour will get inactive and a *Get-Back* behaviour will navigate the robot back *home*. However, if the stimulus of the *Explore* behaviour is active (the robot still doesn't know enough places, or hasn't visited some of the almost forgotten ones) it will eventually reach a fatigued state. In that case it will stop exploring and the *Get-Back* behaviour will also take the robot back *home*. Therefore this maintains the robot in a limited neighbourhood of *home*, which reduces the probability of getting lost by accumulation of errors in dead-reckoning navigation. Due to the robustness of the approach we have implemented a variation of the fatigue function, so that fatigue is only accumulated when the robot is navigating through unknown (new) places. This allows an increasing radius of exploration around home. In fact this radius is unlimited and in large environments the energy level must also be considered as an input to the fatigue function.

3   Forgetting Old Places

There are important reasons to consider the use of forgetting in a mapping strategy. First, we observe that even though the environment is static the robot does not generate equal trajectories each time it traverses it. This is due to noise in both sensors and actuators. As a consequence, outlier places are created, which will disappear due to forgetting. Second, previous information is bound to get outdated if enough time is elapsed and could therefore be discarded by the robot. Forgetting also provides the means for those outdated descriptions to vanish. Forgetting is then a simple mechanism to throw away obsolete space descriptions, allowing to maintain a constantly updated map. Therefore, it is also a way to keep the size of the map tractable.

Let $w(t)$ represent the weight of some place at time t. In general we want $w(t)$ to decrease with time and proportionally to $w(t)$ itself.

Consider a time interval $\Delta t_{ij} = t_j - t_i$. The weight variation in that interval should then be $\Delta w(t_{ij}) = -\alpha \Delta t_{ij}\, w(t_i)$, where α represents a forgetting constant. Rewriting this equation, we get $\frac{\Delta w(t_{ij})}{\Delta t_{ij}} = -\alpha w(t_i)$. Considering an arbitrarily small time interval, i.e., $t_j - t_i \to 0$, we may write $\frac{dw}{dt} = -\alpha w(t)$. This implies $w(t)$ to be of the form $w(t) = e^{-\alpha t}$. We then have, $\frac{dw}{dt} = -\alpha e^{-\alpha t}$. In a discrete domain, we get

$$w[t+1] = w[t] - \alpha e^{-\alpha t}$$

which is the implementation of forgetting by exponential decay. A new place gets an initial value of $w(t_0) = 1$, as well as when it is revisited.

Place removal from the map can be advantageous if the corresponding portion of the environment has changed. In case the environment has not changed, then the place was missed due to a trajectory drift (whatever the cause: incremental errors in odometry or a different trajectory executed due to noise in perception and/or actuation). In this case, the forgotten place is replaced by another referring approximately to the same location in the environment, which means that forgetting does not imply serious flaws.

However, note that an exponential weight decay has the disadvantage of making it difficult to discover the most frequent places among every place in the map. In fact, since the decay curve is exponential, the weight of every place (frequent or not frequent) decreases from a maximum value (i.e., 1) to near its minimum (i.e., 0) very fast. In other words, it is difficult to differentiate between a seldom visited place recently visited and a very frequent one visited a while ago. Both have small weights after some time. This fact was our main motivation for an improvement. A very frequent place should be harder to forget, while an infrequent one should be more easily forgotten.

For this we considered, as a better alternative, a weight decay with the shape of a sigmoid curve, $w(t) = \frac{1}{1 + e^{-\alpha t}}$. We want that the more frequent the place is, the more difficult it should be forgotten. In this sense and supposing the basic sigmoid as depicted in curve A of fig. 3 we can have the shape of the sigmoid to depend on the number of visits to a place in at least two ways: i) the sigmoid changes from A to B with increasing number of visits, or ii) from A to C, in the same condition. Since the forgetting policy should allow a clear differentiation between a frequent place that is not visited for a while and an infrequent one that was recently visited, we chose form ii) corresponding to a sigmoid modification from A to C, in fig. 3. The approach we followed postpones the forgetting effect proportionally to the number of place visits.

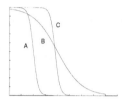

Fig. 3. Sigmoid weight decay. Postponement of forgetting can be achieved by decreasing the derivative, from A to B, or by extending the flat zone on the top part of the curve, from A to C, as the number of visits to the place increases. We chose the later.

The weight decay of a frequent place is thus delayed in time, giving it the opportunity to keep a maximum weight longer. One now has the means to observe which places are more frequently visited, possibly electing some of them to be reliable landmarks (those having weights above a certain threshold value for some time). Such landmarks have at least two advantages: they can act as intermediary and momentary homes, and, for the matter of path evaluation, they constitute highly trustable places. This means that paths across them have less uncertainty. With respect to the first advantage, we remind that path integration error is small near *home*, and that dead-reckoning errors are reset when the robot arrives at *home*. So, if there is the chance of having several of these trustable places throughout the environment, a path between any two far away places may be composed by a set of small paths linking trustable places. That feature, however, will not be explored in this paper.

Note that increasing the delay to forget a frequent place is made on the basis that if the place is frequent its validity in time should be increased. However, such validity should not be stressed too much. After all, a very frequent place can refer to a location in the environment that can also change. So, the robot should maintain the capacity to forget such place. This is done by imposing a saturation limit on how much the sigmoid is shifted right.

We should also emphasize that discarding known places not visited for some time is tricky if the robot has learned a large map. A long time may elapse between two successive passes of the robot by some places and the result would be an undesirable loss of knowledge about parts of the map. This means that the forgetting constant α needs to be chosen carefully depending on the environment the robot is going to live in and on how much information we want it to maintain. Presently, this value is hand-tuned. Soon we intend to express α as a function of known places.

4   Experimental Results

To test these ideas, in a preliminary approach, we ran tests on a simulated Khepera robot [12], performing the previously explained behaviours in a closed environment, depicted in fig. 4. The *Explore* behaviour is, in this case, based on a *Follow-Right-Wall* behaviour.

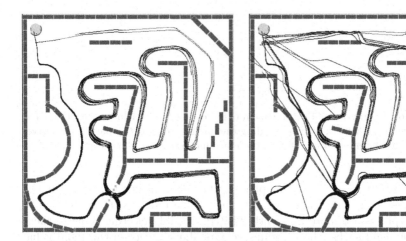

Fig. 4. *Left* - Typical trajectories in test environment. *Home* is at top left corner and 19 trajectories following right wall are presented. The effect of fatigue is clearly visible, occurring each time later. In the 19th trip the robot eventually completes an entire lap without fatigue. A string of small light grey squares indicates a passage that can be closed. *Right* - Navigation tests. Return *home* trajectories are overimposed. After fatigue of the *Explore* behaviour, the robot returns *home* using a direct path. It's always able to get *home* with enough precision. Trajectories are plotted with robot computed coordinates (with errors). That's the reason why it seems the robot crosses walls.

Overall the robot produced the expected behaviour: it leaves *home*, exploring the environment. When it gets fatigued it returns *home* directly, by using dead-reckoning (avoiding obstacles if needed). In spite of errors it is always capable of finding home. In fig. 4-*Right* we have imposed the return trajectories over the wall following trajectories of fig. 4-*Left*.

A place is forgotten by removing it from the map when its weight is residual (10^{-3}). The forgetting factor α was chosen in such a way that a place is forgotten if two consecutive laps are executed without visiting it. In fig. 5 we present the time evolution for a place, with exponential and delayed sigmoid decay. It is clearly visible the difference between the two forgetting curves and the increase in decay delay of the sigmoid curve, each time the robot visits the place. Eventually it is forgotten in both cases. Therefore we use a forgetting function of the form $w(t) = 1 - \frac{1}{1+\exp(-\frac{0.8t-3000}{500}+2.5n)}$, where n is the number of visits to the place.

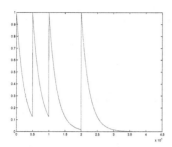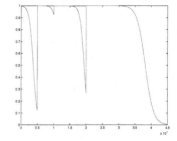

Fig. 5. Evolution of a place weight versus time, as a consequence of forgetting by exponential decay (on the left) and by sigmoid delayed decay (on the right).

Tests were also made to show the effect of forgetting in the behaviour of the robot. A first test was made without fatigue. After the robot got to run around the environment for five laps, knowing all places, we closed the small passage shown in fig. 4-*Left*. The weights of the places on the area in the bottom right part of the environment decreased and eventually they were forgotten by the robot, around trip number 8. In fig. 6-*Left* that decrease in the number of known places can be clearly noticed. By trip number 10, the passage is opened again and the robot quickly reestablishes the total number of salient places of the environment. We closed the passage again in trip 15 and the same forgetting behaviour can be observed.

The results of a test with fatigue are also shown in fig. 6-*Right*. Notice that the vertical scale is different since the robot acquires new places in a more gradual way. When the passage is first closed it doesn't know the whole environment yet. Therefore the number of known places does not decrease too much because new places are still available to visit.

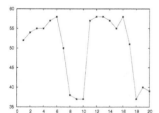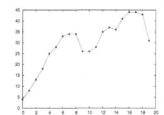

Fig. 6. Number of places known as a function of the number of exploration trips leaving home. A passage is closed on trip 5, then open on trip 10 and then closed again on trip 15. *Left* - without fatigue. *Right* - with fatigue.

The duration of the stay at *home*, when the robot returns, is determined by the recovery time parameter and the activation of the *Explore* behaviour. It leaves *home* again to refresh memories of the known places, in case their weights are low enough to stimulate this behaviour. Exploration of new regions is based on the rules defined in the *Explore* behaviour. In a bifurcation it may explore a branch not travelled before or it may refresh memories of the one it already knows, if places' weights on that branch are low enough.

We also observed that a small α value (slower forgetting) induces a more exploratory behaviour, while a larger α makes the *Explore* behaviour more occupied in refreshing place memories. This is natural since with faster forgetting the robot will be stimulated sooner due to imminent deletion of some places, whereas with slower forgetting there will be more time to explore new areas.

5   Conclusions and Future Developments

Using ethology inspired features in robot behaviour is a line of research being developed for some time now, with important results [5]. In this paper we have presented an original contribution along those lines, adapting and applying the concepts of behaviour fatigue and forgetting to enhance autonomous navigation capabilities for map exploration and maintenance. This is an important basis for long-term longevity robots. Experimental results, though preliminary they are, have proved the viability of the ideas proposed.

Besides the identified capabilities of handling dynamic environments, the advantage of this approach is the possibility of concentrating on three constants, *forgetting factor*, *fatigue time* and *recovery time*, to define a wide range of navigation behaviour. We can define the area the robot is able to explore, how persistent is its memory of the environment and how frequently it is engaged in revisiting the map to refresh its memory, only by tuning those three parameters.

Further work, in a short term, will be focused on tests in real robots (Khepera and Pioneer). From our experience with previous tests the results will be qualitatively similar from the simulator to the robot. The interaction of the *Explore* behaviour with different mission oriented behaviours will also be tested.

Development of the model will study modulation of fatigue by the degree of knowledge the robot has about the places it is in. While the robot is in known zones, fatigue should be slower (instead of none) than when it is exploring new ones. This would put a limit in the area of the environment the robot may explore. Also, rules to define automatic dependencies of the parameters should be developed. Finally the existence of multiple *home* places (again in the sense of a place where the robot can be recharged) will be explored and it should allow a safe mapping of large environments.

References

1. A. Abreu and L. Correia. A fuzzy behavior-based architecture for decision control in autonomous vehicles. In *Proceedings of the 2001 IEEE International Symposium on Intelligent Control - ISIC'01*. IEEE, 2001. Mexico-city, Mexico, September 2001.
2. A. Abreu and L. Correia. A hybrid mapping approach with a fuzzy representation for mobile robots. In *The 11th International Conference on Advanced Robotics - ICAR'03*. IEEE, July 2003.

3. A. Abreu and L. Correia. Forgetting in place learning: an experimental approach. Technical report, 2004.
4. J. Andrade-Cetto and A. Sanfeliu. Learning of dynamic environments by a mobile robot from stereo cues. In *Proc. 2001 IEEE Conference on Multisensor Fusion and Integration for Intelligent Systems*, pages 305–310. IEEE, 2001.
5. R. Arkin. *Behavior-Based Robotics*. MIT Press, 1998.
6. L. Correia and A. Steiger-Garção. A useful autonomous vehicle with a hierarchical behavior control. In F. Morán, A. Moreno, J. J. Merelo, and P. Chacón, editors, *Advances in Artificial Life*, LNAI 929, pages 625–639, 1995.
7. D. Fox, W. Burgard, and S. Thrun. Probabilistic methods for mobile robot mapping. In *Proc. Of the IJCAI-99 Workshop on Adaptive Spatial Representations of Dynamic Environments*, 1999.
8. S. Haykin. *Neural Networks*. Prentice-Hall, 2nd edition, 1999.
9. Z. Kira and R. Arkin. Forgetting bad behavior: Memory management for case-based navigation. Giorgia Tech Mobile Robot Lab, 2003.
10. S. Marsland, U. Nehmzow, and J. Shapiro. Detecting novel features of an environment using habituation. In *From Animals to Animats 6, Proceedings of the 6th Int'l Conf. on Simulation of Adaptive Behaviour, 2000*. MIT Press, 2000.
11. M. Mataric. Navigating with a rat brain: a neurobiologically-inspired model for robot spatial representation. In *Proceedings of the 1st international conference on simulation of adaptive behavior - From animals to animats*. MIT Press, 1991.
12. O. Michel. Khepera simulator package (version 2.0). http://diwww.epfl.ch/lami/team/michel/khep-sim/.
13. A. Pérez-Uribe and E. Sanchez. A comparison of reinforcement learning with eligibility traces and integrated learning, planning and reacting. In *Proceedings of the International Conference on Computational Intelligence for Modelling Control and Automation CIMCA'99*, pages 154–159. IOS Press, 1999.
14. B.-S. Ryu and H. Yang. Integration of reactive behaviors and enhanced topological map for robust mobile robot navigation. *IEEE Transactions on Systems, Man and Cybernetics-Part A: Systems and Humans*, Vol. 29(No. 5):474–485, 1999.
15. S. Sikström. Forgetting curves: implications for connectionist models. *Cognitive Psychology*, (45):95–152, 2002.
16. P.J.B. Slater. *An introduction to ethology*. Cambridge University Press, 1985.
17. S. Thrun. Robotic mapping: A survey. In G. Lakemeyer and B. Nebel, editors, *Exploring Artificial Intelligence in the New Millenium*. Morgan Kaufmann, 2002.
18. O. Trullier, S. Wiener, A. Berthoz, and J. Meyer. Biologically-based artificial navigation systems: Review & prospects. *Progr. in Neurobiology*, 51:483–544, 1997.
19. H. Voicu and N. Schmajuk. Exploration, navigation and cognitive mapping. *Adaptive Behavior*, 8(3/4):207–224, 2000.
20. G. Wyeth and B. Browning. Cognitive models of spatial navigation from a robot builder's perspective. *Adaptive Behavior*, Vol. 6(No. 3/4):509–534, 1998.

Texture Classification
Using the Lempel-Ziv-Welch Algorithm*

Leonardo Vidal Batista and Moab Mariz Meira

Departamento de Informática, CCEN, UFPB, Cidade Universitária
Campus I 58.051-900, João Pessoa, PB, Brazil
`leonardo@di.ufpb.br`

Abstract. This paper presents a new, simple and efficient texture classification method using Lempel-Ziv-Welch (LZW) compression algorithm. In the learning stage, LZW algorithm constructs dictionaries for the horizontal and vertical structure of each class. In the classification stage, texture samples to be classified are encoded by LZW in static mode, using the dictionaries constructed in the learning stage, in vertical and horizontal scanning order. A sample is assigned to the class whose dictionaries minimize the average horizontal and vertical coding rate. The classifier was evaluated for various sample sizes and training set sizes, using 30 Brodatz textures. The proposed method correctly classified 100% of 3000 Brodatz texture samples, and direct comparisons indicated the superiority of the method over several high performance classifiers.

Keywords: Texture classification; Lempel-Ziv-Welch algorithm; pattern recognition.

1 Introduction

Texture is one of the most important attributes used by the human visual system and computer vision systems for segmentation, classification and interpretation of scenes [1]. There has been a great interest in the development of texture-based pattern recognition methods in many different areas, such as remote sensing [2, 3], image-based medical diagnosis [4], industrial automation [5] and biometric recognition [6, 7].

Texture classification is a pattern recognition problem that consists in assigning an unknown input texture sample $\mathbf{x}$ to one of N texture classes C_i, $i = 1, 2, \ldots N$. Discriminating features, or structural or stochastic models, are used to characterize the texture classes, and then classification is performed according to some measure of similarity between $\mathbf{x}$ and each class.

In supervised classification, texture samples known to belong to class C_i, $i = 1, 2, N$, are available. These pre-classified samples are used to construct models or to define discriminating features for each class, in a process known as training or learning. In order to develop efficient texture classifiers, it is crucial to discover discriminating attributes or precise models for the texture classes.

Although easily recognized and intuitively understood by the human visual system, texture is not easy to characterize formally with an acceptable degree of generality. In

---

* This work was supported by CNPQ, a governmental Brazilian institution dedicated to scientific and technological development.

A.L.C. Bazzan and S. Labidi (Eds.): SBIA 2004, LNAI 3171, pp. 444–453, 2004.

the very heart of the question lies the intrinsic difficulty to define what is most relevant to characterize texture, as the answer depends on subjective perceptual considerations and on particular applications. Therefore, texture feature extraction and modeling tends to be a difficult and application-driven task. A popular yet rather vague definition states that textures are spatial patterns formed by more or less accurate repetitions of some basic subpatterns. The placement of these subpatterns can be periodic, quasi-periodic or random [8].

Selecting inadequate features can degrade classification performance, and selecting too many features, even appropriate ones, has negative consequences: increase in processing time and memory requirements, and a potential accuracy degradation due to the statistical phenomenon known as "curse of dimensionality" [9].

Early feature extraction techniques focused on spatial image statistics, such as image correlation, energy features and gray level co-occurrence matrices (GLCM) [10]. More recently, model-based techniques, such as Markov random fields (MRF) [9, 11], and signal processing techniques, such as Gabor and quadrature mirrors filters and wavelet transforms [12] have been widely investigated. An extensive comparison between various signal processing methods for feature extractions concluded that no method is consistently superior to the others [12]. Another evaluation including GLCM, fractal dimension, transform and filter bank features, number of gray level extrema per unit area and curvilinear integration features also led to the conclusion that the performance of these methods is generally similar [13].

After choosing the specific features or models that will be used to characterize texture classes, a classification method must be defined. A large number of classifiers have also been proposed, including neural networks, learning vector quantization (LVQ), support vector machine (SVM) and Bayes classifiers [9]. A multiple SVM classifier, denominate fused SVM, with features generated by discrete wavelet frame transform, compared favorably with single SVM classifiers, Bayes classifiers using Bayes distance and Mahalanobis distance, and the LVQ classifier [14].

Based on the analysis of dozens of filtering methods for texture classification, Randem and Husøy [12] suggest that the development of powerful texture classification methods with low computational complexity is a very useful direction of research. In some applications, such as industrial web inspection, the throughput is enormous and most computer vision solutions require fast methods and special hardware support [5].

Modern lossless data compressors have been applied to classification problems, due to their ability to construct accurate statistical models, in some cases with low computational requirements [15]. A solid theoretical foundation for using LZ78 compression algorithm [16] for classification is well established [17, 18]. However, despite its sound theoretical basis, the application of compression schemes in practical classification problems seems to be rather unexplored and even controversial.

The *prediction by partial matching* (PPM) lossless compressor [15] was applied to text categorization [19]. The conclusion was that although correctly categorizing the majority of the documents, PPM does not compete with the published state-of-the- art machine learning schemes.

However, another work reported that PPM was successfully applied to various text classification problems (language identification, authorship attribution, literary genre categorization and topic categorization) and concluded that PPM performance is comparable to other state-of-the-art-machine learning methods for text categorization

[20]. One problem with PPM is the vast amounts of computational resources it requires [15].

A classifier based on the models built by compression algorithms has several potential advantages over classical machine learning methods: since there is no feature selection, no information is discarded, as the models describe the classes as a whole [19]; there is no need to make assumptions about the probability distributions of the texture classes; the adaptive model construction capability of compression algorithms offers an uniform way to classify different types of sources [19]; the classification rule is very simple [20].

This paper proposes a new, simple and efficient texture classifier based on Lempel-Ziv-Welch (LZW) lossless compression algorithm [21]. The rest of this paper is organized as follows. Section 2 presents the fundamental concepts of entropy and statistical models; section 3 discusses the model construction capability of lossless compression algorithms, which provides a practical way to approximate statistical source models, and presents LZW algorithm; section 4 describes the proposed classifier; section 5 presents the empirical evaluation of the proposed classifier; and section 6 presents a discussion of the results and the concluding remarks.

2   Entropy and Statistical Models

Let S be a stationary discrete information source that generates messages over a finite alphabet $A = \{a_1, a_2,..., a_M\}$. The source chooses successive symbols from A according to some probability distribution that depends, in general, on preceding selected symbols. A generic message will be modeled as a stationary stochastic process $\mathbf{x} = ...x_{-2} x_{-1}x_0x_1x_2$, with $x_i \in A$. Let $\mathbf{x}^n = x_1x_2...x_n$ represent a message of length n. Since $|A| = M$, the source can generate M^n different messages of length n. Let $\mathbf{x}_i^n$, $i = 1, 2, ..., M^n$ denote the ith of these messages, according to some sorting order, and assume that the source follows a probability distribution P, so that message $\mathbf{x}_i^n$ is produced with probability $P(\mathbf{x}_i^n)$.

Let

$$G_n(P) = -\frac{1}{n}\sum_{i=1}^{M^n} P(\mathbf{x}_i^n)\log_2 P(\mathbf{x}_i^n).$$ (1)

$G_n(P)$ decreases monotonically with n [22] and the entropy of the source is:

$$H(P) = \lim_{n\to\infty} G_n(P) \text{ bits/symbol}.$$ (2)

An alternative formulation for $H(P)$ uses conditional probabilities. Let $P(\mathbf{x}_i^{n-1}, a_j)$ be the probability of sequence $\mathbf{x}_i^n = (\mathbf{x}_i^{n-1}, a_j)$, i.e., the probability of $\mathbf{x}_i^{n-1}$ concatenated with symbol $x_n = a_j$, and let $P(a_j | \mathbf{x}_i^{n-1}) = P(\mathbf{x}_i^{n-1}, a_j)P(\mathbf{x}_i^{n-1})$ be the probability of symbol $x_n = a_j$ given $\mathbf{x}_i^{n-1}$. The entropy of the nth order approximation to $H(P)$ [22] is:

$$F_n(P) = -\sum_{i=1}^{M^n} \sum_{j=1}^{M} P(\mathbf{x}_i^{n-1}, a_j) \log_2 P(a_j \mid \mathbf{x}_i^{n-1}) \text{ bits/symbol} . \tag{3}$$

$F_n(P)$ decreases monotonically with n [22] and the entropy of the source is:

$$H(P) = \lim_{n\to\infty} F_n(P) \text{ bits/symbol} . \tag{4}$$

Eq. 4 involves the estimation of probabilities conditioned on an infinite sequence of previous symbols. In practice, finite memory is assumed, and the sources are modeled by an order-$(n$-1) Markov process, so that $P(a_j \mid \ldots x_{-1} x_0 x_1 \ldots x_{n-1}) = P(a_j \mid x_1 \ldots x_{n-1})$. In this case, $H(P) = F_n(P)$.

The concept of entropy as a measure of information is central to Information Theory [22], and data compression provides an intuitive perspective to the concept. Define the *coding rate* of a coding scheme as the average number of bits per symbol the scheme uses to encode the output of a source. A *lossless compressor* is a uniquely decodable coding scheme whose goal is to achieve a coding rate as small as possible. The coding rate of any uniquely decodable coding scheme is always greater than or equal to the source entropy [22]. Optimum coding schemes have a coding rate equal to the theoretical lower bound $H(P)$, thus achieving maximum compression.

For order-$(n$-1) Markov processes, optimum encoding is reached if and only if a symbol $x_n = a_j$ occurring after $\mathbf{x}_i^{n-1}$ is coded with $-\log_2 P(a_j \mid \mathbf{x}_i^{n-1})$ bits [15, 22]. However, it may be impossible to accurately estimate the conditional distribution $P(. \mid \mathbf{x}_i^{n-1})$ for large values of n, due to the exponential growth of the number of different contexts, which brings well-known problems, such as context dilution [15].

3 The LZW Algorithm

Even though the source model P is generally unknown, it is possible to construct a coding scheme based upon some implicit or explicit probabilistic model Q that approximates P. The better Q approximates P, the smaller the coding rate achieved by the coding scheme.

In order to achieve low coding rates, modern lossless compressors rely on the construction of sophisticated models that closely follows the true source model. *Statistical compressors* encode messages according to an estimated statistical model for the source. *Dictionary-based compressors* replace strings of symbols from the message to be encoded with indexes into a dictionary of strings, which is generally adaptively constructed during the encoding process. When *greedy parsing* is used, at each step the encoder searches the current dictionary for the longest string that matches the next sequence of symbols in the message, and replaces this sequence with the index of the longest matching string in the dictionary.

Dictionary-based compressors with greedy parsing, such as LZW, are highly popular because they combine computational efficiency with low coding rates. It has been proved that each dictionary-based compressor with greedy parsing has an equivalent statistical coder that achieves exactly the same compression [15]. In dictionary-based coding, the dictionary embeds an implicit statistical model for the source.

The LZW algorithm [21], derived from the LZ78 algorithm [16], is one of the most successful data compression schemes, due to its modest computational requirements and good compression efficiency [15].

Initially, the LZW dictionary contains all possible strings of length one. The LZW algorithm finds the longest string, starting from the first symbol of the message, that is already present in the dictionary. This string is coded with the index for the matching string in the dictionary, and the string is extended with the next symbol in the message, x_i. The extended string is added to the dictionary and the process repeats, starting from x_i [15].

LZW achieves optimum asymptotic performance for Markov sources, in the sense that its coding rate tends toward the entropy of the source as the length of the message to be coded tends toward infinity [23]. It means that LZW algorithm learns a progressively better model for the source during encoding, and a perfect model for the source is learned when an infinite message has been coded. In practice, since the messages to be compressed are finite, LZW only learns an approximate model for the source.

4   The Proposed Method

Due to their capability to build accurate models, modern lossless compressors can be used as model-based classifiers. Any efficient lossless compressor could be used, but LZW algorithm was chosen for the method here proposed, due to its good compromise between coding efficiency and modest computational requirements [15].

4.1   The Learning Stage

In the learning stage, the number N of classes is defined, and a training set T_i of texture samples ($n \times n$ images) known to belong to class C_i, is selected, $i = 1, 2, \ldots N$. The LZW algorithm sequentially compresses the samples in T_i, following the horizontal scanning order shown in Fig. 1.a, and the resulting dictionary H_i is kept as a model for the horizontal structure of textures in C_i, $i = 1, 2, \ldots N$.

LZW algorithm then compresses the samples in T_i following the vertical scanning order shown in Fig. 1.b, and the resulting dictionary V_i is kept as a model for the vertical structure of textures in C_i, $i = 1, 2, \ldots N$.

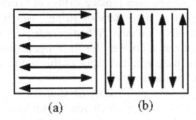

(a)   (b)

Fig. 1. Scanning orders. (a) Horizontal; and (b) Vertical.

4.2 The Classification Stage

In the classification stage, LZW operates in *static mode*. In this mode, one of the dictionaries generated in the classification stage is used, and no new strings are added to the dictionary during the encoding process. Classification is done as follows.

An n x n texture sample $\mathbf{x}$ from an unknown class is coded by the LZW algorithm with static dictionary H_i, following the horizontal scanning order shown in Fig. 1.a., and the corresponding coding rate h_i is registered, $i = 1, 2, \ldots N$. Then the LZW algorithm with static dictionary V_i encodes $\mathbf{x}$, following the vertical scanning order shown in Fig. 1.b., and the corresponding coding rate v_i is registered, $i = 1, 2, \ldots N$.

Let

$$r_i = \frac{h_i + v_i}{2} . \tag{5}$$

Sample $\mathbf{x}$ is assigned to C_i if $r_i < r_j$, $j = 1, 2, \ldots, N, j \neq i$. The rationale is that if $\mathbf{x}$ is a sample from class C_i, the dictionaries H_i and V_i probably embeds the model that best describes its horizontal and vertical structure, thus yielding the smallest coding rates.

5 Experimental Results

Thirty natural textures from the Brodatz album [24], obtained from a public archive, were selected to evaluate the performance of the proposed method. In the experiments, each Brodatz texture constitutes a separate class. All textures have 640 x 640 pixels, with 8 bits/pixel. This corpus is the same used by Li *et al.* [14], thus allowing direct comparison with several state-of-the-art texture classifiers from the literature. The thirty Brodatz textures used are shown in Fig. 2.

Each Brodatz texture was partitioned in n x n non-overlapping subimages, which were taken as texture samples. The samples were separated in two disjoint sets, one for training and the other for testing the classifier. It is important to notice that only with disjoint sets for training and testing it is possible to reach accurate results. Nevertheless, as pointed out by Randen and Husøy [12] and by Li *et al.* [14], the use of overlapping sets is common in the texture classification literature. In these cases, reported results are normally overoptimistic and not attainable in a realistic situation.

Classification accuracy will be assessed by the *correct classification rate* (*CCR*):

$$CCR = \frac{\text{Number of correctly classified samples}}{\text{Number of classified samples}} \times 100\% . \tag{6}$$

In the first experiment, the training set comprised the first three quadrants of each texture, and the test set comprised the last quadrant of each texture. The effect of the sample size in *CCR* was then evaluated for $n = 4, 8, 16, 32$. The results are shown in Table 1.

In the second experiment, the sample size was fixed in 32 x 32. Consequently, there are 400 non-overlapping texture samples in each class. The effect of the training set size in the classifier accuracy was then assessed. For the evaluation, the proportion of training samples in each class was set to 1.25% (5 samples), 2.5% (10 samples),

Fig. 2. Brodatz textures used in the experiments. From left to right and from top to bottom: D1, D3, D6, D11, D16, D17, D20, D21, D24, D28, D29, D32, D34, D35, D46, D47, D49, D51, D52, D53, D55, D56, D57, D65, D78, DD82, D84, D85, D101, D104.

3.75% (15 samples), 5% (20 samples), 6.25% (25 samples), 7.5% (30 samples), 8.75% (35 samples) and 10% (40 samples). In each case, all samples not used for training were used for testing. Table 2 summarizes the results of the proposed method, along with the results [14] for the single and fused SVM classifier, the Bayes classifiers using Bayes distance and Mahalanobis distance, and the LVQ classifier. The features used by the SVM, Bayes and LVQ classifiers are local energies computed in the discrete wavelet frame transform domain, with five decomposition levels. Fig. 3 presents a graphical comparison of the *CCR* achieved by the proposed method and by fused SVM *versus* training set size.

Table 1. *CCR* achieved by the proposed method for various sample sizes.

Sample size (n x n)	CCR (%)
4 x 4	80.6
8 x 8	97.9
16 x 16	99.7
32 x 32	100.0

Table 2. *CCR* achieved by the proposed classifier, Bayes classifer with Bayes distance (Bayes-Bayes), Bayes classifer with Mahalanobis distance (Bayes- Mahalanobis), LVQ, single SVM and fused SVM, for various training set sizes.

Number of training samples per class	CCR (%)					
	Bayes-Bayes	Bayes-Mahalanobis	LVQ	Single SVM	Fused SVM	Proposed classifier
5	79.5	78.7	69.7	78.2	78.4	93.8
10	86.5	86.2	80.0	87.5	87.9	96.2
15	87.9	87.7	83.9	89.6	90.2	98.4
20	90.3	90.2	87.0	91.8	92.5	99.2
25	91.2	91.2	88.2	91.4	92.9	99.3
30	91.8	91.9	89.6	94.6	95.1	99.3
35	92.1	92.1	90.2	94.9	95.9	99.7
40	92.7	92.6	90.4	95.8	96.3	99.7

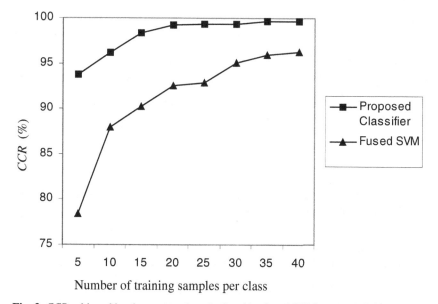

Fig. 3. *CCR* achieved by the proposed method and by fused SVM *versus* training set size.

6 Discussion and Conclusion

This paper proposed a new simple and highly accurate texture classification scheme based on the LZW algorithm.

In the evaluation of the effect of sample size over classification accuracy, Table 1 shows a substantial increase in CCR from $n = 4$ to $n = 8$. This should be expected, since in many cases the structure of the textures is not adequately captured by very small texture samples. The proposed method achieved $CCR = 100\%$ with 32 x 32 texture samples.

From the second experiment, summarized in Table 2 and Fig. 3, the superiority of the proposed method over the single and fused SVM, the Bayes classifiers using Bayes distance and Mahalanobis distance, and the LVQ classifier is evident, and it is still more remarkable for very small training sets. With only five 32 x 32 training samples for each class the proposed method achieved $CCR = 93.8\%$, while the second best method in this situation, Bayes classifier with Bayes distance, achieve $CCR = 79.5\%$. This shows the capability of the proposed method to learn and generalize from very small training sets. This is ratified by noticing that the proposed classifier achieved $CCR = 99.7\%$ with only 35 training samples.

Future directions of research include making the classifier invariant to rotation, scale and illumination; adapting the method for other image classification and segmentation problems; and adapting the method for texture synthesis.

References

1. Porat, M., Zeevi, Y. Y.: Localized Texture Processing in Vision: Analysis and Synthesis in the Gaborian Space. IEEE Transactions on Biomedical Engineering, Vol. 36, Issue: 1 (1989) 115-129
2. Dell'Acqua, F., Gamba, P.: Texture-based Characterization of Urban Environments on Satellite SAR Images. IEEE Transactions on Geoscience and Remote Sensing, Vol. 41, Issue 1 (2003) 153-159
3. Augusteijn, M. F., Clemens, L. E., Shaw, K. A.: Performance evaluation of texture measures for ground cover identification in satellite images by means of a neural network classifier. IEEE Transactions on Geoscience and Remote Sensing, Vol. 33, Issue 3, (1995) 616-626
4. Southard, T. E., Southard, K. A.: Detection of Simulated Osteoporosis in Maxillae Using Radiographic Texture Analysis. IEEE Transactions on Biomedical Engineering, Vol. 43, Issue 2, (1996) 123-132
5. Kumar, A., Pang, G. K. H.: Defect Detection in Textured Materials Using Optimized Filters Systems. IEEE Transactions on Man and Cybernetics, Part B, Vol. 32, Issue 5 (2002) 553-570
6. Jain, A. K., Ross, A., Prabhakar, S.: An Introduction to Biometric Recognition. IEEE Transactions on Circuits and Systems for Video Technology, Vol. 14, Issue 1 (2004) 4-20
7. He, X., Hu, Y., Zhang, H., Li, M., Cheng, Q., Yan, S.: Bayesian Shape Localization for Face Recognition Using Global and Local Textures. IEEE Transactions on Circuits and Systems for Video Technology, Vol. 14, Issue 1 (2004) 102-113
8. Baheerathan, S., Albregtsen, F., Danielsen, H. E.: New Texture Features Based on the Complexity Curve. Pattern Recognition, Vol. 32, Issue 4, (1999) 605-618
9. Duda, R. O., Hart, P. E., Stork, D. G.: Pattern Classification. 2nd ed. Wiley Interscience, New York (2000)

10. Bovik, A. (ed.): Handbook of Image and Video Processing. Academic Press, San Diego London (2000)
11. Cohen, F. S., Fan, Z., Patel, M. A.: Classification of Rotated and Scaled Textured Images Using Gaussian Markov Random Field Models. IEEE Transactions on Pattern Analysis and Machine Intelligence, Vol. 13, Issue 2 (1991) 192–202
12. Randen, T., Husøy, J. H.: Filtering for Texture Classification: a Comparative Study. IEEE Transactions on Pattern Analysis and Machine Intelligence, Vol 21, Issue 4 (1999) 291-310
13. du Buf, J. M. H., Kardan, M., Spann, M. Texture Feature Performance for Image Segmentation. Pattern Recognition, Vol. 23, Issues 3-4, (1990) 291-309.
14. Li, S., Kwok, J. T., Zhu, H., Wang, Y.: Texture Classification Using the Support Vector Machines. Pattern Recognition, Vol. 36, Issue 12 (2003) 2883-2893
15. Bell, T. C., Cleary, J. G, Witten, J. H.: Text Compression. Prentice-Hall, Englewood Cliffs (1990)
16. Ziv, J., Lempel, A.; Compression of Individual Sequences via Variable-Rate Coding. IEEE Transactions on Information Theory, Vol. 24, Issue 5 (1978) 530-536
17. Ziv, J.: On Classification with Empirically Observed Statistics and Universal Data Compression. IEEE Transactions on Information Theory, Vol 34, Issue 2 (1988) 278-286
18. Ziv, J., Merhav, N.: A Measure of Relative Entropy Between Individual Sequences with Application to Universal Classification. IEEE Transactions on Information Theory, Vol. 39, Issue 4 (1993) 1270-1279
19. Frank, E., Chui, C., Witten, I. H.: Text Categorization Using Compression Models. Proceedings of the Data Compression Conference - DCC'2000, Salt Lake City (2000) 555-555
20. Teahan, W. J., Harper , D. J.: Using Compression Based Language Models for Text Categorization. J. Callan, B. Croft and J. Lafferty (eds.): Workshop on Language Modeling and Information Retrieval, ARDA'2001, (2001) 83-88
21. Welch, T. A.: A Technique for High Performance Data Compression. IEEE Computer, Vol. 17, Issue 6 (1984) 8-19
22. Shannon, C. E.: A Mathematical Theory of Communication. Bell Syst. Tech. J., Vol. 27 (1948) 379-423
23. Savari, S.A.: Redundancy of the Lempel-Ziv-Welch Code. Data Compression Conference, 1997. DCC '97. Proceedings , (25-27 Mar 1997) 191 –200
24. Brodatz, P.: Textures: A Photographic Album for Artists and Designers. Dover, New York (1966)

A Clustering-Based Possibilistic Method for Image Classification

Isabela Drummond[1] and Sandra Sandri[2]

[1] Instituto Nacional de Pesquisas Espaciais, SJCampos SP 12227-010, Brasil
isabela@lac.inpe.br
[2] Campus Univ. Automata de Barcelona, Bellaterra 08193, Spain
sandri@iiia.csic.es

Abstract. This work proposes a general image classification method, based in possibility theory and clustering. We illustrate our approach with a CBERS image and compare the results obtained by applying our method to other classification methods.

Keywords: image classification; clustering; possibility theory; similarity relation.

1 Introduction

Image classification is one of the most important tasks in image processing. When samples of pixels from each of the classes known to exist in an image are available, the process most often employed is what is called *supervised image classification*. When a single band is considered, this process can be usually decomposed as follows [6]:

1. An image **I**, with h x v pixels $(x, f(x))$, is selected, where x is the position of the pixel and $f(x)$ is the radiometric value of x, taken from a given scale Ω (usually $\Omega = \{0, 1\}$ or $\Omega = \{0, .., 255\}$).
2. A set of n classes $\mathbf{C} = \{c_1, .., c_n\}$ is selected.
3. A set of n input samples I_i, $i = 1, .., n$ is selected, one for each class. Each $I_i \subseteq \mathbf{I}$ is a set of pixels of **I**, that are classified by an expert as belonging to class c_i. Similarly, a set of n validation samples is selected.
4. Information is extracted from the classified input samples, which is then used to classify the image.
5. A post-classification algorithm may be applied to the classified image, re-classifying pixels according to the classification of its neighbours.
6. The quality of the classification is verified by checking how many of the pixels in the validation sample are correctly classified.

The implementation of item 4 may vary enormously. In the probabilistic method known as *maximum likelihood*, classification is implemented in the following manner (see [3]). First, an histogram h_i is constructed for each class c_i, from the samples I_i, having Ω as domain. Then, a probability distribution p_i is

A.L.C. Bazzan and S. Labidi (Eds.): SBIA 2004, LNAI 3171, pp. 454–463, 2004.
© Springer-Verlag Berlin Heidelberg 2004

estimated to each c_i from h_i (usually p_i is supposed to be Gaussian, although other distributions can be used [10]). Based on these distributions, Ω is divided into n intervals T_i, one to each class c_i. Finally, all pixels $(x, f(x))$ of the image are classified using the intervals T_i, in such a way that if $f(x)$ belongs to the interval T_i then $(x, f(x))$ is classified in class c_i. This approach has two inconvenients worth mentioning. First of all, it is not always possible to find a parameterized probability density function effectively adequate to each class histogram. Apart from that, the partitioning of Ω may generate an erroneous classification of many pixels, to which it is not always possible to obtain the correct classification through an eventual post-classification.

Other approaches employ possibility and fuzzy sets theories, either directly [6] or using some kind of expert system [7],[8]. The approach used in [6] for single band classification derives possibility distributions from the sample histograms to first create an imprecise classification of the image, which gets more and more precise as a neighbourhood algorithm is recurrently applied to it. In this approach, each pixel is labeled with a set, called a simple class if the set is a singleton, and a compound class, otherwise. At the end of the process, each pixel is labeled with a singleton, i.e. a precise class. In [8], for multi-band classification, rules of thumb are used to derive a possibility distribution for each class in each band. Then, each pixel $(x, f_i(x))$ in each band l is associated to a possibility distribution of classes; the closest to 1 is the degree of $f_i(x)$ in relation to class c, the more possible it is that c is the correct class of the pixel. Finally, for each pixel in the image, the possibility distributions related to each band are aggregated using some kind of fuzzy operator, such as min.

Here we propose a possibilistic approach to multi-band images classification. First of all, we clusterize the espectral response elements of the sample of each class. In this way, we obtain a set of centers for each class, which can be seen as the class prototypes. We then apply a similarity relation to each of these centers, thus "enlarging" the classes. To classify a pixel in the image, we verify its likeness to each class, by using the distance of the espectral response of the pixel to the class prototypes. We then use an heuristics to determine if the pixel should be labeled with a compound or to a simple class. Finally, we use the neighborhood algorithm from [6] to obtain the final classification.

This paper is organized as follows. Section 2 brings some basic definitions. Section 3 presents the proposed general model and Section 4 discusses some of its possible implementations. Section 5 brings the conclusion.

2   Basic Issues

2.1   Fuzzy Sets and Possibility Theories

In (classical) set theory, each subset A of an universe U can be expressed by means of a membership function $A : U \rightarrow \{0, 1\}$, such that $A(a) = 1$ (respec. $A(a) = 0$) expresses that $a \in U$ belongs (respec. does not belong) to A. A *fuzzy set* [11] is useful when one needs to model an ill-defined quantity. The membership function of a fuzzy set A is a mapping $A : U \rightarrow [0, 1]$, where

[0,1] can be any bounded scale. A fuzzy set A of U is said to be "precise" when $\exists a \in U$ such that $A(a) = 1$ and $\forall x \neq a$, $A(x) = 0$, and "crisp" when $\forall x \in U, A(x) \in \{0,1\}$.

Possibility theory [12] is closely related to fuzzy sets theory and allows to deal with ill-known quantities. A possibility distribution is a mapping $\pi : U \to \{0,1\}$, associated to a variable x, whose actual value is unknown. When $\pi(a) = 1$ (respec. $\pi(a) = 0$), it is completely possible (respec. impossible) that a is the actual value of x. Although very often confounded in the literature, these theories are not the same; fuzzy sets theory is comparable to sets theory, whereas possibility theory is comparable to probability theory.

The intersection and union of two fuzzy sets, or two possibility distributions, are performed respectively by t-norm and t-conorm operators, which are commutative, associative and monotonic mappings from $[0,1]$ to $[0,1]$. Moreover, a t-norm $\top$ (respec. t-conorm $\bot$) has 1 (respec. 0) as neutral element. The most well-known conjunctive and disjunctive operators are the min (t-norm) and the max (t-conorm). Other operators are, for instance, the families of means, situated between the min and max (e.g. the arithmetic mean).

A similarity relation S on a domain U is a binary fuzzy relation, i.e. a mapping $S : U \times U \to [0,1]$ that satisfies the following properties[1]:

(i) $\forall v \in U, S(v,v) = 1$ (*reflexivity*);
(ii) $\forall v, v' \in U, S(v,v') = S(v',v)$ (*symmetry*).

The application of a similarity relation S on a fuzzy term A, denoted by $S \circ A$, creates a "larger" term *approximately_A*. Formally, we have:

$$(S \circ A)(v) = \sup_{v' \in U} \min(S(v,v'), A(v')). \tag{1}$$

The set of similarity relations on a given domain U forms a lattice (not linearly ordered) with respect to the point-wise ordering (or fuzzy-set inclusion) relationship. The top of the lattice is the similarity $S_\top$ which makes all the elements in the domain maximally similar: $S_\top(v,v') = 1$ for all $v, v' \in U$. The bottom of the lattice $S_\bot$ is the classical equality relation: $S_\bot(v,v') = 1$ if $v = v'$, $S_\bot(v,v') = 0$, otherwise. The higher a similarity is placed in the lattice (i.e. the bigger are their values), the less discriminating it is.

A frequently used family of similarity functions for $U = \mathbf{R}$ is the following:

$$S_\alpha(u,v) = F_\alpha(|u-v|) \tag{2}$$
$$F_\alpha(z) = \max(0, 1 - \lambda^{-1} \cdot z)$$

where $\alpha > 0$. This family enjoys a nice property: if A is a trapezoidal fuzzy set represented by the quadruple $< a, b, c, d >$, then $(S_\alpha \circ A)$ yields the trapezoidal fuzzy set $< a - \alpha, b, c, d + \alpha >$. When A is precise, say a point a, then $(S_\alpha \circ A)$

---

[1] Some authors require similarity relations to also satisfy the T-norm transitivity property $(S(u,v) \otimes S(v,w) \leq S(u,w)$ for all $u, v, w \in U$ and some t-norm $\otimes$).

yields the triangular fuzzy set $< a - \alpha, a, a + \alpha >$. When applied to a, the similarity relation:

$$S'_\beta = \begin{cases} 1, \text{if } |u - v| \leq \beta \\ 0, \text{otherwise} \end{cases} \tag{3}$$

yields the interval (a crisp fuzzy set) $[a - \beta, a + \beta]$.

2.2 Fuzzy c-Means Algorithm

The fuzzy c-means (FCM) algorithm is one of the most widely used methods in data clustering and was originally introduced in [1] as an improvement on earlier clustering methods. In this method, each data point belongs to a cluster to some degree that is specified by a membership grade.

Basically, the algorithm consists of 2 phases: a) a center is identified for each cluster; b) a membership function for each cluster is calculated, which takes into account the center of all the clusters. The membership degree of an element to a cluster is based on a similarity measure, e.g. the Euclidean distance between the element and the center of that cluster. The algorithm is applied repeatedly until a satisfactory set of clusters is obtained. The centers of the clusters in the first iteration of the algorithm are usually chosen at random.

Since the original algorithm is considered very sensible to initial conditions, some authors have proposed to use optimization algorithms to create the first set of centers. In [5], an extension of the fuzzy clustering method is proposed, which starts with an overestimated number of clusters, that is gradually reduced. This extension attempts to reduce the sensitivity of the clustering algorithm to the differences in cluster volumes and the data pattern distributions, aiming at decreasing dependency on the random initialization.

2.3 Test Image

In the remaining of this paper we use a 3-band CBERS satellite image [4] to both illustrate and validate our approach. The image has 839×650 pixels (see Figure 1a)) and $\Omega = \{0, .., 255\}$, and was taken from the northeast of Rio Grande do Sul, in Brazil (coordinates UTM: 550.350;6.750.119 and 564.089;6.736.050). The input samples from the 8 classes of interest (areas with Araucaria, Atlantic rain forest, reforested Pinus, field, bare soil, roads, clouds, shadows) are shown in Figure 1b). Both the image and the samples have been taken from [9].

3 General Classification Method

In the following, we propose a supervised method to classify a multi-band non-binary image, based on possibility theory and clustering. We then discuss some measures that are useful to obtain the parameters for specific implementations.

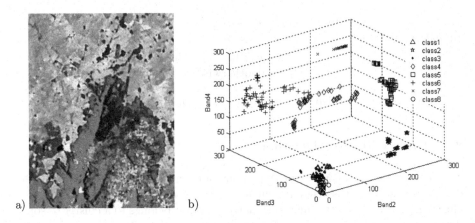

Fig. 1. a) Test image. b)Attribute space of the test image.

3.1   Method

Let $\mathbf{I}$ be a multi-band non-binary image with h x v pixels $(x, f(x))$, $f(x) = (f_1(x), ..., f_m(x))$, where x is the position of the pixel and $f_l(x) \in \Omega$ is the radiometric value of x in band l, $1 \leq l \leq m$. Let $\mathbf{C} = \{c_1, .., c_n\}$ be a set of n classes, and let $I_i \subseteq \mathbf{I}$ be the sample associated to class c_i. Let $P_i \subseteq \Omega^m$ be the set of points associated to $c_i \in \mathbf{C}$ in the attribute space and obtained from I_i, i.e., for each pixel $(x, f(x)) \in I_i$, we have $f(x) \in P_i$. Let $d(p_1, p_2)$ be the distance between points p_1 and p_2 in Ω^m, according to a given metric.

1. For each class c_i, we clusterize the points in P_i, creating k centers[2] (or prototypes) $p_{i,j}$. Let $T_i = \{p_{i,1}, \ldots, p_{i,k}\}$ and $T = \cup T_i$.
2. We associate a possibility distribution $\pi_{i,j} : \Omega^m \to [0, 1]$ to each prototype $p_{i,j} \in T$, and for each point $p \in \Omega^m$ we associate a distribution $\pi_p : T \to [0, 1]$. These distributions are calculated as $\pi_{i,j}(p) = \pi_p(p_{i,j}) = S(p_{i,j}, p)$, where S is a similarity relation.
3. For each pixel $(x, f(x))$ in the image, we obtain the possibility distribution of its class, defined as $\pi_{(x,f(x))} : \mathbf{C} \to [0, 1]$, and calculated as $\forall c_i \in \mathbf{C}$, $\pi_{(x,f(x))}(c_i) = \perp_{1 \leq j \leq k} \pi_{f(x)}(p_{i,j})$, where $\perp$ is a t-conorm.
4. We use some kind of classification criteria to determine a crisp set of classes to associate to $f(x)$, denoted as $class(f(x))$.
5. We associate a class to each pixel $(x, f(x))$ as $class(x, f(x)) = class(f(x))$.
6. We use some kind of neighborhood algorithm to obtain a single class to $(x, f(x))$ using information about the classes associated to pixel $(x, f(x))$ and to the pixels in its neighborhood.
7. We use some kind of index to verify whether the quality of the classification is acceptable, if and when validation class samples are available.

---

[2] To facilitate notation, we here assume, without lack of generality, that a single fixed number of centers is obtained for all of the classes.

We obtain different specific implementations of this general method as we use different values for the items above, such as the clustering algorithm, the similarity relation S, the classification criteria and the neighborhood algorithm.

3.2   Useful Measures and Other Definitions

After the clustering step, some measures can be derived from the clusters, in order to help produce parameters for the similarity relation in specific implementations. The following measures, along with useful definitions, have been used in our work.

- To each center $p_{i,j} \in T_i$, we associate a set $P_{i,j} \subseteq P_i$ with the points in P_i that are closer to $p_{i,j}$ than to any other center of c_i, according to d. Formally, $\forall p \in P_i, p \in P_{i,j}$ iff $\inf_{1 \leq w \leq k} d(p_{i,w}, p) = d(p_{i,j}, p)$.
- To each center $p_{i,j}$, we associate the smallest and largest distance to it, from the elements in $P_{i,j}$, calculated as $d_{min}(p_{i,j}) = \inf_{p \in P_{i,j}} d(p_{i,j}, p)$ and $d_{max}(p_{i,j}) = \sup_{p \in P_{i,j}} d(p_{i,j}, p)$ respectively.
- We calculate the distance between each pair of centers. Let $d_{ext}(p_{i,j}) = \inf_{1 \leq s \leq k, 1 \leq r \leq n, r \neq i} d(p_{i,j}, p_{r,s})$. Set $T_{ext}(p_{i,j})$ denotes the centers that have the highest potential of having points wrongly classified as belonging to class c_i. It is such that $p_{r,s} \in T_{ext}(p_{i,j})$, iff $d(p_{i,j}, p_{r,s}) = d_{ext}(p_{i,j})$.
- Let $d_{in}(p_{i,j}) = \sup_{1 \leq s \leq k, 1 \leq r \leq n, r \neq i} (d_{max}(p_{r,s}) - d(p_{i,j}, p_{r,s}))$. Set $T_{in}(p_{i,j})$ denotes the centers that have the highest potential of misclassifying points of class c_i. It is such that $p_{r,s} \in T_{in}(p_{i,j})$, iff $d(p_{i,j}, p_{r,s}) = d_{in}(p_{i,j})$, $\forall p_{r,s} \in T$.

Table 1 shows the distance measures that were obtained by clusterizing the points in the attribute space, in Figure 1b) above, using FCM with $k = 3$, the Euclidean distance, random matrix initialization and the fuzziness exponent equal to 2.

Table 1. Distance measures for class samples.

	p_{11}	p_{12}	p_{13}	p_{21}	p_{22}	p_{23}	p_{31}	p_{32}	p_{33}	p_{41}	p_{42}	p_{43}
d_{max}	8.11	18.03	6.23	27.91	10.04	3.39	3.16	22.63	15.61	38.32	14.24	51.25
d_{min}	2.04	2.44	1.67	3.85	1.51	1.39	0.62	2.54	3.59	3.12	4.02	20.59
d_{ext}	14.71	22.86	14.22	124.99	145.91	94.91	32.07	14.22	5.95	53.63	114.84	90.60
d_{in}	6.60	4.82	7.98	97.08	135.87	91.52	28.90	-8.41	-9.66	15.31	100.60	39.34

	p_{51}	p_{52}	p_{53}	p_{61}	p_{62}	p_{63}	p_{71}	p_{72}	p_{73}	p_{81}	p_{82}	p_{83}
d_{max}	28.92	8.66	20.31	34.28	32.76	43.02	0.58	14.52	7.29	13.51	16.06	11.41
d_{min}	2.44	1.20	2.77	8.65	5.57	11.59	0.58	1.47	0.29	4.18	1.60	0.44
d_{ext}	96.16	98.57	90.60	53.63	112.12	97.21	114.88	100.06	98.57	8.52	5.95	22.19
d_{in}	67.24	89.91	70.28	19.35	79.35	54.18	114.29	85.54	91.28	-4.98	-10.11	10.78

Ideally, an image should be such that it would be possible to find a small number of class cluster centers $p_{i,j}$, such that $\forall 1 \leq i, j \leq n, \forall 1 \leq r, s \leq k$, $d_{max}(p_{i,j}) \leq d_{ext}(p_{i,j})$, and $d_{in}(p_{i,j}) \leq 0$. When that occurs, we can (theoretically) safely create a hypersphere around $p_{i,j}$ with radius d_{max}, that will contain all the points that belong to that class, without intersections with the hyperspheres associated to any center in any class different of c_i. (Note that just drawing such a compact hypersphere around a center corresponds to applying the similarity relation $S'_{d_{max}}$ to that center.)

Most of the time, however, we may be very far from the ideal situation. Applying this method to the image shown above would probably yield, for no matter the number of centers taken, a very poor classification, due to a large overlap between the classes, and the impossibility of ranking the competing hypotheses. A solution is to use distance metrics that correspond to modeling other kinds of volumes, what augments the complexity of the problem and the consequent cost of solving it. Here we have adopted the use of more discriminating, but still very simple, similarity relations.

4   A Specific Classification Method

In the following, we present a specific classification method that can be derived from the general one, using the measures presented above to create the similarity relations.

We have used the original FCM clustering method as described above in item 1 and $\perp = max$ in item 3. The neighborhood algorithm from [6] was used in item 6 to obtain the final classification. The kappa index [2], a popular measure to evaluate classification performance and which varies between 0 and 1, was employed to assess the quality of the classification (item 7).

Let $p \in \Omega^m$ be a point in the attribute space. Let $\pi_p : T \to [0,1]$ be the possibility distribution of p belonging to class c_i, according to center p_{ij}. Let $p_{a,b}$ and $p_{c,d}, 1 \leq a, c \leq n, 1 \leq b, d \leq k$, be the centers with the hightest possibility degrees in π_p and such that $\pi_p(p_{a,b}) \geq \pi_p(p_{c,d})$. Let $\alpha \in \mathbf{R}, \alpha > 1$, and $\beta \in]0,1]$ be arbitrary values. The following classification criteria algorithm has been used for item 4.

Classification Criteria Algorithm

    if $a = c$
    then $class(p) = c_a$
    else if $\pi_{p_{c,d}}(p_{a,b}) \geq \alpha \pi_p(p_{a,b})$
        then $class(p) = undefined$
        else if $\pi_p(p_{c,d})/\pi_p(p_{a,b}) \geq \beta$
            then $class(p) = \{c_a, c_c\}$
            else $class(p) = c_a$.

To implement item 2 of the general method, we propose to basically use the following similarity relation:

$$S_{\gamma,\lambda} = \begin{cases} 1, & \text{if } |u - v| \leq \gamma \\ F_{\lambda-\gamma}(|u - v| - \gamma), & \text{otherwise} \end{cases} \qquad (4)$$

Note that $S_{0,\lambda} = S_\lambda$ and that $lim_{\lambda \to \gamma} S_{\gamma,\lambda} = S'_\gamma$. Note also that, if fuzzy set A represents a point a, then $S_{\gamma,\lambda} \circ A$ yields a trapezoidal fuzzy set given by $< a - \lambda, a - \gamma, a + \gamma, a + \lambda >$.

Table 2 brings the results of some experiments undertaken using that relation; kappa' and kappa" are the indices obtained, respectively, before and after the neighborhood algorithm is applied. In that table we have $\lambda 1 = min(200, k * dmax), k = 20, \gamma 1 = min(dmax, dext, max(0, din))$ and $\gamma 2 = f(min(dext, dmax * k1), max(din, dmin * k2)); k1 = k2 = 2; f(a, b) = (a + b)/2$. All parameters have been obtained in a trial and error manner.

Table 2. Summary of experiments.

	$S_{(\gamma,\lambda)}$	α	β	kappa' (%)	kappa" (%)
experiment 1	$S_{\lambda 1} \perp S'_{\gamma 1}$	1.2	0.98	75.7	84.7
experiment 2	S_{200}	1.4	0.98	77	83.4
experiment 3	$S_{200} \perp S'_{\gamma 2}$	1.2	0.98	75.7	82
experiment 4	$S_{(\gamma 1, \lambda 1)}$	1.2	0.98	66.7	77.4

We see that, in general, reasonably good results have been obtained without the neighborhood algorithm, but that the application of this algorithm has greatly improved the overall quality.

Table 3 brings the confusion matrix associated with experiment 1, that obtained the best classification. Figure 2 brings the classified image yielded by that experiment.

Table 3. Confusion matrix.

	class1	class2	class3	class4	class5	class6	class7	class8
class1	98	0	18	0	0	0	0	15
class2	0	108	0	0	0	1	2	4
class3	9	0	64	0	0	0	0	5
class4	0	0	6	104	2	11	2	1
class5	0	0	0	4	106	0	0	0
class6	0	0	0	0	0	89	7	0
class7	0	0	0	0	0	5	97	0
class8	0	0	18	0	0	0	0	80
undefined	1	0	2	0	0	2	0	3
sum	108	108	108	108	108	108	108	108

An application of the possibilistic method proposed in [8] for the test image yielded kappa=79%, using min as aggregation operator of the possibility distributions in each band. An approach based on neural networks presented in [9] uses a system that integrates three neural nets models: a Multi-Layer Perceptron - MLP, a Learning Vector Quantization - LVQ, and a Radial Basis Function - RBF. This implementation for the test image yielded kappa=77.2%. We see thus that our best parameterization (kappa=84.7%) performed better for this particular test image.

5   Conclusion

We have presented a general method for image classification, based in possibility theory and data clustering. We also presented a particular implementation of the

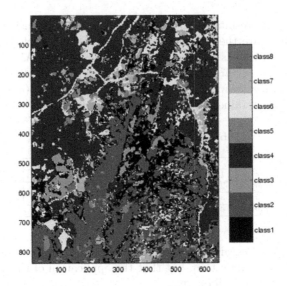

Fig. 2. Classified image.

method, which was applied to a CBERS image. The results obtained show that the approach is very promising. More experiments are needed in order to assess its quality for a large class of images.

We have obtained very good results in the classification of our test image with the use of a simple linear similarity relation. However, more complex functions (e.g. bell-shaped) may yield even better results, without any further cost. Moreover, we have based our tests in the application of similarity relations on class cluster centers, whereas the application of similarity relations to the axis between two class centers might also bring better results, but with an additional cost.

The choice of the clustering method can be very important in our framework. Moreover, clusterizing methods are usually randomic, and the classification, made using one set of centers may largely differ from another one. In the application we have used to illustrate our approach, we have obtained good results by simply using the original FCM, with a small fixed number of representative centers for each sample class. However, that might not be the case in applications in which some classes are much larger or more sparsely distributed than others. Let us suppose a small fixed number of centers is used. Then a large and/or sparse class may have radii so large that it would misclassify points of denser/smaller classes in its vicinity. On the other hand, if a large number of fixed centers is used, the cost may become prohibitive. In such cases, a clustering technique that yields a variable number of centers may become more advantageous.

Although we focus in image classification, this approach can in fact be seen as a general pattern-matching one. In this particular case, the feature space are the pixels spectral response in the various bands. Should we only look for the single prototype that is closer to the pixel spectral response, then the problem would be a type of 1-nearest neighbour classification. The approach proposed here is however more complex, and expected to be more effective in real applications, since characteristics of the clusters themselves are used to help in the classification.

Acknowledgements

The authors are indebted to Cleber Rubert, Viviane Todt Diverio and Paulo Malinski.

References

1. Bezdek, J., Ehrlich, R. e Full, W. FCM: The fuzzy c-means clustering algorithm. *Computers & Geosciences* vol 10, n. 2-3, 191–203, 1984.
2. Bishop, Y. M.; Feinberg, S. E.; Holland, P. W. Discrete Multivariate Analysis: Theory as Practice MIT Press, Cambridge, MA, 1975.
3. Frery, A.C.; Yanasse, C.C.F.; Vieira, P.R.; Sant'Anna, S.J.S.; Renn, C.D. A user-friendly system for synthetic aperture radar image classification based on grayscale distributional properties and context. *Proc. 10th SIBGRAPI*, Campos de Jordão (Br), oct. 1997. *Proc. IEEE*, 1997, p.211-218.
4. Instituto Nacional de Pesquisas Espacias - INPE, 2004. **CBERS Program**, S. J. dos Campos (Br). http://www.cbers.inpe.br/en/index _en.htm
5. Kaymak, U. ; Setnes, M. Extended fuzzy clustering algorithms. In: ERIM Report Series Research in Management ERS2000-51-LIS, Erasmus Research Inst. of Management, 2000. http:/www.erim.eur.nl
6. Malinski, P.; Sandri, S.; Freitas, C. An imprecision-based image classifier. *Proc. FUZZ-IEEE'01* Melbourne (Au), dec. 2001.
7. Moraes, R.M. de; Banon, G.J.F.; Sandri, S.A. Expert Systems Architecture for Image Classification Using Morphological Operators. *Proc. 4th FLINS Int. Conf.*, Ghent (Belgium), in *Intelligent Techniques and Soft Computing in Nuclear Science and Engineering* (D. Ruan, H.A. Abderrahim, P. D'hondt, E.E. Kerre, eds), pp. 271-280, Springer Verlag, ago. 2000.
8. Roux, L.; Desachy, J. Multisource information-fusion application for satellite image classification. in *Fuzzy information Engineering: A Guided Tour of Applications*, (D. Dubois, H. Prade, R.R. Yager - Eds), 1997. p. 111-121.
9. Rubert, C.; Diverio, V. T.; Silva, J. D. S. Integrated Neural System to Identify Targets inside Satellite Images. Submitted.
10. Vieira, P.R.; Yanasse, C.C.F.; Frery, A.C.; Sant'Anna, S.J.S. Um sistema de análise e classificação estatísticas para imagens SAR. In: Primeras Jornadas Latinoamericanas de Percepción Remota por Radar: Técnicas de Procesamiento de Imagenes. Buenos Aires, Argentina, dec. 1996, Workshop Proceedings. ESA, 1997, p.179-185. (ESA SP-407).
11. Zadeh, L. A. Fuzzy Sets, *Information and Control*, v. 8, p.338-353, 1965.
12. R.R. Yager, S. Ovchinikov, R.M. Tong and H.T. Nguyen. *Fuzzy Sets and Applications: selected papers by L.A. Zadeh*, Wiley, 1987.

An Experiment on Handshape Sign Recognition Using Adaptive Technology: Preliminary Results

Hemerson Pistori[1] and João José Neto[2]

[1] Universidade Católica Dom Bosco, Dept. Engenharia de Computação
79117-900 Campo Grande, Brasil
pistori@ec.ucdb.br
[2] Universidade de São Paulo, Escola Politécnica
05508-900 São Paulo, Brasil
joao.jose@poli.usp.br

Abstract. This paper presents an overview of current work on the recognition of sign language and a prototype of a simple editor for a small subset of the Brazilian Sign Language, LIBRAS. Handshape based alphabetical signs, are captured by a single digital camera, processed on-line by using computational vision techniques and converted to the corresponding Latin letter. The development of such prototype employed a machine-learning technique, based on automata theory and adaptive devices. This technique represents a new approach to be used in the far more complex problem of full LIBRAS recognition. As it happens with spoken languages, sign languages are not universal. They vary a lot from country to country, and in spite of the existence of many works in American Sign Language (ASL), the automatic recognition of Brazilian Sign Language has not been extensively studied. ...

1   Introduction

Brazilian census, conducted by IBGE[1] in 2000, reveals an absolute number of 166.000 deaf persons. The most used sign language in Brazil is LIBRAS, which has been officially recognized as a legal communication mean just in 2002[2]. This same law imposes that teachers, special educators and speech therapists be trained for using LIBRAS. The delay in the recognition of brazilian deaf sign language reflects intense and long dated quarrels between oralists and gestualists. Oralists claim that deaf persons should learn the national spoken language, while gestualists defend a bi-linguistic approach. The dominance of the oralist approach until recently (80's) led to extreme measures, as the complete prohibition of sign language in children education [1]. However, two main factors are gradually changing this scenario toward a bi-linguistic approach: (1) the growing acceptance of the richness and importance of the deaf culture, which includes

---

[1] Instituto Brasileiro de Geografia e Estatística (Brazilian Institute of Geography and Statistics)
[2] Brazilian Federal Law number 10.436 - April 24, 2002

A.L.C. Bazzan and S. Labidi (Eds.): SBIA 2004, LNAI 3171, pp. 464–473, 2004.
© Springer-Verlag Berlin Heidelberg 2004

their natural sign language, and (2) scientific discoveries in psychology, indicating that sign communication is essential for early language acquisition and complete development of deaf children [2].

Natural sign languages are not mere transcription of spoken languages. Instead, they are evolving systems, as expressive as any other language, encompassing complex lexical, syntactical and semantical substructures, with specificities absent in oral languages, like spatiality and iconicity [1]. However, as it happens with spoken languages, natural sign languages are much more comfortable, flexible and expressive than written languages. Deaf persons communicate by signs much faster than by writing or typing [3]. Hence, all justifications for researches in computer speech technologies also applies to sign languages, including text-to-sign and sign-to-text translators and human-computer interaction based on sign languages. Besides, as sign languages are not universal - they vary from country to country, sometimes comprising many different dialects inside the same country - sign languages translators are also important research goals to be pursued: an estimate of the number of sign languages around the world ranges from 4000 to 20000 [4].

The specific features of gestural languages turns it impossible to fully reuse algorithms and methods developed for the speech recognition domain. That is seldom recognized by computer scientists and engineers who neglect the cooperation of deaf communities and specialists in this kind of work [1]. The present work is just a first step toward the construction of a LIBRAS-to-Portuguese text converter, which will be used, in the future, as a front-end for applications such as a LIBRAS-to-Speech translator, or to LIBRAS-controlled interfaces. It comprises a simple prototype editor which may be trained to understand alphabetical hand signs corresponding to Latin letters, captured by a single digital camera, and a software framework allowing the integration of different machine learning and computer-vision techniques. Such editor is intended to be used both as a testbed for different techniques and as a dataset capturing tool, where body signs and corresponding portuguese text will be collected to form a huge database of samples, similar to Purdue's RVL-SLLL ASL database for automatic recognition of American Sign Language [5].

Our editor is already being used experimentally on a novel machine learning approach, based on adaptive decision trees (AdapTree [6]), which has as one of its main advantage the fact of being incremental, allowing the dynamic correction of errors even after the training phase (by the user himself), unlike many classic approaches, for instance, traditional feed-forward artificial neural networks with backpropagation.

The next section presents some previous work on the automatic recognition of sign language, followed by a brief introduction to the brazilian sign language. Section 4 introduces the adaptive technology and the machine learning approach used in our work. The prototype and some related experiments are shown and commented in sections 5 and 6. Results analysis, conclusions and future works are discussed in the last section.

2   Related Work

Despite some recent work on the recognition of head movements, like nods and shakes [7], which are very important in sign communication, most of works concentrates on hand movement and shape tracking. Besides being an important feature for sign language recognizers, hand tracking has important applications in human-computer interaction, virtual reality and sign compression. Applications include hand-controlled computer games [8], TV-set control by hand movements [8], video-conference compression techniques for deaf communication [3] and pointing devices that replace the traditional mouse.

The two major classes of hand tracking systems are: (1) data-glove-based, which rely on electromechanical gloves for virtual reality, comprising several sensors for detecting the position of wrists, hands, fingertips and articulations [9] and (2) vision-based, that works on continuous frames of digital images containing the hands [10–13]. The first group usually provides faster and more accurate systems, but the non-intrusive vision-based approach experiments growing interest with recent advances and larger availability of digital cameras, powerful micro-processors and computational vision techniques. Vision-based techniques may also benefit from the use of hand marks (such as colored gloves) [14] and infra-red cameras, which facilitate the identification of human-body parts with noisy backgrounds, but in some degree, at the expense of lower non-obstructiveness and hardware availability.

Works on hand-tracking which are focused on sign language recognition are also frequent, and are available for several different languages such as Australian, Chinese, German, Arabic and American Sign Language [9, 12]. Most of current sign language recognition systems typically include four modules: (1) hands segmentation, (2) parameter extraction, (3) posture recognition and (4) dynamic gesture recognition.

At the segmentation phase, hands are extracted from the background. This task may be very hard if bare hands are required with complex background, but techniques based on luminescence-invariant skin color detection [15], pre-stored background images and subsequent image differencing are showing promising results [11]. Parameter extraction reduces the size of the searching model by detecting interesting features in the segmented hand, such as position and relative angle of fingers and fingertips, hand center and direction, vectors from the hand center to the board, image moments and orientation histograms [16, 12, 14].

Posture and gesture recognition involves searching for the sign model which best fits the extracted parameters. Gesture models must deal with temporal information and much work has been done in the adaptation of speech recognition techniques, based on Hidden Markov Chains, to such problems [9, 15]. Machine learning techniques are also being used both in posture- and gesture-recognition, including artificial neural-networks and neuro-fuzzy networks [12]. Some other recognition techniques include principal component analysis [17], elastic graph matching and Kalman filters [13].

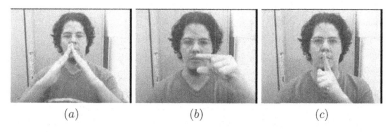

(a) (b) (c)

Fig. 1. Examples of Iconic Signs used in LIBRAS. (a) Home (b) Small (c) Keep Silent

3   Brazilian Sign Language

The Brazilian Sign Language, LIBRAS, is a complex, structured and natural Brazilian language, whose origin is found in the French Sign Language [18]. As it happens with spoken languages, sign languages naturally evolve to take advantage from its basic communication mean, the relation between space and body gestures in the case of sign languages, in order to make communication efficient. For instance, different positions in the space in front of a LIBRAS user may be assigned to different subjects of discourse, which may be referenced afterward, simply by pointing operations. Another feature of LIBRAS, important for its visual nature, is the use of symbols with iconic meaning: figure 1 shows LIBRAS gestures used to represent *home*, *small* and *keep silent*, respectively.

Though full LIBRAS communication includes head, main body, arms and movements of other body parties; hand shapes, position (with respect to the body of the signer) and movement are essential to LIBRAS, as they are used as basic elements from which more complex sentences may be constructed. A set of 46 basic hands shapes, or configurations, are found in LIBRAS. This set includes the 19 alphabetic "static" symbols presented in figure 2 (signs for letters h,j,k,x,y and z involve hand movements and are not shown). In LIBRAS, fingerspelling, the use of alphabetic sequences to form words is restricted to special cases, such as the communication of acronyms and proper nouns. However, alphabetic symbols appear as components in a variety of other signs. The sentence *what is your name*, for instance, is expressed by doing the sign for the q letter (referring to the interrogation *what* - "qual", in portuguese) near the mouth followed by an horizontal hand movement, shaping the letter n (referring to *name* - "nome"), from left to right, near the chest. The later example also illustrates the importance of the position and movement of the hands. More information on LIBRAS, including a LIBRAS-English dictionary, may be found in [18].

4   Adaptive Devices

The prototype editor developed in this work includes a module that learns to recognize certain hand signs by analyzing a set of examples previously interpreted by a human. Even during execution, eventual system recognition errors may be

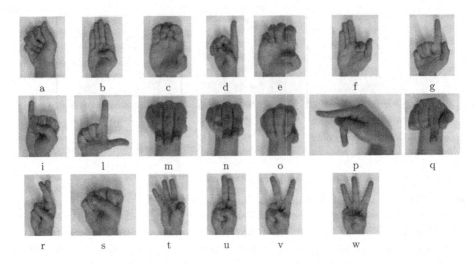

Fig. 2. Some LIBRAS alphabetic symbols

corrected by the user, simple by typing the letter and showing the corresponding hand sign. The ability of the system to evolve its recognition capability by dynamically changing its internal structure when new examples arrive is modeled, in the current work, using adaptive device theory. It is out of the scope of this paper to detail the full complexity of this theory but the next paragraphs give a brief introduction to the topic, referencing some works where more information may be found.

A rule-driven adaptive device [19] is a formal tool obtained by empowering some device whose operation relies on static rules, such as finite state automata, with an adaptive layer which transforms the former device's rules into dynamic ones. Such adaptive layer, which preserves much of the syntax and semantics of the subjacent mechanism, is based on simple deletion and insertion actions that operate on the subjacent mechanism's set of rules and is activated while the subjacent mechanism operates. In this way, the initially static structure of the subjacent device becomes dynamic, although the whole device is essentially expressed in terms of the subjacent formalism.

Figure 3 shows an adaptive automaton that recognizes the context-dependent language $a^n b^n c^n$. The subjacent mechanism, figure 3.(a), follows the standard representation for finite-state automata, with the exception of the $[.F]$ label attached to the transition consuming the symbol a. This label indicates that an adaptive function, called F (figure 3.(b)), is expected to be executed just after performing the transition to which it is attached. Adaptive functions are described using a notation inherited from semantic nets, with variables being denoted by a question mark prefix ($?x$, $?y$ and $?z$). The asterisk prefix indicates generators: new, unique, symbols that should be reinstantiated each time the adaptive function is executed ($*n_1$ and $*n_2$). Vertical parallel arrows give the function execution direction, from the pattern that should be matched and extracted to the pattern that should be included into the subjacent structure. The illustrating example works as follows: each time some symbol a is consumed, the adaptive function F finds the single empty transition in the automaton, removes it and inserts two new transitions for consuming the substring bc, with an empty transition strategically placed between them.

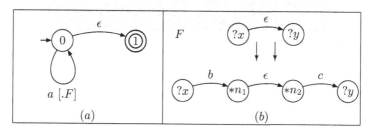

Fig. 3. Adaptive Automaton for $a^n b^n c^n$. (a) Subjacent Mechanism (b) Adaptive Layer

The adaptive technique is already being applied in the solution of problems in areas as diverse as grammatical inference, automatic music composition, natural language processing, robotics and computer vision [20, 19] with subjacent mechanisms that includes context-free grammars, structured pushdown automata, Markov chains, decision tables, Petri-nets and decision trees[3]. In the work reported in the present paper, adaptive decision trees, which are basically an adaptive automata that grows on a tree-like structure, have been used in the implementation of our machine learning strategy. The main features of adaptive decision trees, which elect it as a good alternative are: (1) efficient learning phase, even with large training sets and (2) incremental learning capabilities [6].

5   Development

We have implemented a prototype fingerspelling LIBRAS editor in Java by integrating to our algorithms three auxiliary software packages: an image processing environment, the ImageJ[4]; SUN library for time-based devices, the Java Media Framework (JMF); and a toolkit that support the development and confrontation of different machine learning and data-mining algorithms, WEKA[5]. The choice of reusing existing packages, all of them freely available from Internet, besides facilitating future maintenance and integration to other systems, allowed a very short and cheap development schedule for the whole environment.

Our prototype works as follows: initially, there is a training phase, when users must hand-sign letters to a camera, with one hand, and use the other-hand to

---

[3] Extensive information on adaptive technology may be found at http://www.pcs.usp.br/~lta. A free graphical IDE for experimenting adaptive automata may be downloaded from the same site.

[4] ImageJ is available at http://rsb.info.nih.gov/ij/

[5] WEKA is available at http://www.cs.waikato.ac.nz/~ml/WEKA/

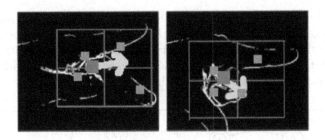

Fig. 4. Parameters extracted from two different handshapes

type the same letter. Training image capture keeps running until a second click is issued. This procedure is then repeated, several times, for all desired letters: usually, the more examples are input, the higher the achieved accuracy. After a special reserved key is pressed, the system enters the next phase, where an adaptive decision tree is induced (learned), and the user may start the finger-spelling section, in which no typing is needed. The learning module may be recalled whenever a wrong guess is detected by the user (the system types a wrong symbol - different from that which is being signed), just by typing (two times - one to start and other to stop collecting image frames) and simultane-ously signing the correct symbol. The ability of the system to incorporate new training instances and improve its performance during its operation phase is a differentiated feature of our incremental learning approach.

Besides the simple editor and the learning module, the prototype comprises a further digital image processing unit that pre-processes the image and extracts some attributes. The first image processing step involves the application of a So-bel edge detector. More sophisticated edge detectors, like Canny's, has also being tried, but limitations, due to real-time processing requirements, lead us to choose Sobel. Next, the image is binarized by using the iterative threshold technique, proposed by Riddler and Calvard [21]. An homogeneous, white, background (as in figure 2) and a fixed hand position were provided so that handtracking was not the issue in the current work.

Parameters extraction is based on image moments [16] with a novel approach that consists in dividing the image in equal-sized rectangular regions, and iter-atively calculating the image moments for each region. This strategy increases the parameter set with some local information, which may be important for dis-criminating some handshapes. Figure 4 illustrate 12 parameters that our method extracts from three different hand signs. The grid, in red, is placed in the center of mass of the image and a new center of mass (red rectangle), calculated on the points inside the grid, delivers the first two parameters (x and y coordinates of the center). The next parameters capture the direction of the hand (illus-trated as green arrows) and may easily be calculated as the standard deviation of the points with respect to the center of mass. The blue rectangles complete the parameter set, and correspond to the center of mass of each grid region.

Table 1. Comparative Results

	AdapTree	C4.5
Ratio of correctly classified instances	95.02%	95.23%
Learning Time	0.25s	0.29s

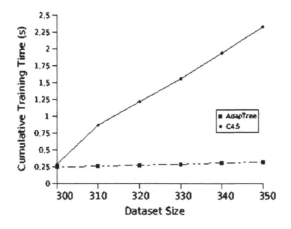

Fig. 5. Cumulative training time for an increment of 10 instances

6 Experiments

For a first test of the learning algorithm performance, we collected a few images
from 9 different signs and created some datasets in WEKA's file format (arff).
Using the WEKA benchmark utilities, our machine learning algorithm, Adap-
Tree, has been compared to Quinlan's C4.5, an state-of-art decision tree learning
algorithm. Table 1 presents the ratio of correctly classified instances (RCC) for
both algorithms, using WEKA's random split test, with a 66% cut, for a dataset
containing 270 instances (30 for each sign). This test randomly chooses 66% of
the dataset instances for training the learning scheme and applies the learned
model to the remaining 34% instances. Table 1 also shows the average training
time. These experiments indicates that the performance of AdapTree and C4.5
is not significantly different, in a non-incremental environment.

The graphic in figure 5 shows the cumulative training time when a set of
10 new training instances are presented to each of the compared algorithms.
In contrast to C4.5, AdapTree does not need to rebuild the tree, from scratch,
each time new instances are obtained. The superiority of AdapTree over C4.5,
regarding incremental learning, becomes evident in the graphic.

7 Conclusion

In this work we presented a prototype for a fingerspelling LIBRAS editor, an innovative way for parameter extraction based on the iterative calculation of image

moments and a new machine learning approach. Such learning schema was chosen because this work is part of a larger project that aims to develop incremental learning approaches, mixing symbolic and sub-symbolic learning strategies. The current solution still lacks some robustness in face of different context training instances, although, it has the advantage of being incremental allowing continuous training and adjustments. An indirect result of this project was the integration of different free-software packages into a single framework for the application of machine learning techniques into machine vision tasks, involving time-based devices (like webcams). Changing the learning algorithm is very easy, due to the integration with WEKA. A prototype based on artificial neural networks, for instance, may be easily achieved, using WEKA's implementation.

The prototype should now be enhanced with a handtracking phase, possibly based on skin-color and image differencing [11]. The next version of the prototype will be developed with the help of deaf specialists in order to determine a representative LIBRAS dataset of training instances to be captured from different signalers, and in several environment conditions, in order to form a huge database for the brazilian sign language, similar to the one already available for the american sign language [5].

References

1. Braffort, A.: Research on computer science and sign language: Ethical aspects. In: Gesture Workshop. (2001) 1–8
2. Schirmer, B.: Language and literacy development in children who are deaf. Macmillan Publishing Co, New York, NY (1994)
3. Schumeyer, R., Heredia, E., Barner, K.: Region of interest priority coding for sign language videoconferencing. In: IEEE First Workshop on Multimedia Signal Processing, Princeton (1997) 531–536
4. Woll, B., Sutton-Spence, R., Elton, F.: Multilingualism - the global approach to sign languages. In: The Sociolinguistics of Sign Languages. Cambridge University Press, Cambridge, UK (2001)
5. Martínez, A., Wilbur, R., Shay, R., Kak, A.: Purdue RVL-SLLL ASL database for automatic recognition of american sign language. In: Proc. IEEE International Conference on Multimodal Interfaces. (2002)
6. Pistori, H., Neto, J.J.: Decision tree induction using adaptive FSA (to appear). CLEI Electronic Journal (2004)
7. Erdem, U.M., Sclaroff, S.: Automatic detection of relevant head gestures in american sign language communication. In: Proceedings of the International Conference on Pattern Recognition - ICPR 2002, Québec, Canada (2002)
8. Freeman, W.T., Tanaka, K., Ohta, J., Kyuma, K.: Computer vision for computer games. In: 2nd International Conference on Automatic Face and Gesture Recognition, Killington, VT, USA (1996) 100–105
9. Fang, G., et al: Signer-independent continuous sign language recognition based on SRN/HMM. In: Gesture Workshop. (2001) 76–85
10. L.Bretzner, I.Laptev, T.Lindeberg: Hand gesture recognition using multi-scale colour features, hierarchical models and particle filtering. In: Proceedings of the Fifth IEEE International Conference on Automatic Face and Gesture Recognition (FGR'02), Washington, USA (2002) 423–428

11. Martin, J., Devin, V., Crowley, J.: Active hand tracking. In: In IEEE Third International Conference on Automatic Face and Gesture Recognition, FG '98, Nara, Japan (1998)
12. Al-Jarrah, O., Halawani, A.: Recognition of gestures in arabic sign language using neuro-fuzzy systems. Artificial Intelligence **133** (2001) 117–138
13. Stenger, B., Mendonça, P.S., Cipolla, R.: Model-based hand tracking using an unscented kalman filter. In: Proc. British Machine Vision Conference. Volume I., Manchester, UK (2001) 63–72
14. Davis, J., Shah, M.: Recognizing hand gestures. In: Proceedgins of the Third European Conference on Computer Vision (ECCV), Stockholm, Sweden (1994) 331–340
15. Kapuscinski, T., Wysocki: Hand gesture recognition for man-machine interaction. In: Proceedings of the Second International Workshop on Robot Motion and Control, Bukowy Dworek, Poland (2001) 91–96
16. Freeman, W.T., Anderson, D.B., Beardsley, P.A., Dodge, C.N., Roth, M., Weissman, C.D., Yerazunis, W.S., Kage, H., Kyuma, K., Miyake, Y., ichi Tanaka, K.: Computer vision for interactive computer graphics. IEEE Computer Graphics and Applications **18** (1998) 42–53
17. Martin, J., Crowley, J.L.: An appearance-based approach to gesture recognition. In: Proc. of 9th Int. Conf. on Image Analysis and Processing, Florence, Italy (1997)
18. Capovilla, F.C., Raphael, W.D.: Dicionário Enciclopédico Ilustrado Trilíngue da Língua de Sinais Brasileira. Editora da Universidade de São Paulo, São Paulo, Brasil (2001)
19. Neto, J.J.: Adaptative rule-driven devices - general formulation anda case study. In: CIAA'2001 Sixth International Conference on Implementation and Application of Automata, Pretoria, South Africa (2001) 234–250
20. Costa, E.R., Hirakawa, A.R., Neto, J.J.: An adaptive alternative for syntactic pattern recognition. In: Proceeding of 3rd International Symposium on Robotics and Automation, ISRA, Toluca, Mexico (2002) 409–413
21. Ridler, T.W., Calvard, S.: Picture thresholding using an iterative selection method. IEEE transactions on Systems, Man and Cybernetics (1978)

Recent Advances on Multi-agent Patrolling

Alessandro Almeida[1], Geber Ramalho[1], Hugo Santana[1], Patrícia Tedesco[1],
Talita Menezes[1], Vincent Corruble[2], and Yann Chevaleyre[2]

[1] Universidade Federal de Pernambuco, Centro de Informática
Cx. Postal 7851, 50732-970,Recife – PE Brasil
Phone: +55 8132718430
{all,glr,hps,pcart,trm}@cin.ufpe.br
[2] Université Paris 6, Laboratoire d'Informatique de Paris VI
Boîte 169 – 4 Place Jussieu75252, Paris Cedex 05
{Vincent.Corruble,Yann.Chevaleyre}@lip6.fr

Abstract. Patrolling is a complex multi-agent task, which usually requires
agents to coordinate their decision-making in order to achieve optimal performance of the group as a whole. In previous work, many patrolling strategies were
developed, based on different approaches: heuristic agents, negotiation mechanisms, reinforcement learning techniques, techniques based on graph-theory
and others. In this paper, we complement these studies by comparing all the approaches developed so far for this domain, using patrolling problem instances
that were not dealt with before (i.e. new map topologies). The final results constitute a valuable benchmark for this domain, as well as a survey of the strategies developed so far for this task.

Keywords: autonomous agents and multi-agent systems, coordination and patrolling

1 Introduction

Patrolling is the act of walking around an area in order to protect or supervise it [1].
Informally, a good patrolling strategy is one that minimizes the time lag between two
visits to the same location. Patrolling can be useful for domains where distributed
surveillance, inspection or control is required. For instance, patrolling agents can help
administrators in the surveillance of failures or specific situations in an Intranet [2] or
detect recently modified or new web pages to be indexed by search engines [3]. Patrolling can be performed by multiple agents, requiring coordinated behavior and
decision-making in order to achieve optimal global performance.

Despite its high potential utility and scientific interest, only recently multi-agent
patrolling has been rigorously studied. In the context of an international AI project,
we initiated pioneering work on this issue, proposing different agent architectures and
empirically evaluating them [4, 5, 6]. In this paper, we put together, summarize and
compare the recent advances, pointing out the benefits and disadvantages of each one,
as well as the situations where they are most appropriate. This kind of comparative
study of different AI paradigms for multi-agent patrolling has not yet been done.
Moreover, in order to provide a more precise and richer comparison of the current
approaches, we introduce novel patrolling scenarios corresponding to some environment topologies, which are thought to be representative instances of the task.

A.L.C. Bazzan and S. Labidi (Eds.): SBIA 2004, LNAI 3171, pp. 474–483, 2004.

Section 2 of this paper describes the patrolling task; section 3 presents various approaches to this task. The experimental results and comparative study are described in section 4. Finally, section 5 presents conclusions and discusses future research.

2 The Patrolling Task

In order to obtain a generic, yet precise, definition of the patrolling task, we represent the terrain being patrolled as a graph, where the nodes correspond to specific locations and the edges to possible paths, as illustrated in Fig. 3. The main advantage of adopting this abstract representation is that it can be easily mapped to many different domains, from terrains to computer networks. Given a graph, the patrolling task studied in the remainder of this paper consists in using agents moving at an equal speed to continuously visit its nodes, in a way that minimizes the interval between the visits to any node.

One of the contributions of our previous work [4] was the identification of *evaluation criteria* for patrolling, since no patrolling related works [7, 8] have proposed performance measures. Considering that a cycle is a simulation step, the *instantaneous node idleness* (or simply idleness) for a node n at a cycle t is the number of cycles elapsed since the last visit before t (i.e. the number of cycles the node n remained unvisited). The *instantaneous graph idleness* is the average idleness over all nodes in a given cycle. Finally, the *average idleness* is the mean of the instantaneous graph idleness over a t-cycle simulation. Another interesting measure is the *worst idleness*: the highest value of the instantaneous node idleness encountered during the whole simulation. In order to better evaluate the contribution of each agent when the population size varies, the idleness can be *normalized* by multiplying its absolute value by the number of agents divided by the number of nodes in the graph.

There are some variations in the patrolling task. For instance, the terrain may contain mobile obstacles or assign different priorities to some regions. In some cases, such as military simulations, agent communication can be forbidden.

3 Survey on Current Approaches

In this section, we give an overview of the approaches taken by our research groups in the investigation of the patrolling task. The current approaches for multi-agent patrolling are based on three different techniques: (1) *Operations research algorithms*, in particular those used for the Traveling Salesman Problem (TSP); (2) Non-learning Multi-Agent Systems (MAS), involving classic techniques for agent coordination and design; and (3) Multi-Agent Learning which, using Reinforcement Learning, allows the agents to continuously adapt their patrolling strategies . In this work we will not compare our findings to the results obtained in robot patrolling [9], since the latter results were rather concerned with dealing with challenges inherent to the complexity of the real world, such as the necessity for robots to recharge.

3.1 Pioneer Agents

The pioneer work on the patrolling problem, as formulated above, has been done by Machado *et al.* [4]. In their article, they proposed several multi-agent architectures varying parameters such as agent type (reactive vs. cognitive), agent communication (allowed vs. forbidden), coordination scheme (central and explicit vs. emergent), agent perception (local vs. global), decision-making (random selection vs. goal-oriented selection). The choice of the next node to visit is basically influenced by two factors: (1) node idleness, which can be either shared (generated by all agents) or individual (based on the visits of a single agent); (2) field of vision, which can be local (agent's neighborhood) or global (entire graph). The experiments they conducted showed two interesting facts: first, agents moving randomly achieved very bad results. Second, agents with absolutely no communication ability (and whose strategies consisted in moving towards the node with the highest idleness) performed nearly as well as the most complex algorithm they implemented.

In our experiments (Section 4), we will the compare the most efficient architecture of each approach with the following two agents: (a) *Conscientious Reactive*, whose next node to visit is the one with the highest individual idleness from its neighborhood; (b) *Cognitive Coordinated*, whose next node to visit is the one with the highest shared idleness from the whole graph, according to the suggestions given by a central coordinator. This coordinator is responsible for avoiding that more than one agent chooses the same next node.

3.2 TSP-Based Single-Cycle Approach

Consider a single agent patrolling over an area. The simplest strategy which comes to mind would be to find a cycle covering all the area, and then to make the agent travel around this cycle over and over. In our case, in which areas are represented by nodes in a graph, the cycle is defined as a closed-path starting and ending on the same node and covering all nodes possibly more than once. It was shown in [6, 10] that, for a single agent, the optimal strategy in terms of worst idleness is this cyclic-based one, where each cycle is calculated as the optimal solution for the Traveling Salesman Problem. The idea is then to reuse all the classic and solid results from the operations research and graph theory in determining the cycle.

One way to extend the single-agent cyclic strategy to the multi-agent case is to arrange agents on the same closed-path such that, when they start moving through it, all in the same direction, they keep an approximately constant gap between them. Although this multi-agent extension is not optimal, it can be shown [6, 10] that a group of agents performing it can achieve a performance, according to the worst idleness criterion, which is lower or equal to $3 \times opt + 4 \times \max_{ij}\{c_{ij}\}$, where opt is the optimal value for the worst idleness and c_{ij} is the length of the edge connecting nodes i and j. Fig. 1 illustrates two agents patrolling two graphs according to this TSP single-cycle approach. It is expected that this strategy will perform better in topologies like (a) than in (b), since the worst idleness is influenced by the longest edge (c_{ij}).

We call *Single-Cycle* the agents following this TSP single-cycle strategy. They will be compared with other agents in Section 4.

3.3 Heuristic Agents

In our initial work [4], a cognitive agent reaches a node using the shortest path. However, the average idleness of the graph would be lower if the agent had taken longer paths, which passed through idler nodes instead. Suppose an agent is located in node *v* (Fig. 2), and has chosen node *w* as objective. The shortest path is *v-a-w* (length of 100), which passes through node *a*, whose idleness is 10. However, the path *v-b-w*, which is just slightly longer (length of 101), passes through the idler node *b* (with idleness 99). This second path, which is much idler, should be chosen. That is the idea behind the *Pathfinder Agents* [5].

(a)   (b)

Fig. 1. TSP Single-cycle patrolling strategy.

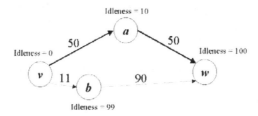

Fig. 2. Example of idleness vs. distance dilemma.

Besides improving the path-finding technique, we have also enhanced the agent's decision making. In previous work [5], the next-node choice criteria could be either random or based on node idleness, where an agent chose the node with the highest idleness. However, if the node with the highest idleness was too far from the agent, it would be better to choose a nearer node with high idleness. In other words, the choice of the goal node should be guided by a utility function that takes into account the cost (distance) and the reward (idleness). Imagine an agent located at node *v*. In this case, the node with the highest idleness (*w* with idleness 100) is relatively far from the agent (distance of 100). However, *b* (with idleness of 99) is much nearer (distance of 11). Node *b* should be chosen. This is the idea behind the *Heuristic Agents* [5]. These new variations of the decision-making process and the path-finding were applied to the previous pioneer agents [5].

In the experiments section we will compare other agents with the *Heuristic Pathfinder Cognitive Coordinated Agent*, which uses both advanced decision-making and path-finding, as well as the guidance of a central coordinator.

3.4 Negotiation Mechanisms for Patrolling

We removed the communication restrictions of the previous works [4], allowing the patrolling agents to exchange messages freely. These agents may need to interact to reach their objectives, either because they do not possess enough ability or resources to solve their problem, or because there are interdependences (both of resources and of results) between them [11]. In this approach, negotiations have been implemented as market-based auctions [11]. They are simple interaction scenarios, which makes them a good choice for reaching agreements [12].

In this light, a typical patrolling scenario has each agent randomly receiving graph nodes to patrol. Each agent tries to get a set of nodes very near to each other (to minimize the gap between two visits, and increase the agent's utility). When the agent detects a node that it cannot visit within a reasonable amount of time, it initiates an auction. The other agents (bidders) then check whether there is a node in their own set that can be traded by the offered one. If such a node is found, the corresponding bidder offers it as a bid. The auctioneer then chooses the best bid (i.e. the node that is nearest from the others in its set) and makes the deal with the bidder.

Following the incremental process suggested in [4], we developed new agents whose utility function only considers the distance between nodes. The main diference between them is the way the agents perform their auction. In our work, auctions are either one or two shot, private value and sealed-bid. We have investigated various market-based MAS architectures; the most eficient are detailed below:

1. Two-Shot-Bidder Agent (TSBA) – only bids for nodes that increase its utility function. It promotes a two-shot auction, and thus increases the chances of getting better offers.
2. Mediated Trade Bidder Agent (MTBA) – in this architecture, there is a broker agent, which informs the auctioneer which agents can be good bidders and which nodes they can trade.

We then enhanced these agents with the decision-making process for choosing the next node and the path finding algorithm presented in 3.3. This has resulted in the following architectures: *Heuristic Cooperative Bidder, Heuristic Mediated Trade Bidder* and *Heuristic Two-shots*. We have also developed the *Heuristic Pathfinder Cooperative Pathfinder Bidder, Heuristic Pathfinder Mediated Trade Bidder*, and *Heuristic Pathfinder Two-shots Bidder*. Section 4 shows the results obtained with these most efficient architectures.

3.5   Reinforcement Learning in Patrolling

Reinforcement learning (RL) is often characterized as the problem of learning how to map situations to actions, in order to maximize some numerical rewards [13]. In [14], we developed adaptive agents that learn to patrol using RL techniques. In order to enable these agents to adapt their patrolling strategies automatically via RL, we mapped the patrolling problem into the standard RL framework, namely the Markov Decision Process (MDP) formalism [13]. This consisted in defining a state and action space for each agent individually, and in developing proper models of instantaneous rewards which could lead to a satisfactory long term performance. Then, a standard RL algorithm, Q-Learning [13], was used to train individual agents.

Two different agent architectures were considered in this study: the Black-Box Learner Agent (BBLA), in which the agents do not communicate explicitly, and the Gray-Box Learner Agent (GBLA), in which the agents may communicate their intentions for future actions. The action space is the set of actions that let the agent navigate between adjacent nodes in the graph. For the BBLA, the state space is represented by: a) the node where the agent is located; b) the edge where it came from; c) the neighbor node which has the highest idleness; d) the neighbor node which has the lowest idleness. The GBLA has the same state representation, plus the information from the communication of intentions: e) the neighbor nodes which other agents intend to visit. These simple state definitions (comprising 10.000 and 200.000 possible states for BBLA and GBLA respectively for the maps studied) are feasible even with traditional Q-Learning implementations.

A function for the instantaneous reward, which showed to be particularly well suited for the average idleness criterion, was the idleness of the node visited by the agent. We showed that this reward model implements the concept of *selfish utility*, and we compared it with other utility models, such as the *team-game utility* and the *wonderful life utility* [14], that try to take into account indication of the global (systemic) performance. The selfish model, combined with the GBLA architecture, showed the best performance among the RL architectures so far.

In the experiments section we will compare *GBLA* with the other agents.

4 Experimental Results

This section presents the methodology used in order to make possible comparisons between the best MAS of each subsection of section 3. It details the set-up of the experiments, the proposed scenarios, the results obtained and a discussion about them.

4.1 Experimental Set-Up

All experiments were carried out using the same simulator, previously developed by our research groups. The experiments were performed on six maps, which are shown in Fig 3. Black blocks in the maps represent obstacles. White blocks are the nodes to be visited. The edges of the graphs are shown in blue. The best architectures of each approach, indicated in the last paragraph of sections 3.1 to 3.5, were compared for each Map. Each MAS was simulated with populations of five and fifteen agents. For each pair (map, architecture) we ran 10 experiments. At each experiment, all the agents start at the same node, but this starting node varies across the 10 experiments.

Regarding the problem of choosing the appropriate number of cycles for a simulation, a reasonable approach is to visit each node k times. In the worst case, a node will stay WI iterations without being visited, where WI is the worst idleness of the simulation. Hence, each simulation run for 15000 cycles, 15 times the experimentally observed WI (1000).

4.2 Results

Fig. 4 and Fig. 5 show the results for all maps and agent architectures, for populations of 5 and 15 agents, respectively. The y-axis indicates the average graph idleness: the smallest the idleness, the better is the performance of the architecture.

It is clear from these graphics that Single Cycle (SC) obtains the best performance for all cases, except in the islands map with 15 agents (where Heuristic Pathfinder Cognitive Coordinated (HPCC) wins) and in the corridor with 15 agents (where there

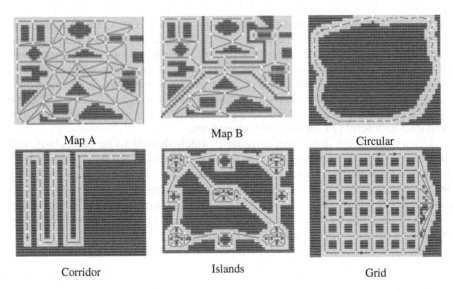

Fig. 3. Maps with different corresponding graph topologies on our simulator.

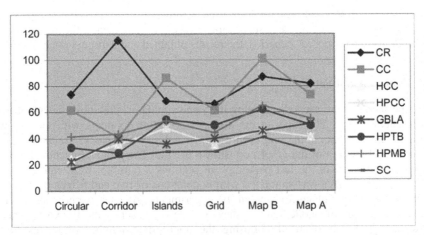

Fig. 4. Results for a population of five agents (where CR = Conscientious Reactive, CC = Cognitive Coordinated, HPCC = Heuristic Cognitive Coordinated, GBLA = Gray-Box Learner Agent, HPTB = Heuristic Pathfinder Two-shots Bidder, HPMB = Heuristic Pathfinder Mediated Trade Bidder, SC = Single-Cycle).

is a draw). On the other extreme, the pioneer agents, Conscientious Reactive (CR) and Cognitive Coordinated (CC), have the worst performances. Regarding the remaining architectures, for 5-agent population and all graphs, HPCC and Gray-Box Learner Agent (GBLA) have the second best performance (followed by Heuristic Pathfinder Two-shots Bidder (HPTB)). For 15 agents and all graphs, HPCC, HPTB and GBLA have an equivalent performance.

It is also interesting to analyze the influence of graph topologies and population size on architectures' performance. To understand these points, Fig. 6 shows the results using the normalized average idleness (Cf. Section 2), as well as its standard deviation. These results are the mean of the results of all maps.

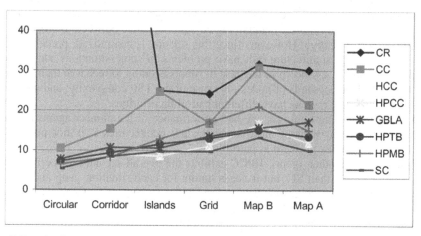

Fig. 5. Results for a population of fifteen agents. For sake of readability, we have hidden the first two results of CR, which were 73,71 and 107,01, respectively.

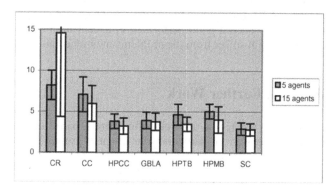

Fig. 6. Normalized average idleness with their standard deviations. These results are the mean of all maps.

With respect to graph topology influence, SC, GBLA and HPCC exhibit the best, and equivalent, performance variation (the standard deviation varies from 0.77 to 0.99). The negotiating agents' performance varies more according to the population size: HPTB has a standard deviation of 1.26 for 5 agents, and Heuristic Pathfinder Mediated Trade Bidder (HPMB), 1.63 for 15 agents. CC and CG are still the worst architectures from this perspective (their standard deviations go from 1.79 to 10.24). Finally, regarding population variation, SC and GBLA exhibit the most stable behavior, i.e., the same performance no matter the number of agents. The others vary their performance (for the best or the worse): adding agents to the population improves the normalized performance, but retracting agents, worsens it.

4.3 Discussion

The most striking finding is the outstanding performance of SC for the three discussed points of view (the only exception occurred in the island map, as theoretically expected, since this graph contains long edges). This excellent performance can be explained by its centralized and explicit coordination scheme (one agent following another in an optimum line and maintaining an equal distance between them), which is intuitively very effective. However, since this scheme is centralized, predefined and fixed, this kind of architecture will have problems in some situations such as: dynamic environment, as shown in the case of robots needing to recharge their batteries [9]; huge graphs (thousands of nodes), because of the TSP complexity; and patrolling task where different regions have different patrolling priorities.

Another interesting finding is the bad performance of the pioneer agents (CR and CC), indicating that without more sophisticated architectures it is not possible to tackle such a complex problem as patrolling.

Concerning the other agents, HPCC exhibits the overall second best performance. It is more adaptive than SC, but it needs tuning for each situation (map and population), to balance the weight of distance and idleness in path finding and decision-making. Like SC, HPCC has also limitations in huge graphs because of pathfinding complexity. GBLA, which has the third overall best performance (even slightly loosing for HPTB with 15 agents), shows a great adaptation capacity, even when the population size varies. Moreover, it is the only architecture using local information, which is a plausible scenario for some applications. The drawback of GBLA is its training cost, which can be prohibitive in huge graphs. The negotiating agents (HPTB and HPMB) do not show such a good performance, except in corridor and circular maps. However, they do not suffer from the problems mentioned above.

5 Conclusions and Further Work

Despite its vast applicative potential and scientific interest, patrolling has only fairly recently begun to be addressed. In particular, our research groups had been working on this task using different approaches [4, 5, 6, 10, 13], but had not yet compared them with a richer benchmark. This article presents an overview of the recent advances in patrolling and it introduces an original comparative study among them, pointing out benefits and disadvantages of each one. Such comparison serves not only as a benchmark and guideline for new multi-agent patrolling approaches, but also for improving the current ones.

In the near future, we intend to deepen our comparative study, finding better explanations for the current architecture behaviors. We also plan to introduce new scenarios and MAS architectures, in particular more dynamic scenarios, huge graphs, and graphs containing regions with different priorities.

References

1. Abate, F.R.: The Oxford Dictionary and Thesaurus: The Ultimate Language Reference for American Readers. Oxford Univ. Press (1996)

2. Andrade, R.d.C, Macedo, H.T., Ramalho, G.L., Ferraz, C.A.G.: Distributed Mobile Autonomous Agents in Network Management. Proceedings of International Conference on Parallel and Distributed Processing Techniques and Applications (2001)
3. Cho, J. Garcia-Molina, H.: Synchronizing a database to Improve Freshness. Proceedings of 2000 ACM International Conference on Management of Data (SIGMOD) (2000)
4. Machado Empirical Analysis of Alternative Architectures. Multi-Agent Based Simulation (2002) 155-170, A., Ramalho, G., Zucker, J.D., Drogoul, A.: Multi-Agent Patrolling: an
5. Almeida, A.: Patrulhamento Multi-Agente em Grafos com Pesos. MSc. dissertation. Universidade Federal de Pernambuco (2003)
6. Chevaleyre, Y.: The patrolling problem. Tech. Rep. of Univ. Paris 9. (2003) available at http://l1.lamsade.dauphine.fr/~chevaley/patrol
7. Pottinger, D.: Coordinated Unit Movement. Game Developer, Vol. January (1999) 42-51
8. Pottinger, D.: Implementing Coordinated Unit Movement. Game Developer, Vol. February (1999) 48-58
9. Sempé, F. Auto-organisation d'une collectivité de robots: application à l'activité de patrouille en présence de perturbations. PhD Thesis. Université Paris VI (2004)
10. Chevaleyre, Y. & Sempé, F. A theoretical analysis of multi-agent patrolling strategies. Submitted to the International Conference on Autonomous Agents and Multi-Agents Systems (AAMAS) (2004).
11. Faratin, P., Sierra, C., Jennings, N.: Using Similarity Criteria to Make Issue Trade-Offs in Automated Negotiations. Artificial Intelligence Journal, 2, (2002) 205-237
12. Faratin, P., Sierra, C., Jennings, N.: Negotiation Decisions Functions for Autonomous Agents. International Journal of Robotics and Autonomous Systems, 24, (1998), 159-182
13. Sutton, R., Barto, A.: Reinforcement Learning: An Introduction. Cambridge (1998)
14. Santana, H., Ramalho, G., Corruble, V., Ratitch, B.: Multi-Agent Patrolling with Reinforcement Learning. International Conference on Autonomous Agents and Multi-Agents Systems (AAMAS) (2004)

On the Convergence to and Location
of Attractors of Uncertain, Dynamic Games

Eduardo Camponogara*

Departamento de Automação e Sistemas, Universidade Federal de Santa Catarina
Caixa Postal 476, Florianópolis SC 88040-900, Brasil
camponog@das.ufsc.br

Abstract. The delegation of decision making to distributed control agents has been a standard approach to operating large, complex systems. The performance of these multi-agent systems depends as much on the decomposition of the overall operating task as on the interplay between the agents. To that end, game theory has served as a formalism to model multi-agent systems, understand the innerworking of their agents, and analyze issues of convergence (stability) and location of attractors (optimality). This paper delivers simple transformations and algorithms that allow altruistic agents to induce convergence to Nash equilibrium points, and draw these attractors closer to the set of Pareto efficient solutions, of dynamic games whose agents' problems cannot be anticipated.

1 Motivation

Having its roots in the pioneering research of Von Neumann and the insightful notion of equilibria later introduced by Nash, game theory has played a part in a number of scientific fields, ranging from the analysis of economic markets to the understanding of population growth [1, 2]. More recently, it has served as a tool to specify control policies for robots in dynamically changing environments [7], a model to design multi-agent systems and understand the interplay of their agents [3], and a formalism to analyze the operation of dynamic networks with networks of distributed control agents, in which the tasks of agents are specified separately rather than obtained from the decomposition of an overall task [4, 6].

Either in application domains or within the formalism of game theory, issues such as the existence of equilibria (Nash or fixed point) and algorithms for the agents that draw their decisions to these attractors are recurring themes. To that end, this paper extends our preceding work [8, 5] to the domain of uncertain, dynamic games, that is, dynamic games where the problems of the decision makers evolve in time. Section 2 presents the formalism of uncertain dynamic games, introducing simple yet effective problem transformations to i) stimulate convergence of the agents' iterative solutions to Nash equilibria (the altruistic factors for convergence) and ii) draw these attractors to optimal operating points known as Pareto efficient solutions (the altruistic factors for attractor location).

* Partially supported by CNPq (research grant number 552248/02-9).

A.L.C. Bazzan and S. Labidi (Eds.): SBIA 2004, LNAI 3171, pp. 484–493, 2004.

Section 3 narrows the focus to games whose agents' objectives are quadratic functions and looks into the issue of convergence. Section 4 tackles the issue of attractor location in uncertain quadratic games, providing a thorough analysis of convergence and rate of convergence of an algorithm that altruistic agents can implement to draw the attractor towards Pareto optimal solutions.

2   Background

This section introduces the essentials of (infinite) uncertain, dynamic games to pave the way for the following developments. In these games, the players can choose their decisions from an infinite set, their goals or pay-off functions cannot be fully anticipated, and their decisions evolve in time, in part due to the time-varying nature of their goals but also as a consequence of the iterative processes that they use to reach their goals. Time is divided in a sequence of non-overlapping time intervals or windows, indexed by variable t, during which the agents' goals are time-invariant, so switching between goals can occur only at the extremes of the time windows. Each of a set of M agents is told what has to be done but not how to reach its goal, i.e. the behavior of the agent is specified as an optimization problem. The agents' iterative search for the optimal solutions to their problems gives rise to a dynamic game. Thus, two issues of concern are *stability*, which refers to the convergence of the agents' decisions to fixed points (Nash equilibria), and *optimality*, which refers to the distance between the location of these attractors and the globally optimal solutions (the Pareto solutions). Hereafter, $x_m \in \Re^{n(m)}$ is the vector with the decisions under the authority of the m-th agent, where $n(m)$ is the dimension of agent m's decision vector, and $x = (x_1, \ldots, x_M) \in \Re^n$ is the vector of all decisions.

Definition 1. $\mathcal{P}_m = \{P_m^1, \ldots, P_m^{k(m)}\}$ *is agent m's family of problems, each of which has the form:*

$$P_m^k : \underset{x_m}{\text{Minimize}} \; f_m^k(x_m, y_m) \tag{1}$$

where: x_m is the vector with the decisions under control of the m-th agent; y_m is the vector with the decisions of the other agents; f_m^k is a twice continuously differentiable function; and $k(m)$ is the number of problems.

Definition 2. $\mathcal{F}_m = \{f_m^1, \ldots, f_m^{k(m)}\}$ *is agent m's set of cost functions.*

Definition 3. $P_m(t) \in \mathcal{P}_m$ *is a random variable with the problem being solved by agent m during time window t, and whose probability of taking on a particular value is given by the distribution Pr_m. (Thus, $Pr_m(P_m(t) = P_m^k)$ is the probability that agent m behaves according to P_m^k for the duration of interval t.) Correspondingly, $f_m(t) \in \mathcal{F}_m$ is a variable with the objective function of $P_m(t)$.*

Definition 4. $P(t)$ *is the random variable that results from the aggregation of the elements of $\{P_m(t)\}$, that is, $P(t) = (P_1(t), \ldots, P_M(t)) \in \mathcal{P} = \mathcal{P}_1 \times \ldots \times \mathcal{P}_M$.*

Assumption 1 *The reaction set $R_m(t, y_m)$ of agent m to the decisions of the others consists, for the length of window t, of the solutions to $P_m(t)$ that satisfy the first-order optimality conditions, i.e. $R_m(t, y_m) = \{x_m : \nabla_{x_m} f_m(t, x_m, y_m) = 0\}$. Further, the agent's reaction function $G_m(t)$ arises from the choice of one element from $R_m(t)$, thus $x_m(t, k+1) = G_m(t, y_m(t, k))$ is the resulting iterative process, where $x_m(t, k)$ is the k-th iterate of x_m (within time window t) and $G_m(t)$ is a function such that $G_m(t, y_m) \in R_m(t, y_m)$.*

Definition 5. *$G(t) = (G_1(t), \ldots, G_M(t))$ is the parallel, iteration function induced by the reactions of M agents, within time window t, implying that the parallel iterative process is $x(t, k+1) = G(t, x(t, k))$, where $x(t, k)$ denotes the k-th iterate of the decisions of the agents.*

From the above definitions, a Nash equilibrium point can be defined as a vector $x^*(t)$ such that $x^*(t) = G^t(x^*(t))$, meaning that no agent has any incentive to deviate from its decision $x_m^*(t)$ provided that the other agents stick to their decisions. Often we will use the time index t as a superscript rather than a function parameter, e.g. G^t might be used in place of $G(t)$. Convergence depends as much on the agents' problems as on the iterative processes they use to solve their problems. One or more agents can promote, possibly induce, convergence to a Nash point by performing simple transformations to their problems. The factors that render these transformations are henceforth referred to as altruistic factors for convergence and the agents that implement them, altruistic agents.

Definition 6. *A vector $\alpha_m \in \Re^{n(m)}$, $\alpha_m > 0$, is referred to as agent m's altruistic factor for convergence. Agent m is competitive if $\alpha_m = 1$.*

Definition 7. *$\alpha = (\alpha_1, \ldots, \alpha_M)$ is the vector of all convergence factors.*

Proposition 1. *If agent m uses convergence factor α_m, during time window t, so as to replace $f_m(t) \in \mathcal{F}_m$ by $\tilde{f}_m(t) = f_m(t, D(\alpha_m)^{-1}x_m, y_m)$, where $D(\alpha_m)$ is a diagonal matrix of dimension $n(m) \times n(m)$ whose diagonal corresponds to the entries of α_m, then the agent's reaction becomes $x_m^{t,k+1} = D(\alpha_m)G_m^t(y_m^{t,k})$.*

Definition 8. *$G_m^t(\alpha_m, y_m) = D(\alpha_m)G_m^t(y_m)$ is agent m's iteration function under altruism.*

Proposition 2. *Let $\alpha = (\alpha_1, \ldots, \alpha_M)$ be a vector with the altruistic factors. If the agents modify their problems according to Proposition 1, G^t is Lipschitz continuous, and $\|\alpha\|_\infty < 1$, then the iterative process effective within window t, $x^{t,k+1} = D(\alpha)G^t(x^{t,k})$, becomes more contractive by a factor of at least $\|\alpha\|_\infty$.*

In view of the above developments, the altruistic agent m can promote convergence and increase the rate of convergence by choosing a suitable factor α_m. Not unlike the convergence factors, altruistic agents can play a part in the issue of optimality by transforming their problems with altruistic factors for location.

Definition 9. *For the m-th agent, a vector $\beta_m \in \Re^{n(m)}$ is referred to as its altruistic factor for attractor location. Agent m remains competitive if $\beta_m = 0$.*

Definition 10. $\beta = (\beta_1, \ldots, \beta_M)$ *is the vector with the factors for attractor location of all the agents.*

Proposition 3. *If the m-th agent applies the altruistic factor β_m to replace its objective function $f_m(t)$ by $\tilde{f}_m(t) = f_m(t, x_m - \beta_m, y_m)$, then its reaction becomes $x_m^{t,k+1} = G_m^t(y_m^{t,k}) + \beta_m$.*

Definition 11. $G_m^t(\beta_m, y_m) = G_m^t(y_m) + \beta_m$ *is agent m's iteration function under altruism for attractor location.*

Proposition 4. *Let $\beta^t = (\beta_1^t, \ldots, \beta_M^t)$ be a vector with the altruistic factors for attractor-location within time window t. (The competitive agent m keeps $\beta_m^t = 0$.) If the agents modify their problems as delineated in Proposition 3, then the resulting iterative process inherits the same contraction properties of the original process while, on the other hand, the attractor is relocated at the point $x^*(t, \beta)$ that solves the equation $x = G^t(x) + \beta^t$.*

According to the above proposition, the convergence properties of the iterative process are invariant to the influence of the altruistic factors for location. This allows an altruistic agent m to search within the space of β_m for improved solutions without meddling with convergence.

3   Uncertain, Quadratic Games

Quadratic games are a special case of the general class of games where the agents' objectives are quadratic functions, whose definition and specifics follow below.

Definition 12. *In the domain of uncertain, quadratic games, each element of $\mathcal{P}_m$ is of the form:*

$$P_m^k : \underset{x_m}{\text{Minimize}} \; f_m^k = \tfrac{1}{2} x^T A_m^k x + {b_m^k}^T x + c_m^k \tag{2}$$

where: x_m is the vector with agent m's decision variables; $x = (x_1, \ldots, x_M)$ is the vector with all of the decisions; A_m^k is a symmetric and positive definite matrix; b_m^k is a vector; and c_m^k is a scalar.

The decomposition of A_m^k into submatrices and b_m^k into subvectors allow us to put (2) into the form:

$$P_m^k : \underset{x_m}{\text{Minimize}} \; \tfrac{1}{2} \sum_{i=1}^{M} \sum_{j=1}^{M} x_i^T A_{m,i,j}^k x_j + \sum_{i=1}^{M} {b_{m,i}^k}^T x_i + c_m^k \tag{3}$$

With the aim of facilitating the developments, the random variable $P_m(t)$ with the problem for window t will be replaced by the triple $(A_m(t), b_m(t), c_m(t))$. Then the iterative process of agent m for the length of window t becomes:

$$x_m^{t,k+1} = G_m^t(y_m^{t,k}) = -A_{m,m,m}(t)^{-1} [\sum_{j \neq m} A_{m,m,j}(t) x_j^{t,k} + b_{m,m}(t)]. \tag{4}$$

By aggregating the iterative processes of all the agents we obtain the overall iterative process G^t, which consist of the iterative solution of the linear equation:

$$A(t)x^{t,k+1} = -B(t)x^{t,k} - b(t) \tag{5}$$

where: $A(t) = diag(A_{1,1,1}(t), \ldots, A_{M,M,M}(t))$, $K(t) = [A_{m,m,j}(t) : m = 1, \ldots,$ M, $j = 1, \ldots, M]$, $B(t) = K(t) - A(t)$, and $b(t) = [b_{1,1}(t) \ldots b_{M,M}(t)]^T$. The solution to (5) leads to the iterative process:

$$x^{t,k+1} = G^t(x^{t,k}) = -A(t)^{-1}[B(t)x^{t,k} + b(t)]. \tag{6}$$

3.1   Inducing Convergence

In the event of agent m becoming altruistic, its iterative process takes the form:

$$x_m^{t,k+1} = G_m^t(\alpha_m, y_m^{t,k}) = -D(\alpha_m)A_{m,m,m}(t)^{-1}[\sum_{j \neq m} A_{m,m,j}(t)x_j^{t,k} + b_{m,m}(t)].$$

The aggregation of the iterative processes induced by altruistic agents, where the competitive agent m sets $\alpha_m = 1$, consists of solving the equation $A(t)D(\alpha)^{-1}$ $x^{t,k+1} = -B(t)x^{t,k} - b(t)$, which leads to the overall iterative process $G^t(\alpha)$:

$$x^{t,k+1} = G^t(\alpha, x^{t,k}) = -D(\alpha)A(t)^{-1}[B(t)x^{t,k} + b(t)]. \tag{7}$$

Proposition 5. *If $H = D(\alpha)A(t)^{-1}B(t)$ has $|||H||| < 1$, for a matrix norm $||| \bullet |||$ induced by some vector norm $|| \bullet ||$, then the iterative process (7) induces a contraction mapping that converges linearly to an attractor $x^*(t, \alpha)$.*

This proposition asserts that the agents can induce convergence, for the sake of stability, by setting sufficiently small values to their altruistic factors $\{\alpha_m\}$.

4   Relocating Attractors in Quadratic Games

This section focuses on the issue of moving the attractor of a convergent, quadratic game towards Pareto efficient solutions. It looks into the specifics of altruistic factors, analyzes the influence of these factors on the attractor's location, and then delivers an algorithm to draw an attractor to the closest location to the Pareto optimal set, according to a criterion that quantifies closeness. An altruistic agent m for attractor location will solve a variant of its original problem:

$$P_m(t, \beta_m) : \text{Minimize } \tfrac{1}{2} \sum_{i=1}^{M} \sum_{j=1}^{M} [x_i - \beta_{m,i}]^T A_{m,i,j}(t)[x_j - \beta_{m,j}] +$$
$$x_m \quad + \sum_{i=1}^{M} b_{m,i}(t)^T [x_i - \beta_{m,i}] + c_m(t) \tag{8}$$

where $\beta_{m,m} = \beta_m$ is the vector with agent m's altruistic factor and $\beta_{m,j} = 0$ for all $j \neq m$, and the remaining variables and parameters are identical to those of $P_m(t)$. The iterative solution of problem $P_m(t, \beta_m)$ gives rise to the agent's iterative process, namely:

$$
\begin{aligned}
x_m^{t,k+1} = G_m^t(\beta_m, y_m^{t,k}) = \\
= -A_{m,m,m}(t)^{-1}[\sum_{j \neq m} A_{m,m,j}(t)x_j^{t,k} + b_{m,m}(t)] + \beta_m.
\end{aligned}
\tag{9}
$$

As in the previous section, the full iterative process $G^t(\beta)$, which spells out the way the altruistic agents behave assuming that any competitive agent m holds $\beta_m = 0$, can be obtained from the equation $A(t)[x^{t,k+1} - \beta] = -B(t)x^{t,k} - b(t)$, where $A(t)$, $B(t)$, and $b(t)$ were defined in the preceding section, and $\beta = (\beta_1, \dots, \beta_M)$. The corresponding iterative process is:

$$
x^{t,k+1} = G^t(\beta, x^{t,k}) = -A(t)^{-1}[B(t)x^{t,k} + b(t)] + \beta.
\tag{10}
$$

For every $P(t) \in \mathcal{P}$, we will assume that the corresponding $A(t)$ and $B(t)$ satisfy $|||A(t)^{-1}B(t)||| < 1$, for some matrix norm $||| \bullet |||$ induced by some vector norm $|| \bullet ||$, which ensures that G^t as well as $G^t(\beta)$ are contraction mappings. In turn, this assumption guarantees that the agents' iterative processes are convergent within any time window.

4.1   Predicting the Location of the Attractor

By rearranging the terms of (10), the location of the attractor $x^*(t, \beta)$ can be expressed as a linear function of its original location (when $\beta = 0$) and the elements of $\{\beta_m : m = 1, \dots, M\}$. Formally, the location of the attractor is:

$$
\begin{aligned}
x^*(t, \beta) = -[I + A(t)^{-1}B(t)]^{-1}[A(t)^{-1}b(t) - \beta] = x^*(t, 0) + Z(t)\beta = \\
= x^*(t, 0) + Z_1(t)\beta_1 + \dots + Z_M(t)\beta_M.
\end{aligned}
\tag{11}
$$

Notice that $[I + A(t)^{-1}B(t)]$ admits an inverse because $|||A(t)^{-1}B(t)||| < 1$. Let $\Psi \subseteq \{1, \dots, M\}$ denote the set with the ids of the agents that behave altruistically. These agents can organize themselves to learn their individual influence on the attractor's location: for each $m \in \Psi$, agent m can systematically perturb the value of each entry of β_m, sense the location of the resulting attractor $x^*(t, \beta)$, and then compute Z_m^t from these measurements. (Notice that the altruistic agents can identify (11) by just sensing the location of the attractor, without having to be informed about the other agents' prevailing problems.)

4.2   Minimizing the Expected Value of the Agents' Objectives

Because multi-objective problems do not have one optimal value, but rather a set of nondominated solutions, the choice between Pareto efficient solutions is up to the decision-maker. One way of improving the location of the attractor is to minimize the expected value of a function of the agents' objectives, another is the maximization of the minimum decrease of their objectives. We have conducted full-fledged analyses of both criteria, including algorithms and conditions for convergence, but herein we focus on the former metric. The task of minimizing the expected value of the agents' cost functions can be expressed as:

$$\tilde{P}(t) : \underset{\beta^t}{\text{Minimize}} \ \sum_{m=1}^{M} E_{Pr_m} \left[w_m f_m(t, x^*(t, \beta^t)) \right] \tag{12}$$

where: $w = (w_1, \ldots, w_M) \in \Re^M_+$ is a vector with non-negative weights spelling out the relative importance of the agents' objectives; $f_m(t)$ is the variable with agent m's problem, whose probability of being f^k_m during time window t is $p^k_m = Pr_m(P_m(t) = P^k_m)$; $\beta^t = [\beta^t_1, \ldots, \beta^t_M]$ is the vector with altruistic factors; and $x^*(t, \beta^t)$ is the location of the attractor according to (11). Through algebraic manipulation of (12), $\tilde{P}(t)$ can be recast as:

$$\tilde{P}(t) : \underset{\beta(t)}{\text{Minimize}} \ \tilde{f}(t, \beta(t)) = \tfrac{1}{2}\beta(t)^T \left[\sum_{m=1}^{M} w_m \sum_{k=1}^{k(m)} p^k_m Z(t)^T A^k_m Z(t) \right] \beta(t) +$$

$$\left[\sum_{m=1}^{M} w_m \sum_{k=1}^{k(m)} p^k_m \left(b^k_m + A^k_m{}^T x^* \right)^T Z(t) \right] \beta(t) +$$

$$\sum_{m=1}^{M} w_m \sum_{k=1}^{k(m)} p^k_m \left[\tfrac{1}{2} x^{*T} A^k_m x^* + b^k_m{}^T x^* + c^k_m \right]$$

where $x^* = x^*(t, 0)$. For a suitable matrix $\tilde{A}(t)$, vector $\tilde{b}(t)$, and scalar $\tilde{c}(t)$, $\tilde{P}(t)$ can be put in a more compact form:

$$\tilde{P}(t) : \underset{\beta(t)}{\text{Minimize}} \ \tilde{f}(t, \beta(t)) = \tfrac{1}{2}\beta(t)^T \tilde{A}(t)\beta(t) + \tilde{b}(t)^T \beta(t) + \tilde{c}(t) \tag{13}$$

It is worth pointing out that $Z(t)$ has full column rank—notice that that $Z(t)$ is a subset of the columns of $[I + A(t)^{-1}B(t)]^{-1}$. This remark and the fact that A^k_m is positive definite, for all m and k, lead us to conclude that $\tilde{A}(t)$ is positive definite.

Two standing issues are the computational cost to put together $\tilde{P}(t)$ from the elements of $\mathcal{P}$ and its distributed solution by altruistic agents. With respect to the first issue, it is simple to deduce that the number of arithmetic operations (additions and multiplications) to obtain $\tilde{A}^t$, $\tilde{b}^t$, and $\tilde{c}^t$ is of the order $O(4Mkn^3)$, where $k = \max\{k(m) : m = 1, \ldots, M\}$. If the altruistic agents employ Strassen's algorithm for matrix multiplication and share the computational burden, the cost can be reduced to $O(4\lceil M/|\Psi|\rceil kn^{2.81})$ per altruistic agent.

After obtaining $\tilde{P}(t)$, the altruistic agents can solve this problem by coordinating their effort: in turns, each agent m computes β^t_m to reduce $\tilde{f}(t)$ and then implements the revised altruistic factor in its iterative process, thereby drawing the attractor to an improved location. To compute β^t_m, agent m solves a reduced form of $\tilde{P}(t)$:

$$\tilde{P}_m(t, \beta^t) : \underset{\beta^t_m}{\text{Minimize}} \ \tfrac{1}{2}\beta(t)^T \tilde{A}(t)\beta(t) + \tilde{b}(t)^T \beta(t) + \tilde{c}(t) \\ \text{where} : \beta^t_k \text{ is held constant for all } k \neq m \tag{14}$$

In what follows, we formalize the procedure outlined above and demonstrate that the series of solutions yielded by the agents, as they solve the set of problems $\{\tilde{P}_m(t, \beta^t) : m \in \Psi\}$, converges to a solution to $\tilde{P}(t)$. Theoretical insights into the rate of converge are also established.

Procedure 1: Solving $\{\tilde{P}_m(t, \beta^t) : m \in \Psi\}$

- The altruistic agents compute the elements of $\{Z_m^t : m \in \Psi\}$.
- The agents compute $\tilde{A}^t$, $\tilde{b}^t$, and $\tilde{c}^t$ to assemble $\tilde{P}^t$.
- Let the iteration index be $k = 0$ and set $\beta^{t,k} = 0$.
- The agents take turns, in any sequence, each time performing the steps:
  - Let $m \in \Psi$ correspond to the agent of the turn.
  - Agent m solves $\tilde{P}_m(t, \beta^{t,k})$ obtaining an optimal solution β_m^t.
  - Obtain $\beta^{t,k+1}$ from $\beta^{t,k}$ by replacing $\beta_m^{t,k}$ with β_m^t and set $k \leftarrow k+1$.
  - Agent m implements the revised β_m^t in its iteration function, allowing the agents to reach the improved attractor $x^*(t, \beta^{t,k+1})$.
  - Agent m transfers the turn to the next agent in the sequence.

The proposition and its corollary that follows establish the rate at which the solution iterates produced by the altruistic agents converge to a solution to $\tilde{P}(t)$.

Proposition 6. *Consider a dynamic game whose iteration function G^t is contractive. Let $\{\beta^{t,k}\}$ be the sequence of iterates produced by the altruistic agents as they follow Procedure 1, but in which they schedule their iterations so that agent m runs if and only if $\|\nabla_{\beta_m^t} \tilde{f}(t, \beta^{t,k})\|_\infty = \|\nabla_{\beta^t} \tilde{f}(t, \beta^{t,k})\|_\infty$. If the agents use the steepest-descent algorithm and compute the optimal step to solve $\tilde{P}_m(t)$, then $\tilde{f}(t, \beta^{t,k+1}) \le \left(1 - \frac{1}{n} \frac{\lambda_{min}}{\lambda_{max}}\right) \tilde{f}(t, \beta^{t,k})$, where λ_{min} is the minimum eigenvalue of $\tilde{A}(t)$ and λ_{max} is its maximum eigenvalue.*

Proof. The altruistic agents succeed in following Procedure 1 since G^t is contractive, rendering (11) a precise prediction of the attractor's location. Thus the value of $\tilde{f}(t, \beta^t)$ predicted by β^t will be the same attained at the attractor $x^*(t, \beta^t)$. This allows the analysis to be confined to the sequence $\{\beta^{t,k}\}$. Without loss of generality, we can drop the index t and assume for the sake of simplicity that $\tilde{f}$, as defined in $\tilde{P}(t)$, is minimized at $\beta^* = 0$ and that $\tilde{f}(\beta^*) = 0$. Thus:

$$\tilde{f}(\beta) = \tfrac{1}{2}\beta^T Q\beta, \ \ \nabla\tilde{f}(\beta) = Q\beta, \text{ and } \nabla^2\tilde{f}(\beta) = Q,$$

where $Q = \tilde{A}(t)$ is symmetric and positive definite. Let $m \in \Psi$ correspond to the agent of the turn. Its iteration can be described by:

$$\beta^{k+1} = \beta^k - \delta^k I_m \nabla\tilde{f}_k \tag{15}$$

where: $\tilde{f}_k = \tilde{f}(\beta^k)$; I_m is an $n \times n$ diagonal matrix, such that $I_m \nabla\tilde{f}_k = [0, \ldots, 0, \nabla_{\beta_m} \tilde{f}_k, 0, \ldots, 0]$ (i.e., I_m projects the gradient onto the space of β_m); and δ^k is the step in the direction $-I_m \nabla\tilde{f}_k$. For this problem, (15) becomes:

$$\beta^{k+1} = \beta^k - \delta^k I_m Q\beta^k = (I - \delta^k I_m Q)\beta^k \tag{16}$$

Denote $g^k = Q\beta^k$ and $h^k = I_m Q\beta^k$. If $h^k = 0$, then agent m cannot improve the current solution β^k. So we assume that $h^k \neq 0$, making this iteration an element of $\{\beta^{t,k}\}$. First, we compute the optimal step δ^k as follows:

$$
\frac{d}{d\delta^k} \tilde{f}(\beta^k - \delta^k h^k) = \frac{d}{d\delta^k} \left[\frac{1}{2}(\beta^k - \delta^k h^k)^T Q (\beta^k - \delta^k h^k) \right]
$$

$$
= \frac{d}{d\delta^k} \left[\frac{1}{2} \beta^{k^T} Q\beta^k - \delta^k h^{k^T} Q\beta^k + \frac{1}{2}(\delta^k)^2 h^{k^T} Q h^k \right]
$$

$$
= -h^{k^T} Q\beta^k + \delta^k h^{k^T} Q h^k = 0
$$

which implies that the optimal step is $\delta^k = \frac{h^{k^T} Q\beta^k}{h^{k^T} Q h^k} > 0$. From the step δ^k, the value of the objective at the next iterate can be computed:

$$
\tilde{f}(\beta^{k+1}) = \frac{1}{2} \left[\beta^k - \delta^k h^k \right] Q \left[\beta^k - \delta^k h^k \right]
$$

$$
= \frac{1}{2} \left[\beta^{k^T} Q\beta^k - 2\delta^k h^{k^T} Q\beta^k + (\delta^k)^2 h^{k^T} Q h^k \right]
$$

$$
= \frac{1}{2} \left[\beta^{k^T} Q\beta^k - 2 \left(\frac{h^{k^T} Q\beta^k}{h^{k^T} Q h^k} \right) h^{k^T} Q\beta^k + \left(\frac{h^{k^T} Q\beta^k}{h^{k^T} Q h^k} \right)^2 h^{k^T} Q h^k \right]
$$

$$
= \frac{1}{2} \left[\beta^{k^T} Q\beta^k - \frac{(h^{k^T} g^k)^2}{h^{k^T} Q h^k} \right] = \left[1 - \frac{(h^{k^T} g^k)^2}{(\beta^{k^T} Q\beta^k)(h^{k^T} Q h^k)} \right] \frac{\beta^{k^T} Q\beta^k}{2}
$$

$$
= \left[1 - \frac{(g^{k^T} I_m g^k)^2}{(g^{k^T} Q^{-1} g^k)(g^{k^T} I_m Q I_m g^k)} \right] \tilde{f}(\beta^k). \tag{17}
$$

Because Q is symmetric, it admits a decomposition $Q = S^T D S$, where $S^T = S^{-1}$ and $D = diag(\lambda_1, ..., \lambda_M)$, with λ_m being an eigenvalue of Q. ($n(m) = 1$ for each agent m and $M = n$.) Substituting the decomposition for Q in (17) we obtain:

$$
\tilde{f}(\beta^{k+1}) = \left[1 - \frac{(g^{k^T} I_m g^k)^2}{(g^{k^T} S^T D^{-1} S g^k)(g^{k^T} I_m S^T D S I_m g^k)} \right] \tilde{f}(\beta^k)
$$

$$
= \left[1 - \frac{(g^{k^T} I_m g^k)^2}{((\tilde{g}^k)^T D^{-1} \tilde{g}^k)((\hat{g}^k)^T D \hat{g}^k)} \right] \tilde{f}(\beta^k) \tag{18}
$$

where $\tilde{g}^k = S g^k$ and $\hat{g}^k = S I_m g^k$. We can deduce from (18) that

$$
\tilde{f}(\beta^{k+1}) \leq \left[1 - \frac{(g^{k^T} I_m g^k)^2}{\frac{1}{\lambda_{min}}((\tilde{g}^k)^T \tilde{g}^k)\lambda_{max}((\hat{g}^k)^T \hat{g}^k)} \right] \tilde{f}(\beta^k)
$$

$$
= \left[1 - \frac{(g^{k^T} I_m g^k)^2}{\frac{\lambda_{max}}{\lambda_{min}}(g^{k^T} g^k)(g^{k^T} I_m g^k)} \right] \tilde{f}(\beta^k)
$$

$$
= \left[1 - \left(\frac{\lambda_{min}}{\lambda_{max}} \right) \left(\frac{g^{k^T} I_m g^k}{g^{k^T} g^k} \right) \right] \tilde{f}(\beta^k)
$$

$$\leq \left[1 - \left(\frac{\lambda_{min}}{\lambda_{max}}\right)\left(\frac{\|\nabla_{\beta_m}\tilde{f}_k\|_\infty^2}{n\|\nabla\tilde{f}_k\|_\infty^2}\right)\right]\tilde{f}(\beta^k) = \left[1 - \frac{1}{n}\frac{\lambda_{min}}{\lambda_{max}}\right]\tilde{f}(\beta^k)$$

where λ_{min} is the minimum eigenvalue of Q and λ_{max} is its maximum.   □

Corollary 1. *The altruistic agents produce a sequence of iterates* $\{\beta^{t,k}\}$ *that induces linear convergence of the sequence* $\{\tilde{f}(t, \beta^{t,k})\}$ *to the optimal objective* $\tilde{f}(t, \beta^*(t))$ *at the rate* $\left(1 - \frac{1}{n}\frac{\lambda_{min}}{\lambda_{max}}\right)$.

The corollary shows that the rate of convergence depends on $\tilde{P}(t)$ and its decomposition in $\{\tilde{P}_m(t)\}$: convergence speed increases as the agents' influences on $\tilde{f}(t)$ become more homogeneous; and the relative effort of each altruistic agent tends to decrease as the number of agents increases, if compared to the effort of solving $\tilde{P}(t)$ with a single agent, but the price is slower convergence rate.

5   Final Remarks

The developments heretofore have addressed the issues of convergence to and location of attractors in uncertain, dynamic games with emphasis on quadratic games. Simple, but effective problem transformations have been designed for altruistic agents that intend to induce convergence and improve the location of attractors, in particular an algorithm was designed for quadratic games whose convergence speed was examined. For quadratic games, we have already developed but not yet published a convergent algorithm that maximizes the minimum decrease in the objective of all or a subset of the agents, and also provided applications in model predictive control. For general games, we have conceived a trust-region-based algorithm whose convergence properties are under investigation.

References

1. Aumann, R. J., Hart, S. (Editors): Handbook of Game Theory with Economic Applications, Vol. 1. North-Holland, Amesterdan (1992)
2. Basar, T., Olsder, G. J.: Dynamic Noncooperative Game Theory. Society for Industrial and Applied Mathematics, Philadelphia, PA (1999)
3. Bowling, M., Veloso, M. M.: Rational and convergent learning in stochastic games. In Proc. of the 17th Int. Joint Conf. on Artificial Intelligence (2001) 1021–1026
4. Camponogara, E., Jia, D., Krogh, B. H., Talukdar, S. N.: Distributed model predictive control. IEEE Control Systems Magazine **22** (2002) 44–52
5. Camponogara, E.: Altruistic agents in dynamic games. In Advances in Artificial Intelligence, Lecture Notes in Artificial Intelligence **2507** (2002) 74–84
6. Camponogara, E., Talukdar, S.: Designing communication networks for distributed control agents. European Journal of Operational Research **153** (2004) 544–563
7. LaValle, S. M.: Robot motion planning: a game-theoretic foundation. Algorithmica **26** (2000) 430–465
8. Talukdar, S. N., Camponogara, E.: Network control as a distributed, dynamic game. In Proc. of the 34th Hawaii Int. Conf. on System Sciences, IEEE CS Press (2001)

Norm Consistency in Electronic Institutions

Marc Esteva[1], Wamberto Vasconcelos[2],
Carles Sierra[1], and Juan A. Rodríguez-Aguilar[1]

[1] Institut d'Investigació en Intel·ligència Artificial, CSIC, Campus UAB
08193 Bellaterra, Spain
{marc,sierra,jar}@iiia.csic.es
[2] Dept. of Computing Science, University of Aberdeen
AB24 3UE, Aberdeen, UK
wvasconc@csd.abdn.ac.uk

Abstract. We elaborate on the verification of properties of electronic institutions, a formalism to define and analyse protocols among agents with a view to achieving global and individual goals. We formally define two kinds of norms, *viz.*, the *integrity norms* and *obligations*, and provide a computational approach to assess whether an electronic institution is *normatively consistent*, that is, we can determine whether its norms prevent norm-compliant executions from happening. For this we strongly rely on the analysis of the dialogues that may occur as agents interact.

1 Introduction

An important aspect in the design of heterogeneous multiagent systems concerns the *norms* that should constrain and influence the behaviour of its individual components [1–3]. Electronic institutions have been proposed as a formalism to define and analyse protocols among agents with a view to achieving global and individual goals [4, 5]. Norms are a central component of electronic institutions. As such, it is fundamental to guarantee that they are not wrongly specified, leading to unexpected executions of electronic institutions, and that an electronic institution indeed complies with its norms.

In this paper we propose a definition for norms and a means of assessing whether an electronic institution is *normatively consistent*. In other words, given an electronic institution specification, we want to determine whether its norms prevent norm-compliant executions from taking place. For this purpose we strongly rely on the analysis of the dialogues that may occur as agents interact by exchanging illocutions in an electronic institution. Since the execution of an electronic institution can be regarded as a multi-agent dialogue, we can analyse such dialogue to assess whether it abides by the institutional norms. Hence, execution models of electronic institutions can be obtained as dialogue models. Thus, our approach can be regarded as a model checking process based on the construction of models for the enactment of electronic institutions. Hereafter, the purpose of the verification process is to evaluate whether such models satisfy the institutional norms.

A.L.C. Bazzan and S. Labidi (Eds.): SBIA 2004, LNAI 3171, pp. 494–505, 2004.
© Springer-Verlag Berlin Heidelberg 2004

In the next section we define the components of an electronic institution. In Section 3 we introduce a precise definition of norms and subsequently show how they can be verified. Finally in Section 4 we present our conclusions, compare our research with related work and give directions for future work.

2   Electronic Institutions

Electronic institutions (EIs) structure agent interactions, establishing what agents are permitted and forbidden to do as well as the consequences of their actions. Next, we put forth definitions of the components of an EI – these are more thoroughly described in [6]. We assume in this paper the existence of a finite and non-empty set $Ag = \{ag_1, \ldots, ag_n\}$ of unique agent identifiers $ag_i \neq ag_j, i \neq j, 1 \leq i, j \leq n$.

2.1   Dialogic Frameworks and Dialogues

In the most general case, each agent immersed in a multi-agent environment is endowed with its own inner language and ontology. In order to allow agents to interact with other agents we must address the fundamental issue of putting their languages and ontologies in relation. For this purpose, we propose that agents share, when communicating, what we call the *dialogic framework* that contains the elements for the construction of the agent communication language expressions. Furthermore the dialogic framework also defines the roles that participating agents can play.

Definition 1. *A dialogic framework is a tuple* $DF = \langle O, L_O, P, R \rangle$ *where* O *stands for an ontology (vocabulary);* L_O *stands for a content language to express the information exchanged between agents using ontology* O; P *is the set of illocutionary particles; and* R *is the set of internal roles.*

Within a dialogic framework the content language allows for the encoding of the knowledge to be exchanged among agents using the vocabulary offered by the ontology. The expressions of the agent communication language are defined as below:

Definition 2. *The language* $\mathcal{L}_{DF}$ *of a dialogic framework* $DF = \langle O, L_O, P, R \rangle$ *is the set of expressions* $\iota(ag, r, ag', r', p, t)$ *such that* $\iota \in P$; $ag, ag' \in Ag$, *the set of agent identifiers;* $r, r' \in R$; $p \in L_O$ *a variable-free expression of* L_O; $t \in I\!N$ *is a time tag.*

That is, the language of a dialogic framework is the collection of all the grounded, variable-free expressions that agents employing the dialogic framework may exchange. Intuitively, $\iota(ag, r, ag', r', p, t)$ denotes that agent ag incorporating role r sent to agent ag' incorporating role r' contents p at instant t.

We also need to refer to expressions which may contain variables. We provide the following definition with this aim:

Definition 3. *The pattern language $\mathcal{L}^*_{DF}$ of a dialogic framework $DF = \langle O,$ $L_O, P, R \rangle$ is the set of expressions $\iota(ag^*, r^*, ag'^*, r'^*, p^*, t^*)$ such that $\iota \in P$; ag^*, ag'^* are agent variables or agent identifiers from the set Ag; r^*, r'^* are role variables or role identifiers in R; $p^* \in L_O$ is an expression which may contain variables; and t^* is either a time variable or a value in $\mathbb{N}$.*

Henceforth we shall refer to $\mathcal{L}_{DF}$ expressions as *illocutions*, represented generically as **i**, and to $\mathcal{L}^*_{DF}$ expressions as *illocution schemes*, represented generically as **i***. It follows from the definitions above that $\mathcal{L}_{DF} \subseteq \mathcal{L}^*_{DF}$.

Although a dialogic framework defines a set of illocutions that agents may exchange, we consider that agents, as human beings, engage in conversations. Conversations structure agents' interactions, by imposing an order on the illocutions exchange and represent the context where exchanged illocutions must be interpreted. As a conversation evolves, a *dialogue*, an ordered sequence of all illocutions exchanged among agents, is generated.

Dialogues represent the history of conversations and the analysis of the properties of a conversation can be conducted on the basis of its dialogues. We hence formally introduce the notion of dialogue as a core element upon which we carry out the analysis of conversations and, ultimately, of dialogic institutions:

Definition 4. *Given a dialogic framework DF and its language $\mathcal{L}_{DF}$, we define a dialogue over $\mathcal{L}_{DF}$ as any non-empty, finite sequence $\langle \mathbf{i}_1, \ldots, \mathbf{i}_n \rangle$ such that $\mathbf{i}_i = \iota_i(ag_i, r_i, ag'_i, r'_i, p_i, t_i) \in \mathcal{L}_{DF}, 1 \leq i \leq n$, and $t_i \leq t_j, 1 \leq i \leq j \leq n$.*

From the definition above we obtain all the possible dialogues that a group of agents using a dialogic framework may have. We next define the set of all possible dialogues of a dialogic framework:

Definition 5. *Given a dialogic framework DF, we define the dialogue set over $\mathcal{L}_{DF}$, represented as $\mathcal{D}_{DF}$, as the set containing all possible dialogues over $\mathcal{L}_{DF}$.*

Clearly, the set $\mathcal{D}_{DF}$ of all possible dialogues is infinite, even though the components of the corresponding dialogic framework DF are finite – the very same illocution can be uttered an infinite number of times with different time stamps.

A single dialogue solely contains only *grounded* illocutions. If we consider instead a sequence of illocution schemes **i***, the very same sequence may produce multiple dialogues as values are bound to the free variables in the illocution schemes. Therefore, we can employ a sequence of illocution schemes for representing a whole set of dialogues that may occur. And thus, we can think of undertaking the analysis of a set of dialogues from the sequence of illocution schemes that generates them.

Definition 6. *Given a dialogic framework DF and its pattern language $\mathcal{L}^*_{DF}$, we define a dialogue scheme over $\mathcal{L}^*_{DF}$ as any non-empty, finite sequence $\langle \mathbf{i}^*_1, \ldots,$ $\mathbf{i}^*_n \rangle$ such that $\mathbf{i}^*_i \in \mathcal{L}^*_{DF}, 1 \leq i \leq n$.*

In order to relate dialogue schemes and dialogues we rely on the concept of *substitution*, that is, the set of values for variables in a computation [7, 8]:

Definition 7. *A substitution* $\sigma = \{x_0/T_0, \ldots, x_n/T_n\}$ *is a finite and possibly empty set of pairs* x_i/T_i, x_i *being a first-order variable and* T_i *an arbitrary first-order term.*

A dialogue scheme and a dialogue are thus related:

Definition 8. *Given a dialogic framework* DF, *we say that a dialogue scheme* $\langle \mathbf{i}_1^*, \ldots, \mathbf{i}_n^* \rangle \in \mathcal{L}_{DF}^*$ *is a scheme of a dialogue* $\langle \mathbf{i}_1, \ldots, \mathbf{i}_n \rangle \in \mathcal{L}_{DF}$ *iff there is a substitution* σ *that when applied to* $\langle \mathbf{i}_1^*, \ldots, \mathbf{i}_n^* \rangle$ *yields (or unifies with)* $\langle \mathbf{i}_1, \ldots, \mathbf{i}_n \rangle$, *that is,* $\langle \mathbf{i}_1^*, \ldots, \mathbf{i}_n^* \rangle \cdot \sigma = \langle \mathbf{i}_1, \ldots, \mathbf{i}_n \rangle$.

The application of a substitution to a dialogue scheme $\langle \mathbf{i}_1^*, \ldots, \mathbf{i}_n^* \rangle \cdot \sigma$ is defined as the application of the substitution σ to each $\mathbf{i}_i^*$, that is, $\langle \mathbf{i}_1^*, \ldots, \mathbf{i}_n^* \rangle \cdot \sigma = \langle \mathbf{i}_1^* \cdot \sigma, \ldots, \mathbf{i}_n^* \cdot \sigma \rangle$. The application of a substitution to $\mathbf{i}_i^*$ follows the usual definition [8]:

1. $c \cdot \sigma = c$ for a constant c.
2. $[\iota(ag^*, r^*, ag'^*, r'^*, p^*, t^*)] \cdot \sigma = \iota(ag^* \cdot \sigma, r^* \cdot \sigma, ag'^* \cdot \sigma, r'^* \cdot \sigma, p^* \cdot \sigma, t^* \cdot \sigma)$.
3. $x \cdot \sigma = T \cdot \sigma$ for a variable x such that $x/T \in \sigma$; if $x/T \notin \sigma$ then $x \cdot \sigma = x$.

The first case defines the application of a substitution to a constant c. Case 2 describes the application of a substitution to a generic illocution scheme $\mathbf{i}^* = \iota(ag^*, r^*, ag'^*, r'^*, p^*, t^*)$: the result is the application of σ to each component of the scheme. Case 3 describes the application of σ to a generic variable x: the result is the application of σ to the term T to which x is associated (if $x/T \in \sigma$) or x itself if x is not associated to terms in σ.

2.2   Scenes

Within the framework of an electronic institution, agent conversations are articulated through agent group meetings, called *scenes*, that follow well-defined interaction protocols. In other words, not all sequences in $\mathcal{D}_{DF}$ make sense, so some structure upon dialogues seems unavoidable.

A scene protocol is specified by a directed graph whose nodes represent the different states of a dialogic interaction among roles. From the set of states we differentiate an initial state (non reachable once left) and a set of final states representing the different dialogue ends. In order to capture that final states represent the end of a dialogue they do not have outgoing arcs. The arcs of the graph are labelled with illocution schemes (whose sender, receiver, content, and time tag may contain variables). We formally define scenes as follows:

Definition 9. *A scene is a tuple* $S = \langle R, DF, W, w_0, W_f, \Theta, \lambda, min, Max \rangle$ *where* R *is the set of scene roles;* DF *is a dialogic framework;* W *is the set of scene states;* $w_0 \in W$ *is the initial state;* $W_f \subseteq W$ *is the set of final states;* $\Theta \subseteq W \times W$ *is a set of directed edges;* $\lambda : \Theta \longrightarrow \mathcal{L}_{DF}^*$ *is a labelling function, which maps each edge to an illocution scheme in the pattern language of the* DF *dialogic framework;* $min, Max : R \longrightarrow \mathbb{N}$ $min(r)$ *and* $Max(r)$ *return the minimum and maximum number of agents that must and can play role* $r \in R$.

We formally define the dialogue schemes of a scene:

Definition 10. *The dialogue schemes* $\mathcal{D}_S^*$ *of a scene* $S = \langle R, DF, W, w_0, W_f, \Theta,$ $\lambda, min, Max \rangle$, *is the set of sequences* $\langle (s^*, w_2, \lambda(w_1, w_2)), \ldots, (s^*, w_n,$ $\lambda(w_{n-1}, w_n)) \rangle$, *where* s^* *is the identifier for scene* S *or a variable, and* $w_1 = w_0$, *and* $w_n \in W_f$.

The dialogue schemes of a scene are the sequence of labels $\lambda(w, w')$ of all paths connecting its initial state w_0 to a final state $w_n \in W_f$. The s and w's are required to precisely identify the context in which an illocution was uttered – this is essential to our notion of norms, as we shall see below.

The dialogue schemes of a scene allow us to obtain all the concrete dialogues accepted by the scene via appropriate substitutions assigning values to all variables of the illocutions. We define the set of all (concrete) dialogues of a scene as follows:

Definition 11. *The dialogues* $\mathcal{D}_S$ *of a scene* $S = \langle R, DF, W, w_0, W_f, \Theta, \lambda, min,$ $Max \rangle$, *is the set of sequences* $\langle (s^*, w_2, \lambda(w_1, w_2)), \ldots, (s^*, w_n, \lambda(w_{n-1}, w_n)) \rangle \cdot \sigma$, *where* s *is the identifier for scene* S, $w_1 = w_0$, *and* $w_n \in W_f$, *and* σ *is a substitution providing values to all variables of the illocution schemes* $\lambda(w, w')$.

The dialogues accepted by a scene are the ground versions of its dialogue schemes, that is, the sequence of labels of a path through the scene with all variables replaced with constants. Given a dialogue scheme we can derive infinite ground versions of it – however, as we shall see below, we provide means to express constraints on the values that the illocutions' variables may have. Extra constraints limit the number of possible applicable substitutions and, hence, concrete dialogues.

2.3   Performative Structures

While a scene models a particular multi-agent dialogic activity, more complex activities can be specified by establishing networks of scenes (activities), the so-called *performative structures*. These define how agents can legally move among different scenes (from activity to activity). Agents within a performative structure can participate concurrently in different scenes.

Definition 12. *Performative structures are recursively defined as:*

- *A scene* S *is a performative structure.*
- *If* PS_1 *and* PS_2 *are performative structures,* $PS_1.PS_2$ *is a performative structure, where* $PS_1.PS_2$ *means that the execution of* PS_1 *is followed by the execution of* PS_2.
- *If* PS_1 *and* PS_2 *are performative structures,* $PS_1|PS_2$ *is a performative structure, where* $PS_1|PS_2$ *stands for the interleaved execution of* PS_1 *and* PS_2.
- *If* PS *is a performative structure,* PS^n *is a performative structure, where* PS^n *stands for* n *executions of* PS, *where* $n \in I\!N, n \geq 0$.

A performative structure defines all the dialogues that agents may have within an electronic institution, by fixing the scenes in which agents can be engaged and how agents can move among them. Notice that the execution of a performative structure must be regarded as the execution of its different scenes. Moreover, executions of different scenes can occur concurrently.

We can define the dialogues accepted by performative structure PS, denoted by $\mathcal{D}_{PS}$ using the definition of performative structures above. For that we must define the operator $\oplus : \mathcal{D}_{PS_1} \times \mathcal{D}_{PS_2} \to \mathcal{D}_{PS_1|PS_2}$ that given two input dialogues d_{PS_1} and d_{PS_2} merges their illocutions taking into account their time stamps. More formally, given dialogues $d_1 = \langle \mathbf{i}_1^1, \ldots, \mathbf{i}_n^1 \rangle$ and $d_2 = \langle \mathbf{i}_1^2, \ldots, \mathbf{i}_m^2 \rangle$, $d_1 \oplus d_2 = \langle \mathbf{i}_1, \ldots, \mathbf{i}_{n+m} \rangle$, where $\mathbf{i}_i = \mathbf{i}_j^1$ or $\mathbf{i}_i = \mathbf{i}_k^2$, for some $j, k, 1 \leq j \leq n, 1 \leq k \leq n$. Furthermore, for any two illocutions $\mathbf{i}_i = \iota_i(ag_i, r_i, ag_i', r_i', p_i, t_i)$ and $\mathbf{i}_l = \iota_l(ag_l, r_l, ag_l', r_l', p_l, t_l)$, such that $1 \leq i \leq l \leq n + m$, then $t_i \leq t_l$. The concatenation operator "$\circ$" over sequences is defined in the usual fashion.

We can now define the dialogues accepted by each performative structure.

Definition 13. *The dialogues $\mathcal{D}_{PS}$ of a performative structure PS are thus obtained:*

- *If $PS = S$, i.e., a scene, then $\mathcal{D}_{PS} = \mathcal{D}_S$ as in Def. 11.*
- *If $PS = PS_1.PS_2$ then $\mathcal{D}_{PS} = \{d_{PS_1} \circ d_{PS_2} | d_{PS_1} \in \mathcal{D}_{PS_1}, d_{PS_2} \in \mathcal{D}_{PS_2}\}$.*
- *If $PS = PS_1|PS_2$ then $\mathcal{D}_{PS} = \{d_{PS_1} \oplus d_{PS_2} | d_{PS_1} \in \mathcal{D}_{PS_1}, d_{PS_2} \in \mathcal{D}_{PS_2}\}$.*
- *If PS is of the form PS^n then $\mathcal{D}_{PS} = \{d_0 \circ \ldots \circ d_n | d_i \in \mathcal{D}_{PS}, 0 \leq i \leq n\}$.*

3   Norms in Electronic Institutions

Agents' actions *within* scenes may have consequences that either limit or enlarge their future acting possibilities. Some actions may create commitments for future actions, interpreted as obligations, and some actions can have consequences that modify the valid illocutions or the paths that a scene evolution can follow. These consequences are captured by a special type of rules called *norms* which contain the actions that will activate them and their consequences. Notice that we are considering dialogic institutions, and the only actions we consider are the utterance of illocutions. In order to express actions within norms and obligations we set out two predicates:

- *uttered*$(s, w, \mathbf{i}^*)$ denoting that a grounded illocution unifying with the illocution scheme $\mathbf{i}^*$ has been uttered at state w of scene S identified by s.
- *uttered*$(s, \mathbf{i}^*)$ denoting that a grounded illocution unifying with the illocution scheme $\mathbf{i}^*$ has been uttered at some state of scene S identified by s.

Therefore, we can refer to the utterance of an illocution within a scene or when a scene execution is at a concrete state.

3.1   Boolean Expressions

In some cases the activation of a norm will depend on the values bound to the variables in the illocution schemes and on the context of the scene (the previous bindings) where the illocution is uttered. With this aim, we incorporate boolean functions over illocution schemes' variables as antecedents and consequents of norms.

The expressions over illocution schemes variables have the following syntax: e_i op e_j; where e_i and e_j are expressions of the appropriate type. The types of variables must be of any basic type: string, numeric and boolean, a type defined in the ontology, or a multi-set of them. We are currently using this reduced set of operators:

- $<, \leq, \geq, >$: $numeric \times numeric \rightarrow boolean$
- $\vee$: $boolean \times boolean \rightarrow boolean$
- $=, \neq$: $\alpha^= \times \alpha^= \rightarrow boolean$ where α represents a basic type or any type defined in the ontology.
- $\in, \notin$: $\alpha^= \times \alpha^= \, multiset \rightarrow boolean$, where α represents a basic type or any type defined in the ontology that may have equality.
- $\subset, \subseteq$: $\alpha^= \, multiset \times \alpha^= \, multiset \rightarrow boolean$, where α represents a basic type of any type defined in the ontology.

Notice that illocutions are tagged with the time at which the illocution is uttered. We consider such tags as numeric, and so, we can apply to them the same operations as to numeric expressions. Hence, order among the utterance of illocutions can be expressed via numeric operators over them.

Moreover, when a scene is executed we keep all the bindings produced by the uttered illocutions. Therefore, we can make reference to the last one or to a set of bindings for a giving variable(s) and use this in the expressions mentioned above. We can apply the following prefix operators to obtain previous bindings:

- $!x$: stands for the last binding of variable x.
- $!^k_{w_i w_j} x$: stands for the multi-set of all the bindings of variable x in the k last subdialogues between w_i and w_j. $!^1_{w_i w_j} x$ is represented as $!_{w_i w_j} x$ for simplicity.
- $!^*_{w_i w_j} x$: stands for the multiset of the bindings of variable x in all subdialogues between w_i and w_j.
- $!^k_{w_i w_j} x$ ($cond$): stands for the multi-set of all the bindings of variable x in the k last sub-dialogues between w_i and w_j such that the substitution σ where the binding appears satisfies the $cond$ condition.

3.2 Integrity Norms and Obligations

We now put forth formal definitions for two types of norms in electronic institutions, the integrity norms and obligations. In both definitions below we can also have $uttered(s, \mathbf{i}^*)$ subformulae.

Definition 14. *Integrity norms are first-order formulae of the form*
$$\left(\bigwedge_{i=1}^n uttered(s_i, w_{k_i}, \mathbf{i}_{l_i}) \wedge \bigwedge_{j=0}^m e_j \right) \rightarrow \bot$$
where s_i are scene identifiers, w_{k_i} is a state k_i of scene s_i, $\mathbf{i}_{l_i}$ is an illocution scheme l_i of scene s_i and e_j are boolean expressions over variables from illocution schemes $\mathbf{i}_{l_i}$.

Integrity norms define sets of actions that *must not* occur within an institution. The meaning of these norms is that if grounded illocutions matching the illocution schemes $\mathbf{i}_{l_1}, \ldots, \mathbf{i}_{l_n}$ are uttered in the corresponding scene states, and expressions $e_1, \ldots, e_m$ are satisfied, then a *violation* occurs ($\bot$).

Definition 15. *Obligations are first-order formulae of the form*

$$\left(\bigwedge_{i=1}^{n} uttered(s_i, w_{k_i}, \mathbf{i}_{l_i}^*) \wedge \bigwedge_{j=0}^{m} e_j \right) \rightarrow \left(\bigwedge_{i=1}^{n'} uttered(s_i', w_{k_i}', \mathbf{i}_{l_i}'^*) \wedge \bigwedge_{j=0}^{m'} e_j' \right)$$

where s_i, s_i' are scene identifiers, w_{k_i}, w_{k_i}' are states of s_i and s_i' respectively, $\mathbf{i}_{l_i}^*, \mathbf{i}_{l_i}'^*$ are illocution schemes l_i of scenes s_i and s_i' respectively, and e_j, e_j' are boolean expressions over variables from the illocution schemes $\mathbf{i}_{l_i}^*$ and $\mathbf{i}_{l_i}'^*$, respectively.

The intuitive meaning of obligations is that if grounded illocutions matching $\mathbf{i}_{l_1}^*, \ldots, \mathbf{i}_{l_n}^*$ are uttered in the corresponding scene states, and the expressions $e_1, \ldots, e_m$ are satisfied, then, grounded illocutions matching $\mathbf{i}_{l_1}'^*, \ldots, \mathbf{i}_{l_n'}'^*$ satisfying the expressions $e_1', \ldots, e_{m'}'$ must be uttered in the corresponding scene states.

Obligations assume a temporal ordering: the left-hand side illocutions must have time stamps which precede those of right-hand side illocutions. Rather than requiring that engineers manually encode such restrictions, we can automatically add them – given our definition above, we can add the extra boolean expressions $t^* \geq t_i^*, 1 \leq i \leq n, t'^* \leq t_j'^*, 1 \leq j \leq n', t^* < t'^*$ to our obligations, where t^*, t_i^* and $t'^*, t_j'^*$ are the time stamps of, respectively, $\mathbf{i}_i^*$ and $\mathbf{i}_j'^*$, t^* being the greatest value of time stamp on the left-hand side illocutions (that is, the time stamp of the latest illocution) and t'^* the lowest value of time stamp on the right-hand side illocutions (that is, the time stamp of the earliest illocution).

3.3   Semantics of Norms

In order to define the semantics of our norms and obligations we need first to define the meaning of the predicates $uttered(s, w, \mathbf{i}^*)$ and $uttered(s, \mathbf{i}^*)$. We shall employ a function $\mathbf{K} : \mathbf{i}^* \times \mathcal{D} \times \sigma \mapsto \{\mathbf{true}, \mathbf{false}\}$, that maps illocution schemes, dialogues and substitutions to $\mathbf{true}$ and $\mathbf{false}$[1].

Definition 16. *The semantics of $u = uttered(s, w, \mathbf{i}^*)$ or $u = uttered(s, \mathbf{i})$ wrt a set of dialogues $\mathcal{D}$ and a substitution σ, $\mathbf{K}(u, \mathcal{D}, \sigma) \mapsto \{\mathbf{true}, \mathbf{false}\}$, is:*

1. $\mathbf{K}(uttered(s, w, \mathbf{i}^*), \mathcal{D}, \sigma) = \mathbf{true}$ *iff there is a dialogue* $\langle (s, w_1, \mathbf{i}_1^*), \ldots,$ $(s, w_n, \mathbf{i}_n^*) \rangle \cdot \sigma \in \mathcal{D}$ *with* $(s, w_i, \mathbf{i}_i^*) = (s, w, \mathbf{i}^*)$, *for some* $i, 1 \leq i \leq n$.
2. $\mathbf{K}(uttered(s, w, \mathbf{i}^*), \mathcal{D}, \sigma) = \mathbf{true}$ *iff there is a dialogue* $\langle (s, w_1, \mathbf{i}_1^*), \ldots,$ $(s, w_n, \mathbf{i}_n^*) \rangle \cdot \sigma \in \mathcal{D}$ *with* $(s, w_i, \mathbf{i}_i^*) = (s, w_i, \mathbf{i}^*)$, *for some* $i, 1 \leq i \leq n$.

Our predicates are true if there is at least one dialogue $\langle (s, w_1, \mathbf{i}_1^*), \ldots, (s, w_n, \mathbf{i}_n^*) \rangle \cdot$ σ in $\mathcal{D}$ with an element $(s, w_i, \mathbf{i}_i^*)$ (an illocution of the dialogue without its

---

[1] We distinguish between the constants "⊤" and "⊥" which are part of the syntax of formulae and the truth-values **true** and **false**. Clearly, $\mathbf{K}(\top, \mathcal{D}, \sigma) = \mathbf{true}$ and $\mathbf{K}(\bot, \mathcal{D}, \sigma) = \mathbf{false}$ for any $\mathcal{D}$ and σ.

substitution σ applied to it) in it that is syntactically equal to $(s, w, \mathbf{i}^*)$. In the case of $uttered(s, \mathbf{i}^*)$ we do not care what the value of w is.

In the definition above, we can understand σ as parameter whose value is determined, confirmed or completed by the function. The substitution σ plays an essential role in finding the truth value of our boolean expressions.

We also need to define a semantic mapping for our boolean expressions e over illocution scheme variables. We shall use the same $\mathbf{K}$ function introduced above, extending it to cope with expressions e as introduced previously.

Definition 17. *The semantics of a boolean expression e wrt a set of dialogues $\mathcal{D}$ and a substitution σ, $\mathbf{K}(e, \mathcal{D}, \sigma) \mapsto \{\mathbf{true}, \mathbf{false}\}$, is*

$$\mathbf{K}(e_1 \ op \ e_2, \mathcal{D}, \sigma) = \mathbf{true} \ iff \ \mathbf{K}'(e_1, \sigma) \ op \ \mathbf{K}'(e_2, \sigma)$$

The "op" operators are all given their usual definition. For instance, $\mathbf{K}(x \in Ag, PS, \sigma) = \mathbf{true}$ iff $\mathbf{K}'(x, \sigma) \in \mathbf{K}'(Ag, \sigma)$, that is, the expression is true iff the value of variable x in σ belongs to the set of values comprising set Ag. The auxiliary mapping $\mathbf{K}' : e \times \sigma \mapsto \Im$, where $\Im$ is the union of all types in the ontology, is defined below.

Definition 18. *The value of a non-boolean expression e wrt a substitution σ, $\mathbf{K}'(e, \sigma) \mapsto \Im$, is:*

1. $\mathbf{K}'(c, \sigma) = c$ *for a constant c.*
2. $\mathbf{K}'(x, \sigma) = T', \mathbf{K}'(T, \sigma) = T', x/T \in \sigma.$
3. $\mathbf{K}'(f(T_1, \ldots, T_n), \sigma) = f(\mathbf{K}'(T_1, \sigma), \ldots, \mathbf{K}'(T_n, \sigma)).$
4. $\mathbf{K}'(\text{Set}, \sigma) = \{c_0, \ldots\}, \text{Set}/\{c_0, \ldots\} \in \sigma.$

Case 1 defines the value of a constant as the constant itself. Case 2 describes how to obtain the value of an arbitrary variable x appearing in illocution schemes. Case 3 describes how functions are evaluated: the meaning of a function is given by the application of the function to the value of its arguments. Finally, case 4 defines the value of a set as the set of values associated with the set name in the substitution σ – sets are treated like any other ordinary constant.

We finally define the meaning of our norms, depicting how the logical operators "$\wedge$" and "$\rightarrow$" are handled in our formalisation. Our atomic formulae are u or e, denoted generically as Atf; $Atfs$ denotes a conjunction of atomic formulae, $Atfs = Atf_1 \wedge \cdots \wedge Atf_n$. The logical operators are defined in the usual way:

Definition 19. *The semantics of a norm is given by*

1. $\mathbf{K}(Atfs_1 \rightarrow Atfs_2, \mathcal{D}, \sigma) = \mathbf{true}$ *iff* $\mathbf{K}(Atfs_1, \mathcal{D}, \sigma) = \mathbf{false}$ *or* $\mathbf{K}(Atfs_1, \mathcal{D}, \sigma) = \mathbf{K}(Atfs_2, \mathcal{D}, \sigma) = \mathbf{true}$
2. $\mathbf{K}(Atfs_1 \wedge Atfs_2, \mathcal{D}, \sigma) = \mathbf{true}$ *iff* $\mathbf{K}(Atfs_1, \mathcal{D}, \sigma) = \mathbf{K}(Atfs_2, \mathcal{D}, \sigma) = \mathbf{true}$

Case 1 depicts the semantics of the "$\rightarrow$" operator: it yields **true** if the formulae on its left and right side evaluate to the same truth-value. Case 2 captures the semantics of the conjunction "$\wedge$": it yields **true** if its subformulae yield **true**. The base cases for the formulation above are u and e, whose semantics are represented in **Defs. 16** and **17** above.

3.4   Verification of Norms

We want to verify that the set of dialogues $\mathcal{D}_{PS}$ of a performative structure PS satisfies a set of norms $\mathcal{N}$, that is, $\mathcal{D}_{PS} \models \mathcal{N}$. One option is to verify that there exists at least one dialogue in $\mathcal{D}_{PS}$ such that
- All integrity norms are satisfied, that is, the performative structure does not contain situations in which a violation occurs.
- There are no pending obligations, that is, all acquired obligations (right-hand side of an obligation) are fulfilled.

We notice that the verification of norms in e-institutions as formalised in this work amounts to a restricted kind of first-order theorem proving. The restriction however does not affect the complexity of the task and attempts to automate it are limited by the semi-decidability of first-order theorem proving [9, 8]. Notwithstanding this theoretical result, we can adopt some practical simplifications to make the verification decidable: if we assume the sets from our ontology are all finite, then the verification process amounts to theorem proving with propositional logics, which is decidable. Our previous formalisation naturally accommodates the proposed simplification: an initial substitution $\sigma_0 = \{\mathsf{Set}_1/\{c_1^1, \ldots, c_{n_1}^1\}, \ldots, \mathsf{Set}_m/\{c_1^m, \ldots, c_{n_m}^m\}\}$ formally represents all sets from our ontology – it is essential to our approach that all sets be finite collections of constants. We can define our finite verification of a norm N wrt the set of dialogues $\mathcal{D}$ of a performative structure as $\mathbf{K}(N, \mathcal{D}, \sigma_0 \cup \sigma) = \mathbf{true}$, that is, we would like to obtain a substitution σ which (added to the initial σ_0) makes N hold in $\mathcal{D}$. Since the value of all variables should ultimately come from a set Set_i in our ontology and given that all these sets are finite and part of the initial substitution σ_0, then we can obtain σ that assign values to each illocution scheme variables – provided there are such values that satisfy the boolean expressions in N. We can extend this definition to cover sets of norms $\mathcal{N} = \{N_1, \ldots, N_p\}$: $\mathbf{K}(\mathcal{N}, \mathcal{D}, \sigma_0 \cup \sigma) = \mathbf{true}$ iff $\mathbf{K}(N_1, \mathcal{D}, \sigma_0 \cup \sigma) = \cdots = \mathbf{K}(N_p, \mathcal{D}, \sigma_0 \cup \sigma) = \mathbf{true}$.

The substitution $\sigma_0 \cup \sigma$ functions as a *model*: by using its values for the illocution scheme variables, we can construct a subset $\mathcal{D}'_{PS} \subseteq \mathcal{D}_{PS}$, $|\mathcal{D}'_{PS}| = 1$ (*i.e.* exactly one dialogue scheme), such that $\mathcal{D}'_{PS} \models \mathcal{N}$. The only dialogue scheme in $\mathcal{D}'_{PS}$ consists of a single path through the scenes of the performative structure. This dialogue, together with its substitution *sigma* provides a norm-compliant execution for the institution.

The complexity of our verification is an exponential function on the number of values for each variable, in the worst case. The verification works by choosing a value for the illocution scheme variables from the appropriate sets and then checking the boolean expressions which might relate and constrain such values. A similar technique has been employed in [10] to obtain models for the enactment of e-institutions. This process can be made more efficient by using standard techniques from constraint logic programming [11].

We can now define means to obtain models $\mathcal{D}'_{PS} \subseteq \mathcal{D}_{PS}$ for a given performative structure and set of norms. We employ the relationships $\mathbf{D}$ and $\mathbf{K}$:

$$\mathbf{model}(PS, \mathcal{N}, \mathcal{D}'_{PS}) \leftarrow \mathcal{D}'_{PS} \subseteq \mathcal{D}_{PS} \wedge |\mathcal{D}'_{PS}| = 1 \wedge \mathbf{K}(\mathcal{N}, \mathcal{D}'_{PS}, \sigma)$$

That is, we obtain individual dialogue schemes from $\mathcal{D}_{PS}$ (one at a time) and then check via $\mathbf{K}$ if it satisfies the set of norms $\mathcal{N}$.

The *correctness* of our definitions can be formulated as: if **model**$(PS, \mathcal{N},$ $\mathcal{D}'_{PS})$ then $\mathcal{D}'_{PS} \models \mathcal{N}$. Whereas the *completeness* can be stated as: if $\mathcal{D}'_{PS} \models \mathcal{N}$ then **model**$(PS, \mathcal{N}, \mathcal{D}'_{PS})$. It is important to notice that if σ_0 contains only finite sets, then our **model** relationship is correct and complete, and its complexity is an exponential function on the number of illocution scheme variables and their possible values.

4   Conclusions, Related Work and Directions of Research

We have presented a formal definition of norms and shown how norms can be employed to verify electronic institutions. We provide a computational approach to assess whether an electronic institution is *normatively consistent*, that is, whether there is at least one possible enactment of it (by heterogeneous agents) in which norms will not be subverted. Given an electronic institution we can also determine whether its norms prevent any norm-compliant executions from happening.

Electronic institutions provide an ideal scenario within which alternative definitions and formalisations of norms can be proposed and studied. In [12] we find an early account of norms relating illocutions of an e-institution. In [13] we find a first-order logic formulation of norms for e-institutions: an institution conforms to a set of norms if it is a logical model for them. Our work is an adaptation and extension of [12] but our approach differs in that we do not explicitly employ any deontic notions of obligations [1]. Our norms are of the form *Pre* → *Obls*, that is, if *Pre* holds then *Obls* ought to hold. The components of *Pre* and *Obls* are utterances, that is, messages the agents participating in the e-institution send. This more pragmatic definition fits in naturally with the view of e-institutions as a specification of virtual environments which can be checked for properties and then used for synthesising agents [14, 15].

We are currently investigating means to automatically verify our norms, building dialogue schemes and sets of substitutions that can be used to restrict the behaviour of agents taking part in the enactment of an institution. We describe in [16] an initial approach to implementing our verification.

Work is also underway to fully define the operational semantics of an electronic institution using our notion of norms. A team of administrative agents (the so-called "governors") will interface external agents with the institution, thus ensuring that norms are complied to. An enactment of an institution consists on the dialogues taking place among the external agents (interfaced by the governors) and that conform to the norms.

References

1. Dignum, F.: Autonomous Agents with Norms. Artificial Intelligence and Law **7** (1999) 69–79
2. López y López, F., Luck, M., d'Inverno, M.: Constraining Autonomy Through Norms. In: Proceedings of the 1st Int'l Joint Conf. on Autonomous Agents and Multiagent Systems (AAMAS), ACM Press (2002)

3. Verhagen, H.: Norm Autonomous Agents. PhD thesis, Stockholm University (2000)
4. Esteva, M., Rodríguez-Aguilar, J.A., Sierra, C., Garcia, P., Arcos, J.L.: On the Formal Specification of Electronic Institutions. Volume 1991 of LNAI. Springer-Verlag (2001)
5. Rodríguez-Aguilar, J.A.: On the Design and Construction of Agent-mediated Electronic Institutions. PhD thesis, IIIA-CSIC, Spain (2001)
6. Esteva, M.: Electronic Institutions: from specification to development. PhD thesis, Universitat Politècnica de Catalunya (UPC) (2003) IIIA monography Vol. 19.
7. Apt, K.R.: From Logic Programming to Prolog. Prentice-Hall, U.K. (1997)
8. Fitting, M.: First-Order Logic and Automated Theorem Proving. Springer-Verlag, New York, U.S.A. (1990)
9. Enderton, H.B.: A Mathematical Introduction to Logic. 2nd edn. Harcourt/Academic Press, Mass., USA (2001)
10. Vasconcelos, W.W.: Expressive Global Protocols via Logic-Based Electronic Institutions. In: Proc. 2nd Int'l Joint Conf. on Autonomous Agents & Multi-Agent Systems (AAMAS 2003), Melbourne, Australia, ACM, U.S.A (2003)
11. Jaffar, J., Maher, M.J.: Constraint Logic Programming: A Survey. Journal of Logic Programming **19/20** (1994) 503–581
12. Esteva, M., Padget, J., Sierra, C.: Formalizing a Language for Institutions and Norms. Volume 2333 of LNAI. Springer-Verlag (2001)
13. Ibrahim, I.K., Kotsis, G., Schwinger, W.: Mapping Abstractions of Norms in Electronic Institutions. In: 12th. Int'l Workshop on Enabling Technologies: Infrastructure for Collaborative Enterprise (WETICE'03), Linz, Austria, IEEE Computer Society (2003)
14. Vasconcelos, W.W., Robertson, D., Sierra, C., Esteva, M., Sabater, J., Wooldridge, M.: Rapid Prototyping of Large Multi-Agent Systems through Logic Programming. Annals of Mathematics and A.I. **41** (2004)
15. Vasconcelos, W.W., Sierra, C., Esteva, M.: An Approach to Rapid Prototyping of Large Multi-Agent Systems. In: Proc. 17th IEEE Int'l Conf. on Automated Software Engineering (ASE 2002), Edinburgh, UK, IEEE Computer Society, U.S.A (2002) 13–22
16. Vasconcelos, W.W.: Norm Verification and Analysis of Electronic Institutions. In: Procs. AAMAS'04 Workshop on Declarative Agent Languages and Technologies (DALT'04), New York, USA (2004)

Using the $\mathcal{M}$OISE$^+$ for a Cooperative Framework of MAS Reorganisation

Jomi Fred Hübner[1], Jaime Simão Sichman[1], and Olivier Boissier[2]

[1] LTI / EP / USP
Av. Prof. Luciano Gualberto, 158, trav. 3
05508-900 São Paulo, SP
{jomi.hubner,jaime.sichman}@poli.usp.br
[2] SMA / SIMMO / ENSM.SE
158 Cours Fauriel
42023 Saint-Etienne Cedex, France
Olivier.Boissier@emse.fr

Abstract. Reorganisation within a multi-agent system may be managed by the agents themselves by adapting the organisation to both environmental changes and their own goals. In this paper, we propose an organisation-centred model for controlling this process. Using the $\mathcal{M}$OISE$^+$ organisation model, we are able to define an organisational structure bearing on a reorganisation process along four phases: monitoring (when to reorganise), design (ways of building a new organisation), selection (how to choose an organisation), and implementation (how to change the current running organisation). The proposed reorganisation scheme is evaluated in the robot soccer domain where we have developed players that follow the team organisation specified in $\mathcal{M}$OISE$^+$. A special group of agents may change this organisation, and thus the team behaviour, using reinforcement learning for the selection phase.

Keywords: Autonomous Agents and Multi-Agent Systems, MAS organizations, groups, and societies; reoranization.

1 Introduction

The organisation of a Multi-Agent System (MAS) can be seen as a set of constraints that a group of agents adopts in order to easily achieve their social purposes [3]. The Fig. 1 briefly shows how an organisation could explain or constrain the agents' behaviour in case we consider an organisation as having both *structural* and *functional* dimensions. In this figure, it is supposed that an MAS has the purpose of maintaining its behaviour in the set P, where P represents all behaviours which draw the MAS's social purposes. In the same figure, the set E represents all possible behaviours in the current environment. The MAS's organisational structure is formed, for example, by roles, groups, and links that constrain the agents' behaviour to those inside the set S, so the set of possible behaviours $(E \cap S)$ becomes closer to P. It is a matter of the agents, and not of the organisation, to conduct their behaviours from a point in $((E \cap S) - P)$ to a point in P. In order to help the agents in this task, the functional dimension contains a set of global plans F that has been proved efficient ways of turning the P behaviours active.

A.L.C. Bazzan and S. Labidi (Eds.): SBIA 2004, LNAI 3171, pp. 506–515, 2004.

Being well organised is a valuable property of an MAS, since it helps the system to assure its efficacy and efficiency [5]. Our general view of the organisation for an MAS, depicted in the Fig. 1, allows us to state a minimal condition for an MAS to be well organised: $E \cap S \cap F \cap P \neq \emptyset$, i.e., the behaviours which lead to the social purpose achievement are allowed by the organisation in

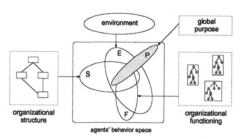

Fig. 1. The organization effects on a MAS

the current environment. However it is almost impossible (indeed undesirable) to specify an organisation where the allowed agents' behaviours fit exactly the set P, since this set also depends on the environment. Different environments require different sets of P behaviours. Moreover, if the sets S and F are too small, the MAS will have adaptation problems to little environmental changes due to the extinction of the agents autonomy by the organisation. On the other side, if S and F are too big, the organisation will not be effective since the agent's behaviours are not sufficiently constrained.

Identifying a good size for the set of organisational allowed behaviours is indeed another way of conceiving one important MAS problem: how to conciliate collective constraints with the agent autonomy. Normally MAS methodologies are concerned with this problem in the MAS design phase (e.g. [14]). However, even if the MAS has an initial good organisation, dynamic changes either in the environment or in the global purposes may cause the looseness of the organisation suitability. Moreover, if we consider the organisation unchangeable, the agents which have several experience and information about the organisation can not contribute to its adaptation. They loose the autonomy regarding its organisation. In other words, this problem could be expressed as how to conciliate an agent centered (AC) point of view with an organizational centered (OC) point of view [8]. This situation brings the *reorganisation* problem up: how the agents themselves might change their current organisation [10].

If we assume that (i) there is no better organisation for a context [4] and (ii) different organisations will give different performances for a system [5], an MAS needs to be capable of reorganising itself in order to well suit in its environment and to efficiently achieve its goals. Our objective is therefore to propose a reorganisation model and its specification (Sec. 3) based on the $\mathcal{M}$OISE$^+$ (Sec. 2). We will thus show how the reorganisation itself could be expressed and controlled in an OC point of view. Before comparing this proposition to related works (Sec. 5), we give a short description of a case study related to soccer robot simulation (Sec. 4).

2   Reorganisation Within $\mathcal{M}$OISE$^+$

The $\mathcal{M}$OISE$^+$ (Model of Organisation for multI-agent SystEms) follows the general view of the organisation depicted in the Fig. 1 and therefore considers the organisational structure and functioning. However, this model adds an explicit deontic relation among these first two dimensions to better explain how an MAS's organisation collaborates for the social purpose and make the agents able to reason on the fulfilment of their obligations or not [7]. These three dimensions form the Organisational Specification (OS). When a set of agents adopts an OS they form an Organisational Entity (OE) and, once created, its history starts and runs by events like other agents entering and/or leaving the OE, group creation, role adoption, mission commitment, etc. The reorganisation is therefore a process which changes the current state of the OS or OE into a new one. Notice that there is a wide spectrum of change types. It can be, for instance, the adoption of a role by an agent (which changes only the OE) or a change in some group's set of roles (a change in the OS).

While we can identify two kinds of *changing objects* (OS or OE), we can also identify some types of *changing processes*:

1. Predefined changes: the reorganisation is already planed and is expressed, for example, as a temporal organisation model [2]. For example, a soccer team has previously accorded to change its formation at the 30 minutes of the match.
2. Controlled (*top-down*): the system does not know when it will reorganise, but when the reorganisation is necessary, it will be carried out by a known process (e.g. the team has an expert system that controls the reorganisation). This process might be performed in two ways: (*i*) an *endogenous* approach where the system's agent (centralised) or agents (decentralised) will carry out the reorganisation; or (*ii*) an *exogenous* approach: the MAS user will control the reorganisation process.
3. Emergent (*bottom-up*): there is not any kind of explicit control on the reorganisation. The reorganisation is performed by some agent according to its own methods.

Since we are concerned with a controlled reorganisation, the reorganisation process is composed by four phases: monitoring, design, selection, and implementation [10]. The problems inherent of these phases are detailed hereafter in sequence.

The Monitoring Phase. The monitoring phase identifies a situation where the current organisation does not satisfy the needs of the MAS. In other words, the current organisation constrains the agents' behaviours to those which do not fit the behaviours that draw the social purpose. Such situations may happen, for instance, when the environment has changed, the MAS purpose has changed, the performance requirements are not satisfied, the agents are not capable of well playing their roles, a new task request arrives and the current organisation is not appropriate, etc.

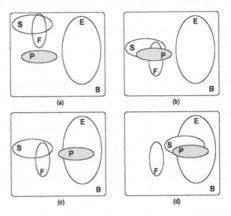

Fig. 2. Some organisational fails

In the Fig. 2, the characterisation of some of these situations are depicted. Given that a well organised system is characterised by $E \cap S \cap F \cap P \neq \emptyset$ and it is not considered changing either P (the purpose) or E (the environment), this figure depicts four fail situations. In the Fig. 2 situation (a), the purpose behaviours are not allowed neither by the environment nor by the organisation. In (b), the P's behaviours are allowed by the organisation, but the environment does not allow them; the reorganisation does not solve this two first fails. In (c), it is possible to achieve the social propose in the current environment, but the organisation does not allow it; thus the reorganisation process can solve this problem. In (d), the social purpose can be achieved in the current configuration, but the functional specification does not collaborate to it; again the reorganisation process can solve the problem.

The main problem in this phase is *how to identify whether the social purpose is not being achieved because the current organisation does not allow it*. Many other reasons may cause the unaccomplishment of the MAS purpose (e.g. the social purpose is impossible to be achieved, $P = \emptyset$). In some cases to change the organisation is not helpful (e.g. situations (a) and (b) of the Fig. 2).

The Design Phase. Once a modification need is identified during the monitoring phase, the next step intends to develop a set of possible alternatives for the current organisation.

The Selection and Implementation Phase. This phase selects one of the alternatives generated by the previous phase. The main problem is the *definition of the criteria to evaluate which proposal is more promising*. The problem in the implementation phase is how to change the current running organisation without causing many drawbacks. For example, how an agent will deal with the fact that the role it is playing was removed in the new organisation? What it will do with the commitments adopted under this extinguished role? As far as we know, there is no current work in progress addressing these problems.

As we briefly see, the reorganisation process is a complex and multi-faceted problem. Moreover, each application domain has its own set of problems leading to different technical solutions for the reorganisation phases (case based reasoning, learning, negotiation, etc). In the next section we present a reorganisation model that could express the logic of the reorganisation process and constrains the agents participating to the reorganisation to follow this logic.

3   Reorganisation upon $\mathcal{M}$OISE$^+$

The reorganisation model proposed here does not solve all the problems presented in the previous section. However it attempts to be an *open* proposal for the reorganisation process with the following assumptions: i) a $\mathcal{M}$OISE$^+$ organisation type is assumed; ii) only reorganisation at the specification level is considered (nevertheless many properties of this proposal can be applied on the entity level reorganisation); iii) the reorganisational phases are performed in an endogenous and decentralised approach.

As we conceive the reorganisation as one cooperative process among others in an MAS, we may thus describe it by the specification support given by $\mathcal{M}$OISE$^+$ itself. Following this trend, the next sections describe a group and a social scheme where the reorganisation process is performed.

Reorganisation Group. The reorganisation process is performed by a set of agents that play roles inside a group created from the group specification defined in the Fig. 3, this group is identified by `ReorgGr` (the graphical notation of the $\mathcal{M}$OISE$^+$ specification language is not detailed here, the reader is referred to [7] for more information). The *soc* role is the root of the role hierarchy, thus every role defined in a $\mathcal{M}$OISE$^+$ organisation inherits its properties.

The agent that assumes the *OrgManager* role is to be in charge of managing the reorganisation process, it is able to change the current state of the MAS's organisation (OS and OE). It also has authority on the *soc* agents and so on all agents.

Monitored is an abstract role[1] which is specialised by roles defined in the application organisation. All agents that will be monitored must play a *Monitored* sub-role and thus are under the *Monitor* agent authority since the *Monitor* role has authority on the *Monitored* role.

Reorg is also an abstract role which allows us to easily distinguish the *OrgManager* from the other roles in this group. Thus we can state, for example, that the *Reorg* and therefore all its sub-roles has permission to communicate with the *OrgManager*.

The *Historian* agent maintains the history of the organisation – a kind of useful information for the monitoring and design phases. Every change either in the OE (role adoption, commitment with missions, goal achievement, etc.) or in the OS (role creation, link creation, change in the cardinalities, etc.) is registered by this agent. The *Historian* will ask the *OrgManager* to inform him all changes it has executed. The agent which adopts this role could be the same that adopts the *OrgManager* role, since they are compatible.

The *Designer* role contains the com-mon properties for designers. Agents

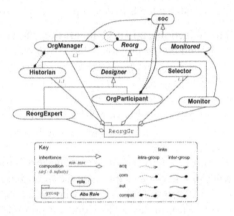

Fig. 3. The reorganisation group

playing *ReorgExpert* role have the ability (and the obligation) to analyse the current organisation, identify its problems, and propose alternatives. They are invited to partic-ipate to the `ReorgGr` just for the reorganisation process as a kind of outside analysts which are able to see the organisation from a global point of view. Conversely, every agent that plays a role in the MAS is also permitted to play the *OrgParticipant* role, since *OrgParticipant* is compatible with the *soc* role. These agents have practical knowledge about the way the organisation works. They are inside analysts and see the organisation from a local point of view.

Finally, the agent that plays the *Selector* role is responsible for the selection of one proposal from the reorganisation proposals developed by the *Designer* agents.

The set of agents that will play these roles is called *reorgConf*. While some of the reorgConf agents must be developed for each specific domain (such as the monitor, selector, and designers), some of them can be used in many applications (such as the OrgManager and the Historian). All of them must follow the behaviour constraints de-fined by the `ReorgGr` group and the reorganisation scheme defined in the next section.

---

[1] Abstract roles have only a specification purpose, no agent can play them.

Reorganisation Scheme. The reorgConf that has instantiated the `ReorgGr` will perform the reorganisation as defined in the scheme shown in the Fig. 4. This scheme is controlled by the *OrgManager* agent which has the obligation for the scheme's root goal. The reorganisation scheme decomposes the root goal in four sub-goals (monitoring, design, selection, and implementation) that have to be achieved in sequence by the agents compromised with the scheme's missions ($m_1, m_2, ..., m_6$). In the $\mathcal{MOISE}^+$, when an agent assumes a role (*ReorgExpert*, for instance) and some scheme is created (the reorganisation scheme, for instance), this agent has obligation or permission for this scheme's missions as stated in the deontic specification (the table of the Fig. 4, for instance).

Monitoring Phase. The method that *Monitor* agents will use to achieve their *monitoring* goal (in the mission m_2) is a domain dependent matter. Nevertheless, the $\mathcal{MOISE}^+$ may help this phase since the organisation description comprises the following useful information for monitoring: the social purpose is explicitly defined and can be verified by some monitor, the schemes are defined by goals which can also be checked, the global plans have a success rate, the well formed status of the structure can be checked, and it is possible to define roles like

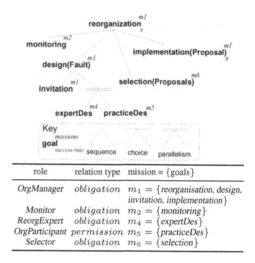

Fig. 4. The reorganisation scheme

role	relation type	mission = {goals}
OrgManager	*obligation*	$m_1 = \{$reorganisation, design, invitation, implementation$\}$
Monitor	*obligation*	$m_2 = \{$monitoring$\}$
ReorgExpert	*obligation*	$m_4 = \{$expertDes$\}$
OrgParticipant	*permission*	$m_5 = \{$practiceDes$\}$
Selector	*obligation*	$m_6 = \{$selection$\}$

Historian and *Monitored* – and the power these roles have/give – which are useful to collect information for the monitoring.

Once one *Monitor* has decided that a reorganisation is required, the *monitoring* goal holds and the next goal (*design*) is allowed. The *Monitor* must send a message to the *OrgManager* telling him the problem that has been identified. This problem description will replace the $Fault$ argument of the *design* goal.

Design Phase. In order to achieve the m_1's *design* goal, the *OrgManager* will firstly invite some agents to play the *Designer* roles (its m_1's *inviteDes* goal). The agents which accept the *ReorgExpert* role ought to commit to the mission m_4 and therefore try to achieve the m_4's *expertDes* goal (design a new organisation by expertise). Conversely, the agents which accept the *OrgParticipant* role are permitted (not obligated) to commit to the mission m_5. In case the *OrgParticipant* commits to the mission m_5, it ought to try to achieve the goals *practiceDes* (design new organisation by experimental knowledge).

Designer agents may use many methods and tools to achieve their goals. In the `ReorgGr`, each method can be implemented as an agent and the *OrgManager* can invite as many *Designers* as it thinks is enough. In other words, the proposed approach is

open: as many agents can play the *Designer* role, many tools (eventually very different) can be used in the reorganisation process. Rather than stating how the *Designers* will make their proposals, this group states the social conditions for participating in the reorganisation process.

In order to achieve its goal, a *Designer* has to write a *plan of changes* and send it to the *OrgManager*. The plan of changes have to modify, step by step, the current organisation to a new organisation. It is formed by actions like add/remove a role, a mission, an obligation, or a group specification. The plan of changes also have one of the following *focus* (the part of the current OS the plan intends to modify): all the current OS, a specific group or role belonging to the Structural Specification (SS), a specific scheme or mission belonging to the Functional Specification (FS), or relations in the Deontic Specification (DS).

The concept of plan of changes has two main advantages. Firstly, it defines step by step how the OS will be changed. Thus, when a *Designer* proposes a plan of changes it also has to deal with implementations issues like "add the role x and after remove the role y, or remove the role y and after add the role x?". The second advantage is the possibility of change only some part of the OS (the plan of changes focus), for instance the *Designer* may change the schemes without changing the roles.

The Selection and Implementation Phases. As in the two previous phases, the selection is also domain dependent. In the next section, a selection strategy is suggested. Once the *Selector* agent has selected one plan of changes, the *OrgManager* will perform this plan in order to reorganise the system.

Although implementation issues are not covered in this paper, the implementation of the reorgConf agents is helped by the $\mathcal{M}\text{OISE}^+$ architecture, available at http://www.lti.pcs.usp.br/moise. This architecture is composed by some general propose agents (as OrgManager), a communication infrastructure, and an agent architecture that follows the $\mathcal{M}\text{OISE}^+$ organisational specification and can be extend for specific applications. However, it is important to note that the agents must *follow* the organisation constraints and not be implemented based on it (as suggested by some MAS methodologies) since the organisation may change during the agent's life.

4   Case Study

In order to evaluate the implementability of the proposal, we have done some reorganisation experiments on a small size robot soccer league using the TeamBots simulator [1]. A robot team that follows a $\mathcal{M}\text{OISE}^+$ specification was developed. The agent architecture is based on a multi-layer approach. The top layer is the *organisational layer* which links the agent to the organisation. It enables the agent (a) to know the OS (groups, roles, schemes, ...); (b) to produce organisational events like group creation, role adoption, and mission commitment; and (c) to know its obligations and permission regarding position on the organisation. The *deliberative layer* is responsible for choosing a role and a mission for the agent. Having a mission and therefore its goals, this layer set the motor schema of the reactive layer that achieves the selected goal. The *reactive layer* perceives the environment and reacts to it according to its current motor schema [9].

Roughly, the initial organisational structure of this team is formed by five possible roles and their field area (Fig. 5). The team also has a reorganisation sub-group as defined in Sec. 3. The FS is formed by schemes that describe how to score a soccer goal. The agents missions is a set of goals associated to motor schemas that defines the robots' behaviour [9]. The team environment is composed by the match score, the match time, and the opponent. This team starts each match with a predefined OS and, during the match, is able to change its OS in order to better fit to the environment.

The reorgConf of the team is composed by one monitor, nine designers, and one selector. The monitor agent is very simple, it starts a reorganisation each 24,000 simulation steps. Since a match has 120,000 steps, we have 5 reorganisations each match. This monitoring strategy is justified by the exploration property of the Reinforcement Learning (RL) algorithm used by the selector agent.

The design phase is performed by 9 designer agents playing the *ReorgExpert* role. For instance, one designer always proposes a plan to change the current OS to a new OS where the players area is increased; other designer also focus on the SS and proposes to change the team formation to 1x1x3 (1 back, 1 middle field, and 3 attackers); another designer chooses to focus on the FS and proposes to change the players goals; etc.

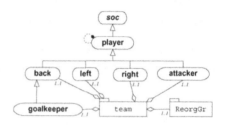

Fig. 5. Example of the team structure

The problem is therefore to find out the best sequence of reorganisations that lead the team to win, for instance "in the begin, select the proposal of the 1x1x3 designer, after select the proposal of the designer that use to decrease the area of the goalkeeper, ..., and, near the end of the game, if we are winning, select the proposal of the 1x4 designer". Since this problem can be seen as a Markov Decision Process (MDP) where the environment transition model is unknown, we can use the Q-Learning algorithm to find out the decision policy [12], i.e, in each reorganisation which designer proposal must be selected. After learning this policy, it can be used in the selection phase to choose the reorganisation plan with maximum expected reward.

For the Q-Learning specification, a state s is a pair formed by the game score and the reorganisation time (first, second, ..., fifth reorganisation). The opponent, the TeamBots package best team, is fixed, so it is not included in the state representation. The actions set A is composed by the action of selecting the proposal of designer i ($1 \leq i \leq 9$) and not change the organisation. The reward r of choosing a designer proposal is the number of goals the team scored minus the number of suffered goals after this proposal has been implemented. At each reorganisation, the selector agent updates the Q-values by the following rule: $Q(s, a) \leftarrow Q(s, a) + \alpha \left(r + \gamma \max_{a' \in A} Q(s', a') - Q(s, a) \right)$ where s and a represent the last reorganisation state and action, α is the learning rate (the initial value is 0.2 and decays 0.0001 each match), γ is the future discount rate (we use 0.9), and s' is the next state in case the action a' is performed (see [12] for RL algorithm's parameters). Based on the current state s'', the selector then chooses the next action by the following function

$$\epsilon - greedy(s") = \begin{cases} \text{ramdom action from } A & \text{if } rv < \epsilon \\ \arg\max_a Q(s", a) & \text{otherwise} \end{cases}$$

rv is a random value $(0 < rv \leq 1)$ and ϵ $(0 \leq \epsilon \leq 1)$ is the exploration rate (it starts with 0.5 and decays 0.0001 each match).

The Fig. 6 shows the team final score along 2000 matches when using Q-Learning to learn to select the designer proposals. It takes about 480 matches to learn a good selection policy, i.e., a good sequence of reorganisations during a match. Thus, with this particular reorgConf, we have an MAS that learns to reorganise itself according to its environment (the opponent). The selection and implementation problems presented at the Sec. 2 are solved in our proposal by the RL and the concept of plan of changes. Of course, this case study does not aim at the soccer problems, but it has exemplified how the proposed reorganisational model could be successfully applied.

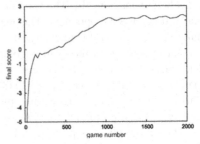

Fig. 6. Learning results

5   Related Work

Lots of work has been done on reorganisation in MAS. Some, as in [13], use an exogenous approach where the user itself reorganise the whole system. Other, like our proposal, use an endogenous approach where the agent themselves modify the organisation. To our knowledge, none of these approaches make clear and explicit the organisation controlling the reorganisation process itself. The reorganisation process is usually hard coded in the MAS itself.

For example, the proposal of [6], a centralised reorganisation process with change focus on the FS (described by TÆMS), uses a diagnostic expert system to identify organisational fails and to propose a solution. Its monitoring phase identifies those fails when the system does not behave as expected by its functional model. Our proposal does not have a specific monitoring approach and thus we can have an MAS that *explores* new organisations even in cases no organisational fails occurs (Sec. 4).

The proposal of [11] has a more flexible monitoring phase. Any agent, a soccer player, can identify in the environment the opportunity for reorganisation. The reorganisation is composed by a change in the team formation (a structural reorganisation in $\mathcal{M}$OISE$^+$ terms) and in the current plan (functional level). Our proposal, besides the explicit organisational model, enable us to consider another modification objects, the deontic specification for instance (our proposal can maintain the same roles and change only their obligations to plans).

6   Conclusions

This paper has presented a general view of the reorganisation problem under the $\mathcal{M}$OISE$^+$ point of view. The main contribution is a reorganisation model where the agents have autonomy to change their organisations. This process is based on an OC point of view throughout the specification of a dedicated reorganisation group.

The $\mathcal{M}\text{OISE}^+$ organisational model has been shown as a good support for the specification of an MAS's organisation which intends to reorganise itself because (i), as an organisational description, it gives useful information for the monitoring and design phases and (ii), as a specification tool, it allows us to define the reorganisation process with valuable properties: (a) the openness for many types of monitoring, design, and selection; (b) the definition of special roles like the *OrgManager* and *Monitored*; and (c) the specification of the reorganisation through the $\mathcal{M}\text{OISE}^+$ enable any $\mathcal{M}\text{OISE}^+$ agent to understand and participate in the reorganisation.

References

1. T. Balch. Teambots, 2000. `http://www.teambots.org`.
2. T. Carron and O. Boissier. Towards a temporal organizational structure language for dynamic multi-agent systems. In *Proceedings of the MAAMAW'2001*, Annecy, 2001.
3. V. Dignum and F. Dignum. Modelling agent societies: Co-ordination frameworks and institutions. In P. Brazdil and A. Jorge, editors, *Proceedings of the EPIA'01*, pages 191–204, Berlin, 2001. Springer.
4. J. Galbraith. *Organization Design*. Addison-Wesley, 1977.
5. L. Gasser. Organizations in multi-agent systems. In *Pre-Proceeding of the MAAMAW'2001*, Annecy, 2001.
6. B. Horling, B. Benyo, and V. Lesser. Using self-diagnosis to adapt organizational structures. In *Proceedings of the Agents'01*, 2001.
7. J. F. Hübner, J. S. Sichman, and O. Boissier. A model for the structural, functional, and deontic specification of organizations in multiagent systems. In G. Bittencourt and G. L. Ramalho, editors, *Proceedings of the SBIA'02*, pages 118–128, Berlin, 2002. Springer.
8. C. Lemaître and C. B. Excelente. Multi-agent organization approach. In F. J. Garijo and C. Lemaître, editors, *Proceedings of II Iberoamerican Workshop on DAI and MAS*, 1998.
9. R. R. Murphy. *Introduction to AI robotics*. Bradford Book/MIT Press, 2000.
10. Y. So and E. H. Durfee. An organizational self-design model for organizational change. In *Proceedings of AAAI93 Workshop on AI and Theories of Groups and Organizations*, 1993.
11. P. Stone and M. M. Veloso. Task decomposition and dynamic role assignment for real-time strategic teamwork. In J. P. Müller, M. P. Singh, and A. S. Rao, editors, *Proceedings of the ATAL-98*, pages 293–308, Berlin, 1999. Springer.
12. R. S. Sutton and A. G. Barto. *Reinforcement Learning: An Introduction*. Bradford, Cambridge, 1998.
13. M. Tambe, D. V. Pynadath, and N. Chauvat. Building dynamic agent organizations in cyberspace. *IEEE Internet Computing*, 4(2), 2001.
14. M. Wooldridge, N. R. Jennings, and D. Kinny. A methodology for agent-oriented analysis and design. In *Proceedings of the Agent's 99*. ACM, 1999.

A Paraconsistent Approach
for Offer Evaluation in Negotiations

Fabiano M. Hasegawa, Bráulio C. Ávila, and Marcos Augusto H. Shmeil

Pontifical Catholic University of Paraná – PUCPR, Brazil
{fmitsuo,avila,shm}@ppgia.pucpr.br

Abstract. The mission of an organization stands for its goals and also leads corrections likely to occur in the posture adopted by the organization before the society. In order to fulfill the goals of the organization, this one needs to interact with other components of the society. Within an organization each individual responsible for the sale and purchase of either commodities or services detens knowledge concerning possible values of the criteria used to represent a determined commodity or service which may be either offered or accepted in a negotiation. So, an offer may be seen as an inconsistency aroused between the previous knowledge owned by the negotiator and the offer. This article presents a *Paraconsistent Approach* based on a heuristic of multi-value decrement followed by formalization into Evidential Paraconsistent Logic to assess offers in a negotiation session. When compared to the *Utility Value Approach*, the paraconsistent one converges toward the negotiation ending with fewer interactions.

1 Introduction

Within an organization, each individual responsible for the sale and purchase of commodities or services detens knowledge concerning possible values of the criteria used to represent a determined commodity or service which may be either offered or accepted in a negotiation. This knowledge is part of the organizational knowledge that stands for the "truth" about the world, the world from the organization's point of view.

In a negotiation, an offer may arouse a conflict with the previous knowledge owned by the negotiator. This conflict may be seen as an intra-case inconsistency. Racine and Yang [1] have identified two types of inconsistencies that may occur in a case base. The inter-case inconsistency occurs when two or more similar cases in the same base arouse contradictions. In the intra-case inconsistency the case which is stored in a base arouses contradiction with the previous knowledge of such case.

This work describes a new approach based on a multi-value heuristic followed by formalization into Evidential Paraconsistent Logic (*EPL*) [2, 3] to evaluate the offers in a negotiation. The *EPL* is used to represent the rules and offers that describe how consistent the offer is according to the individual knowledge of the

A.L.C. Bazzan and S. Labidi (Eds.): SBIA 2004, LNAI 3171, pp. 516–525, 2004.

negotiator. If an offer is consistent and is "true" for the negotiator, it is then accepted. The ARTOR – ARTificial ORganizations [4] – is a Multiagent System (MAS) which simulates a society of organizations – each organization owns agents responsible for the operations of purchasing and selling either commodities or services. Within this MAS a new approach is undertaken by the supply executor and by the selection executor agents which are, respectively, responsible for the operations of purchase and sale.

Section 2 presents how a negotiation using the *Utility Value Approach* is achieved in the ARTOR. In section 3 the *Paraconsistent Approach* is detailed and explained. Section 4 presents the results of tests as well as the comparison between the *Paraconsistent Approach* and the *Utility Value Approach*. Finally, in section 5 some conclusions are inferred.

2   Negotiation in ARTOR

The ARTOR provides an environment which simulates a society of artificial organizations by accounting for both the intra-organizational and inter-organizational dimensions [4]. Each organization is composed of three classes of agents: the cover agent which stands for the organization, the administrator agent responsible for planning and coordination and the executor agent responsible for operational tasks. Another important component of the society is the Newsstand, a public blackboard known by every organization. The Newsstand is used for news exchanging – about business – among organizations.

2.1   Offer Evaluation

In the ARTOR, the commodity or service the organization is willing to sell is represented by a Criteria List (CL) [4]. The CL composed of Selection Criteria (SC) which determines the dimensions used to describe and evaluate the commodity or service. The CL is defined by[1]:

$$CL_{product1}(SC_1, SC_2, ..., SC_n)$$

Each SC has a weight according to its utility for the organization – a type of SC may be more important than other. The utility, in Economics, is an analytical concept which represents a subjective pleasure, the advantage or the satisfaction derived from the consumption of commodities, and explains how consumers divide their limited resources among the commodities consumed [5].

The offer utility value is used to evaluate the offer and according to the result it will be either accepted or not, and it is defined by the sum of all utility values of the dimension instances of the CL:

$$offer\_utility = \sum_{i=0}^{j} instance\_utility_i.$$

The instance utility value is obtained as follows:

---

[1] This representation of the CL was modified to bear continuous values.

$$instance\_utility = (Pr_i \times relative\_instance\_value)$$

The relative instance value for a continuous SC is the relative position of the value in the domain of values of the SC_i. If the relative instance value is positioned on the side that better satisfies – the side indicated by $\{left, right, none\}$ in relation to the value that satisfies – the relative value will be positive, otherwise it will be negative. The relative instance value of a discrete value will be 1 if it exists in the domain of the values, otherwise the relative value will be -1.

3   Paraconsistent Approach for Offer Evaluation

The ParaLog_e [6, 7] is an interpreter of *EPL* based on *Annotated Paraconsistent Logic* [2, 3, 8]. The *EPL* is infinitely valued and its truth values belong to the lattice $\tau = \langle |\tau|, \leq \rangle$, where:

$$|\tau| = \{\mu 1 \in \Re | 0 \leq x \leq 1\} \times \{\mu 2 \in \Re | 0 \leq x \leq 1\}.$$

In the *EPL* a preposition p owns two annotated values $p : [\mu 1, \mu 2]$. The annotated value $\mu 1$ is the favorable evidence to p and the value $\mu 2$ is the contrary evidence to p.

It is possible to obtain from the $[\mu 1, \mu 2]$ the Contradiction Degree (*CtD*) and the Certainty Degree (*CD*) in which the preposition lies [2]. The *CtD* stands for the distance between the inconsistent ($\top$) and the undetermined ($\bot$) truth values. The *CD* stands for the distance between the true (t) and the false (f) truth values.

3.1   Paraconsistent Approach Architecture

The offer evaluation by using the *Paraconsistent Approach* – see Figure 1 – begins when an offer is received by the agent executing the selection. First the offer is translated into facts that use the representation formalism of the *EPL* – Subsection 3.2. after this operation the rules of evaluation are created, having as a basis the facts – Subsection 3.2. So it is obtained as output a text file that contains the facts that represent the offer and the rules of evaluation. The text file is loaded in the Paralog_e and a query of the rules is made. The outcome of this query is the favorable evidence ($\mu 1$) and the contrary evidence ($\mu 2$) in relation to the offer. The *CD* and the *CtD* are obtained from $[\mu 1, \mu 2]$ and they are converted into discrete values by the algorithm Para-Analyzer – Subsection 3.3 – into resulting logical status. The resulting logical status is used to assess the offer. If the resulting logical status is t then the offer is accepted. Otherwise, a decrement value is chosen according to the resulting logical status and used in the creation of a counter-offer.

3.2   Translating Offers to the EPL Representation Formalism

The *paraconsistent_mapping* module is responsible for translating the $SC's$ of an offer into evidential facts. It is also responsible for creating the rules that will

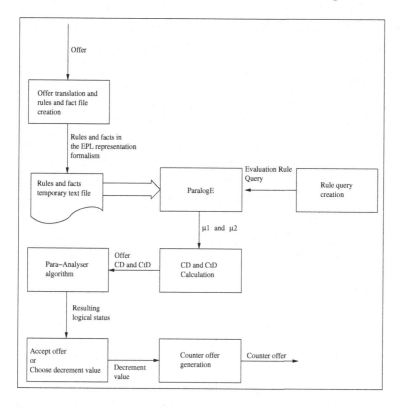

Fig. 1. Offer evaluation architecture through *Paraconsistent Approach.*

evaluate the offer. The value of a SC is mapped into evidential values $[\mu1, \mu2]$ according to the organization PS and the restrictions[2].

If the SC belongs to a discrete domain so the SC instance value is mapped into evidential values as follows:

- $SC\_ID(Value) : [1,0]$ if $Value \in \{element_1, element_2...element_N\}$;
- $SC\_ID(Value) : [0,0]$ if $Value \notin \{element_1, element_2...element_N\}$;
- $SC\_ID(Value) : [0,1]$ if the value fits a restriction for the SC.

If the SC belongs to the continuous domain then the SC instance value is mapped into evidential values as follows[3]:

- $SC\_ID(Value) : [\mu1, \mu2]$ is equal to e, where $e \in E$ ($e = [\mu1, \mu2]$) according to the index k obtained by the function $P(x)$;
- $SC\_ID(Value) : [1,0]$ if $S\_less \leq S\_more$ and $Value > S\_less$ and $Value > S\_more$;

---

[2] The restrictions indicate, for a determined SC, which values are not accepted. The restriction may be applied to bigger, smaller or equal values to a determined value.

[3] The S_less is the value that less satisfies and S_more is the value that more satisfies.

- $SC\_ID(Value) : [0,1]$ if $S\_less \leq S\_more$ and $Value < S\_less$ and $Value < S\_more$;
- $SC\_ID(Value) : [1,0]$ if $S\_less > S\_more$ and $Value < S\_less$ and $Value < S\_more$;
- $SC\_ID(Value) : [0,1]$ if $S\_less > S\_more$ and $Value > S\_less$ and $Value > S\_more$;
- $SC\_ID(Value) : [0,1]$ if the value fits a restriction for the SC.

The function $P(x)$ returns the index k which is associated to the element e ($e = [\mu1, \mu2]$) – belonging to the set E – which corresponds to the evidential values, of the instance value, in relation to the PS contained in the individual knowledge base of the negotiator agent. The function $P(x)$ is defined by[4]:

- $P(x) = -1$ if $x < S\_less$;
- $P(x) = 0$ if $x = S\_less$;
- $P(x) = \frac{10}{(S\_more - S\_less)} \times \frac{(Value\_SC - S\_less)}{Un}$ if:
  - $S\_less \leq x \leq S\_more$;
  - $S\_less \geq x \geq S\_more$.
- $P(x) = 10$ if $x \geq S\_more$.

The evidential values contained in the set E [5] were created through an idiosyncratic heuristic. The offer evaluation in the *Paraconsistent Approach* uses a set of rules which are composed of the facts that represent the SC's of an offer. As in the facts, a rule represented on the formalism of the LPE also owns associated evidential values. The facts are grouped in the rules according to their utility for the organization. Three zones of utility that group the facts were defined by the *utility_zone/2* predicate:

```
utility_zone(high, [10, 9, 8]).
utility_zone(mid, [7, 6, 5]).
utility_zone(low, [4, 3, 2, 1]).
```

Thus, the respect for the utility of the facts is guaranteed. For instance, a fact that represents a SC with low utility and fulfills perfectly what the organizations seeks, will not have much influence on the offer acceptance.

After grouping of the facts in the rules, the evidential values of the rules are obtained in a similar manner to the one used to find the evidential values of the facts. The *rule_evidences(Utl, L)* predicate represents all possible combinations of evidential values that may be used in the rules.

There are ten *rule_evidences(Utl, L)* predicates and each one corresponds to a utility (Utl)[6] associated to a set L, which contains the evidential values[7] to be

---

[4] Un stands for the value of an unit, for instance 30 for value type date.

[5] $E = \{-1 - 0 : 1, 0 - 0 : 0, 1 - 0.1 : 0.0, 2 - 0.2 : 0.8, 3 - 0.3 : 0.7, 4 - 0.4 : 0.6, 5 - 0.5 : 0.5, 6 - 0.6 : 0.4, 7 - 0.7 : 0.3, 8 - 0.8 : 0.2, 9 - 0.9 : 0.1, 10 - 1 : 0\}$.

[6] In this work it was assumed that the minimum utility is 1 and the maximum one is 10.

[7] The values of the evidential values contained in the set L were also created from a idiosyncratic heuristic.

mapped into a rule. The set L, used for the mapping of a determined rule, will be chosen according to the SC of bigger utility.

Once the set L – associated to a utility – was chosen, the rule will take the evidential values indicated by the element l ($l = [\rho1, \rho2]$) of the set L. The element l is found through the index j ($0 \leq j \leq 10$) through the function $R(x)$:

$$R(x) = \tfrac{10}{N} \times \left(\sum_{i=0}^{n} Ev1_i\right)$$

In $R(x)$, N indicates the quantity of facts the rule owns, and $Ev1_i$ is the favorable evidence of each fact belonging to this rule.

The output of the *paraconsistent_mapping* module is a temporary text file[8] which contains the SC's of an offer and the respective evaluation rules.

3.3 Offer Evaluation Through the Para-analyser Algorithm

The offer evaluation is made by the Para-analyser algorithm [2], the Para-analyser algorithm input is the Ctd and the CD and the output is a logical status. It is possible to define a lattice with more logical statuses than the basic set – $\mid \tau \mid = \{\top, t, f, \bot\}$. The more logical statuses the greater the precision in the analysis of the CtD and of the CD. This work uses a lattice with 12 logical statuses – Figure 2.

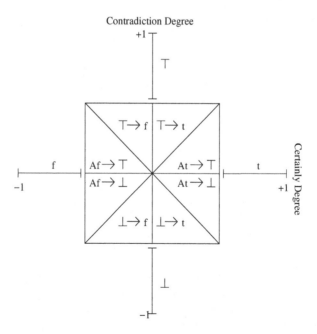

Fig. 2. Lattice with 12 logical status represented in the CtD and CD graphic.

---

[8] Every time the negotiator agent receives an offer the file is erased.

Where:

- $\top$: inconsistent;
- $\top \rightarrow t$: inconsistent toward truth;
- $\top \rightarrow f$: inconsistent toward false;
- t: truth;
- $At \rightarrow \top$: almost truth toward inconsistent;
- $At \rightarrow \bot$: almost truth toward indeterminate;
- f: false;
- $Af \rightarrow \top$: almost false toward inconsistent;
- $Af \rightarrow \bot$: almost false toward indeterminate;
- $\bot$: indeterminate;
- $\bot \rightarrow t$: indeterminate toward truth;
- $\bot \rightarrow f$: indeterminate toward false;

The Para-Analyser algorithm transform the *CtD* and the *CD* into discrete values, interpolating them in the lattice and the convergence point is the resulting logical status. The sensibility of extreme values may be regulated by using the control limits. There are four limit values:

- *Sccv*: *Superior Certainly Control Value* limits the *CD* next to the truth;
- *Iccv*: *Inferior Certainly Control Value* limits the *CD* next to the false;
- *Sctcv*: *Superior Contradiction Control Value* limits the *CtD* next to the inconsistent;
- *Ictcv*: *Inferior Contradiction Control Value* limits the *CtD* next to the indeterminate;

In this work the value used for the *Sccv* was 0.6, and for the other superior and inferior limits 0.5 and -0.5, respectively. According to tests, the increase of the *Sccv* corresponds to an increase of the minimum utility so that the organization accepts the offer. The increase of the *Iccv* corresponds to a decrement in the relaxation when an organization offer anew.

Each resulting logical status may be used to generate either simple or complex actions in the agent. In this work the resulting logical status determines the decrement value which will be used to generate a new offer or counter-offer. The closer a resulting logical status of an offer is to the state t the smaller the decrement to be used in the counter-offer will be.

4   Tests

The scenario used in the tests describes an organization that wishes to buy a determined product in the market. To achieve it the organization broadcasts an announcement urging the society and all organizations interested in providing such a product to contact and begin negotiations. There are two situations that were approached in the tests:

- An organization responds to the announcement;
- Two organizations respond to the announcement.

In the situations presented above, both offer evaluation approaches were used for the organization that wishes to buy the product as well as for the supplier ones.

The values[9] contained in the *PS's* of the organizations were the same ones used in both approaches. The Consumer organization (*CO*) uses the following values:

- *CS*: Size, Possible Values: $\{M, L\}$, Priority: 1;
- *CS*: Model, Possible Values: $\{sport, regular\}$, Priority: 1;
- *CS*: Color, Possible Values: $\{blue, black\}$, Priority: 1;
- *CS*: Price, Possible Values: $\{5, 30\}$, Priority: 10;
- *CS*: Payment Term, Possible Values: $\{0, 120\}$, Priority: 7;
- *CS*: Quantity, Possible Values: $\{50, 80\}$, Priority: 4;

The Supplier organizations (*SO*) uses the following values:

- *CS*: Size, Possible Values: $\{S, M\}$, Priority: 4;
- *CS*: Model, Possible Values: $\{sport, regular\}$, Priority: 4;
- *CS*: Color, Possible Values: $\{blue, black\}$, Priority: 4;
- *CS*: Price, Possible Values: $\{5, 40\}$, Priority: 4;
- *CS*: Payment Term, Possible Values: $\{0, 120\}$, Priority: 5;
- *CS*: Quantity, Possible Values: $\{50, 80\}$, Priority: 10;

According to the strategy used, the initial offer made by the *CO* is the maximization of the continuous values contained in its *PS*. For discrete values the choice is at random, once any value of the set satisfies the *CO*. The values used in the initial offer made by the *CO* is (Size: M, Model: sport, Color: blue, Price: 5, Payment Term: 120, Quantity: 80).

In the tests, the negotiation session was limited to a number of 50 interactions. If at the end of a session a *SO* does not make an offer that the *CO* accepts, so the negotiation is closed without winners.

The decrement value of the *CO* chosen for the *Utility Value Approach* was 5 and for the paraconsistent one $5 - 15$ because they presents a better gain in relation to price and term for payment term that have the two highest utilities for the *CO*. For the *SO* (*SOU*) which uses the *Utilitity Value Approach* the decrement value chosen was 15 and for the *SO* (*SOP*) which uses the *Paraconsistent Approach* the range of values was $4 - 20$. Both values of the *SO's* present a gain in quantity which is the *SC* the one which has more utility.

4.1   Results from Tests

In the tests carried out one could observe that the selection agent that used the *Utility Value Approach* obtained a bigger utility for itself when it negotiated

---

[9] For *SC's* that belong to the continuous domain, the first value corresponds to the value that satisfies less and the second value corresponds to the value that satisfies more.

Table 1. Results of negotiation between the *CO* with decrement value set at 5 and the *SO* with several decrement values, both using the *Utiliti Value Approach*.

CO	SO	Interactions	Utility	Result	Accepted Offer
5	5	23	-4	contracted	[m, sport, blue, 6, 120, 52]
5	10	12	-9	contracted	[m, sport, black, 8, 120, 56]
5	15	24	-28	contracted	[m, sport, blue, 10, 120, 56]

Table 2. Results of negotiation between the *CO* with decrement value ranging 5 − 15 and the *SO* with several decrement values, both using the *Paraconsistent Approach*.

CO	SO	Interactions	CD	Result	Accepted Offer
5-15	2-10	11	0.6	contracted	[m, regular, black, 11, 120, 56]
5-15	5-15	7	0.7	contracted	[m, sport, blue, 8, 120, 56]
5-15	4-20	5	0.8	contracted	[m, regular, black, 8, 120, 64]

Table 3. Results of negotiation between the *CO* with decrement value set at 5 and the *SO* with several decrement values.

CO	SO	Interactions	Utility	Result	Accepted Offer
5	4-20	8	44	contracted	[m, sport, blue, 6, 120, 64]
10	4-20	7	45	contracted	[m, regular, blue, 6, 120, 64]
15	4-20	6	53	contracted	[m, sport, black, 5, 120, 64]

Table 4. Results of negotiation between the *CO* and *SOP* and *SOU*.

CO	SOP	SOU	Interactions	Utility/CD	Winner	Accepted Offer
5	4-20	15	8	44	SOP	[m, sport, blue, 6, 120, 64]
5-15	4-20	15	5	0.8	SOP	[m, sport, blue, 8, 120, 64]

with a supplier agent which used the same approach – see Table 1. However, the same agent obtained an even better result when it negotiated with a supplier agent which used the *Paraconsistent Approach* – see Table 3, in this case both organizations succeeded because the negotiation was ended with fewer interactions and both the *CO* and *SO* reaches a good utility value in the last offer, the same happens when both agents uses the *Paraconsistent Approach* – see Table 2.

5   Conclusions

The *Paraconsistent Approach* converges toward the end of negotiation with fewer interactions when compared to the *Utility Value Approach* – see Table 4. Due to the very nature of a negotiation, it is impossible to infer that the result obtained was the best one.

The use of the *EPL* in this work is due to the formalism representation offered to the problem. The gain in the approach is due to the use of a list of decrement values instead of a set one. The *EPL* allows using the list of decrements in a suitable manner, according to the logical interpretation represented in the lattice – which could be customised.

The time of an offer evaluation using the *Paraconsistent Approach* is 654 milliseconds and the average time of an offer evaluation using the *Utility Value Approach* is 2 milliseconds. As this work aimed at developing a new approach, there was not interest in optimizing the time.

References

1. Racine, K., Yang, Q.: On the consistency management of large case bases: the case for validation. In: Verification and Validation Workshop 1996. (1996)
2. da Costa, N.C.A.e.a.: Lógica Paraconsistente Aplicada. Atlas, São Paulo (1999)
3. Subrahmanian, V.S.: Towards a theory of evidential reasoning in logic programming. In: Logic Colloquium '87, Spain, The European Summer Meeting of the Association for Symbolic Logic (1987)
4. Shmeil, M.A.H.: Sistemas Multiagente na Modelação da Estrutura e Relações de Contratação de Organizações. PhD thesis, Faculdade de Engenharia da Universidade do Porto, Porto (1999)
5. Samuelson, P.A., Nordhaus, W.D.: Economia. McGraw-Hill de Portugal Lda, Portugal (1990)
6. da Costa, N.C.A., Prado, J.P.A., Abe, J.M., Ávila, B.C., Rillo, M.: Paralog: Um prolog paraconsistente baseado em lógica anotada. In: Coleção Documentos. Number 18 in Série: Lógica e Teoria da Ciência. Instituto de Estudos Avançados, Universidade de São Paulo (1995)
7. Ávila, B., Abe, J., Prado, J.: Paralog_e: A paraconsistent evidential logic programming language. In: XVII International Conference of the Chilean Computer Science Society, Chile, IEEE Computer Science Society Press (1997)
8. Blair, H.A., Subrahmanian, V.S.: Paraconsistent foundations for logic programming. Journal of Non-Classical Logic **5** (1988) 45–73

Sequential Bilateral Negotiation

Orlando Pinho Jr.[1], Geber Ramalho[1], Gustavo de Paula[2], and Patrícia Tedesco[1]

[1] Centro de Informática, Universidade Federal de Pernambuco, Recife, PE, Brasil
Phone: +55 8121268430
{ocpj,glr,pcart}@cin.ufpe.br
[2] C.E.S.A.R, Rua Bione, 220, Bairro do Recife, Recife, PE, Brazil
Phone: +55 8134254700
gep@cesar.org.br

Abstract. For some B2C or B2B market places, such as electronic shopping malls, agents representing the buyers could "go shopping" and negotiate with several stores looking for the best deal. To develop agents capable to act in a scenario like this one, it is necessary to deal with several issues that go beyond the bilateral negotiation or auction. In the agent mediated e-commerce literature, there are no in-depth studies on this kind of negotiation, which we call sequential bilateral negotiations (SBNs). The related works provide only superficial insights on multiple bilateral negotiations or are rather concerned with auction models. In this paper, we characterize SBNs, showing the differences between them and auctions or simple bilateral negotiations. We also discuss the main issues on defining a negotiation protocol and designing agents for SBN. In order to achieve a better understanding on SBN and its practical implications, we present a particular implementation of a SBN protocol and an ensemble of agents capable of carrying negotiations under this protocol. This implementation provides experimental results illustrating some nuances of this kind of negotiation model.

1 Introduction

E-commerce enables situations where a user configures an agent to go shopping in the Internet, sequentially negotiating with different Internet seller agents. After each bilateral negotiation (i.e, situation where seller and buyer with contradictory demands must exchange proposals in order to reach an agreement) [4,5,12], this agent should decide whether to make a deal or to continue looking for a better one, probably using the information collected in previous negotiations. We call this kind of negotiation *Sequential Bilateral Negotiation* (SBN). For instance, in a first negotiation, a buyer agent could reach an agreement (let us say $ 10.00) for the price of a CD with a seller S_1. Despite the fact that this value is lower than $12.00, which is the maximum value the buyer is able to pay, the buyer asks S_1 to commit to the agreement for a while and moves to a second negotiation trying to improve its payoff. The negotiation with S_2 is not that successful, reaching the value $11.00 for the CD. Then, the buyer discards this outcome and starts a third negotiation with a seller S_3, reaching an agreement on $ 9.50. Since the buyer agent do not want to spend more time on additional negotiations, it warns S_1 that it found a better offer and closes the transaction with S_3.

Until now, in agent-mediated e-commerce (AMEC) area, multilateral negotiations are modeled mainly as auctions [1,11,17]. The works that could deal with multiple

A.L.C. Bazzan and S. Labidi (Eds.): SBIA 2004, LNAI 3171, pp. 526–535, 2004.

bilateral negotiations do not consider some important issues regarding this type of game [3,5,11]. As discussed later, SBN issues go beyond auction and simple bilateral negotiation.

This paper aims at discussing SBN, presenting questions such as: which interaction protocol is appropriate for SBNs? How can a buyer agent take full advantage of the negotiation history? How does time influence the interactions and the decision-making?

In Section 2, we characterize SBNs, showing the differences between it and auctions or simple bilateral negotiations. In Sections 3 and 4, we introduce, respectively, the main issues on defining a negotiation protocol for SBN, as well as the issues on designing agents capable of acting under this protocol. A particular implementation of a protocol and some agents is presented in Section 5. The experimental results obtained with this implementation are discussed in Section 6, while last Section summarizes the main conclusions and future work.

2   Multiple and Sequential Bilateral Negotiations

In e-commerce, as in the real world, a buyer should be able to negotiate bilaterally with different sellers, offering the same product or service with different conditions, in order to find the best possible deal. A possible model for this scenario, where bilateral negotiations can be performed sequentially or simultaneously is, what we call, *multiple bilateral negotiation* (MBN). In this model, according to the final outcome or partial results of a bilateral negotiation, the buyer can close the deal or try to negotiate with other seller (possibly using the information concerning this and other previous negotiations), until making a better deal or depleting all available sellers.

The simplest way to implement a MBN is through *sequential bilateral negotiation* (SBN), where the buyer agent only starts a new negotiation after having the outcome of the previous one. In fact, the simultaneous model is far more complex than the sequential one and involves issues such as: what to do when there is an imminent deal with a seller and the other negotiations are in different states? How to compare different negotiation's states?

The difference between multiple and simple bilateral negotiations is clear and particularly focused on the fact that, in MBN, the buyer can compare sellers' conditions. Concerning multilateral negotiations such as auctions [1,7,8,15,17], the difference is that they have a protocol defining the game rules considering more than two players. In other words, there is a single negotiation process with more than two players. Alternatively, in a MBN there are several independent (bilateral) negotiation processes, each of them being ruled by a bilateral negotiation protocol.

Moreover, the economic role of auctions is usually to determine the value for rare products and/or maximize the value of the good being offered, favoring one party. On the other hand, MBN concern interaction between opponent parts exchanging proposals to reach an agreement that is good enough for both. This model does not favor any party (sellers or buyers) a priori, making it easier to implement a competitive market.

3   Issues on SBN Protocol

In order to build an environment where agents can perform SBN, it is necessary to deal with some issues involving the definition of a negotiation protocol. In simple bilateral negotiation, when agents reach an *agreement* (concerning the values under negotiation), they immediately make a *deal*, starting then the payment procedures [4,6,14]. In SBN, it is necessary to separate the notions of agreement and deal in order to allow the buyer to continue negotiating with the subsequent seller agents of the market. This is possible with the use of the notion of *Commitment*: when the players reach an agreement, they can make a commitment to keep the negotiated conditions (issue values) until a given *deadline*. After this deadline, the commitment is automatically canceled. Before the deadline, the seller can either *cancel* the commitment (because it reached or intends to reach a better agreement) or *confirm* it, concluding the transaction.

The manner and moment to establish the commitment deadline may vary. The commitment deadline can be either negotiated by the players, informed by the seller agent, or imposed externally by the market. It is also important to consider when the commitment takes place. This can happen before the negotiation begins; when a deal is reached; or through the negotiation process (as one of the issues being negotiated). This has an impact in the agent decision-making, because, if the deadline is predefined by the sellers, the agent may consider this information to decide with whom to negotiate.

4   Issues on SBN Agents

There are several issues to take into account when building agents for SBN, both on the seller and on the buyer sides. From a methodological point of view, we have decided to first focus our studies on the buyers, leaving the sellers for future work. So, we will discuss here the different aspects related to the buyer's decision-making. For instance, the buyer could use the negotiation history to get better deals in the future negotiations. There are at least two approaches to achieve that: machine learning and heuristics. Even though there have been some works (e.g. [2,10,16]) dealing with machine learning in agent negotiation, they have tackled environments that are simpler than the SBN one, since they not consider the information from previous negotiation processes. Our study considered preliminarily only the heuristic-based decision-making, exploring the notion of ultimatum as a bargaining mechanism.

4.1   Using Ultimatum in SBN

In order to get better results in subsequent negotiations, an agent could use the *ultimatum* or change its *reservation value*. An ultimatum is used to indicate that the agent will leave the negotiation if the opponent does not accept its proposal. In SBN, the ultimatum could be used, as a bluff, to force the seller to accept a value lower or equal to the one the buyer obtained in a previous negotiation. Going back to the example in the introduction, the buyer, having already obtained an agreement of $11.00 with seller S_1, could give an ultimatum of $10.00 to seller S_3. Of course, if the agent uses the ultimatum, it takes the risk of having its offer rejected. The higher the expected results are, the higher the possibility that the ultimatum is rejected.

The alternative to ultimatum is to set the agent's reservation value ($ 12.00 in the case of our example) to the one obtained in best agreement so far ($11.00), or even to a lower value (e.g., $10.00). This procedure guarantees that the buyer will not pay more than the best offer obtained. However, it is not assured that this approach will lead to future successful negotiations, since negotiations may vary a lot from opponent to opponent. For instance, given that the buyer will cede less, an agreement may not be reached with a tough opponent. Moreover, the change in the reservation value has necessarily an impact on proposal generation tactics [5] that may not be desired, for instance, in the case the buyer has a winner tactics for the market.

Thus, we think that the ultimatum approach is more adequate than reservation value change, because it does not impose changes in the buyer behavior and allows a more precise estimation of the risks, since they depend basically on the expected payoff improvement. Despite these advantages, the use of ultimatum also raises various issues such as: How to determine the expected gain for a future negotiation? How to decide whether to continue negotiating or to confirm a commitment? How to choose the best commitment available? How to manage time appropriately? The following sections discuss some of these problems, which require a good balance between risk and payoff.

4.2 Time Management and Best Commitment Evaluation

In most models of simple bilateral negotiation, the user can set the *maximum negotiation time* available to the agent to reach an agreement (with a single opponent). The agent acting on the behalf of the user incorporates this time information in the proposal generation tactics and/or in the decision of accepting a proposal. In SBN, the management of time is much more complex, since the given time must be used for the entire *negotiation round*, i.e., the negotiations the agent participates in either until it closes a deal or there are no more sellers available. Each SBN the agent participates in is called a *negotiation round*. The buyer must then manage the time carefully, since the longer the simple bilateral negotiations take, the smaller is their number.

Another impact of time constraint regards the choice of the agreement to be kept under commitment. This occurs when the buyer must choose the *best commitment* amongst those whose deadline has not expired yet. In fact, it is not enough to consider only the commitment with the best associated payoff. The deadlines should be also taken into account. If there is only a small difference in the payoffs, commitments with longer deadlines may be preferred.

4.3 Expected Gain and Future Negotiations

When there are still sellers to negotiate with after an agreement is reached, the buyer needs to decide how much more it expects to gain from the subsequent negotiations. We think that three main factors should influence this decision. The first is the evaluation of the best agreement under commitment: the closest the agreement to the reservation value is, the smaller the expected gain. The second is the number of remaining sellers to negotiate with: the smaller the number of remaining sellers is, the smaller the chances of reaching a better deal, and the smaller the expected gain. The third factor is? the market value of the negotiated item, in the case the buyer is able to infer this information from previous negotiations.

From time to time, especially when a commitment is about to expire, the buyer needs to decide whether to continue looking for better agreements or to confirm the best commitment available so far. This decision may be influenced by four factors: (a) the odds of getting better agreements; (b) the available negotiation time (for closing a deal in the round); (c) the cost of negotiating; and (d) the evaluation of the market profile. The first factor depends on the same elements considered in the estimation of the expected gain (i.e., evaluation of the agreement under commitment, number of remaining sellers and item's market value), although their weights or the calculation procedure may vary. The second factor must be always observed, since the agent cannot violate the time constraint. Concerning the third factor, the cost, it is mainly related to the cases where time is a resource, i.e. where the utility of the agreement might decrease as time goes by [13]. A classical example is buying an ice cream, which tends to melt. Finally, the last factor concerns a possible dynamic evaluation of the progress of the negotiation in the given market place. The buyer may infer whether its negotiation tactics are working well or not. For instance, if the buyer is being tough and the agreements have not been reached, the tactics should change.

5   EmallBargainer

In order to study some practical implications of SBN and achieve a better understanding on the very SBN model, we defined a protocol and agents capable of carrying negotiations under it. Next, we enumerate only some choices and restrictions we imposed, considering the several possible protocols and agents.

We have implemented a protocol that includes the basic actions for bilateral negotiation [5,4], i.e. make a proposal, reject a proposal, make a counterproposal, accept a proposal, give an ultimatum, and abandon a negotiation without reaching an agreement. Besides these actions, the protocol also deals with the notion of commitment, adding the following actions: send a commitment confirmation or cancellation, and accept or reject a commitment confirmation.

Concerning the agents, we have built two types: the agent, called EmallBargainer, which acts on behalf of a buyer; and the other agents representing the sellers. The sellers follow the same strategies for bilateral negotiation proposed by [5] and extended by De Paula et al. [4], but also dealing with the commitment state. It is not in the scope of this paper to detail EmallBargainer's architecture, but let us enumerate the main design choices (most of them simplifications) concerning the issues introduced in Section 4.

EmallBargainer improves its payoff using the ultimatum mechanism. Due to the complexity of the use of ultimatum in multi-issue negotiations [5,12] (there are an infite number of proposals for a given payoff), EmallBargainer deals only with the price of the product. The best commitment is chosen based only on the payoff, disregarding the duration of its deadline. For EmallBargainer, the moment for deciding to confirm or cancel a commitment always occur when the commitment is about to expire. Finally, we determine a maximum duration for each bilateral negotiation, with time constraints on the entire negotiation round.

Besides the basic decision functions involved in a simple bilateral negotiation (e.g., received proposal interpretation, proposal to offer, proposal evaluation) [4,5], EmallBargainer implement two functions: FExpectPayoff, to determine the expected gain; and FAbandon, to decide whether to confirm a commitment or to continue trying better deals, and as discussed in Section 4.3. Intuitively, we defined fexpectPayoff as an increment on the payoff obtained in the best agreement so far. This increment depends only on (a) how far the payoff is to the reservation value (as discussed in Section 4.3) and (b) the *risk profile* of the buyer, the more aggressive the buyer, the greater the expected gain. The ultimatum value is determined by `fex-pectPayoff` just after establishing a commitment (before starting the next negotiation). `fabandon`, whose output is a binary decision, is also based on the buyer profile, the evaluation of the best obtained commitment and a reference value (`ct`) determining the desired result (payoff) for the deal. The buyer profiles and the value of `ct` are given by the user.

6 Experiments with EmallBargainer

6.1 Experimental Setup

We have defined 5 profiles for EmallBargainer (*notbluffer, moderate, conservative, bold and agreessive*). *notbluffer* does not use ultimatums and closes a deal as soon as the first agreement is reached. The other buyers bargain based on a parameterization of the functions `fexpectPayoff` and `fabandon`, going from lesser to greater risk-taking behaviors. It is important to stress that all risk-taking agents (from moderate to aggressive) adopt the same proposal generation tactics, i.e. they concede in the same speed. The difference is the value proposed as the ultimatum and in the decision of abandoning previous commitments. The performance of the buyers corresponds, naturally, to the payoff obtained at the end of each round.

Moreover, we have set up 18 different negotiation rounds in order to obtain more representative data and avoid any bias (i.e., the chances of getting a good deal should be the same, in average, at the end or at the beginning of the rounds). Each round contains 6 sellers with different *agreement ranges* (i.e. the interval between agents' reservation values), which are a key factor for a negotiation to succeed [4].

For each negotiation round, 9 SBN *market scenarios* were defined according to two variables: commitment deadlines (*long, medium and short*, set to 100, 20 and 5 proposals) and sellers' profile (*conceder, linear* and *boulware*). The maximum time for the buyer to finish each bilateral negotiation was set to 16 proposal exchanges. Hence, in short deadline scenarios, a commitment is likely to expire before the end of the next negotiation, whereas, in long deadline ones, the buyer can perform virtually all negotiations of the round. Concerning sellers negotiation profiles, their tactics are 50% imitative and 50% time-dependent, varying the latter, which can be boulware, linear or conceder [5]. In summary, the experiments involve 5 buyers negotiating in 9 market scenarios, each one containing 18 rounds (810 simulations in total).

6.2 Results and Discussion

Fig. 1 shows the average payoff obtained by the different buyers for all rounds and scenarios. From the results it is clear that the *notBluffer* buyer has the lowest performance, indicating that in average it is worthwhile to take risks in SBN. Among the risk-takers, the *moderate* buyer obtained the highest average payoff, as well as the most stable performance. It can also be seen the *aggressive* exhibits the worst average payoff among risk-takers, with a highly instable behavior. All these results correspond to the behavior that is intuitively expected for SBN: taking no risk is a bad strategy, whereas risking too much is sometimes good, but it can also lead to great losses.

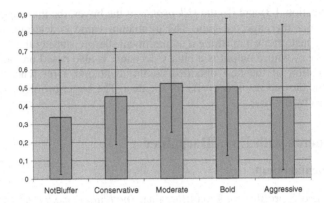

Fig. 1. Average Payoff in all rounds (y-axis indicates buyer's payoff and standard deviation, and x-axis shows the different profiles).

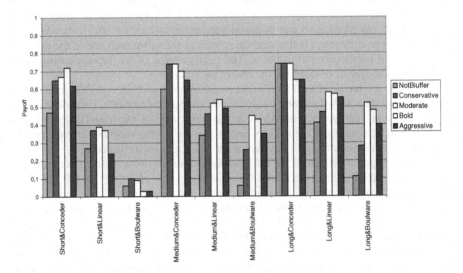

Fig. 2. Results by market scenarios (y-axis indicates buyer payoff and x-axis, the scenario).

Results tabulated by market scenario (Fig. 2) show that, independently of their buying profile, agents get better results in scenarios with longer commitment deadlines, as well as against conceder sellers, as intuitively expected. This figure also shows that, even using simple decision functions (as fabandon and fexpectPay-off), the behavior of EmallBargainer is sensitive to their parameterization, since some buyers perform significantly better than others in some scenarios.

In order to help identify the scenarios that are more favorable to risky behavior, Table 1 shows the difference between the payoff of the most risk-taker agents (*bold* and *aggressive*) and the least risk-taker ones (*moderate* and *conservative*). Form this table it is clear that risky behaviors are better than moderate ones in scenarios with long commitment deadlines and boulware sellers. Moderate behaviors are better suited to two opposite scenarios: long deadlines with conceder sellers, and short deadlines with boulware sellers. In the scenario with short deadlines and conceder sellers, the difference between risky and moderate behaviors is not significant.

To understand these results, it is important to bear in mind that in scenarios with short commitment deadlines, fexpectPayoff is irrelevant, since the buyers hardly ever get the time to conclude a negotiation before the previous commitments expire. In other words, the ultimatum mechanism is useless in these scenarios. On the other hand, in scenarios with long commitment deadlines, fabandon is irrelevant, since the buyers conclude all negotiations of the round before the previous commitments expire. In other words, the buyers have enough time to compare all the commitments and choose the best one.

Table 1. Difference between payoffs ($\text{Payoff}_{\text{Bold}}$ + $\text{Payoff}_{\text{Aggressive}}$ − $\text{Payoff}_{\text{Moderate}}$ − $\text{Payoff}_{\text{conservative}}$) in different negotiation scenarios.

	Conceder	Linear	Boulware
Short	0,02	-0,15	-0,13
Medium	-0,13	0,05	0,07
Long	-0,18	0,07	0,08

For scenarios with long commitment deadlines and conceder sellers, risky behaviors are worse than moderate ones because good agreements are naturally reached against these sellers for all buyers. When risky buyers force agreements, some of the ultimatums are rejected, decreasing their payoff.

For scenarios with long commitment deadlines and boulware sellers, risky behaviors are better than moderate since the only manner of getting good agreements against these sellers is by bargaining (i.e., by sending ultimatums, even though some might be rejected).

For scenarios with short commitment deadlines and boulware sellers, risky behaviors are worse than moderate ones. In fact, since it is difficult to reach good agreements against boulware sellers and since the buyers have no time to send ultimatums, it is not a good strategy to discard good commitments as risky buyers tend to do.

The main findings of the experiments can be summarized as follows:

1. The commitment deadline severely restricts the agent's decision-making process;
2. Although they may be refined, the definitions of fexpectPayoff and fabandon already provide a range of different negotiation behaviors;
3. It is always better for buyers to take some risk in SBN; however, high risks should only be taken in specific scenarios, whereas moderate risks are the best in average;
4. Adaptive mechanisms for adjusting fexpectPayoff and fabandon independently may improve buyers' performance.

7 Conclusions and Further Work

Despite being very common in the real world and feasible for e-commerce B2B or B2C market places, SBN has not yet been studied in depth by the agent community. In this paper, we have characterized SBN and introduced some issues that need to be considered in its implementation. With the aim of better understanding SBN's intricacies, we developed an agent and a protocol for it. This agent, called EmallBargainer, uses ultimatum as a bargain mechanism to take advantage of the information from previous bilateral negotiations. We carried out several experiments in which we could observe the performance of different EmallBargainer profiles in various negotiation scenarios. The results obtained allowed us to draw interesting conclusions about agent profiles and the very SBN model. One of these conclusions is the importance of the commitment deadline as a mechanism for adjusting the competition among sellers.

However, there are still many avenues that the AMEC community could explore in SBN, which is a realistic scenario in e-commerce. As discussed in Sections 3 and 4, one can explore different variations of the negotiation protocol, buyer profiles and strategies. Other open issues concern seller agents, their profiles and strategies. Finally, one could also investigate regulation mechanisms pertaining to markets based on SBN.

References

1. Strobel, M. (2000). "On Auctions as the Negotiation Paradigm of Electronic Markets",EM Journal of Electronic Markets, Vol.10. No.1, pp.39-44.
2. Cardoso, H. L., Schaefer, M. & Oliveira, E. (1999). A Multi-Agent System for Electronic Commerce including Adaptive Strategic Behaviors. In *EPIA'99 - Portuguese Conference on Artificial Intelligence*. Évora.
3. Chavez A., & Maes, P. (1996). Kasbah: An Agent Marketplace for Buying and Selling Goods. In Proceedings of the First Int. Conf. on the Practical Application of Intelligent Agents and Multi-Agent Technology, London.
4. de Paula G. E., Ramos, F. S. & Ramalho, G. L. (2000). Bilateral Negotiation Model for Agent Mediated Electronic Commerce. In Proceedings of the Third Workshop on Agent Mediated Electronic Commerce (AMEC III) in International Conference in Autonomous Agents (Agents 2000) (pp. 1-16). Barcelona.
5. Faratin P., C. Sierra & Jennings, N. R. (1998). Negotiation Decision Function for Autonomous Agents. Int. Journal of Robotics and Autonomous Systems (pp. 159-182).
6. Faratin P., Sierra, C., Jennings, N. R. & Buckle, P. (1999). Designing responsive and deliberative automated negotiators. In Proceedings of the AAAI Workshop on Negotiation: Settling Conflicts and Identifying Opportunities. (pp. 12-18). Orlando, FL.
7. Kersten G., Noronha S. & Teich J. (2000). Are All E-Commerce Negotiations Auctions? In Proceedings of the Fourth Internetional Conference on the Design of Cooperative Systems (COOP'2000). Sophia-Antipolis, France.
8. Lomuscio, A. R., Wooldridge M. & N. R. Jennings (2000) A classification scheme for negotiation in electronic commerce. In *Agent-Mediated Electronic Commerce: A European Perspective*. Springer Verlag. (pp. 1 McAfee, R. P. & McMillan, J. (1987). Auctions and bidding. *Journal of Economic Literature*. (vol. 25, pp. 699-738).9-33).
9. Maes, P., Guttman, R. & Moukas, A.G. (1999). Agents that buy ands sell: Transforming commerce as we know it. *Communications of the ACM*. (pp. 81-84).
10. Matos N., Sierra, C. & Jennings, N. R. (1998). Determining successful negotiation strategies: an evolutionary approach. In Proceedings of the *Int. Conf. on Multi-Agent Systems (ICMAS-98)*. (pp. 182-189). Paris, France.
11. Noriega, P. C. (1997). *Agent Mediated Auction: The Fishmarket Metaphor*. Tesi Doctoral, Universitat Autònoma de Barcelona, Facultat de Ciències.
12. Raiffa H. *The Art and Science of Negotiation*. (1982). Cambridge: Harvard University Press.
13. Rubinstein, A.: Perfect Equilibrium in a Bargain Model. Econometrica, 50(1):97-109. (1982)

14. Sierra C., Faratin, P. & Jennings, N. (1997). A Service-Oriented Negotiation Model between Autonomous Agents. In Proceedings of the 8th European Workshop on Modeling Autonomous Agents in a Multi-Agent World (MAAMAW-97). Ronneby, Sweden. (pp.17-35). Ronneby, Sweden.
15. Smith, C. W. (1989).*The Social Construction of Value*. Berkeley: University of California Press.
16. Wong, W. Y., Zhang, D. M. & Kara-Ali, M. (2000). Negotiating with Experience. *Seventeenth National Conference on Artificial Intelligence*, Workshop on Knowledge-Based Electronic Markets(KBEM). Austin, Texas: AAAI Press.
17. Wurman, P. R., Wellman, M. P. & Walsh, W. E. (1998). The Michigan Internet AuctionBot: A Configurable Auction Server for Human and Software Agents. In Proceedings of the 2nd International Conference on Autonomous Agents (Agents'98). (pp. 301-308). New York: ACM Press.

Towards to Similarity Identification
to Help in the Agents' Negotiation

Andreia Malucelli[1,2] and Eugénio Oliveira[1]

[1] LIACC-NIAD&R, Faculty of Engineering, University of Porto, R. Dr. Roberto Frias
4200-465 Porto, Portugal
malu@ppgia.pucpr.br, eco@fe.up.pt
[2] PUCPR – Pontifical Catholic University of Paraná, R. Imaculada Conceição,1155
80215-901 Curitiba PR, Brazil

Abstract. Enterprise delegates Agents' Negotiation is a simpler task if the enterprises involved in the transaction have homogeneous representation structures as well as the same domain of discourse, thus the use of a common ontology eases semantic problems. However, in real-life situations, real problems involve heterogeneity and different ontologies often developed by several persons and tools. Moreover, domain evolution, or changes in the conceptualisation might cause modifications on the previous ontologies once there is no formal mapping between high-level ontologies. We are proposing a method to be used by an Ontology-Services Agent to make Agents to understand each other despite their different ontologies. The method uses the natural language description of each involved item/product/service and combining statistical, clustering and suffix stripping algorithms finds out similarities between different concepts represented in different ontologies.

Keywords: ontologies, multi-agent systems, similarity identification, negotiation.

1 Introduction

In a decentralized and distributed approach, interoperability refers to the way we communicate with people and software agents, the problems which hampers the communication and collaboration between agents. In B2B transactions, it is a simpler task if the enterprises involved in the transaction have homogeneous representation structures as well as the same domain of discourse, thus the use of a common ontology makes the communication problem easy. The use of a common ontology guarantees the consistency and the compatibility of the shared information in the system. However, in real-life situations, real problems involve heterogeneity and ontologies often developed by several persons continue to evolve over time. Moreover, domain changes or changes in the conceptualisation might cause modifications on the ontology. This will likely cause incompatibilities [1] and makes the negotiation and cooperation process difficult.

A.L.C. Bazzan and S. Labidi (Eds.): SBIA 2004, LNAI 3171, pp. 536–545, 2004.
© Springer-Verlag Berlin Heidelberg 2004

By making the enterprises agents interoperable, we enable them to meet the basic requirement for multilateral cooperation. There are two major types of cooperative interaction which may be identified in a multi-agent system: the first concerns which agents perform which tasks (the task allocation problem) and the second concerns the sharing of information (both results and observations on the outside world) between agents. Purpose heterogeneity is primarily concerned with the former type and semantic heterogeneity with the latter [2].

In B2B transactions, due to the nature of the goods/services traded, these goods/services are described through multiple attributes (e.g. price and quality), which imply that negotiation process and final agreements between seller and supplier must be enhanced with the capability to both understand the terms and conditions of the transaction (e.g. vocabularies semantics, currencies to denote different prices, different units to represent measures or mutual dependencies of products).

A critical factor for the efficiency of the future negotiation processes and the success of the potential settlements is an agreement among the negotiating parties about how the issues of a negotiation are represented in the negotiation and what this representation means to each of the negotiating parties.

Our objective is to help in the interoperability problem, enhancing agents with abilities to provide services to and accept services from other agents, and to use these services so exchanged to enable agents to effectively negotiate together. We are using Multi-Agent System as the paradigm for the system architecture since enterprises are independent and have individual objectives and behavior. The focus here, in this paper, is on ontologies, whose specification includes a term (item/product) that denotes the concept, their characteristics (attributes) with the correspondent types, a description explaining the meaning of the concept in natural language, and a set of relationships among concepts. It is a really weak form of integration, because integration is not the objective of our work. Our approach aims at creating a methodology that assesses semantic similarity among concepts from different ontologies without building on a priori shared ontology. It is one of the services provided [3] by an Ontology-Services Agent (OSAg) for trying to help during the agents' negotiation process.

Next section discusses heterogeneity, interoperability and ontology, including partial ontology examples. Section 3 presents the architecture of the proposed system. The similarity identification method is explained in the section 4 and finally we conclude the paper in section 5.

2 Heterogeneity, Interoperability and Ontology

Heterogeneity is both a welcome and an unwelcome feature for system designers. On the one hand heterogeneity is welcomed because it is closely related to system efficiency. On the other hand, heterogeneity in data and knowledge systems is considered an unwelcome feature because it proves to be an important obstacle for the interoperation of systems. The lack of standards is an obstacle to the exchange of data between heterogeneous systems [4] and this lack of standardization, which hampers communication and collaboration between agents, is known as the interoperability problem [5].

Heterogeneity here, in this paper, means agents communicating using different ontologies. Four types of heterogeneity are distinguished by [4]: (i) **paradigm heterogeneity,** occurs if two systems express their knowledge using different modeling paradigms, (ii) **language heterogeneity,** occurs if two systems express their knowledge in different representation languages, (iii) **ontology heterogeneity** occurs if two systems make different ontological assumptions about their domain knowledge, (iv) **content heterogeneity,** occurs if two systems express different knowledge.

Paradigm and language heterogeneity are types of non-semantic heterogeneity and the ontology and content heterogeneity are types of semantic heterogeneity.

In our proposed system each agent has its own private ontology although about the same knowledge domain, but each ontology was developed by different designers and may expresses knowledge differently.

In literature, ontologies are classified into different types based on different ideas. [6] presents two typologies, according to the level of formality and according to the level of granularity. According to *the level of formality*, three ontologies types are specified: (i) **informal ontology** is the simplest type; it is comprised of a set of concept labels organized in a hierarchy, (ii) **terminological ontology** consists of a hierarchy of concepts defined by natural language definitions, (iii) **formal ontology** further includes axioms and definitions stated in a formal language. According to the *level of granularity*, six ontologies types are specified: (i) **top-level ontology** defines very general concepts such as space, time, object, event, etc., which are independent of a particular domain. (ii) **general ontology** defines a large number of concepts relating to fundamental human knowledge. (iii) **domain ontology** defines concepts associated with a specific domain. (iv) **task ontology** defines concepts related to the execution of a particular task or activity. (v) **application ontology** defines concepts essential for planning a particular application. (vi) **meta-ontology or generic or core ontology** defines concepts, which are common across various domains; these concepts can be further specialized to domain – specific concepts.

In our proposed system, the ontologies are classified in the level of formality as terminological ontologies because they include concepts organized in a hierarchy and the concept definitions are expressed in natural language. According to level of granularity they are classified as domain ontologies, in our case in the specific cars' assembling domain.

Cars' assembling domain is a suitable scenario because it involves several services suppliers' enterprises and consequently several different negotiations. To make it possible the cars' assembly, the service supplier enterprise (cars' assembler) needs to buy several parts/components. For each one of these parts/components there are several potential suppliers, which offer different prices, facilities, quality, delivery time, and others attributes. It is necessary to select among all the interested enterprises the ones which send the best offers and furthermore, it is mandatory a negotiation based on several criteria.

Even with terminology standards used by cars' factories, the same term may have different meanings, or the same meaning may be associated with different terms and different representations. A scenario using this domain will be explored as a study-case. The ontology creation process for our particular domain (cars' assembling domain) involved searching literature on cars' assembling domain and discussion with experts. After careful consideration and test of several different ontology building tools, we have selected the appropriated ones. First we have modeled our ontology by means of UML and then ontology-building tools WebODE [7], Protégé [8] and OntoEdit [9] have been used.

Fig. 1 and Fig. 2 show a part of a UML diagram of the built ontologies. Fig. 1 represents the Customer Enterprise Agent Ontology and Fig. 2 represents the Supplier Enterprise Ontology. Though example we may observe some differences causing interoperability problem during the negotiation process. For example, in the ontology A there are *wheel* and *handwheel* concepts and in the ontology B there is only the wheel concept, here meaning *handwheel*. Other differences as *Motor* x *Engine* and *Tire* x *Tyre* may be observed. The ontologies are composed by concepts, each concept has a set of characteristics, each one of the attributes has a type (not showed in this diagram) and each one of the concepts has relationship with other concepts. The way the Ontology-Services Agent, using a similarity-based algorithm, solves the problem is presented in Section 4.

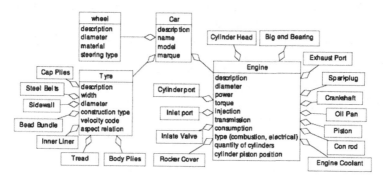

Fig. 1. Ontology A: Part of the Customer Enterprise Agent Ontology.

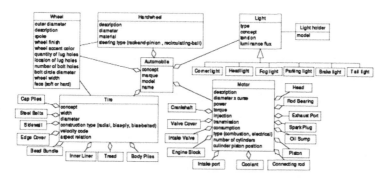

Fig. 2. Ontology B: Part of the Supplier Enterprise Agent Ontology.

3 System Architecture

This framework includes 4 types of agents: facilitator agent, enterprise agents (good/product/services suppliers and customer), and ontology-services agent. The facilitator agent and enterprise agents - suppliers and customers, are cooperating together through a website with the objective of providing or getting goods/products/services, in collaboration, but keeping their own preferences and objectives. An ontology-services agent is involved in all the process for monitoring and facilitating the communication and negotiation between agents.

The **Facilitator Agent (FAg)** is the entity that matches the right agents and supports the negotiation process. The enterprise (customer and suppliers) agents and ontology-services agent have to register themselves to be able to communicate. Each agent has its own private ontology, built in a private and unknown (to the overall system) process. **Customer Enterprise Agents (CEAg)** represent enterprises interested in buying components to build a final product. Several suppliers in the world may have these components with different prices and conditions. Each CEAg sends a message (Identification of Needs) to the facilitator announcing which composed product/service is needed to configure. **Supplier Enterprise Agents (SEAg)** represent enterprises interested in providing some kind of product/service/good. Whenever a needed product, the facilitator agent conveys this announcement to all registered interested supplier enterprise agents. **Ontology-Services Agent (OSAg)** keeps monitoring the whole conversation trying to help when some message is not fully understood by some of the participants. The OSAg service for helping in the similarity identification is explained in the next section. Fig. 3 shows an instance of the multi-agent system. Each Enterprise Agent (Supplier or Customer) has its own architecture and functionalities (some developer will design and build the ontology with some tool and, later, the agent will access the generated file/database).

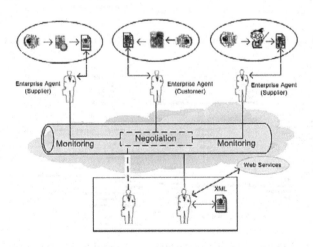

Fig. 3. System Architecture.

4 Similarity Identification

Several different tools and techniques for mapping, aligning, integration, merging [10], [11], [12], [13], [14] of ontologies are available but there is no automatic way to do that. It is still a difficult task and for the success of these processes it is necessary to detect ontology mismatches and solve them. Recent research about ontological discrepancies have been done [4], [15], however none of the available tools tackle all the types of discrepancies [16].

Some problems in finding similarity are related to the following facts: (i) the ontologies use different concept/term names for the same meaning and description. Example: tyre and tire; (ii) the ontologies use the same concept/term name for different meaning and description. Example: wheel and wheel (where one of them means hand wheel), (iii) the ontologies use the same concept/term name for the same meaning. However, the description includes different characteristics (attributes) and relations.

Similarity evaluations among ontologies may be achieved if their representations share some components. If two ontologies have at least one common component (relations, hierarchy, types, etc) then they may be compared. Usually characteristics provide the opportunity to capture details about concepts. In our approach we are using relations and characteristics' types as common components in all the ontologies. There are a set of relations and characteristics that have to be known and used by all the ontologies for initial tests. The concepts are also linked by a number of relations.

The relations used in our approach are: (i) *part_of* relationship, organizes the concepts according to a decomposition hierarchy (composed_by), (ii) *is_a* relationship, a concept is a generalization of the concept being defined, (iii) *equivalent* relationship, the concepts are similar, (iv) *use* relationship, a concept uses functionalities from other concept.

The value types of characteristics used are: (i) *integer*, represents positive and negative integer values (ii) *string*, represents text information (iii) *discrete domain*, represents a set of fixed values (iv) *material*, represents information about what substance the object is made of (v) *numeric*, represents the not integer values.

The OSAg will be monitoring all the communication and negotiation and for helping it will search information in its own ontology, which is a basic ontology built with basic structures in the cars' assembling domain, which will be updated whenever a new concept is discovered. OSAg has also to get additional information from the agents using exchanged messages (see Fig. 4). An example of the structure of one exchanged message between OSAg and SEAg may be observed below, based on the ontologies showed in Fig. 1 and Fig. 2. In the message "ask-about", the OSAg is asking information about the engine concept, and in the "reply" message, the CEAg is answering the questions, filling the template. Each agent has to be able to read its own ontology and understand the template.

ask-about
:sender ontology-services agent
:receiver customer enterprise agent
:language KQML
:content (:concept (engine)
   :description (description)
   :part_of ([ ]∨[concept])
   :is_a ([ ]∨[concept])
   :has_part ([ ]∨[concept])
   :equivalent ([ ]∨[concept])
   :use ([ ]∨[concept])
   :num_characteristics ([ ] ∨ number)
   :num_integer ([ ]∨ number ∧ relevance)
   :num_numeric ([ ]∨ number ∧ relevance)
   :num_discrete_domain ([ ]∨ number ∧ relevance)
   :num_string ([ ]∨number ∧ relevance))

reply
:sender customer enterprise agent
:receiver ontology-services agent
:language KQML
:content (:concept (engine)
   :description (engine is a motor that converts thermal energy to mechanical work)
   :part_of (car)
   :is_a ([ ])
   :has_part (inlate valve, rocker cover, cylinder port, inlet port, engine coolant, con rod, piston, oil pan, crankshaft, sparkplug, exhaust port, big end bearing, cylinder head)
   :equivalent ([ ])
   :use ([ ])
   :num_characteristics (10)
   :num_integer (6, 2)
   :num_numeric ([ ])
   :num_discrete_domain (2,2)
   :num_string (2,0))

Fig. 4. Exchanged messages to get aditional information.

The process is described as follow:

1. CEAg sends a KQML message to the FAg informing about the basic requirement for that particular item/product/service.
2. FAg sends an announcement to the registered SEAg, which probably provide the required item.
3. Each one of the SEAg that provides the item/service required send an advertisement to the CEAg.
4. Some of the SEAg may have the announced item but may not understand it because SEAg may have a different ontology and the item may be specified in a different way. If the SEAg does not understand the announced item, it will send an "unknown" message to FAg. The OSAg, which is monitoring the communication, detects the message and try to help.
5. If 4 occurs, OSAg sends a message to CEAg asking for detailed information about the item required, as showed in the ask-about message example above.
6. After 5, OSAg will exchange messages with the correspondent SEAg asking for the concepts descriptions.
7. Using appropriated algorithms OSAg will find the correspondent concept to the announced item. This process is explained in the subsection 4.1.
8. If some description was not found or more than one was found as similar, new tests are needed to try to find proof of similarity. OSAg will exchange messages with the correspondent SEAg sending and asking for new informations using synonymous, relationships between concepts, type, quantity and relevance of the characteristics.

4.1 Using Description to Similarity Identification

We are proposing the use of metrics, methodologies and algorithms well known in database and information retrieval area for trying to find similarity among the words that compose the concept description.

Usually, in a specific domain, when experts are describing the concepts that form the ontology, they use some technical and specific words, and we may find similar words in the concept descriptions. We are proposing to select the relevant words used in the descriptions and to compare them to find similarities.

To make it easier to understand, consider the example of the KQML message above (Fig. 4), where OSAg asks information about *engine* (the required item), and the CEAg informs about the concept included described in its own ontology "**engine** is a **motor** that **converts thermal energy** to **mechanical work**".

First, it is necessary a process for selecting/extracting the most representative words (showed in bold) from the description, which will represent the concept engine.

engine	motor	converts	thermal	energy	mechanical	work

The OSAg will also extract the most representative words from the description of the concepts in the ontology B, to have also a representation of the concepts. As an example, we now consider two other concepts, *motor* and *tire*, to be compared with engine.

Motor "it is a **machine** that **converts** other **forms** of **energy** into **mechanical energy** and so **imparts motion**".

machine	converts	forms	energy	mechanical	imparts	motion

Tire "**consists** of a **rubber ring** around the **rim** of an **automobile wheel**".

consists	rubber	ring	automobile	wheel

The use of similarity algorithms between the required concept and the candidate concept would not give representative results, because we have semantic similarity and comparing strings would only work for cases as tire and tyre comparison. Using, for example, edit distance [17] for comparing the strings engine and motor we will get the similarity $(1-6/6) = 0$ and comparing engine with tire we will get the similarity $(1-3/6) = 0.5$, where engine and motor have the same meaning and should have a higher similarity value. For solving this problem our purpose is to use a combination of methods to find similarities between the words extracted from the descriptions, and some weights are used for the most representative words.

A similarity matrix is generated between the set of words extracted from required concept description with each one of the set of words extracted from the candidates concepts descriptions. We have two similarity matrix in this example, one among the words extracted from engine and motor descriptions, and another one built with words extracted from engine and tire descriptions. The matrix has its values calculated using edit distance and suffix stripping [18] algorithm.

We are using also in our algorithm, weights for the most relevant words. In the case of a similarity between words equal to 1, a sum of the weight equal to 1 is attributed for the correspondent value in the matrix, and if the required concept word (engine) is contained in the description of the candidate concept, this word gets a weight value of 1 and a result is summed with all the values in the matrix. To have the final result we calculate the matrix sum, but due to the matrix size difference, it is necessary calculate the average, sum the matrix elements and divide by the number of matrix elements.

In our example we got the similarity value between engine and motor of 0.35, where we found 3 identical words and the candidate concept in the description of the required concept. It concludes a difference due to the weights. The similarity value between engine and tire is 0.06. The method calculation shows that engine and motor concepts are more similar than engine and tire.

5 Conclusions

We have proposed a heterogeneous multi-agent architecture suitable for semantic interoperability. Each agent has its own private ontology although in the same knowledge domain. Also each ontology is developed by different designers and expresses knowledge differently. The ontologies are classified regarding the level of formality as terminological ontologies, once their concepts are organized in a hierarchy and the concept definitions are expressed in natural language. According to the level of granularity, they are classified as domain ontologies, in our case in the specific car's assembling domain.

Our approach aims at creating a methodology for extracting similarities from the concept descriptions of the required item and the candidate items to find which one of those candidates may be the requested one. Each agent accesses its own ontology, without building any a priori shared ontology, and sends the needed information to the specific Ontology-Service Agent (OSAg). Relationships among concepts, characteristics, types and synonymous are also important information and may help in the process if the natural language description is not enough to identify the similarities.

A similarity matrix is generated between the description of the required item and the descriptions of the candidate concepts. The matrix has its values calculated using edit distance and suffix stripping algorithm. Rand Statistic is calculated to compare and find out the most promising candidate concept that matches the former unknown concept.

References

1. Klein, M., Kiryakov, A. Ognyanoff, D. and Fensel, D.: Finding and specifying relations between ontology versions. In Proceedings of the ECAI-02 Workshop on Ontologies and Semantic Interoperability http://www.cs.vu.nl/~heiner/ECAI-02-WS/. Lyon, July 22. 2002
2. Roda, C., Jennings, N.R., Mandanu, E.H.: The impact of heterogeneity on cooperating agents. In Proceedings of AAAI Workshop on Cooperation among Heterogeneous Intelligent Systems, Anaheim, USA, 1991

3. Malucelli, A., Oliveira, E., Ontology-Services to Facilitate Agents' Interoperability. In Proceedings of the Sixth Pacific Rim International Workshop on Multi-Agents (PRIMA 2003). Eds. Jaeho Lee, Mike Barley, Springer-Verlag. LNAI 2891, Korea. Novembro. (2003) 170-181.
4. Visser, P.R.S., Jones, D.M., Bench-Capon, T.J.M. and Shave, M.J.R.: An Analysis of Ontology Mismatches; Heterogeneity vs. Interoperability. AAAI'97 Spring Symposium on Ontological Engineering, Stanford (1997)
5. Willmott, S., Constantinescu. I, Calisti, M.: Multilingual Agents: Ontologies, Languages and Abstractions. In Proceedings of the Workshop on Ontologies in Agent Systems. 5th International Conference on Autonomous Agents. Montreal. Canada. (2001)
6. Kavouras, M.: A Unified Ontological Framework for Semantic Integration. In Proceeding of the International Workshop on Next Generation Geospatial Information, Cambridge (Boston), Massachusetts, USA, October (2003) 19-21
7. Arpírez, J.C., Corcho, O., Fernández-López, M., Gómez-Pérez, A.: WebODE in a nutshell. AI Magazine 24(3):37-48. Fall (2003)
8. Gennari, J., Musen, M.A., Fergerson, R. W., Grosso, W.E., Crubézy, M., Eriksson, H., Noy, N.F., Tu, S.W.: The Evolution of Protégé: An Environment for Knowledge-Based Systems Development The Evolution of Protégé: An Environment for Knowledge-Based Systems Development. Technical Report. SMI Report Number: SMI-2002-0943 2002.
9. Sure, Y., Erdmann, M., Angele, J., Staab, S., Studer, R., Wenke, D.: OntoEdit: Collaborative Ontology Development for the Semantic Web. In Proceedings of the First International Semantic Web Conference (ISWC 2002), June 9-12 Sardinia, Italia. 2002.
10. Hakimpour, F., Geppert, A.: Resolving Semantic Heterogeneity in Schema Integration: an Ontology Based Approach. In the Proceedings of the International Conference on Formal Ontology in Information Systems (FOIS 2001) Maine, USA (2001) 297-308
11. McGuinness, D.L., Fikes, R., Rice, J., and Wilder, S.: An environment for merging and testing large ontologies, in Cohn, A., Giunchiglia, F. Selman, B. (eds.), KR2000: Principles on Knowledge Representation and Reasoning, San Francisco (2000) 483-493
12. Noy, N.F. and Musen, M.A.: PROMPT: Algorithm and Tool for Automated Ontology Merging and Alignment. In Proceedings of AAAI'00, Austin (2000)
13. Pinto, H.S.: Towards Ontology Reuse. In Proceedings of AAAI99's Workshop on Ontology Management, WS-99-13, AAAI Press (1999) 67-73
14. Stumme, G and Maedche, A.: Ontology Merging for Federated Ontologies on the Semantic Web. Workshop on Ontologies and Information Sharing. IJCAI'01, Seattle, USA (2001)
15. Klein, M.: Combining and relating ontologies: an analysis of problems and solutions. Workshop on Ontologies and Information Sharing, IJCAI'01, Seattle, USA (2001)
16. Hameed, A. Sleeman, D., Preece, A.: Detecting Mismatches Among Experts' Ontologies Acquired through Knowledge Elicitation. Research and Development in Intelligent Systems XVIII (Proceedings of ES 2001), BCS Conference Series, Springer-Verlag (2001) 9-22
17. Sahinalp, S.C., Tasan, M., Macker, J., Ozsoyoglu, Z.M.: Distance Based Indexing for String Proximity Search. In Proceedings of 19th International Conference on Data Engineering. Bangalore, India. (2003) 125
18. Porter, M.F.: An algorithm for suffix stripping. Readings in information retrieval. Morgan Kaufmann Publishers Inc. San Francisco, CA, USA (1997) 313-316

Author Index

Lecture Notes in Artificial Intelligence (LNAI)

Vol. 3010: K.R. Apt, F. Fages, F. Rossi, P. Szeredi, J. Váncza (Eds.), Recent Advances in Constraints. VIII, 285 pages. 2004.

Vol. 2990: J. Leite, A. Omicini, L. Sterling, P. Torroni (Eds.), Declarative Agent Languages and Technologies. XII, 281 pages. 2004.

Vol. 2980: A. Blackwell, K. Marriott, A. Shimojima (Eds.), Diagrammatic Representation and Inference. XV, 448 pages. 2004.

Vol. 2977: G. Di Marzo Serugendo, A. Karageorgos, O.F. Rana, F. Zambonelli (Eds.), Engineering Self-Organising Systems. X, 299 pages. 2004.

Vol. 2972: R. Monroy, G. Arroyo-Figueroa, L.E. Sucar, H. Sossa (Eds.), MICAI 2004: Advances in Artificial Intelligence. XVII, 923 pages. 2004.

Vol. 2969: M. Nickles, M. Rovatsos, G. Weiss (Eds.), Agents and Computational Autonomy. X, 275 pages. 2004.

Vol. 2961: P. Eklund (Ed.), Concept Lattices. IX, 411 pages. 2004.

Vol. 2953: K. Konrad, Model Generation for Natural Language Interpretation and Analysis. XIII, 166 pages. 2004.

Vol. 2934: G. Lindemann, D. Moldt, M. Paolucci (Eds.), Regulated Agent-Based Social Systems. X, 301 pages. 2004.

Vol. 2930: F. Winkler (Ed.), Automated Deduction in Geometry. VII, 231 pages. 2004.

Vol. 2926: L. van Elst, V. Dignum, A. Abecker (Eds.), Agent-Mediated Knowledge Management. XI, 428 pages. 2004.

Vol. 2923: V. Lifschitz, I. Niemelä (Eds.), Logic Programming and Nonmonotonic Reasoning. IX, 365 pages. 2004.

Vol. 2915: A. Camurri, G. Volpe (Eds.), Gesture-Based Communication in Human-Computer Interaction. XIII, 558 pages. 2004.

Vol. 2913: T.M. Pinkston, V.K. Prasanna (Eds.), High Performance Computing - HiPC 2003. XX, 512 pages. 2003.

Vol. 2903: T.D. Gedeon, L.C.C. Fung (Eds.), AI 2003: Advances in Artificial Intelligence. XVI, 1075 pages. 2003.

Vol. 2902: F.M. Pires, S.P. Abreu (Eds.), Progress in Artificial Intelligence. XV, 504 pages. 2003.

Vol. 2892: F. Dau, The Logic System of Concept Graphs with Negation. XI, 213 pages. 2003.

Vol. 2891: J. Lee, M. Barley (Eds.), Intelligent Agents and Multi-Agent Systems. X, 215 pages. 2003.

Vol. 2882: D. Veit, Matchmaking in Electronic Markets. XV, 180 pages. 2003.

Vol. 2871: N. Zhong, Z.W. Raś, S. Tsumoto, E. Suzuki (Eds.), Foundations of Intelligent Systems. XV, 697 pages. 2003.

Vol. 2854: J. Hoffmann, Utilizing Problem Structure in Planing. XIII, 251 pages. 2003.

Vol. 2843: G. Grieser, Y. Tanaka, A. Yamamoto (Eds.), Discovery Science. XII, 504 pages. 2003.

Vol. 2842: R. Gavaldá, K.P. Jantke, E. Takimoto (Eds.), Algorithmic Learning Theory. XI, 313 pages. 2003.

Vol. 2838: N. Lavrač, D. Gamberger, L. Todorovski, H. Blockeel (Eds.), Knowledge Discovery in Databases: PKDD 2003. XVI, 508 pages. 2003.

Vol. 2837: N. Lavrač, D. Gamberger, L. Todorovski, H. Blockeel (Eds.), Machine Learning: ECML 2003. XVI, 504 pages. 2003.

Vol. 2835: T. Horváth, A. Yamamoto (Eds.), Inductive Logic Programming. X, 401 pages. 2003.

Vol. 2821: A. Günter, R. Kruse, B. Neumann (Eds.), KI 2003: Advances in Artificial Intelligence. XII, 662 pages. 2003.

Vol. 2807: V. Matoušek, P. Mautner (Eds.), Text, Speech and Dialogue. XIII, 426 pages. 2003.

Vol. 2801: W. Banzhaf, J. Ziegler, T. Christaller, P. Dittrich, J.T. Kim (Eds.), Advances in Artificial Life. XVI, 905 pages. 2003.

Vol. 2797: O.R. Zaïane, S.J. Simoff, C. Djeraba (Eds.), Mining Multimedia and Complex Data. XII, 281 pages. 2003.

Vol. 2792: T. Rist, R.S. Aylett, D. Ballin, J. Rickel (Eds.), Intelligent Virtual Agents. XV, 364 pages. 2003.

Vol. 2782: M. Klusch, A. Omicini, S. Ossowski, H. Laamanen (Eds.), Cooperative Information Agents VII. XI, 345 pages. 2003.

Vol. 2780: M. Dojat, E. Keravnou, P. Barahona (Eds.), Artificial Intelligence in Medicine. XIII, 388 pages. 2003.

Vol. 2777: B. Schölkopf, M.K. Warmuth (Eds.), Learning Theory and Kernel Machines. XIV, 746 pages. 2003.

Vol. 2752: G.A. Kaminka, P.U. Lima, R. Rojas (Eds.), RoboCup 2002: Robot Soccer World Cup VI. XVI, 498 pages. 2003.

Vol. 2741: F. Baader (Ed.), Automated Deduction – CADE-19. XII, 503 pages. 2003.

Vol. 2705: S. Renals, G. Grefenstette (Eds.), Text- and Speech-Triggered Information Access. VII, 197 pages. 2003.

Vol. 2703: O.R. Zaïane, J. Srivastava, M. Spiliopoulou, B. Masand (Eds.), WEBKDD 2002 - Mining Web Data for Discovering Usage Patterns and Profiles. IX, 181 pages. 2003.

Vol. 2700: M.T. Pazienza (Ed.), Extraction in the Web Era. XIII, 163 pages. 2003.

Vol. 2699: M.G. Hinchey, J.L. Rash, W.F. Truszkowski, C.A. Rouff, D.F. Gordon-Spears (Eds.), Formal Approaches to Agent-Based Systems. IX, 297 pages. 2002.

Vol. 2691: V. Mařík, J.P. Müller, M. Pechoucek (Eds.), Multi-Agent Systems and Applications III. XIV, 660 pages. 2003.

Vol. 2684: M.V. Butz, O. Sigaud, P. Gérard (Eds.), Anticipatory Behavior in Adaptive Learning Systems. X, 303 pages. 2003.

Vol. 2682: R. Meo, P.L. Lanzi, M. Klemettinen (Eds.), Database Support for Data Mining Applications. XII, 325 pages. 2004.

Vol. 2671: Y. Xiang, B. Chaib-draa (Eds.), Advances in Artificial Intelligence. XIV, 642 pages. 2003.

Vol. 2663: E. Menasalvas, J. Segovia, P.S. Szczepaniak (Eds.), Advances in Web Intelligence. XII, 350 pages. 2003.